THE ENCYCLOPAEDIA OF GREYHOUND RACING

THE ENCYCLOPAEDIA OF GREYHOUND RACING

A COMPLETE HISTORY OF THE SPORT

ROY GENDERS

First published in Great Britain by
PELHAM BOOKS LTD
44 Bedford Square
London WC1B 3DU
1981
Reprinted 1982, 1985, 1986

ISBN 0 7207 1106 1

Typeset by Cambrian Typesetters
Frimley, Camberley, Surrey

Printed and bound in Great Britain by
Butler & Tanner Ltd, Frome and London

CONTENTS

INTRODUCTION

Greyhound racing had only been operating for a year or two when I first became interested in the dogs who took part in it. Betting on them didn't interest me. I was fascinated by their grace of movement and amazing speed and by the intelligent way they moved round a racecourse, with no one on their backs to direct them but always ready to cut inside and move to the front whenever they saw the slightest opening. The track sense of the champions is uncanny.

It was 1929–30, the time of the Depression, and yet there was more interest in sport than ever before or since. Mick the Miller, together with Tom Newman, Dixie Dean and Jack Hobbs, was making the headlines in the sporting press. Mick had arrived on the sporting scene just at the right time, for his wonderful exploits did much to create an interest in greyhound racing everywhere and new tracks were opening every month. As a young Sheffielder I was most fortunate in that 'my' soccer team, Sheffield Wednesday, were then League Champions. In January 1932, only five minutes' walk from Wednesday's famous Hillsborough ground, Sheffield Sports Stadium opened for greyhound racing and speedway, so that now it was possible to see some of the best football in the land and many of the best greyhounds within half a mile of each other. So popular did greyhound racing become in the 1930s that 10,000 paid at each meeting for greyhound or speedway at the Owlerton track, as it is still known. For 6d (2½p) one could see such stars as Vic Huxley and 'Smokey' Strattan performing on the cinder track, and watch greyhounds like Victor Ben Hur and Stansman run at 40 mph on the turfed circuit. Across the city was Bramall Lane, home of another top Football League team, Sheffield United, and then one of Yorkshire's two main county cricket grounds. They were exciting days for a schoolboy, as I was then, and so much high-class sporting entertainment helped to take people's minds off the economic problems of the time.

In the 1940s, whenever RAF leave allowed, it was to Wembley and Jack Harvey's kennels that I made my way. League football and county cricket were no longer played, though many games were arranged on Saturday afternoons as morale-raisers, but greyhound racing drew the crowds in their thousands. By 1940 tracks had opened everywhere – more than a hundred were racing under NGRC rules, and there were as many that did not. Tracks sprang up during the 1930s like mushrooms in an autumn night – at Warrington and Salford, Leeds and Bradford, at Newport in Wales and Stanley in Co. Durham, at Doncaster and Stoke-on-Trent. Newcastle had three tracks, Brough Park, White City and Gosforth; Glasgow had five, Albion, Carntyne, Firhill, White City and Shawfield. Now only the last of these survives. They had opened at exactly the right time, for during the 1940s all enjoyed 'boom' conditions. There was no television, and in any case racing took place on Saturday afternoons to save electricity on the overhead lights. By the end of the 1940s some

50 million paid each year to see greyhounds perform, and Britain's need to import thousands of greyhounds each year was a godsend to the Irish economy. Then, as league football and county cricket got into their stride again, many sports fans were drawn from the greyhound tracks, and from the early 1950s attendances began to fall. This coincided with the development of new town centres after wartime bombings, and when the price of land soared tracks began to close as quickly as they had started up. Today, only about half of those which were active in the 1940s have survived. These include several in London, Perry Barr and Hall Green in Birmingham, the Owlerton track in Sheffield, Powderhall in Edinburgh, Belle Vue and White City in Manchester, Leeds, Derby, Southend, Brighton and Slough. Several new tracks have opened recently, while others, such as Ipswich, Yarmouth and Norton Canes, have come to operate under the NGRC Permit Scheme. Though attendances have fallen to 6 million annually, it is still Britain's second most popular sport.

Greyhound racing continues to give me great pleasure, and if the image of the sport still remains that of the chap in an old raincoat and cloth cap standing near the rails in pouring rain, with a sandwich and a cup of hot Oxo, then that is me. This is how I like my racing, down among the greyhounds from the time they come out of the racing kennels until they go back into them, so that I can see everything they do. I have seen all the greats – Mick the Miller, Brilliant Bob, Bradshaw Fold, Quarter Day, Shove Ha'penny, Ataxy, Model Dasher, Hurry Kitty, Dante, Shannon Shore, Local Interprize, Pigalle Wonder, Mile Bush Pride, Dolores Rocket, Mutt's Silver and Lacca Champion. Each has given me tremendous pleasure in its own way, for every greyhound has a different personality.

The sport has another side that is often overlooked. Since its beginnings, greyhound racing has raised more money for charity than any other sport. During 1979 the White City in London raised more than £100,000 for deserving causes, and every track without exception has contributed most generously to charities. Every year at Owlerton an entire meeting is devoted to raising money for the Injured Jockeys' Fund, and Brough Park raises funds for nearby Cheshire Homes. Brighton, Slough, Southend and Powderhall are other provincial tracks to earn special mention for all they do for worthy causes, and no one is freer in offering both money and time than the bookmakers. They earn much of their livelihood from the sport and put a great deal back into it.

I have often heard it said that greyhound racing is a seedy sport, dominated by those whose only interest is to make money from it and by those who spend their time doping dogs. Nothing could be further from the truth, and no sport has ever been better served by those connected with it. Many of them have spent almost fifty years looking after the interests of followers of the sport and the greyhounds taking part. The racing director at Wimbledon for more than forty years was Con Stevens, and at the White City Major Percy Brown, both highly esteemed men. At Owlerton the original racing manager, who remained until his retirement in 1974, was Sam Vinter, and at Derby for many years was Lieut-Col Prior, who ran things with military precision. Both were completely dedicated to the welfare of the sport. Their places have been taken by others equally respected, such as Squadron Leader 'Bill' Holmes at White City, Jim Layton at Brighton, Norman Russell, for many years at Gloucester, and Vic Abbott at Cleveland Park.

The trainers, too, must be mentioned, for no group of people has made a greater contribution. Again, many have been in from the start and only in recent years have they begun to retire. I am thinking of Paddy McEllistrim of Wimbledon who, now over eighty, retired only recently, and Paddy McEvoy, who trained Daw's Dancer to win the 1953 greyhound Derby and is still a Wimbledon trainer. Others whom I remember with affection include Sidney Orton, the Wizard of Burhill, for nearly forty years a Wimbledon trainer and who died in 1978 aged eighty-three. His son, Clare, is a Wimbledon trainer today. I recall as well the late Paddy Fortune, also a trainer there for forty years. At Wimbledon Dick Ball, hare controller, arrived with Con Stevens before the track opened in 1927 and is still there. The late Stanley Biss, the first trainer whose greyhounds won more than £10,000 in one year for their owners, was for many years at West Ham and Clapton. At Wembley, until the old kennels were demolished in 1974, were several of the greatest trainers in the history of the sport – Leslie Reynolds, Jimmy Rimmer, Jack Harvey and Bob Burls, each of them a household name and brilliant at handling greyhounds; week after week these men kept the dogs under their care at peak fitness, so that they were able to perform at the height of their powers. Between them, these men won every honour the sport had to offer. Each served greyhound racing for almost fifty years and we have every reason to be grateful to them.

The purpose of this book is to record all that I know about the sport, the racing staff and trainers, the greyhounds and their breeders and owners. Since cricket has its Wisden and football its Rothman, it is time that greyhound racing should also have its encyclopaedia. It is a history that covers more than fifty years, and my task has not been an easy one since few records have been kept by the tracks. My thanks are due to Jerry Monk, publicity manager of the Greyhound Racing Association, the pioneers of the sport, who has been most helpful, especially in providing photographs from the White City archives. I have always had the utmost co-operation from the GRA and I am more than grateful to them.

My thanks are due also to the following: Philip Grimstone, assistant racing manager at Brighton and Hove Stadium; G. Bryan, of the racing office at Catford; Vic Abbott, for many years racing manager at Cleveland Park Stadium; W.R. Hiscock, of the Abbey Stadium, Swindon; Dennis Law, for the photograph of and notes about his great dog Tartan Khan; Barry Davis, racing manager at Derby; T.G. Evans, racing manager at Southend; Martin Corrie, press secretary at Wembley Stadium; Mrs Natalie Savva, of the famous Westmead Kennels, for the valuable information she kindly sent me about her champion greyhounds and the photograph of Westmead Champ; Mrs Olive Turner, keeper of the Greyhound Stud Book; Doris Gatling, for the long hours she has spent sorting and typing my copious notes; and Ruth Baldwin of my publisher, Pelham Books. I have also been delighted to hear from the late

Arthur Callanan's mother in Co. Cork, and from G. Boulton who so kindly sent me much interesting material on Mick the Miller.

I am especially grateful to Mrs Lily Moore and to Fr Thomas Brophy, parish priest at Baltinglass, for use of the very rare photograph of his uncle, Fr Martin Brophy, breeder of Mick the Miller.

I must also express my thanks to F.J. Underhill, secretary of the National Greyhound Racing Club, and to H.W. Cox for their patience in answering my many questions; to Bord Na gCon, the Greyhound Racing Board of Ireland; and to Commandant J.M. Fitzpatrick, secretary of the Irish Coursing Club of Clonmel who through the years has provided answers to my many queries. I have enjoyed my greyhound racing in Ireland as much as in England. At one time or another I have been a visitor to most of the Irish tracks and seen many of their finest racing greyhounds but my greatest pleasure has been from the warmth of the hospitality received in the homes of many owners and breeders and of those only remotely connected with greyhound racing. They could not have been kinder and nowhere are the people better informed about greyhounds than in the bars of Longford, Mullingar, Tralee and Clonmel, where I have spent many a happy evening.

The Irish have had the good sense to retain the old race measurements in yards, and even the starting boxes occupy the same position they did when greyhound racing began there in 1927, so that one may compare the times of modern champions winning, say, at Shelbourne Park in 1980 with the times achieved by Mick the Miller in his trials there fifty years earlier. Such continuity makes for greater enjoyment of greyhound racing in our rapidly changing world, and in Ireland the lengths of races can still be counted on the fingers of one hand. In Britain, the change to the metric system was one that no follower of the sport wanted and there are now more than a hundred different lengths to contend with. If it was thought necessary to change to the metric system (and none of the chief greyhound racing countries of the world use this system) it should have been possible for the tracks to race over standard lengths such as 450 or 500 m, 600 m, and 700 m. Now distances are virtually meaningless and the new track records cannot be compared with those run prior to the changeover in 1975.

This book has taken several years to prepare and write, during which time I have checked and re-checked many times all the information I have collected during a lifetime as an enthusiast of the sport. Inevitably, though, there will be inaccuracies and omissions, and to those concerned I apologise. I shall be grateful for any corrections readers are able to make and for any information that should have been included, in the hope that it may appear in a future edition of the book.

Roy Genders
January 1981

ALPHABETICAL LIST OF ENTRIES

A

AGE

A greyhound's age is taken from the first day of the month in which it was born, even if it was actually born on the last day. The minimum age at which a greyhound may run on all tracks controlled by the NGRC is fifteen months.

The age at which a greyhound reaches its peak varies enormously. Dolores Rocket was only two years three months when she won the 1971 Derby, and the 1977 final was dominated by young dogs all under thirty months old; Ballybeg Grand was the oldest at just on thirty months, while Mr R. Bacci's Balliniska Band, who won the event, was only two years one month and the youngest-ever winner of the Derby. Saucy Buck was only one year eleven months. In general a greyhound will usually be at its best when two and a half to three and a half years old, though bitches often take longer than dogs to reach their full potential. Unwin Beauty, that great long-distance bitch, was almost five when she won the Cobb Marathon Bowl, and Robeen Printer the same age when successful in the Winter Stayers Cup at Stamford Bridge. The in-season rest of bitches enables them to race longer than most dogs, but Sherry's Prince was five when he won the third of his consecutive Grand Nationals, and Mick the Miller the same age when winning the St Leger at Wembley, his last race.

Mick lived to the age of thirteen, as did Davesland, winner of the 1934 Derby, and Shove Ha'penny, while Creamery Border was only a few days short of his fourteenth birthday when he died in 1945. More recently, Hi There lived to be fifteen. Those great sires Castledown Lad and Beef Cutlet reached the age of eleven, likewise Border Mutton, Ataxy and Manhattan Midnight. Bitches live a little longer, many up to fourteen or fifteen, and will produce litters to the age of twelve or thirteen when their racing days are over. At this age the

Opposite: Two immortal 'millers': Mick the Miller and Golden Miller.

Waterloo Cup winner Czarina became the mother of the famous Snowball. Direct Lead was ten when she whelped Booked Six, and had another litter afterwards.

Ages to which Some Famous Greyhounds Lived

	years		years
AprilBurglar	10	Hi There	15
Ataxy	11	Junior Classic	10
Beef Cutlet	12	Kilrea Lad	14
Border Mutton	12	Manhattan Midnight	10
Castledown Lad	12	Mick the Miller	13
Davesland	14	Pigalle Wonder	13
Grand Flight II	12	Roeside Creamery	10
Hack Up Chieftan	13	Shove Ha'penny	13

AGENT

An owner (who may have to be abroad for an extended period) may appoint and register an authorized agent to act for him or her in matters connected within the rules of racing.

AILMENTS AND DISEASES

The highly bred greyhound is more prone to ailments and diseases than most other dogs. A greyhound of any class at all is now expensive to buy and to run and it is more important than ever that the dog is kept as free as possible from everyday aches and pains caused when out exercising or when racing, so that he is not off the racing strength for long periods. All credit is due to the trainers who spend long hours grooming and massaging their charges to keep them in peak condition, often for twelve months or more at a stretch, before they need to allow the hounds a well earned rest. If trainers were paid by the hour for the time they spend on each greyhound, the cost of kennelling would be more than doubled and trainers would be wealthier than most of them are.

It is now expensive to rear a young greyhound for track racing. A well bred bitch for breeding may cost several hundred pounds, depending on her track career and pedigree, and the fee for her service when she comes in season may be £100 or even twice that sum. In addition there will be the expense of feeding and care until she whelps, and if she has five pups they will each have

cost at least £80–90. By the time they are ten or twelve weeks old and ready for sale they will have cost another £20–25 each, for although they will have been fed for much of the time on their mother's milk she will have cost £10–12 a week to feed on a nourishing diet with brown bread and biscuits and ample supplies of milk. If the pups are reared to racing age they will have cost at least £200 each, and so no chances must be taken with their health. They will require frequent visits from the vet, who will inoculate them against a number of puppy diseases at the correct age; this, too, costs money. There is also their registration with the English or Irish Stud Book and fees for their naming and markings.

Regular use of the local vet is very important, not only for inoculations. Whenever a dog is off-colour and does not respond quickly to treatment, the vet should be called in. His fee is small compared to the cost of buying a greyhound or rearing a litter of pups, and if he is called in without undue delay the life of a greyhound may well be saved. The two finest greyhounds during the early years of the sport, Mick the Miller and Creamery Border, were both saved by 'Doc' Callanan when their breeders asked him to treat the two dogs when puppies. The fee (if one was charged among friends) was a small price to pay for saving the life of those outstanding greyhounds.

If a greyhound shows signs of being off-colour, first take its temperature. Have someone hold the dog with its body between their legs and with a firm grip on its head or collar. When the dog is still, insert a half-minute thermometer smeared with Vaseline into the dog's rectum for at least an inch, and hold it in place for a full minute. A dog in good health will record a temperature of 101.4° F (38.5° C). If it is above 103° F (39.5° C) or below 97° F (36° C) something is wrong, especially if the animal appears listless and is off its food. Give no exercise and place the dog in a warm isolation kennel, providing him with plenty of clean straw and fresh water, and a coat to wear if the weather is cold. If he does not respond to this treatment within forty-eight hours, call in the vet.

INOCULATION

The chief diseases which attack young greyhounds are distemper in its several forms, hepatitis or jaundice, and leptospirosis or leptospiral jaundice. Each can be fatal, and every puppy should be inoculated against them at an early age. During the first two months of a puppy's life it receives almost complete immunity through its mother's milk, but as soon as taken from its mother, which may be between six and twelve weeks old depending upon the bitch's health and her supply of milk, a puppy should receive its first inoculation as a matter of routine. The first is given at eight to nine weeks and Kavak MiHL will give a general immunity against the main diseases. In another four weeks a second immunization is given, which should see the puppies through to the time of their first trials. It is, however, advisable to have the vet give them a 'booster' immunization when thirteen or fourteen months old, six to eight weeks before they begin trials. They will then be over the effects before they begin racing. As with some humans, inoculations may knock greyhounds off their stride for a few days. They may show signs of shivering and be off their food, and should not be exercised until this condition has passed. Keep them in a warm kennel with plenty of fresh water and the effect will soon pass.

COUGHS

The trouble is caused by a virus which affects the respiratory system and may also damage the lung tissues. It is usually more troublesome during the winter months but an outbreak may occur at any time, and once a dog begins coughing the trouble may quickly spread through the whole kennel range. Any greyhound that starts coughing must be withdrawn from racing and kept in his kennel with plenty of dry bedding. It is also advisable to put on a coat if the weather is cold. Feed plenty of warm, nourishing meat gravy enriched with Oxo or Bovril and give a teaspoonful of brandy in warm milk every four hours. Give exercise only when the day is mild. Let fresh air into the kennel but guard against draughts.

New vaccines from the USA are now being used in Britain to immunize greyhounds from this troublesome ailment, but it is too early yet to say whether they are effective. If a greyhound goes down with a cough, call in the vet without delay and follow his advice. Your vet will also be able to advise on the use of the new vaccines.

DIARRHOEA

This is a common problem with greyhounds and is usually caused by worms or by feeding stale food, or by the dogs picking up stale food when out exercising. It can even be caused by a chill and it does not necessarily mean the animal has contracted distemper or jaundice. The condition needs careful observation and the diarrhoea needs clearing up without delay for nothing pulls a dog down more quickly if unchecked. Diarrhoea is sometimes accompanied by vomiting and may be caused by something the dog has picked up which is causing irritation in the intestines. To clear this, give the dog a dessertspoonful of castor oil and starve him for twelve hours for the oil to have the desired effect. Keep the dog in his kennel and give more straw for warmth. Then give twice daily ten grains of carbonate of bismuth with six drops of chlorodyne, or give a teaspoonful each of port and brandy in a little warm milk twice daily. Repeat these doses until the trouble has cleared, which may take several days, but if by then it has not cleared up call in the vet, for it may be the start of a more serious illness.

Do not give solid food to a dog with diarrhoea – provide nothing more than a little warm milk and then biscuit or brown bread with a little meat extract. Give little or no exercise until the trouble has quite cleared.

If the dog does not respond to either of the simple remedies, it means that he is suffering from a bacterial infection and will need a drug such as Trevetrin, an antibiotic, given under vet's prescription, to clear up the trouble.

DISTEMPER

This disease is caused by a virus and has a number of forms. It is characterized by high temperature, loss of appetite, and a languid condition. The incubation period is eight to ten days, when the dog's nose will be warm and he will shiver, even when the weather is warm. Vomiting and diarrhoea may also occur. Call in the vet immediately.

The distemper will take one of several forms, each of which will cause the dog great distress and will often prove fatal. In any case it will take a racing greyhound some months to recover fully, if it ever does, and for a greyhound to be struck down with distemper when it has begun trials or is about to do so will mean that, even if he recovers in due time, he will have missed possibly the best years of his life as a racing greyhound. Immunization is therefore essential from an early age.

The disease may occur as:

(a) *Catarrhal distemper*, which affects the membrane of the nose, the eyes and possibly the lungs.

(b) *Abdominal distemper*, which affects the intestines.

(c) *Rash distemper*, which affects the upper parts of the abdomen and inside the legs, especially the back legs.

(d) *Cerebral distemper*, which affects the brain and the legs, causing the nose and the pads of the feet to become hard. It is the most dangerous form, usually fatal, and even though a dog may recover it will be of no use for racing. This form of the disease is also known as hard pad.

All forms of distemper are highly infectious, being carried in the saliva of dogs and in urine and faeces. Dogs roaming the streets can pick it up anywhere. For this reason all greyhounds when out walking should be on a lead or chain and the kennels must be kept scrupulously clean, regularly washed down with disinfectant and cleaned out every day, with fresh, clean straw for the dogs to sleep on. Also be sure to keep eating and drinking utensils absolutely clean. Wash them after every meal and see that a daily supply of fresh water is available. Be sure that all types of food fed to dogs is absolutely fresh and free from contamination.

In *catarrhal distemper* there is a discharge from the eyes and nose, and the bronchial tubes may become blocked. Pneumonia may follow in a few days. Warmth is the key to treating this form. Put a warm coat on the animal and give more bedding. If the weather is cold hang a hurricane lamp from the roof of the kennel. Keep the eyes clear of the discharge by regularly bathing them with a warm solution of boric acid, gently applied with cotton wool. The M & B 693 drug will help to control the disease and should be given under vet's prescription. Provide the dog with an invalid's diet consisting of brown bread or biscuit soaked in warm milk or meat juice, to which a little Bovril has been added, but feed no solid meat. Beat up a fresh egg in milk, adding a few drops of brandy, and give this last thing at night when looking in to see that the dog is comfortable. A sick dog may need coaxing with his food and will usually respond to a little extra attention at this time. If a dog refuses to eat, his strength will be maintained by giving a nutrient enema. Use a pint of clean warm water, to which a little salt has been added. Above all keep the dog warm, though this does not mean a stuffy atmosphere. Fresh air must be admitted to his kennel, but not draughts. The ventilator should be opened on the leeward side and should be high off the ground. Give no exercise until the dog's temperature is back to normal and the symptoms have fully cleared. Then give a little gentle exercise, keeping the dog on the lead, whenever the weather is mild. His exercise can be increased a little each day and likewise the food intake, and the dog should have fully recovered within a month or so.

Abdominal or gastric distemper is a more virulent form, characterized by vomiting and loose bowels, in which blood is often present. The dog will have an unquenchable thirst and will take no food. A teaspoonful each of port and brandy in a little warm milk will help to control the diarrhoea. Otherwise give the dog similar treatment as for catarrhal distemper, keeping the animal warm and his kennel absolutely clean. Always burn the straw which is removed from kennels.

With *rash distemper*, the dog will first show signs of shivering and will go off his food. Later, eruptions will appear on his skin, under the legs and on the abdomen. Again, keep the dog warm and give a sloppy but nourishing diet. To relieve the irritation rub the infected parts with ointment containing Gamma BHC.

Cerebral distemper or hard pad is by far the worst form and the most difficult to cure, frequently resulting in death. Even if the dog recovers, the disease may cause paralysis of the limbs or blindness later and the dog will have to be put down. Greyhounds which have hard pad rarely, if ever, race again, so that immunization at the puppy stage should be done as routine. This only became possible in the postwar years when safe and reliable vaccines were discovered, and puppy mortality has since been greatly reduced.

The first symptoms of this distemper are seen when the dog becomes listless and goes off his food. Shivering begins and then fits, and soon he may become unable to stand. Later, the skin of the nose and pads of the feet become hardened and the dog will start to twitch. Even if, by careful nursing, the dog recovers, it will be only partial and a year later the dog may still twitch and shake. Keep the dog warm and get him (by opening his mouth) to take a little brandy and warm milk every three to four hours. If he is going to recover, this will be indicated after two or three weeks by his beginning to take more interest in food. He should then be given biscuit mixed with meat extract or warm milk every three hours. Then begin feeding a little minced meat.

For all greyhounds recovering from distemper, care is as important during the convalescence period as during the illness. Over-exertion is fatal. Do not begin exercising until the dog is completely over the trouble and has begun a proper intake of food. Then exercise only for a few minutes, perhaps twice daily, whenever the weather is mild, and only on the lead. Not for several weeks must the dog be allowed to run loose, but if all seems well increase the exercise a little each day until the dog is ready to rejoin the others for their daily exercise. If the dog succumbs to one of the milder forms of distemper as he nears or has reached racing age, he should be given at least another ten to twelve weeks to recuperate fully, to put on weight and build up his muscles before being given his first solo trial. To push him at this stage will be to undo all the care given him during his illness and convalescence.

Remember that a certificate of inoculation and freedom from illness signed by a vet is required from the owner of any greyhound entering kennels of a licensed track or trainer, and the dogs are required to have booster inoculations every twelve to eighteen months.

Today, the tissue-culture vaccines give more rapid and effective control than the older egg-adapted vaccines, and modern vaccines such as Kavak DiHL, Canilen-D.D, and Epivax TC-plus will also give immunity from hepatitis and leptospiral jaundice, the other most troublesome greyhound diseases.

EARS

Earache will make a dog lie on its side and rub its ear on the turf, or rub its head with its paw to try to ease the pain. The animal may also shake its head and will begin to go off its food. The cause may be some foreign body entering its ear or a cold or chill; alternatively, the dog may have picked up the bacterial infection which gives rise to the trouble known as otitis. Earache may even be caused by parasites, whose presence will be diagnosed by a watery discharge from the ear. Call in the vet at once. He will inspect the ear through magnifying instruments and prescribe accordingly, and will give any treatment necessary. If parasites are the problem, an otodectic mange preparation will be recommended.

The trouble may be due to ear canker, an inflammation of the membrane or skin lining of the ear which causes the dog to shake its head. First give the dog a worming to clear its system of the parasites which caused the trouble, then a few drops of nitrate of soda solution prescribed by the vet should be carefully dropped into each ear. Do this on alternate days for a week or so. The cure is complete when the dog stops shaking and rubbing its head. Have someone hold the dog's head firmly when you are administering the drops. Keep the dog warm and quiet during the next few days to allow the solution to work.

If a dog's ear is sore from rubbing with its paw, dry it with boracic powder or a similar preparation.

ECLAMPSIA

Not a common trouble but a most dangerous one, which may overcome a bitch feeding a large litter. She will be troubled with her breathing and take on a staring expression. Convulsions may follow, which may last for several hours. In a bad attack she may fall into a coma and die. The cause is a simple one – lack of calcium in her diet. From the time of mating a considerable drain has been imposed on the calcium in her body, first in forming her pups and then in the milk they take from her. Additional supplies are essential from the start of pregnancy. Milk contains natural calcium but she will need this supplemented by calcium lactate tablets. Give three or four a day with her feed. In cases of urgency call in the vet, who will inject into her veins a solution of thirty grains of calcium chloride dissolved in one fluid ounce of warm water. This will take immediate effect and will usually save her life.

ENTERITIS

With the recent introduction of more effective vaccines for distemper in young greyhounds, enteritis has become the most common cause of illness and deaths among all classes of greyhound. Possibly without any loss of condition or appetite, a greyhound will vomit food and begin to scour. The incubation period is seven to eight days and the trouble may last for the same length of time. If not taken in hand at once, death may soon follow, for rapid loss of weight and dehydration occur. If treated without delay, within a month the dog should be back racing. Although the dog will lose weight, it will soon be put back with careful feeding. There will be no lasting effect.

Call in the vet at once and he will inject into the veins a dextrose solution which will maintain the dog's strength. Solid food must be avoided for fear of putting undue strain on the dog's stomach. A little warm water containing bicarbonate of soda, or a little warm tea sweetened with sugar, may be given every four hours. The tannic acid in tea will help to stay any discharge of blood in the dog's droppings.

Enteritis often occurs in damp, cold, foggy weather and is most prevalent from December to February. The best prevention is a warm, dry kennel with plenty of dry straw; rub down the dog after exercise or if it gets wet, and feed plenty of hot food.

As the trouble subsides, begin feeding a little beef tea extract mixed with brown bread or any of the recognized brands of milk food. Then gradually build up the dog's strength by providing a more substantial diet such as minced meat with a raw egg and meal or brown bread. Give no violent exercise for several more weeks. Just walk the dog on a lead whenever the day is mild.

In cold, wet weather it is advisable to keep the dog in a warm, dry kennel.

Dysentery is a mild form of enteritis and is treated in the same way. If in doubt as to a greyhound's health, call in the vet. His fee will be small compared to the loss of a high-class dog who may win large sums while racing and even more in stud fees.

EYES

A greyhound's eyes are all-important and weekly bathing in dilute boric acid solution will keep them free from grit which may enter the eyes when running on a sanded surface. It will also ease irritation of the eyelids caused when grit particles become lodged under the lids. If the eyes become inflamed, apply eye ointment made up to the vet's prescription. Place a small amount of the ointment in the inner corner of the eye and gently massage it in over the closed eyelids.

HYSTERIA

This complaint is also known as acidity, because it is caused by a too acid stomach as a result of incorrect feeding. Acidity upsets the function of the stomach and kidneys, causing indigestion and headaches, which in turn bring on hysteria and fits – puppies will run round in circles and bark excitedly before lying or falling down exhausted. They recover after a few minutes but may show similar signs again after a few hours. Acidity also causes eczema, of which prevention is better and easier than cure.

It is most important to feed puppies and adult dogs with wholemeal bread or biscuits, because modern white bread is treated with a bleach called nitrogen trichloride which makes it extremely acid and indigestible. Constipation results and the intestines become troubled with bacteria. In the early days of the sport, hysteria was rare, for most bread was then wholemeal.

Puppies are more prone to hysteria than adult dogs. Feeding them with plenty of milk or Glaxo will provide them with the necessary calcium, and all greyhounds benefit from a small handful of bonemeal or steamed bone flour added to their morning milk feed.

Should an outbreak of hysteria occur, it can be quickly corrected by giving each dog a teaspoonful of this preparation, about half an hour after the morning and evening food for several days when the trouble should have cleared:

Bicarbonate of soda	2 drachms
Tincture of rhubarb	4 drachms
Bismuth	6 drachms

dissolved in six fluid ounces of water.

JAUNDICE

There are two forms: (a) catarrhal jaundice, and (b) infective jaundice, also called leptospirosis, which is worse.

Catarrhal jaundice is diagnosed when the dog is off his food and the whites of the eyes become yellow. This is often accompanied by bleeding gums and a high temperature. Isolate the dog at once, since all forms of jaundice are contagious. Put on a warm coat and increase the bedding. Give two grains of calomel every four hours for two days; then give one grain for the next two days. Place fresh water in the kennel but give no solid food, although a teaspoonful of brandy in a little warm milk every 4 hours will do much to get the dog through his illness.

Infective jaundice or leptospirosis is more dangerous and may be caused by rats, which carry the germ – always keep a sharp lookout for any rat droppings in or near the kennels. If you notice any call in the Local Authority's pest control officer who will exterminate them. This type of jaundice may be spread through a dog's urine. The symptoms are similar to those of catarrhal jaundice but are more severe and the vet should be called in at once. He will give the dog a 10 cc injection of leptospira serum daily for three consecutive days, but as prevention is so much better than cure all pups should be immunized at twelve weeks with Epivax TC vaccine. Older dogs should also receive immunization if they were not given it as puppies.

KENNEL SICKNESS

This is not a disease but a condition, which is dealt with by disinfecting the kennels with formaldehyde, Sterizal or Jeyes' Fluid. The kennels should be left for at least two to three weeks before they are used again, to allow any fumes to escape. It is advisable in any case to give wooden kennels an occasional 'rest' period, leaving the doors and windows open and putting a blow lamp over the inside walls to burn off harmful bacteria. Afterwards, wash down the walls with disinfectant and leave the kennel empty for two to three weeks.

During summer, flies may cause irritation to the dogs. Give the kennels a daily application of a fly-killing aerosol when the dogs are out exercising. Flies, too, spread disease if unchecked.

The dogs' muzzles, leads and collars should be regularly disinfected and their coats washed in a bactericide solution. Dipping each dog's paws into a solution containing hexachloraphene should be done each day as routine when the dogs return from their exercise. It is important to wash feeding utensils after every meal, and for kennel staff to wash their hands in disinfectant after attending to the dogs and before preparing their meals. Regular digging and re-seeding of kennel runs at least once a year will help keep them free of parasites which may enter the dogs' intestines.

Kennel sickness used to be more prevalent than it is today, chiefly because wooden kennels were used for very many years before they were replaced. The use of contract kennels in recent years has done much to reduce the trouble, but everyone who has kennels, whether for boarding or training greyhounds, should always aim to maintain the highest standard of hygiene.

Kennel sickness may be the cause of a greyhound for no apparent reason showing signs of fatigue when coming in from gentle exercise. He will go off his food and in a day or so vomiting and diarrhoea may occur. All forms of exercise must be stopped and the dog should be isolated to prevent the sickness spreading through the kennels. Give the affected dog a teaspoonful each of port and brandy in warm milk and feed no solids for several days. Put on a warm coat and give extra bedding but maintain a fresh atmosphere in the kennel. Prevention, however, is easier than cure, and bouts of kennel sickness should never occur if proper precautions are taken.

MANGE

There are two forms of this irritating and debilitating skin disease – sarcoptic, and follicular or demodectic. Dogs with either kind of mange should be isolated immediately, before treatment commences.

Demodectic mange, the more difficult of the two to cure, is characterized by black discoloration of the skin and the presence of the parasite in the dog's hair. Treatment should be given as soon as the disease is observed, using Cooper's demodectic mange shampoo and ointment.

Sarcoptic mange is caused by a parasite which burrows into the skin, making it wrinkle and thicken. The female lays three or four eggs on the body of the dog which hatch out in about ten days. The larvae then burrow into the skin causing irritation which makes the dog scratch, resulting in sores. It is a very contagious form but is not difficult to control. First give the dog a warm bath containing Cooper's No.2 Skin Shampoo, which includes Gamma BHC. Then rub on to the affected parts an ointment containing Gamma BHC. Leave this on for three days and repeat until the trouble has cleared, which may take two weeks.

As prevention is so much easier than cure, all greyhounds should be given a bath containing Gamma BHC solution every two months. Kennel cleanliness is also important. Use clean straw for bedding and remove and burn it at least every other day. Wash down the walls of the kennels regularly with disinfectant.

NAILS

Greyhounds need more regular attention with their nails than any other breed, for no dog can run well with long nails which will tear if not kept well trimmed, or may result in dislocated toes and cramped feet. A greyhound must feel comfortable when exercising and racing, otherwise he will not run at his best. Inspect the feet and nails every day when the dog returns from exercise and trim back the nails each week – not so far as to cause soreness, but just enough to prevent the nails being a hindrance when running. Special nail clippers are available from good pet shops and should always be carried in a trainer's pocket.

NERVOUSNESS

This is a condition rather than an ailment and is usually caused by the dog being ill-treated or frightened. A long journey unattended may cause a greyhound to show fear on arrival at a kennels. I recall a bitch arriving at my own kennels who began trembling with fear and refused to eat when her food was put in front of her. Eventually a round dish was substituted for the square one we had given her, and the bitch lost all trace of fear and ate ravenously. Evidently where she had come from — and perhaps been ill-treated — a square dish had been used for her food.

The condition calls for a heavy dose of vitamin B1 — as many as fifty tablets on arrival — followed by five or six tablets a day for a month. For the first few days in the kennels, give two or three bromide tablets each evening to quieten the animals before going to sleep, and if possible put the greyhounds in a kennel away from noises such as a barking dog or roadside traffic.

Gentle exercise can begin after a week, and the muscles should be massaged twice daily. After four weeks discontinue the vitamin treatment and add a few drops of Phospherine to the drinking water each day. This preparation was used by a trainer who was a household name in North Country greyhound circles, and he believed it acted as a wonderful tonic.

PARVOVIRUS

Due to lack of knowledge of this killer disease which first made its presence felt in Britain in 1979, and the difficulty of introducing suitable vaccines, many young greyhounds are dying each day from parvovirus. It mostly attacks young dogs, though this is not always the case, and it is so infectious that it may be introduced into kennels by visitors coming to see their greyhounds, or even by tradesmen delivering goods, the virus being taken in on the soles of their shoes. Dogs out exercising may also pick up the disease from the urine or droppings of other dogs. If exercising in the streets, dogs must be kept on a lead and, if possible, taken where few other dogs are seen. A country lane is a better place to exercise a dog than a town street.

The disease was first located by veterinary scientists at Cornell University, USA, late in 1978 and until recently no suitable vaccine had been developed. It had, however, been established that feline enteritis vaccine, used for some years to protect cats from a similar virus. would give part-immunisation to dogs. Fortunately, a vaccine has now been developed specifically for dogs by the Dufa Company of Amsterdam. It is available from vets and costs about £10 for an injection.

The virus attacks all dogs at an early age, often when no more than six or seven weeks old or at about the time the pups are ready to leave their mother. They will become listless, then begin vomiting their food and this is followed by diarrhoea and loss of weight. Soon the virus will affect the heart muscles and this will be followed by total collapse of the animal. Once an outbreak occurs there is no cure and should any pup survive it will be so weakened as to be useless for racing.

Strict cleanliness in the kennels is all-important. The shoes of all who enter should be disinfected and every precaution taken in the kennels. But, most important of all, every young greyhound should be inoculated now that vaccine is available.

RHEUMATISM

The trouble may occur if greyhounds are not immediately rubbed down after exercise, if damp litter is used for bedding, or if the kennels themselves are damp. Straw is more moisture-absorbent than hay and should always be used for bedding. It can be bought by the bale from a farmer or corn merchant, and so is easily stored. It should be kept under cover — shake out one bale at a time when needed. Kennels on low-lying, badly drained land will also cause the dogs to be troubled by stiff or rheumatic joints, and no greyhound can perform well in this condition. Keep the dogs dry at all times. For stiff joints, give an aspirin crushed in milk each day for a week and massage the joint morning and evening with equal parts of Elliman's Embrocation and olive oil.

SCOUR

This is a common trouble with puppies at the weaning stage, as they begin to lap cows' milk and are gradually taken from their mother. The longer they can be left with the bitch, the better, but some bitches soon lose their supply of milk and weaning has to be done earlier than expected. The pups will then be deprived of the iron and potassium salts present in their mother's milk. If this is not replaced in some other way, scouring will take place and soon the pups will lose weight.

The iron which helps to bind the bowels is available in Parrish's Chemical Food, which can be given either in the drinking water or in a milk feed. Give a small teaspoonful daily. As it is quite sweet, the pups will eagerly lap it up.

Much of the valuable mineral salts such as iron and calcium, which the bitch needs to pass on to her pups in her milk, will be picked up from herbage while she is out exercising. For this reason a bitch unable to be on grassland at all during her pregnancy will lack these minerals unless she, too, has additional iron and calcium given in her food. This will make all the difference as to whether the pups will scour or not at weaning time, which is always the most difficult in the life of a greyhound. The reason Irish greyhounds are so good is due in no small way to the richness of the land in mineral salts. For more than fifty years Parrish's Chemical Food has been a great standby in rearing healthy greyhounds, for if scouring is left unchecked it can quickly result in the death of a puppy, which at eight to ten weeks old may have cost £100 in stud fees and to rear.

TICKS

These pests cause irritation to a dog's skin if left unchecked. They may be introduced in the straw used for bedding or may attach themselves to the greyhound while it is exercising in long grass. They feed on the dog's blood, and if you see a dog scratching take a look at that particular part for you can see the pests in the hair with the naked eye. With a piece of cotton wool soaked in methylated spirits or benzol, 'dab' the tick(s), and they will fall to the ground.

Routine washing in a Gamma BHC preparation or dusting the dog's coat with Pybuthrin or derris powder (which do not have the toxic effects of DDT) will keep a dog free of lice and ticks. Kennel cleanliness will also help.

TRACK LEG

This trouble is common among racing greyhounds who run round the bends at high speed, and is caused by the left elbow rubbing the left hind leg. The symptom is a swelling above the hock. Racing greyhounds have either a right- or left-hand galloping action, and it is the left-handed galloper, which puts his weight on the left side as he moves round the track in an anti-clockwise direction, which is troubled by track leg. It may keep a dog off racing for a few weeks.

The best treatment is to apply hot fomentations two or three times daily until the trouble clears up. Then give a gentle massage with a mixture of embrocation and olive oil. But the great healer is rest, so allow the dog very little exercise until it clears — no more than a daily walk on a lead.

WORMS

Puppies pick up worms from an early age and if not quickly and regularly eradicated they will soon reduce the pups to skin and bone. There are three types of worms: hookworms, roundworms, and tapeworms. They are picked up in grass and soil and from faeces, and at some time or other all pups will become infested.

The *hookworm* attaches itself on to the walls of the intestines where it lays its eggs, causing looseness of the bowels. The animal will become thin and go off its food. Fits and hysteria may follow.

The *roundworm* is the most common type and may be from one to six inches long. Suspect roundworms if the pups have bad breath, loose bowels and a rough or staring coat.

Until the introduction of Bayer's Droncit in 1979, *tapeworm* was difficult to treat. The pest is carried to the intestines of the dog by fleas or by eggs laid on grass, or perhaps in the water drunk while the dog is out exercising. The dog soon goes off its food and becomes thin and listless. One tablet of Droncit given after twelve hours' fasting is generally sufficient to expel all tapeworms, and no unpleasant side-effects are known. It used to be normal to dose a dog for tapeworm once a week for three to four weeks, but this lengthy treatment is now unnecessary.

WOUNDS

At any time while racing or out exercising, a dog may receive a gash on its leg, perhaps caused by wire or a sharp piece of wood or even by another dog. It should receive immediate attention. Deep cuts may require stitching and it will be advisable to call in the vet. If the injury can be dealt with satisfactorily without a vet, first clean the wound by gently shaving away the hair from around it. Have someone hold the dog while you do this. Then thoroughly wash the wound with warm water containing Dettol, Lysol or Jeyes' Fluid. If the injury is still bleeding, stop the flow of blood by applying tight pressure above the wound (if on the leg) until the haemorrhage subsides. Then bandage the leg and leave the dog in its kennel for a day or two until the blood clots. Give the dog a teaspoonful of brandy in warm milk and let it rest. If the weather is cold, put on a coat or give extra straw for bedding. An injured dog should always be put in a kennel on its own so that it cannot play with other dogs, which would delay the healing process.

After forty-eight hours, inspect the wound again and clear it of any clotting blood which will harbour bacteria if not removed and might cause septicaemia. Then apply a healing dressing and keep the dog in its kennel for a further forty-eight hours until the wound begins to knit together. A little gentle exercise can then be given each day.

AIR TRAVEL

It is now common practice for greyhounds to be exported by air to all parts of the globe, and for greyhounds to be transported back and forth from England to Ireland by air. The Warrington dog Clady Border set the fashion and is believed to be the first in the British Isles to have travelled by air to a meeting, when in July 1946 he went from Manchester Airport to Belfast to take part in an event at Celtic Park the following day. His trainer, Ken Newham, reported that the dog greatly enjoyed his experience and won the event.

A few weeks later the Irish Derby winner Lilac's Luck, kennelled at Doncaster, flew to Belfast for the National Sprint at Dunmore Park and reached the final.

The *Irish Press* for 30 October 1946 included a photograph of a Pan-American World Airways stewardess with several of twelve Irish greyhounds which had just left the plane upon arrival at La Guardia Airfield, New York, after their flight from Shannon. But Farnane Sweeper was the first to fly the Atlantic, accompanied by his owner, Mike Duffy of Limerick in August 1946.

AMERICA
See Greyhound Racing in America

ANALYSIS OF SAMPLES

Local stewards have power at any time to order an examination and test samples of any greyhound due to take part in, or which has taken part in, any race or trial. They can order a greyhound to be kept under surveillance for as long as necessary for such examination or tests to be made by the taking of any sample of vomit, urine, blood or any body fluid, in the presence of the owner, trainer or kennelhand, or in the presence of a local steward who will ensure that all such samples will be kept secure. Any sample taken will be despatched for analysis as the NGRC stewards may direct. Pending the result, local stewards have power to order the greyhound to be withdrawn from any trial or race. This will be shown on its identity book.

All approved tracks have now installed a chromatography unit, enabling pre-race samples to be taken from all greyhounds running at each meeting, and this is carried out as an additional safeguard for patrons.

APPROVED TRACK

A stadium licensed for racing and approved by the NGRC as being of the standards required for racing.

ARRIAN

Flavius Arrianus was born in Nicomedia in Asia Minor and became a citizen of Athens. Later, through his consular work, he became a Roman citizen and advanced to senatorial dignities. Familiar with the breed since his early days, he wrote the earliest known treatise on the greyhound (the *Cynegeticus*). It was written in the second century AD, when Hadrian was Emperor, though it was not discovered until the late eighteenth century in the Vatican Archives. It was translated by 'A Graduate of Medicine' in 1831 and shows Arrian as a most humane man and great lover of greyhounds.

ATTENDANCES

In 1927, the first full season of track racing

in England, with a full programme at Belle Vue, White City, Harringay and elsewhere, 5,656,686 people paid to go through the turnstiles. Five years later this figure had risen to 20,176,260. Another five years later the 25 million mark had been passed, and by 1945 more than 50 million attended meetings in Britain, with an estimated £5 being spent on betting in that year by each person who visited the tracks, for the tote takings alone were £200 million. Seventy-seven tracks were then licensed by the NGRC. So great were the crowds attending some tracks during the 1940s – as many as 30,000 attended the meetings at White City and Wembley – that the gates were closed long before the first race was started.

By 1960, because so many people now had television, and because a greater variety of outdoor entertainment had become available than during the 1940s and 1950s, attendances had fallen to 14 million from 5,736 meetings in that year and the tote turnover was £54 million. By 1967, although tote turnover from 6,000 meetings had risen to £66 million, attendances were down to 10 million. In 1977, at forty-eight tracks operating under NGRC rules, just over 6½ million attended the 5,847 meetings and tote investment had risen to £70 million. In 1978 total attendances were only just over 6 million from 5,690 meetings. In comparison, in 1970 nearly 900,000 watched the racing at the 1,760 meetings held in the Irish Republic, and almost £10 million was invested on tote betting.

In the USA, greyhound racing is the sixth ranking spectator sport and, though licensed in only twelve of the fifty states, is watched by nearly 20 million each year, the main centres being Massachusetts, Arizona, Kansas and Florida.

Attendances in Britain

Year	Total
1927	5,656,686
1928	13,695,275
1929	15,855,162
1930	17,119,120
1931	17,906,917
1932	20,178,260
1939	26,000,000
1945 (109 tracks)	50,000,000
1960	14,243,808
1967	10,000,000
1971	7,119,398
1975	6,200,118
1976	6,517,864
1977	6,585,491
1978	6,027,327
1979	5,964,323
1980	5,484,781
1981	5,350,000

In Britain in 1978, 48 tracks held 5,688 meetings and the total number of races run was 45,752.

Attendances in the Irish Republic

Year	Total	Meetings
1960	725,500	1,483
1961	800,000	1,612
1962	812,220	1,619
1963	808,818	1,681
1964	841,467	1,814
1965	778,435	1,678
1966	751,768	1,641
1967	752,561	1,702
1968	765,423	1,671
1969	804,733	1,706
1970	868,725	1,760
1971	852,172	1,742
1972	900,129	1,818
1973	973,397	1,946
1974	995,328	1,906
1975	1,074,687	1,971
1976	1,020,492	1,980
1977	895,398	1,828
1978*	951,899	1,950
1979	989,950	1,990
1980	958,072	2,011

* Harold's Cross closed for modernization

In Britain, greyhound racing is the second most widely patronized sport. These are the approximate figures for 1981 for the six most popular spectator sports:

Association football	25,000,000
Greyhound racing: Britain	5,350,000
Ireland	1,000,000
Horse racing: Britain	3,500,000
Ireland	750,000
Rugby football	1,500,000
Cricket	1,250,000
Motor and stock car racing	1,000,000

AUCTION SALES

One method of buying a greyhound is at public auction. You may wish to buy a puppy that has not raced, or a dog with a track record, or perhaps a sire or bitch of good breeding for stud purposes. The greyhound will be sold with a vet's certificate confirming its freedom from illness or injury, and that it is a guaranteed 'non-fighter', unless stated otherwise. Perhaps you will be looking for an older dog which may have been retired from racing through injury but which is otherwise in good health and is being sold as a useful sire, or a bitch which may be retired through injury and is being sold for breeding.

In England, greyhound auctions are held

every month at Hackney Stadium, Waterden Road, London E15, where greyhounds may be purchased for as little as £5 or for more than £1,000. The sales are conducted by IGS (Hackney) Ltd whose managing director is Bill Pountney and auctioneers John Davis and Derek Pugh. The sales are supervised by stewards licensed by the NGRC and there are veterinary surgeons in attendance. Sales commence at 2.00 pm and there are trials of greyhounds at 11.00 am at the Stadium. Many excellent greyhounds have passed through the sales in recent years, including Silver Thoughts who reached the final of the Scottish Derby in 1974 after being purchased for 175 gns. During each year, more than a thousand greyhounds change hands at these auctions.

The sales at Hackney have taken over the auctions held by Freeman, Aldridge Ltd, who for more than 200 years held fortnightly sales of dogs, at first in Upper St Martin's Lane when gun dogs were in vogue and coursing dogs, unwanted by the kennels of wealthy owners, were sold for a few pounds each to followers of the sport. Track racing boosted prices and just before the Second World War Aldridge's moved to bigger premises in William Road, near Euston Station, where for over forty years Harry Lott was the highly respected auctioneer whose own valuation of every dog he sold was of great help to the many potential buyers who crowded the main hall for every sale.

Many famous greyhounds came up for sale at Aldridge's, including Dark Shadow, winner of the Irish St Leger in 1945, and Magic Bohemian, shortly afterwards to become the fastest greyhound in the world over 525 yds. Mrs Sanderson purchased Derryboy Jubilee at Aldridge's for 1,250 gns, the highest price ever paid at Aldridge's. He turned out to be one of the greatest hurdlers ever, repaying his purchase price many times over. But not all greyhounds made such high prices. Gladstone Brigadier was purchased in May 1943 for 125 gns and the next year won the Scottish Derby, while Danielli's son, Train, made only 78 gns when bought during the war years and was to become one of the most successful of all sires, repaying his purchase price a hundred-fold. Another excellent purchase was made when Mr Dent bid 18 gns for Pretty Nell at the Upper St Martin's Lane saleroom in December 1881. She was to become the dam of Bit of Fashion who divided the Waterloo Cup in 1885 and who, in turn, became even more famous as the dam of Fullerton, four times consecutive winner of the Waterloo Cup. The bitch, Kitshine, purchased at Aldridge's for 3½ gns, won the Oaks and Laurels for Mr Presman within twelve months.

Yet for all these successes, Aldridge's achieved special fame for the puppies and saplings (four to fourteen months old) sold at auction and which always created great interest, especially the late Mr D.K. Steadman's litters which earned big money. His litter of seven dogs and three bitches by April Burglar out of Maesydd Maewest sold in March 1943 when twelve months old for 2,180 gns, more than 200 guineas each, but among them was Maesydd Michael, winner of the Waterloo Cup in 1945, and Humming Bee, who won the Hackney Cup at Clapton in 1946, so they were cheap at the price. The last of Beef Cutlet's offspring (out of the bitch May Hasty), whelped in March 1942, made 1,020 gns when sold a year later. The twice Waterloo Cup winner, Swinging Light, one of the greatest coursing dogs of all time, was purchased at Aldridge's as a sapling by Mr Molyneux Cohen, and many an untried greyhound sold at Aldridge's turned out to be a winner.

Aldridge's held greyhound sales every fortnight throughout the year when about 150 dogs were auctioned. Sales commenced at 12.00 noon and ended about 5.00 pm, and 10 per cent was deducted from the sale price for the auctioneer's fee. Catalogues were sent out a week before the sale and cost 6d post free, and each dog's career was given in some detail. Preceding the main sale was a sale of books on greyhounds, stop-watches leather goods and kennel equipment such as coats and mincers.

Back in the present, Messrs Hall, Wateridge and Owen of Shrewsbury hold sales throughout the year at a number of tracks, including the pre-Derby sales at the White City. Others are held at Belle Vue and Shawfield, Glasgow. For all greyhounds sold at over £100 the auctioneers will refund the purchase price and take back the greyhound should it turn out to be a fighter.

In April 1977 White City held their first

public auction of greyhounds since 1939. High prices were obtained, including 4,750 gns paid by Mr David Drinkwater, the highest price paid for a greyhound at auction in Britain. Ella's Champion made 3,100 gns and Sheksburn Mint, 2,200 gns.

One of the most recent and profitable purchases at Shelbourne Park Sales was the dog Jon Barrie who won the 1980 Northern Flat Championship at Belle Vue by four lengths to give his owner, Terry Hawkshaw, the £2,000 first prize. The previous year, the dog won Powderhall's famous Edinburgh Cup, and by the end of 1980 he had won nearly £10,000 so that his purchase price of 1,300 gns was re-paid many times over. In addition, he should be well patronized when retired to stud.

In Ireland, the main auction rooms for greyhounds in the early years of the sport were Goff's of Dublin, while sales have been conducted at Shelbourne Park two days a week throughout the year since the track opened. The tremendous increase in greyhound prices can be seen when it is realized that in 1942 total sales figures at Shelbourne Park amounted to £16,644. Two years later this had increased to £92,000, and by 1946 it was £150,000. By 1970 sales were worth just double that amount, while 1975 saw a figure of 5,182 greyhounds catalogued, of which half sold for £400,000 (about £200 each).

Sales are also held at Cork, Limerick, Clonmel and Thurles. At Limerick one sale is held each month and 1978 saw 600 greyhounds sold for 73,766 gns, about £130 each. Cork also hold one sale a month, and in 1978 624 sold for 104,546 gns, £175 each.

High prices have always been paid for greyhounds at auction in Ireland. In the 1930s the hurdlers Carpio and Stylish Cutlet made 1,000 gns each, and Faithful Kitty £800. In the 1940s Robeen Printer was sold at auction for 2,000 gns and was cheap at the price, and Cold Christmas, winner of the Irish Oaks in 1946 in record time, made 3,000 gns but died soon after reaching England, her great potential unfulfilled. At the Shelbourne Park sales in 1947 the fawn dog Slaney Record sold for 1,500 gns to race in England, and within the year had earned his new owner exactly that sum in prize money. He was also to become one of the great foundation sires of modern track racing. He continued to race in England until the late summer of 1950 when he was more than six years old, and one of the first bitches he was to serve was Dublin Red. From this mating was born Hi There, possibly the greatest sire of all time, sire of Crazy Parachute, in turn sire of Monalee Champion who was to become sire of the 1971 Irish Derby winner, Sole Aim, and of the 1977 winner, Linda's Champion, and others such as Jimsun, winner of the English Derby, sire of Sarah's Bunny. Hi There's mating to Sally's Gossip was to produce Printer's Prince, sire of Yellow Printer and Newdown Heather who, like Monalee Champion, was to take over Hi There's mantle as the greatest of modern sires. Again, Hi There's mating with Prairie Peg gave another prepotent sire in Prairie Flash, in turn sire of Pastorville Badge, dam of An Tain, dam of Irish Derby winner Tain Mor. Prairie Flash was also sire of the Irish Oaks winner Itsamint, grand dam of the 1979 Oaks winner Nameless Pixie. From that one mating with Dublin Red twenty years ago, Slaney Record has carved his name for all time on the record books of modern greyhound racing.

The Shelbourne Park sales are the largest in the world and take place on Tuesday and Wednesday each week. Pre-sales trials commence at 11.00 am and the auctions about two hours later in the comfort of a warm room with bar and restaurant facilities. Catalogues are issued for each sale, giving full particulars of the greyhounds entered. In attendance at every sale and at the pre-sale trials are the Bord Na gCon's stipendiary stewards, to ensure that everything is conducted to the highest standards and in the interests of both buyer and seller.

Sales of Greyhounds at Shelbourne Park in Recent Years

Year	*Sales*	*Greyhounds catalogued*	*Sold*	*Total*
1973	42	5,678	2,190	283,582 gns
1974	43	5,476	2,227	316,600 gns
1975	40	5,182	2,500	390,000 gns
1976	43	5,631	2,239	471,031 gns
1977	41	6,110	2,293	488,091 gns
1978	47	6,957	2,743	678,159 gns
1979	47	6,743	2,200	661,698 gns
1980	44	6,004	2,047	707,987 gns

The average price per greyhound sold under the hammer in 1973 was £136 and in 1978 was £260.

AUSTRALIA

See Greyhound Racing in Australia.

B

BELLE VUE RACECOURSE
See under British Greyhound Racecourses.

BETTING AND LOTTERIES ACT

By the Act of 1934, for the first time the powers of the Racecourse Betting Control Board were extended to cover greyhound racing and the tracks were allowed to set up a tote and to retain 6 per cent of tote takings for their profit and expenses. By 1971, when the Act was amended, the tracks were allowed to retain 12½ per cent which was later increased to 15 per cent. The amendment also permitted the tracks to hold 130 meetings a year instead of two each week, which has helped them meet ever-increasing overheads.

Under the 1934 Act it was stipulated that 'Betting by way of bookmaking or of a totalizator shall not take place . . . in connection with more than eight races . . . during one continuous period not exceeding four hours,' which has continued until the present day. In the 1947 Budget a 10 per cent tax was imposed on all greyhound betting, causing the tote to pay out very much less to the backer, while there was also less for the tracks to retain to pay overheads, for the 10 per cent tax was deductible before the tracks were allowed to deduct their own 6 per cent. This ruling came into force on 1 January 1948, a time when petrol rationing was ending, enabling people to spend more time in their cars, and television starting up which attracted many away from the sport. The decline in attendances was considerable, and by the 1960 amendment to the Act the tax on on-course betting was fixed at 5 per cent and that on off-course at 6 per cent. Though the reduction has been of some benefit to the tracks, the difference between the on-course and off-course tax of only 1 per cent has not been sufficient to bring back those who deserted the sport for other entertainments such as bingo and football pools, which offer considerably more prize money for a small outlay than can be won at a greyhound meeting. In the USA there is no legalized off-course betting and attendances have increased every year since 1920.

In March 1980 an amendment to the Act received Royal Assent, by which greyhound racecourses were permitted to hold up to 130 meetings each calendar year, each meeting to be of ten races (instead of the previously permitted eight races), and on six special days twenty races could be held. Shortage of greyhounds has prevented many of the tracks from holding the maximum number of races permitted during 1980.

BIGGEST WINNING MARGINS

The biggest winning margin for a classic race was eight lengths by Ballyhennessy Seal, which was the margin each time when winning his heat, semi-final and final for the 1945 Gold Collar at Catford. For each run he was quoted 9–2 on. The biggest win in the the Derby was by Monday's News in 1946 when he defeated Lilac's Luck by seven lengths. When taking the London Cup at Clapton in 1943, Blackwater Cutlet covered the 550 yds course in 31.80 secs to win by twelve lengths from Ballykildare with whom he had dead-heated for the Steward's Cup at Walthamstow the week before. In 1945, in the final of the important Golden Crest at Eastville, Bristol Shannon Shore won by ten lengths from Magic Beau in a new record for 500 yds of 28.76 secs. The first race on a British track was won by the dog Mistley by the big margin of eight lengths.

BIRMINGHAM RACECOURSES
See under British Greyhound Racecourses.

BITCH

Bitches possess exceptional stamina, which they have displayed when winning over the longer distances. Famous examples are Queen of the Suir, Bradshaw Fold and Quarter Day in the early years of the sport, and later Astra, Hurry Kitty, Fair Mistress, Clomoney Grand, Cranog Bet, Westpark Mustard and Dolores Rocket. The longer the distance, the better will a bitch perform, out-staying most dogs. However the sprinters' classic, the Scurry Gold Cup, has been won by a bitch on only three occasions – Monachdy Girl in 1952, Lucky

Joan in 1963, and Foyle Tonic in 1968. Four bitches have won the English Derby – Greta Ranee, Narrogar Ann, Dolores Rocket and Sarah's Bunny (1979), and four have won the Irish Derby – Monologue, Brave Damsel, Catsrock Daisy and Penny County (1979). In 1979, for the first time, a bitch took the premier event both in England and Ireland. In the English St Leger, run over a much longer distance, eight bitches have been successful since the first winner, the bitch Burletta, won in 1928.

Bitches usually have a longer racing life than dogs, simply because they obtain a periodical rest when they come in season. This extends their racing career, unless their owners want to breed from them in which case they may be retired early. A greyhound bitch comes in season once a year, and must then be withdrawn from all racing activities. This means she will do no racing for three months every year. It may be necessary for a racing manager, on the instructions of her trainer, to withdraw a bitch before taking part in a classic event or even from the final when she was thought to have a good chance of winning. This will cause disappointment but against this can be weighed the fact that a bitch may well reach peak condition in her training just before she comes in season each year, when she will often outpace the finest dogs to win events considered beyond her reach. A well cared-for bitch will also greatly benefit from her enforced period of inactivity, from which she will return refreshed. This will usually give her anything up to two extra years of racing.

As soon as discharge from her sexual organs is observed, a bitch will be withdrawn from racing, though this may not be done immediately if a bitch is contesting an important event, for she will suffer no ill effects if kept in training for a few more days. But after several days she must take no further part in racing, and be given only short walks on the lead each day for the next two months. She will then gradually be given a little more exercise, and at the end of another month will be ready to race again, though it will usually be another two months before she is back to her old form. The trainer with probably the greatest knowledge of training and looking after bitches was Jack Harvey of Wembley, who had charge of Ballinasloe Blondie, twice winner of the Oaks. He believed bitches to be more affectionate and less highly strung than dogs and therefore easier to train.

A bitch of good pedigree may be used for breeding when her racing days are over, though if this is intended she must not be over-raced. For preference, use for breeding a litter sister or one of similar blood lines who has not been over-raced, if your racing bitch is a champion on the racecourse. Some will retain their speed and stamina for five or six years, and if it is desirable for them to remain in training for most of this time they may not be suitable for breeding when retired from racing.

When a bitch is used for breeding and put to a sire, she becomes a brood bitch, and is called a dam after she has had (whelped) her pups.

See Brood Bitch; Dam.

BLETCHLEY RACECOURSE

See under British Greyhound Racecourses.

BLOOD LINES

During the past twenty or so years, greater attention has been given by greyhound breeders to the successful combination of various blood lines, with the result that the standard of racing has been considerably improved. There are now more good greyhounds than ever, because breeders are giving more care to their choice of brood bitch and sire. In the 1940s and 1950s the bitches sired by Brilliant Bob, and later Mad Tanist, produced the most outstanding female lines, as more recently did Pigalle Wonder and The Grand Fire, and discerning breeders have noted this. But the female side is only half the story. A suitable sire has to be considered, and it is necessary to discover from a careful study of the pedigree of modern champions those whose breeding would be expected to 'nick in' with the blood lines of the brood bitch.

In the early history of the sport, most of the track stock was provided by the great coursing dogs, such as Jamie (sire of the first track star, Entry Badge), Mutton Cutlet, Danielli, and Inler, who appeared at Wembley in the first years of track racing. These were the foundation sires of the sport. Inler passed on his tremendous speed to Tanist, and to the bitch Inler May, dam of a number of magnificent coursing greyhounds.

Faithful Hope	Solar Prince	Champion Prince	Balla's Prince
			Sallywell
		Lisabelle	Sandown Champion
			Miss Nu Look
	Millie Hawthorn	The Grand Fire	The Grand Champion
			Quare Fire
		Glittering Millie	Glittering Look
			Millie's May

Among his other sons were Talon, sire of Mountain Emperor; and Ataxy, sire of the 1940 Derby winner, G.R. Archduke. It was one of Inler's first matings, to Gosha Bead, that produced the flying Ataxy in 1933, and not until Inler was mated to Tranquilla five years later did he produce anything comparable – Tanist, destined to become the greatest sire of the 1940s. Tranquilla was a daughter of Gosha Bead, so here the same blood lines were necessary to produce another champion. Tanist had the same tremendous early pace as Ataxy and won the 1940 Irish Derby, the same year that G.R. Archduke won the English Derby. It was the continuation of these blood lines through Tanist to Mad Tanist and Astra that produced a number of outstanding trackers.

It is worth mentioning that Ataxy's litter brother Altogether, from a mating with Nuttle, sired Monday Next, dam of the Derby winner Monday's News, born in April 1944. Previously Altogether had sired the bitch Cheerful Rattler, dam of Disputed Rattler, born in July 1941. Thus three of the finest greyhounds of the 1940s – Tanist, Monday's News and Disputed Rattler – each had Gosha Bead as their great grand dam, and each of these champions possessed the same tremendous speed from the traps. In turn Tanist, who in his short career proved the fastest of all greyhounds over shorter distances, produced from a mating with Mad Darkie the wonder bitch Astra and her remarkable litter brother Mad Tanist, who, when put to bitches of Castledown Lad blood, was to produce a number of the finest racing greyhounds ever known. It was to give the sport a golden era of magnificent greyhounds the like of which had never been seen before, and who in turn, through sire and dam, were able to transmit their great speed and staying powers to even faster greyhounds.

When put to Could be Worse, Mad Tanist produced The Grand Champion. He in turn sired The Grand Fire, sire of Millie Hawthorn through Glittering Millie, who when put to Solar Prince produced the 1966 Derby winner Faithful Hope, later sire of the 1970 winner, John Silver. The pedigree of Faithful Hope can be seen above. Here the Tanist–Castledown Lad 'nick' (the outstanding combination of two blood lines or crosses) is clearly apparent, for Bella's Prince was by Castledown Lad.

Let us take another example, this time the mating of Mad Tanist to Caledonia Desire. This produced the bitch Mad Prospect who, when put to Hi There, whelped Crazy Parachute, an outstanding tracker and an equally outstanding sire. Hi There's dam was Dublin Red whose sire was Bella's Prince, the son of Castledown Lad. Once again the Tanist–Castledown Lad 'nick' had produced champions.

As a third example, from Solar Prince's mating to Witching Grand (litter sister to Mile Bush Pride) came Supreme Witch who, when put to Crazy Parachute (son of Mad Tanist's daughter, Mad Prospect), whelped possibly the finest litter of all time in Tric Trac, Spectre II, Forward King and Forward Flash. Once again the Tanist–Castledown Lad 'nick' had produced outstanding results.

Yet again we have Castledown Lad's grandson, Champion Prince, who when mated to Prairie Peg sired the great Pigalle Wonder. Prairie Peg was from a mating of Prairie Vixen and Astra's Son (Astra–Paddy the Champion) with The Grand Champion, grandson of Tanist, who appeared on both sides of her pedigree. The 'nick' in blood lines continues. When Prairie Peg was mated to Hi There (great grandson of Castledown Lad on his dam's side), Prairie Flash was born, once again an outstanding tracker and a great sire. When put to Duet Fire, daughter of Duet Leader who all but won the 1956 English Derby, Prairie Flash sired Camira Flash the 1968 Derby winner who, from a mating to One for Minnie, sired Don't Gambol, twice winner of the sprinter's classic, the Scurry Gold Cup.

Since Brilliant Bob of the 1930s, The Grand Fire has had the greatest influence of all sires on the dam lines in modern greyhound breeding. He was the great grandson of Tanist through Mad Tanist and The Grand Champion, and his bitches were able to pass on the wonderful qualities of the Tanist sires when mated with Castledown Lad stock. The Grand Fire bitch Technician, when mated with Booked Out, gave Booked Six. Booked Out's parents were Direct Lead (dam) and Knockhill Chieftain (sire). Direct Lead was sired by Hi There who had the Castledown Lad blood on his dam's side – once again we have the Tanist–Castledown Lad 'nick'. Because of these famous 'nicks', by 1958 there were an unprecedented number of greyhounds of the highest class, who combined tremendous speed with stamina and track sense. Pigalle Wonder took the Derby in that year and Mile Bush Pride was third. Next year Mile Bush Pride was successful, and finished third again in 1960. Third in 1959 was Crazy Parachute.

By 1966 a second generation of these top-class trackers were the champions. Faithful Hope won that year, and in 1967 possibly the six finest greyhounds ever to contest the final fought it out, Tric Trac being the winner with Spectre II as runner-up. All six were of the famous Tanist–Castledown Lad blood lines, five of them sired by Crazy Parachute. The following year the final contestants were almost as powerful, and once again each of the dogs had the same blood lines. This has continued until the present day, more recent winners being Sand Star, John Silver and Patricia's Hope. From a mating of The Grand Fire with Last Landing came the blue, Clomoney Grand, an Easter Cup winner and thought by many to be the finest bitch ever to race in Ireland. From her mating with Prairie Flash she was to produce the great litter which included Albany, winner of the Thurles' Puppy Derby and of many other top events; Kilbelin Style (English Derby 1969 runner-up); Kilbelin Grand (Irish Derby finalist); and Clomoney Jude (winner of the 1969 Pigalle Stakes). A later mating produced the Irish St Leger winner Clomoney Jet.

The pedigree of Clomoney Jet reads:

Clomoney Jet	Prairie Flash	Hi There	Slaney Record
			Dublin Red
		Prairie Peg	The Grand Champion
			Prairie Vixen
	Clomoney Grand	The Grand Fire	The Grand Champion
			Quare Fire
		Last Landing	Man of Pleasure
			Johnny's Gift

The mating of Prairie Flash and Clomoney Grand had The Grand Champion on both the sire's and dam's side – Prairie Peg, dam of Prairie Flash, had Prairie Vixen and The Grand Champion as her parents. The bitch Prairie Vixen was by Astra's Son whose dam was Astra, herself sister of Mad Tanist so that Tanist appears on both sides of the pedigree of Prairie Peg. Hi There was from the bitch Dublin Red; her sire, Bella's Prince, was by Castledown Lad, and so once again we have the successful Tanist–Castledown Lad cross. The best dog sired by Astra's Son was Magourna Reject.

The greatest dogs of modern times, Tric Trac and Spectre II, Pigalle Wonder and Camira Flash, Mile Bush Pride and Crazy Parachute, had similar blood lines on both the sire's and dam's side. They were the result of two great track strains combining for the first time to produce the ideal 'nick'. Until then each of the Tanist and Castledown Lad strains had produced in its own right good greyhounds, but not world-beaters. The coming together of the two classic lines was to revolutionize the sport, and faster and faster times were achieved over all distances. Certainly there were good racing greyhounds before the fusion of the great Tanist–Castledown Lad blood lines. Champions such as Mick the Miller, Brilliant Bob, Ballynennan Moon, Monday's News, Local Interprize, Trev's Perfection, Priceless Border and Endless Gossip were the equal of any Derby winners of the past twenty years, but not until the great Tanist–Castledown Lad blood lines became joined did so many above-average greyhounds appear at any one time.

It is remarkable how, through the entire history of coursing and track racing, the fourth-generation cross of particular blood lines has produced champion progeny with the qualities of their ancestors of four generations before but to a much greater degree. A century ago, a fourth-generation cross of Canaradzo produced Misterton, who won the Waterloo Cup in 1879, and a Herschel cross at the fourth generation produced the 1916 winner, Harmonicon. The first of the great track sires, Mutton Cutlet, had in his pedigree a fourth-generation cross of Farndon Ferry blood, who had won the Waterloo Cup in 1902, and so it has continued. A fourth-generation cross of Tanist, through Mad Tanist, The Grand Champion, The Grand Fire, Prairie Peg and finally Clomoney Grand and Prairie Flash, produced Albany and Clomoney Jet, and these are the blood lines to look for when breeding racing greyhounds.

The part played by Rare Record in modern breeding must not be overlooked. He was to sire Slaney Record, who finished third in the 1947 Derby, won by Trev's Perfection from Monday's News. How often do the runner-up and other placed dogs go unnoticed, when they may have been beaten by only a very short distance and perhaps after being in difficulties through bumping at the turns. Slaney Record was one such dog. His mating with Dublin Red (Bella's Prince, by Castledown Lad) produced the sire Hi There, who has perhaps had a greater influence on modern track racing than any other dog. He was the ideal cross for Tanist bitches. Slaney Record was produced from coursing stock, his sire Rare Record being by Dee Chime, a full brother to Dee Rock, winner of the 1935 Waterloo Cup out of the bitch Olympic Cutlet. Hi There's dam, Dublin Red, was of Castledown Lad blood as we have seen. The mating of Hi There with the Tanist bitch Prairie Peg produced Prairie Flash, and with Drumlock Sheevaun gave us the McAlevey Gold Cup winner Crazy Drumlock, and Direct Lead who, when put to the Tanist dog, Knockhill Chieftain, produced Booked Out, sire of Booked Six.

Rare Record, through his son Slaney Record, through Slaney Record's son and Hi There, a combination of Dee Rock and Castledown Lad blood and with Tanist dams, was to be one of the most important 'nicks' in the sport's history. When mated to the bitch Favide, Rare Record sired a son, Powerstown Prospect, who won the 1962 St Leger; and when put to Maggie Ann, Rare Record produced the great staying bitch Trojan Silver, Cobb Marathon winner in 1966, who, when mated with Faithful Hope, whelped the 1970 Derby winner John Silver. Hi There, put to Sally's Gossip, whelped Sally's Yarn and Printer's Prince, sire of Yellow Printer. Sally's Yarn, through the Tanist-descended bitch Finola, produced Finola's Yarn. Rare Record was perhaps the conveyor of coursing blood (which Tom Morris, secretary of the Irish Coursing Club and owner of the stud dog Mutton Cutlet, said was so essential) needed to join together the Tanist—Castledown Lad blood lines — the catalyst, so to speak.

Special mention should be made here of the bitch Sally's Gossip and of her sire, the English-bred Endless Gossip, son of the two English Derby winners, Priceless Border and the English-bred bitch Narrogar Ann (the latter by Winnie of Berrow, daughter of Beef Cutlet, a son of Mutton Cutlet). The meeting of Priceless Border and Narrogar Ann was perhaps the most important in the history of modern greyhound racing and coursing. Included in the litter was not only the outstanding Endless Gossip (who was later to sire Sally's Gossip, who was dam of Printer's Prince, sire of the world's greatest track and coursing sire of the past decade, Newdown Heather and of Yellow Printer, the fastest ever to race) but also the bitch Edgerley's Gloria. She raced but little, yet when mated to Sandown Champion (by Mad Tanist out of Good Record, by Rare Record) she whelped the bitch Elphin Girl. This little bitch was to produce a son, Holystone Elf, who, when put to the bitch Deb, was to sire the 1962 Waterloo Cup winner, Best Champagne. Three years later, the 1962 winner was to sire the 1965 Waterloo Cup winner, Nicelya Head, and also the runner-up of that year, Galleon's Hold, whose dam Anthea was a grand-daughter of Endless Gossip. Thus the great English Derby winner appears twice in the pedigree of Galleon's Hold.

The following year (1966) Just Better, another son of Best Champagne won the coveted coursing honour and runner-up was Park Plumtree, son of Mighty Fire whose sire was Eton Graduate. Mother of this dog was none other than Narrogar Ann, but this time from a mating to Peter's Poet. This was not the end of the saga, however, for in 1967 the Waterloo Cup winner was HB, owned by Mr Harold Baldock of Sheffield and trained by Teddy Brennan who had been a greyhound trainer at the city's Owlerton track since its opening; and dam of HB was High Dyke Rebecca, litter sister of Best Champagne who whelped the winner from her mating to Old Kentucky Minstrel.

Another bitch in the litter produced by Holystone Elf and Deb was Debbie, dam of How Cool, who from a mating with Ebony Magnet was to whelp the 1970 Waterloo Cup winner Rodney Magnet. In 1971 So Clever won for the Earl of Sefton. The dog had been sired by How Clever, a son of Debbie from a mating with Fourth of July, and the runner up was Holly Tree, whose sire was Galleon's Hold.

In 1972 Hedera ran up. He was a son of Newdown Heather, son of Printer's Prince (by Hi There out of Sally's Gossip). In 1973 Newdown Heather was to sire the Waterloo Cup winner Modest Newdown.

Holystone Elf, Best Champagne, Debbie and her son, How Clever, appeared in the pedigrees of both winner, Hardly Ever, and runner-up, Hollypark Magpie, in 1975 and Galleon's Hold (always the bridesmaid) was grand sire of the 1976 runner-up Henry Tudor. Now appeared another member of the Priceless Border—Narrogar Ann litter in Explosive Gilbert, a dog who was to sire the bitch Barbara Joan who, when mated to Fourth of July, produced July Joan. From a mating with Rocket Ship she whelped Bright Lad, sire of Minnesota Miller who won the Waterloo Cup for Mrs M. Ryan of Ireland in 1976. She was again successful the following year with her dog Minnesota Yank, another son of Bright Lad. Thus Edwin Gocher's idea of mating two Derby winners together was to pay handsome dividends on the coursing field as well as on the track, though he lived only to see Endless Gossip's success. (*See* Endless Gossip *under* Famous Racing Greyhounds).

BOOKE OF ST ALBANS

In 1481 Dame Juliana Berners, prioress of the nunnery of Sopwell, was the first to set down the 'Points of a good greyhound' in her famous *Booke of St Albans*, printed by Wynkin de Worde, Caxton's most famous assistant. It is important, for the 'points' hold good to this day. A greyhound, said the prioress, should have:

A head lyke a snake,
A neck lyke a drake
The feet of a cat
A tail lyke a rat.
A back lyke a beam,
The sides of a bream.

BOOKMAKERS

'Bookies' are present on all greyhound tracks, and with their shouting of the odds for each race bring colour to the tracks as they do to race courses. For their stands, they contribute some half a million pounds to the tracks every year.

When placing a bet with a bookie, the name of a dog in a particular race is given, together with your stake; in return you receive a ticket confirming the transaction and showing the odds obtained. If your selection wins, the ticket is exchanged for the amount due to you; winnings cannot be collected without it.

To off-course bookmakers and backers the starting price of a race is important, and this is made by the press agencies, a representative of whom is present at every meeting. The moment the dogs are put into the traps he compares the prices of at least three bookmakers at the meeting and sets down those prices common to each. As soon as the hare begins to move he hands the sheet to a 'runner' who immediately takes it to the judges' box above the finishing line. The judge will enter the prices on his card, together with the exact time the hare was set off and the result and times of each race. Copies are then sent to members of the press, the track racing office and to the stewards of the NGRC. There can be no alterations; it is final and binding.

In recent years the large betting firms, mostly with a Stock Exchange quotation, have been buying into the sport and have taken over a number of tracks. Ladbroke's acquired Totalisator and Greyhound Holdings in 1974 and later purchased the Perry Barr Stadium and also Leeds Stadium. Another publicly quoted company, Coral Leisure, now owns the Crayford track and those at Brighton and Romford. John Sutton, formerly managing director of GRA Property Trust, left to manage the Brighton track for Coral's, and another GRA stalwart, Arthur Aldridge, Britain's most experienced greyhound racing administrator, joined Ladbroke's to promote the sport with Peter Thompson.

BORD NA gCON

This, the Irish Greyhound Board, began operations in 1958, taking over responsibility for all tracks in the Irish Republic but not in Ulster, where the tracks continue to be administered by the Irish Coursing Club. Bord na gCon's headquarters are at 104 Henry St, Limerick; Des Hanraham is chairman of the Board and Seamus Flanagan chief executive officer.

During its first ten years as administrator the Board allocated more than £1 million in prize money. Dr P. Maguire, first chairman of the Board, travelled extensively in the USA and Europe with a view to increasing the export market for greyhounds, and during the first decade of the Board's existence more than £1 million was obtained for Irish greyhounds sent abroad. During the same period, on-course totalizator betting on Irish tracks amounted to more than £60 million. A new look was given to most tracks, and at Limerick, Shelbourne Park and Harold's Cross facilities both for the dogs and for the public are now equal to those anywhere in the world. A new track was built at Newbridge, where the glass-enclosed bar allows patrons to view the racing, kennels and weighing room in comfort, and in 1972 similar public accommodation was provided at Mullingar and Lifford. In the same year a new hare drive and lighting system were installed at Navan, Longford and Dundalk, and totalizator facilities at Newbridge. Of the eighteen tracks under its jurisdiction, nine are now owned by the Board, which is answerable to the Irish Department of Agriculture for the running and maintenance of the tracks.

More than a million people a year visit the eighteen tracks, and in 1969 the Board was able to purchase the well-known Cork track and also Shelbourne Park, Dublin, which prevented them from falling into the hands of speculators who would have closed the tracks to use the land for building. The purchase of the Cork track for £127,000 seems a tremendous bargain some fifteen years later.

In 1967 Bord na gCon, in conjunction with the Irish Television and Broadcasting Corporation, inaugurated a special Television Trophy to be staged at Shelbourne Park and run over the 750 yds course. Contested in July each year, the event is open to greyhounds from Britain and Ireland and is televized by Radiotelefis Eirann. The Board also sponsors a National Greyhounds Award Scheme, for which the sports editors of all the Irish newspapers meet once a year to select the outstanding greyhounds on the track and the coursing field.

BREEDERS OF FAMOUS GREYHOUNDS

Abbeylara	Larry Kiernan, Granard, Co. Longford
Balliniska Band	Mrs Helen Cusson, Gurrane, Charleville Co. Kerry
Ballybeg Prim	Mr J. Brennan and Dr P. McGovern, Thurles, Co. Tipperary
Bashful Man	Mrs Nancy Dirrane, Kilmallock, Co. Limerick
Beef Cutlet	Mr J. Byrne, Cahir, Co. Tipperary
Bold Work	Michael Foley, Drislane, Donaskeigh, Co. Tipperary
Case Money	Mr C. D'Estelle Roe, Park View, Templemore, Co. Tipperary
Coin Case	Mr Con Ryan, Clongonhue, Cappawhite, Co. Tipperary
Cooladine Super	Charles Kavanagh, Co. Tyrone
Calandra Champ	Denis Clancy Drangan, Co. Tipperary
Creamery Border	Mr Michael Collins, Inniscara, Co. Cork
Dolores Rocket	Mr H.G. White Brookwood, Surrey
Entry Badge	Mr Edwin Baxter, Sarre, Isle of Thanet
Fair Mistress	Mr F. Moore, Larne, Co. Antrim
Fine Jubilee	Mr F. Jephcott, Beoley, Worcestershire
Good Worker	Capt. and Mrs Ward, Challocks, Kent
Hidden Shadow	Mr John Barrett, Feohenagh, Co. Limerick
Hume Highway	Ms Patricia McGrath, Outrath, Co. Tipperary
Hurry on Bran	Mr Liam Dwan, Glenbane, Thurles, Co. Tipperary
Jimsun	Mrs Josephine Walsh, Cromogue, Charleville, Co. Cork
Knockrour Slave	Mr Andy Lynch, Cappoquin, Co. Waterford
Lacca Champion	Mr J.J. O'Sullivan, Kilmore West, Ballyduff, Co. Kerry
Linda's Champion	Mr M. Barrett, Crohane, Ballingarry, Thurles, Co. Tipperary
Lively Band	Mr Larry Clancy, Athboy, Co. Meath
Lone Keel	Mr Archie Gordon, Kilkeel, Co. Down
Mick the Miller	Fr Martin Brophy, Killeigh, Co. Offaly
Mile Bush Pride	Mrs Nora Johnston, Campile, Co. Wexford

Move Gas	Mr R. Liffey Jnr, Dublin
Mutt's Silver	Lawrence Callery Tallagh, Dublin
Nameless Pixie	Mr Ben McAuley Shankill, Co. Dublin
Narrogar Ann	Mr W.J. Reid, Worcestershire
Oran Jack	James O'Brien Lanesboro, Co. Longford
Patricia's Hope	Mick Murphy Castleisland, Co. Kerry
Pampered Rover	Mr Joe Phelan, Co. Kilkenny
Penny County	Mr Con Moore, Thomastown, Co. Kilkenny
Pigalle Wonder	Mr T. Murphy Fiddawn, Inistioge, Co. Kilkenny
Pineapple Grand	Mr Pat O'Sullivan and Mr R. Reidy Ardfert, Co. Kerry
Priceless Border	Mr W.P. O'Kane, Ballymena, Co. Antrim
Quare Times	Mr Billy Quinn, Killenaule, Co. Tipperary
Red Rasper	Mr William O'Donnell, Bruff, Co. Limerick
Spanish Battleship	Mr Tim O'Connor, Killorglin, Co. Kerry
Spectre II	Mr Leo Stack, Duagh, Listowel, Co. Kerry
Suir Miller	Mrs Elizabeth Flood, Ballyslateen, Golden, Co. Tipperary
Tanist	Father Browne, Bray, Co. Wicklow
The Grand Champion The Grand Canal	Mr Paddy Dunphy Castlecomer, Co. Kilkenny
Train	Major G.F. Tennison, Lancashire
Trev's Perfection	Mr H.G. Nunn, Cumbria
Tric Trac	Mr Leo Stack, Duagh, Listowel, Co. Kerry

BRIGHTON RACECOURSE
See under British Greyhound Racecourses.

BRISTOL RACECOURSE
See under British Greyhound Racecourses.

BRITISH-BRED GREYHOUNDS
Though the number of greyhounds racing on British tracks has, since the beginning of the sport, been in the proportion of two-thirds Irish-bred and one-third British, many of the outstanding dogs have been British-bred and -reared. The winner of the first English Derby, Entry Badge, was born in the kennels of Mr Edwin Baxter on the Isle of Thanet; Boher Ash, winner in 1928, was born in Scotland, being the only greyhound owned and trained north of the border to win the English Derby. Bradshaw Fold, the bitch

The late Father Martin Brophy, parish priest of Killeigh, Co. Offaly, who bred and reared Mick the Miller. Photo: Father Thomas Brophy.

who ran up to Mick the Miller in the 1930 Derby, was English-bred, while the great Junior Classic (one-time holder of the world 500 yds record) and Juvenile Classic (a Grand National winner) were bred and reared in Wales. Also British-bred was Jesmond Cutlet, of the famous Beef Cutlet–Lady Eleanor mating, and who in turn was to sire Magic Beau, at one time holder of the world record for the 525 yds course. G.R. Archduke, who won the 1940 Derby, was born at the GRA kennels at Northaw, and the 1947 Derby winner, Trev's Perfection, was born and reared on the Northumberland fells. He was to become the first greyhound ever to win the English, Scottish and Welsh Derbys in the same year, a feat which has been accomplished only twice since. Two years later the English-bred bitch Narrogar Ann won the Derby, and from her mating to the 1948 winner, Priceless Border, she would become the first and so far only Derby-winning bitch whose son (Endless Gossip, winner in 1952) also won the premier event. Rushton Mac, winner in 1955, was English-bred, and Chittering Clapton, winner in 1965, was born on the Cambridgeshire farm of Mr Creek.

Probably the greatest bitch of all time, Dolores Rocket, who won both the Derby and the St Leger in 1971, was born and reared by Mr H.G. White in Surrey. The great Bah's Choice, by Tokio out of Chittering Duchess, became in a trial at the White City on 6 June 1946 the first greyhound to better 29.00 secs over 525 yds. Bah's Choice was also born in Cambridgeshire and must be reckoned one of the three best English-bred greyhounds in the history of the sport. The 'father' of greyhound racing, Mutton Cutlet, was born in Major McCalmont's kennels in the Cotswolds. The great long-distance dogs of the 1940s, Grosvenor Bob and Grosvenor Edwin, were English-born and -reared, as was Ella's Jim, who twice won the wartime substitute St Leger – and no greyhound has ever won the St Leger twice. Those other long-distance champions, Kampion Sailor and Train, were English-bred, and the Scurry Gold Cup winner Country Life came from the home of Dr and Mrs O'Brien in Birmingham.

One of the greatest of English Derby winners, Fine Jubilee, was English-bred, raised at the kennels of Mr Fred Jephcott at Beoley near Worcester. The dog was outstanding in 1936 when he won the Derby by six lengths, one of the biggest winning margins of all time. He was owned and trained by Mrs M. Yate, the only woman to have owned and trained a Derby winner.

Good Worker, who won the English Laurels in 1948, was English-bred and so was Gala Flash, one of the finest dogs of the postwar era, who won the Wimbledon Champion Stakes and ran up in the Cesarewitch in 1945. He was a son of Tokio out of Joyous Ruth and trained by Hardy Wright at Annan, Dumfries-shire.

One of the all-time great bitches, Rio Cepretta, Oaks winner in 1947, was bred at the kennels of Capt. and Mrs Ward at Challocks in Kent and trained by Sid Jennings at Wembley. At the kennels of Mr Phil Rees, also in Kent, the flying Xmas Holiday was born and trained by him to win the Scurry Cup and Laurels in 1976. Mr Arthur Wichello, who owned the dog, also owned his dam, Mary's Snowball. Though both sire and dam were registered with the Irish Stud Book, Xmas Holiday was Kent-born and -bred.

Another outstanding British greyhound was Daemonic Gambol, a son of Don't Gambol from the first litter that the dual Scurry Cup-winner sired. Daemonic Gambol was selected as the best English-bred greyhound of 1974, after winning the Wimbledon two-year-old Produce Stakes and the Oxford Produce Stakes in that year.

BRITISH GREYHOUND RACECOURSES

The courses are arranged alphabetically under track name, which is not always that of the town or city in which they are situated. The following list is provided for easy reference.

Birmingham *see* Hall Green; Perry Barr
Bristol *see* Eastville
Brownhills *see* Norton Canes
Cheltenham *see* Gloucester and Cheltenham
Edinburgh *see* Powderhall
Glasgow *see* Shawfield
Hoddesdon *see* Rye House
Hull *see* Craven Park
London *see* Catford; Clapton; Hackney; Harringay; Walthamstow; Wembley; West Ham; White City; Wimbledon
Manchester *see* Belle Vue; White City
Middlesbrough *see* Cleveland Park
Newcastle *see* Brough Park; Gosforth
Sheffield *see* Owlerton
Wolverhampton *see* Monmore Green

BELLE VUE

The track, in the Gorton district of Manchester, was the first in Britain to open for racing when on 24 July 1926 some 1,700 enthusiasts saw the red dog Mistley (by Jack-in-Office out of Duck), carrying the blue jacket of trap 2, win the first race, run over 440 yds, by eight lengths in 25.00 secs. The first meeting consisted of six races, the first two taking place in daylight, the others under lights, and eight dogs took part in each event. (On 1 January 1928, the rules of racing formulated by the NGRC henceforth allowed only six dogs or fewer to contest a race, and racing was confined to the summer months.) So quickly did the sport take on that the second meeting of 1927 was attended by ten times the number of people as the very first meeting. The first racing director was Major-Gen. T. Anderson and L.V. Browne was Racing Manager (the first in the history of the sport). Among the trainers on the opening night were Tom Fear and Bill Brinkley, who were soon joined by H. (Jack) Harvey who retired in 1975 as the much respected Wembley maestro.

The present track, with its inside hare and large, easy bends, favours the fast, well-built greyhound. Belle Vue had to wait until 1964 before having a Derby winner in the kennels, so emulating the White City track at Manchester which housed the great Wild Woolley early in the sport's history. Belle Vue's 1964 winner, Hack-up Chieftain, owned by Mr Donohue and trained by Len Stagg, was the outsider. Quoted at 20–1 before the race, he defeated the favourite, Die Cast, by a comfortable two lengths in 28.92 secs. This great dog died in 1974 aged thirteen.

Another very popular greyhound at Belle Vue was Crefogue Flash, owned by the Williamson brothers, bookmakers, in partnership with Mr P. Taylor. The dog had previously won the Wimbledon Puppy Derby and was ante-post favourite for the 1971 Derby, but had to be withdrawn through injury. Crefogue Flash was by Newdown Heather out of Duffrey Flash, dam of the Irish Derby winner Monalee Pride, and had been purchased at Shelbourne Park sales for 325 guineas.

A quite outstanding tracker kennelled at Belle Vue was Balliniska Band, owned by Mr Raphaello Bacci and trained by Eddie Moore, who moved to Belle Vue from White City, Manchester, in 1976. The dog was to win the 1977 English Derby – the fiftieth anniversary of the race – in which he equalled Glen Rock's track record of 29.16 secs for the 500 m course. It is interesting to record that in this dog's heat, semi-final and final, the order of finishing of the first three greyhounds (Balliniska Band, El Cavalier and Pat Seamur) was the same each time. Each time the three dogs occupied different traps, so it can truly be said that the 1977 Derby was won by the best dog.

That wonderful bitch of the war years, Disputed Rattler, came over from Ireland as an untried sapling and set Belle Vue alight with her first trial there. Her time of 28.44 secs was only just outside the record for 500 yds set up by Wild Woolley and Jamboree Reveller ten years earlier. While still a puppy she was sent to Wimbledon and placed in the care of Sidney Orton, who for her first open race entered her against the incomparable Ballynennan Moon, whom she defeated. But it was at Belle Vue that she had her first run on a track, and those who saw her will never forget her.

In 1971, when West Ham closed for racing, the Cesarewitch classic was allocated to Belle Vue. The first race was run over the old 880 yds course, but since 1975 the event has been over 815 m. The 1979 Cesarewitch was for the first time sponsored by the Demmy Bookmaking and Leisure Group after Ladbroke's three-year sponsorship had expired. The Demmy Group have increased the first prize money from £2,000 to £3,000, and this will be £3,500 in 1980 and £4,000 in 1981, making the Cesarewitch the richest race run in the provinces.

Since 1927 the Northern Flat Championship has been run here, originally over 500 yds and since 1975 over 460 m. One of the most popular events of the northern calendar, it has been won by many outstanding greyhounds. Hurdle races were included in the very first meeting and have been a feature of racing at Belle Vue ever since. The first was won by Melksham Autocrat, who won by ten lengths at the opening meeting.

During the 1970s more than £500,000 has been spent on modernizing the track and its amenities. The new Mistley Stand provides excellent restaurant and tote facilities, while on the 'popular' side the Chieftain Stand, named after the 1964 Derby winner, offers equally good facilities. In addition, a new range of brick kennels was built in 1970 at a cost of £100,000, providing accommodation for 360 dogs.

In May 1971 the GRA, who still own the track, reintroduced eight-dog racing after a break of forty-four years, but it did not prove popular. Indeed, it could not have been expected to, since even six-dog races are troubled by wide runners and bumping. The new system was abandoned due to falling attendances.

John Kennedy is general manager here and also at the GRA's White City track, while Norman Porter is racing manager at Belle Vue and G. Furness his assistant.

Among the most successful Belle Vue trainers was Stan Mitchell, who moved to Hull in 1973 after which his place was taken by Jean Day. Miss Day had been head kennel girl to Stan Mitchell for more than ten years and her appointment made her the first woman trainer at the track.

Main Events Run at Belle Vue

Gorton Cup	February	460 m
Northern Stayers' Stakes	April	654 m
Northern Flat Championship	July	460 m
* Cesarewitch	October	815 m
Manchester Puppy Cup	November	460 m
Red Rose Marathon	November	815 m

* Classic event

Track Records (1950)

Newceston Ration	500 yds	28.07 secs
Douro	500 yds H	29.45 secs
Killcoran Castle	700 yds	40.83 secs

Track Records (1980),

Balliniska Band	9.4.77	460 m	27.26 secs
Kickham Inn	15.5.78	460 m	27.26 secs
Meanus Dandy	27.8.77	460 m	28.13 secs
Montreen	9.4.77	645 m	39.25 secs
January Prince	14.4.62	645 m	42.00 secs
Visiting Time	6.9.80	815 m	50.88 secs

Winners of Northern Flat Championship 1927–49

1927	Great Chum	29.60 secs
1928	Mutable	29.08 secs
1929	Mutable	29.34 secs
1930	Doumergue	29.17 secs
1931	Ross Regatta	29.14 secs
1932	Wild Woolley	28.49 secs
1933	Deemster's Mike	29.08 secs
1934	Kum on Steve	29.42 secs
1935	Perendar	29.00 secs
1936	First Nobleman	29.16 secs
1937	Demotic Mac	28.66 secs
1938	Italian Primer	28.92 secs
1939	Sporting Offer	28.74 secs
1940–5	not run	
1946	Dante II	28.35 secs
1947	Tonycus	28.09 secs
1948	Clan Cameron	28.68 secs
1949	Behattan Marquis	28.37 secs

Winners of Northern Flat Championship 1968–84

1968	Limits Crackers	28.09 secs
1969	Infatuated	28.23 secs
1970	The Other Green	27.66 secs
1971	Knockmant Pride	28.12 secs
1972–4	not run	
* 1975	Milebush Heron	28.14 secs
1976	Detties Joy	27.91 secs
1977	not run	
1978	Dale Lad	27.54 secs
1979	Ella's Sound	27.45 secs
1980	Jon Barrie	27.85 secs
1981	Thanks Kev	27.67 secs
1982	Oakfield Tracy	27.40 secs
1983	Slender Boy	27.80 secs
1984	Precious Prince	27.99 secs

* Since 1975 run over 460 m

Winners of Northern Stayers' Stakes 1968–84

1968	Booked Six	41.38 secs
1969	Aughgor King	40.43 secs
1970	Meronome	40.18 secs
1971	Knock Off	39.29 secs
1972	Albany Ranger	40.16 secs
1973	Poor Rudolf	39.80 secs
1974	Boreen Spec	40.25 secs
* 1975	Moy Mona	39.72 secs
1976	Wow	39.30 secs
1977	Montreen	39.25 secs
1978	Jim's Image	39.96 secs
1979	Kilbelin Ruler	40.85 secs
1980	Honeygar Kid	40.23 secs
1982	Catsrock Tiger	39.54 secs
1983	Sugar Palm	40.47 secs
1984	Feeling Great	41.36 secs

* Pre-1975 run over 700 yds and known also as the Northern 700'; since 1975 run over 647 m

BLETCHLEY

The track first opened at Groveway in the early 1960s under the direction of Mr Robert Beckett and his son David, and by 1970 had undergone so many improvements that it was granted a licence to race under NGRC rules, since when it has gone from strength to strength. The track is large with wide turns and an inside Sumner hare; in 1970 the surface was sanded. At that time a range of sixty racing kennels was constructed around the paddock, and a new stand and bar built. Greyhounds are supplied by several contract trainers and racing takes place on Thursdays and Saturdays throughout the year. Many of the Westmead greyhounds began here, including the great Westmead County, since the track is handy for the famous kennels run by Nick and Natalie Savva. Another trainer who supplies the track with top-class greyhounds is Wally Ginzel, who had charge of Ashgrove Glen when he broke the track record, while Mrs Edna Wearing trained Trinas Girl to win the 1979 Trafalgar Cup.

The most important event run here is the Milton Keynes Derby, sponsored by Watney Mann, the brewers, and run in October over 620 m with a prize of £1,000 for the winner. A recent winner of the event was Rail Fred, owned locally by Mr R. Gough and trained by J. Corley, a contract trainer. To Bletchley in 1979 came the great bitch Kilmagoura Mist to win the Milton Keynes Derby in 39.10 secs.

Main Event Run at Bletchley

Milton Keynes Derby	September	620 m

BRIGHTON (HOVE);

Situated in Neville Road, Hove, this is one of the pleasantest tracks in England and it was one of the earliest to open its doors to greyhound racing, at the instigation of Charles Wakeling, F. Arnold and Major C. Campbell. The first meeting took place in May 1928, and the first race, run over 550 yds, was won by a dog called Costs, owned by Mr W.G. Hooper, a Brighton solicitor, before a crowd of more than 7,000 who had assembled to watch the start of greyhound racing on the first track to be opened outside London south of the Thames. By modern standards the conditions were primitive – not for ten years was electric lighting installed, though in 1932 a hand-operated tote was available to punters. Six months later tote betting in England was declared illegal, a decision which put the track in jeopardy, but the Betting Act of 1934 revoked the decision just in time.

The first managing director was Charles Wakeling, on whose death Major Campbell, then chairman of Brighton and Hove Albion Football Club, was appointed and remained until his own death in 1958. The beneficiaries of these gentlemen's wills disposed of their controlling interest in the track to the GRA, who appointed Gerald Kearley as general manager and Peter Shotton as racing manager. Both were at Brighton for more than twenty years. They brought in David White as catering manager and the three were to make the track, with its magnificent restaurant seating over 200 people, one of the most go-ahead in Britain. Mr Kearley is now president and Jim Layton racing manager. Racing takes place on Thursday and Saturday evenings throughout the year, with the addition of Tuesdays during the summer. With the closure of Stamford Bridge, Brighton is now the fastest track in Britain and two world records were set there.

In 1940 the kennels were moved to Albourne, north of Brighton, and are now in the capable hands of five experienced trainers, including Mrs Doreen Walsh and the long-serving George Curtis, who moved here from Park Royal when that track closed. Mr Curtis has been a trainer for more than forty years and looked after Brighton's finest dogs, Glin Bridge, Langford Dacoit and Wired to the Moon, the last of whom won the 1977 Scurry Cup. As trainer of 3-times Scurry Cup winner, Yankee Express, he set a record which may never be equalled. But it is as a trainer of hurdlers that he stands supreme and in 1983 trained Sir Winston to win the Grand National classic, the dog being but a novice over hurdles when the event began.

The track, with its all grass 450 m circuit and outside McGee hare is owned and run by Coral Leisure, members of the Bass Charrington Group. Ken Tucker is chairman, and some of the longest-serving members of the Stadium are Bill Holland, who began as starter and is now timekeeper, and Bill Cook, the judge. Both have given more than thirty years of service to greyhound racing.

Situated within easy reach of London, the track has attracted many famous greyhounds, especially to take part in Brighton's most famous event, the Regency Produce Stakes. It is run in May, since 1975 over 680 m, and is a race for stayers. The Regency was first contested in 1948 and was restricted to English-bred greyhounds which were two years old. The track also stipulated that all entries were to be received by 28 February in the year before that in which the race would be run. Towards the end of 1946 the rules were made public. By the end of February 1947 161 litters had been registered, and the following year this had passed the 200 mark. The first prize was £750, which made the event one of the most lucrative at the time. One famous dog to take part in the first Regency was Good Worker, who had previously won the Laurels and whose time of 29.31 secs in his semi-final of the Regency was to stand for a decade. The locally bred Bunny's Hoard, owned by Mr L. Lucas, won the final; he was trained at Brighton by the outstanding Gunner Smith, who, thirty years later, is still at Brighton. He was the trainer of Glin Fane when in 1978 that dog set a new track record for 725 m. For the second Regency there were nine heats (fifty-four greyhounds), and in heat 8 King's Signature, who was to win the event, set a new track record with 29.24 secs.

In 1966 the Regency was opened to all-comers and the course was lengthened from 525 yds to 725 yds. It was won that year by Mrs Eade's Ardvullen and in 1967 by Ever Work, trained by George Curtis at the track. Two years later the Regency was won by the outstanding Brough Park dog Shady Begonia, and in 1975, when it was first run over 680 m, by Glin Bridge. Another fine dog, Westmead Champ, won in 1976, and two years later it was Mr Luckhurst's Ballinamona Sam, trained at Catford by Jim Horsfall.

The track holds most of its valuable open events during the holiday season. The Coral Leisure Stakes and the Sussex Cup, inaugurated in 1972, are both run over 500 m in August. In the same month the Langford

Dacoit Stakes, named in honour of one of Brighton's finest greyhounds, is run over the 725 m course. Another outstanding greyhound kennelled here was Glin Bridge, now at stud and sire of Glin Fane, one-time holder of the 725 m record. A son of Spectre II, Glin Bridge won fifty open races and was second thirty-three times. In one wonderful spell he won fifteen races in a row and, but for being badly hampered in his next race, might easily have set an all-time record for consecutive wins. He set a new track record at Brighton with a time of 39.94 secs for 680 m, and at the White City with 44.03 secs for the 730 m course. Possessing the same wonderful stamina as his sire, he also had the same trackcraft of the champions of the past like Mick the Miller and Monday's News.

An excellent Brighton dog of recent years was the white and black British-bred Deneholme Hunter, by Maryville Hi out of Rocco Lynne. Owned by Mr S. Saxby and trained by Fred Lugg, in 1968 Deneholme Hunter was chosen as best British-bred greyhound of the year, an honour he well deserved. He was to sire Deneholme Chief, winner of the Wimbledon Two-year Produce Stakes of 1973 when only twenty months old. He also defeated Skyhawk in that dog's last race at Brighton.

On 30 June 1973, a year before the metric system became standard on British tracks, the Brighton-kennelled dog Easy Investment clocked the world's fastest time of 28.17 secs for 525 yds, a record which will now stand for all time in Britain. It was at Brighton in 1977, when contesting the Sussex Cup, that Linacre, litter brother to the 1977 Derby winner Balliniska Band, became the first greyhound to break 29 secs for a 500 m course, with a time of 28.99 secs. In 1980 Monday's Bran clocked 28.92 secs for 500 m, a world record for this distance until June, 1983.

Main Events Run at Brighton

Regency Produce Stakes	May	670 m
Schweppes Brighton Belle	June	500 m
Whitbread National Hurdles	July	500 m
Sussex Cup	August	500 m
Coral Leisure Stakes	August	500 m
Variety Club Stakes	August	680 m
Langford Dacoit Stakes	August	725 m
Beaverwood Club Stakes	August	500 m

Track Records (1950)			
Good Worker	1948	525 yds	29.31 secs
Wooty's Kingmaker	1938	525 yds H	30.39 secs
Rath's Record	1949	565 yds	31.50 secs
Grosvenor Edwin	1938	800 yds	46.35 secs
Track Records (1970)			
Kans	1963	525 yds	28.71 secs
Athea Lad	1968	525 yds H	30.34 secs
Deneholme Flash	1969	725 yds	40.20 secs
Track Records (1980)			
Linacre	1976	500 m	28.99 secs
Wotch it Buster	1978	500 m H	29.71 secs
Fair Reward	1980	680 m	40.30 secs
Across the Miles	1979	680 m H	41.43 secs
Princess Glin	1979	725 m	43.22 secs
Langford Dacoit	1978	955 m	58.46 secs

Winners of the Regency Produce Stakes 1968–84

1968	Steer Me Home	41.35 secs
1969	Shady Begonia	40.51 secs
1970	Glory Crazy	40.88 secs
1971	Specfire	40.88 secs
1972	Adamstown Lane	40.83 secs
1973	Pepper Joe	40.81 secs
1974	Chain Gang	40.05 secs
*1975	Glin Bridge	40.19 secs
1976	Westmead Champ	39.78 secs
1977	Bonzo	40.03 secs
1978	Ballinamona Sam	41.74 secs
1979	Jingling Star	40.62 secs
1980	Gallally Magpie	43.78 secs
1981	Fuffylugs	46.84 secs
1982	Paradise Lost	44.65 secs
1983	Aquila Bay	47.41 secs
1984	Mac's Jeanie	45.41 secs

*Pre-1975 run over 725 yds; since run over 670 m

Winners of the Sussex Cup 1972–84

1972	Carry On Hasty	28.32 secs
1973	Mickey Finn	28.65 secs
1974	Clear Reason	28.47 secs
*1975	Abbey Glade	29.63 secs
1976	Gaily Noble	29.23 secs
1977	Linacre	28.99 secs
1978	Sandpiper Dolly	29.52 secs
1979	Monday's Bran	28.96 secs
1980	Maplehurst Star	29.21 secs
1981	Black Armour	30.04 secs
1982	Yankee Express	30.06 secs
1983	The Jolly Norman	30.15 secs
1984	Sammy Bear	29.98 secs

*Pre-1975 run over 525 yds; since run over 500 m

BROUGH PARK

Run by Glassedin Greyhounds Ltd., this Newcastle track is one of the best of provincial racecourses. It opened in 1933, and with Gosforth is the only track in the area still in business, for the White City track at Newcastle, as well as those at South Shields and Gateshead, have long since closed down. The track is about 415 m in circumference with an outside hare, long straights and well banked bends. In 1980 the grass surface was replaced by sand. Considerable improvements have been made in recent years to the main stand, which now provides excellent restaurant facilities for patrons. Paul Richardson and Tony Smith were joint racing managers here in the 1970s. Bob Harwood is general manager and R.J. May, racing manager.

The most important event is the All

England Cup which is the north's most prestigious event, contested since 1946. It is now sponsored by Charles Chisholm & Sons, with £5,000 for the winner. One of the most exciting and most keenly contested of All England Cups was that of 1946, when for the only time in the history of track racing the final of an open event was contested by four dogs each of whom had won a Derby in one of the four countries of the British Isles – Monday's News in England, Lilac's Luck in Ireland, Latin Pearl in Scotland, and Negro's Lad in Wales. The winner was Monday's News, who defeated Latin Pearl by a neck in 29.55 secs.

The All England Cup, contested in November, is one of the last important events of the racing calendar. For this reason, with the classics over, it always attracts the best greyhounds in training before taking their midwinter rest. The 1965 event was won by Kilbeg Kuda, trained by John Bassett, and sire of Kerry's Pal, dam of the 1978 Edinburgh Cup winner, Dale Lad. The winner in 1968 was Pool's Punter, fresh from winning the Irish St Leger and making Mr G. Adams of Sheffield the first English owner to win this event. Pool's Punter also ran up the Irish Laurels to Flaming King. He was one of Oregon Prince's finest sons.

Three years later came Spectre Jockey to win the All England Cup by six lengths from Ivy Jet. He was from Spectre's first litter, which included Spectre's Dream, winner of the 1971 Welsh Derby. Spectre Jockey also won the Evening Standard Challenge Trophy at White City, London, and ran up to Dolores Rocket in the St Leger and to Down Your Way in the Gold Collar. He was trained by Freddy Warrell, also trainer of Down Your Way, who had then held a trainer's licence for only six months. The dog was owned by Mr Warrell's wife, Marion, and during 1971 was the most consistent to run in Britain.

Now run over 484 m, the 1978 Cup was won by Champer's Club, a fawn and white dog by the Derby winner Patricia's Hope, and in 1979 by the flying Burniston Jet from Owlerton, son of another Derby winner, Jimsun.

Also run at Brough Park over the same distance are the Northumberland Cup and the Northumberland Stakes, both worth £500 to the winning owner. The latter, now run over 669 m, is sponsored by Britvic. An early winner of the Stakes, in 1948, was that very consistent dog Whiterock Abbey, who won the Eclipse Stakes at Coventry the same year and reached the final of many other top events. A recent winner of the Stakes was Gan On Kuda, owned and trained by Mrs Marjorie Fenwick; and of the Northumberland Cup, Deal Away, trained by Mrs S. Hayward at Coventry.

The most outstanding greyhound to be kennelled at the track since its opening was undoubtedly Shady Begonia, a white and brindle dog trained by Norman Oliver, who has had long associations with Brough Park. Sired by the great Pigalle Wonder, Shady Begonia reached the final of the 1968 Derby and the Cesarewitch and won the Midlands St Leger and TV Trophy that year. Owned by Mr Bob Dinning, the dog won more than £6,000 in prize money during 1968 and 1969, and won on every track he raced. Another excellent dog kennelled here was the St Leger winner Ramdeen Stuart, also trained by Norman Oliver; he won the 1973 Gold Collar.

Another of Brough Park's most successful trainers is Jimmy Smith, who was in charge of Mr Cyril Young's Irish Airport when the dog won the Yorkshire Puppy Cup at Leeds in 1970 and the North of England Puppy Cup at Brough Park. It was appropriate that he should have done so, for the dog was a son of Kilbeg Kuda who had won the All England Cup three years before. Indeed, Brough Park dogs often performed well at Leeds, and in 1974 Black Caprice, even-money favourite, won the stayers' event, the Ebor Stakes. Jimmy Smith also had charge of the locally kennelled greyhound Cute Chaser, who took the Northumberland Cup for Mr N. Phipps in 1979.

Other contract trainers here are G. Williams and K. Raggatt and Bob Hopper.

Main Events Run at Brough Park

Britvic Northumberland Stakes	August	669 m
Northumberland Cup	September	484 m
North of England Puppy Cup	October	484 m
All England Cup	November	484 m

Track Records (1950)

Kenn Flyer	300 yds	17.31 secs
Ballydancer	520 yds	29.45 secs
Farloe's Pride	520 yds H	31.24 secs
Attorney General	650 yds	39.02 secs

Track Records (1980)

Cooga Hall	23.11.79	277 m	16.92 secs

Hack Up Georgie	29.6.68	480 m	29.59 secs
Lisroe Mike	10.9.76	480 m	29.59 secs
Shady Wonder	12.7.68	614 m	39.13 secs
Cahermone Ruby	26.5.69	680 m	43.24 secs
Seven Wells	3.6 68	864 m	58.40 secs

Winners of the All England Cup 1968–83

1968	Pool's Punter	30.57 secs
1969	Jackpot Painter	30.54 secs
1970	Allied Banker	30.64 secs
1971	Spectre Jockey	30.54 secs
1972	Proud Tack	30.20 secs
1973	Fly Dazzler	30.63 secs
1974	not run	
* 1975	Show Man	29.21 secs
1976	Houghton Rip	29.93 secs
1977	Prince Hill	29.37 secs
1978	Champer's Club	29.30 secs
1979	Burniston Jet	29.45 secs
† 1980	Jon Barrie	30.07 secs
1982	Long Spell	30.92 secs
1983	Squire Cass	30.15 secs

* Pre-1975 run over 525 yds; 1975-9 runover 484 m
† 1980 run over 507 m

CAMBRIDGE

This track first came under NGRC rules in November 1978 and closed in 1984. An excellent small circuit track of 340 m with wide slightly banked bends which eliminated bumping and an outside McGee hare. The outstanding greyhound here was Sport Promoter, owned by Mr J. Crish and trained by the late Pat Mullins who also had charge of the great Lacca Champion when winning the 1978 Derby. Sport Promoter, later owned by Pat and Linda Mullins, reached the final of the 1979 Gold Collar and went through the 1980 event undefeated. He also won the Grand Prix.

After the death of her husband, Mrs Linda Mullins trained Apaka Express to win the Rikasso Champion 2-year Produce Stakes here for Mr I. Lindsey in 1982 and the Mecca Bookmakers Stayers Stakes at Hackney. From this track too came Darkie Fli to win the Laurels in 1983.

Cambridge was the first track to appoint a lady racing manager in Miss Sue Foster.

CATFORD

Situated on the south side of the Thames, this has always had a reputation for being the prettiest of London's tracks, and the one with the greatest variety of races. Racing takes place on Thursdays and Saturdays with additional meetings in summer. The track opened for racing on 30 July 1932, and has always had a member of the Sutton family on its board of directors. It is now owned by GRA Property Ltd.

The classic Gold Collar, inaugurated in 1933, is run here, originally in May and now in September. Of all the classic events, its distance has been changed most often. Run over 440 yds before 1962, the event is now run over 555 m and is worth £5,000 to the winner. With its wide bends and outside McKee hare, the track has always favoured dogs from traps 3, 4, 5 and 6, and in nine of the first ten years of the Gold Collar a dog

Catford Stadium, one of the prettiest of Britain's tracks, home of the classic Gold Collar.

from one of these traps won the event. The first Gold Collar winner was Wild Woolley, who in a heat clocked 25.95 secs for a new track record. He was second only to Mick the Miller as the outstanding greyhound of the early 1930s, and took over Mick's mantle as the most popular dog in Britain when Mick retired in 1931.

From July 1932 until July 1964 the track record holders for the 440 yds course were:

South Tipperary	30 July 1932	27.92 secs
Jazz First	5 August 1932	26.18 secs
Wild Woolley	6 May 1933	25.95 secs
Jack's Joke	14 June 1935	25.95 secs
Fine Jubilee	26 May 1936	25.82 secs
Fine Jubilee	25 May 1937	25.42 secs
Monday's News	31 May 1947	25.41 secs
Polonius	16 March 1953	25.40 secs
Rusty Chain	19 May 1956	25.26 secs
Dangerous Customer	5 July 1958	25.26 secs

The first of Fine Jubilee's track records was set in a heat of the 1936 Gold Collar which he won; he also won the Derby that year. He was back again the following year to knock five lengths off his previous record (one length is calculated at .06 secs), and his time of 25.42 secs was not beaten until 1947 when the great Monday's News clipped it by only .01 secs. Six years later Polonius was to better Monday's News's record, again by only .01 secs. Thus in sixteen years Fine Jubilee's magnificent run – possibly the best ever done by any greyhound anywhere, for no track record held for so long – was beaten by only a short head, and by no more than .02 secs six years later. It gives some idea of the dog's incredible speed during 1936 and 1937.

Mr Rupert Cobb, a local brewer, inaugurated the Cobb Marathon Bowl in 1942. He was a regular visitor to the track, and his other hobby, astrology, brought him to the conclusion that marathon races were most suited to be run here. The event was first run over 810 yds and was then the longest race in England, but so successful was it from the beginning that the Catford management inaugurated even longer events, run over 970 yds and even 1,180 yds, the longest race to be run in Britain. The first winner of the Cobb Marathon was Castledown Prince, whose time of 49.69 secs stood for many years, but he was not the first to break 50.00 secs over the distance, as is often believed. This was achieved by English Warrior back in 1934 when he clocked 49.10 secs, a time which stood for more than a decade before the tiny bitch Alvaston Lulu Belle produced a time of 48.58 secs.

The track record holders over the 810 yds course from 1933 to 1964, were:

Ilene Darling	31 January 1933	53.70 secs
Drintyre	7 March 1933	51.46 secs
Extra Smart	17 June 1933	51.27 secs
Master Ralph	7 August 1933	50.90 secs
Dapifir	29 March 1934	50.35 secs
Real Busy	12 July 1934	50.04 secs
English Warrior	16 August 1934	49.10 secs
Alvaston Lulu Belle	27 July 1945	48.58 secs
Tia Tina	27 September 1958	48.48 secs
Rapid Progress	4 July 1959	48.44 secs
I'm Dogmatic	16 May 1964	48.40 secs

The distance was discontinued in 1974, and I'm Dogmatic's time was never beaten. In thirty-six years English Warrior's time of 49.10 secs was beaten on only four occasions. His run in August 1934 was one of the fastest over a stayers' course anywhere. He also held the 970 yds record here, his time of 60.52 secs, achieved in May 1935, standing for more than thirteen years. This distance was run at Catford from 1935 to 1971, and in all that time only two dogs (Canada's Glory in 1948 and Budget Surplus ten years later) ever bettered it.

Catford has always encouraged hurdle racing and the Stayers' Hurdles, which takes place in January, attracts the best hurdlers. Wimbledon is also strong on hurdle events, and in 1978 the Wimbledon trainer Nora McEllistrim, Paddy's daughter, won the event with Raybet.

The important Greenwich Challenge Cup, an event previously held at New Cross, is run over 555 m in March with a first prize of £800. The bitch Loyal Katie, at 5–2 on, was the lowest-priced winner of recent years when she won for Mr R. Palmer in 1978. The British Breeders' Stakes is run here in September, and in October follows the Ben Truman Stakes with a first prize of £750. It was won in 1978 by a complete outsider, Quakerfield Fun, at 28–1. William Hill, the bookmakers, also sponsor a Nationwide Championship here.

Surprisingly, Catford-trained dogs have had only limited success in the classics. No Catford trainer has won the Derby and only one, M. Thistleton, the Oaks, when Solerina won in 1967. Until 1954 the Gold Collar had been won on only one occasion by a Catford-trained dog – Ardskeagh Ville, trained by Ernie Barker. The 1949 Gold Collar was won by Gay Flash, the Coronation Cup winner and trained by Paddy Milligan, later at Catford. In 1967 A.W. Smith won the event with Stylish Lad, and had further successes in 1969 and 1970. The Gold Collar is now sponsored by John Humphreys, and worth £5,000 to the winner.

Paddy Milligan also won the Gold Collar in 1968 with Shane's Rocket when he was a private trainer at the well-known Beaverwood Kennels in Kent. In that year he trained for Mr Jim O'Connor the outstanding Dusty Trail, who finished third in that year's Derby, won by Faithful Hope in the fastest time ever recorded for the event. Dusty Trail was to win the International and Gimcrack Stakes the same year, and was voted best greyhound of 1968. But it was his great success in the 1967 Catford Breeders' Produce Stakes that finally decided Paddy to throw in his lot with the track. In that year he trained the first three to finish, one of whom was Shane's Rocket. Shane's Rocket (son of Crazy Parachute) was to sire Silly Rocket, who in only one year's racing won the 1973 Welsh Derby, going through unbeaten, and finished third in the Laurels. Twice he broke the track record at Monmore Green.

Paddy Milligan trained Yellow Printer for Miss Pauline Wallis during the early years of that dog's career, but he handled no finer greyhound than Gay Flash, the brindle and white bitch by Fiontra Frolic, owned by Mr Goodwright, who gave Paddy his third Gold Collar. She also won the Coronation Cup that year (1979) and took the Future Champion Stakes at Rochester before the untimely closure of that much-loved track late in 1979.

Main Events Run at Catford

Stayers' Hurdles	January	555 m
Greenwich Challenge Cup	March	555 m
British Breeders' Produce Stakes	September	385 m
* Gold Collar	September	555 m
Ben Truman Stakes	October	555 m
Cobb Marathon Bowl	December	790 m

* Classic event

Track Records (1950)

Monday's News	440 yds	25.41 secs
Bright Board	440 yds H	26.19 secs
Shadowlands Delight	600 yds	35.20 secs
Derryboy Jubilee	600 yds H	36.31 secs
May Hasty	700 yds	40.03 secs
Alvaston Lulu Belle	810 yds	48.58 secs
Western Dasher	1,180 yds	74.42 secs

Track Records (1972)

Cheathas Artist	1971	420 yds	23.88 secs
Sherry's Prince	1971	420 yds H	24.39 secs
The Phoenix	1972	610 yds	35.08 secs
Sherry's Prince	1972	610 yds H	35.75 secs
Breach's Buzzard	1971	790 yds	45.91 secs
Spots of Luck	1971	1,156 yds	70.94 secs

Track Records (1980)

Westmead Champ	1976	555 m	34.65 secs
Autumn River	1977	555 m H	35.72 secs
Pitman's Brief	1976	888 m	58.47 secs

Winners of the Cobb Marathon Bowl

1942	Castledown Prince	49.69 secs
1943	Patty Dear	50.61 secs
1944	Unwin Beauty	50.98 secs
1945	Handsome and Fair	50.99 secs
1946	Keep Sake	51.97 secs
1947	Missouri	49.36 secs
1948	Moral Hostess	51.57 secs
1949	Santolina	49.62 secs
1950	Santolina	51.04 secs
1951	Beauty's Prince	50.11 secs
1952	Bear Hug	50.39 secs
1953	Rimmell's Pearl	48.65 secs
1954	Lizette	49.93 secs
1955	Macennan James	50.73 secs
1956	Endless Victory	49.37 secs
1957	Paul's Vixen	50.01 secs
1958	Shares Again	49.46 secs
1959	Rapid Progress	50.59 secs
1960	Dancing Daisy	50.43 secs
1961	Westfield Prince	49.32 secs
1962	Rothman's Henriette	50.71 secs
1963	Shady Camellia	50.63 secs
1964	Boothroyden Flash	50.40 secs
1965	Doreen Berry	50.28 secs
1966	Breshen Crackers	51.71 secs
1967	Tanyard Swallow	50.21 secs
1968	Sunrise Rover	50.90 secs
1969	Sovereign Ore	48.70 secs
* 1970	Specfire	49.36 secs
† 1971	Breach's Buzzard	46.61 secs
1972	The Marchioness	46.01 secs
1973	Liam's Toby	47.65 secs
1974	Silver Sceptre	46.27 secs
1975	Edenvale Lady	46.75 secs
	(not run since 1975)	

* In 1970 run over 810 yds
† 1971–4 run over 790 yds; in 1975 run over 790 m

Winners of the British Breeders' Produce Stakes 1933–49

1933	Weston Ranger	27.16 secs
1934	Mick the Cavalier	27.01 secs
1935	Melksham Lassie	26.81 secs
1936	Congleton Lord	26.14 secs
1937	Junior Classic	25.90 secs
1938	Dogberry Galent	26.42 secs
1939	not run	
1940	Creamery Glory	26.38 secs
1941	Glorious Double	26.60 secs
1942	Sea Faring	26.54 secs
1943	Erleigh Hero	26.42 secs
1944	Lacquer's Boy	26.34 secs
1945	Judge's Nip	26.13 secs
1946	Leicester	26.20 secs
1947	Tralibawn	26.61 secs
1948	Southern Stoller	26.10 secs
1949	Trev's Kismet	25.98 secs

Winners of the British Breeder's Produce Stakes 1970–84

1970	Cool Water	25.64 secs
1971	Sutton Stroller	25.55 secs
1972	Silver Mist	24.41 secs
1973	Black Dragonfly	24.12 secs
1974	Westmead Moss	24.15 secs
* 1975	not run	
1976	Pharoah's Alert	24.36 secs
1977	Yahoo	24.12 secs
1978	The Corsair	23.93 secs
1979	The Bluelamp	24.06 secs
1980	Panview	24.14 secs

1981	Lordsbury Mac	23.99 secs
1982	Rikasso Mick	23.99 secs
1983	Celalton Grange	23.68 secs
1984	Is He Busy	23.84 secs

*Pre-1975 run over 440 yds; since run over 385 m

CLAPTON

This was the fourth London track to open, on 7 April 1928. The first managing director was Mr H. Garland-Wells. Joint vice-president of the NGRS until his death in 1948, he was considered one of the most astute of track administrators and was in charge of all other tracks controlled by Clapton Stadium Ltd, which included those at South Shields and Warrington. Sadly all are now closed, and of all those tracks which have closed their doors since the booming postwar years, Clapton's demise has caused most heart-aches to followers of the sport.

The track was as near circular as possible with short straights and wide, easy bends. With West Ham and Stamford Bridge (also closed) it was the fastest track in Britain, and it was the venue for the sprinters' classic, the Scurry Gold Cup, run over 400 yds and first contested in 1928. This event, inaugurated by Clapton's first racing manager, Major C. Moss, is held in greater respect by patrons of greyhound racing than any other classic. It has been won by the finest sprinters in the history of the sport – those dogs with the ability to shoot from the traps as if fired from a gun, accompanied by the roar of a packed stadium. What memories they revive – Cruseline Boy and Brave Enough, Creamery Border and Brilliant Bob, Rimmell's Black and Local Interprize, Gorey Airways and Carry On Oregon. Only three bitches have won the event: Monachdy Girlie, in 1952, after which her owner, Mr W. Carter, presented a trophy to be contested each year as the National Sprint Championship, which became almost as popular as the Scurry Cup; Lucky Joan, in 1963; and Foyle Tonic five years later. Two dogs were to win both the Scurry Cup and National Sprint in the same year – Rolling Mike in 1953, and George Flintham's Demon King in 1954.

Surprisingly, almost twenty years were to elapse before a Clapton-trained dog took the Scurry Cup. This was in 1947, when Stanley Biss had charge of Rimmell's Black whose time of 23.11 secs was a new track record. Biss won it again the following year with another black dog, Local Interprize. While at West Ham before the Second World War, he had trained Bradshaw Fold and Queen of the Suir to win the Oaks. In 1933 he was the first trainer to win £10,000 prize money in one year. But his greatest successes came when he moved to Clapton, for Rimmell's Black won the Laurels in 1947 and Local Interprize the Gold Collar in 1948 and 1949. In 1948 Stanley Biss became the first trainer to win £20,000 prize money in one year. He died in March 1952, shortly after Local Interprize retired, and this loved and respected trainer, one of the greatest in the history of the sport, was much missed by Clapton patrons.

Jimmy Jowett of Clapton was another wonderful handler of greyhounds. He trained the Scurry Cup winners of 1952 and 1953 and had another double in 1959 and 1960 with George Flintham's Gorey Airways, the first puppy ever to win the event. No trainer has had more than Jowett's four wins, but John Bassett came close and set a record by training three in a row. During the 1960s no trainer had more successes. His dogs won every honour except the St Leger, and in 1963 he was chosen Trainer of the Year after Lucky Boy Boy won the English Derby. That year he trained four classic winners, including Lucky Joan to win the Scurry Cup and Dromin Glory to win the Cesare-witch and Scottish Derby. No man ever trained more classic winners in one year. His greyhounds were the most successful to race in Britain that year, for besides the classics Dromin Glory won the Birmingham Cup, the Select Stakes, the Prince Philip Cup, the Daily Mirror Cup and the Evening Standard Cup, while Lucky Joan won the Midland Puppy Derby, the Inaugural Stakes and the Coronation Stakes. In 1964 Bassett trained Salthill Sands to win the Scurry Cup, Lucky Boy Boy to win the Select Stakes, and Dromin Glory to win the Elite Stakes. In 1965 he again won the Scurry Cup with After You, the Cesarewitch with Lucky Montforte, and the Birmingham Cup with Arthur's Jet. Then, before Clapton closed, he had charge of the flying Yellow Printer when that dog set a world 525 yds record at White City and won the Irish Derby, the Spring and Summer Cups and the Wood Lane Stakes. In 1975, as a private trainer, he came close to winning the Derby again when Sally's Cobbler ran up to Tartan

Khan. His sire, Cobbler, had reached the 1971 Derby final, and in that year he ran up for the Pall Mall.

Before moving to Wimbledon, Paddy McEvoy was a Clapton trainer and in 1956 trained Dunmore King for Jack McAllister, which he followed in 1961 by training Palm's Printer when he won the Derby for Mr Alf Heale. The dog was to win the Scurry Cup the same year and was the only dog ever to win both events.

Another Clapton trainer of considerable repute was Adam Jackson, a Co. Kildare man who came to England in 1955 as head kennelman to Paddy McEvoy, becoming a trainer in his own right five years later. From here he took the Cambridgeshire-bred Chittering Clapton to the White City to win the Derby by six lengths in 1965. Seven years later he had charge of the twice-winner Patricia's Hope, when the great dog won the event for the first time. The dog also went on to win the Scottish and Welsh Derby in the same year, a feat accomplished by only two other dogs, Trev's Perfection and Mile Bush Pride.

The Clapton kennels, situated at Claverambury Farm, Waltham Cross, taken over by the track in 1938, always had 200 greyhounds in residence, which had the run of 200 acres of magnificent parkland. It was at Clapton that the Conal hurdle was perfected, which was considered much safer for greyhounds than the older types. It has been installed at all tracks since 1950. In 1959 Clapton Stadium Ltd was the subject of an abortive takeover bid, but on 1 January 1974 the track closed for racing.

Track Records (1950)			
Return Fare		400 yds	22.89 secs
Mount Divis		400 yds H	24.08 secs
Blackwater Cutlet		550 yds	31.80 secs
Macaroni II		550 yds H	33.02 secs
Poetic Boy		760 yds	45.29 secs
Track Records (1970)			
Don't Gambol	1971	400 yds	22.29 secs
Prince Chancer	1954	550 yds	31.76 secs
Yellow Printer	1968	575 yds	32.67 secs
Lucky Hi There	1964	760 yds	43.88 secs
Movealong Margo	1968	934 yds	55.20 secs

CLEVELAND PARK

Owned by National Greyhounds Ltd, this Middlesbrough track opened on 19 May 1928 and has continued to provide high-class racing ever since. Less than a year before the Stadium site was a field of allotments covering about ten acres. Although without the benefit of sophisticated modern earth-moving equipment the complex was completed within that time, with an excellent stand and club house, accommodation for 15,000 people, and parking for 600 cars, though in those days few people arrived in their own transport.

More than 5,000 passed through the turnstiles on that opening night when eight races were run, all over 500 yds, with two over hurdles. As usual then, the spectators were entertained before the racing began by a military band. Before each race the greyhounds came on to the track to a fanfare from buglers in hunting pink. The timekeeper and stewards were housed in something like a tobacco kiosk in the centre of the arena. The hare was then on the outside. Admission prices were 5s (25p) to the main stand, where one could get a sandwich and cup of hot Oxo, and 1s (5p) to the 'popular' part. Both prices included a race card.

The champion at Cleveland Park that first summer was an Irish dog called Brilliant Gambler. He was to give many brilliant performances over all distances and set track records over 470 yds and 650 yds; of his first fifteen races he won seven and was second five times. When racing resumed in April 1929 the dog was sold, but in August that year he returned to the track for the first open invitation event run under NGRC rules. Once again Brilliant Gambler showed his superiority, winning over 470 yds in 27.29 secs to establish a new track record.

Other outstanding greyhounds kennelled at Cleveland Park were Degrease, purchased for a fiver, and who went on to win many hundreds of pounds; Lonely Spot; Racing Law, who was still winning when over eight years old; Hanslope Arnold; and Cheerful Chinaman, who won 126 races at the track.

Racing takes place on Wednesday and Saturday evenings throughout the year and there is speedway racing on Thursdays, so the Stadium is kept fully occupied. Many of the greyhounds are track-owned but there are sponsored open events such as the Ladbroke Stayers' Stakes. The general and racing manager for some years was Vic Abbott. It is now Mike Middle. The all-grass track is a 375 m circuit with wide, well banked turns and an inside Sumner hare. Handicap races are a feature here.

Track Records (1950)

Brilliant Gambler		470 yds	27.29 secs
Dusky Guy		518 yds	30.27 secs

Track Records (1970)

Lincoln's Inn	1970	288 yds	16.18 secs
Idle Sailor	1966	500 yds	28.48 secs
Maylin Justice	1962	700 yds	41.83 secs

Track Records (1980)

Kippling's Fox	1976	282 m	17.55 secs
Lazy John	1978	478 m	29.59 secs

COVENTRY

The present track is not the one operated for many years in Lythalls Lane by Alan Sanderson, where George McKay trained many of the best greyhounds in Britain for Mrs Hilda Sanderson. That track closed in 1964 and on 19 September 1978 dog racing was started at the Brandon Stadium in Rugby Road, on the south side of the city close to the M1. Brandon had already staged stock car and speedway racing for some years, so excellent amenities were there from the start. It is an all-sand track of 410 m circuit and an outside McGee hare, while punters are provided with a modern computerized tote, bar and restaurant facilities. Midland Sports Stadiums Ltd., are the owners and racing manager is Sean Doyle. Racing takes place on Tuesday and Friday evenings over 260 m, 460 m and 670 m.

Most of the outstanding dogs in Britain raced at the old Lythalls Lane track. Robeen Printer, kennelled here, was purchased at Shelbourne Park sales in 1944 for 1,650 gns, the highest price ever paid for a bitch at auction. For Coventry's famous Eclipse Stakes, which attracted the best in Britain, she tied with Prancing Kitty in that never-to-be-forgotten final of 1945, and in April that year she broke the track record over 725 yds at Wimbledon by twenty lengths, which gives some idea of her quality. At Coventry, also in 1945, Model Dasher set a new track record over 750 yds which was never bettered.

The Brandon Stadium has recommenced the Eclipse Stakes, run in August and now worth £1,000 to the winner. Since its inauguration in 1938, when Catherine of Waterhall and Demotic Mack dead-heated, bitches have dominated the event. The Stakes was not run between 1939 and 1942, because the club house was almost completely destroyed in the devastating air raid on Coventry, but the event was resumed in 1943, when Model Dasher won. The following year the winner was Winnie of Berrow, who was to become the dam of the 1949 Derby winner, Narrogar Ann. 1945 saw the tie between Robeen Printer and Prancing Kitty, winner of that year's Oaks, and in 1947 Castledown Tiptoes was successful, her time for the event standing for many years. She had won the Puppy Oaks the previous year. The event again went to a bitch when run in 1979 for the first time at the new venue; that year's Derby winner, the great Sarah's Bunny, won in brilliant style. She started 6–4 on favourite to give trainer Geoff de Mulder his first Eclipse Stakes winner. He was following in the footsteps of George McKay, who trained Robeen Printer, later became racing manager at Coventry and then went on to Leicester in that capacity.

Geoff de Mulder is now a contract trainer at Coventry. Amongst other trainers here are Bertie Gaynor, Ken Hancox, Christine Cooper and Barbara Tompkins who trained John Silver to win the English Derby in 1970 and I'm Slippy to win the event again in 1983. Females have held the stage at Coventry since the time of Lady Godiva, outstanding greyhounds kennelled at the Old Lythalls Lane track including those great bitches Shaggy Lass, Simone, Castledown Tiptoes and Robeen Printer.

Main Events Run at Coventry

Spring-time Stakes	March	460 m
Eclipse Stakes	August	460 m

Track Records (1980)

Ballagarrow Jet	1979	260 m	16.06 secs
Brainy Prince	1979	460 m	28.23 secs
Solar Shamrock	1979	670 m	42.54 secs
Eternal Mist	1978	870 m	56.68 secs

CRADLEY HEATH

Racing began here in December 1947. Situated as it is in North Staffordshire, the track has been widely patronized by dog lovers of the Black Country, but at no time in its history has the sport enjoyed greater popularity at Cradley Heath than during 1980, due chiefly to the untiring efforts of Sean Doyle, racing manager until his departure at the year end to take up similar duties at Coventry. During 1980 many improvements were carried out to the running track and to its amenities. The Golden Hammer was the maint event associated with the track but was not run between 1973–82. An outstanding winner of recent years was Thrush's Song, who won from

Little Country in 28.30 secs for the 500 yds course, the fastest time for the event. The dog was trained at Perry Barr by Ted Baldwin who also handled Price Wise when the dog won the 1979 Puppy Derby.

Most important event now run at Cradley Heath is the Elsinore Silver Stakes, worth £500 to the winner and won in 1978 by Westmead Tulip, owned by Natalie Savva and trained on this occasion by Tommy Atkins, a contract trainer at Reading.

In 1983 the Golden Hammer was happily re-introduced.

Main Event Run at Cradley Heath
Elsinore Silver Stakes April 462 m

Winners of the Golden Hammer (500 yds)

1968	Shannon Water	27.96 secs
1969	Discretions	28.20 secs
1970	Thrush's Song	28.30 secs
1971	Big Crash	28.89 secs
1972	Fleet Fox	28.90 secs
1983	Roman Spring	28.36 secs

CRAVEN PARK

The Hull track, almost oval, with wide, well banked bends and long straights. For many years V. Holland was racing manager. It is now Roy Thickett who was his general manager. The Stadium is owned by Hull Kingston Rovers R.F.C. A good, fast track with excellent facilities, including a newly opened restaurant, Craven Park first opened for racing in 1928. There is an inside Sumner hare and racing takes place on Thursday and Saturday evenings.

One of the main events, run in October, is the Art Wells Super Stakes, worth £500 to the winner, which takes place over 462 m. A recent winner was Sligo Swallow, privately trained by J. Booth and owned by Mr Bill Hough. The Hair Belle Trophy is a popular event which was won in 1978 by Burniston Jet, the Owlerton dog, trained by Ron Hookway. This excellent dog also won the William Hill Trophy at Hall Green and was one of the best provincial greyhounds of 1978 and 1979. Other important events staged at Hull are the Charles Key Memorial Trophy, one of the most valuable in greyhound racing, and the Jack Lawlor Trophy.

The leading trainers at Craven Park are G. Lilley; Sylvia Cooke, who had charge of the outstanding Lisamote Exile; John Tollafield; and Ray Jones, trainer of Glebe Blackie, a consistent winner over 462 m and 647 m, which are the principal distances run here. Mr Jones also had charge of By Trouble when the dog won the 1978 Edinburgh Sprint at Powderhall.

It was at Craven Park in April 1946 that the great Lilac's Luck set a new 700 yds record when defeating the wonderful little bitch Alvaston Lulu Belle.

Main Events Run at Craven Park
Charles Key Memorial Trophy
Jack Lawlor Trophy
Art Wells Super Stakes
John Hudson Trophy

Track Records (1950)

Spring Shower	14.8.48	295 yds	16.47 secs
Promotive	5.10.50	500 yds	28.22 secs
Miley's Bridge	29.5.48	700 yds	40.53 secs

Track Records (1970)

Spring Shower	14.8.48	295 yds	16.47 secs
Galbally Gallop	20.6.63	500 yds	28.04 secs
Clonalvy Sue	16.7.64	700 yds	40.30 secs

CRAYFORD

The Crayford and Bexleyheath Greyhound Stadium, to give it its full name, is situated at Crayford in Kent and is reached by train from Waterloo and Charing Cross. The track opened in 1935 and in 1977 came under Ladbroke's management. The running track is about 400 m in circumference with long straights and fairly sharp turns, but excellent banking eliminates excessive bumping. There is an outside Sumner hare and an all-sand surface. Racing takes place on Mondays, Thursdays and Saturdays. Dave Bowman is racing manager and Stan Wolfe general manager.

There is an excellent car park, and right from the start viewing has been entirely under cover. Crayford has the largest totalizator board in Britain and excellent restaurant facilities. A great variety of racing takes place here – over 462 m, 650 m and 880 m, over which course the New Year Marathon is run in January. The Stayers' Stakes is run over 650 m in May, sponsored by Wilkinson Sword, with £500 for the winner; the bitch Iris of Mayfair won the 1978 event. The Britvic Hurdle Cup is also run here and was won in 1978 by that great hurdler Topothetide, owned by Mr and Mrs Denis Parish and trained at Harringay by Tommy Foster. Topothetide also won that year's Grand National. The *Daily Express* Hurdles, another popular event, is run in February, and like the Britvic Hurdles carries a prize of £300 for the winner. Winner of the *Daily Express* Hurdles in

1978 was the Portsmouth dog Prince Rover, who also won the 1978 March Hare Hurdles at Crayford. Carlsberg Lager sponsor a number of events, and Crayford's last racing manager, Tony Smith did much to bring in new sponsors. The most important event run here is the Crayford Vase, now sponsored by Courage's brewery, with £1,000 for the winner.

One of the longest races in Britain, over 1,068 m, is run here, usually in May; in 1978 it was won by the game Yarmouth bitch Bookfield Sarah, who defeated the fine Crayford dog Welsh Cobbler. Another outstanding dog to win at Crayford in that year was the £10,000 purchase Noble Brigg, who had previously won the Irish National Sprint at Dunmore Park. He was to set a new track record at Crayford for the 650 m course when winning the Ladbroke's Trainers' Championship.

Crayford moved to the contract trainer system early in 1971, with trainers Paddy Coughlan, who was previously at Arms Park, Cardiff; Terry O'Sullivan, who has been at Crayford since 1955; John Gibbons; John Honeysett; and Eric Parsons, whose father and grandfather were associated with Harringay during the early years of the sport. The Crayford track was, in fact, the first in Britain to follow the American idea of having greyhounds trained by contract trainers with kennels away from the track, and with whom a contract is made annually. The method has since been taken up by most tracks licensed by the NGRC and has worked well.

One of the finest dogs ever trained here was Flying Pursuit who gave John Gibbons his first classic success when winning the 1980 Laurels and Flying Duke, trained by P. Coughlan to win the Grand Prix for Mr Byrne.

Main Events Run at Crayford

New Year Marathon	January	880 m
Daily Express Hurdles	February	462 m
March Hare Hurdles	March	462 m
Courage's Spring Trophy	March	650 m
Crayford Vase	August	462 m
Ike Morris Puppy Cup	July	462 m

Track Records (1950)

Rover's Companion	440 yds	26.02 secs
Hetton Ring	500 yds	28.89 secs
Go the Bell	530 yds	30.36 secs
Cannuck's Wish	530 yds H	31.29 secs

Track Records (1980)

Bray Vale	2.6.80	240 m	14.77 secs
Pigeon Flyer	14.8.78	462 m	28.04 secs
London Rover	14.4.80	462 m H	28.88 secs
Cormacruiser	31.3.80	648 m	40.26 secs
Howl On Rodger	28.3.79	648 m H	41.45 secs
Salina	2.6.80	870 m	55.31 secs
Keem Princess	6.12.80	1056 m	69.35 secs

Winners of the Crayford Vase 1968–84

1968	Ambiguous	29.10 secs
1969	Quarrymount Bill	28.69 secs
1970	Lord Phil	29.21 secs
1971	Mad Risk	28.77 secs
1972	Fragrant Flyer	28.41 secs
1973	Kilmac Chieftan	28.58 secs
1974	Money Again	28.92 secs
* 1975	London Spec	28.41 secs
1976	Gin and Jass	28.54 secs
1977	Colonel Pearloma	28.70 secs
1978	Proud Time	28.40 secs
1979	Fearna Cobbler	28.38 secs
1980	John's Luck	28.47 secs
1981	Deel Joker	28.11 secs
1982	General Fun	29.02 secs
1983	Sammy Bear	28.58 secs
1984	Gortatlea Brigg	28.17 secs

*Pre-1975 run over 500 yds; since run over 462 m

DERBY

This Midlands track, which began racing in 1934, must be unique among greyhound tracks for it was built inside the thick walls of the ancient Derby prison, on the prisoners' exercising ground. It is one of the smallest tracks, with a circuit of only 380 yds; it has quite sharp bends, but they are sanded and well banked so that bumping is reduced to a minimum. Amenities are good and the kennels adjoin the stadium. Recently the club room has been modernized and is now very comfortable. The whole arena, tucked inside its thick walls, presents an intimate atmosphere and the highest standards of racing have always been maintained.

The racing manager here for many years was Lieut-Col Prior, who felt that greyhounds always raced better at night, under lights. He therefore ensured that the lighting here was always first-class. In the early years Derby raced mostly track-owned greyhounds all of which were looked after by one trainer, Harvey Broadbent. Now a number open events with good prize money encourage some of the north's best dogs to enter. The most important event is the Arnold Dennis Stakes, sponsored by the Owlerton and Derby bookmaker of that name, with a £500 prize and handsome trophy for the winner. Derby is the venue for one of the longest races in Britain, over 934 m (almost

1000 yds). In 1979 it was won by the Cambridge dog Gloss, trained by Miss Godwin, in 61.05 secs. It is not often that a race lasts for more than a minute.

The track is owned by Derby Greyhound Stadium Ltd. Its general manager from 1970 to 1979 was George Coleman, now replaced by Terry Corden. Barry Davis is racing manager. Racing takes place on Wednesday and Saturday evenings, with additional Mondays in summer, mostly over 246 m, 420 m and 764 m. Some greyhounds are supplied by contract trainers including Doug Kenny and Terry Munslow, while those kennelled at the track are looked after by Tom Harrison, Frank Heald, Peter Corbett and P. Murphy. The best dog to win here in recent years was Derby Pleasure, who in 1979 won thirty-four races in top grade.

Main Event Run at Derby

Arnold Dennis Trophy	April	420 m

Track Records (1970)			
Cheerful Cricket		270 yds	15.21 secs
Rich Tea		460 yds	25.51 secs
Spectre II		650 yds	36.49 secs
Track Records (1980)			
Illinois Riki	1979	246 m	15.14 secs
Pacey	1979	420 m	25.79 secs
Dyrnham Star	1975	590 m	36.95 secs
Derange Me	1978	764 m	49.40 secs
Gloss	1979	934 m	61.05 secs

EASTVILLE (BRISTOL)

The Bristol track opened in July 1932 and has always been in the forefront of provincial tracks. It is also the home of Bristol Rovers Football Club, and has a spacious car park and excellent restaurant facilities. The track is 400 m in circumference with long straights and well banked, graduated bends, so that fast times are recorded. The first general manager was Lieut-Col Forsdike, who was to become secretary of the NGRC. The present general manager is Ian Stevens and the racing manager Ken Whitrow, who has been at Eastville since the late 1950s. Racing takes place on Monday and Friday afternoons over 470 m, 670 m and 874 m, and five contract kennels make up the racing strength, providing about thirty dogs each. The track has recently had its turf removed and sand laid to a depth of 14 ins, which makes for faster times than were possible on the original sand, which was a surface layer. Sadly, in August 1980, the stand and all records were destroyed by fire.

The most important event run here since the track opened is the Golden Crest. Indeed it was, with the Eclipse Stakes run at the old Coventry track and the All-England Cup at Brough Park, the most important provincial event and has always attracted the best dogs in training. One of the outstanding performances was that of Shannon Shore in 1945, when the Golden Crest was run over 500 yds, for he defeated one of the fastest dogs in England, Magic Beau, by ten lengths in 28.76 secs. The following year Shannon Shore again reached the final, but after setting a new track record of 28.66 secs in his semi-final met in the final another outstanding dog, Rimmell's Black, who won by a neck from Tan Gent after the two had raced neck-and-neck throughout. The following year Rimmell's Black again reached the final and in his semi-final clipped .01 secs off Shannon Shore's record, but he was beaten in the final by Funny Mick, whom he had defeated in the semi-final.

Several other great dogs of the 1940s won the Golden Crest. Wireless Delight was successful in 1943 and Fair and Handsome the following year. Wireless Delight was by Wireless Rally out of Erin's Green; also in that litter was Erin's Fury, a bitch who won the Coronation Stakes in 1944 when she was elected champion bitch of the year. More recently an outstanding dog to have won the event was Discretions, owned by Mr and Mrs Haden and trained by Dave Geggus. He won in 1968, setting a new track record. That year he also won the Catford Cup and Birmingham Cup, and in a short career smashed four track records. Ten years later Dolla Arkle, a 2–1 favourite, was to take the trophy and the £2,000 prize for his owner, Mr G. Holt, and his trainer, Jim Coleman who came back in 1979 as trainer of the winner, Our Rufus. The race is now run over 470 m in July.

Also run at Eastville is the Western Two-year-old Produce Stakes, of which the most important winner was undoubtedly the bitch Narrogar Ann. She had just run her first race, at Oxford, and had contested the Coronation Stakes at Wembley without success, but in the 1948 Produce Stakes she was joined by three others from the same litter and three of them were to win their respective heats -- Narrogar Tommy, Narrogar Ann and Narrogar Dusty, the last-named winning by ten lengths. All three took the first three places in the final, won by a short head by Narrogar Ann from Narrogar Dusty, and this outstanding bitch went on to win the Derby the following year, becoming only the second bitch to do so. She was later to be dam of another Derby winner, Endless Gossip. Both Narrogar Ann and her son were English-born and -bred. In 1978 Paddy McEvoy, a legend in his lifetime, who as long ago as 1953 trained Daw's Dancer to win the Derby for Mr D. Fitzgerald, was at Eastville to win the Produce Stakes, now valued at £1,225, with the even-money favourite Ricky O.

The Ernest Thornton-Smith Trophy, run in August, over the marathon 874 m course, was won in 1978 by another excellent bitch, Eternal Mist, owned and trained by Mr Richard Iremonger. From Eastville in 1982 went the great Donna's Dixie, trained and owned by Mr H Kibble, to take the Golden Collar at Catford.

Main Events Run at Eastville

Con-John Trophy	May	670 m
Golden Crest	July	470 m
Western Two-year-old Produce Stakes	July	470 m
Ernest Thornton-Smith Trophy	August	874 m

Track Records (1950)

Flintfield Grosvenor	500 yds	28.50 secs
Red Nuxer	500 yds H	29.21 secs
Glen Ranger	525 yds	29.64 secs
Model Dasher	600 yds	35.11 secs
Shaggy Lass	700 yds	40.61 secs

Track Records (1970)

Discretions	500 yds	27.85 secs
Red Nuxer	500 yds H	29.21 secs
Nobody's Pick	730 yds	42.29 secs
Hop's Pal	932 yds	54.80 secs

Winners of the Golden Crest 1944–9

1944	Fair and Handsome	28.00 secs
1945	Shannon Shore	28.69 secs
1946	Rimmell's Black	28.67 secs
1947	Funny Mick	28.69 secs
1948	Freckled Major	29.81 secs
1949	Flintfield Grosvenor	28.83 secs

Winners of the Golden Crest 1970–81

1970	Moordyke Spot	28.74 secs
1971	Clonarrow Piper	28.83 secs
1972	Royal Spitfire	28.86 secs
1973	Maureen's Ben	28.61 secs
1974	Last Rocket	28.75 secs
* 1975	Daemonic Gambol	28.74 secs
1976	Countryman	28.78 secs
1977	Rathduff Spring	28.58 secs
1978	Dolla Arkle	28.62 secs
1979	Our Rufus	28.39 secs
1980	Jack's Asleep	28.25 secs
1981	Astral Cloud	28.34 secs

*Pre-1975 run over 500 yds; since run over 470 m

GLOUCESTER and CHELTENHAM

This track, which opened its gates for racing in 1933, is small, with only a 430 yds circuit, but is fast, with sanded bends and undersoil heating which enables racing to take place whatever the weather. Racing is on Thursday and Saturday evenings each week, and also on Monday in summer, and it is well attended. The distances run are 462 m, 647 m and 860 m, with hurdles events over the shorter course. Amenities are good and a large car park caters for those who come from the Cotswolds and other outlying districts where there has always been a keen interest in greyhounds. There is an inside Sumner hare.

At one time the Grand National of the West was run here in July. In 1948 it was won by that excellent hurdler Appleford Peter, who set a new track record in winning his heat and went on to take the Christmas Vase at Wimbledon. He was trained by Arthur Shelton who was for many years a respected trainer at the track. This event has not been run since 1965.

Mr Norman Russell was for many years racing manager.

One of the first of Gloucester's trainers was Ron Mills, a kennel boy with Jack Harvey before going to Gloucester in 1940 where he remained until the track closed. In 1983 he trained Roman Spring to win the Golden Hammer at Cradley Heath, showing that he had lost none of his expertise. Also at Gloucester was Janet Dickenson who joined as a contract trainer in 1972 and had charge of that fine bitch, What Now.

The track closed in 1984.

Track Records (1950)

Spring Shower	1948	500 yds	28.01 secs
Joy's Heartbreak	1948	500 yds H	29.24 secs
Bundle of Fun	1948	650 yds	37.25 secs

Track Records (1970)

Square Gift	1962	500 yds	27.79 secs
Halfpenny King	1965	500 yds H	28.72 secs
Old Berry Jewel	1962	700 yds	39.75 secs

Track Records (1980)

Doverdale Lady	1976	860 m	54.79 secs

GOSFORTH

This Newcastle track is the home of the county rugby club, and was opened for racing in May 1932. From the beginning most other club houses, for the plate glass front of the south stand at Gosforth provided an uninterrupted view of racing and the amenities are first-class.

The track is almost square, because the rugby field is in the centre, so the bends are graduated and wide; there are short straights on all four sides and fast times are run. The circumference of the track is 400 m, and it has an inside Sumner hare. Racing takes place on Wednesday and Friday evenings each week and the racing manager is Mr Joe May.

Main Event Run at Gosforth

Fennturn Leger	December	614 m

Track Records (1950)

Carefree Rambler	1948	475 yds	27.82 secs
Jersey Belle	1948	520 yds	29.95 secs

HACKNEY

The Stadium is in east London and started racing in 1932. It is a fine, big, galloping track of 430 m circumference, with long straights and well banked bends, while the all-sand surface permits fast times even in the winter. There is an outside Sumner hare. Michael Marks is the racing manager, and the track, owned by Brent Walker Ltd, has always been noted for its go-ahead innovations which have kept it in the forefront of greyhound stadia. Photo-electric timing gear, an invention of its chief electrician, George Crookbank, was first installed at Hackney, and from his ideas the General Electric Co. produced new timing equipment with a view to eliminating hand timing (though timing is also done by hand in case the electric system goes wrong). The first ray-timing of the Derby at White City took place in 1953. Excellent bar and restaurant facilities add to the enjoyment of racing here, which takes place on Tuesdays, Thursdays and Saturdays over 304 m, 523 m and 740 m.

The Mecca Bookmakers' Winter Stayers' Stakes, run over the 740 m course in January, was won in 1978 by the great Paradise Spectre at 3–1 on. Owned by Mr Roger and trained by Pat Mullins, the great black also won the Grand Prix at Walthamstow that year. The 1979 event was won by Mrs Maud's great dog Aglish Boss, trained at Southend by G. Baggs. In March is run the Ladbroke's Golden Sprint over 304 m, the most important two-bend sprint in Britain and worth £1,000 to the winner. In 1978 the Oaks winner Ballinderry Moth, trained by Barney O'Connor, was successful, and the bitch proved herself the fastest in training that year. Sampson's Pal, trained by Pat Mullins, won in 1979. Over the 484 m course is run the William Hill Sixer, worth £1,000 and won in 1978 by Mrs Tozer's brilliant Wired to the Moon. Also over the 484 m course is run the One Thousand Guineas, now sponsored by Mecca Bookmakers and previously run at Park Royal until that track closed. Ashmore Fun won in 1979. The last event of the year is the William Hill Lead, run in December and won in 1975 by the great brindle Baffling Bart, sired by The Grand Silver. He won his heat, semi-final and final from a top-class field, and early the following year went on to win the Steel City Cup at Owlerton and ran up to Mutt's Silver (neck) for the White City Cambridgeshire. He won thirty open events and was rarely, if ever, out of the first two.

At one time the Armhurst Cup was the premier event run here. It was won in 1948 by Don Gypsy, one of the most consistent dogs ever to run who set a new track record when beating Funny Mick in the final. The next year the event was won by West End Dasher, who had run up to Local Interprize for the Welsh Derby the previous year. Another important event was the Gilbert Trophy, run over 550 yds, which was won in 1946 by the Derby winner Monday's News and three years later by another Derby winner, Narrogar Ann, when she set a new track record.

Racing takes place on Tuesday and Thursday afternoons and Saturday mornings.

Main Events Run at Hackney

William Hill Sixer	January	484 m
Mecca Bookmakers' Winter Stakes	January	740 m
Ladbrokes' Golden Sprint	March	304 m
Mecca Bookmakers' Thousand Guineas	October	484 m
William Hill Lead	December	523 m

Track Records (1950)

Don Gypsy	1948	500 yds	27.93 secs
Narrogar Ann	1949	550 yds	31.09 secs

Track Records (1980)

Clear Reason	1. 3.75	304 m	18.02 secs
London Spec	27. 3.76	484 m	29.02 secs

Drynham Star	22. 2.75	523 m	31.48 secs
Wired to Moon	10.12.77	523 m	31.48 secs
Sound Wave	12. 1.80	523 m	31.48 secs
Monday's Style	24.10.74	669 m	41.80 secs
Tally Ho Sabrina	7. 4.80	740 m	45.88 secs

HALIFAX

The Stadium had been operating as an independent track for more than forty years when in 1975 it began racing under the NGRC permit scheme, but has now closed for racing. The track was a large one, more egg-shaped than oval, and is fast, with the minimum of bumping at the bends. Jack Wardman, the general manager, introduced the Festival of Racing which took place in July and attracted some of the north's finest greyhounds. Early in 1978 Mr David Collins, a local businessman, purchased the track and installed new photo-finish and ray-timing equipment and built a modern club house, but the track stopped racing under NGRC rules in 1979.

The finest dog ever trained and kennelled here was Amber Sky, who in 1977 won the Scottish Derby, the first classic won by a Halifax dog. His trainer was Peter Beaumont who shortly afterwards moved to Elland Road, Leeds and was there until the track closed.

HALL GREEN

This south Birmingham track is owned by the GRA has always been one of the best in the Midlands. The track, which opened in 1927, has always provided patrons with first-class racing. In 1970 extensive alterations were made to the club house including a splendid restaurant with four-tier seating for more than 100 patrons, so that all the diners get an excellent view of the racing. A new track surface has been provided, and there is now better banking at the bends with the result that the track has become one of the fastest in Britain. Much of the enclosure was also glassed in to give patrons winter protection. These improvements cost about £250,000.

The general manager is David Burkett. Sidney Wood, deputy chief racing manager for all GRA stadia, is racing manager. Since 1970 the track kennels have been replaced by outside contract trainers and the system has worked well. Racing takes place on alternate Monday evenings, and on Wednesday and Saturday each week throughout the year. The track is of turf with sanded bends and has an outside McGee hare. Racing takes place whatever the weather, because undersoil electric heating has been installed.

The most important events run here are the Midland Flat Championship over 474 m, in August, and the Midland Grand National over hurdles. The Midland Flat carries a first prize of £2,000 while the hurdles event is now sponsored by Courage's brewery. The 1979 BBC TV Trophy final was also contested at the track over the 815 m course. Here, too, is run the Midland Oaks, won in 1979 by Mrs Perry's Shiloh Jenny, trained at Hall Green by R. Wilkes.

Followers of greyhound racing at Hall Green when the track first opened will remember the wonderful performances in 1936–7 of the track-kennelled dog Grosvenor Edwin, who was the champion stayer of all England. He was to lose only once over 700 yds – in 1937, when Jesmond Cutlet beat him by just over a length on his home course, after one of the greatest races of all time. That year Grosvenor Edwin won the Wembley Gold Cup over a similar distance and came back to win it again the following year, while his litter brother, Grosvenor Bob, took the St Leger in 1937 and ran up to Jesmond Cutlet in the Cesarewitch. These three were the greatest long-distance dogs the sport had ever known until Model Dasher, kennelled at another Birmingham track, Perry Barr, appeared on the scene a few years later. Grosvenor Bob and Edwin were from Macoma's daughter, Wonderful Expression, from her first mating to Golden Hammer. From a second mating she produced Grosvenor Ferdinand, who won the Gold Collar in 1939. A later mating to Grand Flight II produced the fine bitch Wonder Flyer who, but for the war years, might have won more than one of the bitches' classics.

The magnificent Westown Adam took the Nationwide Supreme Champion Marathon here in 1979. Trained by Natalie Savva, that great stayer had won in 1978 the TV Sportsview Trophy at Walthamstow, the Stow Marathon, and the Mullard Stakes at White City. He was again a finalist in 1979 for the TV Trophy, run at Hall Green. By taking the Supreme Champion Marathon he proved himself a worthy successor to Grosvenor Edwin and the finest stayer in Britain of the past decade.

One of the contract trainers at Hall Green for some years has been Geoff de Mulder, who trained Jimsun to win the 1974 Derby for his father, the late Joe de Mulder, for many years a great greyhound racing enthusiast who owned a number of outstanding dogs. Five years later Geoff was in charge of Sarah's Bunny, the fourth bitch to win the event. Owned by Mr and Mrs Roy Hadley, she won by a length from the 1978 winner, Lacca Champion, with Desert Pilot, also trained by Geoff de Mulder, and owned by his father, in third place. Sarah's Bunny was sired by Jimsun, which gave Geoff de Mulder the honour of being only the second person to train both a Derby winner and the son or daughter of a Derby winner.

Main Events Run at Hall Green

Midland Stayers' Stakes	March	663 m
Midland Flat Championship	August	474 m

Track Records (1950)

Demotic Mac	1937	500 yds	28.30 secs
Patlander	1934	500 yds H	29.42 secs
Jersey Creamery	1948	700 yds	40.40 secs
Border Rambler	1939	700 yds H	42.30 secs

Track Records (1971)

Bresheen Legacy	1971	500 yds	27.73 secs
Sherry's Prince	1971	500 yds H	28.38 secs
The Grand Canoe	1965	700 yds	39.42 secs
Border Rambler	1939	700 yds H	42.30 secs
Black Myross	1971	880 yds	50.90 secs

Track Records (1980)

Foxy Cooper	1977	259 m	15.45 secs
Pat Seamur	1977	474 m	28.49 secs
Autumn Berlin	1978	474 m H	29.39 secs
Let Him Go	1977	606 m	37.65 secs
Katie Toughnut	1977	663 m	40.88 secs

Winners of the Midland Flat Champ 1970–84

1970	Kilronan Jet	28.00 secs
1971	Cash for Harry	27.93 secs
1972	Short Cake	27.50 secs
1973	Casa Miel	27.76 secs
1974	Lady Devine	28.76 secs
* 1975	Sun Chariot	28.87 secs
1976	Westmead Border	29.22 secs
1977	Shiloh Jenny	28.84 secs
1978	Shiloh Jenny	28.83 secs
1979	Loughlass Champ	29.04 secs
1980	Creamery Pat	28.97 secs
1981	Houghton Sinbad	29.05 secs
1982	Rikasso Hiker	28.97 secs
1983	Beau Geste	29.02 secs
1984	Golden Sand	28.91 secs

*Pre-1975 run over 525 yds; since run over 474 m

HARRINGAY

Situated in north London and easily reached by tube, Harringay was the second London track to open, on 13 September 1927, and the third in Britain. It has always been owned by the GRA. The running track is of average size with long straights and easy, graduated bends. A wide variety of racing, over several distances and over hurdles, has always been a feature here, while the amenities are among the best anywhere. Racing takes place on Monday and Friday each week, and on alternate Tuesdays. The general manager is Ernest Farrant, who took over when Bill Holmes moved to the White City; the racing manager is P.J. Saunders. Harringay has always been most helpful to those connected with the sport, and November is designated Harringay Owners' Month, with special events contested and over £2,000 added to prize money by sponsors – trophies presented by Guinness, Schweppes, Skol Lager and John Haig Whisky. In September each year the British Breeders' Festival is held here. There are trade stands and a parade of stud dogs, brood bitches and retired champions. The Festival concentrates on publicizing British-bred greyhounds and does much to stimulate interest in them.

The track was built on the site of a London refuse tip and presented considerable difficulty in its construction, but the excellent drainage enables racing to take place the whole year round, no matter what the weather. Indeed, during the severe winter of 1978–9, when no horse racing took place for several weeks, greyhound racing from Harringay was televized on Saturday afternoons and did much to popularize the sport with those who had not previously seen greyhounds racing.

Here is run over 475 m the classic event for bitches, the Oaks, though before 1959 it was run at the White City. Perhaps the outstanding bitches to have won the Oaks during the 1960s were Cranog Bet and Shady Parachute, both trained by Phil Rees. Cranog Bet won the event in 1963 and 1964 and Shady Parachute in 1968, when she became the first to break 29 secs over the 525 yds course, her time of 28.89 secs beating Pigalle Wonder's track record of 29.03 secs, set in the 1958 Pall Mall. Shady Parachute had been purchased for only 300 gns and won prize money to the value of £8,500 during her career.

Another outstanding Oaks winner of recent years was Kilmagoura Mist, who won in 1978 and went on to win the 1979

St Leger at her home track, Wembley. Four bitches have won the Oaks twice, but few who have won the premier event for bitches have been successful in other classics, and vice versa. Dolores Rocket won the Derby and St Leger – the only bitch to do so – but did not win the Oaks. Indeed, none of the bitches which won the Derby was also successful in the Oaks. Queen of the Suir, who twice won the English Oaks, also won the Irish event – the only bitch to have done so – but only Kilmagoura Mist has won the English Oaks and another English classic, the St Leger. She was by Yanka Boy and was quoted 10–1 against her winning the Oaks, becoming one of the biggest outsiders to win. The Oaks now carries a prize of £2,000 for the winning owner, and in 1977 Switch Off became the first Harringay-kennelled greyhound to win the event since the war, when she won for trainer Jim Singleton. He came to Harringay in 1936 when Jack Harvey and Harry Buck were trainers here. Then, after spells at the White City and Stamford Bridge, he moved back to Harringay, retiring early in 1979.

Apart from the Oaks, the most important event run at Harringay is the Pall Mall, inaugurated in 1935 and perhaps the most important event of the racing calendar not given classic status, even though it always attracts the best dogs in training. The first Pall Mall was won by Mr Keen's outstanding dog Shove Ha'penny by a head from George Flintham's Grand Flight II. Two years later the event was won by a dog trained by Jack Harvey, who had just moved to Harringay from Belle Vue. Bill France, another Harringay trainer, won the event in 1946 with the great Dante II, since when no Harringay trainer has been successful. Indeed, it was not until 1973 that a Harringay-trained dog (by Ted Parker), Case Money, was to win another important event when he took the St Leger. Before the war, Jack Harvey won the Derby and Gold Collar with Davesland, and Jim Wright won the St Leger with Greta's Rosary and Gayhunter in 1938 and 1939. During the 1930s, Harringay trainers were particularly successful in the classics. Jim Kennedy won the 1930 Scurry Gold Cup with Barlock, and Harry Buck did so with Brave Enough in 1931.

Shortly after his success in the first Pall Mall, C.W. Ashley moved from Stamford Bridge to Harringay and trained Orluck's Best to win the 1938 Scurry Cup. This great dog was to sire the even greater Monday's News, who won the Pall Mall in 1947. The following year Night Breeze took the Oaks and the Pall Mall and gave Stanley Biss his only success in the latter event. Two years later Jack Harvey had his second success, this time with George Flintham's Ballycurreen Garrett, and ten years later this trainer was in charge of the Pall Mall winners Mile Bush Pride and Clonalvy Pride. Mile Bush Pride took all before him in 1959, winning the Derby, the Scottish and Welsh Derbys, the Cesarewitch and the Pall Mall. But in Clonalvy Pride Jack Harvey had an equally fine dog, who won the St Leger two years later when almost five years old and in 1960 had reached the final of the Derby, for which he was 2–1 co-favourite. But it was at stud that Clonalvy Pride was to earn everlasting fame as sire of Yanka Boy, in turn sire of Nameless Pixie, winner of the Irish Oaks and, from a mating with An Tain, of Dark Mercury, sire of the 1979 Irish Derby winner, the bitch Penny County. Clonalvy Pride figures in the pedigree of nearly every top greyhound of the 1970s.

No Harringay greyhound has ever won the Laurels, and only twice the Derby – Jack Harvey with Davesland in 1934, when he defeated Grey Raca, Wild Woolley and Brilliant Bob; and C.W. Ashley in 1940 with G.R. Archduke. This was the only occasion on which the Derby has been run away from the White City, and it was appropriate that the winner should be kennelled and trained at Harringay.

Perhaps the most outstanding dog to be kennelled at Harringay was Dante II who, until moved to Bob Burls at Wembley early in 1947, was trained here by Bill France. Besides his Pall Mall success he won the Northern Flat at Belle Vue and the O.A. Critchley Memorial Stakes, and ran up to Tonycus for the Grand Prix.

Another outstanding winner of the Pall Mall in more recent years was Camira Story, owned by Mr V. Hart and trained at Clapton by Adam Jackson. He won in 1971 in a time of 28.39 secs, second only to the track record of 28.30 secs set by Yellow Printer in 1968. In the Pall Mall of that year this great dog twice set a new track record, winning his heat in 28.71 secs and his semi-final in 28.60 secs, when he defeated Mr and Mrs Greatorex's Local Motive by five lengths. But, as so often happened to Yellow Printer, Camira Story was beaten by a neck in the final, and the winner was Local Motive. Also taking part in the event that year were Camira Flash, the Derby winner, and the Leeds record-breaker Lisamote Precept.

Over the 660 m course is run the prestigious Ladbroke's Golden Jacket Invitation Stakes, worth £2,000 to the winner and won in 1978 by Mrs R. Marks's Black Legend, trained by Ted Dickson at Slough. Over the same distance is run the Harringay Gold Vase, with a prize of £500 for the winner. The longest race here is the Nipa Lassie Marathon, run over 830 m and worth £500 to the winner. The event is sponsored by Mr Bill Crowe, owner of the great marathon bitch Nipa Lassie. The first winner of the event was the bitch Princess Glen, who produced the same gameness as Nipa Lassie, who finished third in the 1978 St Leger, behind Westmead Power and Rhu.

The National Sprint, run at Clapton until that track closed, is now run at Harringay and was won in 1979 by Mr Gidrey's Knockrour Brandy.

Harringay also gives prominence to hurdle events, the most important being the *Daily Mirror* Hurdles, run over 475 m. The *Daily Mirror* has always been generous in its sponsorship of greyhound racing and in the amount of interest it has taken in the sport. A recent winner was Mr P. Leeper's Out all Night. Success in the Scottish Grand National of 1979 came to the Harringay trainer Frank Melville, when Scintilla's Rock won the event, sponsored by the *Scottish Daily Express*. This much respected trainer also trained Tilbrook Value and Elton Smasher to finish second and third. It was at Harringay in 1972 that Sherry's Prince, trained by Colin West at West Ham, clocked the world record time of 29.02 secs for the 525 yds hurdles, which he was to better on a later visit. Here, too, was kennelled the great dog Train, who within two months of his arrival at the track in July 1940 had lowered the 525 yds track record and had won his first three races there. He was later to beat Ballynennan Moon three times in four races.

Main Events Run at Harringay

Daily Mirror Hurdles	February	475 m H
Ladbroke's Golden Jacket Stakes	February	660 m
Pall Mall	April	475 m
Harringay Gold Vase	July	660 m
National Sprint Championship	September	414 m
Oaks	November	475 m
Harringay Marathon	November	830 m

Track Records (1950)

Demotic Mac	500 yds	28.46 secs
Kilganny Bridge	500 yds	29.53 secs
Fish Hill	525 yds	29.40 secs
Dark General	525 yds H	30.22 secs
Alvaston Lulu Belle	700 yds	40.44 secs

Track Records (1970)

Welcome Home	500 yds	28.41 secs
Yellow Printer	525 yds	28.20 secs
Sherry's Prince	525 yds H	29.02 secs
Westpark Quail	700 yds	39.89 secs
Hiver Whitenose	880 yds	50.43 secs

Track Records (1980)

Sampsons Pal	31.8 79	414 m	24.77 secs
House Party	23 10 78	475 m	28.37 secs
Derby Wonder	23 2 80	475 m H	29.13 secs
Westlands Steve	13.12 80		
Drynam Star	21 2 76	660 m	40.14 secs
Howl on Rodger	5.10.79	660 m H	41.38 secs
Miss Kilkenny	3.10.77	830 m	51.79 secs
Welsh Cobbler	3.11.78	891 m	56.38 secs

Winners of the Pall Mall

		Trainer	Track	
1935	Shove Ha'penny	C.W. Ashley	Stamford Bridge	30.97 secs
1936	Safe Rock	F. Wilson	Rochester	31.01 secs
1937	Golden Safeguard	H. Harvey	Harringay	30.22 secs
1938	Roeside Creamery	J. Harmon	Stamford Bridge	30.43 secs
1939–44	not run			
1945	Shannon Shore	L. Reynolds	Wembley	29.86 secs
1946	Dante II	W. France	Harringay	30.30 secs
1947	Monday's News	F. Farey	(Private)	30.10 secs
1948	Night Breeze	S. Biss	Clapton	30.03 secs
1949	Drumgoon Boy	F. Davis	(Private)	29.71 secs
1950	Ballycurreen Garrett	H. Harvey	Wembley	30.02 secs
1951	Westbourne	N. Merchant	(Private)	29.97 secs
1952	Marsh Harrier	H. Mills	(Private)	29.82 secs
1953	Home Luck	S. Martin	Wimbledon	29.49 secs
1954	Rushton Mac	F. Johnson	(Private)	30.26 secs
1955	Duet Leader	T. Reilly	Walthamstow	29.42 secs
1956	Silent Worship	J. Bassett	(Private)	29.42 secs
1957	Clara Prince	P. McEvoy	Clapton	29.44 secs
1958	Pigalle Wonder	J. Syder Jnr	Wembley	29.03 secs

		Trainer	Track	
1959	Mile Bush Pride	H. Harvey	Wembley	29.26 secs
1960	Clonalvy Pride	H. Harvey	Wembley	30.18 secs
1961	Jockey's Glen	M. Sandeeson	(Private)	29.15 secs
1962	Hurry On King	T. Johnston	West Ham	29.67 secs
1963	Cahara Rover	G. de Mulder	(Private)	29.74 secs
1964	Poor Linda	Nora Gleeson	Wimbledon	29.70 secs
1965	Clonmannon Flash	R. Hookway	Owlerton	29.41 secs
1966	Dusty Trail	P. Milligan	(Private)	29.40 secs
1967	Castle Fame	J. Pickering	White City	29.48 secs
1968	Local Motive	J. Kinsley	Wembley	28.86 secs
1969	Bread Soda	W. Wilson	Owlerton	28.80 secs
1970	Moordyke Spot	S. Martin	Wimbledon	28.74 secs
1971	Camira Story	A. Jackson	Clapton	28.88 secs
1972	Forest Noble	P. McEvoy	Wimbledon	28.85 secs
1973	Carrig Shane	J. Lancashire	(Private)	28.57 secs
1974	Blackwater Champ	P. Payne	(Private)	28.53 secs
* 1975	My Dowry	Miss Heasman	(Private)	29.11 secs
1976	Gin and Jass	W. Drinkwater	(Private)	28.81 secs
1977	Greenfield Fox	E. Dickson	Slough	28.71 secs
1978	Ballinderry Moth	B. O'Connor	Walthamstow	28.80 secs
1979	Sampson's Pal	P. Mullins	(Private)	28.91 secs
1980	Lift Coming	R. Hawkes	Walthamstow	28.94 secs
1981	Creamery Pat	R. Chamberlain	(Private)	28.62 secs
1982	Sugarville Jet	J. Honeyset	Harringay	28.58 secs
1983	Yankee Express	G. Curtis	Brighton	28.55 secs
1984	Game Ball	J. Fisher	Reading	28.23 secs

*Pre-1975 run over 200 yds; since 1975 run over 475 m

Winners of the National Sprint Championship 1970–84*

1970	Don't Gambol	22.59 secs
1971	One Last Day	23.07 secs
1972	Hazelbury Silver	22.77 secs
1973	Gigli's Star	22.91 secs
† 1974	Star Vega	26.71 secs
1975	On Its Own	27.31 secs
1976	What's the Score	27.56 secs
**1977	Glazepta Work	24.88 secs
1978	Sampson's Pal	24.94 secs
1979	Knockrour Brandy	24.90 secs
1980	Knockrour Brandy	25.19 secs
1981	Ballybeg Sport	24.60 secs
1982	Not run	
1983	Ballybeg Sport	25.19 secs
1984	Floating Petal	25.41 secs

* 1970-3 run at Clapton; 1974-6 run at Portsmouth, 1977-80 run at Haringay
† Pre-1974 run over 400 yds; 1974-6 run over 435 m
** Since 1977 run over 414 m

HENLOW

This track has been operating successfully under the NGRC permit scheme since 1975. Racing takes place on Mondays and Fridays and J. Smith is racing manager. Several open events attract some of the best dogs in training. The Capital Car Factors' Sprint is run here in September over 318 m, with a prize of £1,000 for the winner. In 1979 the event went to Mr C. Francis's dog, Belfast Bound. In August over the 484 m course is contested the Hemeling Lager Derby, with a similar first prize. In 1979 this was won by Mr Kovac's Lough Lass Champ, who shortly afterwards took the Midlands' Flat Championship at Hall Green.

Main Events Run at Henlow

Hemeling Lager Derby	August	484 m
Capital Car Factors Sprint	September	318 m

IPSWICH

This track first came under NGRC permit rules in 1974 and has since become one of the best attended in the provinces, because it serves the greater part of southern East Anglia, long famed for its interest in greyhounds. The management take pride in their excellent, superbly maintained grass track with its well sanded bends. Racing takes place on Wednesday and Saturday evenings over 277 m, 437 m, 647 m and 832 m. The track has recently built a fine new stand at a cost of over £100,000, and installed a new computerized tote. Like all the smaller and more remotely situated tracks, Ipswich plays a valuable role in encouraging local breeders who can race their greyhounds and give them trials without having to travel long distances and without having to compete with the wealthier owners who dominate the big city tracks.

The director of racing at Ipswich is Tom Stanley, previously at Rayleigh until that track closed, and the racing manager is W.D. Davis. The Suffolk Derby is run here over 437 m in late August, and the Suffolk St Leger in November. Both attract some of the best dogs in training. The Suffolk Derby is worth £1500 to the winner, who in 1979 was Mr Fitzgerald's John's Luck the 2–1 favourite, trained by John Coleman for his Wembley patron. The event is sponsored by Tollemache and Cobbold's brewery.

Main Events Run at Ipswich

Suffolk Derby	September	440 m
Suffolk St Leger	November	625 m

Winners of the Suffolk Derby (1974–81)

1974	Bealkiller Diver	27.73 secs
1975	Black Flint	28.82 secs
1976	Surmount Lark	28.44 secs
1977	Secret Crook	27.07 secs
1978	Clean Winner	26.60 secs
1979	John's Luck	27.04 secs
1980	Taciad	27.78 secs
1981	Bann Merry	27.04 secs

LEEDS (Closed March, 1982)

Situated in Elland Road, the Stadium has a small track of some 400 yds circumference, with wider bends at one end than at the other, where sharp turns make the track more suited to small, compact greyhounds. The track opened for racing in 1934 and for many years, before his transfer to Hull, V. Holland was the popular racing manager. He was followed by Harry Bridge who was here for twelve years until Tim Hale took over on 1 January 1981. In 1969 a new stand was erected with huge plate glass windows through which the racing can be seen in comfort. Racing takes place on Mondays, Thursdays and Saturdays. Derek Bowman is now Racing Manager.

Early in 1978 the track kennels were demolished and the Stadium switched to contract trainers. Completely new trainers were engaged, for stalwarts like Jim Brennan and Tommy Brown retired at that time after many years of excellent service, and Joe Kelly moved to Owlerton. He trained 2,500 winners during his twelve years at Leeds and there were few years when he did not put out 200 winners. In addition he trained Brilane Clipper and Lisamote Precept to win the Scottish Derby in successive years, a feat which no other trainer has accomplished.

One of the new contract trainers is Peter Beaumont, who trained Mr Ted Lord's Lime Lane to win the important Ebor Stakes in 1979, after the dog had been moved from Belle Vue. This was only the third time a Leeds-trained greyhound had won this event. Before moving to Leeds Peter Beaumont was a trainer at Halifax, where he had charge of Amber Sky when this dog won the 1977 Scottish Derby by one and a half lengths from Skilful Boy, becoming the only Halifax-trained greyhound to win a classic race. Another of Leed's contract trainers is Ray Andrews who had charge of the Leeds dog Jon Barrie when he won the 1979 Edinburgh Cup at Powderhall; this dog went far in the 1979 Derby too. Jon Barrie, owned by Terry Hawkshaw, a Leeds businessman, was also to win the 1980 Northern Flat Championship at Belle Vue, worth £2,000 to the winner, and the William King Cup at Shawfield to bring his total winnings to more than £9,000, a record for any dog racing at Leeds.

The premier event at Leeds is the Ebor Stakes, run over the longer distance and worth £1,000 to the winner. The event was won in 1978, just before he retired, by Jim Brennan with his charge Be Splendid, owned by Mrs Emily Walker of Outwood. In one of the most thrilling races ever seen at Elland Road he defeated the 1978 St Leger winner Westmead Power by a short head in 40.94 secs.

Over the shorter distance is run the Tetley's-sponsored Qualifying Event which attracts the best dogs from all over Britain. A popular winner of recent years was the 1978 Scurry Cup winner Greenfield Fox, trained by Ted Dickson at Slough. The Britvic Yorkshire Hurdles is run over the same course and in 1978 was won by Mr and Mrs Parish's Grand National winner Topothetide, trained by Tommy Foster at Harringay.

Another event which always creates much interest is the Yorkshire Puppy Cup, run in September, which is a pointer to those greyhounds which may be expected to perform well in the main events the following year. Perhaps no dog created a better impression when winning the event than Irish Airport, who in 1970 broke the long-standing track record. Another outstanding puppy was Carhumore Speech, who in 1977 became the only greyhound ever to have won the Yorkshire, Midland and Wimbledon Puppy Derbys, and he ran up two Scurry Gold Cups. After his puppy successes £10,000 was refused for him, but injury brought his career to a premature close.

One of the finest dogs to have raced at Leeds was Elland Rumba, a brindle weighing 75 lbs. Since he was Newdown Heather's litter brother his magnificent achievements are readily understood.

Wherever he raced he slammed the opposition by many lengths, for example when he set a new track record early in 1970 for the 650 yds course, running from scratch in a graded race and winning by seven lengths in 37.10 secs. His career was cut short by injuries when destined to win the sport's highest honours.

Another of the great Leeds-kennelled dogs was Lisamote Precept, Scottish Derby winner of 1968 and a winner on fifteen tracks in two years. A fawn weighing 75 lbs, he was by the Hi There sire Hi Spark out of The Grand Fire bitch Lisamote Queen – yet another instance of The Grand Fire making his influence felt through the dam line.

Track Records (1950)

Hepicoleum	325 yds	17.95 secs
Chatterton	512 yds	29.04 secs
All Out	743 yds	44.02 secs

Track Records (1970)

Fly Dazzler) Princess Quail)	500 yds	27.92 secs
High St Boy	500 yds H	28.95 secs
Shady Pagoda	650 yds	36.85 secs
Gleneagle Comedy	700 yds	40.16 secs

Winners of the Ebor Stakes 1970–81

1970	Colonel Imp	37.27 secs
1971	not run	
1972	Dramatic Ace	37.92 secs
1973	Pit Lamp	36.95 secs
1974	Black Caprice	37.52 secs
* 1975	Star Port	37.08 secs
1976	Ardbeg Star	37.42 secs
† 1977	Kinard Cross	39.98 secs
1978	Be Splendid	40.94 secs
1979	Lime Lane	40.63 secs
1980	Torry Kotty	41.85 secs
1981	Lois Lane	41.02 secs

*Pre-1975 run over 650 yds; 1975-6 run over 600 m † 1977–80 run over 650 m

MAIDSTONE

One of the few tracks to open in recent years, it is owned by Todos Promotions and opened on October 16th, 1981. Situated on the London Road, it is an all-sand circuit of 375 m circumference with an outside Sumner hare. Mr Tom Jones is general manager with Steve Hibbard racing manager. Racing takes place on Tuesdays and Fridays with Saturday racing in summer, main event being the Watney Combe Stakes run in May over 454 m and valued at £500. First winner was Alfa My Son, owned and trained by Mr L. Steel of Ipswich. The dog also won the BBC TV Trophy at Belle Vue and was one of the best dogs in training that year. Amongst many good greyhounds trained at the track, outstanding was House of Crystal, trained by Mr J. Wood for his wife. It took the Nipa Lassie Marathon at Harringay in 1983, run over 830 m. But the finest dog to be kennelled here is Whisper Wishes, trained by Charlie Coyle for owner Mr J. Duffy. Mr Coyle had the dog for only 6 months before he won the 1984 English Derby, last to be run at White City, to give his sire, Sandman, a unique double for in the same year he sired the Irish Derby winner, Dipmac. Once again, the influence of Pigalle Wonder in the dam's line is prominent in the pedigree of Whisper Wishes.

MILTON KEYNES

The track first opened on July 25th, 1963 but did not come under the rules of the NGRC until 1983. It is an all-sand track of 375 m with an outside Sumner hare and racing takes place on Thursdays and Saturdays over 440, 620 and 815 m. Main events are the Spring Cup run in March over 440 m and won in 1983 by Mr Sullivan's Valient Point, and the Autumn Cup, sponsored by Whitbreads and run in October over 620 m. It was won in 1983 by Miss Morrow's Northway Comet in 39.16 seconds but fastest over this distance is Tartan Sarah, best daughter of Tartan Khan and trained by Jim Edmonds.

MONMORE GREEN

Now owned by Ladbroke's, this track is situated on the outskirts of Wolverhampton and began racing in 1932, since when it has remained one of the best of provincial tracks with excellent amenities while it has always attracted the best dogs to its open events. In 1969 Monmore Green opened a magnificent new stand with a plate glass frontage and a tiered restaurant. A fast galloping track of 450 yds circumference, with long straights and easy turns, it has an outside Sumner hare, and outside runners always do well here. Racing takes place on Monday, Thursday and Saturday evenings.

In 1975 the BBC TV Trophy was run here over the 815 m course. It was one of the most exciting events ever staged at the track, and in a thrilling finish was won by a neck by the 7–4 favourite, Lizzie's Girl, from another long-distance bitch, Silver Lipstick, in a new track record of 52.16 secs.

The most important event run at Monmore Green is the valuable Skol Champion of Champions, worth £3,000 to the winner and run over 484 m. In 1979 it was won by Mr V. Bailey's Duke of Avon, trained at Walthamstow by Tommy Reilly. Over the same distance is run the Schweppes Classic Prospects Stake. The Britvic Midland Marathon, run over 815 m and worth £600, was won in 1978 by the Perry Barr bitch Judy Gee, owned by Mr Eacock and trained by Andy Agnew who also trained Jim's Image when that fine performer won the Pride of the Midlands Trophy, run over the 647 m course. Other sponsors here are Carbo Engineering and Haig Whisky.

In 1946 the great bitch Hurry Kitty ran to set a new track record for 300 yds at Monmore Green, although she was essentially a stayer. Another excellent bitch, Coynes Castle, also a long-distance expert, set a new record for the 475 yds course in the same year.

Main Events Run at Monmore Green

Britvic Midland Marathon	May	815 m
Skol Champion of Champions	July	484 m
Midland St Leger	July	484 m
Midland Classic Prospects	November	484 m

Track Records (1950)

Hurry Kitty	1946	300 yds	17.17 secs
Coyne's Castle	1946	475 yds	27.14 secs
Kilpeacon Bride	1948	525 yds	30.09 secs
Baytown Express	1944	525 yds H	30.90 secs

Winners of the Britvic Midlands Marathon (815 m)

1978	Judy Gee	52.68 secs
1979	Westown Adam	52.36 secs
1980	Keem Princess	52.46 secs

NORTON CANES

Situated at Brownhills West, near Cannock in Staffordshire, this compact and pleasant track is well placed to serve the Black Country and it began racing under the NGRC permit scheme in 1975. Racing takes place on Wednesday and Friday evenings and also on alternate Mondays in summer, over 265 m, 440 m and 672 m. The all-grass track has sanded bends and an outside Sumner hare, and there is a comfortable licensed club house with buffet bars.

In October the Norton Canes Derby is held, over 440 m and worth £1,000 to the winner; The Champion Bitch Stakes, run in May, was won in 1978 by the Oaks winner Ballinderry Moth, trained at Walthamstow by Barney O'Connor and owned by Mr Dick Francis. In the same month is run the Bookmakers' Stakes, won in 1978 by Autumn Belin, owned by Mrs Tasker and trained by her husband, Harry. They also owned Pat Seamur before parting with the two champions to stand at stud. A recently inaugurated event is the Charles Southall Memorial Sweepstake, to commemmorate the founder of the track who died in 1978 and was its general manager until then. Charles Southall's son Brian has taken over as general manager and maintains the high standards set by his father. Steve Pardoe is racing manager.

Main Events Run at Norton Canes

Charles Southall Memorial Stakes	April	440 m
Champion Bitch Stakes	May	440 m
Norton Canes Puppy Derby	October	440 m

Winners of the Norton Canes Puppy Derby 1975-80

1975	Information	27.64 secs
1976	Brookhouse Gent	27.84 secs
1977	Autumn Belin	27.85 secs
1978	Shuna	27.16 secs

NOTTINGHAM

In 1970 the old White City track here was sold for development, but on 24 January 1980 a new track opened under the management of Sheffield Sports Stadium Ltd who operate the Owlerton track. Director of racing at both tracks is Terry Meynell, who moved to Owlerton from Brough Park on Sam Vinter's retirement in 1973. The racing manager is Jim Woods, from Harringay. The new track is at Colwick Park, near Nottingham's horse racecourse, and cost £250,000 to equip, with a fine stand containing bar and buffet facilities and a modern computerized totalizator. There is an all-sand surface and outside Sumner hare and the track is large, with graduated turns so that fast times can be expected. Racing takes place on Thursday and Saturday evenings over 485 m, 650 m and 715 m. Four contract trainers have been engaged to supply the greyhounds – C. Lister, T. Smith, Christine Lawlor and Mrs Coppin.

OWLERTON (SHEFFIELD)

This track, owned by Sheffield Sports Stadium Ltd and situated in Penistone Road Sheffield, was opened in 1932. Many highly dedicated and respected men have been connected with greyhound racing at Owlerton and the track has always been an important one. Terry Meynell, the present chief of racing, took over from Sam Vinter who retired in 1973 after forty years at

Owlerton.

The track has a large circuit of 475 yds, with long straights and wide, well banked bends, and is most suited to the strong galloping greyhound. There is an inside Sumner hare and the restaurant facilities are excellent. It was one of the first tracks to instal photo-finish equipment, and in 1979 the running surface was removed and replaced with special sand which, with the wide turns, has almost entirely eliminated bumping. Recently a new computerized tote was installed, so that in every respect the track has maintained its reputation of providing the racing public with nothing but the best. Racing takes place on Friday and Saturday evenings, and additionally on Tuesdays from early April to the end of October.

In the early years of the sport Mr Alf Morton provided the track with several outstanding greyhounds of his own breeding, for he had at stud on his Derbyshire smallholding the Irish St Leger winner Marching through Georgia, who was to sire many fine northern greyhounds. In the late 1930s Alf Morton's Victor Ben Hur was the Owlerton champion, able to give up to 12 yds in a graded race and come from behind to win in the last few strides. His mantle was later taken on by Duffy's Arrival, the best dog to be trained here until the arrival of the great litter bred in Ireland by Leo Stack, which included Tric Trac, Spectre II and Forward King. The first two were to take first and second place in the 1967 Derby, the only litter brothers ever to do so, while Forward King was to win the 1968 St Leger. This great dog was trained by Teddy Brennan, who was at Owlerton on the opening night in 1932 and retired more than forty years later. No one knew more about greyhounds

Trainers R. Hookway, E. Brennan and J. Brennan with four of Owlerton's most famous greyhounds (from left): Spectre II, Tric Trac (1968 English Derby winner), Forward Flash, and Haich Bee (1967 Waterloo Cup winner). Photo: Telegraph & Star, Sheffield.

than Irish-born Teddy, and no trainer was more respected by those owners who raced at Owlerton. Teddy's record of training the St Leger winner of 1968 and also the Waterloo Cup winner (HB) in the same year may never be equalled. He came to England from Ireland in May 1927 with a batch of Irish greyhounds destined for the Southend track, one of the first to open. The following year he moved to the White City, Liverpool, long since closed, and he was at Owlerton in time for its opening. Of all the dogs he trained, Teddy Brennan rated Matchlock, 1954 Cesarewitch winner, the best.

The years 1967 and 1968 were exciting ones at Owlerton. Ron Hookway trained both Tric Trac and Spectre II for Mr Nat Pinson, who owned them both, and in the entire history of the greyhound Derby no other trainer has handled the first two dogs to cross the winning line. Wherever and whenever he ran Tric Trac tended to set new records, and he even came out of retirement after his Derby success to win Wimbledon's Champion of Champions Stakes. Spectre II was equally successful, winning the 1967 TV Sportsview Trophy at Brighton and the Midlands St Leger at Monmore Green before being retired to stud, where he was to join Newdown Heather, Monalee Champion and Clonalvy Pride, the greatest sires of the 1970s. Hookway, elected Trainer of the Year in 1968, followed his Derby success with the two great sons of Crazy Parachute by winning the 1970 Cesarewitch, the last to be run at West Ham, with another Owlerton dog, Gleneagle Comedy, owned by Mr E. Petty. Ron Hookway died in 1984.

Other fine dogs to run at Owlerton were Cash for Dan, also a winner of the TV Trophy, and who once held the 880 yds record at the track; and Ballybeg Flash, who won the All England Cup at Brough Park and set track records at Owlerton over 525 yds with a time of 28.44 secs and over 550 yds with 29.85 secs, the only dog to break 30 secs for the latter distance.

The finest dog trained by Harry Crapper is surely On Spec, the 33/1 outsider to win the 1983 English Derby and who all but did so, losing by only a neck in the most thrilling finish ever and beating other fine dogs in Debbycot Lad and Game Ball. And to show just how good he was, he trounced a top class field a few weeks later to win the Scottish Derby for Mr & Mrs Raper.

Another excellent Owlerton greyhound of recent years was Burniston Jet, trained by Ron Hookway. The first of Jimsun's offspring to show similar pace to his sire, he was whelped in 1975. Owned by Mr J. Chance, he won the Bass Cup at Owlerton in 1978 and the following April won the Steel City Cup, the track's major event, by a short head from Wheeler's Big Boy, with Desert Pilot a neck behind. In his semi-final Desert Pilot had set a new 500 m record when beating Noble Brigg by six lengths in 29.65 secs. In 1979 Burniston Jet won the All England Cup at Brough Park, the Arnie Dennis Stakes at Derby, and the William Hill Trapper Championship at Hall Green. In that year he was undoubtedly one of the finest dogs in Britain.

Harry Crapper has enjoyed tremendous success in his first years as an Owlerton trainer for he had charge of that great bitch Caribbean Queen, who was practically unbeatable over the 650 m course, and Little Tullig, winner of the Manchester Puppy Derby at Belle Vue in 1978.

Bass Charrington sponsor the Bass Cup, worth £1,000 to the winner. One of the first winners of this event was the bitch Priory Hi, owned by Mr L. Andrews and trained by his son. She had previously contested the Supreme Championship at the White City, finishing third behind Skyhawk and the dual Derby winner, Patricia's Hope. The Bass Cup is run over 500 m and Owlerton is to be complimented on changing the old 525 yds course to 500 m, a figure that should have been standardized on all racetracks. The 1975 Bass Cup was won by the Leeds greyhound Company Cash, owned by Miss L. Horner, and in so doing the dog set a new record over the 500 m course at the track. The 1979 event was won by Harry Crapper's charge Jebb Rambler, owned by Mrs Norton. He set a new track record with a time of 29.61 secs, and in that year also won the Midlands Grand Prix at Leicester. He rivalled Burniston Jet in consistency and ability.

Also run at Owlerton is the Partisan Cup, worth £1,000 to the winner, and in August the White Rose Trophy is run over the 650 m course. It was won in 1979 by Mr Eisenberg's Brainy Prince, trained by

Geoffrey de Mulder who is no stranger to Owlerton.

Other well-known Owlerton trainers are Jimmy Brennan, who came from Leeds, and Billy Wilson who trained Bread Soda, the 20–1 outsider, to win the 1968 Pall Mall for Mr J. Ellis.

The original kennels were situated at Wardsend Farm, a short distance from the track, where the dogs were housed in a range of stone buildings. Towards the end of the 1930s a new range of high-quality brick-built kennels was erected at the Stadium, and has been used ever since. Each kennel range accommodates sixty greyhounds and there have always been four trainers at the track.

Main Events Run at Owlerton

Stainless Metal Trophy	March	650 m
Partisan Cup	April	500 m
Steel City Cup	April	500 m
White Rose Trophy	August	650 m
Bass Cup	October	500 m

Track Records (1950)

Silver Wire	300 yds	16.70 secs
Victor Ben Hur	500 yds	28.02 secs
Latin Pearl	525 yds	29.25 secs
Gaullsmill Again	525 yds H	30.67 secs
Victor Ben Hur	700 yds	40.28 secs

Track Records (1970)

Victor Ben Hur	500 yds	28.02 secs
Tric Trac	525 yds	28.48 secs
Bingo Basher	525 yds H	29.76 secs
Leinster Elm	700 yds	39.04 secs
Rainbow Trout	770 yds	43.12 secs
Poor Barney	880 yds	49.70 secs

Winners of the Bass Cup 1968–82

1968	Cu Luain	29.24 secs
1969	Red Lake	29.08 secs
1970	Brilane Clipper	30.34 secs
1971	Dramatic Ace	30.26 secs
1972	Priory Hi	30.01 secs
1973	Carrig Shane	30.26 secs
1974	Lady Devine	30.68 secs
*1975	not run	
1976	Lucky Arrival	30.24 secs
1977	Sheskburn Mint	29.12 secs
1978	Burniston Jet	28.89 secs
1979	Jeb Rambler	29.61 secs
1980	Gentle Star	29.61 secs
1982	Long Spell	29.48 secs

Winners of the Steel City Cup 1970–81

1970	Westpark Toots	30.66 secs
1971	Toremore Flash	31.20 secs
1972	Kuda's Honour	29.88 secs
1973	Priory Hi	30.42 secs
1974	Gone the Time	30.26 secs
*1975	Company Cash	29.65 secs
1976	Tilbrook Herald	29.21 secs
1977	Gan on Paddy	29.58 secs
1978	Westmead Manor	30.08 secs
1979	Burniston Jet	29.99 secs
1980	Desert Pilot	29.38 secs
1981	Heres Gay	29.58 secs

*Pre-1975 run over 550 yds; since run over 500 m

OXFORD

Now owned by Northern Sports Ltd, who also owned the Ramsgate track, Oxford Greyhound Stadium has a large population to draw upon. Racing takes place on Friday and Saturday evenings each week, with Tuesday meetings in summer, and there is an all-sand track with an outside Sumner hare. An excellent club house with bar and first-rate catering adds to the evening's enjoyment, and being easily accessible from London, Oxford has little difficulty in filling its open events. The track is a 430 yds circuit with wide, easy bends which reduce bumping to a minimum.

The first greyhound meeting to be held on this site was on 7 April 1939, the date of the official opening of the Stadium. The opening ceremony was performed by Lord Denham, at that time chairman of the Greyhound Racing Board of Control as it was known and senior steward of the NGRC. The managing director of the Stadium at that time was L.V. Calcutt and the racing manager G. Parker. The track closed in autumn 1977 and reopened for racing under the present management in June 1978.

It was at Oxford in 1945 that Winnie of Berrow set a new track record shortly after winning the Eclipse Stakes at Coventry. She was whelped in 1940, was then more than five years old, and had not begun racing until she had whelped a litter of six pups. By the great Beef Cutlet, she was mated to Dutton Swordfish in 1946 when her racing career was over and whelped a large litter. It was at Oxford on 27 March 1948 that the English-bred bitch Narrogar Ann, one of that litter, ran her first race and was beaten half a length by the dog Wexford, a consistent winner at the track. Apart from her owner, few who saw Narrogar Ann run could have believed she would be the Derby winner of 1949. Four months later she was at Oxford again, and at 6–1 was once more beaten into second place. At the same meeting, Come up First won the Varsity Cup in a thrilling finish, beating Northam Star by a short head and setting a new track record. Two weeks later, Narrogar Ann was to win the Western 2-Year Produce Stakes at Eastville and gave some indication of her potential.

Oxford's main event is now the Oxfordshire Stakes, contested in October over

450 m, the seventeenth event being won in 1979 by Mr Alexander's Faoides Choice trained by Mrs G. Lynds. The previous year the event was won by the locally owned and trained Ballybeg Blaze, of whom Mrs M. Holloway was both owner and trainer. The event is worth £1,000 to the winner.

The summer of 1980 was one of great excitement to all who attend the track for it was the first time in its history that Oxford had a representative in the English Derby Final. This was Young Breeze, owned and trained at Oxford by Jack Coker, whose dog ran brilliantly to finish in third place. He had previously won the 1979 Haig Cambridgeshire with Tic'n Tot. In October 1980 further success came when the Oxford-trained Silver Duchess ran up both the Puppy Derby and the Oaks at Wimbledon.

At Oxford Joe Farrand still trains greyhounds as he has done there for the past fifty years and no trainer is more respected. Other trainers are Vicki Holloway and Maurice Massey. Brian Ward is Racing Manager.

Main Event Run at Oxford

Oxfordshire Stakes	October	450 m

Track Records (1950)

Gortnagory	1948	290 yds	16.16 secs
Don Gipsy	1949	500 yds	28.04 secs
Latest Surprise	1947	525 yds	29.55 secs
Come Up First	1948	715 yds	40.72 secs

Track Records (1970)

Discretions	1968	500 yds	27.70 secs
Drealistown Leader	1963	500 yds H	29.60 secs
Come up First	1948	715 yds	40.72 secs

Track Records (1980)

First General	450 m	26.97 secs
Hunday Doss	450 m H	28.35 secs
Ballybeg Delight	645 m	39.92 secs
Gan on Rita	845 m	54.13 secs

Winners of the Oxfordshire Stakes 1968–81

1968	Shady Peacock	28.08 secs
1969	Manton Tim	28.79 secs
1970	Moordyke Spot	28.31 secs
1971	Dactars Speed	28.47 secs
1972	Kybo Venture	28.38 secs
1973	Arctic Tern	28.33 secs
1974	Crown Walter	27.76 secs
* 1975	By Chance	27.76 secs
1976	Mister Little	27.30 secs
1977	Rathduff Spring	27.03 secs
1978	Ballybeg Blaze	27.43 secs
1979	Faoides Choice	27.27 secs
1980	Deal Joker	27.66 secs
1981	Bright Tiger	27.57 secs

*Pre-1975 run over 490 yds; since run over 450 m

PERRY BARR (Closed 1984)

Situated at Birchfield in the north of Birmingham, the track opened in April 1928 and was taken over by Ladbroke's in 1976. The running track was one of the best in Britain, being 450 yds in circumference with very wide, graduated bends which almost entirely eliminate bumping and suit the big, strong greyhound. It was surfaced with sand.

In June 1970 fire destroyed the main stand, which was rebuilt and reopened exactly a year later with excellent restaurant and bar facilities. Soon after Ladbroke's took over, more than £100,000 was spent on improving the lighting, the bends being lit by tall columns and the straights by additional lights from the stands, so that the track was one of the best for night racing in Britain. It also had a number of sponsors such as Skol Lager who stage the Champion of Champions event in July. Perry Barr was the first provincial track to instal automatic ray-starting and timing and the photo-finish equipment which has done more than anything to eliminate controversy about the winner of a close-finishing race. A very fine X-ray room with the most modern equipment ensures that every greyhound receives the best possible care and attention.

The racing director of the Ladbroke stadia is Arthur Aldridge, who has spent a lifetime in the sport and is widely respected. His father, Sidney Aldridge, was kennel manager at the GRA Kennels, Northaw, and after the Second World War Arthur went to Powderhall and then to Manchester as racing manager. He was GRA's director of racing before joining Ladbroke's in 1976. No man has wider experience of greyhound racing. The racing manager at Perry Barr from its opening to 1960 was J. Poole, who maintained a high standard of racing which has continued ever since. The present racing manager is John Rowe, previously at Leicester, and John Moore is general manager.

Racing takes place on Tuesdays, Thursdays and Saturdays, and among Perry Barr's large number of sponsored events the Birmingham Cup and the Perry Barr Trophy, which have been run since 1939, are the most important, always attracting the best dogs in Britain. The Birmingham Cup is now run over 475 m (before 1975, over 525 yds) and is worth £1,000 to the winner. The Perry Barr Trophy is run over 650 m and is valued at £500. One of the greatest dogs to win the Birmingham Cup was Monday's News, who won the Derby in the same year, 1946. At Birmingham, he won by one length from Lemon Flash, a dog that had cost £3,000 and which died soon after. The following year, the Perry Barr Trophy was won by another great performer, Slaney Record, who was kennelled at the track. An unlucky dog, he ran up for the Laurels and finished third in the Derby. He is best remembered for his siring of Hi There, the result of a mating to Dublin Red – perhaps the most important mating in the whole history of greyhound racing. Hi There was to sire Crazy Parachute; Printer's Prince, sire of Newdown Heather; and Printer's Present, sire of Dusty Trail. Crazy Parachute was to sire Monalee Champion, sire of Sole Aim and Black Banjo and many other champions of modern greyhound racing.

But one of the greatest dogs ever kennelled at Perry Barr was Model Dasher, who came over from Ireland in 1943 and had his first trials at the Birmingham track. He was then purchased by Mr Bithel for 100 gns and within twelve months had won the Midland Puppy Championship and broken track records at his home track as well as at Wembley, Eastville and Coventry, besides winning the substitute St Leger in 1944, and the Birmingham Cup. He was trained by Tommy Baldwin, who was in at the beginning of track racing in Birmingham and is now in retirement in Wales. His place at Perry Barr was taken by his son Frank who had charge of that fine dog Discretions (Prairie Flash–Sheila at Last) when he set a track record at Perry Barr. More recently he trained Tails to win the Birmingham Cup of 1978. This great dog, one of Jimsun's first sons, won his first three races at Perry Barr when only sixteen months old and might have emulated his sire but for serious injury.

Another of Perry Barr's outstanding dogs was Black Mire, who won the Spring Cup at Wembley in 1951 in a thrilling finish. He was left in the traps, and until the last bend the Scottish Derby winner Rushton Smutty led all the way by at least four lengths, but by a great effort Black Mire threw himself over the line to win by inches.

Nor must the name of Country Life be forgotten. He, too, was kennelled at Perry Barr and in 1944 won the Midlands Puppy Championship, beating Prancing Kitty by a short head. He went on to win the Scurry Gold Cup and ran up to Burhill Moon in the Laurels.

Another of the outstanding Perry Barr dogs of that time was Negro's Lad, trained by Ernie Toseland, and who won the Welsh Derby in 1946. The bitch Pineapple Grand was also kennelled here and achieved fame. Owned by Mr Michael Cleary and trained by Frank Baldwin, the fawn bitch was to win the Bookmaker's Trophy at Monmore Green and the Laurels of 1975. She also won Wembley's Spring Cup that year.

More recently Rambler's Jet, trained by Mrs Solomon and sired by Tullig Rambler, set a new track record here over 500 m with a time of 31.16 secs when winning his heat for the Mitton Mermaid Trophy, and he bettered this when winning the final in 31.04 secs. Shortly afterwards he set a new record at Rochester for the 480 m course with a time of 28.79 secs when winning the Master Brew Derby.

Besides the Perry Barr Trophy, which is a race for stayers, the Perry Barr Bookmakers' Marathon is run over 725 m, and of recent winners Westgrove Haig, trained by Geoffrey de Mulder, stamped himself as a stayer of ability. Another outstanding Perry Barr dog was Instant Gambler, trained by Mrs Barbara Tompkins, and who won the Wood Lane Stakes at White City in 1978. Other Perry Barr trainers who have enjoyed considerable success in recent years are Ralph Smith, Bertie Gaynor and Andy Agnew, trainer of Jim's Image (son of the Derby winner Jimsun), who won the 1978 Perry Barr Trophy for Mr Jack Randall, the Midlands Stayers Stakes at Hall Green and the Northern Stayers at Belle Vue. He also trained Judy Gee, winner of the Britvic Midlands Marathon at Monmore Green.

Trainer Colin McNally achieved every trainer's ambition of winning a classic event when in 1971 Breach's Buzzard won the Grand Prix. His owner, Mrs Judy Pattinson of Uppingham, is one of the few people to have bred and owned a classic winner.

In 1978 Bertie Gaynor went one better when he became one of the few trainers to have first and second in a classic event when Jet Control, kennelled at Perry Barr, won the Laurels and Night Fall was runner-up. In a thrilling race, Jet Control came through at the finish to win by three-quarters of a length with Pigeon Flyer a further length behind, in third place.

Track Records (1950)

Model Dasher	500 yds	28.24 secs
Brindled Beggar	500 yds H	29.25 secs
Halston Parade	525 yds	29.57 secs
Holiday Thrill	525 yds H	30.83 secs
Model Dasher	700 yds	40.18 secs

Winners of the Birmingham Cup (1939–49)

1939	Black Johnny	29.76 secs
1940	S.M. Hector	30.05 secs
1941–2	not run	
1943	Farloe Best	29.68 secs
1944	Model Dasher	29.80 secs
1945	Duffy's Arrival	30.14 secs
1946	Monday's News	30.35 secs
1947	Funny Mick	30.09 secs
1948	Baytown Stork	30.34 secs
1949	Kilcaskin Mail	30.52 secs

Winners of the Birmingham Cup 1971–80

1971	Jellicoe Mist	29.79 secs
1972	Cowboy Joe	29.57 secs
1973	Mel's Pupil	29.23 secs
1974–6	not run	
1977	Blackwater Glade	29.79 secs
*1978	Tails	29.48 secs
1979	Mohane	31.01 secs
1980	not run	

* Since 1978 run over 500 m

PETERBOROUGH

Situated in Fengate, within sight of the lovely cathedral, the track is owned by Peterborough Sports Stadium and began operating under NGRC rules in March, 1983. The circuit is of 370 m circumference with an all-sand surface and racing takes place on Tuesdays and Saturdays over 420, 605 and 790 m. The finest dog to be associated with the track is Creamery Cross, trained and owned by Mr A. Briggs who, in 1983 took all before him including the Thanet Gold Cup at Ramsgate; the coveted Edinburgh Cup; and the East Anglian Derby, all in eight weeks.

POOLE

The most southerly track in Britain, it opened in May 1961 and also caters for speedway racing. Its instigators were Mr Charles Knott Snr and his son Mr. C.J. Knott, the cricketer. The Knotts originally controlled the excellent Southampton greyhound track which adjoined the cricket ground. It closed in 1960, and shortly afterwards the Poole Stadium was opened with D.J. Poole as racing manager. Today Ernie Walsh is the racing manager.

Racing takes place on Thursday and Saturday evenings each week and in summer draws holidaymakers from nearby Bournemouth and other resorts.

The top trainer at Poole in 1980 was Rita Randall, with Pat Clarke almost as successful.

In 1980 the Knotts sold their controlling interest in the track.

PORTSMOUTH

This pleasant and friendly track was opened in 1930 and has always maintained a high standard of racing. In 1932 the track was bought by the late Joe Childs, the jockey. On his death it was inherited by his son, F.A. Childs, who was tragically drowned in 1960. In 1972 the track was purchased by the GRA, since when Bill Francis, previously at Park Royal and Clapton, has been racing manager. He is now ably assisted by Dennis Stow.

A number of important events take place here, including the F.A. Childs Memorial Trophy, run over 435 m in July, a recent winner of which was Charisma King, trained by Mrs P. Walsh at Brighton. The Club Tiberius Trophy is contested over 603 m, and was won in 1978 by an outstanding Portsmouth dog, The Grand World, bred by Mr Paddy Dunphy in Ireland and trained at the home track by Peter Isaac. The same trainer also had charge of Prince Rover when he won the Daily Express Hurdles at Crayford that year for Mr P. Byrne.

Racing takes place with an inside Sumner hare on Tuesdays, Fridays and Saturdays in the evenings. There is an excellent licensed restaurant and several bars are located around the track.

Among Portsmouth's trainers pride of place must go to Hugo Spencer, who in 1978 completed forty years of service. Both his parents were trainers of racing greyhounds during the early years of the sport. Dedicated to the fifty or more greyhounds in his charge at Portsmouth, Hugo Spencer has had little time to enter his dogs in 'open' events but he trained Hi There Merry to win the Scottish Derby, and Spectre's Dream the 1971 Welsh Derby. At Portsmouth it is believed that the dogs in his care have won more than 10,000 races, more than any single trainer has achieved on any other track in Britain, a record of which Portsmouth is justly proud. Charles Curtis was another highly respected trainer here until his untimely death following a road accident in 1969.

In July 1946 one of the fastest bitches of all time, Shaggy Lass, came to Portsmouth to win her open event by ten lengths and to set a new record for the 655 yds course with a time of 38.34 secs. In more recent years an outstanding dog was Northwood Double, who in winning the F.A. Childs Trophy in 1977 set a record for the 435 m course with a time of 26.95 secs. He also ran up to Greenfield Fox for the Scurry Gold Cup, losing by only a short head after setting a new track record in his heat. He was one of Sole Aim's finest sons.

Main Events Run at Portsmouth

Club Tiberius Trophy	July	603 m
F.A. Childs Memorial Trophy	July	438 m

Track Records (1950)

Clam	470 yds	27.30 secs
Tuathal Teachtmar	470 yds H	28.29 secs
Shaggy Lass	655 yds	38.34 secs

Track Records (1970)

Hi There Merry	1962	470 yds	26.68 secs
Laurdella Guest	1964	655 yds	37.63 secs
Woodville Fortune	1964	850 yds	50.54 secs

Winners of the F.A. Childs Memorial Trophy 1973–81

1973	Bright Boffin	27.08 secs
1974	Cosmic Jet	27.33 secs
* 1975	What's the Score	27.30 secs
1976	Bold Flight	27.08 secs
1977	Northwood Double	27.08 secs
1978	Charisma King	27.41 secs
1979	Please Sir	27.43 secs
1980	Hill Sand	27.20 secs
1981	Flying Pursuit	27.19 secs

*Pre-1975 run over 470 yds; since run over 438 m

POWDERHALL

Situated in Beaverhall Road, Edinburgh, it has remained in the forefront of greyhound racing tracks, both for its amenities and for its standard of racing, since it opened its gates in 1927. Owned by the GRA, there is no more pleasantly situated track in Britain and none where higher standards are maintained. In 1970 an extensive programme of modernization was begun, and the track is now one of the finest in the British Isles. Chief among the improved facilities is the Silver Hound Restaurant with its plate glass front, which provides about 100 diners with a magnificent view of the entire race. In addition there are seven bars situated in all parts of the Stadium. The modernization has been carried out under the watchful eye of the general manager, W.J. (Bill) Glennie, one of the most astute managers in the sport. Stuart Strachan came to Powderhall as racing manager in 1978. The Powderhall Owners' Association is active in organizing charity events and speedway racing takes place on Friday evenings.

Racing takes place on Thursday, Saturday and alternate Tuesday evenings and only in the worst weather, such as early 1979, does it not take place, since one of the most important innovations here is the electrically heated 'blanket' laid beneath the track surface, which provides ideal running conditions in winter. Easy bends and long straights make for fast times. The greyhounds are kennelled at nearby Dalkeith, where 200 dogs can be accommodated under ideal conditions.

The first of the important events run here is the Scottish Grand National, which takes place in April over 465 m hurdles and in 1978 was won by the Grand National winner Topothetide, the 5–2 on favourite kennelled at Harringay. The busiest time of year at Powderhall is September, when the famous Edinburgh Cup is run over 465 m, the Edinburgh Sprint over 241 m, and the Scottish St Leger over the 650 m course.

Since its inauguration in 1933 the Edinburgh Cup, until 1975 run over 500 yds, has always been considered one of the top events of the British greyhound racing calendar and has always attracted the best dogs. The great Jesmond Cutlet was here in 1937 after winning the Scottish Derby at Carntyne, and he was to take the Edinburgh Cup back to London just before winning the Cesarewitch in October. A decade later Dante II won the Cup, beating the Scottish Derby winner Latin Pearl by one length in 28.57 secs. In 1969 another outstanding dog, Rockfield Era, trained at Carntyne, defeated Mr Cyril Young's Kilbelin Style by a length. By Mad Era, sire of Sherry's Prince, Rockfield Era was to sire I'm a Smasher, winner of the 1978 Gold Collar, and finalist the following year. Rockfield Era proved himself one of the outstanding sires in the history of the sport when his son, Ballybeg Prim, won the Irish 1975 Cesarewitch and St Leger and ran up for the English Derby in 1976.

Another great dog seen at Powderhall in 1969 was Booked Six, who in the Scottish St Leger set a new 700 yds record with a time of 39.84 secs, beating 40 secs here for the first time. The 1978 Cup was won by Geoffrey de Mulder's charge, Dale Lad, and his owner, Mr J. Eisenberg, received a prize of £2,500. Dale Lad also won the 1978 Select Stakes at Wembley, beating the Derby winner Lacca Champion. By Bright Lad out of Kerry's Pal, whose sire was Kilbeg Kuda, grandson of Shaggy Lad, Dale Lad raced for only twelve months when a broken hock compelled his retirement to stud where he stands at the kennels of Mrs Valerie Ineson at Clayton West, Huddersfield.

The only Scottish-trained greyhound ever to win the English Derby, Boher Ash, was kennelled at Powderhall. Owned by Mrs Mollie Stokes and trained by Tommy Johnston, in 1928 he won the second Derby at 5–1 by less than half a length from Fabulous Figure, with Musical Box a neck behind in what was one of the most exciting of all Greyhound Derbies.

Main Events Run at Powderhall

Edinburgh Cup	September	465 m
Edinburgh Sprint	September	241 m
Scottish St Leger	September	650 m
Tennent Marathon	October	824 m

Track Records (1940)

Telepathy	1931	440 yds	25.38 secs
Jesmond Cutlet	1937	500 yds	28.20 secs
Rich Cream	1938	500 yds H	29.23 secs
Robin's Reward	1933	700 yds	41.15 secs

Track Records (1950)

Gold Deposit	1948	440 yds	25.14 secs
Jesmond Cutlet	1937)	500 yds	28.20 secs
Kildrid Hero	1948)		
Rich Cream	1938	500 yds H	29.23 secs
Don Gipsy	1947	700 yds	41.05 secs

Track Records (1970)

Houghton Spur	1968	400 yds	24.77 secs
Shady Begonia	1968	500 yds	27.85 secs
Rory's Pleasure	1961	500 yds H	28.64 secs
Booked Six	1969	700 yds	39.84 secs
Poor Mick	1967	880 yds	50.84 secs
April Event	1966	940 yds	56.12 secs

Track Records (1980)

Bray Vale	30.8 79	241 m	14.41 secs
Tory Mor	23.8 75	465 m	27.67 secs
Ann's Chancer	19 7.80	465 m H	28.96 secs
Paradise Spectre	22 9.77	650 m	40.09 secs
Portland Dusty	29.10.79	824 m	52.23 secs

Winners of the Edinburgh Cup (1933–84)

		Trainer	Track	
1933	S.L.D.	J.W. Tallantire	Powderhall	28.64 secs
1934	Tosto	A. Patterson	Powderhall	28.72 secs
1935	Good Redress	A. Jonas	White City, London	28.62 secs
1936	Banksell	J. Dickenson	Manchester	28.64 secs
1937	Jesmond Cutlet	D. Hawkesley	Catford	28.30 secs
1938	Wattle Bark	A. Jonas	White City, London	28.82 secs
1945	Gourna Bridge	W. Sidney	Carntyne	28.25 secs
1946	Dante	W. France	Harringay	28.51 secs
1947	Clan Cameron	W. McLean	Powderhall	28.57 secs
1950	Stoneyhill Sweep	H. Ward	Powderhall	28.39 secs
1951	Rushton Smutty	F. Johnson	(Private)	28.16 secs
1952	Foolish Billy	H. Heyes	White City, London	28.20 secs
1953	Polonius	T. Reilly	Walthamstow	28.07 secs
1954	Rushton Mac	F. Johnson	(Private)	27.81 secs
1955	Rushton Mac	F. Johnson	(Private)	28.39 secs
1956	Belinga's Customer	R. Melville	Wembley	28.82 secs
1957	Northern King	H. Harvey	Wembley	28.22 secs
1958	Pigalle Wonder	J. Syder Jnr	Wembley	28.10 secs
1959	Pigalle Wonder	J. Syder Jnr	Wembley	28.08 secs
1960	Skibbereen Rocket	G. Rodgerson	Powderhall	28.38 secs
1961	Faithful Charlie	J. Irving	(Private)	28.02 secs
1962	Monforte Jo Jo	G. Barnett	(Private)	28.29 secs
1963	We'll See	T. Johnston	Carntyre	28.03 secs
1964	Ocean Roll	W. Weir	(Private)	28.07 secs
1965	Clonmannon Flash	R.Hookway	Owlerton	28.14 secs
1966	I'm Quickest	R. Singleton	White City, London	28.33 secs
1967	Negro Harpist	J. Irving	(Private)	27.94 secs
1968	Kerry Long Ago	S. Milligan	(Private)	28.04 secs
1969	Rockfield Era	S. Doyle	Shawfield	28.40 secs
1970	The Other Green	J. Irving	(Private)	28.10 secs
1971	Supreme Fun	S. Ryall	(Private)	28.08 secs
1972	Say Little	C. McNally	Perry Barr	27.91 secs
1973	Deelside Silver	T. Kane	(Private)	28.14 secs
1974	Bealkilla Diver	P. Mullins	(Private)	28.20 secs
* 1975	Tory Mor	S. Milligan	(Private)	27.67 secs
1976	Gaily Noble	J. Coleman	Romford	28.24 secs
1977	Linacre	E. Dickson	Slough	27.91 secs
1978	Dale Lad	G. de Mulder	Coventry	28.07 secs
1979	Jon Barrie	R. Andrews	Leeds	28.25 secs
1980	Jelly Crock	M. Travers	Ireland	28.35 secs
1981	Deel Joker	B. Gaynor	Perry Barr	28.07 secs
1982	Brief Candle	P. Hancox	Perry Barr	27.98 secs
1983	Creamery Cross	A. Briggs	Peterborough	28.18 secs
1984	Creamery Cross	A. Briggs	Peterborough	28.35 secs

*Pre-1975 run over 500 yds; since 1975 run over 465 m

RAMSGATE

Dumpton Park Stadium is owned by Northern Sports Ltd and racing takes place on Wednesday and Saturday evenings each week. The track is opposite the railway station and has a large car park. Patrons are provided with excellent bars and buffets, while the all-sand surface allows racing to take place all the year. One of the best running tracks in the south, it has a 400 m circumference with long straights and banked turns which make it suitable for all types of greyhounds. There is an inside Sumner hare and the glass-fronted stand enables racing to be viewed to advantage and in comfort. In July the Thanet Gold Cup is run here over 465 m, and is worth £1,000 to the winner. Recent winners include Timeless, trained by Jim Coleman who was successful in 1978, and Noon Time, owned by Mr C. Linney and trained by Jack Sherry at Walthamstow, who won in 1979. One of the best dogs in training that year, Noon Time also won the John Humphreys and Tony Morris Stakes at Crayford, run in April.

It was to Ramsgate in August 1948 that Good Worker came after his Laurels win, and set a new track record with a time of 28.72 secs for the 500 yds course.

The racing manager is Jeff Jeffcote, whose enterprise has made this one of the most popular venues in the south both for punters and for owners.

Main Events Run at Ramsgate

Thanet Gold Cup	July	465 m;

Track Records (1950)

Glum	1948	440 yds	25.70 secs
Good Worker	1948	500 yds	28.72 secs
Crissie Tanist	1947	600 yds	35.31 secs
Key Stone	1947	600 yds H	41.46 secs

Winners of the Thanet Gold Cup 1977–84

1977	Lively March	28.31 secs
1978	Timeless	28.42 secs
1979	Noon Time	28.24 secs
1980	Gurrane Purdo	28.09 secs
1981	Heres Gay	28.74 secs
1982	Westpark Clover	28.57 secs
1983	Creamery Cross	27.24 secs
1984	Cawarra Lad	27,57 secs

READING

This track is easily accessible by car and train from London. It has excellent amenities and a car park for 600. The directors are Bill Dore, Reg Fearman, F. Higley and Len Silver, and the racing manager is Martyn Dore.

The GRA closed the old Reading track on 1 January 1974, and eighteen months later Allied Presentations Ltd opened a new track in Bennet Road, operating under NGRC rules. The first meeting was held on 10 June 1975, and racing now takes place on Thursday and Saturday evenings, on an all-sand track and with an outside Sumner hare. The gradually banked turns make for fast running, and in September the Berkshire Cup is contested here over 465 m, for a first prize of £2,000. The winner in 1978 was that excellent dog Cougar Prince, trained by Ted Dickson at Slough. The 1979 event was won by Rathvilly Night, trained at the track by Tommy Atkins. Over the 635 m course is run the Hunt Cup, which was previously run at the old Reading track. This event takes place in February, a time when few top-class events are taking place in Britain, and so there is always a full entry of top greyhounds. In 1978 the event was won by Mr A. Katz's Westmead Manor, trained by Natalie Savva at Bletchley. This fine dog also won the Steel City Stakes at Owlerton. Another trainer here is Jerry Fisher who in 1983 tooks Jo's Gamble to Belle Vue and won the Cesarewitch, the first classic to be won by a Reading dog.

The old Reading track had the largest racing circuit in England, 400 yds races being run with only one bend, and fast times were a feature. Patrons will remember with affection Mr A. Vivien's great dog Bally Rambler, who in one year (1946) broke the 400 yds record set by Guideless Joe fifteen years earlier and set also a new record for the 550 yds course.

Main Events Run at Reading

Berkshire Cup	September	465 m
Hunt Cup	February	635 m

ROMFORD

It was through the foresight and enthusiasm of a local businessman, Mr Archer Leggett, and his brother-in-law that greyhound racing came to Romford in 1929, when they put down £400 to equip a small piece of land near the Crown Hotel in London Road and set up a track without any accommodation for patrons or greyhounds. No more than 500 enthusiasts came to the track on five evenings a week to see privately trained greyhounds follow a hare driven by the engine of an old Ford car, yet so successful was the venture that after a year's racing the landlords doubled the £4 a week rent. It was then decided to buy a nearby field and to build a track with amenities for the ever-growing band of racing enthusiasts. Another £600 was raised and a stand was built, complete with a hand-operated totalizator and an electrically-operated hare. On 20 September 1931 the Romford Stadium came into operation, and enjoyed attendances of more than 1,000 at each meeting. In 1935 four others joined the three original directors to form Romford Stadium Ltd with a capital of £17,000; extra stands were built, together with a range of high-quality kennels. Ten years later, with crowds of more than 2,000 at every meeting, a Stock Exchange quotation was obtained for 200,000 shares offered to the public at 10s 6d each. The company also owned the Dagenham track, which they sold in 1963 for £185,000, but Archer Leggett remained at Romford as managing director until 1976 when Coral's, the bookmakers and leisure group, purchased a controlling interest.

Coral's immediately set about making Romford one of the finest tracks in Britain and within two years had built a new stand and installed first-class accommodation with a magnificent plate glass-fronted restaurant, a new tote and hare. The track itself was completely relaid, with better banking at the bends and a sand surface.

The present managing director is John Sutton, and the general manager George 'Bunny' Gough, who joined Romford in 1960 after being racing manager at Powderhall and Harringay. The racing manager is J. Simpson, previously at Crayford, and he has introduced a wide variety of races from 400 m to 925 m. He is ably assisted by five contract trainers with great experience and owners who are happy to allow their dogs to be entered for most of the events run at the track.

Romford Stadium is easily reached from Liverpool Street Station and is only a few minutes' walk from the local station. Racing takes place there on Tuesday and Saturday evenings throughout the year, with the addition of Thursday from early April to late September. Four distances usually make up the race card – 400 m, 575 m, 750 m and 925 m, which is one of the longest in the racing calendar. There is an outside McKee hare and a sand surface. The introduction of a computer-operated tote has led to increased tote betting.

Inside the members' clubroom at Romford Stadium.

The trophy presented to the winner of the Essex Vase, the main event of the year run at Romford Stadium.

The Essex Vase, which has been run since 1930, is the premier event and is now sponsored by Charrington's. The winning owner gets £3,000. The event is run in July over 575 m and some of the finest greyhounds have taken part. None was finer than Dolores Rocket, who on 6 July 1971 clocked a new record time of 36.06 secs for the 650 yds course (it did not become 575 m until 1975). A fortnight before, she had set a new record for a bitch over 525 yds at the White City, and a fortnight later was to set a new 700 yds record at Wimbledon.

A contestant for the 1946 Essex Vase, won by Humming Bee, was the dog Mott's Regret, who did not even get a place in the final. Few who saw him eliminated in the semi-finals would have believed him capable of winning the Greyhound Derby, let alone the Essex Vase, but he did exactly that in 1947, shortly after being bought by Fred Trevillion, his owner and trainer from early 1947 and who renamed him Trev's Perfection. This dog was also the first to win the Scottish and Welsh Derbys – the Triple Crown. Another triumph was the Gold Collar at Catford.

Another outstanding dog to win the Essex Vase was Bermuda Fun, who won in 1978. He was owned by Messrs J. and D. Coleman and trained at the track by Ken Usher. It was also a Romford-trained dog, Bedford, who won the BBC TV Trophy at Walthamstow in 1966 as a 20–1 outsider. He was trained by Bob Thomson who is now paddock steward at the track. Romford also kennelled the wonderful long-distance bitch Go Ahead Girl, trained by Terry Duggan. She won seventeen consecutive races over the stayers' course and, when within sight of Westpark Mustard's twenty in a row, was unluckily beaten in a match at Eastville. Mr Duggan was then one of five contract trainers to supply the track with greyhounds. He trained Lauries Panther.

One of the best greyhounds to be trained at Romford was Ace of Trumps, owned by Mr Jim Fletcher and trained there by Jim Coleman before he moved to Wembley as a contract trainer. In 1969 Ace of Trumps became the first Romford dog to win a classic event when he won the Scurry Gold Cup, beating Lovely Morning by a neck.

The first of the main events to be run is the Greater London Challenge Cup, in March, over 750 m, and with a prize of £500. Over the same distance, in September, is run the Wheatley-Triad Stakes with a first prize of the same value. But probably the best night's racing takes place in May on press night, when the dogs in each race contest a trophy presented by a national newspaper or magazine.

Main Events Run at Romford

Greater London Challenge Trophy	March	750 m
Essex Vase	July	575 m
Farewell Stakes	August	575 m
Wheatley-Triad Stakes	September	750 m

Track Records (1950)

Tan Gent	1946	460 yds	26.08 secs
Cheerful Chairman	1939	460 yds H	27.60 secs
Pastorale	1941	550 yds	32.58 secs
Passe-partout	1941	550 yds	32.58 secs
Pearl's Choice	1947	650 yds	37.66 secs

Track Records (1970)

Ace of Trumps	1969	460 yds	25.18 secs
Derry's Calm	1970	460 yds H	26.14 secs

Dolores Rocket	1971	650 yds	36.06 secs
Gypsy Jerry	1968	650 yds H	37.47 secs

Track Records (1980)

Just Clear	10 8.78	1978	400 m	24.21 secs
Bermudas Fun	11.7.78	1978	575 m	35.15 secs
Attila	11.7.78	1978	750 m	41.13 secs
Langford Dacoit	27 7.78	1978	925 m	59.56 secs

Winners of the Essex Vase 1968–84

1968	Dick's Dilemma	36.49 secs
1969	Torry's Gay Lady	36.54 secs
1970	Quail's Glory	36.38 secs
1971	Dolores Rocket	36.06 secs
1972	Fit Me In	36.59 secs
1973	Kenneally's Moor	36.91 secs
1974	Cowpark Yank	36.70 secs
* 1975	Handy High	36.62 secs
1976	Westmead Myra	36.69 secs
1977	Xmas Holiday	37.40 secs
1978	Bermuda's Fun	35.15 secs
1979	Black Heaven	35.55 secs
1980	Taranaki	35.82 secs
1981	Sugarville Jet	35.68 secs
1982	Glenmoy Raven	36.03 secs
1983	Winning Line	35.36 secs
1984	Wheeler's Tory	35.45 secs

*Pre-1975 run over 650 yds; since 1975 run over 600 m; since 1978 run over 575 m

RYE HOUSE

The Stadium is in Hoddesdon, Hertfordshire, near the A10 at Rye Park, and is also reached by rail from London's Liverpool Street Station. The track, owned by Carter and Bailey Ltd, is operated under the NGRC permit scheme by which a number of independent tracks with facilities up to the required standards are now racing under NGRC rules.

Racing takes place on Wednesday and Saturday evenings each week and the track is a fast one with an inside hare and sanded bends. There are excellent bars and buffets and racing can be viewed from the comfort of a new stand.

The most important event, the Sovereign Stakes, run in October over a sprinters' course of 281 m and sponsored by the Rye House bookmakers, attracts many of the best dogs in training to compete for the first prize of £2,000. Among recent winners was Knockrour Brandy, who won in 1978. He obtained his tremendous pace through his dam from the Irish sire, Knockrour Again. Knockrour Brandy also took the National Sprint at Harringay for his owner, Mr A. Gidney, and trainer, Mrs F. Greenacre, in 1979, to confirm the opinion of racegoers that in 1978–9 the dog was one of the fastest ever over the sprint distances. In two years Knockrour Brandy won over £5,000 in prize money and broke four track records. A blue brindle, whelped September 1976 he is now at stud.

In 1979 Flying Pursuit, owned by Mr J. McCormack, was the first dog to 'break' seventeen seconds over this distance with a time of 16.97 secs. This he did in the Sovereign Stakes and, trained by John Gibbons at Crayford, the dog went on to win the 1980 Laurels. Mrs Pateman is a trainer here and in 1983 won the Thames Silver Salver for her patron, Mr L. Harrington with his dog, Daily Message.

The racing manager here is Gerry Bailey.

Main Event Run at Rye House

Sovereign Stakes	October	281 m

Track Records (1980)

Tiger Jazz	1978	281 m	16.91 secs
Oulartwick Kibo	1976	484 m	29.88 secs
Askinvillar King	1976	670 m	43.12 secs

Winners of the Sovereign Stakes

1976	Raheen Sam	17.13 secs
1977	Paddock Boy	17.05 secs
1978	Knockrour Brandy	17.17 secs
1979	Flying Pursuit	16.97 secs
1980	Greenfield Chief	17.00 secs
1981	Skipping Scot	17.03 secs
1982	Valiant Point	17.17 secs
1983	Upton Rocket	16.99 secs
1984	Upton Rocket	16.70 secs

SHAWFIELD

Situated at Rutherglen, Shawfield is the only Glasgow track to have survived the great days of the 1940s and 1950s when Carntyne staged the Scottish Derby and the Albion and White City tracks were also flourishing. Since 1972 the Scottish Derby has been held at Shawfield, which is well served by buses from the city centre. The Scottish St Leger used to be run here, but when Shawfield staged the Scottish Derby from 1972 the St Leger was transferred to Powderhall. The track opened November, 1932.

A big, galloping circuit of 430 m, with 125 yd straights and well-banked bends almost eliminating bumping, it has always been one of the fastest tracks in Britain and the amenities here are first-class. Owned by the GRA, it was one of the first tracks to instal ray timing and photo-finish equipment and has always been run to the highest standards. In 1977 the track installed totalizator aggregating equipment by which any number of denominations can be dealt in.

Racing takes place on Tuesday, Thursday and Saturday each week over 300 m, 480 m and 500 m. The Scottish Derby is contested in August over 500 m, and is worth £2,500 to the winner. In 1978 this was Pat Seamur, trained by Geoffrey de Mulder, and the dog was to win the Cambridgeshire in the same year. In May 1970 Bright Lad set a new track record here for 300 yds, and seven years later his son Amber Sky won the Scottish Derby for his trainer, Peter Beaumont of Halifax. Another of Bright Lad's sons was Dale Lad, who won the Edinburgh Cup at Powderhall and took the William King Cup at Shawfield at 2–1 on. He was one of the fastest ever to the first turn and ante-post favourite for the 1978 Derby. The William King Cup is contested in July and is worth £1,000 to the winner.

Also run at Shawfield is the St Mungo Cup, worth £500 together with a large, handsome trophy. It was won in 1978 by the Perry Barr champion All Wit, trained by Frank Baldwin. All Wit was a finalist for the 1978 Derby, won by Lacca Champion. By Monalee Champion out of the Newdown Heather bitch, Dunally, there is no better bred dog in Britain and he is now at stud at a fee of £150. The St Mungo Cup was run at Carntyne until that track closed, and was won in 1946 by Monday's Son who had won the Scottish Derby the previous year.

Two outstanding greyhounds to race at Shawfield in the 1940s were the bitches Mad Midnight and Coyne's Castle, two of the greatest ever to run over long distances. Mad Midnight set a world record here for 700 yds with a time of 39.88 secs.

At Shawfield on 20 March 1972 was recorded the only triple dead heat ever run in Britain, when over the 535 yds course Turkish Maid, Thurles Queen and War Girl crossed the line together as shown on the photo-finish camera.

The racing manager is Ross Searle.

Main Events Run at Shawfield

St Mungo Cup	May	480 m
William King Cup	July	500 m
Scottish Derby	August	500 m

Track Records (1950)

Fin Mackree	1947	525 yds	29.07 secs
Our Tansy	1947	700 yds	39.53 secs

Track Records (1970)

Bright Lad	1970	300 yds	16.60 secs
Rushton Smutty	1951	500 yds	27.60 secs
Minorcas Glass	1956	500 yds H	28.75 secs
Biddy's Fire	1964	525 yds	28.75 secs
Morganstown View	1958	525 yds H	30.30 secs
Our Tansy	1947	700 yds	39.53 secs

Winners of the St Mungo Cup 1970–83*

1970	Ballybeg Flash	29.00 secs
1971	Glittering Man	28.86 secs
1972	not run	
1973	Pit Lamp	29.30 secs
1974	Blessington Boy	28.70 secs
† 1975	Lianda Rebel	29.20 secs
1976	Broken Secret	30.79 secs
1977	Broken Secret	30.12 secs
1978	All Wit	30.70 secs
1979	Kilbelin Ruler	30.84 secs
1980	Decoy Duke	31.03 secs
1982	Pineapple Barrow	30.22 secs
1983	Go Winston	30.01 secs

† Pre-1975 run over 500 yds; since 1975 run over 48
* 1970-4 run at Carntyne; 1975-80 run at Shawfield

SLOUGH

Owned and maintained by the GRA since 1966, this excellent track was opened in 1928 as a result of the enterprise of Mr George Bennet, son of the owner of the local Dolphin Hotel. The Dolphin Trophy is a popular event held here each year. In 1938 the track was purchased by Clapton Stadium, and in 1959 it came under the wing of New Clapton Stadium Ltd, with E. and H. Luper as joint managing directors and John Collins as racing manager. Then, when the Clapton Stadium closed down, the other tracks owned by the company were also sold. Several were closed for greyhound racing but fortunately the Slough track came under the banner of the GRA and attracts excellent support, chiefly because it is less than twenty miles from central London and easily reached by bus and train. With Brighton, it has the highest tote turnover of any track in Britain outside London. John Edmonds is general manager with Peter Regan, racing manager.

The running track has a circumference of 365 m with long straights. Racing takes place on Tuesday and Saturday evenings each week and alternate Thursdays. The most important event now held at Slough is the sprinters' classic, the Scurry Gold Cup, which was transferred from Clapton in 1974. Now worth £3,000 to the winner, it is run over 442 metres and takes place in April, being the first of the year's classics. Contesting the event in 1976 were those outstanding dogs, the Derby winner Mutt's Silver, and the Laurels winner Xmas Holiday, who won the event that year and finished third the following year, two lengths behind Wired to the Moon, winner in 1977, with Carhumore Speech in second place.

Perhaps the outstanding dog to be kennelled here in recent years was Greenfield Fox, who won the Laurels and went through the event by winning every heat. He also won the Pall Mall and Scurry Gold Cup. Greenfield Fox was trained by Ted Dickson, one of the immortals among greyhound trainers, who in 1977 was elected Greyhound Trainer of the Year. Ted Dickson began training greyhounds as a kennel boy to Norman Chambers in his native Edinburgh when the Powderhall track opened. He took out a private trainer's license in the 1960s and joined Slough in 1970. Apart from his classic successes in 1977, nothing gave him more pleasure than appearing once again at Powderhall in charge of Linacre when that outstanding dog won the Dodge City Cup and the £5,000 prize for his owner.

Run over the same 442 m course at Slough is the Ben Truman Sprint, sponsored by the brewers, who also sponsor the Ben Truman Stayers' Stakes, run over 593 m. Both are run in May and a recent winner of the latter event was Mr and Mrs Boddy's dog Kudas Joy, trained by Ted Dickson.

The Buckinghamshire Cup, run over the stayers' course, is the premier event after the Scurry Cup and has been contested since the track opened. It is worth £500 to the winner. In its early years the Cup was run over 475 yds, and one of the most exciting dogs to win the event was Glin Lad who won by six lengths in 1946 when quoted 6–4 on. Another of Slough's legendary trainers is Jimmy Jowett, who went there when Clapton closed, and later trained Owner's Guide to win the 1978 Buckinghamshire Cup. Two long-serving trainers were Arthur Cudmore, who was in at the start and remained a trainer there for thirty years, and Paddy Pierce. Hazel Walden and Ray Iremonger replaced them upon retirement.

Main Events Run at Slough

Scurry Gold Cup	April	442 m
Ben Truman Sprint	May	442 m
Ben Truman Stayers' Trophy	May	593 m
Champagne Trophy	May	807 m
Buckinghamshire Cup	August	593 m

Track Records (1950)

Oola Rattler	1946	275 yds	15.51 secs
Parish Model	1947	475 yds	26.71 secs
Cadet Captain	1946	475 yds H	27.69 secs
Diamond Jim	1946	675 yds	39.42 secs

Track Records (1970)

Shamrock Clipper	1966	460 yds	25.62 secs
Rory's Pleasure	1961	460 yds H	26.57 secs
Quail's Glory	1970	640 yds	36.42 secs
Gladness	1968	880 yds	50.97 secs

Track Records (1980)

Northwood Double	1978	442 m	26.74 secs
Owner's Guide	1979	593 m	37.20 secs
Westpark Putter	1978	807 m	52.13 secs

Winners of the Buckinghamshire Cup 1968–80

1968	Dick's Dilemma	37.72 secs
1969	Jeannie's Wonder	37.00 secs
1970	Albany Grand	36.99 secs
1971	Coset Fire	36.53 secs
1972	Adamstown Fire	36.37 secs
1973	Ashgrove Tric	37.06 secs
1974	Delroney Leader	37.14 secs
* 1975	Houghton Girl	37.28 secs
1976	Thade is Out	38.49 secs
1977	Black Legend	37.87 secs
1978	Owner's Guide	37.57 secs
1979	Full Again	37.33 secs
† 1980	Rikasso Pancho	30.51 secs

* Pre-1975 run over 640 yds; 1975-9 run over 603 m
† 1980 run over 593 m

SOUTHEND

The Essex track opened its gates for greyhound racing in September 1931 and has remained one of the foremost of Britain's provincial tracks. In 1970 considerable improvements were made, including the building of a new stand and restaurant with tiered seating to enable diners to watch the racing. The track is almost circular, with wide and easy bends. It was at Southend that the first colour television pictures of a greyhound race were filmed, for the track had brighter lighting than anywhere else. So forward-looking has the management always been that Southend is one of the few British tracks where attendances and tote takings have risen continuously since the 1970s.

Racing takes place on Thursday and Saturday (also Monday in the summer) each week throughout the year, and the most important event is the well-known Thames Silver Salver, now run over 277 m in July. Since its inauguration in 1933 it has always attracted the best sprinters in training. Until 1965 it was run over 600 yds; then, for ten years, over 300 yds. In 1935 Border Mutton came here with Paddy McEllistrim, only recently (1975) retired as a Wimbledon trainer, to win the event. The dog was to race for more than four years and was the most versatile greyhound in the sport's history, contesting in all more than 150 races over all distances on the flat and over hurdles. Border Mutton was again a winner of the Silver Salver in 1936, being the only dog to win the event twice. Two years later that immortal bitch Quarter Day won the event. In 1946 the great Shannon Shore won by six lengths from Tan Gent in 27.89 secs and in the same year came Monday's News, recent winner of the Derby, to win The Overture by six lengths and set a new track record. The following year another Derby winner, Priceless Border, won the Silver Salver, beating Rimmell's Black by eleven lengths to show just how good he was, for this dog had won the Laurels only a month earlier. Two years later Red Wind set a new record of 27.78 secs when winning the event. In 1971 Don't Gambol, fresh from winning his second Scurry Cup, was entered for the Silver Salver and set a new track record for the 300 yds course, but when leading in the final broke a toe and pulled up lame. More recently Geoffrey de Mulder brought Superior Champ to contest the 1978 event and won £1,000 for his owners, Mr D. Matthieson and Mr G. Hendry. The following year Pat Mullins brought Kerry Smile from Cambridge to win and in 1980 H. Crapper of the Owlerton track, Sheffield, took the £1,200 first prize for Mrs. J. Gascoigne with the dog Ballyderg Fox, the 2–1 on favourite who won by a neck from Brandy Darr.

A trainer at Southend from its opening until his retirement in 1970 was Stanley Gray, whose dogs won the Wembley and Wimbledon Spring Cups and a host of open events at his home track. Other trainers here are Albert Skelton, Ted Windsor and Tony Dennis. Terry Evans is racing manager.

Main Event Run at Southend

Thames Silver Salver	July	277 m

Track Records (1950)

Royal Canopy	1948	300 yds	16.90 secs
Red Wind	1949	500 yds	27.78 secs
Sprightly Peter	1948	500 yds H	28.72 secs
Royal Canopy	1948	525 yds	29.49 secs
Drastic O'Leer	1949	700 yds	40.04 secs

Track Records (1980)

Knockrour Brandy	2.7.79	277 m	16.45 secs
Graceful Fellow	26.5.73	462 m H	28.61 secs
My Royal	30.4.79	484 m	29.03 secs
Fosters Folly	12.6.80	484 m	29.03 secs
Shyan Trader	26.5.79	484 m H	29.94 secs
Montini's Flash	1.11.79	647 m	39.67 secs
Billys Glory	22.8.74	705 m	43.97 secs
Maldon West	12.8.78	913 m	57.66 secs

Winners of the Thames Silver Salver

1933	Just Oblige	28.93 secs
1934	Hymer Puritan	28.88 secs
1935	Border Mutton	28.88 secs
1936	Border Mutton	28.74 secs
1937	Top of the Carlow Road	28.92 secs
1938	Quarter Day	28.66 secs
1939	Flying Jockey	29.26 secs
1940-45	not run	
1946	Shannon Shore	27.89 secs
1947	Priceless Border	28.04 secs
1948	Good Worker	28.64 secs
1949	Red Wind	27.78 secs
1950	Dick's Symphony	28.47 secs
1951	Irish Hooligan	28.52 secs
1952	Minorca's Hope	28.21 secs
* 1953	Uskane Lad	17.15 secs
1954	Morgan's Hillside	17.13 secs
1955	Big Buffer	17.05 secs
1956	Majestic Matador	17.15 secs
1957	Howardstown Cu	16.80 secs
1958	Tickled Pink	16.70 secs
1959	Red Kestrel	17.04 secs
1960	Chamois	17.01 secs
1961	Hi Tivoli	16.45 secs
1962	Knockalisheen Prince	16.86 secs
1963	Mossdale Paddy	16.80 secs
1964	Sapphire Prince	16.74 secs
1965	Geddy's Flash	16.65 secs
1966	Near the Fire	16.81 secs
1967	Rosslad King	16.71 secs
1968	Deise Leads	16.88 secs
1969	Lovely Morning	16.80 secs
1970	Don't Gambol	16.56 secs
1971	Fireside Reject	16.76 secs
1972	An Toileanagh	16.61 secs
1973	Carrig Shane	16.49 secs
1974	Over Protected	16.72 secs
† 1975	Chief Stuart	16.78 secs
1976	Mutts Silver	16.99 secs
1977	El Patrone	16.79 secs
1978	Superior Champ	16.62 secs
1979	Kerry Smile	16.62 secs
1980	Ballyderg Fox	16.70 secs
1981	Woodland Chimes	16.48 secs
1982	Sand Style	16.60 secs
1983	Daily Message	16.79 secs

*Pre-1953 run over 600 yds; 1953-74 run over 300 yds † Since 1975 run over 277 m

SWINDON

The Abbey Stadium is at Blunsdon on the outskirts of the town and came under NGRC rules in April 1968. Racing takes place on Monday and Wednesday evenings, and on occasional Saturdays in summer, over 480 m, 530 m, 685 m and 943 m. The facilities are excellent; E.W. Nelson is general manager and W.R. Hiscock racing manager. When the Knowle track at Bristol closed, its well-known Silver Plume event was transferred to Swindon, to become its main event, run in June.

During the 1960s one of the most popular dogs to race there was Just Cruising, who won many races when more than six years old. Later The Grand Show, trained by Mrs K. Lee, was a consistent winner. By Wonder Valley out of April Twilight, he was

Opposite: Walthamstow trainer Dave Geggus with Sole Aim, winner of the 1970 Laurels and the 1971 Irish Derby. Photo: Pictorial Press Ltd, reproduced by permission of Walthamstow Stadium.

bred in Ireland by Mr Paddy Dunphy and always put up a fine performance.

Another successful trainer here is Mrs Hazel Walden, who also supplies the Slough track with greyhounds trained at her kennels near Newbury. She trained the flying Piledriver to break Swindon's track record in 1973, and he finished third in the final of the British Breeders' Produce Stakes that year. Great things were expected of him but a few weeks later he died.

Greenfield Fox, trained at Slough by Ted Dickson, was here in 1977 to set a new 530 m record, and he went on to win the Scurry Gold Cup at his home track the following year.

Main Event Run at Swindon

The Silver Plume (Arkell's)	October	685 m

Track Record Holders (1980)

Dave's War	1979	480 m	28.49 secs
Greenfield Fox	1977	530 m	31.58 secs
Bright Cut	1976	685 m	42.38 secs
Eternal Mist	1980	943 m	60.18 secs

WALTHAMSTOW

Situated on the north-eastern side of London, this track began on some ground in Chingford Road used as a rubbish dump by local residents. It opened on 19 June 1933 with William (Billy) Chandler, its builder, as managing director. He was succeeded by his son Charles and the track has been managed with the same flair and ability by his sons in turn; the Chandlers retain a controlling interest and it has continued to be one of the best-run tracks in Britain. In 1936 a magnificent ballroom was added to the amenities and in 1971 a new stand was built with a luxurious restaurant which enables diners to view the evening's entertainment through the huge plate glass window that runs the entire length of the enclosure. There are totalizator counters at either end of the room.

Bill Chandler, always known as 'the Guv'nor', died in 1950, leaving seven sons and a daughter, and the Chandler bookmaking empire and Walthamstow Stadium passed to his son, Charles. It later passed to Charles's brother, Percy, who is managing director and is assisted by William and Jack, with Charles's son, Charles Jnr, as chairman.

1978 saw a takeover bid by Coral Leisure backed by some members of the Chandler family. It resulted in a thirty-three-day hearing in the High Court after which judgment was given in favour of the ruling faction of the Chandler family.

Since the early 1950s Mrs Frances Chandler, Charles Chandler's wife, has been one of the most successful owners of greyhounds ever. She has followed the tradition begun by several other wives of track owners in buying nothing but the best to put before the patrons. For many years they provided the sport with a succession of wonderful greyhounds. The first of these far-sighted ladies were Mrs Hilda Sanderson, wife of the managing director of Coventry Stadium and Mrs Cearns, wife of Wimbledon's chairman. Shortly afterwards Mrs Chandler enjoyed comparable success with her dogs, winning the Laurels in 1970 and the Irish Derby in 1971 with Sole Aim, the English Cesarewitch and St Leger in 1953 with the great Magourna Reject, one of the outstanding stayers of all time. Both dogs were trained at Walthamstow, Sole Aim by Dave Geggus who died in December 1979 while still a trainer there, and Magourna Reject by Tommy Reilly.

In 1956 Barney O'Connor came to Walthamstow from Co. Galway to accept a long-standing invitation by Charles Chandler (son of the founder) to become a full-time trainer. He remained at Walthamstow for over twenty years. That year Dunmore King won the Derby and Barney O'Connor came with his charge, although in those days the regulations required the dog to be placed in the care of an officially registered track trainer; consequently Paddy McEvoy is credited as the dog's trainer. Seventeen years later Barney O'Connor achieved his life's ambition to win an English classic when Black Banjo won the 1973 Laurels. He later became the only trainer to win the English and Irish Grand Nationals, which he did with Mr Pat Browne's Indoor Sport; this great dog beaten by only a short head for the Scottish National. In 1976 Barney O'Connor had charge of Ballinderry Moth.

During the 1950s Tommy Reilly was one of the most successful of all trainers. Not only did he handle Magourna Reject with considerable ability to win the 1953 St Leger and Cesarewitch, but he also won the Laurels that year with Polonius. Only one other trainer – Phil Rees – had ever won three classics in one year. Tommy Reilly also trained Loyal Accomplice to win the Gold Collar in 1951 and Dunstown Warrior in 1959. Graham Sharpe is another experienced trainer here.

Walthamstow used to be one of the slowest and most difficult of tracks to run on, with the inside hare favouring dogs from trap 1, but some years ago the surface was sanded and the bends improved to give greater banking, since when the track has become much faster. Not surprisingly, Walthamstow-kennelled dogs have always performed best at Wimbledon, with its equally tight bends, and greyhounds trained at the two tracks have the best record of Laurels winners. No Walthamstow-trained greyhound has ever won the Derby, but Sole Aim won the Irish Derby. Racing manager for more than forty years was Jim Watson, who on his retirement in 1979 was succeeded by Ray Spalding.

Racing takes place on Tuesday and Saturday each week and on alternate Thursdays, and the October Grand Prix, now sponsored by the Courage brewery, is the classic allocated to this track. Though contested since 1946, it was not given classic status until 1971, though it has always attracted the best dogs in training. Until 1975 it was run over 525 yds, the standard distance; it has since been run over the longer distance of 650 m, with a prize of £5,000 for the winner.

The 1947 Grand Prix was perhaps the finest, when two great greyhounds ran their hearts out in the final, which was won by Monday's News, Derby winner of the previous year, by two lengths from the 1948 Derby winner, Priceless Border. These two were among the outstanding greyhounds of all time.

Amongst the dogs in the 1946 Grand Prix was Mott's Regret, who did not reach the final. Those who saw him eliminated in his heat could never have dreamed that here was the Derby winner of 1947, the peerless Trev's Perfection, renamed when purchased by Fred Trevillion, his owner and trainer.

Long established as Walthamstow's main event for stayers is the June-run Test, run over 700 yds until 1974, and now over 640 m. It is sponsored by Carling Black Label Lager with £1,000 as the first prize together with a silver-plated tray. Many famous greyhounds have won the event, none more so than Model Dasher, who won the event in 1944 when 8–1 on favourite. The following year Kampion Sailor won from Stylish Nancy – both he and Model Dasher were among the finest stayers of all time. Not many would class the magnificent Monday's News with these two marathon performers, yet he won the Test the year after and was well able to manage the 700 yds.

There was irony in the fact that the first race that Trev's Perfection won for his new owner was the Circuit at Walthamstow, then run over 500 yds, now over 475 m, and sponsored by Holsten Lager with a prize of £2,500 for the winner. The longest race is the Chingford Marathon, run over 820 m, and won in 1977 by the outstanding stayer Langford Dacoit, Spectre's grandson. A recent winner was Pigeon Flyer, voted best English-bred greyhound of 1978, who was second in the Laurels the following year.

For many years the late Harry Briggs was the much-respected racing manager. Today Ray Spalding is in charge of racing.

Main Events Run at Walthamstow

Chingford Marathon	February	820 m
The Holsten Test	June	640 m
Holsten Circuit	July	475 m
Waltham Forest Marathon	July	820 m
Courage Grand Prix	October	640 m
Stow Marathon	November	820 m
The Chase	October	475 m

Track Records (1950)

Ballyhennessy Seal	1944	500 yds	28.59 secs
Shaggy Lass	1945	500 yds	28.55 secs
Ballynennan Moon	1942	525 yds	29.92 secs
Baytown Blackbird	1946	525 yds H	30.52 secs
Stylish Nancy	1945	700 yds	40.92 secs
Kilbelin Dancer	1948	700 yds	40.81 secs

Track Records (1980)

Blissful Hero	1978	475 m	28.72 secs
Paradise Spectre	1977	640 m	39.50 secs
Todos Liza	1969	820 m	51.58 secs

Winners of the Stow Marathon 1970–81

1970	Following Day	53.12 secs
1971	Breachs Buzzard	52.80 secs
1972	The Marchioness	52.73 secs
1973	not run	
1974	Weston Showman	52.55 secs
* 1975	not run	
1976	Hycroft Lyric	52.87 secs
1977	Top Touch	52.99 secs
1978	Weston Blaze	51.99 secs
1979	Royston's Supreme	52.12 secs
1980	Pineapple Choice	52.28 secs
1981	Decoy Boom	52.26 secs

* Pre-1975 run over 880 yds; since 1975 run over 820 m

Winners of the Carling Test 1968–83

* 1968	Fully Booked	41.01 secs
1969	Precious Dan	52.87 secs
1970	Curraheen Lady	52.25 secs
1971	Bill the Pig	52.60 secs
1972	Westmead Lane	52.95 secs
1973	not run	
1974	Chain Gang	52.63 secs
† 1975	Silver Sceptre	52.09 secs
1976	not run	
1977	Blue Angel	52.87 secs
1978	not run	
** 1979	Jingling Star	40.43 secs
1980	Mr Squeeze	40.20 secs
1981	Valient May	40.22 secs
1982	Westmead Gem	40.33 secs
1983	Go Winston	40.07 secs

* Run over 700 yds in 1968; over 880 yds 1974
† 1975–77 820 m ** Since 1979 over 640 m

WEMBLEY

The history of Wembley Stadium as a sports arena is known the world over for here is staged the soccer event of the year, the FA Cup Final which takes place in May, and the Rugby League Cup Final later in the month. It was here that the 1948 Olympic Games were held and in 1966 the World Cup Final for football which saw England victorious. The Stadium was originally constructed as the centre-piece for the British Empire Exhibition, which was staged at a cost of £12,000,000, soon after the ending of the First World War, on a site covering 220 acres. The Stadium was built to the design of Sir Owen Williams and was completed in exactly three hundred days. It was built on top of a hill from which it can be seen for miles around; 250,000 tons of soil were removed to level the site and 25,000 tons of cement were used in its construction. It was completed in time to stage the 1923 FA Cup between Bolton Wanderers (the winners) and West Ham United and cost £750,000. A year later, the Stadium and the exhibition were officially opened by Their Majesties King George V and Queen Mary.

The exhibition, built to show the world the splendours of the empire, and lavish in its construction, lost money in spite of almost 100,000 people passing through its gates every hour from the day it opened, and in October 1925 it was closed and the site placed in the hands of the official receiver. Though nearly bankrupt himself, the speculator Mr Jimmy White offered to purchase the lot, the stadium included, for £300,000 – an offer which was accepted, though White had no idea of what to do with his purchase and he could find no buyers. But for the foresight of a young man, Arthur Elvin, the son of a Norwich policeman, who was an assistant in a tobacco kiosk during the exhibition earning £4 a week, Wembley Stadium would have been pulled down and sold for scrap, together with the rest of the buildings. Elvin had other ideas, however. He bought the exhibition buildings from White and within a few months had made a profit of £20,000 from the sale of the materials. He then asked White to sell him the stadium which had no other use than to stage the FA Cup Final on one day a year; though this event was watched by more than 100,000 people, it yielded a profit of less than £5,000. He agreed with White on a price of £120,000 and was given ten days to find the money. But White died suddenly, killed by his own hand rather than face bankruptcy proceedings, and his executors called in the money in full to pay off his debts, giving Elvin only a few days to find it. This was 1926, however, and the new sport of greyhound racing had reached Britain. Not to be put off, Elvin contacted several City financiers with plans to open the stadium on several days a week for speedway and greyhound racing as well as to use it to stage other sporting events and they agreed to put up £25,000 each. Wembley Stadium Ltd came into being and purchased the arena from Elvin for £150,000. He took his profit in shares and was appointed managing director of the company. Within four months, the Stadium had opened for greyhound racing, the first meeting taking place on 10 December 1927, when the dog Spin, owned by Mrs Allcoat and trained by Tom Cudmore, won the first race from trap 4. The runner-up was more interesting, for it was a dog called Second Brigade whose joint owners were Mr Stanley Biss and Mr Ken Appleton, both to become trainers of many famous greyhounds in the early years of the sport.

During the 1970s the Stadium had a complete refit to conform to safety requirements, and the restaurant facilities were modernized, a programme costing more than £2 million. Racing now takes place on Monday and Friday evenings. Originally the dogs followed a trackless inside hare, but this was replaced early in 1952 by the outside Magee hare which has been in operation ever since.

If the White City was the Mecca of greyhound racing, Wembley is its Ascot, and has always provided a high standard of comfort for its patrons. No track has been more fortunate in its officials and trainers, for until the mid-1970s many of them had been there since 1927. Captain Arthur Brice was the first director of racing, a position he held for twenty years. He was also judge of the Waterloo Cup for a quarter of a century and no one knew more about greyhounds. He was followed by John Joliffe as racing manager, who also was there for twenty years, after which Jack Tetlow became head of racing.

After serving with the RAF during the war, John Joliffe went back to Wembley as racing manager. On his retirement he was succeeded by Jack Tetlow, another long servant at Wembley who first went there in 1930 as a programme seller. Of all the greyhounds John Joliffe had seen running at the Stadium, he thought the best was Mile Bush Pride who was kennelled there and trained by Jack Harvey. Jack Tetlow retired at the end of 1973, after forty-three years at Wembley, the last five as racing manager. He thought that of all the greyhounds he had seen racing, from Mick the Miller when he won the St Leger to Ardine Flame who broke the track record there, Future Cutlet was the best, the finest greyhound that ever raced and the best looker. Many would agree.

It was to the Wembley management in 1928 that Major Jack Paget suggested the idea of holding an 'open' race to be competed for by greyhounds from other tracks, and after meeting the stewards of the NGRC Captain Brice agreed. It was the first trophy to be presented, and the beginning of 'open' greyhound racing events in Britain.

Col Middleton Perry was veterinary surgeon from the first meeting until 1967 when Mr Lawson took over, ably assisted by Miss Vera Birtles. Wembley has always had trainers of the highest integrity. The first were Bob Burls, at Wembley fifty years later, Sidney Probert, Jim Syder Snr, Alf Mulliner and Tom Cudmore. Soon afterwards came veterinary surgeon and trainer Arthur Callanan from Ireland; he was later to become racing manager at Shelbourne Park, Dublin. At Wembley he became known as 'Doc' because of his great skill in treating young greyhounds given up by their owners as too sickly to rear. He was in charge of the great Creamery Border, in 1934 'the fastest dog on earth' but who was originally sent to him as a sickly puppy in need of considerable care.

The late Leslie Reynolds came here from the White City in 1940 and for many years was a 'slipper' at Waterloo Cup meetings. His first classic win was with Fret Not when the five-year-old dog won the St Leger in 1932. But he was not the oldest Leger winner – Mick the Miller was older by three months when he won the event the year before. Leslie Reynolds had three Leger winners in five years at what was to become his home track, the others being Bosham in 1934 and the speedy Ataxy in 1936. Surprisingly, in view of his wonderful record in the Derby, for which he trained five winners in seven years, Reynolds never trained another St Leger winner after 1936. He joined the Wembley staff during the Second World War and remained until his death in 1960. At Wembley he had several of the greatest dogs under his care that the sport has known, such as Priceless Border in 1948, and Shannon Shore, with whom he won the 1946 Laurels. He trained the bitch Narrogar Ann to win the Derby in 1949, and she was only the second bitch to do so. The Reynolds-trained Ballylanigan Tanist and Endless Gossip won the Derby in 1951 and 1952.

At Wembley since the early days was Harry (Jack) Harvey, whom many consider to have been the most knowledgeable of all greyhound trainers. Like Stanley Biss he had a wonderful way with bitches, who require great attention to their seasonal rests if they are to come fit at exactly the right time, since there is little margin for error. Jack was a trainer at Belle Vue when the sport began and he then moved to Harringay, where he had charge of Davesland when that dog won the 1934 Derby, beating such outstanding dogs as Grey Raca, Wild Woolley and Brilliant Bob. He also trained the great Mile Bush Pride who won the event for Mr Noel Purvis twenty-five years later. In his long career Jack Harvey created the wonderful record of having had a greyhound in the Derby final on twenty-four occasions.

He was equally successful in the St Leger, which was the third of the classic races to be inaugurated, in 1928, when Burletta, trained at Wembley by Alf Mulliner, won over the 700 yds course which since 1975 has been changed to 655 m. Harvey moved to Wembley in 1937, but had to wait until 1949 before training a St Leger winner when the bitch Lovely Rio was successful. Then followed four wins in eight years between 1954 and 1961; the 1961 event was won by one of the greatest in the sport's history, Clonalvy Pride, whose time of 39.64 secs was bettered by only one dog, O'Hara's Rebel, when the St Leger was run over 700 yds. Jack Harvey also won the first Pall Mall run at Harringay in 1935 with Shove Ha'penny, his favourite of all the dogs he trained. Shove Ha'penny went to Wembley with him and remained there in retirement until he died in 1946.

Among the best-known owners of greyhounds at Wembley were Mr George Flintham, Mr Noel Purvis and Mr Norman Dupont, who for thirty years provided Wembley with some of the finest dogs the sport has known. Money was no object and they wanted to provide only the best. George Flintham was in at the start, winning his first open event in 1929, and one of his earliest champions was Grand Flight II. No more honest dog ever raced; he was to win the Cesarewitch in 1935 and was beaten only a short head by Shove Ha'penny for the Pall Mall. Some other outstanding greyhounds owned by George Flintham were Quarter Day, one of the greatest bitches ever to race, Grosvenor Bob, Ballycurreen Garrett, Mighty Hassan and Gorey Airways, who twice won the Scurry Cup, the first time as a puppy. Although George Flintham's greyhounds won every classic the Derby always eluded him, to his intense disappointment. He had very bad luck with that fine dog Galtee Cleo who, drawn in trap 1 and installed favourite, was beaten in the 1953 Derby by Daw's Dancer by half a length. Three years before, his Ballycurreen Garrett also reached the Derby final, but after being badly hampered at the first turn finished last. He, too, started favourite. This outstanding dog was to win the 1949 Wimbledon Puppy Derby, which Mr Flintham had also won in 1939 and 1940 with Keel Border and Grosvenor Flexian, both trained by Joe Harmon.

Jack Harvey trained for Mr Noel Purvis; in the 1950s, he handled his greyhounds brilliantly and during that decade they won every classic. Mr Purvis began buying late in 1949, at Clonmel, when he purchased five of the dogs contesting the National Puppy Cup there, but none did more than win the odd open event in England. Coolkill Chieftain was the first of his greyhounds to win a big event, the Laurels in 1954, and the following year Title Role won the St Leger and Barrowside the Grand National. Barrowside was one of the fastest dogs of all over hurdles, and he ran up for the Derby in 1955 with Coolkill Chieftain in third place. Noel Purvis was to crown a most successful few years as an owner when he purchased the wonderful Mile Bush Pride, one of the greatest of all time, who was twice third in the Derby and won the event in 1959. At this time Jack Harvey's head kennelman was Charlie Green, who had been at Wembley since the 1930s. Several great dogs were in his care, including Prairie Flash, Coolkill Chieftan, Barrowside and Mile Bush Pride.

Norman Dupont became a steward of the NGRC and later a director of Brighton Stadium. His first expensive buy was Quare Customer who reached the final of the 1950 Derby and was beaten into second place by the brilliant Ballymac Ball, but Mr Dupont did not have long to wait before winning the premier event. Next year Ballylanigan Tanist, trained by Leslie Reynolds, won in the record time for the Derby of 28.62 secs. This dog was also to win the Laurels.

Another of the great Wembley trainers of the 'fabulous fifties' was Jim Syder Jnr, who was to win the Derby with the magnificent Pigalle Wonder. The dog was originally named Prairie Champion, but whichever name he carried he was indeed a champion. His owner, the late Mr Al Burnett, owned the Pigalle club in Piccadilly and was always seen at Wembley and the White City wearing silk suits and smoking cigars of Churchillian dimensions. It was a unique era on the greyhound tracks of England.

Another of the great Wembley trainers of the early days was Sidney Probert, who had the fabulous Future Cutlet in his charge. Beaten a neck in the 1932 Derby, Mr Evershed's champion won the event the following year, beating Beef Cutlet by a short head in one of the greatest of all Derbys. Mr

Probert also won the St Leger with The Daw, and was considered one of the best of all greyhound handlers.

Then there were the Syders, father and son. Jim Syder Snr trained So Green, winner of the first Puppy Derby at Wimbledon, and Wattle Bark which won the 1937 Derby for Mrs Dent. It was his son, also Jim, who achieved a similar success with Pigalle Wonder twenty years later. The dog also dead-heated for the Cesarewitch. In 1955 Jim Syder Jnr trained Firgrove Slipper to win the Gold Collar, but if he had trained no other greyhound but Pigalle Wonder, Jim Syder's name would endure as long as track racing, for Al Burnett's champion broke track records wherever he ran.

Bob Burls was another of the Wembley masters in the training of greyhounds. He was there for nearly fifty years, and was the longest-serving trainer in the sport's history. Mr Burls had charge of Bah's Choice, the first dog to 'break' 29 secs for the 525 yds course, and of Dante II, later renamed Dante the Great, who won the 1947 St Leger in 39.70 secs, a new track record and record for the event. His time stood for fourteen years, until Clonalvy Pride clocked 39.64 secs in 1961; this was bettered only by another Burls dog, O'Hara's Rebel. His time of 39.54 secs was not a track record, however – this was 39.28 secs, achieved by Lucky Hi There in 1964, a time never beaten over 700 yds at Wembley. This fine dog took the St Leger that year, and in 1965 the TV Trophy, run over 880 yds. Five years after Dante's triumph Mr Burls had another St Leger winner in Funny Worker. Then came O'Hara's Rebel in 1967 and Crefogue Dancer in 1969, whose time of 39.65 secs for the St Leger was bettered only by two other dogs. The Derby eluded Bob Burls, even though he trained so many fine greyhounds. Among these was Mrs Lily Aubrey's wonderful white and black bitch Miss Taft, who ran in 115 races during her long career, winning fifty-five and being placed second twenty-five times, an achievement of great consistency due largely to Bob Burls' care and handling. Miss Taft was chosen as Bitch of the Year for 1967.

In 1949 Ronnie Melville came to Wembley as a trainer. He remained for twenty years until his place was taken by Tommy Johnston who performed a unique feat in training three consecutive winners of the Coronation Stakes (1970–2), Drive On equalling the fastest time yet achieved for the event (29.17 secs). He trained Kilbelin Style for Mr Cyril Young when the dog ran up for the 1969 Derby, won by Sand Star. The dog was an outstanding tracker but, as Tommy said, the most difficult of dogs to train. Tommy Johnston was trainer of the legendary Skyhawk in the early 1970s, and the bitch Westpark Mustard when in 1974 she beat Mick the Miller's long-standing record of nineteen consecutive wins.

Jack Kinsley was Bob Burl's head kennelman for more than twenty years before taking over as a trainer in the 1960s when Jim Syder Jnr left. Another of the Wembley trainers was Jimmy Rimmer who was a 'slipper' at the Waterloo Cup for many years, but his first job was to assist his elder brother Jack at the White City, Manchester, during the 1930s, when he had charge of the fabulous Wild Woolley who won the Derby and followed in Mick the Miller's footsteps for popularity.

Today the legendary Wembley trainers are there no longer, nor are greyhounds kennelled there. In 1973 the kennels, which were situated left of the famous twin towers, were demolished and the 250 greyhounds were put with contract trainers, one of them being Adam Jackson, previously at Clapton and who in 1982 trained three classic winners in Duchess of Avon and Hubert's Shade (2).

Although the St Leger, run in September, is Wembley's most important race (for further information *see* Classic events), other events staged there have long been considered among the premier events of the racing calendar. The Coronation Stakes confined to bitches, starts the year and is run in February over 490 m. It is followed by the Inaugural Sweepstakes. Many fine greyhounds have won the Coronation Stakes but none more popular than those wonderful bitches Bradshaw Fold, who won the event in 1931, followed by Queen of the Suir in 1932 and 1933, and Disputed Rattler in 1943. In April the famous Spring Cup is run, won in 1930 and 1931 by Mick the Miller and in 1944 by Ballyhennessy Seal. In May the Marathon Stakes, now run over 850 m, takes place. A recent winner of this event was Westpark Kale, trained by John

Coleman, a Wembley contract trainer originally at Romford. John Coleman trained Meadlands to win the Gold Cup in 1978; this race is run over 655 m in June. In July is run the Summer Cup, won in 1946 by the great Bah's Choice who only a few days earlier had become the first dog ever to break the 29 secs barrier for 525 yds, which he did at the White City. In 1947 the Summer Cup was won by the St Leger winner of that year, Dante II. In recent years John Coleman has turned out many greyhounds in peak condition for the race, and has followed in the footsteps of the great Wembley trainers of the past.

In October is run the important Trafalgar Cup, inaugurated in 1929. Made of solid silver, the Cup is one of the sport's finest trophies. The first winner was So Green, winner of the first Wimbledon Puppy Derby. He was trained at Wembley by Jim Syder Snr and was a son of the Waterloo Cup finalist Running Rein. So Green also reached the final of the 1930 Derby, won by Mick the Miller. Then came Seldom Led's victory in the Second Trafalgar Cup; he was later to beat Mick the Miller in the sensational re-run of the 1931 Derby. Seldom Led ran sixty-two races and won exactly half of them; he was one of the three or four best greyhounds of his day. Wild Woolley won the Trafalgar Cup in 1931 and was to win the premier classic later. Then came George Flintham's Grosvenor Bob, the 1937 St Leger winner, and his great bitch Quarter Day who won the Oaks in 1938. Until recent years the Trafalgar Cup was an event for greyhounds of not more than twenty months, but in 1973 it was opened to greyhounds of not more than two years old. It has always been a pointer for those dogs who were later to stamp their names on classic events – Gay Hunter and Magourna Reject both took the Cup and returned to Wembley to win the St Leger; Ballinasloe Blondie was twice winner of the Oaks and one of the best bitches of all time; and Paul's Fun and Duleek Dandy both won the Derby. Now run over 490 metres, the event was won in 1978 by an outstanding puppy called Off Shore Diver, trained by Charlie Coyle and owned by Mrs G. Costello. A son of Bright Lad whelped in October 1976, the dog defeated one of Sally's Cobbler's first sons to race, The Corsair, by three lengths in 29.32 secs. Another outstanding winner in recent years was the bitch Hunsdon Pride, carrying the famous Hunsdon prefix of George and Michelle Findlay.

Ron Fraser is racing manager, assisted by Chris Palmer, who has been at Wembley for many years.

Main Events Run at Wembley

Super Stork Stakes	January	850 m
Coronation Stakes	February	490 m
Spring Cup	April	490 m
Marathon Stakes	May	850 m
Gold Trophy	June	655 m
Double Diamond Select Stakes	July	655 m
Summer Cup	July	490 m
* Ladbroke's St Leger	September	655 m
Trafalgar Challenge Cup	September	490 m
Empire Stadium Stakes	October	490 m H
Greyhound Breeders' Forum Stakes	October	490 m
John Manley Stakes	October	490 m H
Victoria Sporting and Racing Stakes	October	490 m

* Classic event

Track Records (1950)

Bah's Choice	525 yds	29.04 secs
Dark General	525 yds H	30.09 secs
Dante II	700 yds	39.70 secs
Gananocque Ranger	990 yds	58.32 secs

Track Records (1960)

Pigalle Wonder	1958	525 yds	28.78 secs
Dark General	1946	525 yds H	30.09 secs
Dante II	1947	700 yds	39.70 secs
Saucy Lad	1960	700 yds H	40.85 secs
The Popular Streak	1959	990 yds	57.87 secs
Chantilly Lace	1960	990 yds	57.87 secs

Track Records (1970)

Pigalle Wonder	1958	525 yds	28.78 secs
Sherry's Prince	1969	525 yds H	29.81 secs
Lucky Hi There	1964	700 yds	39.28 secs
Saucy Lad	1960	700 yds H	40.85 secs
Miss Taft	1967	880 yds	50.78 secs
Poor Mick	1968	900 yds	51.84 secs
The Popular Streak	1959	990 yds	57.87 secs
Chantilly Lace	1960	990 yds	57.87 secs

Track Records (1980)

Bray Vale	8.6.79	275 m	16.22 secs
Myroyal	3.9.79	490 m	29.01 secs
Westlands Steve	9.1.81	490 m H	29.83 secs
Black Earl	19.5.80	655 m	39.73 secs
Roystons Supreme	3.9.79	710 m	43.40 secs
Jolly United	1.1.80	850 m	53.13 secs

Winners of the Coronation Stakes

1928	Bearded Biddy	30.23 secs
1929	Silent Lassie	30.91 secs
1930	Toftwood Misery	30.45 secs
1931	Bradshaw Fold	30.50 secs
1932	Roving Joan	30.65 secs
1933	Queen of the Suir	30.06 secs
1934	Queen of the Suir	30.03 secs
1935	Gillyflower	30.33 secs
1936	Ripe Cherry	30.33 secs
1937	Beckbury Moth	30.31 secs
1938	Quarter Day	30.03 secs
1939	Quarter Day	29.34 secs
1940	not run	

Winners of the Coronation Stakes

1941	Duna Taxilas	29.57 secs
1942	Satin Beauty	29.46 secs
1943	Disputed Rattler	29.80 secs
1944	Erin's Fury	29.63 secs
1945	Prancing Kitty	29.36 secs
1946	Trev's Castle	29.65 secs
1947	Crissie Tanist	29.39 secs
1948	Major Movement	29.48 secs
1949	Baytown Stream	29.45 secs
	...	
1959	Princess Jester	29.51 secs
1960	Mink Muff	29.65 secs
1961	Just Sherry	29.37 secs
1962	Dainty Spark	29.38 secs
1963	Lucky Joan II	29.57 secs
1964	Precious Pam	29.71 secs
1965	Drumsough Princess	29.59 secs
1966	Roman Vale	29.86 secs
1967	Trudy's Bird	29.49 secs
1968	Breda's Feathers	29.17 secs
1969	Cal's Pick	29.57 secs
1970	Mannon Ranger	30.16 secs
1971	Drive On	29.17 secs
1972	Tarralina	29.88 secs
1973	Flonic Amy Jo	29.55 secs
1974	Shara Flash	29.69 secs
* 1975	Irish Lawn	30.08 secs
1976	Paradise Peg	29.44 secs
1977	Elteen Queen	29.92 secs
1978	Westmead Trophy	30.16 secs
1979	Gay Flash	29.82 secs
1980	Kildangan Wind	29.96 secs
1981	Balaclava Charge	29.69 secs
1983	Lannon Lass	29.65 secs
1984	Sandy Sally	30.08 secs

*Pre-1975 run over 500 yds; since run over 490 m

Winners of the Gold Cup 1929–49

1929	Chain Mail	41.52 secs
1930	War Cloud	41.45 secs
1931	Maiden's Boy	41.42 secs
1932	Maiden's Boy	41.46 secs
1933	Jubilee Jim	41.15 secs
1934	Scallywag II	41.11 secs
1935	Mick the Moocher	41.12 secs
1936	Satan's Baby	41.30 secs
1937	Grosvenor Edwin	41.07 secs
1938	Grosvenor Edwin	40.96 secs
1939	Catherine of Waterhall	40.17 secs
1940	Muskerry Cream	39.90 secs
1941-3	not run	
1944	Model Dasher	40.01 secs
1945	Kampion Sailor	40.19 secs
1946	Lilac's Luck	40.06 secs
1947	Mad Midnight	40.03 secs
1948	Northam Star	40.65 secs
1949	Rising Tide II	40.60 secs

Winners of the Gold Cup 1968–84
Re-named Gold Trophy 1981

1968	Forward King	39.81 secs
1969	Special Cognac	40.19 secs
1970	Monalee Peter	39.92 secs
1971	Pallas Melody	39.58 secs
1972	Pepper Joe	39.93 secs
1973	Scintilla Champ	40.26 secs
1974	Streaky Sheila	40.28 secs
* 1975	Glin Bridge	40.09 secs
1976	Paradise Peg	40.07 secs
1977	Westpark Kale	40.14 secs
1978	Meadlands	40.28 secs
1979	Royston's Supreme	40.37 secs
1980	Black Earl	39.97 secs
1981	Linkside Liquor	43.53 secs
1982	Big Dom	43.76 secs
1983	Minnie's Matador	43.50 secs
1984	Blue Shirt	43.76 secs

* Pre-1975 run over 700 yds; since run over 655 m; since 1981 run over 710 m

Winners of the Spring Cup 1930–50

1930	Mick the Miller	30.56 secs
1931	Mick the Miller	30.04 secs
1932	Future Cutlet	29.81 secs
1933	Goofy Gear	30.46 secs
1934	Black Warrior	30.75 secs
1935	Suil King	30.47 secs
1936	Suil King	30.31 secs
1937	Shandy Gaff	30.15 secs
1938	Sheehan	30.18 secs
1939	Greta's Rosary	30.39 secs
1940	Junior Classic	29.60 secs
1941	Rochester Clipper	29.92 secs
1942	Dearlaw	30.48 secs
1943	Flying Dart II	29.59 secs
1944	Disputed Rattler	29.58 secs
1945	Ballyhennessy Seal	29.45 secs
1946	MacRamble	29.72 secs
1947	not run	
1948	Whiterock Abbey) Don Gypsy)	29.68 secs
1949	West End Dasher	29.62 secs

Winners of the Spring Cup 1968–80

1968	Butcher's Tec	29.27 secs
1969	Ballyseedy Star	29.61 secs
1970	Hymus Silver	29.87 secs
1971	Dolores Rocket	29.30 secs
1972	Proud Gomble	29.56 secs
1973	Shara Dee	29.25 secs
1974	Mountleader Gold	29.31 secs
* 1975	Pineapple Grand	29.78 secs
1976	Knockrour Bank	29.01 secs
1977	Linacre	29.20 secs
1978	Head Prefect	29.82 secs
1979	Law Lad	30.02 secs
1980	Linkside Champ	29.62 secs

* Pre-1975 run over 500 yds; since 1975 run over 490 m

Winners of the Summer Cup 1968–80

1968	Yellow Printer	29.20 secs
1969	Northern Glow	29.02 secs
1970	Valiant Boy	29.04 secs
1971	Cobbler	29.15 secs
1972	Westmead County	29.56 secs
1973	Butcher's Flash	29.39 secs
1974	Mores Hero	29.50 secs
* 1975	Tory Mor	29.25 secs
1976	Doon Fantasy	29.56 secs
1977	Hubert's Consort	29.17 secs
1978	Pat Seamur	29.02 secs
1979	Desert Pilot	29.33 secs
1980	Super Glow	29.54 secs

* Pre-1975 run over 500 yds; since 1975 run over 490 m

Winners of the Trafalgar Challenge Cup 1929–49

1929	So Green	30.48 secs
1930	Seldom Led	30.76 secs
1931	Wild Woolley	30.84 secs
1932	Mikado Beauty	31.02 secs
1933	Grey Raca	30.86 secs
1934	Black Lion Favourite	30.93 secs
1935	Esksell	30.55 secs
1936	Grosvenor Bob	30.22 secs
1937	Quarter Day	30.62 secs
1938	Gayhunter	30.44 secs
1939–40	not run	
1941	Laughing Lieutenant	30.12 secs
1942	Jubilee Time	30.97 secs
1943	Dark Tiger	30.18 secs
1944	Wandering Lad	30. 12 secs
1945	Ballymactanist	29.68 secs
1946	Shadowlands Delight	30.20 secs
1947	Mad Birthday	29.73 secs
1948	Baytown Colonel	29.73 secs
1949	Ballycurreen Garrett	30.39 secs

Winner of the 1972 Summer Cup at Wembley, Westmead County.

Winners of the Trafalgar Challenge Cup 1968–81

1968	Active Host	29.73 secs
1969	Sherwood Glen	29.47 secs
1970	Toda's Kingpin	29.67 secs
1971	Todos Imp	29.56 secs
1972	Stow Welcome	29.44 secs
1973	Coin Case	29.55 secs
1974	Pineapple Grand	29.08 secs
* 1975	The Snow Queen	29.34 secs
1976	Hunsdon Pride	29.33 secs
1977	Homely Girl	29.30 secs
1978	Off Shore Diver	29.32 secs
1979	Trinas Girl	29.53 secs
1980	Sailor May	29.45 secs
1981	Careless Dragon	29.24 secs

*Pre-1975 run over 500 yds; since run over 490 m

Winners of the Empire Stadium Stakes 1930–47

1930	Smart Fashion
1931	Rule the Roost
1932	Long Hop
1933	Scallywag II
1934	Long-fellow
1935	Era Jem
1936	Red Car
1937	Border Mutton
1938	Lenin's Ring
1939	Printer
1940	Juvenile Classic
1941	Tact
1942	Still Moving
1943	Frating Dan
1944	Derryboy Jubilee
1945	Nilo
1946	not run
1947	Obstinate Invader

Winners of the Empire Stadium Stakes 1970–81

1970	Petronius	41.56 secs
1971	not run	
1972	Clinker Pat	41.61 secs
1973	Mad Cavalier	41.56 secs
* 1974	Secret Armour	30.49 secs
† 1975	Try It Blackie	30.22 secs
1976	Black Pengola	31.05 secs
1977	Meanus Dandy	30.16 secs
1978	Meanus Dandy	30.46 secs
1979	Bowery Music	30.67 secs
1980	Lourdelle Wizard	30.49 secs
1981	Westlands Steve	29.98 secs

*Pre-1974 run over 700 yds; run over 525 yds in 1974 † Since 1975 run over 490 m

WEST HAM

It was a sad day when the West Ham track closed in May 1972, for it was one of the first London tracks to open, and with Stamford Bridge (closed July 1968) was the fastest track in Britain, at one time holding eight world records. It was the longest track in Britain with a circumference of 562 yds, with long straights and wide, well-banked bends so that bumping and fighting were virtually unknown. For that reason alone, followers of the sport always enjoyed their racing at West Ham. It had the unique distinction of its entire running track being of turf laid on wood raised 12 ins above ground level, so that even on the wettest winter days racing always took place and fast times were run. 'Time' variations were also very small, which made for easier forecasting. It had more accommodation than any other British track, and could hold 100,000 spectators, all able to enjoy a clear view of the dogs right the way round the track.

A number of the finest greyhound trainers were connected with the track in its early years. Perhaps the most famous of them was Stanley Biss, later to transfer to Clapton (also now closed). Stanley Biss was one of the greatest handlers of bitches. No one understood their moods and peak periods of racing better, and when on the last day of 1933 he needed that excellent bitch Queen of the Suir to win £100 or more for him to become the first trainer to win £10,000 for his owners in one year, there were few who doubted that the 'Queen' would not win her race. She did, winning a first prize of £125, which enabled Stanley Biss to achieve his ambition.

When at Clapton in 1947, and trainer of the great Local Interprize, Stanley Biss became the first trainer ever to win £20,000 for the owners of his greyhounds. In that year he had under his care another great bitch, Rio Cepretta, but none could rival the great Queen of the Suir who won the English and Irish Oaks – the only bitch ever to do the double.

Stanley Biss began racing by entering a greyhound in co-ownership with Ken Appleton, in the first meeting at Wembley, and these two became the most successful West Ham trainers before the Second World War. In 1940 Ken Appleton won the Laurels at Wimbledon with April Burglar, who was to sire a Waterloo Cup winner when retired to stud.

In later years Tommy Johnston was an outstanding trainer at West Ham, winning the Gold Collar in 1963 with Music Guest, while in the previous year he took the Pall Mall with Hurry on King. When West Ham closed he transferred to Wembley and took the 1979 St Leger with Kilmagourna Mist.

In 1928, soon after the track opened, it was allocated the last classic event of the season, the Cesarewitch, and only the St Leger was then run over a longer distance. Until the war, apart from 1936 when it was run over 550 yds, the event was run over 600 yds, then over 500 yds during 1945–50 before reverting to 600 yds.

Mick the Miller won the event in 1930 and his winning time of 34.01 secs in his heat was a world record. The following year the great Future Cutlet achieved the first of his two Cesarewitch successes; he was the only dog ever to win twice. In 1934 Brilliant Bob made it four classics in one year when he won the event. Ataxy won in 1936; the famous bitch Hurry Kitty in 1945; Local Interprize in 1948; and Magourna Reject in 1953, with two Derby winners, Pigalle Wonder and Mile Bush Pride, winning in consecutive years, 1958 and 1959. The 1971 Cesarewitch, the last to be run at West Ham, was won by Whisper Billy at 50–1, the biggest outsider in the history of the event. Owned by Lady Houstoun-Boswall, the dog was trained by Charlie Coyle and it defeated the 33–1 Rosemount Gunner. They are believed to be the two biggest long odds for win and place in the history of track racing.

For all the stars who contested the Cesarewitch, the most popular greyhound to run at West Ham was the brilliant black bitch Bradshaw Fold, trained by Stanley Biss and owned by Mr A.R. Hughes of Manchester. Jewel, as she was affectionately called by those who handled her, was the winner of the Coronation Cup in 1931 and Mick the Miller's great rival. Wherever these two great stars raced, they drew the crowds in their thousands. At West Ham in March 1930 she covered the 700 yds course in 40.04 secs, a world record time which stood for sixteen years until Lilac's Luck clocked 39.88 secs in 1946. It was also at West Ham, in 1935, that Ataxy clocked 33.50 secs for 600 yds, a world record for that distance which stood for ten years.

At West Ham was also run the Cambridgeshire, a race which all greyhound owners love to win. It used to be run over 400 yds and the final took place on or near the last day of each year to round off the racing calendar. It was won by many good sprinters, such as Terry's Monarch and Honey Boy Finnegan – those who perhaps could not quite make the final of the Scurry Gold Cup. Since the track closed the race has been run at the White City, and continues to attract the best sprinters.

Track Records (1950)

Cook's Sandhills	1942)	400 yds	21.91 secs
Wireless Time	1943)		
Selsey Cutlet	1940	525 yds	29.26 secs
Drumgoon Boy	1949	550 yds	30.53 secs
Juvenile Classic	1940	550 yds H	31.40 secs
Ataxy	1935	600 yds	33.50 secs
Longfellow II	1933	600 yds H	34.94 secs
Lilac's Luck	1946	700 yds	39.88 secs
Loughnagare	1930	1,000 yds	61.16 secs

Track Records (1970)

Come on Wonder	500 yds	30.17 secs
Sherry's Prince	550 yds H	30.89 secs
Cal's Pick	600 yds	32.72 secs
Park Nightingale) Westmead Villa)	700 yds	38.96 secs
Spotted Nice	880 yds	49.35 secs

WHITE CITY, London (Closed September 1984)

This Stadium, at Shepherd's Bush, was built to stage the 1908 Olympic Games. Its name derives from the brilliant whiteness of the ferro-concrete buildings. In 1908 an Italian marathon runner called Dorando both won and lost a gold medal. He collapsed just before reaching the finishing line over which he was helped by sympathetic spectators. Although he was first home he was later disqualified. To commemorate the event the Dorando Marathon for greyhounds is held on Derby night each year. It is a race for six greyhounds, run over 962 m, and is the longest race in the calendar.

In 1926 the GRA took over the track, following the success of their first venture into greyhound racing at Belle Vue. New covered terracing and a restaurant were built, and on 20 June 1927 the first greyhound meeting in London took place. The dog Charlie Cranston won the first race, having covered the 525 yds course in 30.86 secs. In July that year the Prince of Wales and Prince George (later King George VI) attended a race meeting. Ten years later, the world's largest tote came into operation at the White City, and it was here in 1945 that the first photo-finish camera in Britain was used. The Stadium was and is used for various other sports, including athletics and showjumping.

Soon after the start Major Percy Brown became racing manager, and remained at White City until 1976. A dedicated man, he served the GRA for more than fifty years. Publicity manager for many years was Reg Howell, who also served the interests of other sports at other GRA stadia. E.J. Monk, formerly racing manager at Wimbledon, has now taken his place. Squadron Leader

White City Stadium, where greyhound racing first began in London.

W. 'Bill' Holmes and R.J. Rowe, both widely experienced, are respectively general manager and racing manager.

The White City track is the largest in Britain, with a 500 yds circumference, 120 yds straights, and wide, sweeping turns which enable fast times to be recorded. The Derby is run over 500 m, while the longer events are run over 680 m and 730 m, and marathons over 962 m. The Oaks was originally held here before it was moved to Harringay in 1959. The Grand National, the classic event for hurdlers, is run in April over the 500 m course. In 1972 it was won for the third consecutive year by Sherry's Prince. The Sherry's Prince Hurdles event, contested on Derby night, attracts the best jumpers in Britain. Apart from the Dorando Marathon, already mentioned, another important race run on Derby night is the BBC2 Chase.

So great had been the enthusiasm for the new sport of greyhound racing in the north that 10,000 people turned up at that first meeting at the White City, and they went away well satisfied with the entertainment. With its spacious club house providing restaurant accommodation for 1,000, and excellent terracing all round the Stadium, White City became known as the Mecca of greyhound racing. It was only right that it should stage the premier event of the racing calendar, the greyhound Derby, which first took place on July 1927 over the 500 yds course, the only time it was run over the shorter distance. The £1,000 prize was won by Mr Edwin Baxter's Entry Badge, litter brother of the famous dam Edna Best, named after a popular actress of the day. Their sire was the celebrated Jamie, also sire of Mutton Cutlet. That Entry Badge, trained by Joe Harmon, might well become the first winner of the Derby was fairly obvious when, at the first meeting at White City, in June, he had beaten the Belle Vue 'stars' very decisively over the 525 yds course. In the Derby final he was quoted 4–1 on, the shortest odds of any dog to contest the Derby. He beat Ever Bright by more than six lengths, which no Derby winner has bettered, although Monday's News and Lucky Boy Boy equalled this winning margin.

The first Derby to be run over 525 yds was that of 1928, won by a Scottish-trained dog, Boher Ash, for the first and only time. His owner, Mrs Stokes, became the first lady to win a classic event. In 1929 came Mick the Miller, who won the event again the following year; on both occasions he started

Indian Joe after winning Spillers 1980 Jubilee Derby. Trainer John Hayes of Ireland holds the dog; the owner, Alf McLean, stands in the centre.

at 2–1 on, but whereas the amount won by Boher Ash in 1928 was £1,500 (equal to ten times the amount in purchasing power today), Mick won only £700 in 1929. Even in 1946 Monday's News winning sum was only £1,000, and it was not until 1960, when the 25–1 outsider Duleek Dandy won, that the first prize went up to £2,000. In 1965 this had become £5,000, and £10,000 by 1970 when John Silver won. In 1973 Spiller's, the petfood manufacturers, took over the sponsorship of the event and by 1977 the prize money totalled £40,000, with £17,500 going to the winner, and the following year the prize money was more than £50,000. For the first time the winner received £20,000. The sum of £35,000 was awarded to the winner (Indian Joe) of the 1980 Jubilee Derby. In 1978 the event was won by Mrs Pearce's Lacca Champion, one of only three greyhounds to have won each of his heats and semi-final in addition to the final.

Twelve races make up the Derby meeting, which is now televized, and attendances are more than 30,000. The heats begin early in May on various tracks throughout Britain, and there are always a number of Irish entries. The roar of the crowd when the traps are released is unlike that at any other time and to some dogs is very disconcerting. Many greyhounds, including Shady Begonia, have failed to produce top form in a Derby final because of the terrifying noise.

One dog who was always quite untroubled by the crowd was Mick the Miller, who came over to England with his owner, Father Brophy, an Irish village priest, in the early summer of 1929. Mick arrived on the scene at exactly the right time, in the years of the Depression, when people of all walks of life were looking for a bit of glamour to distract them from day-to-day worries. He was a character, a dog possessing almost human intelligence, who could extricate himself from an almost impossible situation and win from yards behind. People loved him. When Mick retired, Wild Woolley and Brilliant Bob followed in his footsteps, but no dog had quite the same appeal as Mick and when he was nearing his nineteenth consecutive race without defeat he drew the crowds as no dog has done before or since. He was just what the sport needed to establish itself and the White City owes him a great debt. After running an impressive trial, the dog was auctioned there and then, and was bought by A.H. Williams, a London bookmaker, for 800 guineas. Within weeks he had won the Derby for his new owner.

The year's racing at White City starts with the Longcross Cup, run over 680 m, and in March come the press-sponsored events – the *Sunday Times* Marathon, run over 962 m; the *Daily Express* Trophy; and the *Daily Mirror* Trophy, won in 1978 by the previous year's Derby winner Balliniska Band. In May the important Mullard Stakes is run, worth £2,000 to the winner, as well as the *Evening Standard* and Joe Coral Cup, won in 1978 by the outstanding Glen Rock. The semi-finals and final and the consolation final of the Derby take place during June, and in October the Haig-sponsored Cambridgeshire is now run here.

In addition to Joe Harmon, who trained the first Derby winner, among the earliest White City trainers was Arthur Jonas, who in 1935 had charge of Greta Ranee, the first bitch to win the Derby. It was not until 1968, when Randolph Singleton trained Camira Flash to win the event, that it was again won by a White City trainer. During its entire history the Derby has been practically monopolized by dogs trained either privately or by trainers with kennels at Wembley and the now closed Clapton track. Also at the White City in the 1930s was Leslie Reynolds, who trained Fret Not to win the 1932 St Leger and who had charge of Bosham when he won the 1935 Gold Collar and reached that year's Derby final. The previous year this great dog had taken the St Leger, and in 1934 only Brilliant Bob was his equal – he had a trainer who understood his whims, just as Sidney Orton did with Brilliant Bob, and when Leslie Reynolds left White City for Wembley the GRA lost an outstanding trainer of greyhounds. With him at White City was Les Perry, who trained Satan's Baby to win the 1935 St Leger. The following year Reynolds was again successful, this time with the brilliant but temperamental Ataxy.

During the 1970s White City trainers have had considerable success with their dogs. In 1971 Randolph Singleton had charge of Black Andrew when he won the

Laurels, the first and only time the classic has been won by a White City dog. He also trained Killane Flash to win the Grand National. In 1974 Cute Caddie won the St Leger for Dave Kinchett, and three years later Stormy Spirit won for Joe Pickering, a highly successful White City trainer since he took over from Bert Hayes in 1957, and still there. He had charge of Our Tim when winning the Trafalgar Cup at Wembley, and We'll See when taking the Scottish Derby. Then Rostown Genius won the Cesarewitch for him and Casa Miel the Scurry Cup, among other successes, but still Joe Pickering remains one of the most modest men in the sport, unaffected by his position as one of the all-time greats.

It was at White City on 6 June 1946 that Bah's Choice, in a trial, became the first dog ever to break 29 secs for the 525 yds course anywhere when he clocked 28.99 secs. Twenty-two years later Yellow Printer set a new world record for 525 yds at the track, with a time of 28.30 secs, and in June 1971, in a heat for the Derby, Clohast Rebel reduced this to 28.28 secs, which remained unbeaten over this course.

The 1984 Derby, sponsored by the *Daily Mirror* was the last to be run at the White City. It was won by Whisper Wishes (a white and black son of Sandman) owned by Mr John Duffy of Co. Donegal and trained by Charlie Coyle to give the Maidstone track its first classic winner. The dog was a worthy winner for he had come through each round undefeated, a tribute to his breeder and rearer, Mr Martin Conroy of Mullawn, Co. Wexford. Whisper Wishes was in trap 4 and 7/4 favourite.

The last race run at White City took place at 10.15 pm on September 22nd, 1984 and was won from trap 3 by a blue brindle bitch, Hastings Girl owned by Messrs. Roberts & Gruszka and trained by Tommy Foster. A few days later, the demolition contractors moved in and soon the once proud stadium was a heap of rubble.

Track Records (1950)

Priceless Border	525 yds	28.64 secs
Quare Times	550 yds	30.38 secs
Shaggy Lass	725 yds	41.43 secs
Ryan's Rose	800 yds	45.69 secs

Track Records (1960)

Outside Left	500 yds	27.55 secs
Priceless Border	525 yds	28.64 secs
Shaggy Lass	725 yds	41.43 secs
Gypsy Boy	725 yds H	41.84 secs

Track Records (1970)

Outside Left	1958	500 yds	27.55 secs
Yellow Printer	1968	525 yds	28.30 secs
Sherry's Prince	1971	525 yds H	29.10 secs
Monalee Champion	1967	550 yds	29.82 secs
Sherry's Prince	1969	550 yds H	30.62 secs
Cash for Dan	1969	725 yds	40.16 secs
Gypsy Boy	1959	725 yds H	41.84 secs
Lively Mandy	1970	800 yds	44.89 secs
Cash for Dan	1969	880 yds	49.44 secs
Greenville Fauna	1968	1,025 yds	58.60 secs

Track Records (1980)

Mutt's Silver	268 m	15.70 secs
Balliniska Band	500 m	29.16 secs
Glen Rock	500 m	29.16 secs
Moon View	500 m H	30.09 secs
Sally's Cobbler	680 m	40.85 secs
Topothetide	680 m H	42.56 secs
Glin Bridge	730 m	44.03 secs
Westown Adam	962 m	59.81 secs
Portland Dusty	962 m	59.81 secs

Winners of the Cambridgeshire 1968–83*

1968	Joan's Boy	34.48 secs
1969	Ballyseedy Star	33.88 secs
1970	Sir Ginger	33.49 secs
1971	Bob's Return	33.54 secs
† 1972	First Case	30.38 secs
1973	Coin Case	30.42 secs
1974	Myrtown	30.17 secs
** 1975	Adioss	29.64 secs
1976	Mutt's Silver	30.38 secs
1977	Boherglass Swell	29.30 secs
1978	Pat Seamur	29.41 secs
1979	Tic'n Tot	29.45 secs
1980	Under Par	29.41 secs
1981	Thanks Kev	29.67 secs
1982	Astrosyn Doll	29.83 secs

*1968–71 run at West Ham †Pre-1972 run over 600 yds; 1972–4 over 550 yds; ** Since 1975 over 500 m

Winners of the Longcross Cup 1970–82

1970	Tullyallen	30.42 secs
1971	Mona's Flash	41.42 secs
1972	Brookside Prince	41.37 secs
1973	Commutering	40.87 secs
1974	Westpark Mustard	41.03 secs
* 1975	Westmead Bounty	42.23 secs
1976	Sally's Cobbler	40.85 secs
1977	Fly by Night	42.99 secs
1978	Black Legend	41.81 secs
1979	Beaverwood Tony	42.53 secs
1980	Musical Lady	41.18 secs
1981	Decoy Boom	42.20 secs
1984	Game Ball	39.78 secs

*Pre-1975 run over 725 yds; since run over 680 m

Winners of the Wood Lane Stakes 1968–81

1968	Yellow Printer	28.91 secs
1969	Avondhu Iron	29.16 secs
1970	Tullyallen	29.44 secs
1971	Linmaree	28.85 secs
1972	After the Show	29.24 secs
1973	Skyhawk	29.05 secs
1974	Myrtown	28.68 secs
* 1975	Sampson's Flash	29.98 secs
1976	Princeley Moment	29.41 secs
1977	Sivibo	30.17 secs
1978	Instant Gambler	30.42 secs
1979	Our Rufus	30.02 secs
1980	Jon Barrie	29.99 secs
1981	Corrakelly Air	30.58 secs

*Pre-1975 run over 525 yds; since run over 500 m

WHITE CITY, Manchester (Closed 1982)

Owned by the GRA since it opened in 1930,

this track is the junior to Belle Vue and has usually taken second place in the amount of publicity it has received through the years. The track is a circuit of 450 yds with wide, well banked turns and an inside Sumner hare. Excellent restaurant facilities are available from which the racing may be viewed in comfort. Racing takes place on Monday, Wednesday and Friday afternoons. The racing manager for a decade was Charles Birch, who then moved to Harringay and the White City, London, before becoming general manager of the Northaw Kennels, completing fifty years' service with the GRA in 1979. The present racing manager is E. Thomas with Ian Travis as his assistant. One of the contract trainers is Rita Issacs, who was at Salford until that track closed. She was the first woman trainer to be engaged at the White City.

The most important event held here is the Manchester Cup, run in March over 485 m, which was won in 1979 by Kilbelin Ruler, owned by Mrs Ramage and Mrs Robb and trained at White City by George Barnett. The event is worth £500 to the winner. The previous year the Cup was won by Clashing Breeze, owned by Mr R. Bacci and trained by Eddie Moore. In 1977 they had won the Derby with Balliniska Band for the Belle Vue track, where Eddie Moore had moved. At White City Eddie had trained the great Myrtown, owned by Mrs Helen Kirwan. The dark brindle ran up to Jimsun in the final of the 1974 Derby and won the Manchester Cup the following year when he again reached the final of the Derby, won by Tartan Khan.

Eddie Moore also trained at White City Always a Monarch, another dog owned by Helen Kirwan, who must be considered one of the unluckiest owners of all time. In the 1970 Laurels, Always a Monarch won his first and second round heats and his semi-final, as did Sole Aim who beat him by a short head in the final, though only after a photo decision. If ever a classic should have resulted in a dead heat it was this one.

The Mancunian Cup is run over the 670 m course in September. The 1979 event was won by Eddie Moore with the 14–1 outsider More Smut. Over the same course in October is contested the Cock o' the North, worth £600 and won in 1979 by Remarkable Lad, trained by Harry Bamford at Belle Vue. Winner of the event in 1970 was Forward King, from one of the greatest litters of all time that also included Tric Trac and Spectre II. For nearly two years he roamed the Yorkshire moors living on whatever he could find, yet he went on to win the English and Scottish St Legers, the only dog ever to do so, and also won the Wembley Gold Cup and Cock o' the North from a top-class field. In all he won more than £5,000 in prize money. The Northern Oaks is run in August, and over the 810 m course in December the Mecca Bookmakers' Christmas Marathon is contested.

Perhaps the greatest greyhound to be kennelled at White City was Mr Sam Johnson's Wild Woolley, trained by Jack Rimmer, eldest of the Rimmer brothers who were in at the beginning of the sport and have continued almost until the present when Jimmy, the youngest brother and for many years a Wembley trainer, retired after the old kennels were pulled down and Wembley changed to contract trainers. Wild Woolley won the 1932 Derby when he defeated Future Cutlet by a neck, and so outstanding were these two that they were ten lengths in front of the other runners. Wild Woolley was also to contest the next two events, on both occasions finishing in third place, and was the first winner of the Gold Collar at Catford.

At the White City during the early days, until he moved to Belle Vue in 1960, was Len Stagg, who in 1964 handled Hack Up Chieftain when as a 20–1 outsider he won the Derby for Mr S. Donohue. At White City Len Stagg had trained the fine bitch Jersey Creamery, who set a new track record in September 1948. She won her heat and semi-final of the 1948 Oaks, but was beaten in the final by Night Breeze who also went on to win the Pall Mall and ran up for the Wembley Spring Cup the following year. Another outstanding bitch trained by Len Stagg was Kilbelin Dancer, a daughter of Bella's Prince, and who won the Winter Stayers' Trophy at Stamford Bridge in January 1949.

Main Events Run at White City, Manchester

Manchester Cup	March	485 m
Northern Oaks	August	485 m
Mancunian Cup	September	670 m
Cock o' the North	October	670 m
William Hill Trapper	November	485 m

Track Records (1950)

Coynes Castle	1946	500 yds	28.55 secs

Jersey Creamery	1948	525 yds	29.65 secs
Dark Hissop	1946	700 yds	41.07 secs
Clady Border	1946	725 yds	42.26 secs

Track Records (1980)

Bunker Prince	15. 8.80	255 m	15.15 secs
Myrtown	5. 5.76	485 m	28.76 secs
Beamons Feat	30.10.69	485 m H	30.00 secs
Strebor Gem	10. 6.73	485 m H	30.00 secs
Croghan Hostess	13.10.69	670 m	41.12 secs
Rozels Blue Girl	15. 6.64	810 m	50.63 secs

Winners of the Manchester Cup 1968–81

1968	Special Mortell	29.92 secs
1969	Desert Kuda	29.86 secs
1970	Always a Monarch	29.49 secs
1971	John Silver	29.50 secs
1972	Allowdale Era	30.24 secs
1973	Fly Dazzler	29.08 secs
1974	Deise Valiant	29.12 secs
• 1975	Myrtown	29.00 secs
1976	El Teide	29.99 secs
1977	Chensu Mula	29.56 secs
1978	Clashing Breeze	29.85 secs
1979	Kilbelin Ruler	30.03 secs
1980	Cushie Snowball	30.09 secs
1981	Oakdene Sonny	29.75 secs

•Pre-1975 run over 500 yds; since run over 485 m

Winners of the Cock o' the North 1969–81

1969	Shady Begonia	41.58 secs
1970	Seafield Flash	41.74 secs
1971	Brookside Prince	41.42 secs
1972	Waggy Champion	42.03 secs
1973	Thomond Girl	41.89 secs
1974	Chickery Tip	42.33 secs
• 1975	Wow	41.91 secs
1976	Dear Charmer	42.50 secs
1977	Ballybeg Grand	41.27 secs
1978	Sheskburn Mint	41.55 secs
1979	Remarkable Lad	41.99 secs
1980	Honeygar Kid	41.36 secs
1981	Honeygar Kid	41.70 secs

•Pre-1975 run over 725 yds; since run over 670 m

WIMBLEDON

This course is one of the important Ws – *White City, Wembley, Walthamstow and Wimbledon – which have provided London-based enthusiasts with the best greyhounds and the finest amenities since the sport began. Racing was first held at this track on 19 May 1928. The site was a difficult, marshy one, and by the time the Stadium was ready to open South London Greyhound Racecourses Ltd, the consortium which had purchased the site, were in financial difficulties. W.J. Cearns, whose firm had done the building, put in a large sum, took a place on the board, and saved the venture. His son John is now managing director.

The first race was won by Mr J.H. Baker's World of Roses, trained by Harry Leader, while in the same race were two dogs jointly trained – an unusual procedure – by Biss and Appleton. Stanley Biss was the first trainer of greyhounds to earn an international reputation, but soon left Wimbledon for Clapton. Ken Appleton went to West Ham where he, too, quickly made a name as a trainer of champions. Another name on that first seven-race programme, as timekeeper, was Con Stevens, who was to remain at Wimbledon as first racing manager, then director of racing, for almost fifty years. W.J. Cearns and Con Stevens, with the assistance of several outstanding trainers, were to bring Wimbledon world-wide acclaim for the quality of its dogs, and the efficient manner in which racing was conducted made a big impact on patrons. In at the beginning also was the late Paddy McEllistrim, who arrived from his native Ireland with some greyhounds for Harry Leader and applied for a trainer's job at the track without any recommendation other than his love of dogs. He was to remain there for more than forty years and his name will be remembered as long as the sport lasts.

Con Stevens not only suggested the name for Wimbledon's classic event, the Laurels, inaugurated in 1930, but introduced in his first year as racing manager the three important hurdles events – the Gold Cup, the Perpetual Challenge Trophy and the Christmas Vase. It was Con Stevens' opinion that hurdles racing made a greater contribution to the sport than anything else, providing variety and excitement, and after the introduction of the Conal-type hurdle any danger in jumping was eliminated.

Wimbledon's trainers were famous throughout the greyhound world. Paddy McEllistrim won every honour except the Derby. 'Paddy Mac', as he was affectionately called, was in charge of Cruiseline Boy when he won the first Scurry Gold Cup in 1928, and he was over eighty when Spotted Rory won the 1971 St Leger. Among his greatest successes were hurdles events, his first love, and he had charge of the outstanding hurdler Printer, subsequently amazingly successful as a sire, and also of the flying Tanist, another of the great track sires.

Paddy Fortune was a famous and much loved Wimbledon trainer. He trained Highland Rum to win the 1939 Derby and his death in 1958 at a relatively early age robbed the sport of a delightful character. His place was taken by Nora Gleeson, who won the 1966 Laurels with Super Fame to become the first woman trainer of a Laurels

*With the closure of White City, the Greyhound Derby was held at Wimbledon in 1985.

winner. Paddy McEllistrim's place was taken by his daughter, another Nora.

In 1928 Sidney Orton arrived at Wimbledon and so successful did he become that he was soon known to the sporting world as the 'Wizard of Burhill' (where the track has its kennels). He started his long career as paddock steward and became a trainer in 1929. He was a trainer for thirty years and in 1930 had Mick the Miller when the great dog won his second Derby. Orton was also in charge of him during the dog's great run of nineteen consecutive wins. In 1934 he had another champion in Brilliant Bob, whom Orton considered the most difficult dog he ever handled but, after Mick, the best. Orton's first full year as a trainer was quite remarkable, for he achieved what most trainers attempt but rarely achieve in a lifetime. Not only did he train the Derby winner, but also Kilbrean Boy to win the first Laurels. Then, beginning with Brilliant Bob's win in 1934, he trained four Laurels winners in five years. Top of Carlow Road, the 1936 winner, was the first dog he trained for Mrs W.J. Cearns, wife of Wimbledon's chairman, and who during the next two decades was to own many outstanding dogs, including Ballyhennessy Sandhills who set up more 500 yds records than any other dog until Pigalle Wonder some twenty years later. Another favourite trained by Orton and owned by Mrs Cearns was Ballynennan Moon, while Burhill Moon won the 1946 Laurels. On Orton's retirement in 1959 his son Clare took over his father's kennels and in 1967 trained Carry on Oregon, the fastest dog to be kennelled at Wimbledon since Ballyhennessy Sandhills and Ballymac Ball, to win the Laurels and Scurry Gold Cup.

Joe Harmon came to Wimbledon in 1936 from White City where he had been a trainer for ten years. While at Wimbledon he looked after the great Junior Classic, taking him to the 1939 Derby final won by another Wimbledon dog, Highland Rum, and to the final of the 1938 Gold Collar, which he won.

Joe Harmon died just after the outbreak of the Second World War, and Stan Martin took over his kennels. He had charge of the great Ballymac Ball, one of the fastest dogs in the sport's history, Laurels winner in 1949 and 1950 and of the Derby also in the latter year. Stan Martin had already trained Ballyhennessy Seal when the dog won the 1945 Derby, and he too was one of the fastest ever to race. During the first six years after the war Stan Martin was England's most successful trainer.

The Hannafin brothers were also among the successful Wimbledon trainers. Jerry had charge of the great Ford Spartan when the dog won the Derby and the Laurels in 1957. He also trained Conna Count when the dog won in 1964. The following year the dog won again but this time Paddy McEvoy was the dog's trainer; he retired in May 1983. Paddy was at Clapton from 1953 until 1964, during which time he trained three Derby winners – Daw's Dancer in 1953, Dunmore King in 1956 and Palm's Printer in 1961. At Wimbledon he trained Ambiguous to win the Laurels, and for a long time has been one of the most successful and respected of trainers. Another Wimbledon trainer was George Waterman, who trained Mighty Wind to win the 1964 Gold Collar at 33–1, the all-time outsider for the event.

In more recent years Phil Rees came to Wimbledon after being a private trainer and in 1968 had charge of Shady Parachute when she won the Oaks and was chosen bitch of the year. In the Oaks she clocked 28.89 secs, beating Pigalle Wonder's 29.03 secs, and was the first to break 29.00 secs at Harringay. Phil Rees has often talked of her nervous temperament compared with that of Cranog Bet, whom he also trained. That bitch had a wonderful temperament, was lovable and easy to train, cost only 300 gns and earned more than £8,500 in prize money. In 1968 and 1969 Mr Phil Rees was elected Trainer of the Year. Previously he had trained Oregon Prince, who in 1960 set a new world record at Stamford Bridge with a time of 27.16 secs for 500 yds, and the following year won the Chelsea Cup and Welsh Derby after finishing second in the English event. Mr Rees always considered this flying machine to be the finest dog he ever trained or saw racing. But another animal of whom he thought most highly was Mr F. Wood's Always Present, who broke Yellow Printer's 525 yds record at Harringay in 1969.

Racing nowadays takes place at Wimbledon on Monday and Friday each week, and a special bus takes patrons to Plough Lane from Wimbledon and Tooting

Broadway Underground Stations. In March 1972 the GRA bought the track.

The Laurels (*see* Classic events) has been run here since 1930 and been won by most of the finest track greyhounds, including Brilliant Bob, Future Cutlet, Beef Cutlet, Wild Woolley, Ballyhennessy Sandhills, Burhill Moon and Shannon Shore. Four times the Laurels has been won twice consecutively by the same dog: Ballyhennessy Sandhills in 1937 and 1938; Ballymac Ball in 1949 and 1950; Duet Leader in 1955 and 1956; and Conna Count in 1964 and 1965.

One of the most popular events to be staged here was the Wimbledon Produce Stakes, run over 500 yds, which always attracted the best British-bred greyhounds under twenty months. However, the event ceased in 1973, when Daemonic Gambol was successful. In 1972 Deneholme Chief won after beating Forest Noble in his semi-final. In the final he defeated Westmead County in 27.92 secs, the fastest time for the event, to win the £2,000 prize. The dog won ten of his first fourteen races and put up an outstanding performance wherever he ran.

The Puppy Derby is run in October for greyhounds not yet two years old. It was first contested in 1929 when it was won by So Green who started 6–4 favourite and was trained at Wembley by Jim Syder Snr. The following year Paddy McEllistrim trained his first and only Puppy Derby winner, when Mountain Loafer won for Mr J. Savage. In 1937 the great Junior Classic took the magnificent gold cup, and in 1939 Mr G.H. Flintham enjoyed the first of his four wins when Keel Border, trained by Joe Harmon, won easily. The great sire of coursing greyhounds, Laughing Lieutenant, won in 1941 and Prancing Kitty three years later. She was the first and only bitch to win the Laurels until Pineapple Grand thirty years later. Mr Flintham again won the Puppy Derby in 1949 with Ballycurreen Garrett, trained by Jack Harvey at Wembley, who had three in a row for he trained the 1950 winner Rushton Smutty and Moreton Ann to win in 1951. The biggest outsider in recent years was Mrs Wichello's Purdy's Pursuit in 1978, quoted at 20–1 before the race. He was trained by Phil Rees Jnr, who took over his father's kennels at the track on his retirement in 1975. Phil Jnr had charge of Muskerry Air when the dog won the W.J. Cearns Memorial Trophy in 1978. Run in August over 660 m, this race is worth £600 to the winner. But perhaps the greatest of all winners of this event was the flying Oregon Prince, trained by Phil Rees Snr, who won in 1960. The following year he ran up for the Derby and was to become a great track favourite and an even greater sire.

The Puppy Oaks is confined to bitches not yet two years old. The only greyhound to win both puppy events was Castledown Tiptoes, for whom £3,000 was paid shortly after her second success, the highest price ever paid for a bitch. The 1980 Puppy Oaks, sponsored by Joe and Mary Quinn, was won by Devilish Dolores who also took the senior event, thus emulating the great Cranog Bet.

Wimbledon has always encouraged hurdle racing and has had many of the sport's top hurdlers in the kennels. After the Grand National, the Christmas Vase is perhaps the most prestigious event, first being run in 1929 when Mrs Arundel Kempton's Fond Fashion was the winner. Sidney Orton and Paddy McEllistrim each had four winners, one of the best being the latter's Sprightly Peter, who won the Christmas Vase in 1949 and the Gold Cup and Perpetual Challenge Trophy that year and again in 1950, in which year he set a record of 28.88 secs for the 500 yds hurdles. Other outstanding hurdlers to win the Christmas Vase were Derryboy Jubilee in 1945, when he was the best hurdler in Britain, and Sherry's Prince, who in winning the Wimbledon Gold Cup in 1971 set a new world record for 500 yds hurdles of 27.83 secs. The great Gypsy Win took the Gold Cup two years in succession, in 1943 and 1944.

The Challenge Trophy is an event unique to Wimbledon. It is run over 460 m and the track management select their champion hurdler to race against other hurdlers chosen by a panel of pressmen from all parts of Britain. The 1969 champion was Paddock Jet, but surprisingly he was beaten by Murhur Blackie, also of the home track and trained by Clare Orton.

Among other important events staged at Wimbledon is the Winter Cup, run in

February, and won in 1978 by Balliniska Band who had won the 1977 Derby. He was quoted 2–1 on before the race, the result of which was never in doubt. The Spring Cup is run in March, and the Gold Cup over hurdles in April. In June is run Wimbledon's longest race, the Key, over 868 m. The first Key, in 1936, was over 725 yds. It was won in that year by Book Reporter, by Editor's Book out of Housekeeper. Editor's Book was the first winner of Ireland's International Cup, run at Powerstown Park, while Housekeeper was litter sister of Cook, dam of Creamery Border, so Book Reporter was 'bred in the purple'. The following year the event was won by the bitch Brave Queen, whose dam was the equally famous Burette, dam of the great Beef Cutlet who was to sire the 1942 winner, Wallace C.

It was often said that the Scurry Cup winner Creamery Border would sire only sprinters, but nothing was further from the truth for he was sire of two winners of the Key – Keel Border, who won in 1940, and Merry Two Star who came first in 1943, and both were well able to stay 725 yds and further. In 1944 the great Model Dasher won the Key, followed by two wonderful bitches, Robeen Printer in 1945 and Maggie Sallie in 1946. Both also won the Stayers' Plaque, run over the same distance, in the same years, while Unwin Beauty won the event in 1944 and Shaggy Lass in 1947; May Hasty had won in 1941. These five bitches were among the greatest ever to race on a greyhound track. One of the most powerful greyhounds to have contested the Key was Rapid Choice, St Leger runner-up of 1951. In winning his heat for the Key by twelve lengths he set a new track record, and he won the final by six lengths from Forest Town Queen. The Brighton stayer Langford Dacoit won in 1978, fresh from setting a new track record over 955 m at his home track, and he was on offer at 4–1. He was a son of the unlucky Spectre Jockey who ran up for the Gold Collar and St Leger.

The Challenge Trophy is run in August. The important *Sporting Life* Juvenile Championship is run over 460 m in December and in 1978 was won by the Leeds-trained dog Prince Hill, owned by Mrs M. Pearce and trained by Jim Kelly.

Following in the steps of the great Wimbledon trainers of the past is Eric Pateman who had charge of Hurry On Bran when the fine brindle ran up for the 1980 Derby.

Main Events Run at Wimbledon

Winter Cup	February	460 m
Spring Cup	March	490 m
Gold Cup	April	460 m H
* Laurels	May	460 m
The Key	June	868 m
W.J. Cearns Memorial Trophy	August	660 m
Perpetual Challenge Trophy	August	460 m H
Ben Truman Puppy Derby	October	460 m
Sporting Life Juvenile Trophy	December	460 m
Schweppes Christmas Vase	December	460 m

* Classic event

Track Records (1950)

Lone Keel	275 yds	15.43 secs
Wily Captain	440 yds	25.02 secs
Juvenile Classic	440 yds H	25.73 secs
Ballyhennessey Sandhills	500 yds	28.08 secs
Sprightly Peter	500 yds H	28.88 secs
Grosvenor Edwin	700 yds	40.58 secs
Markham's Brandy	700 yds H	41.84 secs
Robeen Printer	725 yds	41.51 secs

Track Records (1970)

Chi Chi's Joker	1968	440 yds	24.82 secs
Shady Parachute	1968)	500 yds	27.57 secs
Moordyke Spot	1970)		
Ballinatana Special	1961	500 yds H	28.37 secs
Dolores Rocket	1971	700 yds	39.58 secs
January Prince	1961)	700 yds H	41.36 secs
Prince Cheetah	1961)		
Following Day	1970	880 yds	50.79 secs
Meteoric	1964	940 yds	54.13 secs
Bushane Star	1969	1140 yds	66.86 secs

Track Records (1980)

Travara Rock	12.12.80	252 m	15.15 secs
Ramblers Jet	7. 5.80	460 m	27.52 secs
Dine Out	12.12.80	460 m H	28.29 secs
Jingling Star	27. 7.80	660 m	40.61 secs
Laurdella Wizard	1.9.80	660 m H	42.33 secs
Princess Glin	14.9.80	868 m	54.76 secs
Lynns Pride	28.3.80	1068 m	70.72 secs

Winners of the Key 1936–48

1936	Book Reporter	40.80 secs
1937	Brave Queen	40.70 secs
1938	Sally Maid	41.04 secs
1939	Ballydancer	41.42 secs
1940	Keel Border	41.20 secs
1941	Rahinisky Champion	40.81 secs
1942	Wallace C	41.63 secs
1943	Merry Two Star	41.03 secs
1944	Model Dasher	42.17 secs
1945	Robeen Printer	41.53 secs
1946	Maggie Sallie	42.06 secs
1947	Ben Silver	42.39 secs
1948	Baytown Finch	42.20 secs

Winners of The Key 1970–81

1970	Swift Silver	55.05 secs
1971	Swift Silver	54.88 secs
1972	Iver Flash	54.67 secs
1973	Country Maiden	55.67 secs
1974	Leading Pride	54.49 secs
* 1975	not run	
1976	Sindy's Flame	54.54 secs
1977	Moonlight Mod	54.34 secs
1978	Langford Dacoit	54.25 secs
1979	Portland Dusty	55.30 secs
1980	Salina	55.15 secs
1981	Regal Girl	55.38 secs

*Pre-1975 run over 940 yds; since run over 868 m

Winners of the Spring Cup 1929–46

1929	Elm Branch	29.08 secs
1930	Brisbane	29.48 secs
1931	Rory of the Hill	29.33 secs
1932	Altamatzin	28.99 secs
1933	Wild Woolley	29.61 secs
1934	Happy Form	29.78 secs
1935	Curly's Fancy II	28.37 secs
1936	Mitzvah	29.56 secs
1937	Shandy Gaff	29.18 secs
1938	Lone Keel	28.48 secs
1939	Ivyhouse Champion	28.97 secs
1940	Selsey Cutlet	28.57 secs
1941	Lights o' London	29.37 secs
1942	Ballynennan Moon	29.05 secs
1943	Farloe Best	28.86 secs
1944	Jazzer Smith	28.05 secs
1945	Fair Marquis	28.67 secs
1946	Fair and Handsome	28.99 secs

Winners of the Spring Cup 1970–81

1970	Shady Antionette	40.31 secs
1971	Dolores Rocket	39.66 secs
1972	Puff Pastry	40.80 secs
1973	Starline Lady	40.21 secs
1974	Cowboy Jo	41.16 secs
* 1975	Glin Bridge	42.07 secs
1976	Dyrnham Star	40.18 secs
1977	Oaken Lad	41.82 secs
1978	Sindy's Prospect	41.48 secs
1979	Owners Guide	42.59 secs
1980	Little Lamb	40.95 secs
1981	Nails Tails	41.38 secs

*Since 1975 run over 660 m

Winners of the W.J. Cearns Memorial Trophy 1969–81

1969	Always Present	28.75 secs
1970	Bell Solo	28.10 secs
1971	Sole Aim	27.96 secs
1972	Mullas Shore	28.54 secs
1973	Mel's Pupil	27.74 secs
1974	Carry on Bimbo	28.45 secs
* 1975	Sandispec	40.66 secs
1976	Monalee Customer	40.99 secs
1977	Miss Kilkenny	40.89 secs
1978	Muskerry Air	40.82 secs
1979	Clountie Comment	41.03 secs
1980	Murray's Champion	41.36 secs
1981	Flower Noel	40.92 secs

*Pre-1975 run over 500 yds; since run over 660 m

Winners of the Gold Cup 1929–49

1929	Honeyman's Last	29.76 secs
1930	Firework	29.81 secs
1931	Smart Fashion	29.75 secs
1932	Lock Audacity	31.09 secs
1933	Bronze Dragon	29.87 secs
1934	March On	29.27 secs
1935	Kilganny Bridge	29.46 secs
1936	Wild Storm	29.37 secs
1937	Terry's Hope	29.23 secs
1938	Lenin's Ring	29.18 secs
1939	Printer	29.18 secs
1940	Captain Moonlight	29.71 secs
1941	Dangerous Rally	30.03 secs
1942	Winterhead Big	30.05 secs
1943	Gypsy Win	29.58 secs
1944	Gypsy Win	29.17 secs
1945	Derryboy Jubilee	29.33 secs
1946	Red Nuxer	28.94 secs
1947	Scoff That	29.43 secs
1948	Listoke Invader	29.40 secs
1949	Sprightly Peter	29.48 secs

Winners of the Gold Cup 1970–80

1970	Peaceful Home	28.99 secs
1971	Sherry's Prince	28.83 secs
1972	Derry Palm	29.33 secs
1973	Crimson's Grove	29.13 secs
1974	Gurteen Prince	29.55 secs
* 1975	Bansha Pride	28.24 secs
1976	Try it Blackie	28.67 secs
1977	Belated Silver	28.35 secs
1978	Moreen Penguin	29.11 secs
1979	Toms Chance	29.06 secs
1980	Cladagh Colina	29.65 secs

*Pre-1975 run over 500 yds; since run over 460 m

Winners of the Puppy Derby

		Trap	*Trainer*	*Track*	
1929	So Green	2	J.P. Syder	Wembley	30.73 secs
1930	Mountain Loafer	6	P. McEllistrim	Wimbledon	30.00 secs
1931	Lavaka	2	J. Hannafin	Wimbledon	30.00 secs
1932	Mikado Beauty	5	J.P. Syder	Wembley	29.81 secs
1933	Denham Robin	1	*Mrs. Westerley	(Private)	29.31 secs
1934	(Maiden's Delight	3	*Miss Young	(Private)	28.87 secs
	(Tosto (dead heat)	6	Sidney Orton	Wimbledon	28.87 secs
1935	Flying Youle	1	*Mrs M. Yate	(Private)	29.26 secs
1936	Berwick Law	1	L. Parry	Powderhall	29.63 secs
1937	Junior Classic	2	Joe Harmon	Wimbledon	28.86 secs
1938	Grosvenor Ferdinand	2	S. Rolfe	(Private)	29.04 secs
1939	Keel Border	3	Joe Harmon	Wimbledon	29.08 secs
1940	Grosvenor Flexion	2	Joe Harmon	Wimbledon	29.45 secs
1941	Laughing Lieutenant	1	H. Hayes	White City	29.41 secs
1942	Clow's Top	5	S. Jennings	Wembley	28.99 secs
1943	Allardstown Playboy	5	J.S. Biss	(Private)	29.32 secs
1944	Prancing Kitty	4	W. Weaver	Catford	29.20 secs
1945	Lee Ripple	6	J.S. Biss	Clapton	28.81 secs
1946	Castledown Tiptoes	1	S.J. Orton	Wimbledon	29.09 secs
1947	Mad Birthday	6	J.S. Biss	Clapton	28.56 secs
1948	Saft Alex	6	F. Toseland	Perry Barr	28.72 secs
1949	Ballycurreen Garrett	5	H. Harvey	Wembley	29.21 secs
1950	Rushton Smutty	1	H. Harvey	Wembley	28.96 secs
1951	Moreton Ann	3	H. Harvey	Wembley	28.59 secs
1952	Lizette	4	P. Fortune	Wimbledon	28.75 secs
1953	Lancelot	1	P. Fortune	Wimbledon	28.96 secs
1954	Gulf of Darien	3	H. Harvey	Wembley	28.31 secs
1955	Glacier Metal	3	P. Fortune	Wimbledon	28.74 secs

1956	Ford Spartan	5	D. Hannafin	Wimbledon	28.02 secs
1957	Sean's Pal	2	T. Reilly	Walthamstow	28.21 secs
1958	Verra Black Nose	5	D. Hannafin	Wimbledon	28.08 secs
1959	Violet's Duke	3	B. O'Connor	Walthamstow	28.04 secs
1960	Oregon Prince	6	P. Rees	(Private)	28.59 secs
1961	Dancing Point	2	C. Orton	Wimbledon	28.35 secs
1962	Cloudbank	1	D. Geggus	Walthamstow	27.96 secs
1963	Pineapple Joe	1	D. Hannafin	Wimbledon	27.95 secs
1964	Bad Trick	1	F. Curtis	Portsmouth	28.46 secs
1965	Morden Mist	4	C. Orton	Wimbledon	28.27 secs
1966	Wattlehurst Rogue	1	J. Jowett	Clapton	28.58 secs
1967	Breach's Bill	3	*Mrs. Pattinson	(Private)	28.10 secs
1968	Winter Hope	4	D. Dare	(Private)	28.53 secs
1969	Sherwood Glen	2	J. Booth	(Private)	28.27 secs
1970	Crefogue Flash	5	S. Mitchell	Belle Vue	27.99 secs
1971	Tawny Satin		T. Johnston	Wembley	28.22 secs
1972	Seaman's Pride		S. Milligan	(Private)	27.78 secs
1973	Handy High		S. Milligan	(Private)	28.17 secs
1974	Tory Mor		S. Milligan	(Private)	28.40 secs
†1975	Knockrour Bank		J. Coleman	Wembley	27.72 secs
1976	Carhumore Speech		L. White	(Private)	28.17 secs
1977	Ruakura's Mutt		C. Coyle	(Private)	27.65 secs
1978	Purdy's Pursuit		P. Rees Jnr.	Wimbledon	27.83 secs
1979	Price Wise		E. Baldwin	Perry Barr	27.70 secs
1980	Desmond's Fancy		H. Coker	Oxford	28.22 secs
1981	Special Account		Mrs. N. Savva	Cambridge	27.79 secs
1982	Mountleader Mint		T. Duggan	Romford	27.82 secs
1983	Rhincrew Moth		Miss Gwynn	Ipswich	27.53 secs
1984	Ben's Champion		E. Bateman	Wimbledon	27.61 secs

*Owner-trainer; † Until 1975 run over 500 yds; since 1975 over 460 m

YARMOUTH

This track opened in 1940, at the instigation of Mr L.W. Franklin. For thirty-five years the track conducted its racing independently, but in January 1975 it joined the NGRC permit scheme. At this time Mr Franklin was joined by his sons Martin and Stephen, who have continued to run the venture with the same flair and competence as their father.
In 1970 a new raceview bar was constructed at a cost of £20,000 and the track was given a special sand surface so that racing could take place whatever the weather. Colour-corrected track lighting was also introduced. Early in 1975 the raceview bar was extended and several other bars provided around the arena, which now has under-cover accommodation for 3,000 people. The track has always provided excellent facilities for greyhound trials and dogs come from far and wide to take part. Racing takes place on Tuesday and Saturday in winter and on Monday, Wednesday and Saturday from April until the end of September.

The most important event, the East Anglian Greyhound Derby, is held in September and attracts some outstanding greyhounds. Until 1975 it was run over 500 yds, since then over 462 m and is worth £2,000 to the winner. The 1978 winner was Our Rufus, owned by Mrs N. Simmons and trained by Jim Coleman at Wembley. Over the same distance is run the Madge Lambert Memorial Trophy, won in 1978 by Mrs Simmons' dog March Supreme. The Sterling Dog Food Trophy is run over 659 m in August.

In 1980 Yarmouth won a classic event for the first time when the bitch Linkside Liquor, trained by Gordon Bailey, took the Cesarewitch in the fastest time recorded for the event. Another trainer enjoying success at Yarmouth in Ray Cross.

Main Events Run at Yarmouth

Madge Lambert Memorial Trophy	July	462 m H
Sterling Dog Food Trophy	August	659 m
East Anglian Derby	September	462 m

Winners of the East Anglian Derby 1975–83

1975	Another Gear	28.36 secs
1976	Hubert's Town	28.57 secs
1977	Westmead Dance	28.24 secs
1978	Our Rufus	28.30 secs
1979	Our Rufus	28.44 secs
1980	Kilrickle Star	28.44 secs
1981	Swift Band	28.83 secs
1982	Swift Rapier	28.24 secs
1983	Creamery Cross	28.28 secs

BRITISH GREYHOUND RACING BOARD

The Board came into being on 24 April 1979, and is intended to be a link between the NGRC and those racecourses which perform under NGRC rules. The chairman is Lord Mancroft, and the deputy chairman Prof. A. Steele-Bodger. Other members include Major-General J.H. Majury, senior steward of the NGRC; two representatives of NGRC Racecourse Promoters, Mr E.J. Aaronson and Mr Ian Stevens; a greyhound owner, Mr A. Hammond; a trainer, Mr J. Coleman; and a breeder, Mr Reg Young. The Board will take over full responsibility for making representations to the government or members of parliament on all matters affecting greyhound racing in Britain, such as totalizator rules and regulations, on-course bookmakers' rules, rules of racing, etc.

A consultative body has been set up to meet quarterly under the chairman or deputy chairman, to discuss matters concerning the sport and which need attention. This body, to be known as the Greyhound Racing Consultative Body, comprises those elected to the BGRB and in addition Major R.W. McMath; a trainer, Mr Paddy Milligan; two veterinary surgeons, Mr E. Westcott and Mr J.H. Prole; Mr Arthur Aldridge and Mr J. Carter; an on-course bookmaker, Mr D. Tyler; Mr K. Guy, a stipendiary steward of the NGRC; and the body's secretary, Mr Fred Underhill. Messrs Aaronson and Stevens were elected by the NGRC Racecourse Promoters to represent the association on the consultative body, and the secretary will also act for the BGRB and the NGRC as at present.

The NGRC will continue to be responsible for the day-to-day running of the sport, its conduct and welfare, and will implement the rules of racing whenever necessary.

BROADCASTING

Wembley Stadium was the first track from which a greyhound race was broadcast by the BBC. Surprisingly, this took place as late as Easter Monday 1940, when Raymond Glendenning broadcast the Spring Cup Final, which was won by the finest dog of the time, Junior Classic, from Majestic Sandhills.

Since that time, though greyhound racing is Britain's second most popular sport, scant attention has been given to it by the BBC. It was not until 1970 that the first regular broadcast was made from Radio London by Neil Martin, then editor of the *Greyhound Magazine*, in a special programme devoted to the sport. This was later to become a nightly 'spot', put out at 6.15 pm, which covered news items of the greyhounds and selections for the night's racing on the London tracks. In 1974, these broadcasts were taken over by Mike Palmer, for Neil Martin was finding the daily chore too time-consuming for the editor of so popular a magazine. Mike Palmer has continued ever since and he is assisted by the popular *Daily Mail* greyhound journalist Jim Bailey who sums up the week's racing on Saturday.

The popularity of Radio London's broadcasts persuaded other radio stations to follow their lead. Radio Birmingham has Norton Jones as commentator and he gives daily selections for the tracks in the Midlands. On Saturdays Radio Manchester puts out a ten-minute programme on affairs concerning the two Manchester tracks. Radio Orwell, at Ipswich, covers the East Anglian scene, with news of the tracks at Ipswich, Yarmouth and Cambridge.

BROOD BITCH

A bitch becomes a brood bitch when she is to be used for breeding and put to a sire (stud dog). After whelping a litter she becomes a dam. When a bitch has been heavily raced, she may be irregular in her periods when she comes in season, which may be two or three times a year rather than only once, though generally one of these periods will be a false one when no results would come from mating. Some bitches may not come in season until they are several years old, while others do so at an early age. Drishogue was not two years old when she first came in season and was put to Manhattan Midnight, the outcome of which was the great Rimmell's Black. An Tain, bred in Thurles by Mrs Lilly Lanigan, was only just two when she was put to Yanka Boy; her litter included Quick Thought, a bitch who was to break the track record over 525 yds and 550 yds at Enniscorthy. Also in the litter was Dark Mercury, winner of the McAlinden Gold Cup, who was to sire the 1979 Irish Derby winner Penny County. The next year An Tain was mated to Monalee Champion Crazy Parachute—Sheila at Last, one of the greatest of sires, and the result was the great Tain Mor, who was three years old when he won his first race, in the first round of the 1976 Irish Cambridgeshire, in which he remained undefeated. He then went on to take the Irish Derby in similar style. An Tain died after whelping this litter.

One of the outstanding brood bitches in track-racing history was Miss Islington, English born and bred like so many splendid bitches such as Winnie of Berrow and Narrogar Ann. When aged four years, Miss Islington whelped a litter of four from her mating to George Flintham's Grand Flight II, one of which was Ella's Jim, twice winner of the wartime St Leger. Each year, until she was more than ten years old, Miss Islington produced a litter of top-class greyhounds and her last litter, by Briar Wood – again four – resulted in the bitch Ella's Excellence who was rightly named for she excelled on the coursing field. Miss Islington lived to be fourteen and remained in perfect health throughout her life. A big upstanding blue, she was owned by Mrs Ella Lewy of Eynesford, Kent.

Having selected a bitch of suitable blood lines for brood purposes (*see* Blood lines), and having made sure she has not been over-raced, several weeks before she is due in season (if the information is available) dose her for worms with one of the oily preparations which are not too violent, giving the medicine according to the makers' instructions and preferably on an empty stomach. Do not worm her when once she has been mated.

After worming her, put her on to a special diet, for she must be in top condition when put to the stud dog (*see* Sire) and during her gestation period. Give her milk in the morning, with dried rusks or brown bread. For her second meal, which should contain meat to provide her with protein, make up some stock from bones obtained from the butcher, and feed this with a proprietary dog food containing a large proportion of meat, and biscuit or brown bread. Keep the water in which vegetables have been cooked for the household and add this to the stock. Mashed carrots and potatoes are also valuable and are better than greens which tend to cause wind. It is noticeable that when greyhounds receive a daily quantity of potatoes in their diet they rarely contract enteritis. The Irish use them and their dogs rarely suffer from stomach upsets. Add a teaspoonful of wheatgerm oil and cod liver oil on alternate days. As to amounts, give her a good bowlful morning and evening, but each bitch will have different eating habits; some can manage on quite small amounts, while others are ravenous eaters. But she must not be thin when put to the dog, nor must she be perceptibly overweight. She will, however, lose weight after whelping and weaning her pups, and so must be a little over- rather than underweight at the time she goes to the dog. Most important of all, never cut down her daily supply of fresh milk which is the most important of all foods for brood bitches and one of the chief reasons why greyhounds do so well on farms.

Give her plenty of gentle exercise at regular times and see that her kennel is draughtproof and that she always has plenty of fresh straw. Before she is put to the dog she must be well accustomed to her quarters, where she will remain until she has whelped and weaned her litter. Moving her about will be detrimental to her whelping.

Shortly before she comes in season she may grow restive and go off her food, but these conditions will quickly right themselves once the discharge begins. Watch for these signs carefully. At first the discharge will be colourless and her genitals will swell. Her exercise must now consist only of gentle walking on the lead and she must not come in contact with other dogs at the kennels or outside. She should also be put on to an invalid's diet. Beat a raw egg into her morning milk feed (greyhounds love raw eggs), and on alternate evenings substitute fish or meat. If you are not putting a bitch to a stud dog, possibly because she is considered too young, or not fit, or maybe has come in season at the wrong time of year, give her exactly the same treatment and see that she has no hard exercise until at least ten weeks after coming in season.

Within five or six days of the colourless discharge appearing it will become coloured, which will continue for about the same length of time. The bitch must then be taken to the stud dog. 'Stonehenge' said she should be mated about the tenth day, just as the discharge begins to diminish, but Mr Montagu-Harrison, an expert on breeding and showing greyhounds, says the mating should take place on the thirteenth day after the discharge is first seen. However with greyhounds the 'heat' period varies greatly; some bitches are ready to be put to the dog after nine or ten days of the first signs of discharge, while others may take up to twenty or twenty-one days before they are ready. Inspect the bitch's genitals every day, for it is important to mate her at exactly the right time.

If possible, take the bitch to the chosen sire yourself or send her with some capable person she knows well, especially if she is a bitch of nervous disposition. Take her by car or by train on a lead and wearing a warm coat. Make sure she does not come in contact with another dog, and keep in touch for several days before with the owner of the dog to which she is to be taken. Let the owner know exactly when the bitch will be arriving, preferably the day before she is due to be served, and if she can stay in the kennels overnight all the better. This will give ample time for a good service to take place and afterwards both sire and bitch can rest before you collect her. Both animals must be given time to get used to each other, and if the bitch can stay in the kennels for a day or two afterwards this is an ideal arrangement. You will pay for her keep, in addition to the stud fee which is payable at the time. A good service will be a matter of satisfaction to the owners of both the stud dog and bitch, for if she does not conceive a return mating is given free of charge, but valuable time will have been lost and a bitch gets older every day. Often when a bitch arrives at the home of a stud dog she will have nothing to do with him, and vice versa. It may take a day or two until she stands for him, and it is therefore important that the bitch has not been left too long before she is taken for a service. Bitches that come in season during August–October present problems with breeding, since they will have their pups at the most difficult time for weaning them, but if a bitch comes in season only once a year one has no option but to have her mated. It is important that the owners of stud dogs and bitches give the utmost attention to the mating procedure. Both animals must be in top condition and time must be allowed for the mating to be successful. Shyness is the cause of so many 'misses', and coursing men of old would insist that dog and bitch were closed up together, out of sight of humans, for several hours until a satisfactory service had taken place. Certainly a bitch should not be mated in front of anyone but her owner or someone who knows her well.

Once embryonic life is established (in about three weeks) the bitch can safely be given a little more exercise. Indeed Mr J.S. Nelson's bitch Costly Gift was heavy in whelp to Mad Tanist when she jumped into a drain when out exercising and came out with a dog fox in her mouth! Three weeks later she whelped a large litter including Russell Lupin, a big winner at Celtic Park, Belfast. The famous bitch Flirt ran up for the 1847 Waterloo Cup a few days before whelping a litter, one of which was War Eagle. They treated their greyhounds rough in those days but apparently without doing them any harm. To keep her stomach muscles in condition, the bitch should be exercised often, and above all see that her sleeping quarters are always kept clean and dry. Her food should be as varied and tasty as possible.

Give her a little meat every other day and add to her evening meal a teaspoonful of bonemeal, which will supply her with the extra calcium she needs to pass to her pups to make strong bones. To her morning milk feed add a teaspoonful of Parrish's Chemical Food, which supplies extra iron to prevent scouring (*see* Ailments and diseases) among her pups after birth. Give her as much concentrated food as possible without extending her stomach, and keep carbohydrates to a minimum. She should be kept adequately covered, neither too fat nor too thin. If feeding horsemeat, put it through a mincer to make it more digestible, and mix it with stock and brown bread. Add an Oxo cube to give it more flavour. Serve her food nicely moist, and during the last three weeks of pregnancy give her an extra milk feed at noon. She may whelp a litter of ten to twelve pups and will need plenty of her own milk to do them well. If not given sufficient milk during the last three weeks, she may not have enough for her own needs. Keep up the supplies of wheatgerm oil and cod liver oil, and reduce her exercise about ten days before whelping. This will be after sixty-three days, possibly a day or two longer, but if she has not begun to deliver her pups by then call in the vet.

Just before she is due to begin whelping she will become restless and go off her food, and there will be a slight discharge from her vagina. If the weather is cold, close her up in her kennel and put down fresh straw, which should be covered with sacking on that part of her kennel, raised just above floor level, where she sleeps and will have her pups. If the weather is really cold put on a coat, though it may get in the way when she whelps and should not be used unless really necessary. Keep her warm and quiet and look in every two or three hours day and night to see that she is all right. Usually a bitch will present no trouble with her whelping, which mostly takes place throughout one night.

Some bitches make excellent mothers and are never more content than when with a litter of pups, nursing them for at least eight weeks and even longer. A good brood bitch from a great dam line will be worth her weight in gold to a greyhound breeder, and should not be sold unless really necessary.

A word should be said here about the amount of racing a bitch should do, if she is to be used for breeding afterwards. As little as possible is the answer. Irish breeders usually retain a bitch of good breeding from a litter and part with the dogs. The form that the litter brothers show on track or coursing field will be a reliable guide to the quality of the bitch. She may be given a few races to prove her ability, but if she proves a champion one must decide either to keep her in training with a view to her winning several top events and maybe a classic, or to use her for breeding. Bitches that have had a long career in racing rarely, if ever, produce top-class stock, and the same can be said of sires. Great racing bitches of the past such as Robeen Printer, Queen of the Suir, Greta Ranee, Fair Mistress and Disputed Rattler produced nothing of note. Their names figure in no pedigree of top-class greyhounds. There are, of course, exceptions. Winnie of Berrow raced over an extended period, then produced Narrogar Ann who won the Derby and in turn was mother of another Derby winner, Endless Gossip. Cranog Bet, twice winner of the Oaks, was another. After she finished racing she produced Itsamint, winner of the Irish Oaks, who in turn produced the 1979 Irish Oaks winner Nameless Pixie. But the great dams of the past never raced, or did so but little. I am thinking of December Girl, dam of Bradshaw Fold, who was a house pet, as was Harrow Glamour, dam of the Derby winner Ford Spartan. Nor is it on the whole advisable to bring a bitch back into training after she has had a litter. Winnie of Berrow did so with little effect, and Alvaston Lulu Belle, one of the greatest in track history, set a new 700 yds track record at Harringay late in 1946 after whelping a litter of eight, but died in February 1948, a year later. The bitch Shady Bunny, litter sister to Shady Parachute, won the Greenwich Cup at New Cross after whelping a litter to Faithful Hope. When next she came in season she was put to Russian Gun and had a litter of seven pups but in general it is not good to ask a bitch to perform on the track and to be used for breeding at the same time. A short period of racing followed by a rest, and then possibly a mating to a sire, is all that is necessary to confirm her potential as a dam, and if she proves a good mother and whelps a good litter she should be kept for breeding.

See Bitch; Dam; Weaning.

BROUGH PARK RACECOURSE
See under British Greyhound Racecourses.

BROWNHILLS RACECOURSE
See under British Greyhound Racecourses.

BUFFALO BILL
The person who had most to do with the introduction into America of greyhounds, which were the foundation stock on which greyhound racing was developed there, was the legendary Buffalo Bill, William F. Cody. His friend General James Custer, also a breeder of greyhounds, asked Cody to bring him back from a visit to England with his Wild West Show in 1889 a well bred dog and a bitch, from which Custer might breed. Cody purchased from Col. North's famous kennels the dog Dingwall, which had that year run up for the Waterloo Plate, and the bitch Miss Kitten. Whether or not Cody kept them or had half the resulting litter is not known, but several of the pups, among which was Border Ruffian, appeared in the *American Greyhound Stud Book* in the name of W.F. Cody.

C

CAMBRIDGE RACECOURSE
See under British Greyhound Racecourses.

CARROLL'S IRISH DERBY
See Classic Events in Ireland.

CATFORD RACECOURSE
See under British Greyhound Racecourses.

CELTIC PARK RACECOURSE
See under Irish Greyhound Racecourses.

CESAREWITCH
English Cesarewitch *see under* Classic Events in Great Britain; Irish Cesarewitch *see* Classic Events in Ireland.

CHALLENGE

On 27 February 1945 the *Greyhound Owner* gave details of a challenge by Miss Kitty Kwasnik of Salford, Lancashire, on behalf of her bitch Hurry Kitty, for the title of fastest greyhound in England against all comers for the then huge sum of £5,000, in an open event to be run at the West Ham Stadium in March of that year. For various reasons the challenge, which was directed primarily against Burhill Moon and Shannon Shore, was not taken up.

CHAMPION GREYHOUND OF THE YEAR

This scheme was inaugurated in Ireland in 1965 by Bord na gCon, who each year ask a panel of leading sports journalists in the Republic to select the outstanding greyhound of track and coursing field. A handsome trophy is presented to each winner by the Minister of State for Agriculture in June at Shelbourne Park.

	Track	Coursing
1965	Ballyowen Chief	Mourne Monarch
1966	Hair Dresser	Rusheen Gallant
1967	Yanka Boy	no award
1968	Russian Gun	Proud Prince
1969	Own Pride	Quiet Dandy
1970	Mark Antony	Hack up Fenian
1971	Ivy Hall Flash	Fancy Stuff
1972	Cat's Rock Daisy	Asdee Stranger
1973	Romping to Work	Move on Swanky
1974	Lively Band	Move on Swanky
1975	Ballybeg Prim	Lusty More
1976	Tain Mor	Quarrymount Riki
1977	Linda's Champion	Master Myles
1978	Pampered Rover	Ashmore Fairy
1979	Nameless Pixie	Gay Comfort
1980	Indian Joe	Ashmore Melody
1981	Parkdown Jet	Knockash Rover
1982	Supreme Tiger	Little Scotch
1983	I'm Slippy	Swanky Star

CHANGE OF NAME

Early in 1938 Mrs Cearns, wife of the Wimbledon managing director, purchased the dog Joker of Waterhall from Miss Merritt's famous Waterhall kennels and renamed him Ballyjoker. Within six months he was to win the Wembley Summer Cup, the All-England Cup and the Cesarewitch, and was one of the greatest of Beef Cutlet's many outstanding sons.

Perhaps the most famous change of a greyhound's name was that of Mr Thomas Murphy's Prairie Champion, by Champion Prince—Prairie Peg. After clocking 29.10 secs in a 525 yds trial at Harold's Cross in 1957 this dog was bought by Mr Al Burnett, owner of the Pigalle Club in London, and under the name of Pigalle Wonder won for him the 1958 English Derby and nearly £8,000 in prize money.

Equally interesting was the change of name of another English Derby winner, Trev's Perfection, from Mott's Regret. He first raced for Miss N. Roth, for whom he won a number of open races during 1946. At the end of the year, after recovering from severe illness, he was bought by Mr Fred Trevillion for whom he won in 1947 the English, Scottish and Welsh Derbys, the first time the triple was ever accomplished. He also won the Catford Gold Collar in the same year to establish himself as one of the all-time greats. Trev's Perfection was first named Highland Perfection, and is one of the few examples of a greyhound racing under three different names.

Another change of name concerned Super Fun, who under that name raced for Mr Alf McLean in Ireland, and when sold to Mr Harry Gover to race in England did so under the name of Supreme Fun, because there was already a dog called Super Fun registered to race in England. He was also an excellent tracker and later, like Pigalle Wonder, became an equally fine sire.

After winning several races in Ireland as a puppy, Flashing Maxie was sold to Mr and Mrs R. Grant for 1,000 gns to race in

England, and they changed his name to Don't Gambol. They had bought one of the all-time bargains, for he was to win the Scurry Gold Cup classic on two occasions, as well as many other top-class events.

In recognition of his wonderful performances, the owner of Dante II had his name changed to Dante the Great when his racing days were over. Other well-known greyhounds to have had a change of name are Lone Seal from Manhattan Moonshine, Manhattan Midnight from Roeside Prince, and Laurels winner Burhill Moon who was originally called Island Rebel.

Great Record, son of two Derby winners, Mick the Miller and Greta Ranee, was originally named Glasgow Rangers. Councillor's Rock, bought by Fred Trevillion for £1,000 with a view to his winning the 1947 Derby, was renamed Trev's Councillor. He was to be disqualified for fighting and took no part in the Derby, won by Trev's Perfection, for whom Mr Trevillion had paid £900 as Mott's Regret.

The 1980 winner of the *Daily Mirror* sponsored Grand National run at the White City, London, in April was Gilt Edge Flyer who was originally named Young Toby.

In the first race to be run in Ireland, at Celtic Park, Belfast, in April 1927, the dog in trap 6, R. Matthew's Real McCoy, was previously called Ocean Blizzard. Sired by Guard's Brigade, he ran up to Mutual Friend.

CHANGE OF OWNER

The NGRC Rules of Racing state that, subject to the approval of the NGRC Stewards, every change of ownership of a registered greyhound shall be registered on the application of the proposed transferee. Application for registration shall be preceded by registration of the change with the appropriate stud book(s) and the appropriate documents shall be produced to the racing manager of an approved racecourse or to a qualified employee thereof appointed by him. The registered owner shall make available all documents necessary for registration of the change and shall ensure that the NGRC are notified. Registration of the change shall not be effective until the application is received and approved by the NGRC.

There have been many changes of ownership of greyhounds but it is only on rare occasions that change of ownership takes place during an important open event. Perhaps the most famous instance was Mick the Miller who was bought by London bookmaker A.H. Williams for £600 after the dog had won his early heat for the 1929 Greyhound Derby. After winning the event, Mick was again sold, this time for £2,000 to Mrs Arundel Kempton for whom he won the event the following year.

More recently, in 1969, the Callanan Cup, run at Harold's Cross, was won by Finola's Yarn for Cyril Young who purchased the dog mid-way through the event. So outstanding was the dog that he was quoted 6–4 on his winning the final which he did, coming through the event undefeated.

The 1980 Golden Jubilee Greyhound Derby, run at the White City, was won by the Irish dog Indian Joe who had been bought for a reputed £45,000 by Alf McLean, the Belfast bookmaker, after the dog won his first-round heat in near-record time. Indian Joe was troubled by lameness throughout the event and, but for his trainer John Hayes calling in the services of Mark Glennister of London, an expert in ultrasonic physiotherapy, it is unlikely that he would have run in the final. He reached the 1979 Irish Greyhound Derby final and joins Pigalle Wonder, Lilac's Luck, Hack up Chieftain, The Grand Canal, Myrtown, Black Banjo, Spider Hill and Ivy Hall Flash in reaching the English and Irish Derby finals.

CHARITIES

Since it began, no sport has made a greater contribution to deserving causes than greyhound racing. HRH The Duke of Edinburgh has been impressed by the fund-raising powers of the sport, and early in 1968 graciously accepted the gift of the dog Camira Flash. It was presented to him by Frankie Vaughan, on behalf of the Water Rats' Club of Great Britain, with the hope that any winnings the dog might earn would go towards the Duke's Award Scheme. Within a few months Camira Flash had won the English Derby! In a short career he amassed about £8,000 on the track and earned at least that sum when at stud. Ten years later His Royal Highness accepted the dog Playfield Royal on behalf of his Playing Fields Scheme and, even if not as successful as Camira Flash, the dog helped to swell its funds.

The Wimbledon track has organized a number of events on behalf of the National Playing Fields Association, while the Owlerton track in Sheffield each year stages an event on behalf of the Injured Jockeys Fund. Brighton organizes a meeting on behalf of the Variety Club of Britain's Children's Charity Fund, the Variety Club Stakes being an important event of the Brighton calendar. This track also holds an event run on behalf of the Sussex Youth Association, and every year at Brighton since the track opened several thousands of pounds have been raised for deserving causes.

Nor must the wonderful efforts of the Brough Park Stadium, Newcastle, in raising funds for the Cheshire Home at Matfen go without special mention. When it was found necessary to raise £30,000 needed to convert Matfen Hall to a Cheshire Home, ex-Squadron Leader Jimmy Rush AFC, a steward of the NGRC and a long-time friend of Group-Captain Leonard Cheshire VC, set about the task in earnest, and his greatest helpers were the directors and staff of Brough Park Stadium. At one meeting alone more than £1,500 was raised, and every year since considerable sums have been raised for the Home. In addition, on a number of occasions the patients have been entertained in royal fashion at the track, with the local bookmaking fraternity providing food and wine in the restaurant.

Early in 1978 the secretary of the GRA was able to present to the Queen's Silver Jubilee Appeal Fund a cheque for £25,000, collected from those who visited the GRA tracks during the year. In the same year £50,000 was raised at the White City alone for deserving causes. The special press-sponsored meeting brought in £10,000. For the Grocers' Benevolent Fund a similar sum was obtained, and £8,000 for the Heart Foundation. During 1979 more than twice that sum was distributed to charities, thanks to Bill Holmes, general manager of White City, including in his programmes additional events for good causes. In 1979 HRH Princess Margaret visited White City to support, in her role as president, the Sunshine Fund for Blind Children, and presented the Princess Margaret trophy to the winning owner of a specially sponsored event.

During recent years Perry Barr Stadium has raised money for the Sutton Coldfield Handicapped Children's Association, and at Hall Green a ten-race programme is run each year for the Variety Club of Great Britain when Mr J. Scobie of A1 Paper generously doubles the amount raised.

Crayford holds an annual Ladbroke's Injured Jockeys' Stakes, run over 650 m. A sponsored sweepstake in aid of the Injured Jockeys' Fund is run every year, and among those who have sponsored greyhounds in recent years are the Marquess of Zetland, Lord Oaksey, Lord Masham and Lord Bolton. At Wimbledon a meeting is arranged annually for the Multiple Sclerosis Fund, and in 1978 Harringay donated £1,000 to the fund for the Guide Dogs for the Blind. Powderhall are most enthusiastic in raising money for the hospitals and for medical research. They hold meetings for the Kidney Machine Appeal and for Edinburgh's Eastern General Hospital. Portsmouth are active in raising money for Penguin Club Charities, especially for leukemia research.

The greyhounds themselves, the providers of so much excitement and entertainment, are not forgotten. Many tracks also raise money for retired greyhounds, to enable them to live in the comfort they deserve when their racing days are over.

In 1979 a total of almost a quarter of a million pounds was raised for charities on British greyhound tracks.

CHELTENHAM RACECOURSE
See under British Greyhound Racecourses.

CIGARETTE CARDS

The first issue devoted to greyhound racing was put out by Carreras in their Black Cat cigarettes in 1926, the first year of the sport, as a set of fifty-two cards in both large (twenty-cigarette packets) and small (ten-cigarette packets) sizes, called the Greyhound Racing Game. They can still be obtained from specialist dealers in cigarette cards, together with the rules of the game, which in those days tobacconists supplied free of charge. The game is played on a greyhound track, with the dogs making their way round by jumping over obstacles which resemble fences on the hunting field rather than hurdles! Indeed, huntsmen take part in the game.

Early in 1927 and 1928 there appeared two more issues connected with the sport, called Greyhound Racing series I and II. Each comprised twenty-five small-size cards of famous greyhounds and were issued by Ogden's in their Robin cigarettes. In 1934 Churchman's produced a set of fifty Racing Greyhounds in full colour. In 1935 Irish Player's Navy Cut cigarettes contained a series of fifty cards called Famous Irish Greyhounds, with descriptions of the greyhounds on the reverse side. They are now scarce, since only a limited number was printed for the Irish market.

The last set to be issued was Racing Greyhounds, put out late in 1939. This was in fact one of the last of all cigarette card issues, since cigarette cards were discontinued early in 1940 because paper was more urgently needed to make cartridge cases. The cards appeared in B. Morris & Sons' Forcast cigarettes, and are black and white photogravure of excellent quality. They cover all the famous greyhounds of 1938–40, including those who reached the 1939 Derby final, except Junior Classic, a sad omission. They are as follows:

1. Quarter Day
2. Ballyhennessy Sandhills
3. Grosvenor Bob
4. Roeside Creamery
5. Lone Keel
6. Juvenile Classic
7. Valiant Bob
8. Bealtaine
9. Duna Taxmaid
10. Gayhunter
11. Keerie's Pride
12. Melksham Numeral
13. Demotic Mack
14. Jesmond Cutlet
15. Baltinglass Hope
16. Roeside Scottie
17. Lemon Produce
18. Printer
19. Charming Prince
20. Greta's Rosary
21. Black Peter
22. Carmel Ash
23. Highland Rum
24. Mister Mutt
25. Musical Duke

Among the greyhounds depicted were several of the all-time greats, and on the back of each card is a description of the greyhound and his or her record almost to the end of 1939. The honour of being the first card was given to Quarter Day, perhaps the greatest bitch of all time over middle distances. Card no.2 is Ballyhennessy Sandhills, twice winner of the Laurels, who raced for little over a year, during which time he won more than £5,000. Card no.3 is of Grosvenor Bob, who was born and bred in Kent and owned by G.H. Flintham for whom he won the Trafalgar Cup in 1936. In 1937 he reached the Derby final in which he finished third. In that year he won the St Leger, and the following year set a new world record for 525 yds at White City with a time of 29.22 secs, beating Wattle Bark's 29.26 secs achieved when winning the Derby in 1937.

Roeside Creamery and Roeside Scottie were litter brothers, from a litter by Deemster's Olive sired by Creamery Border which also included Manhattan Midnight. Roeside Creamery was one of the fastest ever to run, twice setting a new national record over 500 yds at his home track, Stamford Bridge, and he won the Pall Mall in 1938. 'Scottie' won the 1938 Scottish Derby and was a Laurels finalist that year, while Manhattan Midnight reached the final of the 1937 Derby.

Lone Keel was one of the greatest ever. He was raised at Kilkeel, Co. Down, and owned by Jack Walsh for whom he won the 1938 Derby, beating Melksham Numeral (card no.12) by half a length, with Wattle Bark a short head behind in third place. In reaching the final Lone Keel had won every round. Melksham Numeral was another English star, born and reared at the famous Melksham kennels of Henry Sawtell in Wiltshire. He was one of the unluckiest dogs, reaching the final of several important events without ever winning one.

Juvenile Classic, Printer and Valiant Bob were outstanding over hurdles, each being included among the best half dozen hurdlers ever, and each was at its peak during the late 1930s and in the early months of the war. Juvenile Classic won the Grand National in 1938 and reached the final the following year. Valiant Bob won the Grand National for his Cork owner, W. Mackesy, in 1939.

Duna Taxmaid was by Ataxy and bred and reared in England. In 1939 she set a new record at Wembley for 700 yds with a time of 40.38 secs, beating her sire's record by .01 secs. She also came within a few inches of winning the 1940 Derby, being beaten only a neck by another Ataxy offspring, G.R. Archduke, which would have made her the second bitch to have won the Derby. Only Greta Ranee had done so well, and in the whole history of the classic only Narrogar Ann, Dolores Rocket and Sarah's Bunny, in addition to Greta Ranee, have bettered her performance.

Gayhunter may not be so well known, but he set a new national record over 525 yds, beating Grosvenor Bob's 29.22 secs by .01 secs, and he finished second to Greta's Rosary for the 1938 St Leger. Demotic Mack was another English-bred dog who just missed the highest honours. He was bred at Birmingham by Mr and Mrs Mackenzie and reached the Derby final in 1938 and also in 1939, when Highland Rum beat the Scottish-bred Carmel Ash by two and a half lengths, both dogs starting 2–1 joint favourites. Highland Rum was bred by his owner, J. Harty, not in Scotland as his name might imply but at Dungarvan, Co. Waterford, and came to England to contest the Derby after winning each of his five races at Clonmel. He was only once beaten, for he was retired to stud after his Derby success and became a successful sire.

CLAPTON RACECOURSE
See under British Greyhound Racecourses.

CLASSIC EVENTS IN GREAT BRITAIN

See also Classic Winners; and entries for the various tracks at which these events are run.

CESAREWITCH
Always the last classic of the year, it was inaugurated in 1928 and allocated to the West Ham track where it was run, apart from the war years, until the track closed in May 1972. The event then transferred to Belle Vue, the first time a classic had been run in the north. Many of the greatest greyhounds have won this event and some wonderful finals have been established. The Cesarewitch trophy is the finest ever designed. West Ham's own creation, it is made of silver, stands 3 ft high and weighs over 300 oz. Today it must be one of the most valuable trophies presented on any sporting occasion.

For the first eight years it was run over 600 yds. Its first winner was Dick's Son. Then came Five of Hearts, whose sire was the great Jamie, also sire of Mutton Cutlet and of Entry Badge, winner of the first greyhound Derby in 1927. The following year Mick the Miller added the Cesarewitch to his second Derby. He won the St Leger the following year at the age of five, and no other dog except Future Cutlet has ever won a classic race in three consecutive years, and none has won a classic when over five. In 1931 Future Cutlet had the first of his two Cesarewitch wins, being the only greyhound ever to win the event twice – he was again successful in 1932, and in 1933 went on to win the Derby, the oldest dog to do so. He had also won the Laurels in 1931 – thus, like Mick the Miller, winning four classics.

Brilliant Bob added the Cesarewitch to his 1934 achievements in the Laurels and Scurry Gold Cup. He had also won the Irish St Leger the previous year, making him one of the few greyhounds to win a classic in both countries. In 1948 Local Interprize was to emulate Brilliant Bob by winning three classics – the Gold Collar, the Scurry Cup and the Cesarewitch – in the one year, and like 'Bob' he also reached the final of the Derby. Brilliant Bob's win in 1934 was achieved in 33.80 secs, a time which was not beaten for the 600 yds course until Prionsa Luath seventeen years later.

The 1935 Cesarewitch was won by Mr George Flintham's Grand Flight II, when he defeated two outstanding greyhounds, Shove Ha'penny and Ataxy, who was to win the event the following year and also the St Leger. In 1935 the first of Lady Eleanor's wonderful sons from her matings to Beef Cutlet was born. This was Jesmond Cutlet, trained at Catford, who won the 1938 Cesarewitch (beating Grosvenor Bob) after winning the Scottish Derby and Edinburgh Cup the previous year. Another of Beef Cutlet's sons was Ballyjoker, bred at Miss Merrett's famous Waterhall Kennels from the Future Cutlet dam, Jeanne of Waterhall. Ballyjoker was to complete a magnificent six months' running with his Cesarewitch triumph, during which time he won the Wembley Summer Cup, the All England Cup at Brough Park, and the O.A. Critchley Memorial Stakes at the White City. Then came the war, and during 1939–1944 the Cesarewitch was not held.

Between 1945 and 1950 it was run over 550 yds. The great bitch Hurry Kitty won the 1945 event, the first bitch to do so. Her dam's sire was none other than the Cesarewitch winner of a decade earlier, the great Brilliant Bob. Hurry Kitty's nine and a half lengths' margin when winning the final from Gala Flash was the biggest in the history of the race or of any classic. She had won her first-round heat by twelve lengths from Jonwell Shamrock and her semi-final by six lengths. In 1946 Cesarewitch finals were run in one year, for although the heats and semi-final had been run in 1945, owing to adverse weather and shortage of fuel for electricity greyhound racing was curtailed during December 1945, and the 1945 final was run on 9 January 1946. Five outstanding greyhounds contested it. Besides the winner and runner-up, in third place was the Laurels winner Burhill Moon; fourth was Kilcora Master; and fifth was the Oaks winner Prancing Kitty. Such was Hurry Kitty's power and stamina, however, that she won by nearly ten lengths.

Two more wonderful bitches contested the 1947 events – Rio Cepretta and Izadaisy. Both reached the final, which was won by Red Tan who beat Izadaisy by a neck, with Parish Model in third place, half a length behind. 1948 was the year that Local Interprize won three classics, including the Cesarewitch, in which he beat Freckled Major by just under two lengths in 30.88 secs, the first time 31 secs had been beaten over the 550 yds course. The 1949 Cesarewitch was won by the fawn dog Drumgoon Boy, who in his heat and semi-final set new track records. In his heat he beat the Derby winner Narrogar Ann by six lengths in 30.54 secs, and he bettered this by 0.01 secs when winning his semi-final. In the final he equalled his own track record.

The St Leger winner Magourna Reject won in 1953, and in 1955 Gulf of Darien became the first to break 33 secs for the event, winning in 32.99 secs. Five years later came the wonderful final which ended in a dead heat between Pigalle Wonder and Rylane Pleasure, the only occasion that a classic race in Britain has ended in a dead heat. The following year saw the great Mile Bush Pride add this event to his Derby success, to crown a wonderful year for Mr Noel Purvis, his owner. His time of 32.66 secs was the fastest ever over the 600 yds course.

Two years later Prairie Flash, trained by Jack Harvey, came first, and few who saw him win could ever have believed that he was to be one of the most important sires in the history of greyhound racing. His dam was Prairie Peg, also dam of Pigalle Wonder from a previous mating with Champion Prince. Prairie Flash was from her mating with Hi There and he was to sire Don't Gambol, twice winner of the Scurry Gold Cup, and Camira Flash, winner of the English Derby.

Another great sire, Silver Hope, won the 1967 Cesarewitch. He was to sire Patricia's Hope, winner of the Derby in 1972 and 1973, and Lively Band, sire of the 1977 Derby winner Balliniska Band and his litter brother Linacre. The 1968 event was won by another outstanding bitch, Cal's Pick, trained by Jack Harvey at Wembley. In fact Wembley-trained greyhounds have won the Cesarewitch more than those from any other track, and in 1955–9 won it consistently.

Since 1972, when West Ham closed for racing, the Cesarewitch has been run at Belle Vue and there was no better choice of new venue. The general manager at Belle Vue is John Kennedy who was for many years chief engineer at West Ham, so it must give him great pleasure that the classic is now thoroughly re-established at Manchester. The race still takes place in October but is now run over 815 m and is one of the longest in the racing calendar, a real test of a dog's stamina. The event is now sponsored by the Demmy Leisure Group of Manchester, who in 1979 put up a winner's prize of £3,000, to be increased to £4,000 in 1981. Those who saw the early champions win the wonderful trophy (still presented to the winning owner) and a prize of £500 will be delighted to know that this major event goes from strength to strength. The 1979 winner, Royston's Supreme, owned by Mr R.J. Todd and trained by Adam Jackson of Wembley, established himself as the best greyhound of the year, for he also reached the final of the St Leger and was runner-up to Frame That for the Grand Prix. He won the Cesarewitch by three-quarters of a length from Clountie Comment, Brighton's favourite, in 51.47 secs.

Another outstanding bitch, Linkside Liquor, won in 1980. She was trained by Gordon Bailey at Yarmouth to give his track its first classic success.

Winners of the Cesarewitch

1928	Dick's Son	32.38 secs
1929	Five of Hearts	34.82 secs
1930	Mick the Miller	34.11 secs
1931	Future Cutlet	34.03 secs

Winners of the Cesarewitch

1932	Future Cutlet	34.11 secs
1933	Elsell	34.22 secs
1934	Brilliant Bob	33.80 secs
1935	Grand Flight II	33.97 secs
*1936	Ataxy	31.24 secs
1937	Jesmond Cutlet	34.56 secs
1938	Ballyjoker	34.02 secs
1939–44	not run	
*1945	Hurry Kitty	31.26 secs
*1946	Colonel Skookum	31.28 secs
*1947	Red Tan	31.30 secs
*1948	Local Interprize	30.88 secs
*1949	Drumgoon Boy	30.53 secs
*1950	Quare Customer	30.80 secs
1951	Prionsa Luath	33.77 secs
1952	Shaggy Swank	34.03 secs
1953	Magourna Reject	33.24 secs
1954	Matchlock	33.03 secs
1955	Gulf of Darien	32.99 secs
1956	Coming Champion	33.02 secs
1957	Scoutbush	33.05 secs
1958	Pigalle Wonder) Rylane Pleasure)	33.06 secs
1959	Mile Bush Pride	32.66 secs
1960	Rostown Genius	33.29 secs
1961	Prairie Flash	32.91 secs
1962	Dromin Glory	32.97 secs
1963	Jehu II	33.15 secs
1964	Clifden Orbit	33.08 secs
1965	Lucky Monforte	33.00 secs
1966	Rostown Victor	34.06 secs
1967	Silver Hope	32.99 secs
1968	Deen Valley	33.29 secs
1969	Cal's Pick	32.98 secs
1970	Gleneagles Comedy	33.25 secs
1971	Whisper Billy	32.96 secs
†1972	Westmead Lane	51.65 secs
1973	Country Maiden	52.43 secs
1974	Westbrook Quinn	52.17 secs
1975	Silver Spectre	52.31 secs
1976	Moy Summer	51.32 secs
1977	Montreen	51.64 secs
1978	Shortland Blue	51.20 secs
1979	Royston's Supreme	51.47 secs
1980	Linkside Liquor	51.22 secs
1981	Kinda Friendly	52.68 secs
1982	Liga Lad	51.83 secs
1983	Jo's Gamble	50.90 secs
1984	Mobile Bank	52.92 secs

*Run over 550 yds; all others until 1972 over 600 yds † Since 1972 run over 815 m

ENGLISH GREYHOUND DERBY

It was only right that the premier event in the greyhound racing calendar, and the first event to be given classic status, was allocated to the White City, headquarters of the GRA and the first track to open in London. The first Derby took place in July 1927, only a month after the White City held its first meeting. This was the only time the event was run over 500 yds; thereafter until 1975 it was over 525 yds, and since 1975 has been run over 500 m. The first winner was Mr Edwin Baxter's Entry Badge, the first outstanding dog in the history of the sport, who was unbeaten during the first full year of greyhound racing. Entry Badge was kennelled at the White City and trained by Joe Harmon. He started at 4–1 on, the shortest odds of any Derby contestant, and won from trap 5.

In 1928 Boher Ash became the first and only Derby winner from Scotland when he won over 525 yds, and his owner, Mrs M. Stokes, was the first lady to win the Derby. The winner's prize in 1928 was £1,500, and it was not until twenty years later, when Priceless Border won in 1948, that this amount was again awarded. It was not exceeded until 1960 when Duleek Dandy earned its owner, Mrs B. Dash, £2,000 when winning at 25–1, the biggest odds ever quoted against a Derby winner. Almost every year since then the winner's prize money has increased, and in 1971 £10,000 was received by the White brothers for Dolores Rocket's wonderful win. In 1977, the fiftieth anniversary of the Derby (though the event did not take place between 1941 and 1944), the winner, Balliniska Band, received £17,500, and the following year Lacca Champion earned his owner £20,000. The greatly increased prize money in recent years is the result of the generosity of Spiller's, who in 1973 sponsored the event for the first time. The total prize money each year now exceeds £50,000.

Derby night is a great occasion; the race is watched by more than 40,000 people and by millions more on television, for since 1977 it has been put out live by the BBC. The magnificent silver Derby trophy presented to the winning owner resembles the FA Cup and is of similar value. The GRA put on twelve races and military bands entertain the crowd. Among other important events run on this occasion are the Derby Consolation final for the unlucky semi-finalists, the Dorando Marathon, and the Sherry's Prince Hurdles.

The first of Mick the Miller's Derby wins was in 1929, shortly after his arrival from Ireland. In fact, the first-round heat of the Derby was his first official race in England after running a trial at the White City, when he was purchased by Mr A.H. Williams for 800 gns. In his first heat Mick clocked the amazing time of 29.82 secs, which was not bettered in any Derby heat until Wild Woolley clocked 29.72 secs in the 1931 final. Soon after Mick's first Derby triumph he was bought by Mr Arundel Kempton for 2,000 gns as a present for his wife, in whose name he was to win the Derby the following year. She remained his owner until he died in 1939. Mick's second Derby was won from a very strong field – Bradshaw Fold, the first great racing bitch, ran up, and also in the race was that fine dog So Green. Mick actually achieved the Derby three years in succession for he won in 1931, only for the event to be ruled 'no race'. This was due to Ryland R fighting, and this dog did not take part in the re-run. At five years old it was clearly out of even Mick's powers to run and win after only a short rest, and it would have been better if he had been withdrawn from the re-run.

In 1932 and 1933 the amazing contests took place between Wild Woolley, Future Cutlet and Beef Cutlet, each about equal in ability, and they must be included among the all-time greats. Then came Davesland, trained by Jack Harvey, who won in 1934 and had his twenty-fourth Derby finalist in 1971; and Brilliant Bob, another great dog. In 1935 the event was won for the first time by a bitch, Greta Ranee, who defeated Curly's Fancy and Bosham, both outstanding dogs. Fine Jubilee won in 1936 from Curly's Fancy (a most unlucky dog) and Grand Flight II, Mr Flintham's first champion. When winning in 1937 Wattle Bark set a new national record with a time of 29.26 secs, and he almost won again the following year, finishing only half a length and a short head behind Lone Keel and Melksham Numeral respectively.

Monday's News, probably the most popular winner since Mick the Miller, was successful in 1946. A small dog of amazing intelligence, he was able to move round the bends at tremendous speed and would nip inside to the rails at the slightest opportunity. His time of 29.34 secs was a new final record, which was broken the following year when Trev's Perfection became the first dog to break 29 secs in the final. He was also the first to do the treble, winning the English, Scottish and Welsh Derbys that year. He was to beat two fine dogs in Monday's News, who ran up, and Slaney Record. In 1948 Priceless Border set a new final record with 28.78 secs, beating Local Interprize by two lengths with the bitch Sheevaun in third place. It was the first victory in Leslie Reynolds' amazing run of five Derby wins in seven years. Priceless Border was never beaten and was the first

Mrs Yate with her 1936 Derby winner, Fine Jubilee. Photo: GRA.

and only greyhound to start as odds-on favourite for the Derby and go through the entire event with an odds-on quotation. The betting was 2–1 on his winning the final.

Narrogar Ann won in 1949, and in 1950 Ballymac Ball set a new final record, which was broken in 1951 when Mr N. Dupont's Ballylanigan Tanist beat the favourite, Black Mire. Then came Endless Gossip, the finest English-bred greyhound ever to race and the first Derby winner to be bred from two former Derby winners, Priceless Border and Narrogar Ann. He was trained by Leslie Reynolds and started as even money favourite. He, too, was to set a new final

Opposite: HRH The Duke of Edinburgh with Camira Flash, accompanied by Frankie Vaughan who presented the greyhound on behalf of the Water Rats of Great Britain. The dog was to win the 1968 English Derby. Photo: GRA.

record of 28.50 secs. The following year, photo-timing was used for the first time in a Derby final and Paddy McEvoy enjoyed his first success, with Daw's Dancer. The splendid Paul's Fun, at 2–1 on, won in 1954. The 1955 Derby final was made up of six outstanding contestants, with Barrowside the 2–1 on favourite, but the winner was Mr and Mrs F. Johnson's Rushton Mac, also trained by them. Behind him at the finish were Barrowside, Coolkill Chieftain, Gulf of Honduras, Home Straight and Duet Leader, each to become a power when retired to stud. Duet Leader ran up the following year to Mr Jack McAllister's Dunmore King. Then came a trio of outstanding winners, each of whom must be included among the twenty best greyhounds ever to race in Britain. They were Ford Spartan, the 1957 winner; Pigalle Wonder, who was successful in 1958; and Mile Bush Pride, trained by Jack Harvey and who won for Mr Noel Purvis in 1959.

The two favourites, Palm's Printer and Oregon Prince, fought it out in 1961, and the former, Alf Heale's dog, won by just over a length. The Grand Canal won for its Irish owner–trainer, Paddy Dunphy, the following year, and in 1964 Hack Up Chieftain took the honours for Belle Vue when quoted at 20–1, being one of the biggest outsiders to win the event. Faithful Hope, trained by Paddy Keane when at Clapton, won in 1966 and set a new photo-time record. The following year saw the litter brothers Tric Trac and Spectre II, owned by Nat Pinson of Sheffield and trained by Ron Hookway at Owlerton, finish first and second, a feat without precedent in the Derby or any other classic event.

The Duke of Edinburgh's Camira Flash, the first greyhound owned by royalty to race in public, won the coveted trophy in 1968. The dog was trained by Randolph Singleton at White City and all prize money and stud fees were donated to the Duke of Edinburgh's Award Scheme. In 1969 Sand Star won for his breeder, trainer and owner, Mr Hamilton Orr of Northern Ireland, and the dog won each of his heats and semi-final. In the final he beat the powerful Kilbelin Style. Then came John Silver's victory. He was a son of Faithful Hope, and therefore the second winner sired by a former Derby winner, and was trained by Barbara Tomkins. In 1971 Dolores Rocket won from a high-class field which included Supreme Fun, Leap and Run, Moordyke Champion, Cobbler, and Ivy Hall Flash. Patricia's Hope won in 1972 and 1973, joining Mick the Miller who had until then been the only greyhound to win two Derbys.

1975 was Tartan Khan's great year, in which he also won the St Leger and the Scottish Derby. A year later Mr Roy Lancaster's Mutt's Silver was successful, winning by two and a half lengths from a strong field which included Ballybeg Prim, the runner-up, Westmead Champ and Xmas Holiday. In 1977 Balliniska Band, trained by Eddie Moore, took the honours for Belle Vue and established himself as the best dog of the year. Then came Lacca Champion's win in 1978, and this great dog ran up to the bitch Sarah's Bunny the following year. Sarah's Bunny was the third winner to be sired by an earlier Derby winner – in this instance Jimsun, the 1974 winner.

Only two people have ever won both the English and Irish Derbys. Miss Pauline Wallis, in joint ownership with Sir Robert Adeane, won the English event with Faithful Hope in 1966 and the Irish Derby with Yellow Printer in 1968.

Winners of the English Greyhound Derby

		Trap	*Trainer*		
*1927	Entry Badge	5	J. Harmon	White City	29.01 secs
1928	Boher Ash	1	T. Johnston	Powderhall	30.48 secs
1929	Mick the Miller	4	P. Horan	Shelbourne Park	29.96 secs
1930	Mick the Miller	1	S. Orton	Wimbledon	30.24 secs
1931	Seldom Led	4	A. Green	West Ham	30.04 secs
1932	Wild Woolley	6	J. Rimmer	White City, Manchester	29.72 secs
1933	Future Cutlet	3	S. Probert	Wembley	29.80 secs

		Trap	Trainer		
1934	Davesland	4	H. Harvey	Harringay	29.81 secs
1935	Greta Ranee	3	A. Jonas	White City	30.18 secs
1936	Fine Jubilee	3	Mrs M. Yate	(Private)	29.48 secs
1937	Wattle Bark	6	J. Syder	Wembley	29.26 secs
1938	Lone Keel	3	S. Wright	(Private)	29.62 secs
1939	Highland Rum	6	P. Fortune	Wimbledon	29.35 secs
+1940	G.R. Archduke	1	C. Ashley	Harringay	29.66 secs
1941–4	not run				
1945	Ballyhennessy Seal	1	S. Martin	Wimbledon	29.56 secs
1946	Monday's News	3	F. Farey	(Private)	29.34 secs
1947	Trev's Perfection	2	F. Trevillion	(Private)	28.95 secs
1948	Priceless Border	1	L. Reynolds	Wembley	28.78 secs
1949	Narrogar Ann	2	L. Reynolds	Wembley	28.95 secs
1950	Ballymac Ball	4	S. Martin	Wimbledon	28.72 secs
1951	Ballylanigan Tanist	1	L. Reynolds	Wembley	28.62 secs
1952	Endless Gossip	6	L. Reynolds	Wembley	28.50 secs
1953	Daw's Dancer	5	P. McEvoy	(Private)	29.20 secs
1954	Paul's Fun	3	L. Reynolds	Wembley	28.84 secs
1955	Rushton Mac	2	F. Johnson	(Private)	28.97 secs
1956	Dunmore King	3	P. McEvoy	Clapton	29.22 secs
1957	Ford Spartan	1	J. Hannafin	Wimbledon	28.84 secs
1958	Pigalle Wonder	1	J. Syder Jnr.	Wembley	28.65 secs
1959	Mile Bush Pride	4	H. Harvey	Wembley	28.76 secs
1960	Duleek Dandy	4	Mrs B. Dash	(Private)	29.15 secs
1961	Palm's Printer	1	P. McEvoy	Clapton	28.84 secs
1962	The Grand Canal	5	P. Dunphy	(Private)	20.09 secs
1963	Lucky Boy Boy	1	J. Bassett	Clapton	29.00 secs
1964	Hack Up Chieftain	1	T. Stagg	Belle Vue	28.92 secs
1965	Chittering Clapton	6	A. Jackson	Clapton	28.82 secs
1966	Faithful Hope	3	P Keane	Clapton	28.52 secs
1967	Tric Trac	1	R. Hookway	Owlerton	29.00 secs
1968	Camira Flash	4	R. Singleton	White City	28.89 secs
1969	Sand Star	4	H. Orr	(Private)	28.76 secs
1970	John Silver	2	Mrs B. Tompkins	(Private)	29.01 secs
1971	Dolores Rocket	2	H.G. White	(Private)	28.74 secs
1972	Patricia's Hope	5	A. Jackson	Clapton	28.55 secs
1973	Patricia's Hope	5	J. O'Connor	(Private)	28.68 secs
1974	Jimsun	2	G. de Mulder	Hall Green	28.76 secs
†1975	Tartan Khan	2	Mrs Lynds	(Private)	29.57 secs
1976	Mutt's Silver	4	P. Rees	Wimbledon	29.38 secs
1977	Balliniska Band	5	E. Moore	Belle Vue	29.16 secs
1978	Lacca Champion	3	P. Mullins	(Private)	29.42 secs
1979	Sarah's Bunny	6	G. de Mulder	Hall Green	29.53 secs
1980	Indian Joe	6	J. Hayes	Ireland	29.68 secs
1981	Parkdown Jet	6	Ger McKenna	Ireland	29.57 secs
1982	Laurie's Panther	1	T. Duggan	Romford	29.60 secs
1983	I'm Slippy	4	Mrs B. Tompkins	Coventry	29.40 secs
1984	Whisper Wishes	4	C. Coyle	Maidstone	29.43 secs

*1927 run over 500 yds; 1928-74 run over 525 yds; + 1940 run at Harringay
†1975 onwards, run over 500 m

Below: Winners of the first five English Greyhound Derbies: Entry Badge, 1927; Boher Ash, 1928; Mick the Miller, 1929 and 1930; and Seldom Led, 1931. 1972–82 sponsored by Spillers; 1983–84 sponsored by the Daily Mail. Opposite: Recent champions of the English Greyhound Derby.

Spillers Greyhound Derby Winners

Patricia's Hope, 1972 and 1973.

Jimsun, 1974.

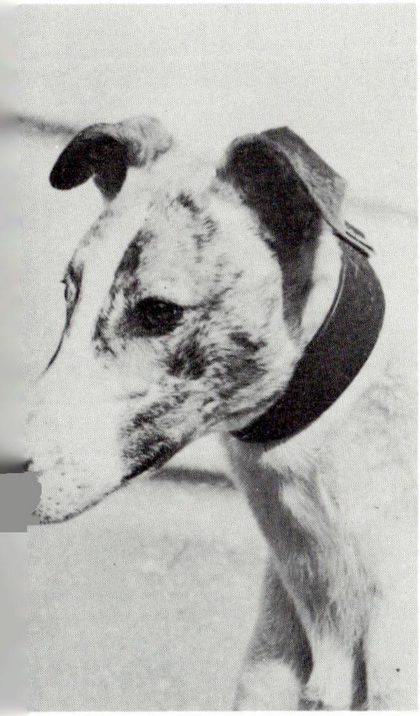

Tartan Khan, 1975.

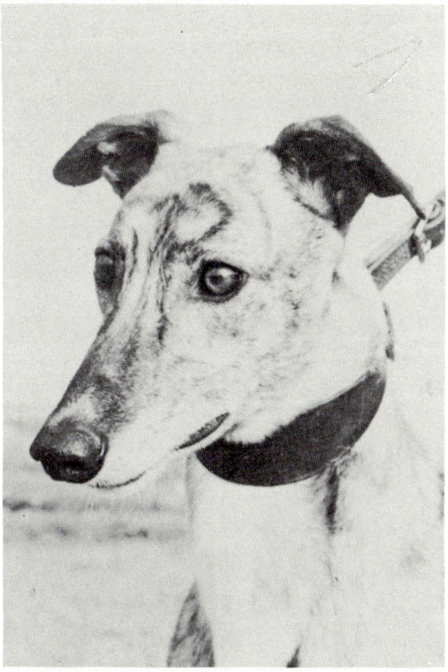

Mutt's Silver, 1976.

Balliniska Band, 1977.

Lacca Champion, 1978.

Sarah's Bunny, 1979

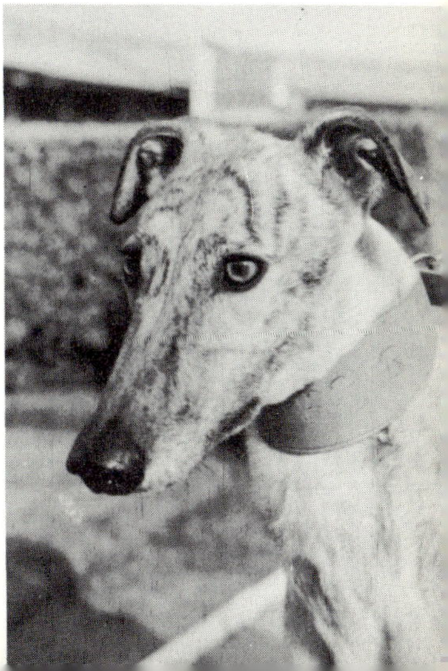

FACTS and FIGURES of the English Greyhound Derby

The only Scottish-owned greyhound to win the English Derby was Boher Ash in 1928 when he defeated Fabulous Figure by half a length. His time of 30.48 secs was the slowest for the Derby over the 525 yds course.

The fastest time for the event was Endless Gossip's 28.50 secs, recorded in winning the 1952 final; and Ballylanigan Tanist's 28.62 secs of the previous year was the next fastest. Both dogs were trained by Leslie Reynolds.

The first greyhound to break 29.00 secs for the event was Trev's Perfection when winning in 1947 with a time of 28.95 secs.

The biggest winning margin was seven lengths by Monday's News in 1946, followed by six and a half lengths by Lucky Boy Boy in 1963 (also achieved by Entry Badge in 1927).

The closest race was Future Cutlet's short-head victory over Beef Cutlet in 1933. As there was no photo-finish then, many thought a dead heat should have been given because the dogs were so close and there were some spectators not right opposite the line who believed Beef Cutlet was the winner. Ford Spartan and Mile Bush Pride also won by a neck.

The first bitch to win the Derby was Greta Ranee in 1935. Other bitches to win were Narrogar Ann in 1949, Dolores Rocket in 1971, and Sarah's Bunny in 1979.

Biggest favourite (shortest odds) to win was Entry Badge who was 4–1 on, followed by Mick the Miller 9–4 on when winning in 1930, and Priceless Border and Paul's Fun 2–1 on when winning in 1948 and 1954. Longest odds were Duleek Dandy 25–1 in 1960 and Tartan Khan also 25–1 in 1975. Both won comfortably. Hack up Chieftain won at 20–1 against in 1964.

Three greyhounds reached the final three times – Mick the Miller in 1929, 1930 and 1931, winning the first two years; Wild Woolley in 1932, 1933 and 1934, winning in 1932 and being third on the other two occasions; and Mile Bush Pride in 1958, 1959 and 1960, winning in 1959 and finishing third on the other occasions.

Mick the Miller and Patricia's Hope were the only dogs to have won the Derby twice; but Future Cutlet nearly did so. He reached two finals, winning one by a short head and losing the other by the same margin. So did Wattle Bark, winning in 1937; Monday's News, winning in 1946; and Lacca Champion, winning in 1978 and running up in 1979. Curley's Fancy also reached two finals, finishing second and third, and is the unluckiest greyhound not to have won the event. Others to contest two finals were Celtic Chief, Local Interprize (one of the best dogs ever to race), Duet Leader, Shady Parachute and Myrtown.

Only four trainers have won the Derby more than once: Jack Harvey with Davesland in 1934 and Mile Bush Pride in 1959; Paddy McEvoy with Daw's Dancer in 1953, Dunmore King in 1956 and Palm's Printer in 1961; Stan Martin with Ballyhennessy Seal in 1946 and Ballymac Ball in 1950; Geoffrey de Mulder with Jimsun in 1974 and Sarah's Bunny in 1979; and Leslie Reynolds with Priceless Border in 1948, Narrogar Ann in 1949, Ballylanigan Tanist in 1951, Endless Gossip in 1952 and Paul's Fun in 1954. His five wins in seven years will surely stand for all time.

One father and son have trained Derby winners: Jim Syder Snr with Wattle Bark in 1937 and his son Jim with Pigalle Wonder in 1958.

To the late Leslie Reynolds belongs a unique record in having trained the Derby-winning son (Endless Gossip) of two Derby winners (Priceless Border and Narrogar Ann). And to Geoffrey de Mulder belongs the distinction of having trained both sire (Jimsun) and daughter (Sarah's Bunny) to win the premier classic.

Three English Derby winners also completed the Triple Crown, winning the Scottish and Welsh Derbys in the same year. They were Trev's Perfection in 1947; Mile Bush Pride in 1959; and Patricia's Hope in 1972. Rushton Mac, bred, trained and owned by Mr and Mrs Johnson in Cheshire, won the English and Welsh Derbys in 1955 and the Scottish Derby in 1954. Only three greyhounds have contested the final of both the English and Irish Derbys. In 1945 Lilac's Luck won the Irish event and the following year ran up to Monday's News for the English Derby; in 1958 Pigalle Wonder won the English Derby and in 1960 finished third in the Irish event, and in 1979 Indian Joe reached the final of the Irish Derby and won the 1980 English Derby.

On three occasions the Derby has been won by a dog whose owner was also its breeder and trainer: in 1962 by The Grand Canal for Mr P.J. Dunphy of Ireland; in 1969 by Sand Star for Mr Hamilton Orr of Ireland; and in 1971 by Dolores Rocket for Mr H.G. White. Besides these three, there have been five others to have owned and trained a Derby winner though they did not breed it. These were Mr Trevillion with Trev's Perfection; Mr F. Johnson with Rushton Mac in 1955 (in part-ownership with Mrs M. Johnson); Mr J. O'Connor who partly owned and trained Patricia's Hope who won in 1973 for the second time; and the only two women to train and own the winner were Mrs M. Yate and Mrs B. Dash.

When Mr Phil Rees (Wimbledon) trained the 1976 Derby winner, he also trained the winners of the Scurry Gold Cup and the Cesarewitch in the same year. Only one other trainer has trained three classic winners in the same year: the Walthamstow trainer Mr Tommy Reilly in 1953, but he did not train the Derby winner. He was in charge of Magourna Reject who won the Cesarewitch and St Leger that year, and Polonius who won the Laurels. Surprisingly no Walthamstow-trained dog has ever won the Derby.

The only women to have owned and trained a Derby winner were Mrs M. Yate with Fine Jubilee in 1936 when he won by six lengths, one of the biggest winning margins; and Mrs B. Dash who owned and trained the 25–1 outsider, Duleek Dandy, to win the first £2,000 Derby prize in 1960. The only other lady trainers of a Derby winner are Mrs B. Tompkins with John Silver and Mrs Lynds with Tartan Khan.

Endless Gossip was the first Derby winner to have been sired by a Derby winner (Priceless Border) and was the only winner to be sired by two previous winners, his dam being Narrogar Ann, who won in 1949. Other Derby winners sired by a Derby winner are John Silver (1970) whose sire was Faithful Hope (1966) and Sarah's Bunny (1979) whose sire was Jimsun (1976).

The record of the dam Millie's Hawthorn is unique for she had a hand in six Derby finals in eight years. From a mating with Solar Prince she was dam of the 1966 winner, Faithful Hope, who in turn was sire of the 1970 winner, John Silver. From a mating with Clonalvy Pride, she was mother of Silver Hope (whose litter brother was Yanka Boy) who reached the 1967 final and who in turn was sire of the 1972 and 1973 winner, Patricia's Hope. In 1968 Millie's son, Winning Hope, reached the final. Silver Hope was also sire of Lively Band who won the Irish Derby and whose son, Balliniska Band, won the 1977 English Derby.

The oldest dog to win the Derby was Future Cutlet in 1933 when aged four and a half years and the youngest were Daw's Dancer and John Silver who were both twenty-two months old.

When Patricia's Hope won in 1972 and 1973, the order in which each dog finished was the same each year: traps 5, 4, 6, 1, 3, 2. Though the St Leger has not, in its forty-eight years, ever been won by a greyhound from trap 5, it took twenty years (1927–47) before a dog from trap 2 won the Derby. This was Trev's Perfection who won in 1947, and from the first Derby, when a dog from trap 5 was successful, until Daw's Dancer won from trap 5 in 1953, twenty-one Derbys had been contested.

Equally remarkable is the fact that when Trev's Perfection won the English and Scottish Derbys in 1947, he beat the same five dogs each time. They were Monday's News, Slaney Record, Trev's Jackie, Lacken Invader and Patsy's Record.

For the only time in its history, the English Derby of 1939 was contested by greyhounds from England, Scotland, Ireland and Wales. Highland Rum, the winner, was born in Co. Waterford, Ireland; the runner-up, Carmel Ash, was Scottish-born; Demotic Mack, in third place, was born in Birmingham; and Junior Classic was born and reared at Llandaff, South Wales. Mister Mutt, the other finalist (there were only five runners), was from Co. Carlow, Ireland.

Mutt's Silver's win by a head from Ballybeg Prim in 1976 gave trainer Phil Rees of Wimbledon three different classics in a row. In three months he won the Scurry Gold Cup with Xmas Holiday in April; the Laurels in May with the same dog; and the Derby in June. This had never before been achieved nor has it since been equalled by any trainer in the history of the sport.

Only three men have trained both an English and Irish Derby winner: John Bassett; Paddy Keane who trained Faithful Hope to win the English Derby in 1966 and he won the Irish Derby with Pampered Hero in 1978; and Ger McKenna.

For the first time in the history of track racing, bitches won both the English and Irish Derby in the same year (1979) when Sarah's Bunny took the White City event and Penny County won at Shelbourne Park.

GOLD COLLAR

Now worth £5,000 to the winner and sponsored by the Catford bookmaker John Humphreys, the Gold Collar has always been run at Catford though its distance has been altered several times. It was inaugurated in 1933. The first race, run over 440 yds, was won by Wild Woolley (winner of the Derby later that year) at 3- 1 on. Trained by J. Rimmer at White City, Manchester, Wild Woolley was one of the sport's outstanding greyhounds in its early years. Badly baulked at the first turn in the final, Wild Woolley hung on to the leader, Deemster's Mike, and managed to cut inside him at the final turn to win by a length from this fine dog. The following year Davesland won this event, and also the Derby; two years later Fine Jubilee repeated the performance. It was again to be won by a Derby winner, Ballyhennessy Seal, in 1945, and by Trev's Perfection two years later, so that in the first eleven Gold Collars a Derby winner was successful five times. In 1938 the peerless Junior Classic, trained by Joe Harmon, won the event and reached the Derby final the following year. Each of the dogs that won both the Derby and the Gold Collar was descended from Macoma, Mick the Miller's litter brother, through his son Silver Seal, while Junior Classic was from Macoma's daughter, Lady Eleanor.

In 1948 and 1949 came Local Interprize, the only dog ever to win the event twice. One of the greatest ever to race in England, he was trained at Clapton by Stanley Biss, top trainer during the 1940s when his only rivals were Sydney Orton and Stan Martin, neither of whom ever won the Gold Collar. Until 1970 it had been won by more privately trained dogs (thirteen) than any other classic. Only one trainer, A.W. Smith, was successful with more than one dog, although Stanley Biss won it twice with the same dog, which shows how difficult it is to win the Gold Collar.

Only one greyhound, Bosham, has ever won the Gold Collar and the St Leger; and only one has won the Gold Collar and Laurels Wild Woolley. There has been only one dog to win the Gold Collar and the Scurry Gold Cup — Local Interprize, who almost won both events twice. No bitch had won the Gold Collar until Gayflash was successful in 1979. She was trained by Paddy Mulligan, who had won the event with Shane's Rocket in 1968. The Gold Collar has not been won by a Derby winner since 1947. The longest odds winner was the 33- 1 Mighty Wind in 1964; the shortest were Wild Woolley in 1933 and Silent Worship in 1957, both 3–1 on.

Winners of the Gold Collar

		Trap	*Trainer*		
1933	Wild Woolley (D)	4	J. Rimmer	White City, Manchester	26.63 secs
*1934	Davesland (D)	3	H. Harvey	Harringay	32.70 secs
*1935	Bosham	6	L. Reynolds	White City	32.84 secs
1936	Fine Jubilee (D)	4	Mrs M. Yate	(Private)	26.00 secs
1937	Avion Ballerina	1	J. Hannafin	Wimbledon	25.87 secs
1938	Junior Classic	6	J. Harmon	Wimbledon	25.77 secs
1939	Grosvenor Ferdinand	6	F. Rolfe	(Private)	25.92 secs
1940	Cash Balance	5	S. Probert	Wembley	25.74 secs
1941–4	not run				
1945	Ballyhennessy Seal (D)	3	S. Martin	Wimbledon	25.45 secs
1946	King Silver	2	C. Crowley	Clapton	25.88 secs
1947	Trev's Perfection (D)	3	F. Trevillion	(Private)	25.52 secs
1948	Local Interprize	6	S. Biss	Clapton	25.71 secs
1949	Local Interprize	1	S. Biss	Clapton	25.88 secs
1950	Islandeady	4	H. Copsey	(Private)	26.07 secs
1951	Local Accomplice	6	T. Reilly	Walthamstow	25.63 secs
1952	Hectic Birthday	4	B. Melville	Wembley	25.41 secs
1953	Mushera Silver	3	L. Gould	(Private)	25.70 secs
1954	Ardskeagh Ville	5	E. Barker	Catford	25.86 secs
1955	Firgrove Slipper	6	J. Syder Jnr	Wembley	26.35 secs
1956	Ponsford	1	Miss N. Collins	(Private)	25.69 secs

1957	Silent Worship	1	J. Bassett	(Private)	25.50 secs
1958	Five Up	4	R. Chamberlain	(Private)	25.43 secs
1959	Dunstown Warrior	5	T. Reilly	Walthamstow	25.77 secs
1960	Catch Cold	4	D. Hannafin	Wimbledon	25.56 secs
1961	Long Story	6	P. Rees	(Private)	25.69 secs
1962	Super Orange	5	Miss P. Heasman	(Private)	25.51 secs
†1963	Music Guest	5	T. Johnston	West Ham	33.36 secs
†1964	Mighty Wind	2	G. Waterman	Wimbledon	33.36 secs
†1965	Friday Morning	6	R. Chamberlain	(Private)	33.73 secs
†1966	Dark Symphony	1	P. Collett	(Private)	33.21 secs
†1967	Stylish Lad	5	A.W. Smith	Catford	33.75 secs
†1968	Shane's Rocket	3	P. Milligan	(Private)	33.39 secs
†1969	Surprising Fella	5	A.W. Smith	Catford	33.40 secs
†1970	Cameo Lawrence	5	A.W. Smith	Catford	33.84 secs
†1971	Down Your Way	4	H. Warrell	(Private)	33.10 secs
+1972	Rathmartin	5	S.C. Orton	Wimbledon	35.36 secs
+1973	Ramdeen Stuart	1	N. Oliver	Brough Park	35.04 secs
+1974	Leader's Champion	1	D. Geggus	Walthamstow	35.02 secs
1975	Abbey Glade	4	G. Curtis	Brighton	34.97 secs
1976	Westmead Champ	2	Miss P. Heasman	Hackney	35.02 secs
1977	Westmead Power	1	Mrs N. Savva	Bletchley	34.98 secs
1978	I'm a Smasher	1	J. Coleman	Wembley	35.31 secs
1979	Gayflash	5	P. Milligan	Catford	35.08 secs
1980	Sport Promoter	5	P. Mullins	Cambridge	35.06 secs
1981	Laughing Sam	6	Mrs P. Goode	Hall Green	35.50 secs
1982	Donna's Dixie	6	H. Kibble	Eastville	35.19 secs
1983	Rathduff Tad	5	T. Dennis	Southend	35.13 secs
1984	Wheeler's Tory	2	P. Wheeler	Private	35.05 secs

*Run over 540 yds; †Run over 570 yds; Other races run over 440 yds until 1970, and since 1975 over 555 m (D) also won English Greyhound Derby

GRAND NATIONAL

This event for hurdlers, the first of the year's classics, joins the Greyhound Derby and the Oaks in seniority for it was first run in 1927, the year the White City, London, opened for greyhound racing. Originally it was designated to be run at Harringay but has always been run at the older of the GRA tracks and is now sponsored by the *Daily Mirror*. It is run in April over 500 m and is the most popular event in the racing calendar after the Derby for everyone loves to see a good jumper perform. Previously, the Grand National was run over 525 yds except for the first, which was over 500 yds and won by the dog Bonzo. The following year saw Cormorant successful. He had been purchased in Ireland for £1,000 a few weeks before the event and was the first great hurdler to excite the public with his magnificent jumping. Cormorant was almost ungradable on the tracks wherever he raced and also won the Welsh Grand National at Cardiff the same year. He was to sire Killing Pace, who finished second to Rule the Roost in the National of 1931. Cormorant's litter brother, Carpio, was also an outstanding hurdler.

The 1930 National was won by one of Mutton Cutlet's first and finest sons, Stylish Cutlet, who was the first to 'break' 31.00 secs over the 525 yds hurdles course. He too cost £1,000. Two years later, Long Hop won the event. He was Macoma's first son to reproduce his sire's ability over hurdles. Macoma, litter brother of Mick the Miller, was one of the finest hurdlers of his day and was to sire several of the finest hurdlers the sport has known. But none was greater than Long Hop who in 1932 won the National at the White City, the Empire Stadium Stakes at Wembley and the Wimbledon Challenge Trophy – all tracks came alike to him.

Long Hop was out of the bitch Bright Emblem who, when put to Macoma a second time, whelped the equally courageous Scapegoat, owned by Miss I. Lake and trained at the White City by A. Jones. Macoma's influence was later to reappear in his great-grandson, Derryboy Jubilee, son of Fine Jubilee who in turn was a son of Silver Seal, sire also of Lone Seal and Trev's Despatch, each of whom sired a Derby winner. Derryboy Jubilee, who began racing on the flat with little success, became a champion when tried over hurdles and, though he took no part in any Grand National because it was wartime, he won the Empire Stadium Stakes, the Wimbledon Challenge Trophy and The Chase in 1944 as well as Wimbledon's Gold Cup the following year.

In 1937 Flying Wedge won the National

but by only a short head from that great all-rounder Border Mutton, one of Mutton Cutlet's last and finest sons. So fast was Border Mutton in finishing, coming from behind along the final straight, that there were those watching who thought he had in fact won, and if the photo-finish camera had been installed at the White City in those days it might well have reversed the judge's decision or at least given the race a dead heat.

The year 1938 saw the first of Juvenile Classic's two National wins, and during the next three years he was to prove one of the all-time greats over hurdles. Together with Junior Classic, his litter brother, he was from the amazingly successful Beef Cutlet–Lady Eleanor combination which had also produced Jesmond Cutlet and Epinard from an earlier mating. Junior and Juvenile Classic were well named for they were indeed of classic stock and two from one litter with such outstanding capabilities were not seen again until Tric Trac and Spectre took the first two places in the 1966 Derby. Juvenile Classic again won the National in 1940, the last time it was run until the war ended, and his time of 30.30 secs was easily the fastest since its inauguration.

Between Juvenile Classic's two successes, Valient Bob won in 1939 for W. Mackesy of Cork, and in the first year after the war (1946), Barry from Limerick set the seal on his great ability as a jumper. The great hurdler Printer, at his best during the war years, had no opportunity of adding the National to his many hurdling achievements which must place him amongst the all-time greats.

The year 1950 was a vintage one for hurdlers and at the White City, Blossom of Annagurra, a dog which cost £100, defeated another wonderful hurdler in Dangerous Prince who, in winning his heat by fourteen lengths, had set a new national record with a time of 29.39 secs, being the first dog to 'break' 30 secs over hurdles. This record stood for twenty years when Sherry's Prince clocked 29.02 secs at Harringay to set a new national record. Sherry's Prince was one of the sport's finest hurdlers, his record of three successive Grand Nationals in 1970, 1971 and 1972 unlikely ever to be equalled. Twice he won the Long Hop Hurdles at the White City where he was kennelled and trained by Colin West for his second and third National wins.

In six years, between 1971 and 1976, Mr West trained six National winners, a record which has never been equalled.

The dog Topothetide took over from Sherry's Prince as champion, winning in 1978 and 1979, both times as the odds-on favourite. He also won the Scottish Grand National in 1978, a feat which Sherry's Prince never achieved.

The 1980 *Daily Mirror* Grand National was won by Gilt Edge Flyer, the 5–4 on favourite who defeated Westlands Steve by the considerable margin of nine lengths in 30.22 secs for the 500 m course. He had previously won his semi-final by six lengths.

In 1981 and 1982, trainer Norah McEllistrim achieved the 'double' of Grand National Winners.

Winners of the Grand National 1927–49

1927	Bonzo	31.42 secs
1928	Cormorant	31.16 secs
1929	Levator	31.09 secs
1930	Stylish Cutlet	30.94 secs
1931	Rule the Roost	31.17 secs
1932	Long Hop	31.44 secs
1933	Scapegoat	31.20 secs
1934	Lemonition	30.84 secs
1935	Quarter Cross	30.76 secs
1936	Kilganny Bridge	30.70 secs
1937	Flying Wedge	30.61 secs
1938	Juvenile Classic	30.35 secs
1939	Valiant Bob	30.50 secs
1940	Juvenile Classic	30.23 secs
1941–5	not run	
1946	Barry from Limerick	30.61 secs
1947	Baytown Pigeon	30.67 secs
1948	Jove's Reason	30.37 secs
1949	Blossom of Annagurra	30.20 secs

Winners of the Grand National 1970–84

1970	Sherry's Prince	30.02 secs
1971	Sherry's Prince	29.22 secs
1972	Sherry's Prince	29.80 secs
1973	Killone Flash	29.35 secs
1974	Shanney's Darkie	29.43 secs
* 1975	Pier Hero	30.40 secs
1976	Weston Pete	30.60 secs
1977	Salerno	30.43 secs
1978	Topothetide	30.23 secs
1979	Topothetide	31.60 secs
1980	Gilt Edge Flyer	30.22 secs
1981	Bobcol	30.64 secs
1982	Face the Mutt	30.71 secs
1983	Sir Winston	31.09 secs
1984	Kilcoe Foxy	30.32 secs

*Pre-1975 run over 500 yds; since run over 500 m

GRAND PRIX

This event, run at Walthamstow since its inauguration in 1946, usually early in October, is one of the most important events of the racing calendar. An event for forty-eight greyhounds, it began over the standard 525 yds course, which twenty years later was increased to 700 yds. In

1975 the event was first run over 640 m. In its early days the Grand Prix carried a first prize of £500, second only in value to the Derby, and when it was given classic status in 1971 this was increased to £2,000. Since the race has been sponsored by Courage's the winner's prize has been increased to £5,000, which after the Derby and St Leger is the highest in the sport.

The first event was won by Mrs Dent's good greyhound Tonycus, who defeated the great Dante II by three quarters of a length, and also another fine greyhound, Monday's News, who finished third. The following year Monday's News was on the top of his form, and in winning the event he beat the fastest dog in the world, Priceless Border, who went on to win the Derby in 1948.

Walthamstow dogs have dominated the event in recent years. In 1969 it was won by Mrs Berridge's Chame Sparrow, trained at the home track by Barney O'Connor. The following year a home dog was again successful when Baton, trained by J. Durkin, won. In 1977 the St Leger winner, Stormy Spirit, contested the event and in a thrilling finish was beaten into 2nd place by Paradise Spectre. In 1978 Paradise Spectre, whose sire, Spectre II, was also sire of Stormy Spirit, was again successful for Mr P. Roger and his trainer, Pat Mullins. The 1979 Grand Prix was equally exciting when Frame That, trained by Ted Dickson at Slough, defeated the Cesarewitch winner, Royston's Supreme, by one and a half lengths, with Brainy Prince a head behind, and in fourth place, less than a length away, Black Earl. Both the winner and Black Earl were sired by Rita's Choice, at one time kennelled at Walthamstow. Among the best long-distance performers of the year, both Grand Prix finalists also reached the final of the St Leger, which was won by Kilmagoura Mist who defeated Mrs Mark's Black Earl by a short head.

LAURELS

The name of this classic was suggested by Con Stevens, racing manager and then director at Wimbledon since the track opened in 1928 until he retired almost fifty years later. It was an original idea, for the other classics take their names from the horse racing classics – 'Laurels' was an excellent choice for laurel wreaths were used to adorn Roman heroes.

The race was first run over 500 yds, but in 1975 this was changed to 460 m. The Laurels follows the Scurry Gold Cup, the first of the season's classics and the shortest; the Laurels is next in distance, so that by the time the Derby final is run early in July the dogs have grown used to longer distances. Later come the St Leger and the Cesarewitch, over still greater distances.

The Laurels is unique in the number of times it has been won by a Derby winner and for the times it has been won by the same dog twice; also for the number of times the race has been won by home-kennelled greyhounds. During the first forty years greyhounds kennelled at Burhill were successful on fifteen occasions, but since then only Xmas Holiday has won the event. The first twelve races were dominated by greyhounds trained at Burhill by Sidney Orton. He trained the first winner, Kilbrean Boy, in 1930, and his last success was with Burhill Moon in 1945. His son Clare trained the 1967 winner, the great Carry On Oregon. In the eight years 1953–60, dogs trained at

Winners of the Grand Prix 1968–84

		Trainer	Track	
1968	Carmen John	J. Mills	(Private)	41.16 secs
1969	Chame Sparrow	B. O'Connor	Walthamstow	40.75 secs
1970	Baton	J. Durkin	Walthamstow	40.39 secs
† 1971	Breeches Buzzard	C. M'Nally	Perry Barr	40.00 secs
1972	not run			
1973	Pendy's Mermaid	D. Geggus	Walthamstow	40.65 secs
1974	Ballyglass Hope	D. Thornton	(Private)	40.58 secs
* 1975	not run			
1976	Mandalay King	G. de Mulder	Hall Green	40.21 secs
1977	Paradise Spectre	P. Mullins	(Private)	40.03 secs
1978	Paradise Spectre	P. Mullins	(Private)	40.19 secs
1979	Frame That	E. Dickson	Slough	39.57 secs
1980	Sport Promoter	J. Gibbons	Crayford	40.17 secs
1981	Rathduff Solara	A. Dennis	Southend	40.71 secs
1982	Hubert's Shade	A. Jackson	Wembley	38.73 secs
1983	Flying Duke	P. Coughlan	Walthamstow	40.49 secs
1984	Sunrise Sonny	G. Curtis	Brighton	40.00 secs

* 1975 onwards, run over 640 m; previously over 700 yds † Given classic status in 1971

Walthamstow by Tommy Reilly won on four occasions.

The first dog to win the event twice in succession was Mrs W.J. Cearns' Ballyhennessy Sandhills, in 1937 and 1938. Her dog was at that time the fastest in the world, and in July 1938 he set a national record for the 500 yds course which stood for many years. Until Pigalle Wonder nearly twenty years later no dog achieved a greater number of consistently fast times. In 1949 and 1950 the Derby winner Ballymac Ball, trained by Stan Martin, recorded two consecutive wins. His 1950 time of 28.19 secs was the fastest until the fabulous Endless Gossip clocked 27.96 secs two years later – the first dog to break 28 secs for the event.

The second Laurels, run in 1931, was won by the superb Future Cutlet. He was to lose the Derby by only a neck to Wild Woolley the following year, and was still at the height of his powers in 1933 when he defeated the Welsh dog Beef Cutlet by a short head to win the Derby with Wild Woolley in third place. Beef Cutlet won the third Laurels and in so doing set a new world record for the 500 yds course. The Laurels final was only his seventh race on a track and he was virtually unknown in London, but what a sensation he created.

Wild Woolley took the fourth Laurels for Belle Vue; then came Brilliant Bob and 'Doc' Callanan's winning bitch Kitshine, who cost her owner just 3½ gns at auction. She was the first of only two bitches ever to win this event – Pineapple Grand was the other, in 1975. It is said that Brilliant Bob ran so badly in his early heats, after coming over from Ireland with a great reputation, that Sidney Orton decided to leave him entirely alone apart from taking him for a gentle walk each day, as he thought the dog was fretting badly. His understanding of the dog, as of all the greyhounds he trained, paid handsome dividends, for Bob ran brilliantly to take the final in record time.

There were other dual Laurels winners besides Ballyhennessy Sandhills and Ballymac Ball. Mrs Chandler's Duet Leader won in 1955 and 1956, and Conna Count in 1964 and 1965. With the victory of Sole Aim by a short head from Always a Monarch in 1970, Mrs Chandler created a record by winning her fourth Laurels. In heat three of the 1970 Laurels Moordyke Spot clocked 27.57 secs to equal Shady Begonia's track record at Wimbledon. The first occasion on which 28.00 secs had been broken at the track was when in his semi-final Ballymac Ball clocked 27.99 secs; he went on to win the event by two lengths from Magna Hasty. The next year Endless Gossip clocked 27.96 secs when beating the previous year's winner, Ballylanigan Tanist, in the Laurels final, to set a new track record.

The 1970 Laurels was one of the best ever contested, for three greyhounds stood out from the other forty-eight. These were Sole Aim, Always a Monarch and The Other Green. Each won both his first and second round heat; Sole Aim and Always a Monarch also won their semi-finals, with The Other Green second in his. The final was won by Sole Aim, a short head in front of Always a Monarch, with The Other Green less than a length away in third place.

The following year Black Andrew won for his owner, Mr T. Smith, who received £5,000 presented by the first sponsors of the event, Williams & Sons Ltd, one of London's largest betting groups. This was the first time in the history of the Laurels that it had been won by a White City greyhound.

It is amazing how the fortunes of a particular trainer or a track come in cycles. The first twenty years was dominated by Wimbledon dogs trained by Sidney Orton and Stan Martin. In the next decade almost every Laurels was won by a Wembley trainer – Leslie Reynolds with Ballylanigan Tanist and Endless Gossip, followed by Jack Harvey with four wins in eight years. Among Jack Harvey's best dogs were Coolkill Chieftain and Clonalvy Pride, both of whom were to make enduring names as sires of champion greyhounds. Clonalvy Pride's time of 27.66 secs was never beaten over the 500 yds Laurels course. He was a son of Solar Prince and sire of Silver Hope, sire of the English Derby winner Mutt's Silver and also of Lively Band, who in turn sired 1977 English Derby winner Balliniska Band. Clonalvy Pride figures in the pedigree of many of the champions of the 1970s.

The greatest greyhounds have contested and won the Laurels, for besides those already mentioned the wonderful Shannon Shore won in 1946 and Rimmell's Black the following year, when handled by Stanley Biss; this was the only occasion on which a Clapton greyhound has won the event. Surprisingly, no Catford dog has ever won it. After Jack Harvey's several successes Wembley had two winners, including one of the greatest Laurels, that of 1969, when Jack Kinsley, one-time head kennel boy to 'Doc' Callanan at Wembley, took the trophy with Mr Joe Edwards' dog Ardine Flame, who won by a neck from the fast-finishing Beaverwood Wind, the favourite.

The only woman to train a Laurels winner was Nora Gleeson with Super Fame in 1966. Those great trainers Paddy Fortune, Paddy McEllistrim and Bob Burls never trained a Laurels winner. Since 1960 the Laurels has been won by a different greyhound and by a different trainer on each occasion, with one exception. Paddy McEvoy won in 1965, when Conna Count won for the second time, and the same trainer took Ambiguous to his Laurels success three years later (when Conna Count won in 1964 he was handled by Jerry Hannafin). All this shows how difficult it is to train a Laurels winner today.

In the 1979 Laurels final, of the six dogs competing five were by Monalee Champion or Monalee King, so that each had Sheila At Last as dam of his grandsire. Monalee Champion was from a mating of Sheila At Last with Crazy Parachute, and three dogs, including the winner, Another Spatter, were from Sheila's mating to Odd Venture, through Monalee King.

Winners of the Laurels

		Trap	Trainer	Track	
1930	Kilbrean Boy	2	S. Orton	Wimbledon	29.20 secs
1931	Future Cutlet	4	S. Probert	Wembley	28.52 secs
1932	Beef Cutlet	4	J. Hogarty	Cardiff	28.47 secs
1933	Wild Woolley	6	J. Campbell	Belle Vue	28.80 secs
1934	Brilliant Bob	6	S. Orton	Wimbledon	28.46 secs
1935	Kitshine	6	A. Callanan	Wembley	29.05 secs
1936	Top of Carlow Road	1	S. Orton	Wimbledon	28.38 secs
1937	Ballyhennessy Sandhills	4	S. Orton	Wimbledon	28.25 secs
1938	Ballyhennessy Sandhills	6	S. Orton	Wimbledon	28.50 secs
1939	Musical Duke	5	J. Crowley	Park Royal	28.42 secs
1940	April Burglar	3	K. Appleton	West Ham	28.56 secs
1941–4	not run				
1945	Burhill Moon	3	S. Orton	Wimbledon	28.42 secs
1946	Shannon Shore	2	L. Reynolds	Wembley	28.26 secs
1947	Rimmell's Black	3	S. Biss	Clapton	28.77 secs
1948	Good Worker	5	S. Daley	Ramsgate	28.49 secs
1949	Ballymac Ball	6	S. Martin	Wimbledon	28.61 secs
1950	Ballymac Ball	6	S. Martin	Wimbledon	28.19 secs
1951	Ballylanigan Tanist	2	L. Reynolds	Wembley	28.37 secs
1952	Endless Gossip	1	L. Reynolds	Wembley	27.96 secs
1953	Polonius	4	T. Reilly	Walthamstow	28.04 secs
1954	Coolkill Chieftain	5	H. Harvey	Wembley	28.05 secs
1955	Duet Leader	1	T. Reilly	Walthamstow	28.25 secs
1956	Duet Leader	1	T. Reilly	Walthamstow	28.13 secs
1957	Ford Spartan	5	J. Hannafin	Wimbledon	27.89 secs
1958	Granthamian	5	H. Harvey	Wembley	28.57 secs
1959	Mighty Hassan	1	H. Harvey	Wembley	28.01 secs
1960	Dunstown Paddy	4	T. Reilly	Walthamstow	28.02 secs
1961	Clonalvy Pride	5	H. Harvey	Wembley	27.66 secs
1962	Tuturama	1	H. Sanderson	(Private)	27.83 secs
1963	Dalcassion's Son	2	T. Hiscock	Belle Vue	28.08 secs
1964	Conna Count	3	J. Hannafin	Wimbledon	28.08 secs
1965	Conna Count	4	P. McEvoy	Wimbledon	28.13 secs
1966	Super Fame	5	Nora Gleeson	Wimbledon	28.05 secs
1967	Carry On Oregon	6	C. Orton	Wimbledon	27.89 secs
1968	Ambiguous	4	P. McEvoy	Wimbledon	28.10 secs
1969	Ardine Flame	2	J. Kinsley	Wembley	27.96 secs
1970	Sole Aim	1	D. Geggus	Walthamstow	28.04 secs
1971	Black Andrew	2	R. Singleton	White City	27.96 secs
1972	Cricket Bunny	4	J. Booth	(Private)	28.11 secs
1973	Black Banjo	4	J.B. O'Connor	Walthamstow	27.93 secs
1974	Over Protected	4	J. Coleman	Wembley	28.00 secs
*1975	Pineapple Grand	1	T. Baldwin	Perry Barr	27.77 secs
1976	Xmas Holiday	3	P. Rees	Wimbledon	27.66 secs
1977	Greenfield Fox	5	T. Dickson	Slough	27.26 secs
1978	Jet Control	2	T. Gaylor	Perry Barr	27.45 secs
1979	Another Splatter	2	J. Pickering	White City	27.75 secs
1980	Flying Pursuit	4	J. Gibbons	Crayford	27.89 secs

1981	Echo Spark	6	J. Cobbold	Ipswich	27.84 secs
1982	Laurie's Panther	4	T. Duggan	Romford	27.79 secs
1983	Darkie Fli	5	F. Stevens	Cambridge	27.87 secs
1984	Amenhotep	6	L. Mullins	Crayford	27.82 secs

*Since 1975 run over 460 m; previously over 525 yds

OAKS

This race is confined to bitches and has been contested since 1927, so that with the Derby it is the oldest classic. Until 1958 it was run at White City, since when it has been transferred to Harringay.

The first Oaks, run over 500 yds, was won by Three of Spades, trained at Harringay by Sid Jennings. Seven years later Harry Buck, also of Harringay, won the Oaks with Gallant Ruth, daughter of Mick the Miller. Since that date no Harringay trainer has won the event. In 1930 Paddy McEllistrim won with Mutton Cutlet's outstanding daughter, Faithful Kitty. Indeed, she was her sire's finest daughter, coupled with Queen of the Suir, Beef Cutlet's litter sister. Fifty years later Queen of the Suir is still the only bitch ever to win the Irish and English Oaks, which she did in the same year, 1932. She won the English Oaks the following year together with that other important event for bitches the Coronation Cup which she won again in 1934. She was then five and for three years had dominated bitches' events. Her record has never been surpassed.

Gallant Ruth won in 1934 when two years old, and was one of the first of Mick's offspring to race and possibly his best. The following year, Kitshine, purchased for 3½ gns at Aldridge's saleroom, won the Oaks. She was by Mick's litter brother Macoma, and was virtually unbeatable that year for she also went undefeated through the Laurels. She was trained by 'Doc' Callanan at Wembley.

Brave Queen won the Oaks for Stanley Biss in 1937 and the following year the event was won by the great Quarter Day, a black bitch owned by Mr George Flintham and trained by Joe Harmon. The Oaks was not run during the war years. In 1945 it was won by Prancing Kitty, Tanist's finest daughter, who in the same year also won the Coronation Cup, as had Queen of the Suir and Quarter Day before her. She was trained by Paddy Fortune who was also to train the lovely Lizette, winner of the Oaks in 1953 and again in 1955 when nearly five years old. She weighed only

Lizette, English Greyhound Oaks winner in 1953 and 1955. Photo: GRA.

48 lbs and was one of the most courageous bitches ever to race.

After Prancing Kitty's success, Stanley Biss was to win the event in the next three years with three of the best bitches of all time: Dumbles Maid, who won in 1946; Rio Cepretta in 1947; and Night Breeze in 1948. Coyne's Castle and Simone, also in the 1946 final, were two of the best bitches ever to race. Dumble's Maid was also outstanding, and was beaten only a short head by Bohernagrag Boy in that year's St Leger. Rio Cepretta was another wonderful bitch, English-bred, and in the Oaks she was up against the equally brilliant Izadaisy whom she beat in her heat. After both had won their semi-finals, she again beat Izadaisy by a head to win the 1947 final.

The 1949 Oaks was won by the black bitch Still Drifting, trained at Wembley by Sidney Probert. She was one of the few good offspring of her sire, Shannon Shore, one of the best middle-distance dogs ever to race, but like Mick the Miller and Future Cutlet before him he had possibly been raced too much to become a potent sire. The 1952 event resulted in a dead heat, only the second occasion that a classic event had ended in this manner.

For the next ten years, beginning with Ballinasloe Mona in 1951, Jack Harvey dominated the Oaks. He trained Lizette when she won for the second time in 1955, and he won again the next year with First But Last. This win gave Noel Purvis the unique distinction of owning both an English Derby winner, Mile Bush Pride, and a winner of the Oaks – the two major classics.

Antartica, trained by Jimmy Jowett at Clapton, won the 1958 event, the last to be held at White City, and Gurteen Scamp won the first Oaks run at Harringay. 1960 saw Stan Martin win his first and only Oaks with Wheatfield Countess, and over the next four years the event was dominated by two outstanding bitches, Ballinasloe Blondie, trained by Jack Harvey, who won in 1961 and 1962, and the great Cranog Bet, trained by Phil Rees who won the next two years. Cranog Bet, owned by Mr and Mrs Gee, was one of the greatest bitches ever to race. She was equally successful as a dam of champions, for from a mating with Prairie Flash she was to whelp the bitch Itsamint, who was to win the Irish Oaks. In turn she was dam of Itsastar from a mating with Yanka Boy. Mated to Monalee Champion, Itsastar whelped the black bitch Nameless Pixie, who ran third in the Irish Derby of 1979; mated to Rita's Choice, Itsastar gave birth to Nameless Star, winner of the 1976 Irish Laurels and St Leger. From a later mating with Monalee Champion, Cranog Bet whelped Itsachampion, winner of the 1972 Irish Cesarewitch, and who in turn was to sire Lacca Champion, winner of the 1978 English Derby. Cranog Bet was by Knockhill Chieftain out of the Glittering Look bitch Don't Bet. Her wonderful running and prowess as the dam of champions made her possibly the greatest bitch in the history of the sport.

Phil Rees was to win the Oaks again in 1968 with another fine bitch, Shady Parachute, owned by Mr H. Knight, and who reached the final of the 1967 and 1968 Derby. She was 6–4 favourite for the 1968 Derby and expected to do the double that year by winning the Oaks, but in the Derby she finished fourth, as she had done the previous year. But she won the International and the Playfield Cup at Wimbledon, and was elected best bitch of the year, which she undoubtedly was. When winning her Oaks final she clocked 28.89 secs, beating the 29.03 secs track record set up by Pigalle Wonder, and was the first greyhound to beat 29 secs at Harringay.

Two years later Perth Pat became the first Oaks winner to be trained and owned by the same person, Mr J. Morgan. This occurred again in 1972, for Decimal Queen was both owned and trained by Mr F.G. Hawkins. She won in the fastest time ever recorded over the 525 yds course.

In 1978 another outstanding bitch won the Oaks, now run over 475 m. This was Kilmagourna Mist, owned by Mr J. Lovett and trained by Wembley's maestro, Tommy Johnston. She was to win the St Leger in 1979. She was by Yanka Boy out of Kilmagoura Fair, whose dam, More Wonder, was by the great Pigalle Wonder out of the bitch Survival, by The Grand Fire, so Kilmagourna Mist was bred in 'the purple'.

The Oaks has been dominated by just two or three trainers – Stanley Biss in the early days, then Jack Harvey, and more recently Phil Rees. They were the recognized masters in looking after bitches. Neither Leslie Reynolds nor Bob Burles nor Sidney Orton ever trained an Oaks winner; Stan Martin only one. The only woman to train an Oaks winner is Mrs J. Thistleton, who trained the 1967 winner, Solerina. Only two people have won the Oaks with two different bitches. Mr W.P. Tabbush won in 1951 with Ballinasloe Mona, and in 1961 and 1962 with Ballinasloe Blondie. He is also the only person to have won the Oaks three times. Mr Cyril Scotland won in 1973 and 1974 with Miss Ross and Lady Devine.

SCOTTISH DERBY

Inaugurated in 1928, it is one of the oldest races in the calendar though it was not given classic status until 1950. It was, however, one of the races all English Derby winners' owners have been keen to win, for with the Welsh Derby it comprises the triple crown, won by only three dogs – Trev's Perfection Mile Bush Pride and Patricia's Hope.

Winners of the Oaks

		Trainer	*Track*	
1927	Three of Spades	S. Jennings	Harringay	29.96 secs
1928	Moselle	J. Quinn	(Private)	30.50 secs
1929	Bewitching Eve	A. Whitcher	Clapton	30.33 secs
1930	Faithful Kitty	S. Biss	West Ham	30.02 secs
1931	Drizzle	H. Woolner	White City	30.00 secs
1932	Queen of the Suir	S. Biss	West Ham	30.89 secs
1933	Queen of the Suir	S. Biss	West Ham	30.23 secs
1934	Gallant Ruth	H. Buck	Harringay	30.22 secs
1935	Kitshine	A. Callanan	Wembley	30.12 secs
1936	Ganial Radiance	A. Hiscock	Belle Vue	29.86 secs
1937	Brave Queen	S. Biss	West Ham	29.62 secs
1938	Quarter Day	J. Harmon	Wimbledon	29.49 secs
1939–44	not run			
1945	Prancing Kitty	P. Fortune	Wimbledon	29.54 secs
1946	Dumbles Maid	S. Biss	Clapton	29.42 secs
1947	Rio Cepretta	S. Biss	Clapton	29.32 secs
1948	Night Breeze	S. Biss	Clapton	29.19 secs
1949	Still Drifting	S. Probert	Wembley	29.48 secs
1950	Caledonian Faith	A. Montfield	(Private)	29.62 secs
1951	Ballinasloe Mona	H. Harvey	Wembley	29.28 secs
1952	Flo's Pet)	P. Fortune	Wimbledon	29.60 secs
	Monachdy Girlie)	J. Jowett	Clapton	
1953	Lizette	P. Fortune	Wimbledon	29.18 secs
1954	Ashcott Winsome	H. Heyes	White City	29.39 secs
1955	Lizette	H. Harvey	Wembley	29.52 secs
1956	First But Last	H. Harvey	Wembley	29.08 secs
1957	Dark Rose	W. Brown	(Private)	29.02 secs
1958	Antartica	J. Jowett	Clapton	29.12 secs
1959	Gurteen Scamp	G. Waterman	Wimbledon	29.90 secs
1960	Wheatfield Countess	S. Martin	Wimbledon	29.33 secs
1961	Ballinalsoe Blondie	H. Harvey	Wembley	29.58 secs
1962	Ballinasloe Blondie	H. Harvey	Wembley	29.68 secs
1963	Cranog Bet	P. Rees	(Private)	29.31 secs
1964	Cranog Bet	P. Rees	(Private)	29.03 secs
1965	Marjone	P. O'Toole	Ireland	29.37 secs
1966	Merry Emblem	M. Bruton	Ireland	29.58 secs
1967	Solerina	M. Thisleton	Catford	29.50 secs
1968	Shady Parachute	P. Rees	Wimbledon	29.38 secs
1969	Shady Bracelet	P. Collett	(Private)	28.63 secs
1970	Perth Pat	J. Morgan	(Private)	28.81 secs
1971	Short Cake	D. Geggus	Walthamstow	28.98 secs
1972	Decimal Queen	F. Hawkins	(Private)	28.60 secs
1973	Miss Ross	T. Johnston	Wembley	28.63 secs
1974	Lady Devine	S. Ryall	Wembley	28.76 secs
1975	Pineapple Grand	F. Baldwin	Perry Barr	28.85 secs
1976	Balinderry Moth	B. O'Connor	Walthamstow	28.60 secs
1977	Switch Off	J. Singleton	Harringay	28.69 secs
1978	Kilmagoura Mist	T. Johnston	Wembley	28.55 secs
1979	Sunny Interval	P. Rees Jnr	Wimbledon	28.77 secs
1980	Devilish Dolores	J. Cobbold	(Private)	28.72 secs
1981	Thanet Princess	D. Hawkes	Walthamstow	28.82 secs
1982	Duchess of Avon	A. Jackson	Wembley	28.72 secs
1983	Major Grove	E. Pateman	Wimbledon	28.59 secs
1984	Sandy Sally	H.J. Coker	Milton Keynes	28.69 secs

The first race run over 500 yds at White City; 1928–48 run there over 525 yds; 1949–79 run at Harringay, until 1975 over 525 yds, thereafter over 475 m

Until the closure of the track in 1972 the event was always run at Carntyne in Glasgow, the finest running surface in Scotland. The track, of 450 yds circumference, had long straights and banked turns and fast times were usually done, while there was little bumping. The Scottish Derby always attracted the best greyhounds in Britain. The first event, run in 1928, was won by Glingerbank who covered the 525 yds course in 30.39 secs. His sire was the illustrious Jamie, sire also of Mutton Cutlet. In 1934 and 1935 Olive's Best won, the only time the event has been won two years in succession, though Ballycurreen Soldier won in 1940 and 1942 and contested the 1941 final.

In 1937 an outstanding greyhound, Jesmond Cutlet, won the event. His sire was the fabulous Beef Cutlet, his dam the Macoma bitch Lady Eleanor, one of the greatest dams in the history of track racing. Jesmond Cutlet followed his success by taking the prestigious Edinburgh Cup at Powderhall. The following year, when four years old, he won the Cesarewitch, and at Hall Green defeated Grosvenor Edwin over 700 yds, the first dog to do so for more than two years. Beef Cutlet was to sire another outstanding greyhound which won the Scottish Derby six years later – Bilting Hawk, a bitch, and only the second of her sex to win the event.

In 1938 Mrs. Adams' Roeside Scottie won the event. He was one of Creamery Border's first sons out of the bitch Deemster's Olive, by Deemster out of Sister Olive. A litter brother of Deemster's Olive was Olive's Best, owned by Mrs A.W. Berkeley, who had won in 1933 and 1934. Creamery Border was to sire another winner three years later – George Flintham's famous Lights o' London, the first black dog in fourteen years to win the event. Lights o' London's dam, Life of Luxury, was by the coursing sire Danielli, and the dog was bred by Mr L. Lucas, a great coursing enthusiast. Misty Law, who won in 1939, was by another great coursing sire, Dee Rock, a Waterloo Cup winner.

The Scottish Derby was run all through the war years and 1945 saw the event won by Mr Wright's Monday's Son. His time of 29.19 secs was by far the fastest for the event. This outstanding dog, from the first mating of the Scurry Cup winner Orluck's Best to Monday Next, has been overshadowed by his brother from a later mating, the incomparable Monday's News, but Monday's Son won not only the Scottish Derby but also the St Mungo Cup, also run at Carntyne, and the Spring Cup at Shawfield, besides finishing third in both the Scurry Cup and Gold Collar.

In 1946 the event went to Latin Pearl, a fawn dog owned by Shawfield Stadium and whose sire was Melksham Nobody, who also sired the 1944 Irish Derby winner Clonbonny Bridge. He won his heat and semi-final, beating Magic Bohemian both times, and he beat this dog again by two lengths to win the final. Monday's Son also reached the final for the second year. A few days later Latin Pearl set a new track record for the 530 yds course at the Darnall track in Sheffield, and that year was one of the best dogs in training. The following year the great Trev's Perfection won the event, winning every round, just as he had in the English Derby. Interestingly, in the final he defeated the same dogs that he had beaten at the White City, thus confirming his superiority over all his rivals.

The 1948 Scottish Derby was expected to go to that outstanding bitch Sheevaun, owned and trained in Scotland, but instead it was won by Western Post, a handsome fawn and white dog by Lucky Post, by Castledown Lad, whelped in April 1945. He won by one and a half lengths from Always There, with West End Dasher half a length behind, to win £500 for his owner–trainer Mr Fred Davis, who had been a private trainer for less than twelve months. Western Post went across to Dublin to beat the best dogs in Ireland when he won the Irish Derby at Shelbourne Park, beating Baytown Colonel into second place and becoming only the second dog to break 30 secs in the event. No other greyhound has ever won the Irish Greyhound Derby and that of another country in the same year.

In 1959 the great Mile Bush Pride won the event. Like Trev's Perfection he also won each round of the triple crown, but it was Royston Genius the following year who became the first to beat 29 secs with a time of 28.92 secs, which remained unbeaten until Dusty Trail set a new Derby final time and a new track record with a time of 28.54 secs, which was never bettered at Carntyne. In 1968 the Leeds dog Lisamote Precept won when trained by Joe Kelly, who became the first trainer to handle two consecutive winners when Brilane Clipper won in 1969.

When Carntyne closed in 1972 the Scottish Derby transferred to Shawfield, owned by the GRA and the only Glasgow track still open. In 1977 the event was won by the Halifax dog Amber Sky, trained by Peter Beaumont, now at Leeds, who defeated Skilful Boy by one and a half lengths. That year the race was run over 480 m. It is now run over 500 m and in 1978 was won by the outstanding Pat Seamur, trained by Geoff de Mulder and owned by Mrs H. Tasker, whose husband was later to become the dog's handler. Pat Seamur defeated Rum Atease, trained by Bertie Gaynor.

One of the finest dogs to win in recent years was On Spec, owned by Mr R. Raper and trained at Owlerton by Harry Crapper. The dog had been narrowly beaten in the English Derby by I'm Slippy a few weeks before.

Winners of the Scottish Derby

1928	Glingerbank	30.39 secs
1929	Cleveralitz	30.87 secs
1930	Captured Half	30.30 secs
1931	Sister Olive	30.65 secs
1932	Laverock	30.10 secs
1933	S.L.D.	30.30 secs
1934	Olive's Best	29.90 secs
1935	Olive's Best	30.16 secs
1936	Diamond Glory	29.99 secs
1937	Jesmond Cutlet	29.83 secs
1938	Roeside Scottie	29.53 secs
1939	Misty Law	29.60 secs
1940	Ballycurreen Soldier	29.40 secs
1941	Lights o'London	29.75 secs
1942	Ballycurreen Soldier	29.94 secs
1943	Bilting Hawk	29.25 secs
1944	Gladstone Brigadier	29.55 secs
1945	Monday's Son	29.19 secs
1946	Latin Pearl	29.53 secs
1947	Trev's Perfection	29.25 secs
1948	Western Post	29.45 secs
1949	not run	
1950	Behatten's Choice	29.28 secs
1951	Rushton Smutty	29.08 secs
1952	not run	
1953	not run	
1954	Rushton Mac	29.20 secs
1955	not run	
1956	Quick Surprise	29.50 secs
1957	Ballypatrick	29.53 secs
1958	Just Fame	29.36 secs
1959	Mile Bush Pride	29.41 secs
1960	Royston Genius	28.92 secs
1961	Hi There Merry	29.11 secs
1962	Dromin Glory	29.09 secs
1963	We'll See	29.19 secs
1964	Hi Imperial	29.24 secs
1965	Clonmannon Flash	29.00 secs
1966	Dusty Trail	28.54 secs
1967	Hi Ho Silver	28.90 secs
1968	Lisamote Precept	28.93 secs
1969	Brilane Clipper	29.00 secs
1970	Brilane Clipper	29.06 secs
1971	not run	
1972	Patricia's Hope	29.22 secs
1973	Dashalong Chief	29.60 secs
1974	Cosha Orchis	29.26 secs
*1975	Drumlara Master	29.30 secs
1976	Flip your Top	30.56 secs
*1977	Amber Sky	29.08 secs
1978	Pat Seamur	30.52 secs
1979	Greenville Boy	30.49 secs
1980	Decoy Sovereign	30.68 secs
1981	Marbella Sky	30.66 secs
1982	Special Account	29.99 secs
1983	On Spec	30.50 secs

*Run over 480 m; pre-1975 run over 525 yds; 1976 and 1978 onwards run over 500 m

SCURRY GOLD CUP

The event was inaugurated and given classic status in 1928, shortly after Clapton Stadium was opened, and took place there every year until the track closed in 1974. The event, now worth £7,000 to the winner, was transferred to Slough where it has since been run over 442 m (at Clapton it was over 400 yds). This is the sprinters' classic, for the race is over in little more than 20 secs and to win it a greyhound must come out of the trap like a bullet for there is no second chance to make up lost ground.

The Scurry has been won only once by a Derby winner, Mr Alf Heale's Palm's Printer in 1961, whose time of 22.63 secs was one of the fastest recorded over 400 yds. Few other greyhounds that have won any of the other classics have also won the Scurry Cup. Only one Gold Collar winner, Local Interprize, also won the Scurry Cup; and two Scurry winners, Brilliant Bob and Rimmell's Black, also won the Laurels. The event has been won by a bitch on only three occasions – Monachdy Girlie in 1952, Lucky Joan in 1963, and Foyle Tonic in 1968. Two greyhounds, Gorey Airways and Don't Gambol, have won the event twice, though Local Interprize came close to doing so when he won in 1948 and ran up in 1949, and Creamery Border won the 1933 event and ran up to Brilliant Bob in 1934 and Jack's Joke the next year. Creamery Border was the only dog to contest three finals until Yankee Express in 1982/3/4, winning each time. Paddy McEllistrim trained the first winner and won again with Country Life. The Famous trainers Sydney Orton, Leslie Reynolds and Jack

Harvey each won the event only once, and Bob Burls was never successful. It was not until Mr Charles Weston's Casa Miel won in 1973 that a White City dog won the event.

Romance surrounds the 1980 winner, Willing Slave, trained by Ted Dickson and owned by Mr S. Bowey, for it is believed that only a very small sum was paid for the son of Nameless Star to perform in graded races at Slough. Under the Slough maestro's care, however, the dog won his heat and semi-final and throughout the event was never led in any race. He started at 20–1 and put up the second-fastest time of the eight heats.

ST LEGER

The stayers' classic is run at Wembley in September, now over 655 m but until 1975 over 700 yds. Since 1978 it has been sponsored by Ladbroke's, who provide £10,000 in prize money for the winner, £2,000 for the runner-up, and £1,000 for third place, making it the second richest event in the racing calendar. On the final night Wembley puts on a twelve-race

Winners of the Scurry Gold Cup

		Trainer		
1928	Cruiseline Boy	P. McEllistrim	Wimbledon	24.91 secs
1929	Loose Card	J. Madden	White City, Manchester	24.13 secs
1930	Barlock	J. Kennedy	Harringay	24.19 secs
1931	Brave Enough	H. Buck	Harringay	23.62 secs
1932	Expert's Boast	S. Jennings	Wembley	23.61 secs
1933	Creamery Border	A. Callanan	Wembley	23.31 secs
1934	Brilliant Bob	S. Orton	Wimbledon	23.47 secs
1935	Jack's Joke	H. Champion	Catford	23.15 secs
1936	Mitzvah	A. Callanan	Wembley	23.29 secs
1937	Hexham Bridge	T. Cowell	Southend	23.37 secs
1938	Orluck's Best	T. Ashley	Harringay	23.24 secs
1939	Silver Wire	T. Green	Derby	23.53 secs
1940–4	not run			
1945	Country Life	P. McEllistrim	Wimbledon	23.50 secs
1946	Mischievous Manhattan	P. Fortune	Wimbledon	23.40 secs
1947	Rimmell's Black	S. Biss	Clapton	23.11 secs
1948	Local Interprize	S. Biss	Clapton	23.04 secs
1949	Burndennet Brook	L. Reynolds	Wembley	23.48 secs
1950	Gortnagory	H. Merchant	(Private)	23.47 secs
1951	Defence Leader	J. Mills	(Private)	22.99 secs
1952	Monachdy Girlie	J. Jowett	Clapton	23.08 secs
1953	Rolling Mike	J. Jowett	Clapton	22.77 secs
1954	Demon King	H. Harvey	Wembley	22.84 secs
1955	Chance me Paddy	J. Linney	Catford	22.85 secs
1956	Belingas Customer	T. Melville	Wembley	22.82 secs
1957	Lisbrook Chieftain	M. Holland	(Private)	23.09 secs
1958	Beware Champ	S. Waterman	Wimbledon	22.71 secs
1959	Gorey Airways	J. Jowett	Clapton	22.95 secs
1960	Gorey Airways	J. Jowett	Clapton	22.48 secs
1961	Palm's Printer	T. Doyle	Clapton	22.63 secs
1962	Hi Darkie	H. Wilkes	(Private)	22.95 secs
1963	Lucky Joan	J. Bassett	Clapton	22.70 secs
1964	Salthill Sand	J. Bassett	Clapton	22.72 secs
1965	After You	J. Bassett	Clapton	22.47 secs
1966	Geddy's Blaze	T. Gudgin	Clapton	22.79 secs
1967	Carry On Oregon	C. Orton	Wimbledon	22.62 secs
1968	Foyle Tonic	P. Keane	Clapton	22.59 secs
1969	Ace of Trumps	J. Coleman	Romford	22.85 secs
1970	Don't Gambol	P. McEvoy	Wimbledon	22.48 secs
1971	Don't Gambol	P. McEvoy	Wimbledon	22.29 secs
1972	Cricket Bunny	P. McEvoy	Wimbledon	22.31 secs
1973	Casa Miel	J. Pickering	White City	22.83 secs
1974	Westmead Valley	N. Savva	(Private)	26.24 secs
*1975	Longnor Lad	B. Parsons	Hall Green	26.77 secs
1976	Xmas Holiday	P. Rees	Wimbledon	26.67 secs
1977	Wired to Moon	T. Atkins	(Private)	26.63 secs
1978	Greenfield Fox	E. Dickson	Slough	27.00 secs
1979	Northway Point	G. Morrow	(Private)	27.20 secs
1980	Willing Slave	E. Dickson	Slough	27.11 secs
1981	Longcross Smokey	P. Rees Jnr	Wimbledon	27.17 secs
1982	Yankee Express	G. Curtis	Brighton	27.19 secs
1983	Yankee Express	G. Curtis	Brighton	26.84 secs
1984	Yankee Express	G. Curtis	Brighton	27.00 secs

* Since 1975 run at Slough over 442 m; previously run at Clapton over 400 yds

programme and it is the second most popular event at the Stadium, after the FA Cup Final.

The first to win the event, inaugurated in 1928, was the bitch Burletta, the forerunner of a number of great bitches to win the classic. Afterwards she was to become one of the sport's most famous dams. After her Leger triumph she was mated with the 1928 Waterloo Cup winner White Collar, and the result was a litter that included Genial Nobleman, the 1933 Waterloo Cup winner, and the bitch White Crocus, who, when mated to Lord Rosebery's Danielli, whelped Hand Grenade, winner of the Waterloo Cup in 1936. Burletta's next mating was to Mr Rowland Rank's Red Robin, and in her litter was Rum Ration, sire of the 1939 English Derby winner, Highland Rum. As if this was not enough, from a second mating to Red Robin she produced the great Rotten Row, who won the Waterloo Cup for Mr Rank in 1937 and ran up the following year. Burletta was trained by Alf Mulliner, one of the early Wembley trainers. The last Wembley-kennelled dog to win was Crefogue Dancer, trained by Bob Burls, in 1969. During the 1970s no Wembley trainer put out a winner of the 'home' event until 1979, and during this time no trainer has won the race twice. In 1979 the sport was dominated by great bitches for the first time since Dolores Rocket won both the Derby and the St Leger. Kilmagoura Mist, trained by Tommy Johnston, won the St Leger by a short head from Black Earl. Many of the greatest long-distance bitches have won the event. In 1938 the St Leger was won for the first time by an offspring of a former winner, when the bitch Greta's Rosary came in first. Her sire was Mick the Miller, who won in 1931.

The most successful St Leger-winning trainers are Jack Harvey (Lively Rio, 1949; Pancho Villa, 1964; Title Role, 1965; Barry's Prince, 1958; and Clonalvy Pride, 1961) and Bob Burls (Dante II, 1947; Funny Worker, 1952; O'Hara's Rebel, 1967; and Crefogue Dancer, 1969). Only four other trainers won the event more than once – Reynolds with three and Toseland (Perry Barr), Wright (Harringay), Parry (White City) and McEllistrim (Wimbledon) with two each. Surprisingly, Leslie Reynolds' three wins in five years came when he was at the White City, before he moved to Wembley – he never won it while at the home track. Reynolds first won the St Leger in 1932 with the dog Fret Not which he trained for one of his patrons during his short stay at Belle Vue and before he moved to the White City. Fret Not was owned by Mr Harry Farrand, and by the time the dog arrived in London was more than four years old. He was to win his first ten races in London and went on to win the Welsh Marathon as well as the St Leger and earned for his owner more than £2,000 in 1932. Harry Farrand's daughter was owner of the outstanding blue dog Douro, one of the greatest hurdlers of all time, whose national record over 500 yds, set up in 1928, remained unbeaten for a decade.

Stanley Biss never won the St Leger, though he won every other classic, and Sidney Orton only won it once – with Mick the Miller in 1931. Mick was the oldest dog to win the event, at five, while Dante II won at the shortest odds, 5–1 on. No greyhound has won the St Leger twice and no dog has won both the English and Irish event, though Rhu came close to doing so, winning the Irish Leger in 1978 and being runner-up to Westmead Power at Wembley that year.

Only three greyhounds have won the Derby and the St Leger. Mick the Miller won the Derby in 1929 and 1930 and the Leger in 1931, two years after his first Derby win; Tartan Khan won both events in 1975; and Dolores Rocket achieved the double in 1971. Only these last two won the two major classics in the same year. In the final, Tartan Khan set a new world, Wembley and St Leger record with a time of 39.45 secs for 655 m. O'Hara's Rebel did the fastest time over the old 700 yds course with 39.54 secs, beating the 39.64 secs set up by Clonalvy Pride in 1961. After Mick the Miller the next most popular winner was Spotted Rory, in 1970, for it was forty-one years since his trainer, Paddy McEllistrim, had trained his first classic winner, Loughnagare, to win the second St Leger in 1929.

The 1978 St Leger was the first sponsored by Ladbroke's and the winning owner, Mrs Mabel Woodward, collected a cheque for £10,000. Her brindle dog, Westmead Power, was by Westmead County out of the Newdown Heather bitch Westmead Damson, and was bred, reared and trained by Nick and Natalie Savva, whose stud dog Westmead County (by Clonalvy Pride) has produced two St Leger winners and two seconds in the 1976, 1977 and 1978 finals. The even money favourite won by two lengths from the Irish St Leger winner, Rhu, in 39.67 secs. Westmead Power is a direct descendant of Castledown Lad through his greatest son Bella's Prince, sire of Champion Prince, sire of Solar Prince, sire of Clonalvy Pride, sire of Westmead County, each of them outstanding at stud and on the track.

The record over the distance is held by Tartan Khan, who won the Leger in 1975.

An interesting little story about the St Leger, not generally known to followers of the sport, concerns the great Ataxy's win in 1936. Arthur Elvin had to borrow a small silver cup – which had already been presented that evening to another winner – for just before the final was due to be run the magnificent gold St Leger trophy was discovered to be missing from its glass case where it was kept under lock and key. Neither the trophy nor the thief was ever found, and the trophy had to be replaced.

Winners of the St Leger

		Trap	*Trainer*		
1928	Burletta	3	A. Mulliner	Wembley	41.91 secs
1929	Loughnagare	2	P. McEllistrim	Wimbledon	42.76 secs
1930	Maiden's Boy	1	A. Young	(Private)	41.48 secs
*1931	Mick the Miller	3	S. Orton	Wimbledon	41.31 secs
1932	Fret Not	2	L. Reynolds	White City	41.35 secs
1933	The Daw	1	S. Probert	Wembley	41.24 secs
1934	Bosham	1	L. Reynolds	White City	41.17 secs
1935	Satan's Baby	3	L. Perry	White City	40.95 secs
1936	Ataxy	4	L. Reynolds	White City	40.39 secs
1937	Grosvenor Bob	4	J. Syder	Wembley	41.13 secs
1938	Greta's Rosary	4	T. Wright	Harringay	40.82 secs
1939	Gayhunter	2	T. Wright	Harringay	41.79 secs
1940–4	not run				
1945	Robeen Printer	6	G. McKay	Coventry	40.03 secs
1946	Bohernagraga Boy	4	J. Syder	Wembley	39.92 secs
1947	Dante II	3	R. Burls	Wembley	39.70 secs
1948	Streets After Midnight	3	J. Parry	White City	40.40 secs
1949	Lovely Rio	2	H. Harvey	Wembley	40.77 secs
1950	Fawn Mack	6	G. Curtis	Park Royal	40.56 secs
1951	Black Mire	3	E. Toseland	Perry Barr	40.19 secs
1952	Funny Worker	6	R. Burls	Wembley	40.50 secs
1953	Magourna Reject	4	T. Reilly	Walthamstow	39.88 secs
1954	Pancho Villa	1	H. Harvey	Wembley	40.99 secs
1955	Title Role	6	H. Harvey	Wembley	40.78 secs
1956	Jakfigaralt	1	J. Myles	Coventry	39.97 secs
1957	Duke of Alva	6	T. Booth	(Private)	40.50 secs
1958	Barry's Prince	4	H. Harvey	Wembley	40.01 secs
1959	Wincott Clifford	1	E. Toseland	Perry Barr	40.25 secs
1960	Jungle Man	4	H. Tasker	(Private)	40.08 secs
1961	Clonalvy Pride	1	H. Harvey	Wembley	39.64 secs
1962	Powerstown Prospect	3	T. Melville	Wembley	40.02 secs
1963	Friendly Lass	6	E. Dennis	(Private)	40.15 secs
1964	Lucky Hi There	4	J. Jowett	Clapton	39.90 secs
1965	Greenane Flash	6	W. Quinn	Perry Barr	40.13 secs
1966	Summer Guest	1	T. France	Harringay	40.03 secs
1967	O'Hara's Rebel	3	R. Burls	Wembley	39.54 secs
1968	Forward King	1	E. Brennan	Owlerton	39.98 secs
1969	Crefogue Dancer	1	R. Burls	Wembley	39.65 secs
1970	Spotted Rory	2	P. McEllistrim	Wimbledon	40.28 secs
*1971	Dolores Rocket	1	H.G. White	(Private)	40.03 secs
1972	Ramdeen Stuart	1	N. Oliver	Brough Park	39.82 secs
1973	Case Money	2	C. Parker	Harringay	39.89 secs
1974	Cute Caddie	2	D. Kinchett	White City	41.17 secs
*+1975	Tartan Khan	3	Mrs G. Lynds	Bletchley	39.45 secs
1976	Westmead Champ	2	P. Heasman	Hackney	39.90 secs
1977	Stormy Spirit	1	J. Pickering	White City	40.22 secs
1978	Westmead Power	2	Mrs N. Savva	Coventry	39.67 secs
1979	Kilmagoura Mist	1	T. Johnston	Wembley	40.04 secs
1980	Fair Reward	2	R. Young	(Private)	40.46 secs
1981	Fox Watch	4	Mrs Jill Holt	(Private)	40.17 secs
1982	Hubert's Shade	5	A. Jackson	Wembley	39.83 secs
1983	Easy and Slow	3	A. Jackson	Wembley	40.37 secs
1984	Gizzajob	4	J. Coleman	Romford	40.28 secs

* Also won the English Derby; + Since 1975 run over 655 m; previously over 700 yds

Opposite: Mrs Frances Chandler with Magourna Reject, 1953 Cesarewitch and St Leger winner. Photo: Pictorial Press Ltd, reproduced by permission of Walthamstow Stadium.

WELSH DERBY

It was not until 1971 that this event was afforded full classic status but since its inception every greyhound that has won or reached the final of the English event has also taken part in the Welsh one, for it has always been every owner's ambition for his dog to win the triple crown. No greyhound has ever won the Irish and English Derby, but three have won the triple crown at home. These were Trev's Perfection in 1947, Mile Bush Pride in 1959, and Patricia's Hope in 1972. Mick the Miller won the English and Welsh Derbys and so did Endless Gossip, Ballylanigan Tanist and Rushton Mac, but the Scottish event eluded them.

The Welsh Derby was first run at White City, Cardiff, in 1928 and was won by Mr J.J. Cronin's dog Cheerful Choice. Mick the Miller added the title to his English Derby success in 1930, and three years later the great Beef Cutlet took the title, his time of 29.56 secs being only .01 sec slower than Mick's incredibly fast time.

During the war years the White City track was closed and the Welsh Derby was not run. In 1945 its venue was Arms Park where Shaggy Lass, one of the greatest bitches of all time, won in 29.75 secs. The following year Negro's Lad won the event and set a new track record of 29.54 secs. Then in 1947 came Trev's Perfection, straight from his successes in the English and Scottish Derbys, to become the first dog in history to win the triple crown. He went through each event undefeated, which stamped him as one of the all-time greats.

In 1948 an equally outstanding dog, Local Interprize, won the Welsh Derby in a new track record time of 29.32 secs; he had previously run up for the English Derby to Priceless Border. Two years later his track record was beaten by .10 sec when George Flintham's Ballycurreen Garrett won, and so credited his owner with having won every major event except the English and Irish Derbys.

In the next two years the Welsh Derby was won by Ballylanigan Tanist and Endless Gossip, two of the sport's finest dogs. Endless Gossip had another champion, Magourna Reject, to defeat in the final; he managed to beat Mrs Chandler's dog by an amazing eight lengths, the biggest winning margin in the history of the race. Ballylanigan Tanist, who also won the English Derby, was one of only five greyhounds ever to reach the finals of the English, Scottish and Welsh Derbys. He came close to winning the triple crown, for in the final of the Scottish Derby he ran up to Rushton Smutty who beat him by three quarters of a length. The following year the event was won by Glittering Look, who was found after the race to have broken a hock and ran no more. He would surely have developed into one of the greatest but for his unfortunate injury; instead he became one of the sires from which many of the great names of the past twenty years were descended.

There was no Welsh Derby in 1954 and 1956. The 1955 event was won by the English Derby winner Rushton Mac, owned and trained by Mr Frank Johnson, only the second person to own and train a winner of the English and Welsh Derbys. Fred Trevillion was the first and only owner–trainer to win the triple crown. Mile Bush Pride did so in 1958, but had a different owner and trainer. This great dog set a new track record at Arms Park, being the first to break 29 secs there, and his time of 28.80 secs was never beaten, although the great Oregon Prince, who won in 1960, came near to doing so, being just one length (.06 secs) slower. I'm Quickest was a popular winner in 1966, for he was possibly the best dog racing in Britain that year.

Not until 1971 was the Welsh Derby finally given classic status, though it had always been recognized as such by greyhound owners. Patricia's Hope won the event and the triple crown in 1973. In 1977 Arms Park closed for greyhound racing, since when the Welsh Derby has not been held, though there are moves to build a new track in Cardiff and the classic may then hopefully be revived.

The most successful trainers of Welsh Derby winners have been Leslie Reynolds with Ballylanigan Tanist and Endless Gossip, Jack Harvey with Ballycurreen Garrett and Mile Bush Pride, and Ernie Toseland of Perry Barr with Negro's Lad and Go Doggy Go.

Negro's Lad, winner of the Welsh Greyhound Derby 1946. Photo: GRA.

Winners of the Welsh Derby

1928	Cheerful Choice	30.73 secs
1929	Black Isle	29.84 secs
1930	Mick the Miller	29.55 secs
1931	Altamatzin	29.88 secs
1932	Reel Tom	29.87 secs
1933	Beef Cutlet	29.56 secs
1934	Valiant Rufus	30.08 secs
1935	not run	
1936	Bully Ring	30.28 secs
1937	Genial Radiance	30.15 secs
1938–44	not run	
1945	Shaggy Lass	29.75 secs
1946	Negro's Lad	29.54 secs
*†1947	Trev's Perfection	29.74 secs
1948	Local Interprize	29.32 secs
1949	not run	
1950	Ballycurreen Garrett	29.22 secs
1951	Ballylanigan Tanist	29.95 secs
*1952	Endless Gossip	29.41 secs
1953	Glittering Look	29.39 secs
1954	not run	
*1955	Rushton Mac	29.40 secs
1956	not run	
1957	Go Doggie Go	29.38 secs
1958	Our Defence	30.27 secs
*†1959	Mile Bush Pride	28.80 secs
1960	Fitz's Star	29.48 secs
1961	Oregon Prince	28.86 secs
1962	Summerhill Fancy	29.07 secs
1963	Fairy's Chum	29.49 secs
1964	Davo's Rink	28.84 secs
1965	Harmony	29.53 secs
1966	I'm Quickest	29.59 secs
1967	Millie's Valley	29.36 secs
1968	Swift Half	29.58 secs
1969	Palla's Joy	29.43 secs
1970	Super Gamble	29.46 secs
1971	not run	
*†1972	Patricia's Hope	29.75 secs
1973	Silly Rocket	29.56 secs
1974	Dankie	29.79 secs
1975	Baffling Bart	29.37 secs
1976	Cameo Colonel	29.63 secs
1977	Instant Gambler	30.01 secs

* Also won English Derby
† Winner of the triple crown 1928–38 run at White City, Cardiff; 1939–77 at Arms Park, Cardiff; thereafter discontinued
Run over 525 yds until 1975; 1975–7 over 500 m

CLASSIC EVENTS IN IRELAND

		Inaugurated		
National Breeders' Produce Stakes	Clonmel	1939	525 yds	April
Trigo Cup (now Guinness Ulster Derby)	Celtic Park	1929	525 yds	May–June
Carroll's Irish Derby	Shelbourne Park	1932	525 yds	July
Grand National	Thurles	1932	525 yds H	August
Guinness National Sprint	Dunmore Park	1943	375 yds	August
Liam Cashman Laurels	Cork	1944	525 yds	August–September
Sean Kelly Oaks	Harold's Cross	1932	525 yds	September
Cesarewitch	Navan	1960	600 yds	September
St Leger	Limerick	1932	550 yds	October

The above classics are run each year at the stadia listed. In the early years of the sport they were run at a different venue each year. The oldest classic is the Trigo Cup, now the Guinness Ulster Derby, though it did not receive classic status until 1944. The first important event to be staged was the Easter Cup, first held in 1928 at Shelbourne Park where it has been held ever since. It has always attracted outstanding greyhounds, yet has never been given classic status although regarded as such by followers of the sport. Six of the classics are now sponsored, which has greatly increased the prize money and given additional prestige to the events. The Irish Derby has been sponsored since 1970 by P.J. Carroll & Co. Ltd, who offer the winner £20,000.

The classics are run between early April and mid-October when the weather is fine and warm and the tracks in the best possible condition for racing. Considerable prestige goes with each trophy, and if the winner is a dog it may be expected to earn a large sum in stud fees for the next five or six years or more. Any greyhound that has come through his heats and semi-final and has been placed first or second in the final must have exceptional stamina, pace and track sense and will be able to command a fee of at least £100 when retired to stud.

The results of the Irish classics are given under the tracks where they are staged; *see under* Irish Greyhound Racecourses.

CLASSIC WINNERS

These greyhounds have been successful in the same event on more than one occasion. An omitted event means that no dog has won it twice.

GREAT BRITAIN		
Cesarewitch	Future Cutlet	1931, 1932
Derby	Mick the Miller	1929, 1930
	Patricia's Hope	1972, 1973
Gold Collar	Local Interprize	1948, 1949
Grand National	Sherry's Prince	1970, 1971, 1972
	Juvenile Classic	1938, 1940
	Topothetide	1978, 1979
Grand Prix	Paradise Spectre	1977, 1978
Laurels	Ballyhennessey Sandhills	1937, 1938
	Ballymac Ball	1949, 1950
	Duet Leader	1955, 1956
	Conna Count	1964, 1965
Oaks	Queen of the Suir	1932, 1933
	Lizette	1953, 1955
	Ballinasloe Blondie	1961, 1962
	Cranog Bet	1963, 1964
*Scottish Derby	Olive's Best	1934, 1935
	Ballycurreen Soldier	1940, 1942
	Brilane Clipper	1969, 1970
Scurry Gold Cup	Gorey Airways	1959, 1960
	Don't Gambol	1970, 1971
	Yankee Express	1982, 1983, 1984
IRELAND		
Derby	Spanish Battleship	1953, 1954, 1955
Grand National	Special	1972, 1973, 1974
Laurels	Spanish Chestnut	1949, 1950
	Knockrour Slave	1979, 1980
Oaks	Peaceful Lady	1952, 1953
St Leger	Monarch of the Glen	1942, 1943
	Time up Please	1971, 1972
Trigo Cup	Magheragh Soldier	1935, 1936, 1937
	Fearless Gaughan	1939, 1940

* Given classic status in 1950

Only one person, Jack McAlister of Ireland in 1946 won three classics in one year with three different greyhounds: Count Lally, the National Sprint; Mad Midnight, the Nat. Produce Stakes; Miltiades, the Trigo Cup.

Opposite: Wembley trainer Jack Harvey with Ballinasloe Blondie. Photo: Wembley Stadium Ltd.

CLOSE FINISHES

One of the closest was in the final of Wembley's Blue Riband in 1981 when a short-head separated each of the first 5 dogs – Arfer Mo; Duke of Hazard; Sugarville Jet; Prince Spy; and Decoy Ranger.

In the 1982 Scurry Cup final at Slough, 3 greyhounds seemed to have dead-heated but the photo showed Yankee Express to have won by a short-head from Lannon Lass with Decoy Ranch, a head behind.

One of the closest finishes in a classic event occurred at White City in the 1959 Derby final, when Mile Bush Pride defeated Snub Nose by a neck, with Crazy Parachute third, a short head away. They were seven lengths ahead of the next dog to finish.

No greyhound was involved in more close finishes than Future Cutlet, usually with his great rival Beef Cutlet. In the 1932 Derby Future Cutlet was beaten a neck by Wild Woolley, and the following year he took the premier event by a short head from Beef Cutlet. In that year's Record Stakes, run over 500 yds at Wimbledon, in a race contested by Future Cutlet, Beef Cutlet, Fallinga, Brave Enough and Goofy Gear, Beef Cutlet reversed the Derby decision and won by a short head, with Fallinga a short head behind them in what was almost a triple dead heat.

In Ireland the 1969 Guinness '600' run at Shelbourne Park came close to a triple dead heat: only a photo separated Itsamint, Own Pride and Sports Ban, who all crossed the line together. The photo showed that Itsamint had won by a short head from Own Pride, with Sports Ban a short head behind, no more than 2–3 ins separating the three greyhounds.

In the final of the 1968 Ulster Derby at Celtic Park the three favourites crossed the line virtually together. The photo-finish camera, however, revealed that Drumna Chestnut had won by a short head from Russian Gun, with April Merry in third place another short head away. In the National Sprint at Dunmore Park later that year Russian Gun took part in an even closer finish, when the litter brothers Newhill Printer and Dry Flash dead heated for first place with Russian Gun only a short head away in third place.

See Dead Heat; Triple Dead Heat.

COLOUR

The standard greyhound colours are black, blue, brindle, red, fawn, white, and ticked – meaning light flecks on a dark coat. The colour of a greyhound is shown in its identity book and appears on the race card immediately below the dog's name in abbreviated form. A blue brindle, for instance, is shown as bebd, a white and brindle as wbd, a red-fawn as rf.

'A good dog cannot be a bad colour,' wrote Stonehenge, and this was a saying of the coursing men of old as well as of track racing enthusiasts of today. During the first twenty-five years of the Waterloo Cup it was won by dogs and bitches with either a red or a black coat, and no white dog was successful until 1861. The first winner with a white coat was Canaradzo, by Beacon out of Scotland Yet, the latter being runner-up to Judge in 1855. It is of interest that Canaradzo had seven white ancestors in his pedigree, a remarkable number in these days. Then came the white and black bitch Chloe who won in 1863, and in 1864 the white and black dog King Death, sired by Canaradzo – it seems that the white colour first became prominent through the influence of Scotland Yet, and although the coursers of old believed that a hare could see a white dog first and so turned towards the other dog, white greyhounds on the track have more than earned their share of top awards. White dogs have always been famed for their staying powers. At Owlerton in the 1940s Stansman won most times in the heaviest going, and for Model Dasher of Perry Barr, the greatest stayer of them all, the heavier the track the better he performed.

Newdown Heather, the world's greatest sire of the 1960s, was predominantly a white and black dog, and so were the outstanding bitch Miss Taft and Ambiguous, winner of the Chelsea Cup and the Laurels in 1968, a year in which three greyhound finalists were predominantly white, with a little brindled colouring. These were the winner, Camira Flash, and Shady Parachute and Shady Begonia. Another outstanding white and brindled greyhound born in that year was Don't Gambol, who was to win the Scurry Gold Cup in 1970 and 1971. Sole Aim, winner of the Irish Greyhound Derby, was of the same colour, as were Hammond and the coursing dog Coxcomb, and since several of these dogs are standing at stud it appears that white dogs will dominate track racing for some years to come.

It was for a son of Sole Aim that one of the highest prices ever was offered for a greyhound. The offer was £30,000, made for Mr D. Lynch's white and black dog Knockrour Slave after winning the Guinness Trophy at Cork by ten lengths in 1979. The price was refused. Another white and black, Top Customer, by Monalee Champion, was sold for £6,000 after clocking 29.27 secs at Limerick in the Guinness Sweepstake.

Yet successes on the coursing field by white greyhounds have been few and far between, and no white dog had ever won the Irish Coursing Derby until Tender Heather in 1969; only three have won the Irish Cup (the equivalent of the Waterloo Cup) – Quite Happy in 1913, First Capture in 1923, and Tender Hero in 1969. To complete an amazing trio of successes in premier Irish coursing events in 1969, the bitch Tender Honey won the Oaks – all three greyhounds were from the same Newdown Heather–Tender Heart litter.

The brindled colouring (a mixture of fawn, black, red and white) did not make its appearance until long after Lord Orford's bulldog crossings had been made, and the first occasion on which a brindled greyhound won the premier coursing event was in 1862 when Roaring Meg, a bitch, defeated Sea Rock. No broken colour greyhound was to win again for another twenty-four years, when the famous Miss Glendyne took the Cup, and three years later the brindled Fullerton, the first dog (as against a bitch) of that colouring to win the event. In the whole history of the Waterloo Cup, from 1836 to 1979, a brindled animal has been successful on only twenty occasions, yet on the racecourse brindled and black dogs have been the most successful.

It is of interest to recall that when Lord Rivers' fifty-two famous coursing dogs were sold in May 1825, twenty-three were black, fourteen were blue, four were blue and white, six were red, and there was only one white dog – so perhaps his lordship did believe that hares turned away from a white greyhound and so made it easier for the others to take her and so win the course.

The first winner of the Greyhound Derby, Entry Badge, was a brindle, as was the great dog Wild Woolley. So too were Mick the Miller, Train, Future Cutlet, Jubilee Time, Monday's News, Trev's Perfection and Mile Bush Pride. Among other famous brindles are Priceless Border, Pigalle Wonder, Ballynennan Moon, Ballymac Ball, Sherry's Prince and Faithful Hope – all greyhounds which have had few equals over the 525 yds (500 m) course in the history of the sport. Lacca Champion, the 1978 Derby winner, is a very dark brindle, almost black. The great trainer Sidney Orton considered that a dark brindle dog was the best of all, with a black a very close second, and there is no denying that, along with brindles, black greyhounds had most success in the earlier years of the sport, especially over the longer distances. Among the successful bitches in this category are Alvaston Lulu Belle, Edna's Hope, Sneem, Disputed Rattler, Quarter Day, Nameless Pixie, Coolkill Darkie and Dolores Rocket; and among dogs Local Interprize, Blackwater Cutlet, Rimmell's Black, Dante, Spectre II, Tric Trac, Sand Star and Poor Mick, all of them outstanding performers over all distances.

It is said that black greyhounds 'lack bone', meaning that they are more lightly built; while there is something in this – the brindles and whites tend to be more heavily built – the blacks certainly have never lacked courage and stamina, as witness their performances on the track over long distances and on the coursing field. Modern greyhound racing owes the black colouring as much as anything to Inler, who with Mutton Cutlet was one of the foundation sires of track stock. Other great blacks of recent years include Time Up Please, who twice won the Irish St Leger; Rushing to Work, twice winner of the Tipperary Cup; Finola's Yarn; Kerryman; Greenane Decca; and Cricket Bunny, winner of the 1973 Scurry Cup.

Many black dogs standing at stud in 1980 were descended from the black Spectre, and will ensure that greyhounds of this colour will rival white greyhounds in the immediate future. These dogs are all black – Tain Mor (1976 Irish Derby), Rita's Choice, Shamrock Sailor, Black Banjo (1973 English Laurels), Brush Tim, Linda's Champion (1977 Irish Derby), Pampered Rover (1978

Irish Derby), Monalee Hiker, Limerick Hero and Paradise Spectre.

A rare colour of greyhounds, the blue (really a slatey grey shade), has been represented by several of the fastest in the history of the sport. The first blue champion was Creamery Border, the fastest breaker of them all, who passed on his colouring and his amazing early speed to a long line of top-class greyhounds, for he was many years at stud and lived to be fourteen. One of his sons was Manhattan Midnight, a blue and also a great sire. Then there was Orluck's Best, Scurry Gold Cup winner of 1938 and later sire of the mercurial Monday's News, Derby winner in 1946. Douro, the famous hurdler, was a blue, so too were Roeside Creamery and Bohernagraga Boy, winner of the 1946 English St Leger. Later came Quare Times, owned by Mrs Quinn, who set a new national record for the 525 yds course in the second round of the 1946 Derby. In turn he was to pass on his blue coat and amazing speed to the bitch Quare Fire, who became grand dam of Mr George Kidd's Clomoney Grand, also a blue and one of the fastest bitches of all time, winning the Easter Cup in 1966. Nor must we forget Astra, twice winner of the Easter Cup, who beat Mad Tanist, Hurry Kitty and Quare Times in doing so. The Irish Derby winner Lilac's Luck, who ran up to Monday's News in the English Derby, was a blue brindle, an even more unusual colour. The 1981 English Derby winner, Parkdown Jet, was a blue and so was Murray's Mixture. In *The Book of the Greyhound* (*see* Bibliography on page 387), Edward Ash said that blue was considered 'a fortunate colour, greatly to be admired, rarely to be obtained', but sixty years ago Adair Dighton ('King Cob' of *The Sportsman*) wrote in his book *The Greyhound and Coursing*: 'Personally I am very much averse to blues,' though on the track such aversion is not borne out by the facts, for the success of the few blues to race has been considerable, though this was long after Mr Dighton's time.

Another famous blue of recent times is Noble Brigg, a January 1977 whelp by Faction Fighter out of Noble Lynn, and bred, trained and owned by Mr A. McCookin of Co. Antrim who won the Irish Coursing Derby in 1963 with Glideaway Dreamer. Noble Brigg, a fine puppy tipping the scales at 80 lbs, won the 1978 National Sprint at Dunmore Park in 23.76 secs. No other coloured dog could match the blues for speed from the traps, like streaks of blue lightning. Cranog Bet was also a blue.

In the early years of organized coursing, red and fawn dogs, along with the blacks, were most successful, and Stonehenge considered black and red dogs with black muzzles the best. By red is meant a bronzy fawn colour, while a fawn dog has a lighter creamy fawn coat. The latter is perhaps the most impressive of all dog colours, but it is rare today to find a top-class track greyhound with a coat of either colouring, for during the past fifty years the leading sires have been blue, black, white and brindle and have, not unexpectedly, passed on their colouring, as well as their particular qualities, to their offspring. Among the exceptions were Hi There and his son Printer's Prince, sire of the flying Yellow Printer, who was also fawn; and the 1970 Derby winner, John Silver. In the 1930s Grand Flight II was a fawn and so were those four wonderful bitches of the 1940s, Robeen Printer, Narrogar Ann, Hurry Kitty and Shaggy Lass, the last two sired by the great Castledown Lad. In the same decade three of the greatest dogs on the coursing field were fawns – Swinging Light, Countryman and Dutton Swordfish, sire of Narrogar Ann. More recently the 1964 Derby winner, Hack Up Chieftain, was a fawn, as was Mr Jimmy O'Connor's fine performer Dusty Trail.

The true red colouring (usually accompanied by a black muzzle) is now rare on the race track, if not on the coursing field, though one may come across the red-fawn dog.

CONSECUTIVE WINS

The longest winning sequence among track greyhounds is said to be that of Nannie Goosegog in Ireland in the early years of racing there. In more recent times Peruvian Style, trained by Tony Fahy, won nineteen races in succession, equalling Mick the Miller's nineteen in a row in England, a record set up in 1930 and which stood for fortyfour years. It was beaten in 1974 by a bitch owned by Mr and Mrs Cyril Scotland and trained by Tommy Johnston, Westpark Mustard, who won twenty consecutive events between 7 January and 28 October, the twentieth being the Mick the Miller Record Stakes at Wembley. This is the longest winning sequence by a greyhound in the British Isles and by a bitch anywhere, but the all-time record for consecutive wins is generally considered to be that of the American dog Real Huntsman, who between 3 April 1950 and 3 June 1951 won twenty-seven races in succession. Whelped in February 1948, the brindle dog was two years old when he began his great series of wins, and he was the only dog to win the American Greyhound Derby, held at Taunton, Mass., on two occasions. In 1950 he won the Flagler Futurity, the Biscayne All-Florida Trophy and the American Derby, repeating this success the following year. In 1971 Izz a Champ had twenty-one consecutive wins, all in eight-dog events, while Real Huntsman's record included four two-dog matches, as did Mick the Miller's.

Mick's record was performed over only five months (and he was then more than four years old), beginning with the semi-final of the Spring Cup at Wembley on 19 March and ending with a match against Faithful Kitty on 20 August. His wins during that time were achieved in the highest company, and apart from the Spring Cup included the 1930 Derby at White City, when he defeated the great Bradshaw Fold by three lengths; the Cesarewitch at West Ham; and the Welsh Derby at Cardiff. It was a sequence of wins unprecedented in the history of the sport in Britain and Ireland for it took in three classics in one year.

The great brindle dog Ballynennan Moon seemed certain to better Mick's record in 1942 when, after winning only eight of his twenty races in Ireland he was bought by Mrs Cearns – wife of the managing director of Wimbledon Stadium, and an astute buyer of greyhounds who had an eye for a champion – while still a puppy, before he had done anything to create attention. On the last day of February 1942 the dog won the Walthamstow Stakes and went on to win the next thirteen races, all of them events open to the best greyhounds in Britain (the classics were not held during the war years). He was then surprisingly beaten by a neck by Laughing Lackey before starting another sequence of eight wins. Then after a short rest he won his next ten races, which made eighteen in a row, only one short of Mick's record. Then he was again beaten into second place by Laughing Lackey. It was his last race, for he pulled up lame in a trial and was retired to stud. Out of his last thirty-four consecutive open races he won thirty-two and was second in the other two. But for these two defeats, both by a whisker, the brindle would have set up a record which might have stood for all time.

Peruvian Style by Kilbelin Style out of Russian Boots, was whelped in 1973 and began his great run of twenty consecutive wins in the Waterford Glass Stakes at Waterford in 1975. He then went through the Harp Lager 525 at Dundalk, and the Shelbourne Leger and Callanan Cup at Harold's Cross; all were top events, though not classics, but the dog showed that all tracks came alike to him. By the time he won the Callanan Cup he had notched sixteen wins in succession. In April 1976 he contested the Truboard Gold Cup, again at the Waterford track. Here he won his first- and second-round heats but had to be withdrawn from the semi-finals owing to a toe injury; it was in October, once more at Waterford, that he reappeared to win his nineteenth race and thus to equal Mick the Miller's record. But once again his toe was giving him trouble. He was withdrawn from the 1976 Waterford Glass Trophy and given another month's rest, reappearing at the Galway track in November where he equalled Westpark Mustard's twenty wins in a row. The following week this game and wonderful dog made his attempt to set a new record at Galway. Thousands made their way to the track, only to be disappointed when the champion failed by a length to set a new record. Perhaps if he had been given longer to recover from his injury he would have won with his customary ease, but it was now winter and since conditions were deteriorating daily it was thought advisable to let him try for the record as soon as possible.

In 1929 Idle Chief won sixteen consecutive graded races at the Slough track, and in 1945–6 Winsome Seal won his first twelve races in England. In 1947 Main Tackle won eleven consecutive graded races at the Albion track, Glasgow, often when giving 12 or 13 yds' start. More recently a white and black bitch, Miss Taft, kennelled at Wembley, won ten consecutive races in 1967, and over the flat no bitch was ever more consistent. In 115 races she won on fifty-five occasions and was second twenty-five times. The record number of consecutive races at Wembley is the seven wins achieved by Moordyke Spot in 1970. At Oxford, the bitch Blissful Pride won 17 consecutive races in 1970–71 before whelping, at 14 years of age, Ballybeg Blaze and Ballybeg Delight, holder of Oxford's 645 m record.

Among hurdlers, the first of the champions over the jumps, Long Hop, who won the Greyhound Grand National in 1932, won sixteen races in a row between 27 August and 14 December that year. For consistent running over hurdles, however, no dog was more successful than Sherry's Prince, who between 9 May 1969 and May 1972 took part in 106 'open' events, winning on seventy-one occasions and being second fifteen times. He won the Grand National three years in succession.

CONSISTENT RUNNING

One of the most interesting features of the sport is the consistent running of those greyhounds who will often clock the same time to within a tenth of a second on several consecutive runs. At Thurles, in March 1973, two bitches came within an inch of recording a double dead heat. Running in the second semi-final of the Spring Sweepstake, Scoby Queen and Beauty Mandy dead-heated for second place and this was confirmed by the photo-finish camera. As only one could go through to the final, comprising the first two from each of the three semi-finals, the two had to run again and once more they were thought to have crossed the line together. The camera, however, showed that Beauty Mandy had won by about an inch, the shortest of short heads. In both races the pattern of running was the same, with Beauty Mandy building up a convincing lead to the final turn and Scoby Queen making a terrific finish on the last straight.

In his heats for the 1977 Greyhound Derby Balliniska Band recorded identical times of 29.24 secs over the 500 m course at the White City, though in the final he clocked 29.16 secs, to equal the track record. At Wembley the Coronation Cup for bitches was won in 1935 and 1936 in the identical time of 30.33 secs, and in 1937 in 30.31 secs. At Enniscorthy the winning times for the Guinness Wexford Leger were the same for three consecutive years – 1971, 1972 and 1973 – when the time for 550 yds was 31 secs; the same time was also recorded for 1975. Over ten years the times were the most consistent ever recorded for an important event (*see under* Irish Greyhound Racecourses).

In hurdle events, between April 1971 and April 1972 Sherry's Prince ran forty-three times, of which he won thirty-three events and was second on five occasions. His last race was the final of the Grand National, which he won for the third time, and thus became the finest greyhound to win the same classic on three occasions in Britain.

CORK RACECOURSE
See under Irish Greyhound Racecourses.

COST OF KEEPING A GREYHOUND

Keeping a racing greyhound today is expensive, for it requires the very best care when in training and the finest food. However, whereas a racehorse costs about £12 a day, a greyhound will cost only £2 a day, and if a dog runs once a week it will earn its keep in appearance money on most tracks and any prize money it wins for finishing first or second will be profit to put against the purchase price. This may be as little as £200 for a young untried greyhound, or even for one that has appeared frequently on tracks but has yet to achieve any great success, though it may well do so when on a new racecourse and in the hands of another trainer. On the other hand a greyhound of open race potential may cost £1,000, and considerably more may be asked for one which has given every indication of its ability to win major events. Such a dog may be kennelled with a private trainer who is able to handle a number of open race dogs for clients and take them around the country to the tracks where the races are staged. At the time of writing (January 1981), the cost of keeping a greyhound with a private trainer is about £12–15 a week, so the dog must be of a standard able to win top-class opens which carry a respectable amount of prize money.

On top of kennel charges there will be travelling expenses and vet's fees, in addition to entrance money for open events.

It now costs over £1 a day to kennel a greyhound with a race track, compared with £2 a week only a few years ago, so here too the dog must be reasonably good. The day when the mediocre greyhound could earn his keep has disappeared. Even so, today's prizes are substantial, with at least £100 awarded for first place in the smallest open events and £50 for second place, while appearance money will be £20–25. But wherever a greyhound is to be raced, on a track (where it is put in the hands of a track trainer) or in open events, remember that it costs exactly the same to keep and train a dog of limited ability as it does a champion, and one should always obtain the best animal within one's means and place it with the best trainer who has room for it in his or her kennels.

COVENTRY RACECOURSE
See under British Greyhound Racecourses.

CRADLEY HEATH RACECOURSE
See under British Greyhound Racecourses.

CRAYFORD RACECOURSE
See under British Greyhound Racecourses.

D

DAM
A bitch becomes a dam when she has whelped her first litter – in other words when she becomes a mother. In the history of greyhound racing the dam has perhaps played a more important part in breeding top-class stock than the sire. The Irish have always believed, and rightly so, that since the bitch has so much more to do in producing the offspring of a mating than the sire she will exert a greater influence on the whelps. Her selection, therefore, should be given at least as much care as that of a sire.

Haphazard choice of brood bitches, though put to expensive and proven sires, resulted in much poor stock in the early years of greyhound racing, but there was then little to go on in choosing suitable dam lines, which had only become apparent on the coursing field. Some bitches, about whose breeding little was known, produced high-class trackers, but these were few and far between, the result of luck rather than selection and in the early days of the sport it mattered little, for rearing costs were small compared with today, and if greyhounds didn't make the grade they could be kept as pets. Frequently owners would purchase a bitch for a few pounds after her racing days were over and send her to a top-class sire in the hope that at least one of her offspring would win a classic event. The bitch might have been over-raced and might never have performed above average, while her breeding might have offered little to recommend her as being capable of producing quality stock. But her pups would be sold at a good price if they carried the name of a popular sire, and it was those who devoted time and money to rearing and training them who would be most disappointed. Yet no matter how good the feeding and care of the pups, the equally important essentials of stamina, speed and track sense are inherited characteristics, and if they are not present in the offspring the time and expense involved in their rearing will be wasted.

Before a brood bitch is purchased for breeding her physical qualities as well as her racing career should be as closely examined as her pedigree. If you own a bitch that is racing you will know a great deal about her – how she has performed, whether she is a fast starter, whether she is a sprinter or a stayer, the latter being more usual with bitches. If she is a sprinter and quick over shorter distances this may show in her pedigree – her sire or her dam may have possessed similar qualities, and if so she should be put to a sire noted for his staying powers, for instance a bitch of Tanist stock to a sire who had Castledown Lad in his pedigree. Stoutness or stamina, and into this category must come gameness, is of first importance, and it is usually bitches that possess these qualities to the full. There have been few bitches as quick from the traps and over the shorter distance races as the best dogs. Only one bitch in the history of the sprinters' classic, the Scurry Gold Cup, has been successful; only one has won the Gold Collar and very few the Laurels, yet several have won the Derby, run over the middle distance, and more still have won the St Leger and Cesarewitch, both run over longer distances. The first St Leger was won by a bitch, Burletta, and others include Greta's Rosary, Robeen Printer, Friendly Lass and Dolores Rocket. In the Cobb Marathon, run at Catford, at one time over the great distance of 810 yds, many bitches have been successful since Patty Dear and Unwin Beauty won in 1943 and 1944 – some good examples are Moral Hostess, Lizette, Shady Camellia and Doreen Berry.

So important do the Irish consider the bitch in breeding that, if a litter is born from a proven sire and dam, it is the dog pups that are sold and rarely the bitches. If the dogs turn out spectacular on the track or coursing field the bitches are rarely, if ever, raced and are retained for breeding. There is then no fear that they will have been over-raced or kept in training too long, which would be detrimental in breeding.

If buying a bitch for breeding, make sure she has not been over-raced and is of the correct blood lines, similar to those which are producing champions from every litter, or that she is of the same breeding as successful trackers, probably litter brothers. If the bitch has not been raced, so much the better. Do not overlook a small bitch so long as she is well built, nor one that may have been injured and could not race or may have been retired at an early age. Stonehenge rightly said, a hundred years ago, 'If you can get a small muscular bitch, of from 45 to 50 lbs, belonging to a winning family whose properties you admire . . . by all means select her.' Experience proves that a bitch of this size usually makes an ideal mother. Mr A. Croxton-Smith, the well-known breeder in the early greyhound racing years, agreed with this and suggested a bitch of about 50 lbs, though one well-known North Country breeder favours a big bitch, one with a broad chest and having plenty of heart room. Mr M. Budd, breeder of the famous 'Magic' litter of the late 1940s, said that to him weight did not matter so much but that he liked a bitch with 'good bone formation, straight back hocks, and good depths across the stifle,' and one that was 'keen, with low running movement'. And she must not have shown fighting tendencies if raced, neither should her brothers or her own sire or dam.

The Irish breeders, who usually keep the best bitch from each litter, put her to a successful sire either the first time she is in season or when she is about two years old; then, within two years, it will be seen how her offspring have fared. If they are successful, the breeder can use the same blood lines again and again, for a bitch that is well cared for and not over-raced can continue to have pups until she is eleven or twelve years old. This was the age of Sheila at Last, one of the greatest of modern dams, from her mating with Crazy Parachute mother of Monalee Champion and Monalee Pride, winner of the 1970 Irish Derby, and from her mating to Prairie Flash mother of Monalee Leader, Irish St Leger winner, part of her last litter. The famous bitch of earlier days, Czarina, winner of the Waterloo Cup, did not have a litter until she was nearly thirteen, when she became the mother of the famous Snowball. The dam of Guard's Brigade was nine when she gave birth to this great Waterloo Cup winner of 1922, and Mrs Ella Lewy's blue bitch Miss Islington was twelve when she whelped a litter to Briar Wood in 1946. She had whelped the long-distance champion Ella's Jim eight years before.

Stonehenge believed that a bitch was at her best for breeding between the ages of four and six, and that sire and dam should be of as near the same age as possible. However when Golden Seal, a Waterloo Cup winner, was born, his sire was ten and his dam four; and Drishogue was not quite two when mated to the eight-year-old Creamery Border sire Manhattan Midnight and produced the great Rimmell's Black.

The gameness of bitches is shown by those who have been allowed to continue their career on track or coursing field after whelping a litter. The supreme example is Awful Foolish who, after racing at Shelbourne Park and whelping a litter to Abbeylara, among which was the bitch Simone, sold for 1,500 gns, came back to race in England and ran up to Maggie Sallie in Wimbledon's Pick. When next in season she was mated to Bah's Choice, but did not race again. Fay Cutlet ran up to Disputed

Rattler in the 1943 Coronation Cup when aged five, after having raised a litter of pups, and the Beef Cutlet bitch Winnie of Berrow did not begin her highly successful career on the track until she had had a litter of six. She contested and won the Coventry Eclipse Stakes, beating the flying Ballyhennessy Seal, and within two years earned £1,600 in stake money when £100 was the top prize for most open events. But she was not finished yet. Mated to the Waterloo Cup winner Dutton Swordfish, her litter included Narrogar Ann who became only the second bitch to win the Derby and who, when mated to the 1948 Derby winner, Priceless Border, whelped Endless Gossip, also a Derby winner and one of the fastest dogs ever to race. Like her dam, Winnie of Berrow, and her grandsire, Beef Cutlet (from Mutton Cutlet), Narrogar Ann had tremendous stamina which was passed on right through her pedigree and long after she died. When mated to Castle Yard, Endless Gossip produced Sally's Gossip, who, when put to Hi There, gave Printer's Prince, sire of Yellow Printer and Newdown Heather, sire of another Derby winner, Dolores Rocket and many other champions.

Mutton Cutlet
|
Beef Cutlet
(won 1932 Laurels)
|
Winnie of Berrow (B)
|
× Dutton Swordfish
(won 1944 Waterloo Cup)
|
Narrogar Ann (B)
(won 1949 English Derby)
|
× Priceless Border
(won 1948 English Derby)
|
Endless Gossip
(won 1952 English Derby)
|
× Castle Yard (B)
|
Sally's Gossip (B)
|
× Hi There
|
Printer's Prince
|
Yellow Printer
(won 1968 Irish Derby)
|
Newdown Heather
|
Sire Dolores Rocket (B)
(won 1971 English Derby)

Dolores Rocket was therefore in direct line to Mutton Cutlet and his sire, Jamie. Each of these dogs and bitches possessed great staying power, as would be expected from the wonderful coursing blood of the English bitch Narrogar Ann, who was the foundation of this great line of racing greyhounds.

In the opinion of Mr Tom Morris, for many years keeper of the Irish Stud Book, it was desirable to use a successful coursing dog or bitch on one side of the mating, to ensure that the enormous stamina of the coursing dogs was combined with the speed of the track greyhounds, for without stamina and staying power the constitution of the greyhound in the years ahead would quickly deteriorate. In Ireland, where coursing still has a wide following, this breeding programme continues, and we may therefore expect the quality of track greyhounds to continue to improve.

Another instance of a brood bitch returning to racing is Shady Bunny, a litter sister to the English Oaks winner Shady Parachute. After whelping a large litter to Faithful Hope she returned to racing, and straightaway won the Greenwich Cup at New Cross. She then came in season again and was mated to the 1967 Irish Derby winner Russian Gun, by whom she had a litter of seven. The 1845 Waterloo Cup was won by the black bitch Titania less than four months after whelping a litter, and Negro's Fire won the Clarke Cup in 1945 after giving birth to Gypsy Fire. There have been other instances, but it is rare for a bitch to go into training again when more than three years old, which both Fay Cutlet and Winnie of Berrow were when they resumed racing.

To sum up, breed from a bitch with all the right physical characteristics and from a successful dam line; one who has not been over-raced and as young as possible in order to have several years' breeding in front of her. This will allow her to be sent back to a certain stud dog should the result of a first mating produce stock worthy of their parents. In this event the dam will enjoy a reputation for producing quality stock early in her life.

The first dams to produce top-class racing stock were English-bred, the daughters of Mick the Miller's litter brother Macoma, the first hurdler to achieve champion status. One was Lady Eleanor, and the other Wonderful Expression. In 1935, from a mating with Beef Cutlet, Lady Eleanor produced one of the greatest litters of all time, including Epinard, His Lordship and Jesmond Cutlet. The last of these was to win the Scottish Derby, and a week or so later the Edinburgh Cup. In the St Leger he ran up to Grosvenor Bob and won the Cesarewitch from his old rival. His mating with Magic Pool produced the wonderful 'Magic' litter; Magic Beau set a new national record for 525 yds at Wembley, and Magic Bohemian did the same at White City. From her second mating to Beef Cutlet, Lady Eleanor produced even finer stock, including two of the all-time greats, Juvenile Classic and Junior Classic, the former the greatest hurdler in the early history of the sport, winner of two Grand Nationals and holder of five national records over hurdles. Junior Classic, who did most of his racing in 1938–9, won more than £4,000 in prize money (worth at least £12,000 today) and was considered one of the greatest of all track runners.

Then came Grosvenor Faith, whose dam was the equally famous Wonderful Expression. When mated with the famous coursing dog Lights o' London, Grosvenor Faith produced in her first litter the great Kampion Sailor. A litter from a second mating to the coursing sire made a record 1,265 gns when sold at Aldridge's, and from a later mating, to Glen Ranger, she produced Keep Sake, the Cobb Marathon winner. From the same litter as Grosvenor Faith were Grosvenor Bob and Grosvenor Edwin, and they were all from Wonderful Expression's mating with Golden Hammer. Grosvenor Bob won the Trafalgar Cup, ran up for the Cesarewitch, and won the St Leger in 1937, whilst Grosvenor Edwin won the Wembley Gold Cup and was one of the greatest stayers in the early years of the sport.

Macoma's influence was felt mostly through these wonderful dams, their offspring being British-born and -bred, but in Ireland in 1935 the great Brilliant Bob, probably the finest dual-purpose dog of all time, had been retired to stud at Billy Quinn's kennels in Co. Tipperary and he was to change the whole course of Irish breeding. Previously the Irish had concentrated on coursing stock, but by the end of the 1930s it was obvious that here was a dog capable of transmitting his wonderful speed and stamina through the female line. Bob was born in 1931 and his sire was Other Days, also sire of Banriogan Dann, mother of Ballynennon Moon.

One of Bob's first bitches to command attention was Brilliant Moon, dam of the International Cup winner, Wireless Rally. Then came Miss McCloud, dam of the great Lost Light, winner of the 1942 Irish Coursing Derby. Really Brilliant, dam of the Tipperary Cup winner Rathclogheen Dancer, was to follow, and one of the last of Bob's daughters was Brilliant Gay, who has perhaps had a greater influence on modern track racing than any other dam. Her first litter, to the champion sire Castledown Lad, produced Hurry Kitty, who was to follow in the steps of her maternal grandsire in winning the English Cesarewitch and who proved herself one of the all-time greats. But it was from a later mating to Castledown Lad's son, Bella's Prince, who was to take over from his sire as the greatest of his time, that history was to be made. The mating of Brilliant Gay and Bella's Prince resulted in Paddy the Champion. Here for the first time was a fusion of the two wonderful sires Brilliant Bob and Castledown Lad, the like of which greyhound racing had not known.

At the same time another outstanding sire had been retired to stud after winning the 1940 Irish Derby – Tanist, son of the coursing sire Inler. This excellent dog had earlier sired Inler May (from a mating with Border Cutlet), dam of one of the greatest coursing litters of all time, which included Shule Aroon, winner of the Irish Cup in 1940; Salisbury, winner of the Coursing Derby; Sneem, winner of the Oaks; and Sprig of Shillelagh, who won the Connaught Cup. Nothing like it had ever been seen before. Inler May was to continue to breed champions from every mating, and her last, to Orluck, produced the Oaks winner Edna's Hope. However it was Inler's mating with Tranquilla that was to dominate greyhound racing in the years ahead, in the same way as did the mating of Brilliant Bob's outstanding daughter Brilliant Gay with Castledown Lad's son, Bella's Prince. It was a combination of these blood lines that was to produce a number of the fastest greyhounds ever seen on track or coursing field.

The Inler–Tranquilla mating produced that superb litter which included Tanist, then the fastest dog in the world; Talon, sire of the great Mountain Emperor; Tact; and Tempestuous. Early in 1942 Mr J. Horan took his bitch Mad Darkie, holder of the 550 yds track record at Cork, to be mated to Tanist. The result was a litter that included Mad Tanner and the wonderful bitch Astra. When her racing days were over Astra was put to Paddy the Champion, and this fusion of Tanist, Castledown Lad and Brilliant Bob blood produced the outstanding dog Astra's Son. Through him the great dam lines were to be perpetuated through his daughter Prairie Vixen, who, when mated to The Grand Champion, gave Prairie Peg. The Grand Champion's sire was Mad Tanist, himself the result of a second mating of Tanist and Mad Darkie. (How the Irish breeders always stick with a proven sire or blood line!) Prairie Peg was discarded from the two matings of Tanist with Mad Darkie, and these, combined with the blood of Castledown Lad and Brilliant Bob through Paddy the Champion, were destined to produce something special. They did. When Prairie Peg was put to Hi There (whose dam Dublin Red was also by Bella's Prince) the result was Prairie Flash, sire of the 1968 English Derby winner Camira Flash from a mating with Duet Fire, whose great grandparents were Negro's Fire and Quare Times. Of the same litter as Prairie Flash (Prairie Peg and Hi There) was Hi Look, dam of Maryville Hi, who was almost as successful a sire as Hi There and Prairie Flash.

From a mating of Prairie Peg and Champion Prince was born the one and only Pigalle Wonder, one of the greatest trackers of all time and an English Derby winner. He in turn was to sire an Irish Derby winner, Russian Gun. Champion Prince (and Hi There's dam) also had the same sire, Bella's Prince, who, it is remembered, figured in the pedigree of Prairie Peg herself.

The same breeding also produced Direct Lead, dam of the Derby winner Sand Star and the great stayer Booked Six. Her pedigree reads:

Direct Lead	Hi There	Slaney Record
		Dublin Red (Bella's Prince)
	Drumlock Sheevaun	Bella's Prince
		Sheevaun

Direct Lead was the result of a mating of Hi There with Drumlock Sheevaun whose sire was Bella's Prince and who was also sire of Hi There's dam, Dublin Red.

Mad Darkie, from a mating to Printer, produced the magnificent staying bitch Mad Printer, winner of the 1943 Oaks; and with Manhattan Midnight gave Mad Midnight, who set a new world record over 700 yds at Glasgow in 1946.

When Mad Tanist was mated with Caledonian Desire (whose sire was Manhattan Midnight) the result was Mad Prospect who, when put to Hi There, produced Crazy Parachute, in turn sire of Kitty True, dam of Own Pride, winner of the Irish Derby in 1969. That amazing litter which included the winner (Tric Trac) and runner-up (Spectre II) of the 1967 English Derby; Forward King and Forward Flash, was the greatest litter of track greyhounds ever produced. Their dam was Supreme Witch, whose mother, Witching Grand, was litter sister to Mile Bush Pride.

Another great dam line, through The Grand Fire, ran concurrently with those of Mad Darkie and Brilliant Gay, and it was to play an equally important part in modern greyhound racing. By the mid-1950s the pattern of successful breeding was clear. There was no longer any excuse for haphazard breeding, and those who took advantage of the lessons learned reaped the rewards, and a long line of top-class greyhounds appeared. For the first twenty-five years of the sport, if just two or three top-quality greyhounds appeared in each season this was all that could be expected, but as the pattern made itself known many dogs of the highest quality were introduced each year to track racing and times got faster and faster. More than this, racing managers were able to put on eight races at each meeting, all contested by greyhounds of a standard unthinkable before the early 1950s.

As Brilliant Bob gave to the sport his superb qualities of speed, stamina and track sense in its early years and passed these on through a number of wonderful dams, so too did The Grand Fire in more recent times. This great sire has figured in almost every pedigree of modern track champions and almost always through the female line. He was sired by The Grand Champion (whose sire was Mad Tanist) out of the dam

Quare Fire, who was the result of a mating of Negro's Fire with the mighty 'blue streak' Quare Times, one of the fastest dogs ever to race. Negro's Fire rivalled Brilliant Gay and Mad Darkie in her exploits as a brood bitch, for when mated to Gypsy Lore in 1941 she produced Gypsy Fire, winner of the 1945 Irish National Cup, and from her mating with Kilrea Lad she whelped Negro's Lad, the 1946 Welsh Derby winner. Put to Carnagh Moon in 1944, she whelped Carnagh Fire and Paddy the Rebel. She had several other litters, all of which produced high-class greyhounds, but it was from her last litter, from a mating to Quare Times, that Negro's Fire produced one of the greatest dams of all time, Quare Fire. From her first mating to The Grand Champion, Quare Fire whelped The Grand Fire, who, when put to Glittering Millie, produced Millie Hawthorn, dam of the Derby winner Faithful Hope, who in turn was to sire another English Derby winner, John Silver. From her mating with Clonalvy Pride, Millie Hawthorn produced the great Yanka Boy, who won the Irish St Leger in record time and became a famous sire.

When mated to Ballinclay Betty, The Grand Fire sired Technician, who, when put to Booked Out (Direct Lead–Knockhill Chieftain), produced Booked Six. Direct Lead was a Hi There bitch, and was also dam of the English Derby winner Sand Star. Another of The Grand Fire's famous dams was Finola, who was mother of Finola's Yarn from a mating with Sally's Yarn, brother of Printer's Prince, sire of Yellow Printer. From a mating of The Grand Fire with the Irish Oaks winner Last Landing came Clomoney Grand, a blue (as was Quare Times), who many believe to have been the fastest bitch of all time; she was the female replica of her great grandsire. When mated to Prairie Flash, Clomoney Grand produced the great litter which included Albany; Kilbelin Style (runner-up for the 1969 English Derby); Kilbelin Grand (Irish Derby finalist); Clomoney Jude; and Albany Grand. From a later mating she produced Clomoney Jet, who was to win the Irish St Leger and become the sire of many outstanding greyhounds.

Quare Fire's mating to the Irish Derby winner Keep Moving produced Quare Fire Again, who, from a mating with Duet Leader, gave Duet Fire, who when put to Prairie Flash, whelped the Derby winner Camira Flash. The dam of Prairie Flash was the great Prairie Peg. Thus the greatest dam lines of modern times figured in the pedigree of Camira Flash – Quare Fire and Quare Fire Again, Prairie Peg and Prairie Vixen, Sallywell and Dublin Red, and, going back further, Astra and Mad Darkie.

In the same litter as The Grand Fire was Favide, dam of Westpark Goldilocks, dam of Frozen Fast who ran up for the Waterloo Cup in 1964. The Grand Fire was sire of Clopook, who reached the final of the 1961 English Derby. Clopook became sire of Newpark Edna, grand dam of Skyhawk, the outstanding English greyhound of 1972. Clopook was also sire of Whittle Down, dam of Whittle Off, mother of Flip Your Top, Scottish Derby winner of 1976. Whittle Down was also dam of Rockfield Era, sire of the great Ballybeg Prim. Another of Clopook's daughters was White May, dam of Miles Apart, the 1975 greyhound of the year and one of the most consistent dogs of the 1970s. In seventy-five races in England and Ireland, he was first on forty-five occasions. When mated to Lisamore Princess, The Grand Fire gave Lisamore Queen, dam of Lisamore Precept who won the Scottish Derby in 1968; and from his mating with Kilcomney Mistress he sired Donore Mistress, dam of Good Brandy, sire of Clohast Rebel.

Yet another of The Grand Fire's wonderful dams was Shane's Judy, who was to achieve fame as the mother of Yellow Streak from a mating to Odd Venture; their daughter, when put to Printer's Prince, gave the world the amazing Yellow Printer, the fastest greyhound since the fabulous Quare Times. Once again we see the fusion of the great dam lines – Printer's Prince by Hi There (Dublin Red) out of Sally's Gossip (Endless Gossip), sire also of the great Newdown Heather, sire of Dolores Rocket and many of the greatest greyhounds of recent times. But perhaps the key to it all was Mad Darkie, through Mad Tanist and his son, The Grand Champion, sire of Prairie Peg and The Grand Fire, whose influence on modern greyhound breeding through the dam has had no equal. The mating of Mad Tanist with Caledonian Desire produced Mad Prospect who, when put to Hi There, gave Crazy Parachute, one of the greatest of all sires. In the blood lines of all modern champions we come back to the mating of Tanist and Mad Darkie, coupled with the blood of Castledown Lad, Rare Record and Brilliant Bob through Brilliant Gay and other outstanding bitches he sired.

To bring the story up-to-date, it is of interest to recall that Tain Mor, winner of the 1976 Irish Derby, was from the bitch An Tain whose sire was Russian Gun, winner of the Irish Derby in 1967. Russian Gun was by Pigalle Wonder, who was the result of a mating of Champion Prince to Prairie Peg. Thus he perpetuates the great dam lines of the past forty years, and their influence is still being felt. There is no doubt that the fusion of the blood of the greatest sires and dams is still being perpetuated through Prairie Peg and her son Pigalle Wonder, for one of the most outstanding of modern dams, Yurituni, was herself a daughter of Pigalle Wonder and dam of Tullig Rambler, sire of Ardfert Rambler (sold for £1,500) from a mating with Monalee Champion (Crazy Parachute—Sheila at Last).

Tullig Rambler was, in turn, sire of the white and blue dog Pat Seamur, who finished third in the English Derby of 1977 and the following year won the Scottish Derby and ran up for the Gold Collar. A later mating of Yurituni with Monalee Champion gave Sole Aim, Irish Derby winner in 1971, who was sire of Columbcille Aim, dam of the 1979 Irish Derby winner, the bitch Penny County. Again, Pigalle Wonder, from a mating with Survival, produced More Wonder, litter sister of Wonder Valley. She was to become dam of Kilmagoura Fair, dam of Kilmagoura Mist, winner of the 1979 English St Leger.

Perhaps the outstanding sire of the 1980s will be Tain Mor, whose dam, An Tain, was by Pigalle Wonder's son, Russian Gun, out of the Prairie Flash bitch, Pastorville Badge. Both Prairie Flash and Pigalle Wonder had the same dam, Prairie Peg, descended from Brilliant Bob through Brilliant Gay and Prairie Vixen. Pigalle Wonder was also sire of Helena's Gossip, who, when put to Odd Venture gave Patricia, dam of Patricia's Hope.

With the exception of Russian Gun and Wonder Valley, it was always in the female line that Pigalle Wonder (like Brilliant Bob thirty years earlier) passed on his amazing speed. He was also to sire Fantastic Prince, who in turn was to sire another outstanding bitch, Catsrock Daisy, winner in 1972 of the Irish Derby and the Easter Cup. The same success came to Pigalle Wonder dams on the coursing field as on the track. He sired April Merry, dam of Merry Newdown, in turn dam of Quiet Lassie, dam of the 1978 Irish Cup winner Castleisland Lad. Again Pigalle Wonder was to sire Lucky Wonder, sire of the bitch Better Get On, dam of the great Master Myles, winner of the 1978 Coursing Derby and sold for £30,000 afterwards, which makes him the most expensive coursing dog in history. He was also the biggest greyhound ever to course or run in public, but he died shortly after his Derby success, through injuries sustained when out exercising.

It is of interest to compare the extended pedigrees of the winner and runner-up of the 1979 English Derby. The winner was the bitch Sarah's Bunny, who defeated the previous year's winner, Lacca Champion, by a length. Both were from sires who were sons of Monalee Champion, who was the grandsire of four of the six finalists. Monalee Champion was by Crazy Parachute out of the bitch Sheila at Last, whose dam was Last Landing. This great brood bitch appears twice in the pedigree of both Sarah's Bunny and Lacca Champion, for, mated to The Grand Fire, she produced the two famous litter sisters Clomoney Grand and Survival. The former, from a mating with Prairie Flash, produced Clomoney Jet who, when mated to Land Rail, produced Sugarloaf Bunny, dam of Sarah's Bunny; and when Survival was put to Pigalle Wonder she produced Martin's Pigalle, dam of Highland Finch, mother of Lacca Champion. Prairie Flash was by Hi There out of another great dam, Prairie Peg, while Pigalle Wonder was from the same dam but this time from a mating to Champion Prince. Again, another prepotent sire, Knockhill Chieftain, appears in both pedigrees: in that of Sarah's Bunny for he was sire of Oregon Prince, sire of Land Rail, the Derby winner's grand dam; and he was also sire (from a mating with Don't Bet) of Cranog Bet, who, when put to Monalee Champion, produced Itsachampion, sire of Lacca Champion. So both pedigrees include the greatest sires who also proved themselves champions on the track; and the greatest dams of modern track champions. They would have been expected to produce champions and they did. The pedigree of Sarah's Bunny reads:

Sarah's Bunny	Jimsun	Monalee Champion	Crazy Parachute
			Sheila at Last
		Lady Expert	Greenane Flash
			Glenogue (Clonalvy Pride)
	Sugarloaf Bunny	Clomoney Jet	Prairie Flash
			Clomoney Grand (litter sister Survival)
		Land Rail	Oregon Prince
			Cloruske Rail (The Grand Fire)

For the pedigree of Lacca Champion, *see under* Famous Racing Greyhounds.

Almost the same sires and dams appear in the pedigree of the 1978 Irish Derby winner, Pampered Rover, but here Sheila at Last and her dam Last Landing (dam of Clomoney Grand and Survival) appear on the dam's side. The great Prairie Peg appears twice in his dam's pedigree and once in his sire's. In place of The Grand Fire (whose dam was Quare Fire) we have the result of Quare Fire's mating with The Grand Champion, which produced Yoblestrap, dam of Dogstown Fame, dam of Time Up Please, sire of Pampered Rover. Thus the Mad Tanist sire, The Grand Champion, appears twice in his sire's pedigree, while Sally's Gossip also comes in as dam of Printer's Prince, sire of the great Newdown Heather. This great dog's entire pedigree consists of the greatest sires and dams of modern track racing. Hi There appears twice, who from his mating to Sally's Gossip produced Printer's Prince and with Prairie Peg (on the dam's side) produced Prairie Flash. Hi There was by Slaney Record out of Dublin Red; Sally's Gossip by the incomparable Endless Gossip (son of Narrogar Ann) out of Castleyard. The Grand Champion again figures in the pedigree, as sire of Prairie Peg from a mating with Prairie Vixen.

As in the pedigree of Lacca Champion, Glittering Look also appears in that of Pampered Rover, as sire of Odd Venture, sire of Shandaroba, who, when put to Pigalle Wonder, gave us Russian Gun, sire of Pampered Rover's dam, Pampered Peggy. Thus both the English and Irish Derby winners of 1978 have virtually the same great sires and dams in their pedigrees, and when retired to stud both champions could be expected to produce champions.

The pedigree of Pampered Rover reads:

Pampered Rover	Time Up Please	Newdown Heather	Printer's Prince
			Pardee
		Dogstown Fame	Wonder Valley (Pigalle Wonder)
			Yoblestrap
	Pampered Peggy	Russian Gun	Pigalle Wonder
			Shandaroba
		Sheila's Prize	Prairie Flash
			Sheila at Last

We have seen that, when Last Landing was mated to The Grand Fire, she produced Clomoney Grand and Survival, both in turn dams of outstanding greyhounds. From a mating to The Grand Prince she produced another of greyhound racing's outstanding dams, Sheila at Last. Not only was she dam of Sheila's Prize, dam of Pampered Peggy, but from an earlier mating, with Odd Venture, she whelped Monalee King, in turn sire of Mel's Pupil, sire of a runner-up in the English Derby, El Cavalier. From her mating to Prairie Flash (whose dam was Prairie Peg) Sheila at Last produced Monalee Pride, winner of the 1970 Irish Derby, and Monalee Gambler, who ran up the Irish Derby the previous year and who won the Easter Cup in 1970.

Another of Sheila at Last's famous sons was Monalee Champion, perhaps the greatest of all sires of racing greyhounds. He was in her last litter, born when she had passed the age of ten, and he was from her mating with Crazy Parachute (Hi There—Mad Prospect). Monalee Champion was to sire Linda's Champion, winner of the 1977 Irish Derby and Tipperary Cup at Thurles; Itsachampion, sire of Lacca Champion; Tain Mor, Irish Derby winner in 1976 and now the sire of champions; Sole Aim, winner of the Irish Derby in 1971 and sire of the St Leger winner Rhu; Nameless Pixie 1979 Irish Oaks winner, and many other champions. Sheila at Last has been one of the most important dams in the history of the sport, perhaps through her own dam, Last Landing.

Last Landing won the Irish Oaks in 1959 and was one of the fastest bitches ever to race. When put to Crazy Parachute she whelped Last Parachute, dam of Free Speech, who from the first bitch he served (Coaster) was to sire Hume Highway, winner of the 1979 National Breeders' Produce Stakes at Clonmel. Last Landing's sire was Man of Pleasure, and it appears that she was the important link in the production of so many modern champions. When put to The Grand Fire she was to whelp Survival, dam of Martin's Pigalle from a mating with Pigalle Wonder. She in turn was dam of Lacca Champion from a mating with Itsachampion. Survival's litter sister was the great bitch Clomoney Grand, one of the fastest ever to race in Ireland. From a mating to Prairie Flash she whelped Clomoney Jet, sire of Sugarloaf Bunny, dam of the 1979 Derby winner Sarah's Bunny.

Another outstanding dam of modern times has undoubtedly been Millie Hawthorn, who between 1968 and 1973 had the greatest influence on the contestants in six English Derbys. Indeed, over a period of five years no other dam has produced so many Derby finalists nor had a greater influence on that event. Her first mating, with Solar Prince, produced Faithful Hope, winner in 1966 in the fastest time ever for a Derby final. The following year, from her mating to Clonalvy Pride, she whelped Yanka Boy and Silver Hope, two dogs that were to have a tremendous influence over track racing in the years ahead. Yanka Boy won the Irish Cesarewitch and St Leger in 1967, while Silver Hope reached the final of the 1967 English Derby. In recent years Yanka Boy has sired Kilmagoura Mist, winner of the 1978 Oaks and the 1979 English St Leger; and Dark Mercury, sire of the 1979 Irish Derby winner Penny County. He was also sire of Itsastar, dam of the 1979 Irish Oaks winner Nameless Pixie. Silver Hope sired Patricia's Hope, winner of the English Derby in 1972 and 1973. The 1968 English Derby final line-up included her son Winning Hope, and the winner in 1970, John Silver, was sired by Faithful Hope, so that Millie Hawthorn was his grand dam. Thus between 1966 and 1973 in only one year, 1971, was her influence not felt in the English Derby. It is, however, through her mating with Clonalvy Pride that her influence continues to be felt on the greyhound racing scene, through her son Yanka Pride and her other son from the same litter – Silver Hope, who was in turn the sire of Lively Band, sire of the 1977 English Derby winner Balliniska Band, and his litter brother Linacre.

The great dams Millie Hawthorn and Prairie Peg have now joined the great bitch Cranog Bet to produce the champions of today. From the mating of the Irish Oaks winner Itsamint (Prairie Flash–Cranog Bet) with Yanka Boy (Clonalvy Pride–Millie Hawthorn) was born Itsastar, who, when mated to Rita's Choice, whelped Nameless Star, winner of the 1976 Irish Laurels and St Leger; and from her mating to Monalee Champion (Sheila at Last) she produced the 1979 Irish Oaks winner Nameless Pixie. Breeding does count, and any bitch of good make-up who has one of the great dams of the past decade in her pedigree can be expected to produce a champion of the future if mated with the right sire.

The following pedigree, given for purposes of comparison, is that of Nameless Pixie:

Nameless Pixie	Monalee Champion	Crazy Parachute	Hi There
			Mad Prospect
		Sheila at Last	The Grand Prince
			Last Landing
	Itsastar	Yanka Boy	Clonalvy Pride
			Millie Hawthorn
		Itsamint	Prairie Flash
			Cranog Bet

If one compares the pedigree of Faithful Hope (*see* Blood Lines) with the one above, its close similarity will be seen. For Clonalvy Pride subsitute Solar Prince, who was the sire of Clonalvy Pride. Itsastar, now the leading dam of racing champions, contains in her pedigree all the successful blood lines of the past decade merging together in this outstanding dam – Solar Prince by Bella's Prince by Castledown Lad; and those outstanding sires of the greatest dams of modern times, The Grand Fire and Pigalle Wonder, through their daughters Prairie Vixen, dam of Prairie Peg, and Millie Hawthorn.

See Blood Lines; Brood Bitch; Sire.

DEAD HEAT

There have been only two dead heats of classic events in England. Flo's Pet and Monachdy Girl dead-heated for the 1952 Oaks, and six years later, the Cesarewitch ended in a dead heat between Pigalle Wonder and Rylane Pleasure. The 1934 Wimbledon Puppy Derby ended in a dead heat between Maiden's Delight and Tosto.

The Metropolitan Cup, run at the now closed Clapton Stadium, ended in a dead heat in two consecutive years, the only time that this has happened in an important event anywhere. The 1939 Cup ended in a dead heat between Nobleman Junior and On the Strait, and the following year in one between Trev's Transport and Congleton Tiger. The 1942 Wembley Gold Cup ended in Patty Dear and Ashfield Star dead-heating, and the 1945 Eclipse Stakes at Coventry resulted in those two outstanding bitches, Prancing Kitty and Robeen Printer, crossing the line together. In 1948 the Wembley Spring Cup was dead-heated by two of the most consistent dogs ever to race, Don Gipsy and Whiterock Abbey. In a semi-final for the 1947 Pall Mall at Harringay, Patsy's Record and Pilgrim John dead-heated.

In Ireland the National Sprint at Dunmore Park, a classic event, has twice resulted in a dead heat – in 1947 between Fair Moving and Hockfield Light, and in 1968 between Dry Flash and Newhill Printer. The first dead heat of a race in Ireland took place at the very first meeting at Celtic Park, on 15 April 1927, when Imperial Jimmy and Keep Whistling crossed the line together. The only time a new track record has been achieved in a race ending in a dead heat was at Galway in 1955, when Spanish Battleship (in his last race in Ireland) and Portahard Lad covered the 525 yds course in 29.98 secs and crossed the line together, the first time 30 secs had been beaten at the track.

The only double dead heat recorded took place at Dunmore Park, Belfast in 1929 when the bitch Maid of Devenish and the dog Ballyhenry Lad dead-heated over 600 yds. The racing manager was approached by their owners for a special re-run at the end of the meeting, just between these two greyhounds. Interest ran high when the announcement was made and the bookies did tremendous business before the race. To the amazement of all present, the re-run was once again declared a dead heat. Another match was arranged for a few days later, when Ballyhenry Lad was the winner by just under a length.

In August 1983 at Gloucester, Entrust and Santa Power dead-heated in two consecutive races in which they took part.

In a feat almost unknown in hurdle events, on August 13th, 1981 at White City, Macintosh Mor at 33/1, dead-heated with Grand National winner, Bobcol in the Bodmin Stakes over 500 m in 30.93 seconds.

DERIVATION OF THE NAME OF THE BREED

Several explanations have been put forward as to the derivation of the name 'greyhound'. Dr Caius, co-founder of Gonville and Caius College, Cambridge, believed the name was derived from the Anglo-Saxon *gre* or *grieg*, meaning 'first in rank' of hounds. Later, *gre* became *gradus*, meaning 'first grade' or 'most important'. In a letter to the German naturalist Conrad Gesner he wrote that 'amongst alle doggs this was the most principalle, occupying the highest place'. A law of Canute, dated 1016, deemed that 'none but a gentleman' was allowed to keep a greyhound, which was held to be above all other breeds, to be kept only by those of royal descent. 'You can tell a gentleman by his greyhound and his hawk', said an old Welsh proverb. King John would accept greyhounds in lieu of taxes, and it is recorded that during his reign William de Brecosa was given three castles in Monmouthshire in return for ten greyhounds and several other dogs, and that one John Engayne was given the Manor of Upminster for rearing and keeping greyhounds for King John. The wife of Robert Bruce of Scotland, when prisoner of Edward I, was – it is said – allowed to keep 'three women servants and three greyhounds'. Edward III, and later Charles II, had the greyhound incorporated into their seals.

In literature Chaucer, who lived during the reign of Edward III, was the first to use the word 'greihound', spelt almost as it is today, in *The Canterbury Tales*: 'Greihounds he had as swift as fowl of flight.'

Shakespeare, in *Henry V*, shows his familiarity with hare coursing in the king's famous speech to his troops before Harfleur:

I see you stand like greyhounds in the slips,
Straining upon the leash. The game's afoot;
Follow your spirit: and upon this charge,
Cry – God for Harry! England! and St George!

In many of his plays which have rural settings Shakespeare mentions the greyhound and coursing, as for instance in *The Merry Wives of Windsor*, in which Master Slender says to Page: 'How does your fallow greyhound? I heard say he was outrun on Cotsall [Cotswold].'

Others believe the dog's name to be derived from 'gaze', alluding to the dog's keen sight when out hunting. Or its name may simply be derived from the soft grey of the eyes of many hounds, as Arrian, the Roman greyhound enthusiast, pointed out, or from the dog's soft grey coat, for the brindle colour was not introduced until Lord Orford crossed the smooth-coated greyhound with the bulldog in the mid-eighteenth century. Arrian wrote:

> I have myself bred up a hound whose eyes are the greyest of grey; a swift, hard-working, sound-footed dog; in his prime a match at any time for four hares. He is moreover most gentle and kindly affectioned. Never before had any dog such regard for myself and friend and fellow sportsman, Megillus . . . . He is the constant companion of whichever of us may be sick; and if he has not seen either of us for but a short time, he jumps up repeatedly by way of salutation, barking with joy as a greeting to us . . . .

DERRY RACECOURSE
See under Irish Greyhound Racecourses.

DESTRUCTION

If in the opinion of a veterinary surgeon a dog is so badly injured (following a fall or road accident), or is so ill, that to prevent further suffering it is necessary for it to be put down while in the kennels of a race track, the veterinary surgeon shall be entitled to do so without the owner's permission, who may be abroad or impossible to contact quickly (rule 58).

DISPOSITION

In *The Courser's Companion* (1830), Thomas Thacker wrote:

> The greyhound is more noted for docility of disposition united with high courage, speed and beautiful shape, than for sagacity or fineness of nose; yet such is the high opinion entertained by some, of the willingness to obey orders, that one character offered to wager any sum that he could train a greyhound to hunt by nose equally with any other dog – to fetch a duck from water, pin a bull or draw a badger.

Arrian has also told of the delightful disposition of his greyhound.

DISQUALIFICATION

Local stewards at all NGRC tracks have the power to disqualify any greyhound which has previously been running on an unapproved track, or which belongs to an owner who may have been connected with such a track in an official capacity or not. A greyhound which interferes with another during a race may be disqualified from taking part in future events. The owner of a disqualified greyhound shall forfeit all rights in that race, but it will not affect the order of finish upon which bets are decided.

A greyhound disqualified for fighting may be reinstated provided it runs at least three clearing trials on separate days, these trials to include at least three other registered greyhounds, and run over a distance of at least 370 m. Details of a greyhound's disqualification and reinstatement will be included in its identity book. Should a greyhound be disqualified for fighting a second time, the stewards may declare it a confirmed fighter and debar it from running at approved racecourses.

Perhaps the most famous incident of a greyhound being disqualified for fighting during a race occurred during the 1931 English Derby, when Mick the Miller won for the third consecutive time, only for it to be called 'no race'. This was due to the dog Ryland R having interfered with another dog, Seldom Led, on the final bend, causing him to finish last. The incident had immediately been reported by the bend stewards. The *Greyhound Mirror and Gazette* of 29 June 1931 wrote:

> The most amazing Greyhound Derby final in the history of greyhound racing was witnessed by a crowd of 70,000 people at the White City on Saturday. Briefly, the original race, run at 9 pm, resulted in Mick the Miller crossing the line first, a head in front of Golden Hammer. The huge crowd cheered until hoarse, whilst Mr and Mrs Kempton, Mr S. Orton and the thousands who had

supported Mick to win were in a delirious enthusiasm. Then came the bombshell and the announcement that No.2. dog, Ryland R, had been disqualified and the race declared void.

Mick was then more than five years old, and when the race was run an hour later it was clear from the start that he had shot his bolt, and he could only finish in fourth place. Seldom Led was declared the winner.

See Fighting.

DISTANCE MEASUREMENTS

The distances for all trials and races shall be marked out by a qualified surveyor, and certificates lodged with the NGRC.

In Ireland all distances in greyhound racing are measured in yards, but in Britain yards were replaced by metres in 1975.

DOCUMENTS

Registration certificates, change of ownership forms and all other NGRC documents are issued entirely for the purpose of the NGRC, and are not title or evidence of legal ownership of a greyhound.

DOGS AT STUD IN GREAT BRITAIN AND IRELAND

See also Sire.

1930–40

	Born	*Parents*	*Fee*
Ataxy	1933	Inler–Gosher Bead	30 gns
Ballyhennessy Sandhills	1935	White Sandhills–Soraca Deas	30 gns
Ballyjoker	1936	Beef Cutlet–Jean of Waterhall	20 gns
Beef Cutlet	1930	Mutton Cutlet–Burette	30 gns
Border Mutton	1933	Mutton Cutlet–Baby Grand	20 gns
Brilliant Bob	1931	Other Days–Birchfield Bessie	40 gns
Creamery Border	1930	Border Line–Cook	30 gns
Danielli	1928	Red Robin–January	40 gns
Dee Rock	1931	Dee Robin–Dicentra	40 gns
Epinard	1935	Beef Cutlet–Lady Eleanor	20 gns
Grand Flight II	1933	Naughty Jack Horner–Little Fawn Biddy	20 gns
Grosvenor Bob	1935	Golden Hammer–Wonderful Expression	20 gns
Inler	1928	Stormont–In Again	20 gns
Macoma	1926	Glorious Event–Na Boc Lei	25 gns
Mick the Miller	1926	Glorious Event–Na Boc Lei	50 gns
Mutton Cutlet	1921	Jamie–Miss Cinderella	10 gns
Rotten Row	1934	Red Robin–Burletta	30 gns
Silver Seal II	1930	Macoma–Yatton Tiny	20 gns
Tallboy	1927	Tall Guardsman–Kaiser's Girl	15 gns
Wattle Bark	1935	Secret Chance–Helena Kane	15 gns
Wily Captain	1934	Lawyer's Fee–Whirlwave	20 gns

1940–50

	Born	*Parents*	*Fee*
Abbeylara	1936	Prudent Turn–That's the Way	25 gns
Another Dancing Willie	1939	Dasher Lad–Dancing Comet	15 gns
*April Burglar	1937	Danielli–Tannyson's Works	20 gns
Ballyhennessy Seal	1944	Lone Seal–Canadian Glory	100 gns
Ballynennan Moon	1940	Mr Moon–Banriogan Dann	100 gns
Bawnmore Lad	1936	Dasher Lad–Doreen	30 gns
Bella's Prince	1941	Castledown Lad–Bella's Witch	12 gns
Briar Wood	1939	Citronwood–Golden Jane	20 gns
Castledown Lad	1934	Meadow Fescue–Tender Cutlet	70 gns
Castledown Prince	1940	Castledown Lad–Walking Peggy	15 gns
Chancellor	1937	Danielli–Final Deal	25 gns
Cherokee Border	1938	Creamery Border–Cutlet's Return	12 gns
Dutton Swordfish	1941	Mellow Outlook–Dutton Oak	25 gns
Ella's Jim	1938	Grand Flight II–Miss Islington	40 gns
Fair Invader	1939	Fair Chevalier–Floating Rose	10 gns
Farloe Border	1938	Valiant Cutlet–Roeside Cook	30 gns
Fawn Cherry	1942	Manhattan Midnight–Merry Cherry	50 gns
Fish Hill	1942	Fishing Smack–Tinker's Hill	30 gns
Glen Ranger	1936	Mick the Miller–Greta Ranee	20 gns
Highland Rum	1937	Rum Ration–Liagh Lady	20 gns
Jesmond Cutlet	1939	Beef Cutlet–Lady Eleanor	50 gns
Jubilee Time	1941	Fine Jubilee–Winning Time	50 gns
Junior Classic	1936	Beef Cutlet–Lady Eleanor	20 gns

* April Burglar was the first track dog to sire a Waterloo Cup winner when Maesydd Michael won in 1946. (April Burglar won the Laurels in 1940.)
Not all these dogs continued at stud until 1950; several died earlier.
The fees of a number of dogs increased in their later years at stud.

	Born	Parents	Fee
Keel Border	1938	Creamery Border–Keel Ruby	20 gns
Kilrea Lad	1935	Song of the Wind–Inler May	30 gns
Kusta Bok	1940	Valiant Cutlet–Karra Katta	15 gns
Laird's Cutlet	1938	Beef Cutlet–War Spy	15 gns
Lawless Bob	1937	Brilliant Bob–Lawless Lassie	25 gns
Lights o' London	1938	Creamery Border–Life of Luxury	40 gns
Lone Seal	1937	Silver Seal II–Lucky Plum	30 gns
Loose Lead	1940	Beef Cutlet–Olympic Maiden	20 gns
Lost Light	1942	Rebel Light–Miss McCloud	20 gns
Maiden's Champion	1941	Inler Iris–Maiden's Beach	30 gns
Manhattan Midnight	1936	Creamery Border–Deemster's Olive	40 gns
Marching Thro' Georgia	1937	Church Parade–Stone Park	20 gns
Model Dasher	1942	Model Whiskey–Dashing Comet	100 gns
Monalia Bob	1936	Brilliant Bob–Monalia	20 gns
Monarch of the Glen	1940	Carolina Prince–Turn of the Glen	30 gns
Mountain Emperor	1942	Talon–Wicklow Heather	35 gns
Printer	1936	Creamery Border–Dumont	25 gns
Rare Record	1940	Dee Chime–Olympic Cutlet	20 gns
Rebel Light	1938	Mr Moon–Rebel Music Mad	40 gns
Roeside Creamery	1936	Creamery Border–Deemster's Olive	20 gns
Ruby Robert	1939	Valiant Cutlet–Whirlpool	30 gns
Running Riot	1936	Tallboy–Rack and Ruin	10 gns
Smartly Fergus	1943	Tanist–Smartly There	30 gns
Still Moving	1939	Sly Mover–Stillorgam	20 gns
Strange Lad	1937	Castledown Lad–Bean Dubh	25 gns
Swinging Light	1939	Dee Rock–Beaut	30 gns
Tanist	1938	Inler–Tranquilla	60 gns
Tempestuous	1938	Inler–Tranquilla	10 gns
Tokio	1936	Danielli–Tonic	15 gns
Train	1938	Danielli–Tiang	50 gns
Trev's Despatch	1937	Silver Seal II–Lady Moonshine	20 gns
Uacterlainn Riac	1940	Creamery Border–Roisin Riac	25 gns
Well Squared	1936	Stockwell Street–Lyntonia Beach	40 gns
Wireless Time	1943	Wireless Rally–Erin's Green	20 gns
1950–60			
April Cavalcade	1942	April Burglar–Maesydd Maywest	10 gns
Astra's Son	1946	Paddy the Champion–Astra	35 gns
Bah's Choice	1944	Tokio–Chittering Duchess	50 gns
Ballybeg Surprise	1947	Mad Tanist–My Little Diamond	25 gns
Ballymac Ball	1946	Lone Seal–Raging Tornado	30 gns
Bella's Prince	1941	Castledown Lad–Bella's Witch	20 gns
Briano	1947	Mad Tanist–Blue Rebecca	20 gns
Castlecoman	1944	Mad Tanist–Smartly There	15 gns
Celtic Chief	1943	Well Squared–Second Row	20 gns
Champion Prince	1949	Bella's Prince–Sallywell	60 gns
Clonahard Border	1943	Ruby Border–Gill's Selected	30 gns
Confey Castle	1946	Smartly Fergus–My Rosette	10 gns
Daring Flash	1945	Tanist–Daring Lady	25 gns
Darkie's Gift	1943	Tanist–Mad Darkie	25 gns
Disputed Dick	1944	Ruby Robert–Drumdillo	20 gns
Endless Gossip	1950	Priceless Border–Narrogar Ann	50 gns
Fire Prince	1948	Bella's Prince–Snowfire	20 gns
Glenview Shaggy	1944	Castledown Lad–Shaggy Shore	20 gns
Glittering Look	1951	Glittering Smack–Knockrour Favourite	30 gns
Imperial Dancer	1947	Bah's Choice–Imperial Girl	30 gns
Kerry Bill	1945	Tanist–Captured Bluebell	15 gns
Little Arthurstown	1945	Fair Invader–Milltown Light	15 gns
Mad Midnight	1944	Manhattan Midnight–Mad Darkie	30 gns
Mad Tanist	1942	Tanist–Mad Darkie	50 gns
Merry Courier	1944	Mad Tanist–Lucky Orna	20 gns
Monday's News	1944	Orluck's Best–Monday Next	30 gns
Paddy the Champion	1943	Castledown Lad–Brilliant Gay	20 gns
Prince Palatine	1946	Shaggy Lad–Negro's Fire	25 gns
Regal Major	1944	Castledown Lad–Brilliant Tan	15 gns
Sandown Champion	1948	Mad Tanist–Good Record	50 gns
Sans Souci	1946	Bella's Prince–Honey Gale	15 gns
Shaggy Lad	1944	Castledown Lad–Shaggy Shore	25 gns
Slaney Record	1944	Rare Record–Honey Gale	15 gns
Smartly Fergus	1943	Tanist–Smartly There	25 gns
Spanish Chestnut	1948	Rebel Abbey–Cordial Moonlight	50 gns
Surely Mad	1948	Mad Tanist–Fly Dancer	20 gns
Tanner Trail	1944	Tanist–Miss Erris	15 gns

The Grand Champion	1949	Mad Tanist- Could Be Worse	60 gns
Trev's Perfection	1944	Trev's Despatch—Friar Tuck	35 gns
Village Major	1946	Mad Tanist—Really Brilliant	20 gns
Winsome Seal	1941	Lone Seal--Friendly	20 gns
1960–70			
Always Proud	1962	Clonalvy Pride—Always a Rebel	40 gns
Ambiguous	1965	Crazy Parachute—The Mistress	30 gns
Bauhus	1969	Solar Prince—Lovely Sister	50 gns
Clonalvy Pride	1958	Solar Prince—Asmena	50 gns
Crazy Parachute	1957	Hi There--Mad Prospect	50 gns
Crazy Salute	1958	Dunmore King--Ballylesson Surprise	25 gns
Dunmore King	1954	Shaggy Lad--Dunmore Dancer	40 gns
Faithful Hope	1963	Solar Prince—Millie Hawthorn	50 gns
Forward King	1965	Crazy Parachute—Supreme Witch	30 gns
Gorey Airways	1958	Imperial Airways--Geff's Linnett	25 gns
Greenane Wonder	1959	Hi There—Prairie Peg	50 gns
Hi There	1952	Slaney Record—Dublin Red	60 gns
Hi There Merry	1967	Hi There--Merry Champion	25 gns
Himalayan Climber	1960	Northern King—Kentucky Duchess	30 gns
I'm Quickest	1964	Skip's Choice—Grattan Star	40 gns
Knockhill Chieftain	1955	Galtee Cleo- Coolkill Mistress	80 gns
Lucky Hi There	1958	Hi There—Olive's Bunny	40 gns
Mad Era	1956	Hi There—Drumloch Sheevaun	40 gns
Maryville Hi	1960	Knockhill Chieftain—Hi Hook	55 gns
Mile Bush Pride	1956	The Grand Champion—Witching Dancer	50 gns
Monalee Champion	1962	Crazy Parachute—Sheila at Last	80 gns
Monalee King	1964	Odd Venture—Sheila at Last	40 gns
Movealong Santa	1966	Champion Tipp—Movealong Sally	60 gns
Newdown Heather	1968	Printer's Prince—Pardee	50 gns
Odd Venture	1959	Glittering Look—Blarney Groves	40 gns
Oregon Prince	1960	Knockhill Chieftain—Burliegh's Fancy	60 gns
Own Pride	1967	Always Proud—Kitty True	50 gns
Pigalle Wonder	1956	Champion Prince—Prairie Peg	60 gns
Prairie Flash	1969	Hi There—Prairie Peg	60 gns
Russian Gun	1964	Pigalle Wonder—Shandaroba	50 gns
Solar Prince	1955	Champion Prince—Lisabelle	50 gns
Spanish Battleship	1951	Spanish Chestnut—Ballyseedy Memory	60 gns
Spectre	1965	Crazy Parachute—Supreme Witch	50 gns
Super Orange	1958	Super Man—Orange Queen	25 gns
The Grand Canal	1959	Champion Prince—The Grand Duchess	50 gns
The Grand Fire	1955	The Grand Champion—Quare Fire	60 gns
The Grand Silver	1960	Prairie Flash—April Twilight	50 gns
Val's Parachute	1962	Crazy Parachute—Val's Orphan	30 gns
1970–80			
Autumn Belin	1975	Kilbelin Style—High Temperature	£150
Ballyseedy Star	1966	Shane's Legacy—Ballyseedy Jay	40 gns
Blissful Hero	1975	Yanka Boy—Blissful Jude	£125
Bright Lad	1967	Rocket Ship—July Joan	£20
Broadford Boy	1972	Lucky Wonder—Broadford That	£150
Camira Flash	1966	Prairie Flash—Duet Fire	35 gns
Camira Story	1969	Sally's Story—Why Wonder	£60
Carhumore Speech	1976	Free Speech—Pat's Glory	£125
Carry on Oregon	1965	Oregon Prince—Gormanstown Wonder	£40
Case Money	1971	Booked Out—Jamboree Judy	£60
Cash for Dan	1970	Movealong Donal—Cash for Carrick	£40
Clohast Rebel	1969	Good Brandy—Clohast Pride	£50
Cosmic Orbit	1977	Flip Your Top—Future Jet	£175
Cragg's Flier	1966	Clonalvy Pride—Cragg's Pet	30 gns
Crefogue Flash	1969	Newdown Heather—Duffrey Flash	£40
Crown Walter	1971	Spectre II—Clomoney Sue	£45
Dale Lad	1976	Bright Lad—Kerry's Pal	50 gns
Deneholme Hunter	1967	Maryville—Rocco Lynne	30 gns
Discretions	1968	Prairie Flash—Sheila at Last	60 gns
Don't Gambol	1968	Prairie Flash—One for Minnie	40 gns
Dusty Trail	1968	Printer's Present—Dolores' Daughter	40 gns
El Cavalier	1977	Mel's Pupil—El Raco	£150
Finola's Yarn	1967	Sally's Yarn Finola	£45
Fionntra Frolic	1976	Myross Again—Grubs Up	£125
Flip Your Top	1973	Own Pride—Whittle Off	£250
Free Speech	1973	Myross Again—Last Parachute	£40
Glenroe Hiker	1976	Monalee Hiker—Glenroe Dasher	£200
Glin Bridge	1972	Spectre II--Shore Susie	£200

	Born	Parents	Fee
Instant Gambler	1975	Its a Champion–Salvina	£200
Itsachampion	1972	Monalee Champion–Cranog Bet	£60
Itsaflash	1969	Prairie Flash–Just Sherry	25 gns
Jeb Rambler	1977	Tullig Rambler–That's the Style	£125
Jimsun	1972	Monalee Champion–Lady Expert	£50
John Silver	1968	Faithful Hope–Trojan Silver	£80
Keep Moving	1974	Westmead County–Merry Flash	£100
Kerry Long Ago	1967	Bauhus–Kerry Piper	30 gns
Kerryman	1969	Newdown Heather–Quiet Knock	£40
Kilbelin Ruler	1976	Millies Express–Kilbelin Heather	100 gns
Knockrour Bank	1975	Clomoney Jet–Damsel's Lass	£125
Knockrour Brandy	1976	Bright Lad–Knockrour Last	£150
Linacre	1975	Lively Band–Certral	£125
Local Motive	1967	Shane's Legacy–Mistaken Minnie	25 gns
Millcock	1971	Spectre II–Kilcox Damsel	£35
Millie's Express	1973	The Grand Silver–Gaultier Millie	£45
Minnesota Miller	1973	Bright Lad–Letesia	£30
Monalee Expert	1970	Monalee Champion–Lady Expert	£80
Moordyk Champion	1974	Monalee Champion–Nelson's Farewell	£60
Mutt's Silver	1974	The Grand Silver–Simple Pride	£250
Our Rufus	1976	Rail Ship–Geraldine Gold	£175
Paradise Spectre	1976	Spectre II–Paradise Wonder	£220
Pat Seamur	1975	Tullig Rambler–Dainty Black	£150
Peruvian Style	1973	Kilbelin Style–Russian Boots	£100
Ploverfield King	1970	Shane's Legacy–Steady Mary	£80
Poor Mick	1965	Crazy Parachute–Dearnside	50 gns
Postal Vote	1969	Dusty Trail–Paddistarr	50 gns
Quakerfield King	1968	Newdown Heather–Motel Paradise	40 gns
Rockfield Era	1971	Mad Era–Whittle Down	£40
Russian Gun	1966	Pigalle Wonder–Shandaroba	£50
Saucy Buck	1975	Sole Aim–Limerick Lass	£125
Say Little	1970	Albany–Newhouse Blue	£60
Shamrock Sailor	1973	Spectre II–Gruelling Point	£50
Skipping Tim	1967	Myross Again–Right on Time	£40
Stormy Spirit	1975	Spectre–Nora Again	£180
Stylish Shane	1967	Shane's Legacy–Jersey Queen	£50
Supreme Fun	1969	Newdown Heather–Top Note	50 gns
Tartan Khan	1972	Spectre II–Chilled Sweet	£100
Time Up Please	1965	Newdown Heather–Dogstown Fame	£100
Tullig Rambler	1969	Monalee Champion–Yurituni	£60
Valiant Ray	1967	Westpark Quail–Jamboree Judy	40 gns
Weston Blaze	1975	Westmead County–Weston Star	£75
Westmead Champ	1974	Westmead County–Hacksaw	£200
Westmead County	1970	Clonalvy Pride–Cricket Dance	£80
Westmead Power	1976	Westmead County–Westmead Damson	£125
Wired to the Moon	1973	Monalee Champion–April Atomic	£200
Xmas Holiday	1974	Supreme Fun–Mary's Snowball	£150
Yanka Boy	1965	Clonalvy Pride–Millie Hawthorn	£85
Yellow Printer	1966	Printer's Prince–Yellow Streak	80 gns

Some of these stud fees may have increased by the time of publication of this book.

DUAL CLASSIC WINNERS

In the fifty-year history of greyhound racing only four dogs and two bitches have won both an English and Irish classic. The first was Queen of the Suir, who won the Irish Oaks in 1932 and the English Oaks in the next two years, and is the only greyhound to have won the English and Irish events. In 1933, when Queen of the Suir was winning the first of her English Oaks, Brilliant Bob was winning the Irish St Leger over 550 yds at Clonmel, and the following year he won the Scurry Gold Cup (400 yds) and Cesarewitch in England. In the same year he also won the Laurels (500 yds) at Wimbledon. Ten years later the great bitch Robeen Printer won the first Irish Laurels at Cork in 1944 and the English St Leger the following year. Then came Burndennet Brook, a black dog who won the Irish National Sprint at Dunmore Park in 1949 and the English equivalent, the Scurry Gold Cup, the same year, a unique record in itself.

In 1971 Sole Aim, trained by Dave Geggus, won the Irish Derby to add to the Laurels he had won at Wimbledon the previous year. He became one of the only three dogs to win the Derby of one country and another classic in another country. I'm Slippy won the English Derby and Irish National Sprint in 1983. None has won the premier event of England and Ireland, though Lilac's Luck came near, winning the Irish Derby in 1945 and running up in 1946 to Monday's News for the English event, won in the record final time of 29.34 secs.

No greyhound has won the English and Irish St. Leger though Rhu won the Irish event in 1979 and ran up the English St. Leger shortly after.

The hurdler, Face the Mutt won the Irish Grand National in 1981 and the English event in 1982.

E

EARLY HISTORY OF THE GREYHOUND

Solomon, in the Old Testament, included the greyhound in his 'four things which are most comely in going', and the greyhound of Solomon's time is embossed on the palm of the ostrich feathers discovered in the tomb of Tutankhamun which shows the dog as being similar to those which race on tracks today. Like others of the tribe, which includes the Persian saluki, the hound of Afghanistan and the borzoi of the Russian steppes, the greyhound originated in the desert lands of southern Arabia and perhaps the Queen of Sheba took with her several of her finest animals on her famed visit to Solomon in Jerusalem about 1000 BC.

The dogs would have reached Egypt with the incense caravans, and the necropolis at El-Ourna near Thebes on the Nile, contains murals which depict greyhounds with the leg and ear featherings of the breed we now call the saluki. When reaching the cooler and more northerly parts of Persia this dog grew a thicker coat and became the Persian wolf-hound; it was used to hunt wolves and bears. Further north still, in the mountainous terrain of Afghanistan, its coat became even thicker and it developed into the Afghan hound, a favourite breed of today. The breed was becoming taller to enable it to see over the rocky ground, and by the time it reached the Crimea the original saluki of southern Arabia was to become taller still and increase the density of its coat to enable it to survive the cold winters. Thus the graceful borzoi was evolved. These dogs were muscular but finely developed to give them maximum speed, for they hunt by sight rather than by scent and in this way lose no time in reaching their quarry. Nor does the breed often bark, which would give away its position.

From the Middle or Near East the grey-hound reached Greece, possibly introduced by Alexander the Great who had annexed Syria to Greece during his early conquests, and it was in Syria that the smooth-haired greyhound is believed to have originated. From then on the breed was used by the Greek nobility for hunting and would soon have reached Italy, from where it may have been introduced into Britain by the Romans.

An illuminated manuscript of the ninth century AD, now in the British Museum, shows a Saxon chieftain and his huntsmen attended by a brace of greyhounds for coursing, which in appearance differ little from the breed today. But long before, during the Roman occupation of these islands, Diana was worshipped as goddess of hunting, for in the pursuit of the hare the people obtained exercise and enjoyment and the food they caught was an important part of their limited diet. Indeed a greyhound was the most important asset they possessed.

That there were two distinct types of greyhound in Britain, the long- and the short-haired, is confirmed by the Elizabethan writer Gervase Markham, who said that the long-haired 'are held most proper for vermin and wild beasts . . . but not the other, which are more smooth and delicately proportioned and are best for pleasure', which shows that by then the smooth-haired greyhound was considered too refined for hunting animals such as the wild boar, deer and wolf which still roamed Britain's forests. Tichel in his *Miscellanies,* also mentions both types, saying that one, the long-haired, which he called the 'gage-hound' was used for stalking deer, the other, the greyhound, for coursing the hare:

See'st thou the gagehound, how with glance
severe
From the close herd, he marks the destined
deer;

How every nerve the greyhound's stretch
displays
The hare, preventing in her airy maze . . .

That the smooth-haired strain was always held in greater esteem in Britain cannot be denied, but it was Lord Orford who was to bring about a greater improvement in the breed in the eighteenth century than at any time since its early history, by crossing the smooth-haired strain with a bulldog. This not only improved its courage and stamina but did much to perpetuate the short, silky coat we now know so well. For the first time, too, there appeared the now familiar brindled coat, a mixture of shades of brown, grey and black in irregular stripes and markings. Previously greyhounds were mostly black or white or a mixture of the two. Lord Orford was to continue with the bulldog cross for seven generations, until he was in possession of what was described at the time as 'the best greyhound ever known'. This is the greyhound we know today. There were those at the time who had grave doubts about Lord Orford's breeding ideas, but he was proved right because his bitch Czarina produced the greatest coursing stock the world had ever known. Czarina's first litter (when thirteen years old) included the dog Claret, later to become the sire of Snowball, owned by Major Topham of the Malton Club in Yorkshire and which was to win four major trophies and thirty courses before being retired to stud. From Claret and Snowball the modern track greyhound was evolved.

One of the first champions possessing the bulldog blood was King Cob, the first dog whose services at stud were available to bitches belonging to the public. It was King Cob breeding that produced the great Master M'Grath, three times winner of the Waterloo Cup, in 1868, 1869 and 1871, while Snowball was to figure in the pedigree of many famous earlier greyhounds including Fly, which through Oliver Twist (narrowly beaten in a Waterloo Cup final) appeared in the ancestry of the brood bitch Fudge. Her son Judge won the Waterloo Cup in 1855 and in turn sired subsequent winners in Maid of the Mill (1860) and Chloe (1863). Indeed all of Judge's daughters proved outstanding on the coursing field and later as dams. It has been said by breeders everywhere that the whole structure of modern greyhound breeding was built upon the bitches sired by Judge, and Judge was the grandson of Snowball, himself the grandson of Lord Orford's bitch Czarina.

EARMARKING

To tighten up the registration of greyhounds born in Ireland, in 1966 the Irish Coursing Club introduced marking of the left ear for all pups up to the age of two months, but the litter must be registered with the Irish Stud Book within fourteen days of whelping, at a fee of 25p; after fourteen days and up to six months, the fee is currently £1. The marking of the bitch must be stated on that part of the declaration of litter form to be filled in by the control steward, who will inspect the bitch and her litter and at the same time earmark the pups. It is stated on the form that 'If the litter or bitch is not available for inspection on request, the Executive Committee may impose a fine or may refuse to accept the litter for registration.' Breeders will know that the declaration of litter form will not be issued until after the certificate of mating is received.

When naming a greyhound with the Irish Stud Book the earmark must be stated, and no greyhound is eligible to race in Ireland until the owner is in possession of an official certificate of registration.

The date of whelping is checked with the date on which the bitch was served, to make sure that it corresponds with the date on the mating certificate issued by the sire's owner or agent. The date of whelping should be sixty-three days or thereabouts from the time of service, and the control steward's inspection form states that: 'I certify that the puppies on inspection looked to be of the age claimed. I further certify I saw the dam which looked to have reared puppies recently. Her earmark agreed with that shown.' Earmarks consist of three letters.

In Britain, as from 1 January 1980, all greyhounds presented for registration for racing at racecourses under the jurisdiction of the NGRC must have an earmark code. This is known as the adult earmarking scheme, and all greyhounds not previously earmarked by the Irish Coursing Club or by an NGRC marking steward under the litter earmarking scheme will be marked at the

racecourse at the time of registration.
The earmark will provide additional identification before racing and if the greyhound is lost or stolen, since the marking cannot be erased. Fees for earmarking puppies are £3 each, and for adult greyhounds £6, both inclusive of VAT. Earmarkings must be done before the age of fourteen months.

EASTVILLE RACECOURSE
See under British Greyhound Racecourses.

EDINBURGH RACECOURSE
See under British Greyhound Racecourses.

ENGLISH GREYHOUND DERBY
See under Classic Events in Great Britain.

EXPORT OF GREYHOUNDS

Greyhounds may be exported to all parts of the world provided the quarantine regulations are observed, and with rabies a constant threat, stringent precautions are now necessary. The chief countries requiring greyhounds for track racing are Britain, which obtains all its stock from Ireland, for which there are no quarantine regulations; Spain; Australia; India; and the USA. Each has its own import regulations. These will be supplied by Spratt's Patent Ltd of Barking, Essex, who carry out the shipping of dogs to all parts of the world. At their kennels, which are licensed by the Ministry of Agriculture to keep dogs in quarantine, all dogs coming into Britain must be held six months as a precaution against rabies.

It used to be a simple matter to export greyhounds to India and Australia. They would take about a month to reach their destination and usually arrived in perfect condition. The cost was about £20 per dog. Today, with containerization, almost no livestock is now taken by boat. Air travel has replaced sea travel and though the time of a journey is much reduced costs are now in the region of £1,000 to export a greyhound to Australia and about £350 to the USA. In addition there is a large increase in quarantine fees, vet's charges and insurance, so that what used to be an easy and inexpensive undertaking is now prohibitive except for the most expensive of greyhounds.

See Air Travel.

EXPORT OF IRISH GREYHOUNDS

Since earliest times the Celts were famed for their greyhounds. The first we hear of Irish-bred dogs reaching England was towards the end of the fourteenth century, when Edward III, a great lover of the breed, sent to Ireland his huntsman Reginald to obtain nineteen greyhounds from various lords, for which he was to pay a halfpenny a day for each dog, presumably towards their keep. The owner of the boat that went over for the dogs was to be paid ten shillings for the double journey, and he would earn it, for to transport nineteen greyhounds in a small, open boat in a sea notorious for its harshness would be no easy task. There could well have been other journeys to Ireland, for so many greyhounds were killed or injured each year in pursuit of stags and wild boar, that the royal kennels were always on the look-out for fresh stock as replacements. Two centuries later it is recorded that one Shane O'Neill, an Irishman, presented Robert Dudley, Earl of Essex, with 'two horses, two hawkes, and two greyhounds', the most important items a man could possess, when asking a favour of Essex.

Some idea of the importance of greyhound breeding to Ireland's economy can be obtained from a few figures. In 1933, when racing had become well established on both sides of the Irish Sea, for the first time more than 1,000 greyhounds were exported to Britain at an average cost of 10 gns each, but in 1946, twenty years after track racing began in England, 7,500 dogs were exported, the average price of which had risen to more than £100 each.

Since then the value of greyhounds exported to Britain from Ireland has passed the £1,000,000 mark each year. Between 1940 and 1945 as many as 15,000 greyhounds were sent to Britain, and by 1976 the annual total was about 5,000, though the value had doubled to an average price of approximately £170 each; 1,500 were exported to the USA, Spain, Italy and Sweden where racing also takes place.

In 1963 the Irish Greyhound Board established a non-profit-making sales agency to develop the US market and at the same time set up an advisory service to inform prospective buyers of the form of those greyhounds racing at the Board's licensed tracks. In 1961 greyhounds to the value of £6,825 were exported to the USA. Ten years later this had risen to almost £150,000.

Export Figures for Greyhounds

Year	*Greyhounds*	*Total value*	*Average value per dog*
1933	1,000	£10,000	£10
1934	2,064	£25,000	£12
1935	3,500	£23,500	£7
1936	1,655	£28,000	£17
1937	2,290	£45,000	£20
1938	3,225	£77,000	£24
1939	2,644	£70,000	£26
1940	1,662	£40,600	£25
1941	2,145	£78,000	£36
1942	2,719	£130,000	£48
1943	3,244	£272,000	£84
1944	4,861	£436,000	£90
1945	7,517	£733,000	£97
1946	10,388	£1,100,000	£106
1947	10,477	£1,063,000	£101
1964	7,595	£1,080,884	£142
1965	7,500	£1,045,000	£140
1966	7,234	£1,100,000	£152
1967	7,252	£1,180,000	£162
1968	7,298	£1,145,000	£156
1969	6,570	£1,010,000	£153
1970	6,076	£1,016,000	£167
1971	6,122	£1,185,000	£193
1972	6,661	£1,251,075	£187
1973	6,297	£809,234	£128
1974	6,200	£817,889	£130
1975	6,672	£884,508	£132
1976	4,983	£763,301	£171
1977	4,860	£719,226	£153
1978	4,745	£760,656	£160

The average price of each greyhound exported to Britain in 1978 was £160. The total value was much the same as in 1945, but the value per dog has increased by about £60. This is a net increase of less than £2 a year, while the cost of breeding (e.g. stud fees, registration fees, feeding and transport) has increased by considerably more.

Total number of greyhounds exported to all countries, including Britain, the USA, Sweden, Spain

Year	*Greyhounds*	*Total value*
1976	7,329	£1,258,648
1977	7,156	£1,204,406
1978	6,607	£1,043,456

F

FAMOUS RACING GREYHOUNDS

ASTRA

A blue, she was one of the fastest bitches ever to race in Ireland and perpetuated her wonderful powers through Astra's Son, sire of Magourna Reject and of Prairie Vixen, dam of Prairie Peg who, from a mating with Hi There, produced an equally great sire in Prairie Flash. Astra was whelped in July 1942, one of a litter that included Mad Tanner; from a second mating of her parents, Tanist and Mad Darkie, came (July 1943) Mad Tanist. Her sire, Tanist, was the greatest sire of the 1940s, while her dam was holder of the 550 yds record at Cork and until she died in March 1948 was the world's greatest dam, producing record-holders from every litter. Astra was bred and owned by Mr J. Horan, who at one time was offered £2,500 (a big sum in the late 1940s) for her but refused, since he knew enough about greyhounds to realize that he had in his possession something far more valuable, something he could never replace.

She soon proved her owner right when she won the Puppy Derby at Harold's Cross in 1944, beating her brother; she followed this by winning the Easter Cup at Shelbourne Park, a race which has always carried the importance of a classic event. In doing so she won by half a length from Hurry Kitty, another wonderful bitch, in the record time for the event of 29.86 secs. This was the first occasion that 30 secs had been broken. In the 1945 Irish Derby at Harold's Cross she won her semi-final from Highland Kid but was beaten in the final by Lilac's Luck and Gun Music, though in an earlier heat she had set a new track record with a time of 29.88 secs, beating her brother's record of a week before and which was again bettered in the 1946 Oaks by an equally wonderful bitch, Baytown Ivy. Astra again contested and won the Easter Cup in 1946, beating the flying Quare Times to equal Odd Blades' record of 1928 and 1929.

She was then retired to stud and her first mating to Paddy the Champion produced Astra's Son. Sadly, it was her only litter, for Astra died in September 1948, the great things expected of her as a brood bitch only partly fulfilled. In Astra's Son, however, she had whelped a dog who was to play a most important part in producing the great champions of the future, for he was to sire the 1953 St Leger winner Magourna Reject, one of the greatest dogs to race in England, and the bitch Prairie Vixen, who from a mating with The Grand Champion produced

Prairie Peg, one of the great foundation dams of modern track racing. From her mating with Hi There she produced Prairie Flash, sire of Albany, Kilbelin Style and Clomoney Jet, and from a mating with Champion Prince the great Pigalle Wonder.

ATAXY

This brindle son of the black Inler out of Gosher Bead was whelped in 1933, and though not endowed with the same gift of track sense as many champions was still one of the fastest greyhounds of all time. His sire, Inler, came over in 1930 during the early years of the sport. Kennelled at Clapton, he made a name as a real flyer from the traps, a quality he passed on to his son Tanist and also to Ataxy, but like all fliers they seemed to move so quickly to the first bend that it was impossible for them to get round it without moving wide. This gave the slower dogs the opportunity of moving inside where they would get round in a shorter distance than those dogs travelling on the outside. The railers like Monday's News, Bah's Choice, Local Interprize and Mick the Miller would always beat a faster dog who could not or had not the sense and ability to move inside at the first opportunity, and Ataxy was no exception. He was often beaten by a slower dog but one who was able to take advantage of his wide running.

Ataxy came over to England in 1935 and contested his first race at Stamford Bridge where his tremendous pace persuaded his owner, Mr C. C. Keen, to place the puppy with Leslie Reynolds, then at White City. Ataxy's first race there was in the first round heats of the 1935 Derby in which he defeated the Scurry Cup winner Jack's Joke. In his second round heat he was in all kinds of trouble and progressed no further. Yet within a week or so, in August, he set the greyhound world alight by breaking two of the White City's long-standing records, first the 550 yds which he covered in 30.97 secs and then the 525 yds which he did in 29.56 secs. No dog had ever held the two records at the same time. He was immediately made favourite to win the Cesarewitch at West Ham, and in his first round heat, though 6–1 on, caused a sensation by beating the great Brilliant Bob by twelve lengths. In round 2 he defeated the St Leger winner Bosham by almost as much, in a new national track record time of 33.67 secs. In his semi-final he defeated Mr Flintham's dog Grand Flight II with similar ease, winning by eight lengths in a new world record time of 33.50 secs, nine lengths faster than Mick the Miller's record of five years earlier. Made odds-on favourite for the final, he got into all kinds of trouble and was well beaten into fourth place by Grand Flight II in 33.97 secs, much to the disappointment of his owner and trainer and all those who had enjoyed his brilliant running throughout the event.

After several weeks' rest, he reappeared early in 1936 to contest the Spring Cup at West Ham, run over 600 yds, which he won with ease; but in his second round heat for the Derby he was found to be lame after being beaten by the ultimate winner, Fine Jubilee. After several months' rest he contested the Daily Mirror Trophy at the White City, run over 725 yds, and after winning his heat in the track record of 41.69 secs once again ran wide in the final to allow his old rival, Grand Flight II, ample room to cut inside and win with ease. It now looked as though Ataxy, the fastest dog ever seen on a track, would not put his name to a single classic race for in every final he had come unstuck. And then, in the Wembley St Leger, he at last came good, winning his heat and semi-final after being so badly bumped throughout that when coming on to the final straight he was well behind the others and only a tremendous final burst of speed enabled him to win. In the final he easily beat the game Shove Ha'penny to set a new national, Wembley and St Leger record of 40.39 secs. It stood for almost ten years, which shows just how good he was, and though possessing exceptional speed from the traps he had the stamina to keep this up over 600, 700 and even 750 yds – only the finest dogs possess this quality. He followed Mick the Miller and Brilliant Bob as the greatest of his time. In the 1936 Cesarewitch, which he should have won the previous year, he was to repeat his St Leger success, winning his heats and easily beating Safe Rock in the final to confirm his superiority over all other dogs in that year. He was retired to stud immediately afterwards, and though nothing like so successful as his near brother,

Tanist, he did become the first St Leger winner, or indeed the first winner of an English classic race, to sire a Derby winner – G.R. Archduke, who won in 1940 at Harringay, his home track, in a record for the track of 29.66 secs.

BAFFLING BART

A brindle dog by The Grand Silver out of Mosaduva, whelped in September 1973, he was one of the most consistent dogs to race in Britain during 1975 and 1976, winning twenty-nine of his thirty-two races in top company. His first race was at Wembley for the Portmagee Cup, which he won; he followed this by taking the May Stakes at White City and the Puppy Stakes at Harringay. He was back at Wembley in June for the Summer Cup which he won in 29.42 secs, and he next contested the Welsh Derby at Arms Park. Running brilliantly throughout, he won his heat, semi-final and final to give him eleven wins from his first eleven races. In the Select Stakes at Wembley he was beaten by Pineapple Grand, one of the few greyhounds capable of beating him; and in the Major Size International at Dundalk he had to be content with third place behind Main Avenue and Shamrock Point, though behind him were the Irish and English Derby winners, Shifting Shadow and Tartan Khan. A week later he was back to winning, this time at Brighton; he also took the William Hill Lead at Hackney, winning all three rounds, before the year-end and three months' rest. In April 1976 he was back at Hackney to win the Keswick Stakes, and at the White City for the Cambridgeshire he reached the final only to be beaten a neck by the Derby winner Mutt's Silver. He continued to run well until early in 1977 when, after taking the Mecca Bookmaker Stakes at Hackney, he was retired to stud where he soon proved himself a first-class sire.

BAH'S CHOICE

One of the finest of English-bred greyhounds, this brindle dog was by Danielli's son, Tokio, bred at the kennels of Mr E. Creek in Cambridgeshire and whelped in July 1944. His dam was Chittering Duchess and the litter included Chittering Choice, sire of the Waterloo Cup winner Peter's Poet; and Chittering Wish, sire of the 1951 Cambridgeshire winner Dead on Dick. Tokio was nine when he sired Bah's Choice,

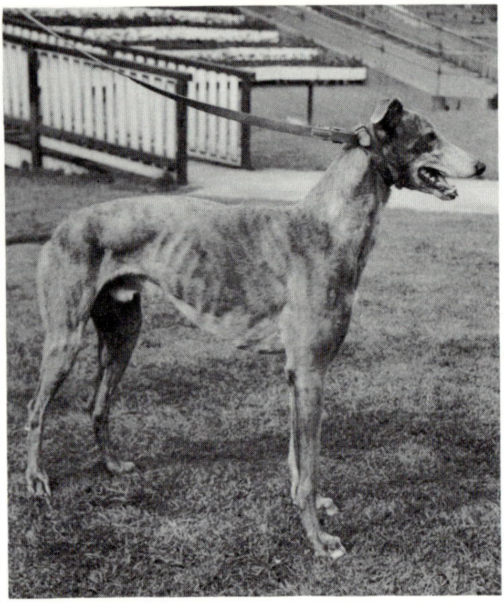

English-bred Bah's Choice.

who was one of his last sons. The dog, who when adult weighed 76 lbs, was originally purchased as a puppy by a West Indian restaurant and night-club owner. Mr E.W. Bah could be seen in his off-duty hours taking a break from entertaining his customers on his Steinway piano by exercising his choice of the litter along the streets of Soho, much to the amazement of those who passed by.

When the dog was old enough to begin trials Mr Bah took him to Catford but after winning only one of his first ten races there he was sold and sent to Wembley. There, in the capable hands of Bob Burls, there was to be a rapid transformation in the dog's abilities. Entered for the Wood Lane Stakes at the White City, he won his heat by two lengths in 29.47 secs, his semi-final in 29.50 secs, and the final, in which he defeated Another Farewell by a short head in 29.48 secs. His track sense and consistent running soon made him a popular dog with the public, and wherever he raced he drew the crowds. When, just two days after his White City win, he clocked 29.04 secs to set a new 525 yds world and track record at Wembley, he began to make headlines in the sporting press. In this race he defeated by six lengths Magic Bohemian, then one of the best dogs in England. Then on 6 June 1946, at White City in a Derby trial, he clocked an incredible 28.99 secs to become the first dog in the world to break 29 secs for this distance, which set a new track record at White City. In his first heat of the Derby he was beaten a short head by Shaggy Lass, but won his heat of round 2 by a neck from Shannon Shore. He failed to get a place in the final, however, and in the Consolation final was beaten four lengths by Quare Times when this dog set a new world record of 28.82 secs, having previously beaten Bah's Choice's own trials record in his second round heat with a time of 28.95 secs, to become the first dog ever to break 29 secs in a race. This was the Derby won by Monday's News by a massive seven lengths from the previous year's Irish Derby winner Lilac's Luck. Just a few weeks before, Monday's News was running in a graded race at Harringay, thus showing how fortunes can turn almost overnight in greyhound racing, as indeed they did for the new owners of Bah's Choice, Max Grant and Solly Jacobs, who had watched the dog being led through the streets of Soho when he was a puppy.

A week later, on 3 August, he won his heat for the Summer Cup at Wembley, by three and a half lengths from Shannon Shore. Behind were Quare Times, Magic Bohemian, Shaggy Lass and Negro's Lad, each a champion in its own right, yet he won the final by three lengths from Parish Model in 29.60 secs. The race was something of a challenge match between Quare Times and Bah's Choice, for the Derby winner was resting before tackling the All-England Cup at Brough Park and no other dogs racing in England could match these two for terrific pace. Yet once again, after he was away to a flying start, Quare Times moved outside at the first bend – he was going so fast that he probably could do nothing else -- but this gave Bah's Choice his opportunity and he always took it. He moved inside in a flash, passed Magic Bohemian on the last bend and won by one and a half lengths to the prolonged cheers of a packed house. Such excitement had the race caused that immediately the result was known Major Percy Brown, racing manager at White City, contacted the owners of the two greyhounds to arrange a return match between these two dogs at White City on August Bank Holiday Monday. Once again it created tremendous interest. It was also a challenge between two of the greatest trainers in the history of the sport, for Quare Times was handled in England by the 'Master of Burhill', the great Sidney Orton, while Bah's Choice was trained by Bob Burls at Wembley. It was also a contest between Wembley and Wimbledon, the two tracks who then had the top trainers and the best greyhounds (only Clapton could approach them in this respect).

Greyhound lovers turned up from all parts of Britain. The two champions were announced with a fanfare of trumpets, like knights on a tilting green, but with only one other dog to do battle against Quare Times, always first from the traps, made no mistakes and set a new world record for the 550 yds course. In the Invitation Stakes run at Coventry on 9 August Bah's Choice had his revenge. He once again beat Quare Times, this time by five lengths, and as usual Quare Times was the odds-on favourite. Bah's Choice set a new track record with a time of 29.45 secs, the record having previously been held by Ballynennon Moon. Entered for the Birmingham Cup at Perry Barr in September he broke a hock in his first round heat and was retired to stud.

In little more than six months' racing after being moved to Wembley he had established himself as one of the outstanding middle-distance dogs in the history of the sport and is an example to those who expect great things from a greyhound as soon as it can begin racing but who do not appreciate that some dogs take longer than others to develop their full potential. Bah's Choice was retired long before he had reached his best. He was favourite for the St Leger at his home track and might well have contested the Derby again the following year. It was rough luck on Mr Bah, for after all his choice of the litter had been the correct one. He had chosen a champion from a very good litter and unfortunately must have sold him for a very small sum.

In early October 1979 another greyhound by the name of Bah's Choice won a race at Harold's Cross, Dublin. The use of this unusual name again is greatly to be deplored for it is too much of a coincidence to have been unintentional.

One of the definitive Bah's Choice's finest sons and one of his first was Imperial Dancer, whelped in November 1947, who possessed the speed and stamina of his sire.

He was a brindle, weighing 73 lbs when racing, and his dam was the great Castledown Lad bitch Imperial Girl, who won twenty-three races in the highest class. As a puppy Imperial Dancer reached the final of the 1949 Irish Cesarewitch but was withdrawn owing to illness. Next year he won the event in the fastest time recorded, 34.25 secs, and ran up for the Easter Cup. Also in 1950 he held the 525 yds track record at both Harold's Cross and Shelbourne Park, and at the latter became the first dog to hold both the 525 yds and 550 yds records together. The 550 yds record had stood for more than ten years.

The pedigree of Bah's Choice reads:

Bah's Choice	Tokio	Danielli	Red Robin
			January
		Tonic	Tabac
			Bontown
	Chittering Duchess	Denham Robin	Deemster
			Beauvallon
		Flint Dairymaid	Hillrow Smash
			De Bula

BALLINISKA BAND

This white and black dog, by Lively Band out of Certral (Newdown Heather), was whelped in May 1975 and won the English Derby when only two years and one month old. He was owned by Mr Raphaello Bacci and trained by Eddie Moore at Belle Vue. His sire, Lively Band, won the 1974 Irish Derby at Shelbourne Park for Mr Cyril Scotland, and was trained by his former owner and breeder, Mr Jack Murphy of Kilmessan, Co. Meath, to win the £10,000 first prize. Winning his semi-final, Lively Band went on to take the final by two and a half lengths from the reliable Windjammer, with Myrtown third. His win compensated his owner for his unlucky defeat in the English Derby that year. This great dog also won the 1000 Guineas at Dundalk and after taking the St Leger at Limerick was elected Greyhound of the Year for 1974.

His outstanding son Balliniska Band won more than £20,000 in prize money during 1977 when he was chosen Greyhound of the Year, an award he richly deserved for that year he won the Puppy Stakes at White City,

Balliniska Bank wins the Spillers English Greyhound Derby 1977. Left to right: trainer Eddie Moore, Geoffrey John (managing director, Spillers Foods Ltd), kennel girl Maxine Aldred (trainer's daughter) Gratella and Patricia Bacci, daughters of Raphaello Bacci, the winning owner who holds the trophy, and Mrs Geoffrey John.

Manchester; was a finalist in the Wood Lane Stakes at White City, London; and finished third in the final of the Pall Mall. He broke the 460 m record at Belle Vue, his home track, and in the Derby final equalled Glen Rock's 500 m record of 29.16 secs to win the premier event by two and a half lengths from El Cavalier with Pat Seamur in third place, after winning all his heats and semi-final. He was an even-money favourite for the final and the first favourite to win for eight years. This fiftieth English Derby was won by a worthy champion.

Balliniska Band had been purchased by Mr Bacci for £2,000 after winning his only race in Ireland by twelve lengths at Cork, and he proved a bargain. In 1977 he won twenty open events and collected more than £20,000 in prize money before his winter rest. Coming out again in March 1978 to contest the Daily Mirror Trophy, run over 500 m at the White City in aid of the Newspapers' Press Fund, he found himself alongside the five finest greyhounds of 1977–8, including the winner of the St Leger, Grand Prix, Oaks, Scurry Cup and Edinburgh Cup. The Derby winner was first from the traps and held on to his lead all the way to win a thrilling race by a neck from his litter brother Linacre, winner of the Edinburgh Cup in 1977.

Linacre was to win the Wembley Spring Cup and finished second in the Welsh Derby and Laurels. He was also the first greyhound ever to break 29.00 secs for 500 m, when he recorded 28.99 secs at Brighton. His sire, Lively Band (by Silver Hope), after two years at stud in Ireland, crossed the Atlantic and was at stud in the USA for several years. Unfortunately he died on the way back home, which was a great loss to greyhound breeding. Another of that great litter whelped in May 1975 was Ballyard Band, who showed magnificent pace and courage in a career cut short by several injuries and is now retired to stud.

The litter brothers' pedigree reads:

Balliniska Band Ballyard Band Linacre	Lively Band	Silver Hope	Clonalvy Pride
			Millie Hawthorn
		Kells Queen	Buffalo Bill
			Miss Ballinclea
	Certral	Newdown Heather	Printer's Prince
			Pardee
		Parlando	Come on Bawnie
			Merry Mistake

BALLYBEG PRIM

A fawn dog by Rockfield Era out of Ballybeg Pride and whelped in March 1973, he was one of the finest middle-distance dogs of all time. He was bred and reared in Thurles, Co. Tipperary by Dr P. McGovern and Mr John Brennan, and trained by Ger McKenna, but for most of his career he was owned by a Lincolnshire farmer, Mr John Bullen. A dog of beautiful proportions, he looked every inch the champion he was. From the same litter was Ballybeg Maid, a brindle who also raced with distinction and was retained for breeding by her original owners. She won the prestigious Thurles 575 in June 1974 when she set a new track record of 31.94 secs, and next month at Kilkenny equalled Clomoney Grand's 525 yds record with a time of 29.00 secs.

Ballybeg Prim developed slowly and it was not until the end of the summer of 1975, when he was two and a half years old, that he first hit the headlines. This was at Navan for the Irish Cesarewitch, run over 600 yds, in which he won his heats and the final in 33.30 secs, a time bettered by only three dogs in the history of the race.

He next contested the St Leger at Limerick, run in September over 550 yds, and here too he went through unbeaten, his time of 30.44 secs being the fastest recorded for the final up to 1979 and it was a new track record. In October he was at Shelbourne Park where he won the important Guinness 600 from a top-class field in 33.40 secs. Later he was selected by a panel of sports editors from the Irish press as national greyhound racing champion of 1975, an honour he well deserved.

Following his winter rest he was entered for the English Derby, and after excellent running in the heats reached the final for which he was made 5–4 on favourite, but was beaten into second place by Mutt's Silver after the two ran neck and neck for the entire race. In October he was back in Dublin for the Guiness 600 which he won for the second successive year, the only dog to do so. He was then retired to stud after two years' racing in which he proved to be a greyhound of outstanding courage and staying ability.

BALLYHENNESSY SEAL

A brindle, whelped in April 1942, by Lone

Seal out of Canadian Glory, he was one of the first of Lone Seal's sons, two of which were to be Derby winners within six years. His dam never raced; because of her breeding she was used entirely as a brood bitch by her owner in Tralee where 'The Seal', as he became affectionately called, was born and reared. There he ran his first trial before the end of June 1943, and in his first race at the track caused no one but his owner to give him a second thought. He did, however, win a sudden death sweepstake shortly afterwards, which must have attracted someone's attention, for a little later he arrived in England to race at Catford under the names of his new owners, Mrs Stowe and Mr Vivian. It is said that they each paid £50 for the puppy and recovered their purchase price in full within two weeks of his arrival when he won the eighteenth Rochester Stakes, his first race in England. He had run well enough to be entered for the Puppy Derby at Wimbledon, where he won his heat by an amazing fourteen lengths in 28.88 secs, one of the fastest times ever recorded at the track, and was made even-money favourite to win the event. In the final, however, he was beaten by a short head by Allardstown Playboy. Towards the end of 1943 the Wimbledon racing manager, Con Stevens, came up with a special invitation race for the puppy champions (a greyhound not two years old) which included Allardstown Playboy; Dark Tiger, the Trafalgar Cup winner; Erlegh Hero, winner of the British Produce Stakes; Model Dasher, the Midlands Puppy Derby winner; and Fawn Cherry, winner of the Irish Puppy Derby. Model Dasher was injured and could not run, so an invitation was sent to the owners of 'The Seal' and it was this dog who won, coming from the traps like greased lightning to win by one and a half lengths in 28.99 secs.

The puppy was now moved from Catford to Wimbledon and placed in the care of Stan Martin. Entered for the May Stakes at Stamford Bridge in 1944 he set a new track and world record when clocking 27.64 secs for the 500 yds course. In mph terms his time was the fastest ever recorded over a track circuit. Then on 28 May in The Circuit at Walthamstow he set a new track record in his heat with a time of 28.62 secs, and improved upon this when winning the final in 28.59 secs. In eight days he had broken three track records and he was only two years one month old. In the Wembley Summer Cup, run over 525 yds, in a race that included Model Dasher, he won by two and a half lengths in 29.29 secs. His next run was in October, again at Walthamstow, for the Steward's Cup. Once again he trapped like a bullet and won by three lengths from Rothman's Arthur. Then just before Christmas, in the eleventh International at Wimbledon, in a race that included Model Dasher, Disputed Rattler and Fish Hill (who had just beaten Train's record at Harringay on his first run in England), Ballyhennessy Seal again went clear of his rivals a few yards from the traps and was never headed, to win by more than six lengths in 28.55 secs. Then, after only a few days' rest, he took the 1945 New Year Stakes at White City, again beating Disputed Rattler, the best bitch in training, and defeated Burhill Moon (in his first major event in England) in the final of the Spring Cup at Wembley.

All tracks came alike to him, and during 1943–5 no dog could compete with him over the middle distances. His style was tailor-made for the Derby, but the Gold Collar, run at Catford over 440 yds, was the first classic to be run after the war. Made 9–2 on his winning his heat, which he did by eight lengths, he won his semi-final by the same distance and in the final repeated this performance when beating Restorer. He raced no more until the Derby in June. In his heat he finished second to Magic Bohemian, but won his semi-final; made even-money favourite to win the event, he did so in torrential rain by five lengths from the game but outclassed Rhynn Castle, the reserve dog with those other fine greyhounds Magic Bohemian, Duffy's Arrival and Celtic Chief many yards behind.

He was next entered for the Laurels at his home track, which he was expected to win in his stride, but after winning his heat and semi-final it was sensationally reported that he was suffering from rheumatism in his hind legs and they were not responding to treatment. His owners withdrew him from the final and he was retired to stud after winning over £3,000 in prize money (the Derby was worth only £1,000 in 1945) and thirteen trophies. He was one of the all-time greats and one of the all time bargains.

BALLYLANIGAN TANIST

This white and brindle flyer, a son of Mad Tanist and the great dam Fly Dancer, inherited his tremendous early pace from his sire, fastest son of the flying Tanist who was the winner of the 1940 Irish Derby in record time and who had himself inherited the great pace of his sire Inler, one of the foundation sires of modern track racing. This same great speed was apparent in Inler's first son, Ataxy, and with Tanist and his son, Mad Tanist, they were the fastest from the traps the sport had ever seen.

Mr Norman Dupont had spent a small fortune on buying greyhounds in his endeavour to win the Derby, but it is said that Ballylanigan Tanist was one of his least expensive buys. Placed with Leslie Reynolds at Wembley, the dog did almost all his racing in the one year, 1951. His first race was for the Derby, in which he won his heats and won the final by two and a half lengths from the favourite, Black Mire, in a new track and final record of 28.62 secs. In his Derby final Ballylanigan Tanist, in trap 1, was off like a bullet and by the first turn was hugging the rails with the race all but won, and although Black Mire never gave up he could not make any impression on Mr Dupont's champion, the outstanding greyhound of 1951. Two weeks later the dog took the Welsh Derby at Cardiff Arms Park and made it a trio of three classics in one year by winning the Laurels, thus establishing himself as one of the greatest middle-distance dogs in the sport's history.

Next night, after winning the Laurels, he set a new track record at White City when winning his heat for the Stewards' Cup, but was beaten in the final by that good dog Rushton Smutty who was to win the Welsh Derby the following year.

Ballylanigan Tanist also came within inches of taking the triple crown, for in the Scottish Derby he ran up, being beaten only a short head. He also set a new world record at Stamford Bridge for 500 yds and for 525 yds, clocking 28.48 secs in the latter, and in the semi-final of the Summer Cup at Wembley he equalled the five-year track record of 29.04 secs, set by Bah's Choice when winning the Summer Cup in 1946.

Ballylanigan Tanist's rival that year was the Perry Barr-trained Black Mire, who won the Wembley Spring Cup in which he defeated another Derby finalist, Rushton Smutty; and the St Leger at Wembley. He also achieved second place in the Derby and was only slightly inferior to the Derby winner throughout 1951.

In 1952 Ballylanigan Tanist again reached the Laurels final, but found Endless Gossip on top form and was beaten into second place by two lengths in 27.96 secs which was the first time that 28.00 secs had been broken in a Laurels final. At Stamford Bridge Ballylanigan Tanist took the Chelsea Cup by four lengths in 27.65 secs and he won the Select Stakes at Wembley by three lengths in 29.93 secs for the 525 yds course. He was then retired to stud.

BALLYMAC BALL

A brindle by Lone Seal out of Raging Tornado, whelped in September 1946, he was one of Lone Seal's last sons, for his sire was ten when he was born. He was endowed with the same amazing speed as his half brother Ballyhennessy Seal, who won the Derby in 1945, and his wonderful track sense was inherited from his great grand sire Glorious Event, sire of Mick the Miller and his litter brother Macoma. After Mutton Cutlet Macoma was the outstanding sire of the early years of the sport, and his son Silver Seal was to sire the 1934 Derby winner Fine Jubilee, while Silver Seal's son Lone Seal was the first to sire two English Derby winners, Ballyhennessy Seal who won in 1945, and Ballymac Ball who won in 1950.

Ballymac Ball was trained throughout his career by Stan Martin at Wimbledon, and his first race in England was at Stamford Bridge on 14 May 1949, when he was beaten one and a half lengths by Local Interprize, but in the June Stakes there he won his heat and the final by half a length from Behattan Marquis in 27.90 secs and gave some idea of his potential. In his heat for the 1949 Derby, however, when quoted 2–1 on, he finished fifth and took no further part in the event, yet in August he was right back to form. He won his heat for the Laurels, beating Eastern Madness by three lengths and setting a new fast time for the event which was also a track record at Wimbledon of 28.03 secs. This he bettered in his semi-final with a time of 27.99 secs, beating Trev's Jubilee by an amazing twelve lengths, with Local

Interprize a further length behind. He was the first to break 28 secs at Wimbledon for 500 yds. Starting at 5–4 on, he left no doubt as to his ability when winning the Laurels final by two lengths from Magna Hasty. He next contested the Thames Silver Salver at Southend, winning his heat and semi-final, but in the final was beaten three lengths by Red Wind in 27.78 secs, a new track record. Red Wind went on to win the Grand Prix a few weeks later and showed the same devastating speed.

Ballymac Ball was then given a long rest and came back refreshed. On 10 December at White City he set a new record for 550 yds with a time of 30.30 secs when beating Good Worker and Narrogar Ann. On Boxing Day he bettered this with a time of 30.27 secs, beating Red Wind, Eastern Madness and Narrogar Ann again. With Narrogar Ann, the Derby winner that year, he was the outstanding greyhound of 1949.

The year 1950 saw him on even better form, winning his heats and the Derby final by three and a quarter lengths from Quare Customer in 28.72 secs, a Derby record, with those outstanding greyhounds Drumgoon Boy, Magna Hasty and Ballycurreen Garrett well behind. Then, for the second successive year, he emulated Ballyhennessy Sandhills by again winning the Laurels, thus crediting his owner, Mr T.F. Nicholls, with three classics. Few other greyhounds ever accomplished this feat. The dog was four years old when he won the Derby and his second Laurels, one of the oldest ever to win these two events. Over the middle distances he was supreme, one of the greatest in the history of the sport.

He was retired to stud after his Laurels win in 1950. One of his best sons was Mr Noel Purvis's Barrowside, winner of the Grand National (his hurdling ability came from Macoma) and who reached the final of the 1955 Derby. Another was the dam Dearnside, mother of the marathon star Poor Mick, the best of all long-distance dogs of the early 1960s. Yet another son was Champion Tipp, sire of Movealong Santa, who in turn was sire of many famous greyhounds. Ballymac Ball was also sire of the bitch Cuckoo Lane, dam of Ivy Hall Rose, who in turn was dam of Ivy Hall Flash, winner of the 1971 Irish Laurels at Cork, so that at stud Ballymac Ball was to have a big influence on the future of track racing. He also figures in the pedigree of the Irish St Leger winner Rhu, for he was sire of Held Over, dam of Ballea Again, who was dam of Rhu's mother, Rigsdale Kuda.

BALLYNENNAN MOON

This brindle was whelped in April 1939, not a particularly good time for a greyhound to be born with war only five months away. Within sixteen months the puppy was to make his first appearance in public and delighted his owner and trainer Mr Billy Quinn, by winning the North Kilkenny Stakes. This was only to be expected for his sire, Mr Moon, was the fastest of Mutton Cutlet's sons, which he proved by winning the International Cup for coursing in 1932, defeating Creamery Border. Mr Moon was then retired to stud and one of his first progeny to win on the coursing field was Model Moon, who in his first season ran into the last four of the Irish Cup and Derby and won the Connaught Cup the following year. Retired to stud, he was mated to the Oaks winner Rebel Music Mad and the result was Rebel Light, who won the coursing Derby in his first season and the following year won the International and the Connaught Cup. In thirty-one courses, Rebel Light was never led. Mr Moon was almost ten when he sired Ballynennan Moon.

At his first run, at Shelbourne Park early in 1941, he competed honestly but without any of the brilliance he later showed. In his first twenty races he won eight times, but in his last race there he broke 30 secs to defeat Roeside Ilene by several lengths and Mr Quinn then negotiated his sale to Mrs Cearns, wife of the managing director of Wimbledon Stadium. He was to be trained by Sidney Orton, following his other stars Mick the Miller and Brilliant Bob.

His first race in England was the Summer Cup at Wembley in August 1941, and after winning his heat he went on to take the final in a very fast time; his performance in his first event greatly impressed the many people who were there to see him. He then contested the August Plate at his home course and by defeating the speedy Lights o' London confirmed his running at Wembley. During September and October the dog was first past the winning line on five occasions but then went down sick, and it was the end of January 1942 before he returned to the racing strength and the last day of February when he took the Walthamstow Stakes. He followed by winning the Wimbledon Spring Cup and in his next forty-eight races he was to win on forty occasions and finish second seven times. It was a year's racing the like of which had never been seen before. He won everything, from 400 yds to 525 yds, and at one point, after finishing first fourteen times in succession, he seemed certain to beat Mick's nineteen wins in succession, but in the fifteenth race he was beaten a neck by Laughing Lackey. He then went on to clock up another eight successive wins during five months of the most brilliant running ever seen. Between his win at Walthamstow in February 1942 and the autumn of 1943 he took part in eighty consecutive weeks of racing; among his outstanding performances were the winning of the Joe Harmon Memorial Stakes, the Charlton Spring Cup, the Wembley Summer Cup, the Coventry Eclipse Stakes and the Stewards' Cup at Walthamstow. It was the height of the war and no classics were run. After a short rest during the winter of 1943–4 he picked up where he had left off, winning his first ten races, and once more seemed set to beat Mick's nineteen in succession when at the White City he was again beaten by Laughing Lackey. He was not to win again, for in the Stewards' Cup he pulled up lame and was retired to stud, being the first to command a 100 gn fee. But he sired nothing of note.

In all, he ran sixty-five of his ninety-one races in Britain and won £4,000 in prize money at a time when first prizes were usually £200. He won thirty-eight trophies and was unplaced only eight times.

BAYTOWN IVY

By the famous sire Manhattan Midnight out of the equally famous bitch Ulster Row, Ivy, as she was known to all followers of the sport in Ireland, can be classed with the greatest bitches ever to race in the Emerald Isle, though the winning of a classic event eluded her. Her racing weight was 58 lbs and she was whelped in 1943. A brindle, she was born in the kennels of Mr Paddy Barry whose greyhounds carried the 'Baytown' prefix.

Ivy first came into prominence when she ran up to Soft Day Matt for the McAlinden Cup at Shelbourne Park, won in 30.12 secs, and she also ran up the following year, this time to Lemon Flash (who was afterwards sold by his owner, Mr Tommy Lennon of Kilkenny for £3,000 to race in England but the dog died shortly after). Entered for the 1946 Irish Derby, Ivy ran brilliantly, winning her heat and semi-final, the latter by the wide margin of four lengths from the ultimate winner, Steve, in what was the fastest time of the three semi-finals. She was made favourite to become only the second bitch to win the Irish Derby but in the final was badly hampered and failed to gain a place.

Then followed the Irish Oaks at Harold's Cross which she was expected to take in her stride. She won her first-round heat by four lengths and her second-round heat by six lengths, knocking .01 secs off Astra's track record of 29.88 secs. It was the author's good fortune to see this magnificent run. She was an odds-on favourite to take the final, yet once again she was defeated, this time by another wonderful bitch, Cold Christmas, who knocked .01 secs off Ivy's new record.

Baytown Ivy was one of the few greyhounds to have held the track record at Harold's Cross and Shelbourne Park, the two Dublin tracks, for she covered the 525 yds at Shelbourne Park in 29.90 secs, being the first to 'break' 30 secs there and beating Quare Times's record of 30.18 secs by almost five lengths.

It was thought, before this record run, that Quare Times was the fastest dog in the world. After it Paddy Barry is reputed to have refused an offer of £3,000 for her to race in England. 'She will never go to England,' he said; 'we think too much of her here.' And though he was many times asked to enter her for the English classics, she never did appear on an English racecourse.

Her last important event before being retired for breeding was at Kilkenny for the Ossory Cup. In her second-round heat she set yet another track record with a time of 29.87 secs, when the Irish Coursing Calendar for 2 November 1946 said: 'She is the fastest bitch of her generation' – as undoubtedly she was. She was now running with amazing speed and intelligence and, after winning her semi-final by six lengths, this time made sure of winning a major event when she took the final by five lengths in 30.03 secs to crown a short but wonderful career.

Ivy was a most handsome bitch with a snake-like head and sharp eyes, while her hindquarters were amazingly well developed for a female. She was one of a group of superb bitches raised in Ireland at that time, others being Prancing Kitty, Robeen Printer and Hurry Kitty, each of whom won classic events on both sides of the Irish Sea. It was a big disappointment to followers of the sport in England that Baytown Ivy herself never made the crossing.

BEEF CUTLET

This brindle son of Mutton Cutlet out of the bitch Burette was born in 1930, soon after greyhound racing had become established. Not only was he one of the fastest and finest dogs ever to run on the track or coursing field, but he passed on all the outstanding qualities of his sire to a new generation of track greyhounds. After reaching the last four of the National Breeders' Stakes at Powerstown in 1932, he was purchased from Mr J.A. Byrne, his breeder, by Sir Herbert Merritt, chairman of Cardiff City Football Club as a present for his daughter, Miss Jane Merritt. Beef Cutlet's first race was at Arms Park, Cardiff, for the Glamorgan Gold Cup which he won; in doing so he set a new track record, covering the 500 yds in 28.41 secs. He was trained first by John Hegarty at the famous Waterhall kennels. Entered for the 1932 Laurels, he won comfortably in 28.47 secs. The time was a new world record for 500 yds and the Laurels final was only his seventh race on a greyhound track. The dog was virtually unknown in England at the time and his victory caused a sensation in greyhound circles. He also took the *Daily Mail* Trophy. He raced no more that year, but in May 1933, over a specially constructed course for the Hunt Cup at Blackpool, which he won by eight lengths, he actually covered 500 yds in 26.13 secs which remains the fastest time ever done for 500 yds and which gave him a speed of over 40 mph. He was quoted 7–1 on his winning! At the White City, Cardiff, which closed in 1936, he covered 525 yds in 29.52 secs, a tremendous time in those days, and then went to the White City, London, for the Derby.

In one of the greatest races ever seen, between the three outstanding dogs of the era, Future Cutlet, Beef Cutlet and Wild Woolley, he was left in the traps and beaten into second place by the shortest of short heads by Future Cutlet, though some who were there contend that it should have been declared a dead heat. But justice was done, for the previous year Wild Woolley had won by no more than a neck from Future Cutlet For the Record Stakes at Wimbledon, where he had won the Laurels the previous year, Beef Cutlet reversed the Derby placings when he beat Future Cutlet by a short head in another thrilling race contested by five of the best dogs in training – Beef Cutlet, Future Cutlet, Goofy Gear, Brave Enough and Fallinga. Three dogs crossed the line virtually together, but Beef Cutlet was judged the winner by a short head from Future Cutlet with Fallinga in third place only a short head away – thus only 5 or 6 ins separated the first three dogs. Beef Cutlet was to win the Welsh Derby, then run at the White City, Cardiff, and was once again beaten into second place by Elsell for the Cesarewitch at West Ham later in the same year. Beef Cutlet would have contested the 1934 Derby but injured himself in a trial at Catford early in the year and was retired to stud.

Among the outstanding progeny he fathered were Laid's Cutlet, Laughing Lieutenant, Epinard, Jesmond Cutlet, Loose Lead, Juvenile Classic and Junior Classic, the last being his most outstanding son and one of the ten best racing greyhounds of all time. One of the last of his offspring was the bitch Winnie of Berrow, who became dam of the Derby winner Narrogar Ann. She was to perpetuate her grand sire's name for, when mated to Priceless Border in 1948, she was to whelp another Derby winner in Endless Gossip, one of the greatest of all time. He was to sire Sally's Gossip who, when mated to Hi There, produced Printer's Prince, sire of the flying Yellow Printer and of Newdown Heather, an outstanding sire of modern track and coursing stock. Beef Cutlet was from a litter that also included Queen of the Suir, one of the greatest bitches in the history of the sport. The great dog died in 1942, aged ten.

Beef Cutlet's breeding was similar to Castledown Lad's, another great sire of the

1940s, but in reverse. Beef Cutlet had Mutton Cutlet on the sire's side and Melksham Tom on his dam's side. It was the reverse with Castledown Lad. Here is Beef Cutlet's pedigree:

Beef Cutlet	Mutton Cutlet	Jamie
		Miss Cinderella
	Burette	Melksham Tom
		Rigadoon

If Junior Classic and Juvenile Classic were Beef Cutlet's finest sons, Ballyjoker was not far behind. Bred at the Waterhall kennels of Beef Cutlet's owner, Miss Merritt, his dam was Jean of Waterhall who was by Mutton Cutlet, and he first caught the eye of followers of the sport when finishing as runner-up to Junior Classic for the 1938 Two-year-old Produce Stakes at Wimbledon. He was then purchased by Mrs Cearns and kennelled at the track under the watchful eye of Sidney Orton. Shortly after his Wimbledon success, Ballyjoker was to win the Summer Cup at Wembley and took the All-England Cup at Brough Park, lowering the track record in each round. Then he went to White City where he won the O.A. Critchley Memorial Stakes, and before the year was out he had won his first classic, the Cesarewitch. He had achieved all this in just seven months.

The year 1939 saw him begin in the same devastating form. First he won the West Ham Spring Stakes, and followed this by taking the Wood Lane Stakes at White City. Then at Wembley he won the Inaugural Stakes, and later in the year set a new national 550 yds record at White City. Again entered for the All-England Cup, one of the north's most important events, he won his way through to the final but had to be withdrawn with a broken bone in a leg. After a long lay-off while his injury healed he came back to racing again in 1940, but never recovered his form and was retired to stud. In two years' racing he had won nearly £3,500 in prize money and a reputation as one of the greatest of middle-distance performers.

BLACKWATER CUTLET

Like Ataxy and Border Mutton, he was a dog for all distances and all tracks, but he raced during the war years when no classics were run and there was only Saturday afternoon racing, so his chances were limited. He was whelped in April 1941, by Woodrow out of Editor's Belle; his sire was by Tallboy and his dam by Editor's Book, and he was trained by Paddy Fortune throughout his career. His first open race in England was the Metropolitan Cup at Clapton, in the final of which he was beaten a short head by the bitch Lizarden. The following week at Wimbledon he was again beaten, this time by a neck, and the great Ballynennan Moon was the victor. At Walthamstow in the final of the Stewards' Cup he dead-heated with Ballykildare, and the following week at Clapton in the London Cup he put up what those who saw the race regard as the finest performance ever achieved by a dog at this track, when he beat Ballykildare by twelve lengths to knock half a second off the track record when covering the 550 yds in 31.80 secs. Then at Walthamstow in the Test, run over 700 yds, he was again successful and completed a wonderful year (1943) by winning the International at Wimbledon, beating Derry's Son.

The following year at Catford, for the Catford Cup, he set another track record when beating the bitch Unwin Beauty by four lengths to record 35.40 secs for the 600 yds course. At Clapton again he took the London Cup when beating Coonavincent Betty in 32.43 secs. He was particularly good on small, difficult tracks like Clapton, and indeed there never was a better performer at this track which is sadly now closed.

BOOKED SIX

A blue brindle, whelped in May 1966, by Booked Out and the famous dam Technician, whose grandsire was Knockhill Chieftain and grand dam Direct Lead, dam of the 1969 Derby winner Sand Star. Direct Lead was ten when Booked Six was born, and it was her last litter but one. She was bred from Hi There and the dam Drumlock Sheevaun, a daughter of the famous Sheevaun, while Technician's sire was The Grand Fire.

Coming to England early in 1968, Booked Six first contested and won the Wills Marathon over 700 yds at Powderhall; he repeated this success the following year when he set a new track record of 39.84

secs, being the first to break 40 secs at this track. He contested the Wills Northern 700 at Belle Vue where he was also successful, and after winning all his heats he took the Grand Handicap at Brough Park in a new course record. In 1969 he won the 932 yds Thornton-Smith Trophy at Eastville and then set a new record at Harringay over 900 yds. At his home track, Clapton, he won the Charles Luper Memorial Trophy, run over 760 yds, and was unbeaten throughout the event. Reaching the final of the St Leger, he was narrowly beaten into second place by Crefogue Dancer in the very fast time of 39.65 secs, and although he did not win a classic event he was voted best racing greyhound of 1969, an honour he well deserved. One of the best stayers of all time, in all he won thirty-five open races and more than £6,000 in prize money, a total that was not swollen by any of the major prizes. During 1969 he won thirteen events from fourteen starts on fourteen tracks, and his gameness and trackcraft were of the highest quality. He was owned by Mr and Mrs A. Fearn and trained at Clapton by Jimmy Jowett.

His sire, Booked Out was also sire of Case Money, who in 1973 won the St Leger at Wembley, winning every round. He also won the Guinness 600 at Shelbourne Park, beating Rail Ship and Rita's Choice in doing so, and in 1973 he was voted Greyhound of the Year in Britain. In that year he won over £7,000 in prize money and the *Evening Standard*'s correspondent wrote: 'After watching his St Leger running, I must rate him one of the very best.'

In the same litter as Direct Lead was a dog who was to earn everlasting fame as sire of the champion hurdler Sherry's Prince, and his name was Mad Era. He was also sire of the Edinburgh Cup winner Rockfield Era, who won equal fame as sire of Ballybeg Prim, one of the greatest ever to race.

The pedigree of Booked Six reads:

Booked Six	Booked Out	Knockhill Chieftain	Galtee Cleo
			Coolkill Mistress
		Direct Lead	Hi There
			Drumlock Sheevaun
	Technician	The Grand Fire	The Grand Champion
			Quare Fire
		Ballinclay Betty	Fire Prince
			Ballinclay Left

BORDER MUTTON

He was one of the last of Mutton Cutlet's sons, whelped in 1933 when his sire was twelve, but he was one of the best all-rounders the sport has known, as good over hurdles as on the flat, and apart from Mick the Miller no greyhound has ever been as popular. From 1935 until the end of 1937 he took part in 166 open events, possibly more than any other dog, and he always gave everything he had, winning seventy of them and finishing, often a very close second, on forty-one occasions. Altogether he won £2,500 and thirty-six trophies, more than any other greyhound, and he won over all distances and on every track he raced.

He was one of a litter that included Border Cutlet, who when mated to Inler May produced the outstanding coursing litter of all time, for Shule Aroon won the 1940 Irish Cup; Salisbury won the coursing Derby of 1939; Sneem the Oaks that year; and Spring of Shillelagh and Shane Bornagh divided the Connaught Cup.

Border Mutton arrived in England in the summer of 1935 and was bought by Mr Proctor Smith who placed him with the Wimbledon trainer Paddy McEllistrim. He first won the Thames Silver Salver at Southend and then took the London Cup at Clapton. Then in the final of the Gold Collar at Catford he was narrowly beaten before taking a well-earned rest. Resuming in March 1936, he ran five races in four days, winning four of them. He was just as successful over hurdles, his best year being 1937 when he won the Empire Stadium Stakes at Wembley and was beaten only a short head in the Grand National, won by Flying Wedge. At the end of the year, after endearing himself to followers of the sport, he was retired, but as so often happens to a dog that has raced so often he was ten before he sired a really good son. This was Country Life, who won the Scurry Gold Cup in 1945 and ran up to Burhill Moon for the Laurels.

BRADSHAW FOLD

Bred in England, she was owned, reared and trained by Mr A.R. Hughes, having been whelpéd in 1928. Her sire was Newville Captain and her dam, who roamed the streets of Manchester and never raced, was December Girl. 'Jewel' as she was affectionately called by all who knew her, was with

Queen of the Suir the most famous bitch of the early years of the sport, and endeared herself to the racing public in the same way that Mick the Miller did for her gameness and intelligence. A black, she was the first of that great tradition of black bitches noted for their outstanding staying qualities – bitches such as Disputed Rattler, Unwin Beauty and Dolores Rocket. In March 1930 she covered the 700 yds West Ham course in 40.04 secs, a world record for the distance which stood for almost twenty years until Lilac's Luck became the first to break 40 secs with a time of 39.88 secs at the track, which by then had been much improved. Whether her record was ever beaten by a bitch at West Ham is not known. In the 1930 Derby Bradshaw Fold was beaten into second place by Mick the Miller, then at the height of his powers, who was the only dog in England that year able to beat her.

Throughout that year she continued to perform well wherever she raced and was on equally good form in 1931, first winning the important Coronation Stakes at Wembley in 30.50 secs; then on her favourite track she reached the final of the St Leger in October, only to be beaten once again by Mick the Miller, running with great brilliance in his last race.

At the year end she retired and ended her life in her owner's home, sleeping in his bedroom and rarely being parted from him until she died of old age in 1939. She was one of the first stars of the early days of track racing, travelling by train all over Britain to take part in open events, arriving only a few hours before she was due to race and always as fresh as a daisy and ready to go. She is remembered with affection.

BRILLIANT BOB

He was bred in Co. Tipperary by Mr Billy Quinn, who later bred and owned Quare Times. When he was a puppy Mr Quinn sold a half share to an Irish farmer, and they were persuaded to part with the dog after he had shown his amazing capabilities only through the persistence of the Wimbledon trainer Sidney Orton who knew of the dog's abilities and had recommended him to his patron, Mr A.J. Dearman.

By Other Days out of Birchfield Bessie and whelped in 1931, Brilliant Bob was well named for he was one of the finest on the track and coursing field in the history of greyhound racing. The dog first came into prominence in 1933 while still a puppy, for he won Ireland's oldest coursing event, the Tipperary Cup. Introduced to track racing in the spring of that year, he ran up for the Easter Cup which is on a par with the classics. Later that year he showed that while possessing tremendous early pace he also possessed the stamina for long distances when he won the 1933 Irish St Leger, run at Clonmel for the only time, clocking 31.53 secs. After a winter's rest he came out again in spring 1934 to contest the Easter Cup and this time made no mistake, winning in the fast time of 30.29 secs. The great Monarch of the Glen could do no better than 30.43 secs when winning the event ten years later.

It was at this stage in his career that his owners were persuaded to part with their champion, who had already done enough to stamp himself as a dual-purpose dog of outstanding brilliance. He now changed hands for £2,000, a large sum in those days, and reached England in time to contest the 1934 Laurels run in May at his home track, Wimbledon. His trainer has told of how moody and off-colour the dog was on his arrival here, and how he decided to give him no training at all but to let him rest and roam about the kennels until he had found his feet. The great trainer's understanding was to pay handsome dividends, for 'Bob' took the event and went on to take two other classics in the same year, a feat never before accomplished.

After his Laurels victory Brilliant Bob next contested the Derby, reaching the final in his usual style, but at the last fence, even though drawn in trap 1, he ran into trouble on the first bend and could do no better than finish fourth behind the three best greyhounds of the year after 'Bob' himself – Davesland, Grey Raca and Wild Woolley.

In the Scurry Gold Cup at Clapton Brilliant Bob soon made amends for his Derby failure, winning his heat and beating the previous year's winner, Creamery Border, in the final in the fast time of 23.47 secs for the 400 yds course.

In October came the Cesarewitch at West Ham, then run over 600 yds and on a totally different style of track, with long straights and wide bends, whereas the Clapton track was almost circular and quite small. Yet to 'Bob' all came alike, and so did all distances, for he won this event too. It was his third classic that year and he had also won the St Leger and Easter Cup in Ireland the previous year. He was then only the second greyhound to have won a classic in England and Ireland, Queen of the Suir being the first.

Retired to stud at the end of 1934, he was to prove himself as effective in siring outstanding stock as on the track. Monalia Bob and Lawless Bob were two of his best sons, but it was through the bitches he produced that he left his own mark on greyhound racing. Among these were Miss McCloud, dam of Lost Light, winner of the 1942 Irish Coursing Derby; Brilliant Moon, dam of the 1939 International Cup winner, Wireless Rally; Really Brilliant, dam of the 1945 Tipperary Cup winner, Rathclogheen Dancer; and Brilliant Gay, dam of Hurry Kitty, who followed in the footsteps of her maternal grand sire by winning the 1945 Cesarewitch. Brilliant Gay was a blue brindle owned by Mrs Cogan and had run up for the Irish Coursing Oaks in 1941. Mated to Castledown Lad early in 1943, she was to whelp Paddy the Champion who was to pass on Brilliant Bob's amazing speed to Astra's Son from his mating to Astra. Yet again Astra's Son was to transmit the ability of his parents and grandparents to another Prairie Vixen, who from a mating with The Grand Champion (sired by Astra's litter brother, Mad Tanist) was sire of the 1955 Irish Oaks winner Prairie Peg who, when mated to Hi There, was dam of Prairie Flash, one of the greatest of modern sires. But it was from the mating of Prairie Peg to Champion Prince (Bella's Prince by Castledown Lad) which produced the English Derby winner Pigalle Wonder that we see the Brilliant Bob influence once more carried through the dam. Pigalle Wonder, when mated to Rather Fancy, produced the bitch Yurituni, who from a mating to Monalee Champion produced Sole Aim, sire of Columbcille Aim, dam of the 1979 Irish Derby winner, the bitch Penny County. Again on the dam's side Prairie Flash, when mated to the great blue, Cranog Bet, produced Itsamint, the Irish Oaks winner who from a mating with Yanka Boy gave Itsastar, the bitch who was to whelp the 1979 Irish Oaks winner, Nameless Pixie. Thus the modern track champions have been bred through the influence of the bitches Brilliant Bob produced, and in turn through Pigalle Wonder.

It is interesting that Brilliant Bob's sire, Other Days (by Melksham Tom), was also sire of the curiously named Banriogan Dann, mother of Ballynennan Moon. Thus even before Brilliant Bob was born the influence of his sire and of Melksham Tom was through the dam line. Thus Other Days was sire and grandsire of two of the greatest dogs in the history of the sport.

The influence of Brilliant Bob over almost fifty years:

Brilliant Bob (1931)
×Civil (B)
|
Brilliant Gay (B)
×Castledown Lad
|
Paddy the Champion
×Astra (B)
|
Astra's Son
×Tae Murex (B)
|
Prairie Vixen (B)
×The Grand Champion
|
Prairie Peg (B)
×Champion Prince
|
Pigalle Wonder
(won 1958 English Derby)
×Rather Fancy (B)
|
Yurituni (B)
×Monalee Champion
|
Sole Aim
(won 1971 Irish Derby)
|
Columbcille Aim (B)
|
Penny County (B)
(won 1979 Irish Derby)

BURNDENNET BROOK

A black dog by Great Climber out of Cherokee Girl, he was whelped in April 1947, and during his only year of racing, 1949, established himself as one of the outstanding sprinters of the decade. Owned by Mr Hugh Gallagher of Belfast, who sent him to Leslie Reynolds, he first contested the important Hunt Cup at the old Reading track and won his heat, semi-final and final, beating Gistra Barcus by a length in 22.05 secs for the 400 yds course. He then returned to Northern Ireland where he was entered for the sprinters' classic, the National Sprint, at Dunmore Park. Here, too, he won his first and second round heats, the third round heat and semi-final before taking the final by two lengths from Dick's Symphony in 23.99 secs, the first time 24 secs had been beaten in the event and the first time a dog had come through every round undefeated. He was back in England for the Scurry Cup at Clapton in August; in his heat he ran up to Local Interprize and in the semi-final to Magna Leader, with Local Interprize taking the other semi-final. But in the final he had age on his side and won by a short head from Local Interprize, who was in his third year of running. Local Interprize lost by an inch, and had he won would have been the only dog ever to win two classics on two occasions for he had already won the Gold Collar twice and the Scurry Cup in 1948. He would also have won six classics, the most by any dog. But on this occasion Burndennet Brook was a worthy winner.

CAL'S PICK

By Any Harm out of Flying Sherry, this outstanding fawn and white bitch was purchased by Mr H.G. Warren for £1,400 at Hackney auction sales and was handled throughout her career by Jack Harvey at Wembley. She first contested the Irish Puppy Derby of 1968, run at Harold's Cross, and after winning her heats and semi-final was made even money favourite to win the event but was beaten in a close finish by the Ger McKenna-trained puppy Always Keen. Always difficult to train, as Mr Harvey said, she was made ante-post favourite to win the 1969 Derby but after a long lay-off due to lameness was eliminated in the early heats. She was fully fit by the time of the Stewards' Cup at Wembley, which she won in 29.88 secs, and put up an amazing performance by taking the 600 yds Cesarewitch at West Ham in 32.98 secs, when she became the first bitch to break 33 secs for the course and the event. Previously, she had won each of her heats and her semi-final, in which Shady Begonia was eliminated.

After winning £3,000 in 1969 with eighteen wins and nine seconds from thirty races, Cal's Pick was chosen Greyhound of the Year for 1969, an honour she had well earned.

CLOMONEY GRAND

By The Grand Fire out of Last Landing, and whelped in 1964, this magnificent blue bitch was, with that other famous blue, Astra, the fastest bitch ever to run on an Irish track and is the foremost example of the many famous bitches produced by her sire and which perpetuated the Inler–Tanist blood lines through the dams he fathered. Her dam, Last Landing, was a grand-daughter of the great Rebel Light, winner of Ireland's coursing Derby, the International and Connaught Cup. Last Landing won the Irish Oaks in 1959 when she proved herself the outstanding bitch of the year. She was purchased for a few pounds as a puppy by Mr George Kidd of Bagenalstown, Co. Carlow, for she was the weed of the litter and it took him all his time to rear her. His patience was amply rewarded when, at only fifteen months, when many greyhounds in England are still on the farm, she won the Hurst Cup at Kilkenny and in doing so broke the track record. She followed this success by taking the Callanan Cup at Harold's Cross, the Waterford Glass International at Kilkenny, and the famous Easter Cup at Shelbourne Park in the very fast time of 29.50 secs.

Expected to be entered for the English Derby, she was instead retired for breeding, and her first litter, to Prairie Flash, produced the outstanding trackers Albany, winner of the Thurles Puppy Derby in 1968 at only fifteen months old; Clomoney Jude, winner of the Pigalle Wonder Stakes in 1969; Kilbelin Style, who ran up the English Derby of 1969; and Kilbelin Grand, finalist in the 1969 Irish Derby. Her next litter by the same sire produced Clomoney Jet, a winner of many top events in Ireland. Thus she proved herself to be one of the greatest dams of all time as well as one of the fastest. In addition she possessed a wonderful track sense which endeared her to everyone.

She was of the same blood lines as the

wonder bitch Prairie Peg, who won the 1955 Irish Oaks in the amazing time of 29.55 secs which was not bettered until Itsamint won fourteen years later in 29.35 secs. Prairie Peg (dam of Prairie Flash) was a grand-daughter of Astra's Son, whose dam was Astra and his sire Paddy the Champion. Thus the greatest racing bitches of modern times, Astra (and her dam Mad Darkie) Prairie Peg and Clomoney Grand, were of the same Tanist–Inler blood lines, the foundation of modern racing stock.

CLONALVY PRIDE
By Solar Prince out of the bitch Asmena, this great dog was the winner of two classic events in England besides being sire of the Irish Derby winner Always Proud, who in turn was to sire another Irish Derby winner, Own Pride. Coming to England in 1960, he first contested the Derby, reaching the final, with that other Wembley favourite and winner in 1959, Mile Bush Pride. The two were made ante-post favourites to win, but in the final, won by Duleek Dandy, Mile Bush Pride finished third with Clonalvy Pride (in trap 3) coming in last, after being badly baulked at the first bend. The Pall Mall followed and he emulated those outstanding dogs Pigalle Wonder and Mile Bush Pride in winning this event. He was made favourite to win the 1961 Derby but found one too good for him in Palm's Printer, though he took the Laurels in the fastest time for the event – 27.66 secs, which remains unbeaten. In fact only six other greyhounds have broken 28.00 secs for the event. He also became one of a select company to beat 40.00 secs for the St Leger, his time of 39.64 secs when winning in 1961 being bettered on only one occasion, by O'Hara's Rebel in 1967. Throughout his career in England Clonalvy Pride was trained by Jack Harvey at Wembley.

At stud he was first mated to Millie Hawthorn, and their son Silver Hope reached the final of the 1967 English Derby (won by Tric Trac) and then sired a dual Derby winner in Patricia's Hope. Silver Hope also sired Lively Band, in turn sire of the 1978 Derby winner Balliniska Band.

Clonalvy Pride is also grand sire of the 1975 and 1978 English St Leger winners, Westmead Champ and Westmead Power, through their sire Westmead County.

COOLADINE SUPER
This fawn dog, by Tranquility Sea out of Cooladine Ruby and whelped in September 1979 was purchased for £15,000 from his breeder, Charles Kavanagh by Mrs Mary McGrath of Coalisland, Co. Tyrone and there is no one with greater knowledge when it comes to selecting a good greyhound. Entered for the important Carroll's International of 1981, at Dundalk, and trained by herself and her husband, Colm, the dog was last out of the traps but so missed bad bumping at the first bend and his terrific pace saw him beat a top class field to win by 2 lengths from Calandra Champ in 29.72 secs over 525 yds. Entered for the Burma-Castrol Puppy Derby shortly after, he reached the final but could only finish 5th, being led all the way by Greenwood Robic keeping close to the rails.

For the 1981 Irish Derby and not yet 2 years old, he reached the semi-finals in which he came up against the best dogs in training and in trap 1 he was never in with a chance being well beaten by Bold Work who went on to win the event. In the Consolation final however, Cooladine Super ran up. He had little more racing until the 1982 English Derby in which, again in trap 1 in his first round heat, unfavourable to a wide runner, he was well beaten after being in all sorts of trouble. For the Irish Derby however, he went through undefeated and had the luck to be drawn in an outside trap in each round. In the final he was soon well clear of the field and though Milwankee Prince chased him all the way, Cooladine Super crossed the line almost 1 metre ahead of the runner up in a time of 29.34 secs.

CRANOG BET
A blue bitch by Mr Leslie McNair's great sire Knockhill Chieftain, out of Don't Bet, she won the first Shelbourne 600 in 1964, but had already in the previous year won the 1963 English Oaks when she came within an ace of breaking 29.00 secs, her time being 29.02 secs, the fastest recorded up to then. She also won the Puppy Oaks at Wimbledon, being the first bitch to complete the 'double' In a heat for the Scurry Gold Cup at Clapton she set a new record with a time of 22.41 secs, and though she did not win the event she was chosen Best Bitch of the Year. In 1964, besides her great win in the

Cranog Bet, twice winner of the English Oaks and one of the fastest bitches ever to race. Photo: GRA.

Shelbourne 600, she again took the English Oaks and was again elected Best Bitch of the Year. During her career Cranog Bet was handled by Phil Rees at Wimbledon.

At the end of 1964 she was mated with Prairie Flash and produced the bitch Itsamint, who was to become as famous as her dam and emulating her in winning the Guinness 600. Her next mating, this time with Monalee Champion, produced Itsachampion, who was to become sire of the 1978 Derby winner Lacca Champion, who ran up the following year to Sarah's Bunny. It is of interest that Itsamint's daughter, Knockhill Silver, ran up to Here's Tat in the 1977 Guinness 600, won in a record 33.26 secs for this event.

Not only was Cranog Bet's tremendous speed perpetuated in her daughter Itsamint, but through her to her grand-daughter Itsastar, who from a mating to Rita's Choice whelped Nameless Star, winner of the 1976 Irish Laurels and St Leger; and when mated to Monalee Champion whelped Nameless Pixie, Irish Derby finalist in 1979 and Oaks winner.

CREAMERY BORDER

This blue dog by Border Line out of Cook was whelped in October 1930 and purchased as a pup by Mr Michael Collins from his friend Tom Culinane, together with his litter brother which he named Sly Mover, for £30, a big sum to lay out during the Depression by one who worked as a butter maker in a small creamery at Inniscara, Co. Cork. Michael Collins' faith in his blue dog, never parting with him no matter how high the offers were, is one of the romances of greyhound racing.

When twelve months old the dog went down with distemper, and since he was not responding to treatment, for his owner had little experience in rearing greyhounds, Mr Collins took the dog to Dublin to his friend, the veterinary surgeon Arthur Callanan, who in an effort to save him, gave the dog day-and-night attention for several weeks and was able to pull him through. After six months' convalescence on his owner's small farm Creamery Border was fit enough to make his first appearance on the coursing field. This was for the Cork Cup in which he was defeated in the semi-final by White Sandhills, the dog without a tail yet who was possibly the greatest coursing dog of all time, winner of the Coursing Derby; the Irish Cup (Ireland's counterpart of the Waterloo Cup); and the Cork Cup, another event enjoying great prestige. Creamery Border next contested Kerry's premier coursing event, the Kingdom Cup at Ballybeggan Park, Tralee, a thirty-two-dog stake which was first contested in 1917. The dog was then two years old and came through the event undefeated to give his owner much satisfaction and some idea of the dog's speed and agility.

It was at this point that Mr Collins was offered what some say was £600, others considerably more, for the dog. It was a most tempting offer, indeed it seemed a fortune to him, but he had other ideas and had no hesitation in refusing, for track racing had by this time become established, and there were considerable financial rewards for greyhounds able to win one of the classic events and then be put to stud.

Perhaps he was also aware that one of the first trainers to arrive at Wembley in 1931 shortly after the track opened was his old and trusted friend Arthur Callanan, already famous for having saved the life of the finest dog of the early days of greyhound racing, Mick the Miller, when he was vet at Shelbourne Park.

What better person to send Creamery Border to than his old friend now at Wembley, thought Michael Collins, who had named his dog from the place where he worked and also in honour of the dog's sire, Border Line. So early in 1933 the dog arrived in England with a note attached to his collar and which said: 'Here he is, do with him whatever you think best.' The dog took up residence at 'Doc' Callanan's kennels at Wembley Stadium. Collins did not have long to wait for his dog to confirm that his decision to keep him had been the right one. After several trials at his home track, in which he gave onlookers indications of his amazing speed, the dog was entered for the Scurry Gold Cup at Clapton where he put up a superb performance, running unbeaten throughout the competition. Winning his heat and semi-final, he went on to win the final by an amazing six lengths from Chesterfield Jewel, with the Oaks winner Queen of the Suir behind them.

It was Michael Collins' belief that if the dog remained in good health, he might also take the Laurels, and in any case he would now be certain to command a big fee at stud when his racing days were over. But after winning his heat for the Laurels the dog pulled up lame in his semi-final and did not finish. It was now necessary to rest him for several weeks, but before the year ended he had broken the 500 yds record at Wimbledon, over the same Laurels course, with a time of 28.29 secs and in so doing defeated the great Brilliant Bob by eight lengths. It was a performance the like of which had never been seen before. His trainer, however, handled the dog with great care, never over-racing him, for he knew full well that Creamery Border was his friend's most valuable asset. So it was decided to keep him in training for the 1934 Scurry Cup, an event he had won the previous year, and having come through to the final once again he was for the second year in succession favourite to win. This time, however, he found Brilliant Bob on his most devastating form, and Creamery Border was beaten into second place. Again he was entered for the event the following year and, once more running with great power, reached the final for a third time, only to be beaten by a short head by Jack's Joke, which caused great disappointment to his connections and to all who saw the wonderful race. The winner's time of 23.15 secs stood for twelve years, which gives some idea of the speed at which the two greyhounds were running. Creamery Border was then nearly five years old, but he was not finished yet. He went on to win the Chelsea Cup at Stamford Bridge, beating Ripe Cherry and setting a new track and world record of 28.01 secs for 500 yds. He ran his last race on 27 September 1935 at Wembley before returning to his owner in Co. Cork to stand at stud.

In her book *Greyhounds and Greyhound Racing*, published in 1934 before Creamery Border had finished racing, Mrs Carlo F. Clark said of him: 'Breeders should watch eagerly for his retirement to stud.' How right she was. One of the first bitches he served was Deemster's Olive, and among the litter were Roeside Creamery, Roeside Scottie and Manhattan Midnight, all blues like their sire. On 28 July 1938 Roeside Creamery set a new world record over 500 yds at Stamford Bridge with a time of 27.86 secs, which stood for more than seven years until it was broken by Ballyhennessy Seal at the same track. Roeside Scottie, aptly named, was to win the Scottish Derby at Carntyne and the Champion Stakes, which his sire had also won.

Manhattan Midnight was bought by Mr James Walsh, and after showing tremendous pace in his trials was made favourite for the 1938 Derby. Winning his heats and semi-final, he was expected to win the premier classic with plenty to spare, but tragedy struck. Moving fast round the first bend and into the lead, he broke a hock and did not finish. Mr Walsh had some compensation for his ill-luck, for the less well-fancied Lone Keel, also owned by him, won by three quarters of a length. Manhattan Midnight was retired to stud and passed on to many outstanding greyhounds the qualities of his sire. Among his first progeny were Mischievous Manhattan, Tonycus, Fawn Cherry and the great Rimmell's Black. The bitch Caledonian Desire was less conspicuous on the track, but when mated to Mad Tanist she whelped Mad Prospect who, when put to Hi There, whelped Crazy Parachute, sire of Tric Trac and Spectre II, who in turn has sired many of the finest stayers of today, thus perpetuating the wonderful qualities of Creamery Border who also sired, in his first year at stud, the great hurdler Printer who in turn sired the outstanding bitches and great stayers Mad Printer and Robeen Printer, as well as the Irish Derby winners Steve and Lilac's Luck.

Later came Lights o' London, sire of the long-distance champion Kampion Sailor, another Irish Derby winner in Uacterlainn Riac; and Ruby Border in 1938. Most of his finest sons came during Creamery Border's first years at stud. Ruby Border was sire of Local Interprize, as fast as his grand sire and also a winner of the Scurry Gold Cup; and Clonahard Border, sire of Priceless Border, 1948 English Derby winner, who in turn sired another Derby winner in Endless Gossip, sire of the bitch Sally's Gossip, dam of Printer's Prince, sire of the fastest ever, Yellow Printer, and of Newdown Heather. Their fantastic speed from the traps came in a direct line from Creamery Border, and Michael Collins, now in his eighties, has lived to see it all come true.

Creamery Border's last litter was one of five dogs and three bitches, whelped by Opel Speed in September 1945, a few months after his death at the age of fourteen and a half. Below are some of the dogs he sired.

CRICKET BUNNY

By Printer's Prince out of Cricket Lady, this black dog had a racing weight of 80 lbs and at 29½ ins tall was one of the biggest dogs ever to race. Whelped in 1970, he was the outstanding dog on English tracks during 1972 and in that year won £7,500 in prize money from his fourteen wins out of twenty races in top company. He was privately trained by Arthur Booth, and his wins included the Laurels and the International at Wimbledon. He continued his wonderful run by winning the Midlands Grand Prix at Leicester and the Scurry Cup for sprinters at Clapton. He was then retired to stud.

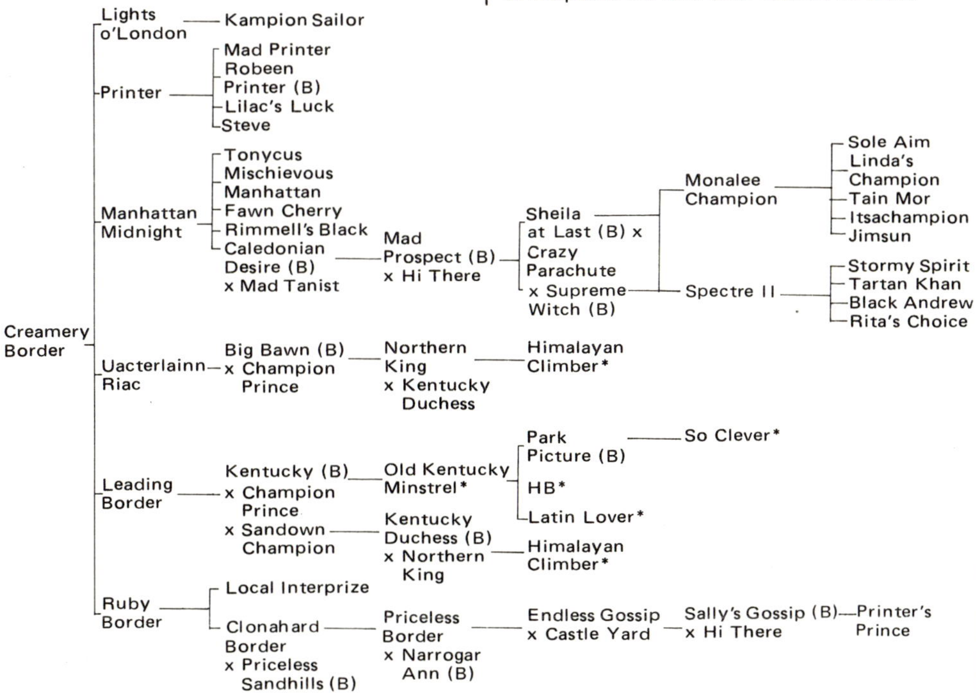

*Waterloo Cup winners

DALE LAD

A brindle dog by Bright Lad out of Kerry's Pal and weighing 72 lbs, he was whelped in May 1976 and began his racing career late in 1977. It lasted exactly twelve months until a broken hock compelled his retirement to stud. With Lacca Champion he was the best dog in training throughout 1978, being handled by Geoff de Mulder for his owner, Mr J. Eisenberg. Early in that year he began a series of top-class open race wins that made him favourite for every event he contested. In June he was at the White City for the Derby, and after his breathtaking displays in the first, second and third round heats he was installed favourite, but in his quarter final heat, drawn in the difficult trap 3, he was unfortunately eliminated after being badly baulked early in the race. In early July he was at Belle Vue for the Northern Flat Championship which he won in 27.56 secs to earn a prize of £1,500, and he was quoted 2–1 on before the final. As a result of his success he was invited later that month to contest the Select Stakes at Wembley, sponsored by Double Diamond with £750 for the winner, a race which included Lacca Champion, Superior Model and Dolla Arkle, winner of the Golden Crest. Here again Dale Lad's devastating early pace saw him in the lead by the first turn and he won by three quarters of a length, with Dolla Arkle in second place. August saw him at Shawfield for the William King Cup, valued at £1,000, and again he made certain of winning by his flying start when quoted at 2–1. The following month took him to Powderhall for the important Edinburgh Cup, valued at £2,500, which he won in a time of 28.07 secs for the 465 m course. He was runner-up for the Midlands Grand Prix at Leicester, and was a finalist for the 1,000 Guineas. His last win of 1978 was at Belle Vue, where he began his great run of successes, when he won the William Hill Nationwide Championship. A few days later, in the same event at the White City, he pulled up lame when leading and was found to have broken a hock. After a winter's rest he came out again in April 1979 and won his first race by twelve lengths, but it was found that he had not fully recovered and was retired. In just twelve months' racing he had won eighteen times and been placed second six times from thirty-two starts, and had won £7,250 in prize money.

Dale Lad. Photo: Valarie Ineson.

He was bred 'in the purple', for Nualas Crazy was by Crazy Parachute out of Sheila at Last and was litter sister of Monalee Champion, while Barbara Joan was by Explosive Gilbert, litter brother of Endless Gossip. The Grand Champion appears twice in his pedigree as sire of Fourth of July and Bermuda's Glory:

Dale Lad	Bright Lad	Rocket Ship	Rocket Fire
			Lady Chee
		July Joan	Fourth of July
			Barbara Joan
	Kerry's Pal	Kilbeg Kuda	KnockrourAgain
			Bermuda's Glory
		Killowen Lace	Clonalvy Pride
			Nualas Crazy

DANTE II

Owned by Mr R. Wynne, who bought him for £400, this black dog was by Well Squared out of Olive's Idol and was whelped in June 1944. Dante II came over as a two-year-old to contest the 1946 Derby, winning his first round heat from the more expensive Model County by a neck and his second round heat by three lengths from that fine bitch Coyne's Castle in 29.26 secs. In his semi-final he finished third to qualify for a final place in which he came up against Monday's News at the height of his powers, who won by seven lengths from the Irish Derby winner Lilac's Luck in a final record time.

In the Northern Flat Championship at Belle Vue he won his heat by one and three quarter lengths, and the final, beating Duffy's Arrival, national record holder for 525 yds, by six lengths in 28.35 secs, only a length outside the track record. Then in the Edinburgh Cup at Powderhall he won his heat and ran up to the Scottish Derby winner Latin Pearl in his semi-final before winning the final by a length in 28.57 secs. In the O.A. Critchley Memorial Stakes at White City he took on the fastest dogs in training; in the final he defeated the expensive Yardley Whistler by a head in 29.36 secs, with Quare Times half a length behind.

At Walthamstow for the Grand Prix, he ran up to Monday's News in his heat and to Tonycus in the final but in the Pall Mall final shortly after he beat Tonycus by a neck in 30.36 seconds, and to complete a wonderful 6 months racing, he defeated a top entry which included Magic Bohemian, to win the Boxing Day Stakes at White City.

He began 1947 on equally fine form and was now trained by Bob Burls at Wembley. His first race was the Wood Lane Stakes at White City in which he won his heat by an amazing 15 lengths in 31.44 secs and the final by 1½ lengths from Parish Model. In June he won his Derby trial stake and his first round heat from Humming Bee but in his semi-final when at 2—1 on, he was beaten into 3rd place by Trev's Perfection, the eventual winner and Slaney Records but he won the Derby Consolation. In the Scottish Derby, he was again beaten by Trev's Perfection.

Dante's next race was the Wandsworth Olympic in which he won his semi-final by 11 lengths from Pushton Ranger and the final by 8 lengths from Shadowlands Delight in 34.67 secs, a new track record. He followed this by winning Wembley's Summer Cup from Quinn's Selection in 29.96 secs, then won his heat of the Birmingham Cup at Perry Barr by 7 lengths but was beaten in the final by Funny Mick. In September, for the St. Leger at Wembley he was on offer at 10/1 on, the shortest odds for a classic event. He won his heat by 14 lengths from Elusive Stranger and his semi-final by 8 lengths in 39.72 secs, a new track record. This he lowered when winning the final, again by 8 lengths in 39.70 secs, beating Shadowlands Delight, with that fine bitch Rio Cepretta in 3rd place. No greyhound, before or since, ever won his heats and the final of a classic event by such large distances.

Dante II ran his last race, the Champion Stakes at White City on December 26th, 1947, in which he was beaten 2 lengths by Priceless Border. He was then retired and to honour a greyhound who weighed only 60 lbs, he was re-named by his owner, Dante the Great. Those who saw him race will never forget his speed and courage.

DECOY BOOM

A fawn bitch, she was one of the all-time greats over long distances, in the same class as Quarter Day, Bradshaw Fold and Disputed Rattler and was of the first litter born to Ka Boom, one of the greatest of all dams, from a mating with Westmead County. Whelped in April 1978, also in the litter was Decoy Sovereign, winner of the Scottish Derby in 1980.

Decoy Boom first came into prominence when winning the Longcross Cup at White City early in 1981 and shortly after, won the Ike Morris Stakes over 730 m at White City and the TV Trophy at Perry Barr. After her seasonal rest, she was back in November to take the Scottish Marathon over 824 m at Powderhall, in her heat, beating Jeff's Love by 6 lengths in a new track record of 52.17 secs. She lowered this to 52.13 secs when beating the bitch, Deliberation by 5 lengths in the final a few days later and soon after, defeated the bitch Rathduff Solara, who had just won the Grand Prix, to win the Stow Marathon. She again defeated her over 730 m at White City to take her winnings for 1981 to more than £10,000, with 21 wins out of 32 marathon races. By a Panel appointed by the Greyhound Trainers Association and the Breeders Forum, she was elected Greyhound of the Year (1981) and best British bred greyhound.

Trained by Joe Cobbold of Ipswich who was elected Trainer of the Year and owned by his wife, Doreen, Decoy Boom broke 5 long distance records in 1981 and in addition to her exploits in Britain, ran up to Straight Free for the Irish TV Trophy run over 750 yds at Harold's Cross. Her sire, Westmead County, winner of the 1972 Wembley Summer Cup, and the St. Leger was one of the sport's top sires of marathon winners. He was also sire of Special Account from a later litter by Ka Boom and who won the 1981 Truman Puppy Derby at Wimbledon, defeating the great Gigolo Diomedes, winner of the Anglo-Irish International that year, by 2 lengths in 27.79 secs with Killacca in 3rd place.

DAVESLAND

By Kick Him Down out of Hasty Go, he was trained by Mr H. (Jack) Harvey when he took up his appointment with the GRA at Harringay Stadium from Belle Vue, and the dog was outstanding during 1934. He won the Derby that year by two lengths from the favourite, Grey Raca; behind them came Wild Woolley, winner in 1932, and the greatest of all greyhounds in 1934, Brilliant Bob. Davesland's time of 29.81 secs was only .01 secs slower than that put up by Future Cutlet in 1933, which gives some idea of his quality. In 1934 Davesland had also lowered Creamery Border's national record for 500 yds with a time of 28.32 secs, and his winning run over 540 yds in 32.70 secs for the Gold Collar at Catford later that year was also a track record. This second classic established him as one of the outstanding trackers of the early years of the sport. He was owned by Mr Frank Brook who bred and reared him at Newmarket and was one of the few to have bred and owned a Derby winner.

DISPUTED RATTLER

A black bitch, by Dasher Lad out of Cheer the Rattler, and whelped in July 1941, she had the stout-hearted Jamie (sire of Mutton Cutlet) and the flying Inler as grand sires in her pedigree. She was one of that famous long line of black bitches, all of whom possessed great staying powers and wonderful courage.

Brought over from Ireland during the war, she ran her first trial at Belle Vue early in 1943 and caused a sensation when she clocked 28.44 secs in her first run over the 500 yds course, only a fraction outside the record held jointly by Wild Woolley for so long and then by Jamboree Reveller. Mr Travis, her owner, who had bought her for only a few pounds (£50 it has been said), knew there and then that she was something out of the ordinary. He gave a half share in her to his daughter, Mrs J. Robinson, and sold the other half to her friend Mrs Gilhooley for a very small sum. Both were dog-lovers and keen followers of the sport, but Mr Travis could not then have envisaged just how much pleasure they would receive from the amazing performances of the bitch.

After winning her first race at Belle Vue, she was entered for her first open event in the Capital, the May Plate at Wimbledon, and like Model Dasher in his first race in London she finished last, beaten as much as ten lengths by Ballynennan Moon. At that point she was written off by those who saw her race. She was, however, there and then placed in the care of Sidney Orton, and her next race found her again in opposition to Ballynennan Moon at their home track. Leading all the way, she confounded her critics with a truly fine performance, but it was at Wembley during the summer of 1943 that she ran so brilliantly to capture the attention of greyhound racing followers during the darkest days of the war.

In June Disputed Rattler enjoyed a run of three consecutive wins at the Wembley track, and but for Wireless Delight beating her by a head in her next outing she would have set a track record of consecutive wins, for she was to go on to win her next eight races there and within a year had won eleven of her twenty-three races at Wembley. In her first race at the Stadium she easily defeated Swanky Ration, and then with a run of 29.32 secs over the 525 yds course came within two lengths of equalling Quarter Day's record of 29.24 secs. There were no classics during the war years, but the Coronation Stakes, run in July, was the most important event for bitches after the Oaks; she won her heat and the final before taking her seasonal rest. She was back at Wembley in February 1944 for the New Year Stayers' Stakes over 700 yds, which she won in 40.18 secs, close to Bradshaw Fold's world record at West Ham. Her next outing was for the Spring Cup at Wembley, which has always attracted the sport's finest performers. The final included Model Dasher, Blackwater Cutlet and Wireless Delight but she won with ease, her time being only .01 secs outside Jubilee Time's record for the 525 yds course. From there she contested the Spring Stakes at the White City, run over 550 yds, a race which included Fawn Cherry, recent winner of the Irish Puppy Derby and sold for a big sum to race in England. But there was no doubt about the outcome. Disputed Rattler, the £50 purchase, beat the field in her usual convincing style.

At the end of May, after her eleventh win from twelve starts at Wembley, she pulled up lame in a race at Harringay with a badly cut foot and was off for almost a year before returning to race. After two outings, though, it was obvious that she was now past her best and her owners wisely retired her while she still retained the affections of the London racing public. She had won twenty-one out of thirty-one races and finished second on five occasions, competing against the finest greyhounds of the war years. Like Mick the Miller before her she had endeared herself to the Wembley patrons by her intelligent racing and tremendous courage. She never accepted that she was beaten and rarely was, always putting in a storming finish even though often well behind as the dogs came round the final bend. She was able to win many of her races by inches when she seemed well beaten a few yards from home, and when less courageous greyhounds would have abandoned the task.

DOLORES ROCKET

Romance surrounds the black bitch and her owners, the White brothers, decorators from Brookwood in Surrey. That she was destined to be successful over middle and longer distances was virtually certain for she was by Newdown Heather, with Mutton Cutlet the greatest sire of track and coursing stock in the sport's history, out of Come on Dolores, a bitch noted for stamina, a winner of the GRA Stakes over 880 yds and of more than £1,000 in prize money. Her dam was owned by Mr Ernest Gaskin who, due to a family bereavement, sold Come on Dolores when she was heavy in whelp to Mr H.G. White and his three brothers for he realized that he would be unable to give her litter the attention it would need.

In March 1969 Come on Dolores whelped a litter of six dogs and one bitch, and the Whites certainly had luck on their side for they sold the dog pups at eight weeks old and retained the bitch with a view to breeding from her later. They called her Dolores Rocket and she was well named.

In her first race, the 1970 Puppy Oaks at Wimbledon, she astonished those who saw her run by winning the final in the fast time of 28.31 secs for 500 yds, starting 3–1 on favourite. It was now obvious that the White brothers had a greyhound of great ability. She then won the Sporting Life Puppy Stakes, beating Crefogue Flash and Supreme Fun, two of the fastest dogs ever to race.

After a seasonal rest she was scarcely back to peak form when the first heats of the 1971 Derby were due to be run. She won her heat in the slowest time of all the heats, and was fortunate to reach the final. In her semi-final she finished third, only a short head in front of Mrs Frances Chandler's Irish Derby winner Sole Aim, but in the final she ran with brilliance, winning by half a length from Supreme Fun, with Leap and Run a further three quarters of a length behind. She had beaten such outstanding greyhounds as Moordyke Champion, Cobbler and Ivy Hall Flash, the favourite. She was only the third bitch to win the Derby, and her time of 28.74 secs

One of the greatest bitches of all time, Dolores Rocket, winner of the English Greyhound Derby and the St Leger, 1971. Photo: GRA.

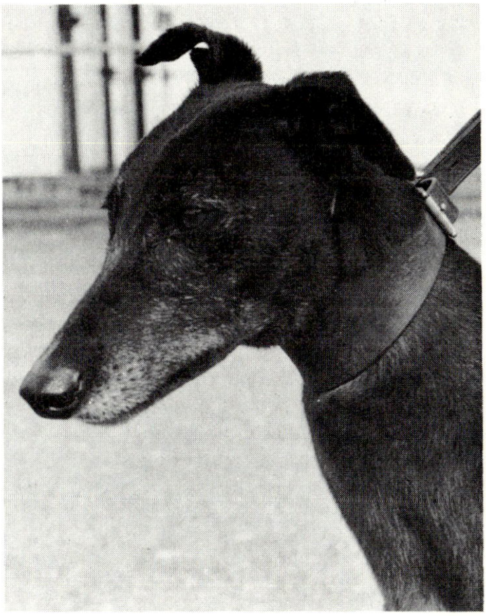

was bettered only by Faithful Hope, who won in 1966 in 28.52 secs, which was never beaten over 525 yds for the event. Her magnificent running speaks well for the way she was trained by her owner, Mr H.G. White, who was only the fifth person to have owned and trained a Derby winner.

Dolores Rocket had bettered her final run in the second round of the Derby on 17 July when she clocked 28.61 secs, the fastest time for a bitch in Britain over 525 yds. Shortly before the Derby, on 6 July, she had set a new record for 650 yds at Romford with a time of 36.06 secs, and before the end of the month had improved upon the 700 yds record at Wimbledon with a time of 39.58 secs. Previously she had won the Spring Cup at Wimbledon, run over 700 yds, and also the Spring Cup at Wembley. But her best was still to come, for in September she became the first greyhound and the only bitch to win the Derby and St Leger in the same year. Coming from behind, she won the St Leger by one and a half lengths from Spectre Jockey in 40.03 secs, which made her the biggest prizewinner in a single year in the history of the sport, and one of the all-time greats.

When mated to The Grand Silver she whelped in January 1975 Sulmac Rocket, winner of the Kent Puppy Salver. In the same litter was Brookwood Maid, winner of the Puppy Oaks of 1976.

Her dam, Come on Dolores, had raced over the stayers' courses, winning twelve of her thirty races and more than £1,000 in prize money for her owner–trainer, Mr Ernie Gaskin. Top marks to the Whites who, realizing her great potential as a brood bitch, sent her to the Belfast bookmaker's wife Mrs Kathleen McKee to be mated to her sire Newdown Heather. She whelped five dogs and three bitches and the rest is well known. But though luck was on the Whites' side in retaining Dolores Rocket, they certainly knew what they were doing in retaining the only bitch in the litter by Come on Dolores and Newdown Heather.

Come on Dolores was a daughter of Knockhill Chieftain out of Sultry Peach by The Grand Fire, an example of The Grand Fire's tremendous pace being passed on through the dam line.

DON'T GAMBOL

A white and brindled dog weighing 70 lbs and whelped in 1968, he was originally named Flashing Maxie and was bred and trained by Mr Richard Kennedy at Bagenalstown in Ireland. With two of the quickest from the traps in his pedigree, Prairie Flash and Oregon Prince, it was only to be expected that he would be endowed with outstanding early pace, but he also possessed gameness and amazing track sense. Not since Local Interprize had there been any greyhound with all these essential qualities which go to make a champion.

In 1969 Flashing Maxie won four of his eight races as a puppy, and after clocking 29.75 secs for the 525 yds run at Harold's Cross he was spotted by the Wimbledon trainer Mr McEvoy, who advised his friends Mr and Mrs Richard Grant to buy him. They paid 1,000 gns and changed his name to Don't Gambol. In 1970 he won his semi-final and final of the Scurry Cup at Clapton, his time of 22.48 secs being only .01 secs outside the national record. In the same year he also won the Wimbledon Owners' Trophy and the Thames Silver Salver at Southend, when he broke the track record. Next year the dog was on even better form, winning the Atalanta Stakes at Charlton and once again the Scurry Cup, this time in a track and national record of 22.29 secs. In winning the sprinters' classic two years in succession he became only the second dog to do so. Then, after winning his heat and semi-final for the Thames Silver Salver, he broke a toe when leading in the final and pulled up lame.

He had done enough to create a name as an outstanding sprinter and was retired to stud after winning twenty-two of his races in England. In 1972, with his injury completely healed, he was brought out of retirement to attempt his third Scurry Cup and almost did the impossible, for he won his heat and semi-final and in the final finished only a length behind the winner, Cricket Bunny, who also won the Laurels that year. He ran thirty-eight races in England in top class and won twenty-five of them. *Sporting Life* described him as the 'greatest sprinter in the history of greyhound racing', coupled with the name of Local Interprize.

One of his first and finest sons was Daemonic Gambol, a fawn of handsome build bred from Mr and Mrs Grant's own bitch Dusk Gambol (by Newdown Heather)

National Sprint Champion Don't Gambol, who won the Scurry Gold Cup in 1970 and 1971.

and whelped in March 1972. Now at stud, Daemonic Gambol won the Wimbledon two-year-old Produce Stakes after winning all his heats, and his time for the final, in which he beat Holkpark Ronson, was a record for the event. He then took the Western Produce Stakes and reached the semi-final of the Gold Collar. He won the Pick, confined to greyhounds kennelled at Wimbledon, and the International, and was voted best English-bred greyhound of 1974.

In January 1974 he took the Winter Cup at Wimbledon; the Golden Crest at Eastville; and the Sussex Cup at Brighton, where he set a new track and national record for 500 m. Once again he won the Pick and International at Wimbledon, and the Greyhound Breeders' Forum Stakes at Wembley.

He came out of his winter rest to contest the 1976 Pall Mall, in which he finished second, and was retired to stud after winning the Laurels consolation final. In all he won £7,500 in prize money and proved himself a great son of a wonderful sire. Both had fantastic speed from the traps. His pedigree is:

Daemonic Gambol	Don't Gambol	Prairie Flash	Hi There
			Prairie Peg
		One for Minnie	Oregon Prince
			Burnt Toast
	Dusk Gambol	Newdown Heather	Printer's Prince
			Pardee
		Dear Millie	Odd Venture
			Millie's Pleasure

DUFFY'S ARRIVAL

At one time the fastest dog in the world over 525 yds, he was whelped in August 1942 and was a fawn dog by Shamrock Prince out of Moon Bride and weighed 67 lbs. He originally raced at Owlerton where he won thirteen out of eighteen races in 1944 when trained by Mr Fred Speck, who shortly afterwards gave up his trainer's licence. Early in 1945 the dog was sent to Aldridge's sales where he was bought for 800 gns by Mrs H. Sanderson and placed on the Coventry track in the care of George McKay. Here the dog made further improvement, reaching the final of the Derby which was won by Ballyhennessy Seal. Following this he won the Catford Stakes over 600 yds and ran up to the wonder bitch Shaggy Lass in the Welsh Derby, who won by three quarters of a length in 29.35 secs. Again he reached the final of the Wembley Summer Cup and the Coventry Eclipse Stakes, but failed to win either event, though at Perry Barr he took the Birmingham Cup, beating Morning Cup by four lengths in 30.14 secs. Two days later, at Wembley, he defeated Burhill Moon and Magic Beau when clocking 29.09 secs to set a new national record for 525 yds, and but for a bump at the first bend would surely have been the first to break the 29.00 secs barrier. Shortly afterwards injury compelled his retirement to stud, but he sired little of note.

DUSTY TRAIL

A fawn dog by Printer's Present out of Dolores Daughter, this fine dog was a model of consistency on the track, earning over £7,000 in prize money and at least that amount at stud, for he sired winners from every dam. During his career he broke 29.00 secs for the 525 yds course on fourteen occasions and was three times a Derby finalist. The dog was owned by a London builder, Mr Jimmy O'Connor, and was whelped in June 1964, his sire being a son of Hi There out of the bitch Faoide who also produced the St Leger winner Powerstown Prospect. Dolores Daughter, his dam, was by Knockhill Chieftain out of the Solar Prince bitch Dolores, whose dam Caramba was by Imperial Dancer (Bah's Choice).

In 1966 Dusty Trail finished third, behind Faithful Hope and Greenane Flash, in one of the most outstanding of all English Derby finals, which was run in record time. From there he ran up to Faithful Hope in the Welsh Derby and took the Scottish Derby at Powderhall when he broke Pigalle Wonder's record time in returning 28.54 secs. He then won ten consecutive open events and went through the Pall Mall undefeated after which he was rightly chosen greyhound of the year in 1966 in front of Faithful Hope and several other champions.

In 1967 he was retired to stud and his first outstanding son was Cameo Laurence, who won the 1970 Gold Collar at Catford. Shortly afterwards another son, Kirkland Darkie, took the McAlevey Gold Cup in Ireland, his time of 28.79 secs being the fastest ever recorded in Ireland over the 525 yds course. When mated to the brindle bitch Paddistar, a daughter of Duet Leader who twice won the English Laurels and reached the final of two Derbys, he fathered Postal Vote, a dark brindle who was whelped in February 1969 and was bought for 500 gns at the June 1970 Shelbourne Park sales by Mrs Betty Hastings. Within weeks he had won £750 and the Irish Cesarewitch at Navan, during which he twice broke the 600 yds record. Soon afterwards he took the £500 Pigalle Stakes and the Easter Cup at Shelbourne Park, in which he showed remarkable track sense. His time of 29.36 secs was the fastest until then recorded for the event. Coming to England for the 1971 Derby he was made ante-post favourite, but failed to reach the final.

Dusty Trail was expertly handled by the Kent trainer Paddy Milligan, who said he was an easy dog to train and one that thrived on affection.

ENDLESS GOSSIP

A brindle dog whelped in 1950, he must be included in the best dozen greyhounds ever

Endless Gossip, winner of the English Greyhound Derby 1952. Photo: GRA.

to have raced in England – with Mick the Miller, Pigalle Wonder, Mile Bush Pride, Brilliant Bob, Dolores Rocket, Patricia's Hope, Sherry's Prince, Future Cutlet, Local Interprize, Carry on Oregon and Ballymac Ball. He was English-bred and perhaps the greatest of all English track greyhounds, with Dolores Rocket the greatest bitch.

His owner and breeder, Mr H.E. Gocher, a retired cattle breeder, was over eighty when he had the idea of breeding a greyhound applying the same genetic theories he had used for many years in raising his prize beef cattle. He believed that he could breed a greyhound to take on and defeat all-comers and did so. He purchased the bitch Narrogar Ann from Mr W.J. Reid, for whom she had won the English Derby in 1949, and put her to Priceless Border, who had won the coveted trophy the previous year. In Narrogar Ann's pedigree were Mutton Cutlet and his son Beef Cutlet, and her sire was Dutton Swordfish, the 1944 Waterloo Cup winner; in Priceless Border's pedigree were Priceless Sandhills and Creamery Border. So on both sides there was a combination of the best coursing and track blood and Mr Gocher was in no doubt about the result for he had given it long and careful study. Both Endless Gossip's parents had been trained at Wembley by Leslie Reynolds, and as a puppy their son was handed to the Wembley maestro in the hope that he would achieve the same success with him. He soon did so. Entered for the 1952 Derby when just two years old, he won his first round heat by an amazing ten lengths in 28.52 secs and was quoted at 4–1 on to win the event, the shortest odds of any Derby winner. In his semi-final he was beaten into third place and only just managed to qualify for the final, in which, however, he made no mistakes, winning by the big margin of four lengths in 28.50 secs, a time which remained unbeaten for more than twenty years when the event came to be run over 500 m.

Two months later, in the Laurels, Endless Gossip took the event in the fast time of 27.96 secs, the first time 28 secs had been broken. So certain was it thought that the dog would win the event that he was quoted 6–1 on, the shortest odds ever quoted on any greyhound for a classic race. In the 1952 Select Stakes at Wembley Endless Gossip made all the running from the moment the traps flew up, and he won by a length from Magourna Reject with Galtee Cleo in third place. These were the three best greyhounds of 1952. His last race was for Wimblédon's Champion Stakes in October 1953, which he again won by a length from Magourna Reject with Galtee Cleo third, and so brought his winnings to more than £5,000.

There are many instances of greyhounds which have proved themselves on the coursing field before becoming track champions; Brilliant Bob was one, but it is rare to hear of a greyhound turning to the coursing field after establishing himself as a champion on the track. However, six months after winning the 1952 English Derby in convincing style and proving himself to be one of the outstanding track greyhounds of all time, Endless Gossip found himself at Altcar in February 1953, competing in the first round of the Waterloo Cup. In every way it was a top-class field and Endless Gossip's appearance added to the interest. In the first round he easily accounted for the bitch Maylin Belle, and gave an impressive display to overcome Laughing Stroller in round 2, only to come up against the Earl of Sefton's outstanding dog, Sucker, in round 3. The two ran neck and neck at the beginning and Endless Gossip looked to be getting the better of the Altcar Cup winner when Sucker found renewed powers and, after a long and severe course, did just enough to earn the judge's verdict amidst great excitement amongst the few spectators who braved the intense cold. Endless Gossip had come up against one of the gamest dogs ever to run at Altcar for, after another gruelling course, Sucker reached the final. Yet, as was only to be expected, he was too exhausted to make any impression on the great Holystone Lifelong who ran out an easy winner of the event. Endless Gossip could so easily have added the premier coursing event to the Blue Riband of the racecourse but on his only appearance at Altcar had done enough to show his outstanding ability behind a live hare as he had behind a stuffed one.

Endless Gossip was one of the most handsome of all greyhounds and in 1952, after winning the Derby and Laurels, he won a challenge certificate at Cruft's. He weighed 70 lbs. At stud he passed on his tremendous pace and track sense to the bitch Sally's Gossip from a mating with Castle Yard, and she was to be one of the foundation dams of modern greyhound racing. Mated to Hi There, Sally's Gossip produced the two great litter brothers Sally's Yarn, sire of Finola's Yarn and the bitch Fallen Ribocco, dam of Easy Investment whose 28.17 secs for 525 yds at Brighton is the fastest time ever recorded in Britain; and Printer's Prince, sire of those fabulous greyhounds Yellow Printer and Newdown Heather. So Endless Gossip had a hand in producing two greyhounds who performed the fastest times ever recorded, while Newdown Heather was sire of Dolores Rocket and many other outstanding greyhounds. In a later mating, to Bealkilla Queen, Sally's Yarn produced the Edinburgh Cup winner Bealkilla Diver. After his early mating to Castle Yard, Endless Gossip was sold to an American breeder and was for some years at stud in the USA.

From the same litter that produced Endless Gossip came the bitch Edgerley's Gloria (both she and her brother took their names from the initials of their breeder, Ernest Gocher) who, when mated to Sandown Champion, produced a bitch named Elphin Girl. She too achieved fame in being the dam of the 1959 Waterloo Cup winner Holystone Elf. Another from the same litter was Explosive Gilbert, a dog who did little on the track but was the great grand sire of Bright Lad, a dog who in recent years has made a name as a sire. His sons include the Waterloo Cup winner Minnesota Miller, Liberty Lad and Thurles Yard, Northern Ireland's outstanding greyhound of 1976 and now a successful sire. Ernest Gocher had indeed done his homework and saw the successful result of his theories in stockbreeding applied to greyhounds. His dream of breeding a champion had come true at the first attempt.

Endless Gossip	Priceless Border	Clonahard Border
		Priceless Sandhills
	Narrogar Ann	Dutton Swordfish
		Winnie of Berrow (Beef Cutlet)

ENTRY BADGE

A handsome brindle weighing 69 lbs when he won the first Derby, he was by the sire Jamie, sire of Mutton Cutlet and the first important sire of racing greyhounds. His dam was Beaded Nora, a daughter of the great coursing dog Hopsack and for whom Mr Edwin Baxter had given 40 gns. So from his breeding alone much was to be expected of this dog.

Mr Baxter will always be remembered with affection by those who have followed greyhound racing from its start, for he was the first of the coursing men to believe that there was a great future for track racing. The name of his dog, Entry Badge, will always be coupled with that of his owner for he was the first great star performer, in a class of his own during the first years of the sport and the winner of the first Greyhound Derby, the first of the classic events to be inaugurated.

Entry Badge was one of three dogs and a bitch born to Beaded Nora in January 1926. It was the year track racing began in Britain, but it was not until June 1927 that the first stadium opened in London for greyhound racing and Entry Badge was there on the opening night at White City, the winner of the first trophy, the White City Cup, which was presented to his owner after he had defeated the more experienced dogs from Belle Vue in convincing style, winning his race by eight lengths in 30.13 secs for the 525 yds course. Previously the dog had shown outstanding ability on the coursing field, reaching the final of the Mentmore Cup for which he was defeated by Lord Dalmeny's dog, Divot, but Mr Baxter always believed that a greyhound had to make greater use of his brains to win on a race track than on the coursing field, and he had no hesitation in sending several of his best coursing dogs to White City to be trained by Joe Harmon.

Entry Badge was one of the fastest ever from the traps and in addition possessed Mick the Miller's intelligence to move to the rails whenever there was the slightest opportunity, while he was always able to steer clear of trouble at the turns. Entered for the first Derby, at the White City, he won his heat and final by six and a half lengths, one of the biggest margins ever, and he started at the shortest odds of 4–1 on his winning. The first Derby was run, for the only time, over 500 yds, and he covered the distance in 29.01 secs. That final was held on 15 October 1927, though since then it has always been held early in July. He had started from trap 5 and not until Daw's Dancer won from this trap in 1953 was a dog again successful from this trap. Mr Baxter's dogs finished first, second and third – Ever Bright ran up, followed by Elder Brother, though only Entry Badge was trained by Joe Harmon. For his success in the Derby Entry Badge had won £1,000 for his owner, a very big sum in those days, and the first £1,000 prize awarded for a greyhound race.

Entry Badge raced for the best part of two years and was beaten only once. In all he won eleven out of twelve races, all in top class, and was odds-on favourite in every race he ran. Always he won them by three lengths or more and in times that would be considered acceptable even today. Within four months of winning the Derby he earned £1,500 in prize money and was the first great champion racing greyhound.

FAIR MISTRESS

She was one of the greatest bitches to race in Ireland, and during 1942 and 1943 ran thirty-one times on the Belfast tracks, winning twenty-one races and being second seven times. She was as popular with the racegoers there as Quarter Day and Disputed Rattler were in England. Whelped in January 1941, she won the Irish Oaks, then run at Limerick, in 1942, beating Kittyhawk in 30.10 secs, the fastest time ever done in the Oaks to that date and a new track record. She then won the National Sprint, then run at Celtic Park, and the Northern Derby at Dunmore Park to establish herself as the outstanding bitch of her time in Ireland. The following year she again won the National Sprint, this time at Dunmore Park, where she equalled the record of 24.03 secs set by Edna's Star and Farloe Border when defeating the Co. Clare dog Mondey. No other greyhound has ever won the National Sprint twice. She also set a track record at Celtic Park for the 375 yds course with a time of 20.52 secs which stood for many years.

On the coursing field she also performed with distinction, reaching the last four of the Belsize Cup in 1943 and 1944, and in the International Cup at Clonmel she was beaten in the semi-final by the ultimate winner, Dancing Model.

FAITHFUL HOPE

This brindle son of Solar Prince out of Millie Hawthorn was born in June 1962 and won the 1966 Greyhound Derby for his owners, Sir Richard Adeane and Miss P. Wallis, when four years old. The outsider for the final and this was one of the most strongly contested of all finals in the history of the race, represented by six outstanding greyhounds – Faithful Hope won by four lengths and in doing so set a new record for photo-timing of 28.52 secs. The dog was handled throughout his career by the Clapton trainer Paddy Keane. Previously Faithful Hope had been successful in the Guinness 600 at Shelbourne Park; reached the Cesarewitch final, and had run up to Rostown Victor and to After You in the Scurry Gold Cup. In a short career he won over £10,000 in prize money, including a record £8,000 in one year.

Retired to stud after 1966 Derby, Faithful Hope was to sire a Derby winner in John Silver, whelped in August 1968 and who won the 1970 event with £10,000 in prize money. 'Silver', owned and bred by Mr Reg Young and trained by Mrs Barbara Tomkins, was one of the few English greyhounds to take the premier event. His grand dam, Millie Hawthorn, from a mating with Clonalvy Pride, whelped (March 1965) Yanka Boy, who in 1967 won the St Leger at Limerick in 30.77 secs, the fastest time then recorded for the event.

John Silver, a fawn dog, was barely twenty-two months old when he won the Derby and was the youngest dog ever to do so, while his sire was the oldest. His dam, Trojan Silver, was also owned by Mr Young and was one of the finest long-distance runners, having won the Cobb Marathon; her sire was Hi There's son, the St Leger winner Powerstown Prospect.

After winning his heat and semi-final of the Cesarewitch at West Ham, John Silver was found to have broken a toe in the final and was retired to stud, though he was allowed a year's complete freedom on his owner's farm before taking up stud duties since he was still only two years old. Yet in spite of his wonderful breeding and his outstanding ability, he was to sire little that would have leave a lasting impression on greyhound racing.

Faithful Hope, 1966 Derby winner in 28.52 secs, the fastest time ever for this event. Photo: GRA.

John Silver	Faithful Hope	Solar Prince	Champion Prince (Bella's Prince)
			Lisabelle
		Millie Hawthorn	The Grand Fire
			Glittering Millie
	Trojan Silver	Powerstown Prospect	Hi There
			Favide
		Maggie Ann	Dunmore King (Shaggy Lad)
			Sitting Pretty

FINE JUBILEE

A son of Silver Seal and a grandson of Macoma, Mick the Miller's litter brother, this fine brindle was whelped in 1934 and first came into prominence when he went through his heats and the final of the Gold Collar undefeated though he was still only twenty months old. The following month he did exactly the same, winning the Derby by the big margin of six lengths when quoted at 6–5 on and in the fastest time yet put up for the event, 29.48 secs. In the Laurels he seemed certain to repeat his performance, but in the final was beaten a short head by Mrs Cearns' dog Top of Carlow Road; if he had won he would have emulated Brilliant Bob who won three classics in the one year In the Champion Stakes and in the O.A. Critchley Memorial Stakes at the White City he was again successful to complete a fabulous year.

At stud he sired Rock Callan, who in 1940 ran up for the Derby and Laurels but won the International that year and again in 1941. Another outstanding son was Derryboy Jubilee, the outstanding hurdler of his time, as one would expect from a great grandson of Macoma; yet another was the fast trapping Jubilee Time, who set a new track record at Wembley and during the war years had the satisfaction of twice beating Ballynennan Moon and Ballyhennessy Seal.

Fine Jubilee was owned and trained by Mrs Marie Yate, the only woman to have owned and trained a Derby winner.

FORD SPARTAN

Romance surrounds this great champion for

he was the result of a lucky mating. When their bitch Harrow Glamour, who I believe was a house pet and had never raced, came in season, her owners took her to Magourna Reject whose services had been booked in advance, but because on the day Harrow Glamour was ready he was already serving another bitch, previously booked and late to come in season, she was immediately put to the 1953 Laurels winner Polonius as she had almost passed her time. Such a result could never have been expected by the owners of the brood bitch, who spent her days in the comforts of a private house rather than in kennels. It was a fairy story come true.

Ford Spartan, a black dog, was owned by F.C. Hill and S.C. Frost and trained at Wimbledon by D.J. Hannafin. It was at this track that the dog first hit the headlines when winning the 1956 Puppy Derby, a classic event for greyhounds under two. Made a 2–1 favourite for the event after winning his heats, he duly obliged his followers and clocked the remarkable time of 28.02 secs, only a neck preventing him from being the first dog since the event was inaugurated in 1929 to break 28.00 secs. The next year Ford Spartan took as his main objective the English Derby, and after winning all his heats was made even-money favourite for the final, which he won in a thrilling race by a neck from Highway Tim in 28.84 secs, which equalled the photo-timing record set up three years earlier by Paul's Fun.

His next classic was the Laurels of 1957; in this, too, he was successful, emulating his sire, and his time of 27.89 secs was the fastest recorded for the event. Only Endless Gossip in 1952 had also broken 28.00 secs, and only Clonalvy Pride, in 1961, has bettered Ford Spartan's time.

Ford Spartan also won the White City Stakes and the Select Stakes and during 1957 no greyhound in Britain was his equal.

FUTURE CUTLET

This brindle dog by Mutton Cutlet out of Wary Guide was whelped in April 1929, and was one of the greatest ever, a dog cast in every respect in the classic mould of a champion. His sire was a dark brindle by Jamie out of Miss Cinderella and was born and raised at Major McCalmont's famous Cotswolds kennels. Whelped in March 1921, Mutton Cutlet contested the Waterloo Cup in 1923, 1924 and 1925 and showed speed and courage without being able to reach the final, though he ran up for the Waterloo Plate in 1924. In 1926 he was bought by Mr Tom Morris, keeper of the Irish Stud book, and put to stud in Ireland at a fee of 10 gns. During the first two or three years he served few bitches, but by the time the dog died in November 1934 he had sired 522 winners on the track and coursing field. He was the sire of Valiant Cutlet, Beef Cutlet and Mr Moon, each of them an important sire in his own right; Beef Cutlet became the sire of the magnificent Junior Classic and Juvenile Classic, Loose Lead and Laird's Cutlet, while Mr Moon was sire of the great Ballynennan Moon. All of these were outstanding racing greyhounds.

Future Cutlet was another of Mutton Cutlet's first-class sons, and although his sire was as English as they come, this son was born and bred in Ireland and purchased for £600, a very large sum in 1930, by Mr W.A. Evershed to race at the newly opened Wembley Stadium. There he was trained by Sidney Probert and entered for the 1931 Laurels, which he won in the fast time of 28.52 secs. He was then only two years old and it was decided that his Derby entry should be delayed until the next year; he was, however, entered for the Cesarewitch over 600 yds at West Ham. Here, too, he was successful in the last classic of the season, and so had won two classics by the time he was two and a half years old, with the best yet to come.

In 1932 he won Wembley's Spring Cup and in spite of his two classic wins odds of 100–1 were quoted against his winning the Derby; but he almost did so. In the final, however, he met the northern flier Wild Woolley, and from the time the traps flew up it was a race just between these two star greyhounds, Wild Woolley getting the verdict by a neck; these two were ten lengths in front of the others as they crossed the line. When winning his heat for the 1932 Derby Future Cutlet set a new track record at the White City with a time of 29.62 secs for the 525 yds course. He also held the record for Wembley over the same distance and in his heat for the 1931 Cesarewitch had set a new national record for the 600 yds course.

Entered in the 1932 Cesarewitch he set

a new world record of 33.78 secs in his semi-final and was again successful, winning in 34.11 secs. Run over 600 yds, only one other classic, the St Leger, is run over a longer course – and by his second win he confounded those who thought that he tended to fade over a longer distance than 525 yds.

By the time he contested the 1933 Derby he was four years three months old, and with Wild Woolley again taking part and the new flier, Beef Cutlet, running brilliantly, it was not thought that Future Cutlet could make amends for his failure the previous year. But again he ran brilliantly, this time with Beef Cutlet, making the running all the way, and the two crossed the line almost together. The result was given in favour of Future Cutlet by the shortest of short heads, but with no photo-finish camera there were many who thought a dead heat would have been the right decision. Future Cutlet was the oldest dog ever to win the Derby and there was no more worthy winner. Later that year, in the Wimbledon Champion Stakes, it was Beef Cutlet who got the verdict by a short head and there was virtually nothing to separate the two.

At the end of that summer Future Cutlet was retired, and before his own death Mr Evershed set up a trust fund for his champion so that he would live in luxury for the rest of his life. Though Sidney Probert thought him a highly strung dog, difficult to train, the dog was only once unplaced during his entire career. He was probably the fastest trapper before Ballyhennessy Seal, and Captain Brice, racing manager at Wembley thought him 'the best looker of them all'. He was a beautifully proportioned dog who never gave anything but a stylish performance. He won four classics in England over a period of three years, and no other greyhound has ever done this over so long a time.

GOOD WORKER

By the Tanist sire Tanimon out of Dolly Meadway, this brindle dog was whelped in March 1946 and was one of a trio of outstanding two-year-olds to race in 1948, the others being Local Interprize and the bitch Sheevaun. The Derby winner, the peerless Priceless Border, was then in his third year. Owned by Mrs E.J. Snell, Good Worker was English-bred and first caught the attention of racegoers at Wembley on 10 January 1948 when winning from a top-class field which included Whiterock Abbey and Patsy's Record, whom he beat by a short head. Also in the race was Honeyboy Finnegan, whom he was again to defeat at Stamford Bridge a few weeks later. He next contested the Regency at Brighton, winning his first and second round heats at 4–1 on and setting a new track record of 29.31 secs. In his semi-final, however, he was beaten by Bunny's Hoard who also took the final, with Good Worker in third place. His next race was in June, when he won his first and second round heats for the Wimbledon Two-year-old Produce Stakes. He also won his semi-final and the final by a length from Lovely Rio to take the £1,000 prize. Three weeks later he was at Wimbledon for the fifteenth Laurels; in his heat he once more beat Honeyboy Finnegan, and in his semi-final he beat Whiterock Abbey and Local Interprize by two lengths. He took the final by a short head from Whiterock Abbey, one of the gamest dogs ever to race. Behind them were Local Interprize and Mad Birthday. He had thus gone through the Produce Stakes and Laurels undefeated, winning seven consecutive races and nearly £2,000 in prize money. Two weeks after his Laurels success Good Worker was at Ramsgate, where he set a new track record with a time of 28.72 secs for 500 yds.

The Thames Silver Salver at Southend was his next race. He ran up in his heat and won his semi-final by three and a half lengths from Sonnie H who had beaten him in his heat. Good Worker was to get the better of his rival when beating him in the final, though only by a short head, to win £500 and so bring his year's total to £3,226, second only to Local Interprize. He would have won more but for being badly hampered in the final of the Anglo-Irish Championship at Belle Vue when, after beating Whiterock Abbey by eleven lengths in their heat, he was beaten two lengths by this great dog.

GRAND FLIGHT II

A fawn dog by Naughty Jack Horner out of Little Fawn Biddy and whelped in 1933, he was one of Mr George Flintham's first greyhounds and one of his best, for he never ran an unsatisfactory race. His best year was 1935, for he won the International at Wimbledon and the Cesarewitch at West Ham over 600 yds, when he defeated Shove Ha'penny in the fast time of 33.97 secs. The flying Ataxy was 9–2 favourite in the Cesarewitch, for he had easily defeated Grand Flight II in the earlier rounds, yet, as so often happened, when it came to the great day Grand Flight surprised the bookies by making up for his lack of pace from the traps by his amazing trackcraft, in which he rivalled Mick the Miller and Brilliant Bob. In the first Pall Mall, run at Harringay, he reached the final only to be beaten by his great rival Shove Ha'penny by a head.

During 1936 he ran consistently, reaching the final of the Derby which was won by the favourite, Fine Jubilee, in 29.48 secs. He also gave a brilliant performance when defeating Ataxy over 725 yds for the *Daily Mirror* Trophy run at the White City, after which he was retired to stud. Though he raced for less than two years he always gave all he had and proved to be one of the most popular greyhounds ever to race. He cost George Flintham only £36 as an untried sapling, and his owner always said Grand Flight II was the best English-bred greyhound he ever owned. The dog lived to the age of eleven and won £3,000 prize money.

GREENFIELD FOX

By Burgess Heather out of Skipping Chick, this outstanding white and black dog, whelped in March 1975, was owned by Mr D. O'Sullivan and kennelled at Slough where he was trained by Ted Dickson. The dog first came into prominence when in March 1977 he set a new track record for the 530 m course at Swindon with a time of 31.58 secs. Later that year he defeated his kennel companion Linacre, also trained by Ted Dickson, by one and a half lengths to win the Laurels in 27.26 secs, the fastest time for the event when run over the 460 m course. The dog had won his heats and semi-final, and in his heat set a new track record with a time of 27.20 secs. In the same year the dog was also successful in the Pall Mall, possibly the most important race in England which does not enjoy classic status.

After a winter rest his next big event was the Scurry Gold Cup, run at his home track, Slough. In this he was again successful, winning his heat and then his final in 27.00 secs, in which he defeated Northwood Double by a head in the best Scurry run at Slough. After a short rest the dog was at Leeds for the Tetley Qualifying Stakes and, quoted 6–4 against, he had no trouble in adding this event to his other successes. It was his last race, and shortly afterwards he was retired to stud.

GROSVENOR BOB and GROSVENOR EDWIN

'Bob' was a handsome fawn dog by Golden Hammer out of the outstanding Macoma dam Wonderful Expression, who in January 1935 whelped a litter that included him and his brother Grosvenor Edwin. Wonderful Expression was herself whelped in 1931, as was the other splendid Macoma dam, Lady Eleanor, who, also in January 1935, whelped Jesmond Cutlet, followed a year later by the litter brothers Junior Classic and Juvenile Classic. The Grosvenor brothers were almost as good as the Classic brothers, which means they were very good indeed.

The Grosvenors were born and raised in Kent and as puppies were purchased by George Flintham. 'Bob' began his career at Wembley where, under Jim Syder Snr., he won 1936 the Trafalgar Cup, an event for greyhounds not more than 2 years old, his time of 30.22 seconds for 525 yds being the fastest until Laughing Lieutenant did 30.12 seconds in 1941. In 1937 'Bob' was entered for the Derby in which he reached the final, being beaten into 3rd place after being badly hampered and by the two best dogs in training, Wattle Bark and Shove Ha'penny.

In the Cesarewitch at West Ham, run over 600 yds, 'Bob' ran up to Jesmond Cutlet, the first of Lady Eleanor's sons to win a classic and by the time the St. Leger was run at Wembley, 'Bob' was ready to tackle 700 yds. Running brilliantly he won his first classic in 41. 13 secs to complete a wonderful year.

Made favourite to win the 1938 Derby after nearly setting a new track and national record in his opening heat with a time of 29.22 seconds, he pulled up lame in his 2nd round heat and was retired to stud.

'Edwin' was equally successful and the

best distance runner before Model Dasher. He was also with Jim Syder and in 1937 took the Gold Cup at Wembley and again the following year, his time of 40.92 secs being a new track record. At West Ham he won the Spring Cup that year but in a 700 yds race at Hall Green, Jesmond Cutlet beat him as he had beaten his brother.

In 1937, two years after whelping 'Bob' and 'Edwin', Wonderful Expression was again mated with Golden Hammer and her litter included another 'star' in Grosvenor Ferdinand. He was to win the Wimbledon Puppy Derby in 1939 and Catford's Gold Collar run over 440 yeds. He was a sprinter: the first offspring of his dam were stayers.

HUBERT'S SHADE

In these times of such high standards in breeding, it is only rarely that a greyhound is good enough to beat such high quality opposition to win more than one classic in the same year but this black dog did so in 1982 and within a few weeks.

Owned by Alan and Flo Cherry and trained by Adam Jackson at Wembley, Hubert's Shade was whelped in May, 1980, his sire being Luminous Lad, his dam Hubert's Fate. He first gave some idea of his ability during the 1982 Derby, reaching the semi-finals and only just failing to qualify for the final won by Laurie's Panther. A few weeks later he became the first greyhound to win the St. Leger from trap 5 in 50 races when, in the final he defeated the Gold Collar winner, Donna's Dixie by a length in 39.83 secs. Beaten into second place in round 1 by Jack Kelly's Liga Lad, winner of the Cesarewitch and who reached the St. Leger final, he won his second round heat and semi-final.

The John Power Grand Prix at Waltham stow followed soon after and in this event he came through undefeated, the final being his 8th consecutive win in classic events, though he was hard pressed to win his semi-final by a neck from Metalina. In the final, for which he was made favourite, he won by the large margin of nearly 5 lengths, beating Glenbrien Ranger in the fast time of 39.73 secs and winning from the outside trap 6.

HURRY KITTY

She was one of those great long-distance runners which appeared in the 1940s, sired by Castledown Lad (others being Shaggy Lass and Coyne's Castle), and her dam was Brilliant Gay, one of the outstanding bitches sired by Brilliant Bob. Any greyhound by Castledown Lad out of a Brilliant Bob bitch was worth its weight in gold. Brilliant Gay had run up for the 1941 Irish Coursing Oaks, and won the Leinster Puppy Stakes at Enniscorthy in 30.50 secs, and so had proved herself on track and coursing field.

Hurry Kitty was a fawn weighing 55 lbs, a good weight for a bitch, and she was whelped in April 1943. Like her dam, she too won the Leinster Puppy Stakes and in exactly the same time as Brilliant Gay. She also finished third in the important Easter Cup at Shelbourne Park, won by Astra in 29.86 secs, after which she was purchased by Miss Kitty Kwasnik for £2,000, then the highest price ever paid for a bitch, though shortly afterwards another Castledown Lad bitch, Castledown Tiptoes, cost £3,000, the highest price ever paid for a bitch in Ireland.

Shortly after arriving in England Hurry Kitty set a new record for 300 yds at Monmore Green, Wolverhampton, with a time of 17.17 secs, and at this track won the second October Stakes by five lengths from the equally expensive Gala Flash. But it was in the Cesarewitch at West Ham, run over 550 yds, that she reached her peak. Winning her heat by twelve lengths from Jonwell Shamrock and her semi-final by six lengths from Kilcora Master, she raced away from the field to take the final by nearly ten lengths from Gala Flash in 31.26 secs; it was the biggest winning margin in the history of this classic event.

After a short rest she was at Wembley for the 1946 Inaugural Trial Stakes and was equally impressive, winning her heat from Fair and Handsome and then the final from Overtime in 30.16 secs. This was her thirteenth race in England and her eleventh win; over all distances she was almost unbeatable, and Miss Kwasnik issued a challenge of £5,000 a side for a match to be staged anywhere in England between her great bitch and any other, but the bitch then went in season, nothing came of the challenge and in fact she raced very little more. She was one of the great trio of the mid-1940s which included Shaggy Lass and Robeen Printer, three of the finest bitches ever to race in England.

INDIAN JOE

A black dog by Brave Bran out of Minnetonka and owned by Kevin Frost of Co. Clare when he started racing, he was whelped in September 1977 at the kennels of Rachel Barry in Limerick and was only twenty-one months old when he ran in the qualifying heats for the 1978 Irish Derby, his first big event. A large dog, weighing 77 lbs, he was beaten by five lengths in his first-round heat, finishing third and only just qualifying for round 2 in which he was again beaten, this time by two lengths into second place. In his quarter-final heat he trapped with his usual tremendous speed and in his favourite trap 6 ran on to win by four lengths from Excellent Choice in 29.22 secs, one of the fastest times of the event. In her quarter-final heat Penny County, the eventual winner, clocked 29.44 secs, and in her semi-final got the better of Indian Joe, beating him by four lengths. But Mr Frost's black went through to the final for which he was drawn in trap 1 and, as was to be expected of him, he found himself in first-bend trouble from which he could not recover. He finished last, but in reaching the final had shown that the youngest greyhound taking part possessed those qualities which must make him a dog to command attention in future. Four weeks later he lined up for the important Carroll's International at Dundalk and once again he had with him Nameless Pixie, Airmount Champ and Distant Clamour, the Derby finalists, who were joined by Tough Decision and Desert Pilot. Again Indian Joe was drawn on the inside, a position not to his liking, but he was out of the traps like lightning and in front on the back straight. It was only in the last few strides that the gallant Distant Clamour got in front, to beat him by less than half a length in 29.53 secs, with Nameless Pixie in third place.

After a winter resting, Joe came to England in May 1980 to contest the English Derby and ran his first qualifying heat at the White City, Manchester. In trap 5 on the outside (which he also favoured, along with trap 6), he was made a 2–1 on favourite and won comfortably, beating Weston Whiskey by four lengths. Ten days later, at the White City, London, he won his first-round heat by one and a quarter lengths, beating Hurry on Bran, and though those who saw the race firmly believed that both dogs were good enough to go right through the event, none could have foreseen that this was to be the order in which they would finish in the final, to be run a fortnight later. The two dogs were again drawn together in the second round but this time the order was reversed. In round 3 Hurry on Bran won his heat by four lengths while Indian Joe could only take third place behind Knockrour Slave and Young Breeze in his heat. Indeed, he was fortunate to go through, for a photo showed that he had beaten Nameless Pixie by only a nose. Again, in his semi-final, the 6–4 on favourite Hurry on Bran had much the better of him, beating Corduroy by two and one third lengths with Indian Joe a further length behind in third place, but he had done enough to qualify for the final of the fiftieth Greyhound Derby, run on 28 June for a world record prize of £35,000 put up by Spillers for the winner. For this Joe was in trap 6 with his great rival in trap 5. Both were wide runners and had been specially 'seeded' to these traps which gave them a considerable advantage. Both were quoted 6–4 against and were joint favourites. Surprisingly they were slow away and there was considerable bumping on the first bend, but Joe continued to run wide, keeping out of trouble, and John Hayes' charge continued in the lead throughout the race to win by a length in 29.68 secs, with Hurry on Bran a worthy runner up and

Indian Joe, 1980 English Greyhound Derby winner.

Young Breeze third. Before the final the dog had been sold to Belfast bookmaker Alf McLean for, it is said, £40,000.

ITSAMINT

One of the great bitches of all time, out of another immortal, Cranog Bet, twice winner of the English Oaks (in 1963 and 1964), Itsamint was owned and trained by Mr Leslie McNair of Newtownards and won for him the 1969 Irish Oaks in the fast time of 29.35 secs. She was then entered for the Guinness 600 at Shelbourne Park, and in one of the greatest races ever seen finished a short head in front of Own Pride, with Russian Gun the same distance away, in 33.69 secs, the three greyhounds crossing the line almost together. The bitch completed a wonderful year when winning the Ulster Cesarewitch at Celtic Park in October by two and a half lengths from Rapid Streak in a new track record for the 600 yds course of 33.34 secs. Only Own Pride could be considered her equal in all Ireland that year.

Previously she had made headlines when taking the 1968 Easter Cup at Shelbourne Park in which she defeated the 1967 Derby winner, the great Russian Gun, by one and a half lengths, with Foyle Tonic, who was to win the 1968 Scurry Gold Cup, in third place.

Itsamint's daughter Knockhill Silver just failed to emulate her dam in winning the Shelbourne 600, for she ran-up to Here's Pat in the 1977 event. From her mating with Yanka Boy Itsamint was to whelp Itsastar, dam of Nameless Pixie, whelped in January 1977 from a mating with Monalee Champion. She was to finish third in the 1979 Irish Derby and won the Oaks that year. Itsastar was also dam of Nameless Star from a mating to Rita's Choice. Nameless Star won the 1976 Laurels at Cork and the St Leger at Limerick before being retired to stud. Itsastar thus perpetuates the great speed of her dam, Itsamint, and of her grand dam, Cranog Bet, twice winner of the English Oaks.

I'M SLIPPY

There have been few greyhounds to win a classic event both in England and in Ireland but this fine dog did so in 1983. A white and brindle by Laudella Fun out of Glencoe Bess and whelped in May, 1981, he is owned by Mr J.J. Quinn of N. Ireland and trained by Barbara Tompkins. He won his heat in the qualifying round at White City, when 220 greyhounds took part, beating On Spec, the Sheffield dog trained by Harry Crapper and whom he was to beat in the final, by 3 lengths in 30.43 secs. In his 1st round heat he beat Cricket's Style by 2 lengths in 29.75 secs. In the 2nd round, he was well beaten 4 lengths by Game Ball, favourite to win the event and who outpaced him along the back straight, but I'm Slippy set a blistering pace to win his quarter final from Speedy Hope. In his semi-final however, he was beaten half a length by Amazing Man, with Real Miller the 33/1 outsider in 3rd place. In the other semi-final Game Ball took first place with Debbycot Lad and On Spec closely behind and these 6 outstanding greyhounds fought out the final now sponsored by the Daily Mirror for a prize of £25,000. In the most exciting final ever run, I'm Slippy, in trap 4, led all the way but so great was the challenge from On Spec and Debbycot Lad that only a neck separated the first three who finished in that order, with Game Ball ¾ length behind. The time was 29,40 secs and it was Barbara Tompkins second Derby winner.

In September the dog was back in N. Ireland to contest the Guinness National Sprint at Dunmore Park, the Irish equivalent of the Scurry Cup and still in peak form, he showed the same devastating speed as he had at White City, being undefeated throughout the event and winning the final by 4 lengths from Ring Beacon in 23.90 secs. This dog, his owner and trainer thus became members of a select few to win a classic event on both sides of the Irish Sea, this being only the second occasion in the sport's history that it had been achieved in the same year.

JON BARRIE

By Clashing out of Famous Heart and whelped in January, 1977 he was one of the finest and most consistent dogs never to have won a classic. Trained by Ray Andrews at Leeds, the dog had been purchased at Shelbourne Park sales in July, 1978 by Terry Hawkshaw for 1,300 gns. In 1979 he ran up for the All England Cup at Brough Park and took the Edinburgh Cup at Powderhall in the fast time of 28.25 secs. In March, 1980 he took the Wood Lane Stakes at White City and on his return to Scotland, the William King Cup at Shawfield but between these events he had contested and won the important sprinters' event, second only to the Scurry Cup, the Northern Flat at Belle Vue worth £2000, beating Cragville Light by 4 lengths. In the Laurels, he finished 3rd in his semi-final behind Life Coming and Dangerous Lad but in the final, Flying Pursuit was away like a bullet and won by 2 lengths from Jon Barrie with Life Coming in 3rd place. Back in Scotland for the Scottish Derby, he won his semi-final by 5 lengths to again reach a classic final, only to be beaten by the fast trapping Decoy Sovereign who held his lead from the start. Contesting the 1980 Edinburgh Cup, Jon Barrie again reached the final but on his occasion was runner up. In less than 2 years racing in top class this game and popular dog won 40 races and more than £10,000 in prize money and endeared himself to all who saw him race.

JUNIOR CLASSIC

He was whelped in January 1936, and was a blue brindle by Beef Cutlet out of Lady Eleanor from their second mating – a combination of sire and dam that produced several of the greatest trackers of all time. From their first mating came Jesmond Cutlet, born in 1935, one of a litter which included Epinard and His Lordship. Jesmond Cutlet, trained at Catford, first gave some indication of the quality of the first offspring of his sire and dam by winning the Wood Lane Stakes at the White City in May 1937, defeating the Derby winner Lone Keel. Shortly afterwards he won the Scottish Derby at Carntyne, his time of 29.83 secs being the fastest ever done at this track up to that date, and he was the first to break 30 secs there. He followed this by taking the Edinburgh Cup at Powderhall and setting a new track record there. Back in London he won the 1937 Cesarewitch, beating his old rival Grosvenor Bob (third in the Derby). But for the St Leger at Wembley the following year the positions were reversed, though he came close to being one of the few greyhounds to win these two long-distance events. Early in 1939 he was moved to West Ham, but was by this time past his best.

In all, Jesmond Cutlet won more than £2,000 in prize money and at least this amount at stud, and among the finest litters ever born was that from his mating with Magic Pool. One of the litter was Magic Beau who died young, but not before he had given indications of his great ability, for over the 525 yds course at Wembley he clocked 29.19 secs to set a new world and track record. Another from the litter was Magic Bohemian, one of the outstanding greyhounds of 1945–6, who finished third in the 1945 Derby, won by Ballyhennessy Seal, and in the same year won the Grand Prix at Walthamstow. At the White City he lowered his litter brother's world record when he covered the 525 yds course in 29.11 secs, which was again lowered the following year by Duffy's Arrival.

The second mating between Beef Cutlet and Lady Eleanor again produced several outstanding greyhounds, and in January 1936, Junior Classic and Juvenile Classic were whelped, the latter distinguishing himself over hurdles as could have been expected from a son of Lady Eleanor, since her sire was the great hurdler Macoma, litter brother of Mick the Miller.

The matings of Beef Cutlet and Lady Eleanor have had no equal in the history of track racing in Britain. Their offspring were British-born and -reared at Llandaff in Wales, and were that country's outstanding greyhounds. They did all their racing in Britain, winning the highest honours on the flat and over hurdles, and only the Derby eluded them. Junior Classic was expected to win the 1939 Derby and when drawn in the lucky no.1 trap was made joint favourite of three to win, but after reaching the final in convncing style he sadly disappointed his supporters and finished last of five runners, an estimated sixteen lengths behind the Irish-bred Highland Rum, the winner, and about fourteen lengths behind the runner-up, Scotland's Carmel Ash. He was never in the picture. Had he won, it would have been the only occasion in which litter brothers had done the double by winning the top event for hurdlers, the Grand National, which was won by Juvenile Classic in 1938 and 1940, and the Derby, which Junior Classic was expected to do. Even so, they are the only litter brothers born in Britain each to have won a classic event, for Junior Classic won the Gold Collar in 1938, so that the two each won a classic in the same year. Both were trained by Joe Harmon.

Before this, however, he had won in 1937 the British Breeders' Produce Stakes in 25.90 secs and the Two-year-old Produce Stakes in a time of 28.43 secs, and at West Ham had covered the 525 yds course in 29.43 secs, a new track record; at Stamford Bridge his time of 27.82 secs for 500 yds was a world and track record. In 1937 he also won the Wimbledon Puppy Derby in 28.86 secs, a time that was not beaten for the event until 1945. Wimbledon was his home track and he always ran there with distinction.

In 1938 he won his only classic, the Gold Collar at Catford, run over 440 yds, and there is no doubt that the shorter distances, up to 500 yds, suited him better. The following year was the year of his Derby failure, but he won the Champion Stakes at Wimbledon and the International, also at his home track, in 29.27 secs for 500 yds. Later that year he also won the Pick. In 1940 he came out of his winter rest and took the Spring Cup at Wembley, confounding those critics who thought that 525 yds was beyond his reach. It was also the first time 30.00 secs had been broken for the event; his time of 29.60 secs was bettered during the next decade only by 0.02 secs, by Disputed Rattler, and by 0.15 secs by Ballyhennessy Seal. The Wembley Spring Cup of 1940 was also the first occasion when a greyhound race was broadcast by the BBC.

Junior Classic was now more than four years old, and had won for his owner, Mr J.J. Cleaver, more than £4,250 at a time when the war was reducing the available prize money. Mr Cleaver also owned Juvenile Classic, who won £2,750 in prize money; the two litter brothers amassed a total of £7,000 during three years' racing.

Juvenile Classic died in his sleep within days of his sixth birthday (Christmas 1942) and Junior Classic ten years to the day after he was born, in January 1946, and his body was preserved for his owner.

At stud, it cannot be said that either dog was really successful, but it must be remembered that they were active during the war years when greyhound breeding was done on a reduced scale and when feeding was difficult. But the name of Junior Classic will always be associated with one of the smallest and most courageous bitches ever to race. Her name was Alvaston Lulu Belle, and she was whelped in 1943. A brindle weighing only 45 lbs, her sire was Junior Classic and her dam Alvaston Heather Belle.

Lulu Belle first caught the attention of racegoers when, at Harringay on 16 July 1945, the first time round the track, she clocked 40.44 secs which was a new record for 700 yds, and she defeated Jonwell Shamrock by five lengths. Then in her heat for the Scottish Derby she beat the ultimate winner, Monday's Son, by a short head; in the final she finished third. A few days later she broke the 810 yds record at Catford with a time of 48.58 secs. This was the longest race in the calendar and she was only a tiny greyhound. She then came in season, and after whelping a litter of eight it was thought her racing days were over. But this was not so, for she contested her second August Stakes at Wembley, over 700 yds, which she won in 40.06 secs. In November 1946 she again ran a magnificent race for the Legion Stakes at Breck Park, being defeated only by a neck by Shannon Shore in 30.36 secs. When she came in season again it was decided to retire her.

Alvaston Lulu Belle was kennelled at Warrington and her trainer was Ken Newham. In her two years' racing she took on the best in the land and endeared herself to all racegoers by her wonderful courage and track sense. She died in February 1948 when only five years old, possibly because of racing again after whelping a large litter. But other bitches have done so and lived to twice her age.

KAMPION SAILOR

This great long-distance dog was a black and was bred and owned throughout his life by Mrs K.V. Snow in Sussex. Sired by Lights o' London, his dam was Grosvenor Faith, whose sire was Grand Flight II and dam Wonderful Expression, so Kampion Sailor was bred to stay. He was whelped in September 1942 and during his career was kennelled with Sidney Orton at Burhill. He began racing in 1944 and for three years only Model Dasher was his equal over the stayers' courses. He started his career by running up to that great dog in the final of the Key at Wimbledon, which gave some idea of his potential, and in 1945 he won the April Stakes at Harringay, beating Duffy's Arrival. He won the 700 yds Wembley Gold Cup by a neck from Half Term in 40.19 secs, coming from behind, and was then at Bristol where he won the Pyramid from a top-class field. At Walthamstow he took the Test by a length from Stylish Nancy in 41.45 secs, and by winning the Grand Victory Stakes at Portsmouth on the last day of the year he earned Sidney Orton the accolade of champion trainer of the year and took his own winnings to more than £1,500, at a time when £200 was a generous prize for an important event.

After a short rest Kampion Sailor returned and began 1946 where he left off, winning the Joe Harmon Memorial Trophy at his home track, beating Ferry Robin by three quarters of a length in 28.37 secs, and he took the Whitsun Cup at Harringay, run over 700 yds, beating Model Country by six lengths in 40.71 secs. Entered for the 1946 Derby he ran up to Quare Times in his heat, to qualify for the semi-final. This was the occasion when Quare Times set a new world record for 525 yds with a time of 28.95 secs, and he was quoted at 3–1 on with Kampion Sailor 25–1 against. In his semi-final Kampion Sailor failed to get a place and so did Quare Times in his semi-final; Shannon Shore beat him by more than twelve lengths so he was in no way disgraced. Afterwards Kampion Sailor was found to have pulled up lame and he did not run again.

Mrs Snow has told of the dog being picked upon by the others of the litter and she had to rear him separately. He also suffered a badly broken leg and it was thought he would never race. Indeed, for twelve months he lived with Mrs Snow in her home and she believed that this was the right choice, rather than have him put down. The dog amply rewarded her with his courageous running, and after his racing career ended he always slept in Mrs Snow's bedroom. In all he won more than £2,500 and ran in seventy-two events, winning twenty-three times and being second on nineteen occasions. A later litter of six saplings by the same sire and dam made 1,265 gns when they were auctioned at Aldridge's.

KILMAGOURA MIST

A brindle bitch by Yanka Boy out of Kilmagoura Star, whelped in June 1976, she has proved herself to be one of the all-time greats by winning the 1978 Oaks and 1979 St Leger and again reaching the final for the 1979 Oaks, losing by only a neck when badly drawn in trap 3. Owned by Mr Jim Lovett and trained by Tommy Johnston, one of the finest trainers of bitches, she first contested the Northern Oaks in August 1978 at White City, Manchester; made even-money favourite, she won the event in the fast time of 29.48 secs. Even so, she was considered to be no more than an outsider when she tackled the Oaks at Harringay in November, yet she won her first round heat by five lengths from Westmead Velvet. She was beaten into third place in her second round heat and in her semi-final, finishing two lengths behind the favourite, House Party, who had won both her heats. In the final it was again House Party who was quickest away and held a nice lead at the back straight, but Kilmagoura Mist, badly drawn in trap 4, gradually moved up and cut inside and had passed the favourite by the second turn to run on to record a comfortable win by a length from House Party in the fast time of 28.55 secs.

After her seasonal rest she was back again for the 1979 season, winning the Milton Keynes Derby, run over 620 m at Bletchley in August and sponsored by Watney Mann with £1,000 for the winner. Here she clearly gave some indication of being well able to go the longer distance, for she won convincingly in 39.10 secs and was entered for the St Leger to be run at Wembley in September, sponsored by Ladbroke's with £10,000 for the winner. Tommy Johnston had the bitch on top form by the time she arrived at Wembley and she won her heat with plenty to spare, but it was Black Earl, a dog by Rita's Choice, who most impressed and was made favourite to take the final. For the decider Kilmagoura Mist was in trap 1; Dangerous Lad in 2; Frame That in 3; Black Earl 2–1 favourite in 4; Colums Corner in 5 (from which trap a dog has never won the St Leger); and Owner's Guide was in trap 6. It was the two dogs from traps 1 and 2 who fought it out the whole way round, Kilmagoura Mist

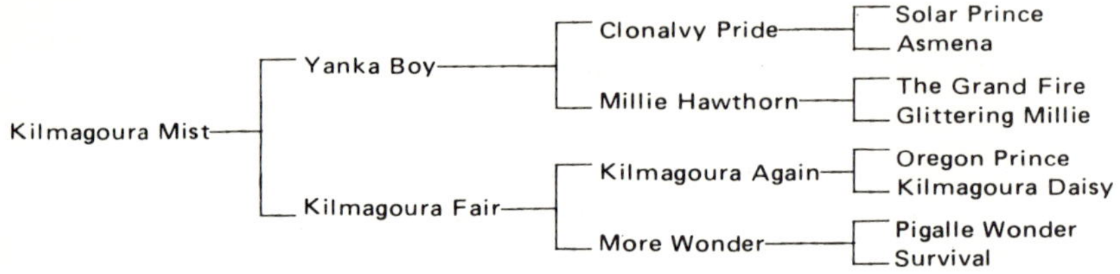

winning by an inch, the shortest of short heads, with Black Earl in second place. The time was 40.04 secs.

The 1979 Oaks followed, with the heats being run in October and the final in November. In her heat Kilmagoura Mist finished behind the Gold Collar winner Gay Flash, but made no mistake when winning her heat in round 2 in the fastest time of 28.63 secs; she also won her semi-final. Once again in the final she was badly drawn in trap 3, with Sunny Interval in trap 4 and Certain Style the 2–1 favourite in trap 6, but though the favourite was first from the traps she was caught on the final straight by the 12–1 outsider, Sunny Interval, who flashed over the line just a neck in front of Kilmagoura Mist. She had failed by inches to join the select band of Queen of the Suir, Cranog Bet and Ballinasloe Blondie who twice won the classic event. Sunny Interval is owned by Mr Ray Lancaster, an executive of *Sporting Life*, and several others. They had already won the 1976 Derby with Mutt's Silver. The pedigree of Kilmagoura Mist is shown above.

KNOCKROUR SLAVE

By Sole Aim out of Knockrour Exile and whelped in April 1977, this remarkable white dog weighing 72lbs was owned and trained by Denis Lynch of Aghabullogue. Since the days of Spanish Chestnut, no greyhound has performed with more brilliance at the Cork track, though elsewhere he had little success. After Knockrour Slave had won the 1979 Guiness Trophy at Cork by an amazing ten lengths, equalling the track record of 29.05 secs in a heat, Mr Lynch was offered £50,000 for the dog, the highest sum ever offered for a greyhound. He did not accept and his judgement was amply rewarded shortly afterwards when Knockrour Slave took the Liam Cashman-sponsored Laurels. At his best over 500–525 yds, no dog ever burst from the traps with greater speed and in the 1979 Laurels at Cork, though beaten in the first two rounds, he won his semi-final by 4 lengths and the final from Airmount Champ after the two had run neck and neck all the way, the 'Slave' pulling ahead in the last few strides to win by ½ length in 29.45 secs. By winning the Laurels again in 1980, by the record margin for the event of 6 lengths and in a new track record of 29 secs, the dog made it three Laurel wins in a row for Denis Lynch for in 1978, he had owned and trained Knockrour Girl to win the event in 29.40 secs, a record unique in the history of the event.

LAURIE'S PANTHER

This fine greyhound, in his short and meteoric career was owned by Mr Laurie James and trained at Romford by Terry Duggan. A black and white dog, whelped in April, 1980 by Shamrock Sailor out of Lady Lucy, his first important race was the Bobby Jack Puppy Cup run at Wimbledon in November 1981 in which he reached the final when he was well beaten into 5th place by the winner, Killacca. His next race was the Christmas Puppy Cup at Romford when, in trap 3, with the centre of the track badly churned up, he finished in 3rd place, 5 lengths behind Seaway Lad. In March he was eliminated from the Pall Mall in the first round and gave no inkling of the brilliance that was to make him a champion in the weeks ahead.

Entered for the Laurels in April, he won his 1st round heat by 3 lengths from Moon Prince and his second round heat by 2½ lengths from Night Miller and Yankee Express in 27.89 secs, with the favourite, Duke of Hazard, who in round 1 had set a new track record on sand, in 4th place. In his semi-final he was badly hampered early in the race and was beaten into 2nd place by Real Good, losing by 1½ lengths. In the final he was fast away and made all the running to win by ¾ length from Decoy Ranch in 27.79 secs, only .01 of a second outside the track record.

In his qualifying heat at Wimbledon for the 1982 Derby, he again defeated Night Miller and this time set a new track record with 27.72 secs defeating Longcross Smokey into 3rd place. In his 1st round heat at White City, he won it by ½ length from Pineapple Barrow in 29.48 secs and was to go through the event undefeated, no mean feat when it is realised that 210 of the best greyhounds in England and Ireland took part and a dog has to race six times to win the event. In round 2, he defeated Clohast Flame by 2 lengths in 29.66 secs and Killimy Ivy by 1¼ lengths in round 3, with Supreme Tiger in 3rd place. In his semi-final, he had a 2 length advantage over Duke of Hazard as he crossed the winning line.

It is always the hall-mark of a high class trainer to keep a greyhound in top form throughout the English Derby which, from the qualifying rounds lasts for a month before the final is run and this is what Terry Duggan did and Laurie's Panther was his first Derby finalist. Drawn in trap 1, the dog was quickly away and clung to the rails throughout, winning by ¾ length from Special Account, another fine dog, with Duke of Hazard only a head behind. It was one of the finest of all Derby finals and won by a worthy champion who was then retired to stud.

LACCA CHAMPION

His sire was Itsachampion and his dam was Highland Finch. This great dog, whelped in March 1976, was to win the 1978 Derby at White City and could well have emulated Mick the Miller and Patricia's Hope in winning two years in succession. In the 1978 event he was made 6–4 favourite after winning every heat and his semi-final, thus becoming only the third dog to do so in the history of the event. In the final he won by one and three quarter lengths from Backdeed Man in the fast time of 29.42 secs and wearing the colours of the difficult no. 3 trap, to earn his owner, Mrs Pearce, a cheque for £20,000. He contested the 1979 Derby, and from more than 200 greyhounds originally entered once again reached the final, in which he was the oldest contestant. Left many lengths behind in the traps, by a tremendous effort he had caught the others at the first bend, only to be badly impeded and to check his stride, again losing valuable ground. Running from trap 5 on the outside, a position he continued to occupy along the back straight and on the final turn, thus covering more ground than those on the inside, he was finally able to cut inside on the last bend and come through the front 100 yds from the winning line, but his age and the difficult run told against him and he did not have enough strength left to make the final effort needed to cross the line in front of the bitch Sarah's Bunny, who was only half his age and who had enjoyed a clear run from the outside trap from start to finish. For several years now the two outside traps, 5 and 6, at the White City have been allocated to the wide runners, while a draw is made for the other traps. Lacca Champion (not then considered to be a wide runner) ran from trap 3 in 1978, and whenever one has seen him he has always made for the inside rail as soon as possible. If he had been allowed to take his chance in the draw and had been fortunate enough to draw one of the inside positions, it is more than likely that he would have again been successful, but never has a gamer dog been seen, nor one with greater courage and track sense since Mick the Miller. A dark brindle, almost black from a distance, and known as 'Little Joe' to his kennel maids, he has been expertly handled throughout his career by trainer Pat Mullins in Cambridgeshire, but he was always a difficult dog to train, taking some time each season before coming to his best. Nor did he enjoy the best of luck when running. He won his heat and semi-final of the 1978 Scurry Cup, only to be crowded out once again in the final, and the same happened to him in the Steel City Cup at Owlerton.

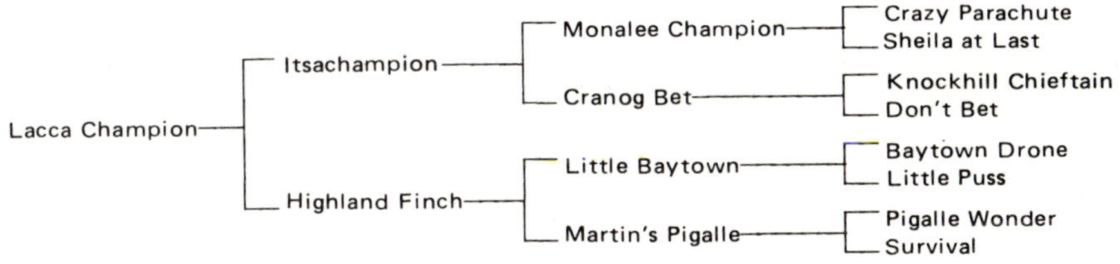

His sire, Itsachampion, was by Monalee Champion out of the great twice Oaks winner Cranog Bet. Monalee Champion was by Crazy Parachute out of another great dam, Sheila at Last, while the great Pigalle Wonder was a grand sire on his dam's side. His grand dam, Survival, was sired by The Grand Fire. Litter sister to Martin's Pigalle was More Wonder, grand dam of Kilmagoura Mist. Survival's litter sister was Clomoney Grand. His pedigree is shown on page 197.

Itsachampion also sired the white and black dog Instant Gambler, winner of the Welsh Derby and the Wood Lane Stakes in 1978 when he defeated five great greyhounds, Linacre, El Cavalier, Balliniska Band, Alfa Boy and Paradise Spectre. He won twenty races in Britain in top class and ten in Ireland, and with Lacca Champion was the best greyhound of 1978.

Itsachampion was possibly the best dog racing in Ireland during 1972, for he won the coveted McAlevy Gold Cup at Celtic Park; the Guinness 600 at Shelbourne Park (only the classics having priority status above these two events); and the Irish Cesarewitch at Navan.

LILAC'S LUCK

A blue brindle son of Printer out of Wilton Sandhills and whelped in December 1943, he was one of the greatest middle-distance dogs of all time and one of the few to have reached the final of both the English and Irish Derby. He was purchased for only £400 at Shelbourne Park sales, and shortly after won the Irish Derby of 1945, beating Gun Music by two lengths in 30.23 secs; he was the first winner of the event to have won his heats and semi-final, which shows how consistent he was. Later that year he won the Trigo Cup (now the Guinness Ulster Derby) in 29.65 secs, a very fast time. Thirty years later Piping Rock's time was less than a length faster. In the 1945 event Lilac's Luck defeated Mad Tanist and Astra, then considered to be Ireland's fastest. He also ran well in the National Sprint before coming to England early in 1946 for an attempt to win the Derby and so become the first to do the double. In his first race at Reading he set a new record for 550 yds with a time of 31.42 secs, and at Wembley won his heat for the Gold Cup by five lengths from Shaggy Lass, which showed

Irish Greyhound Derby winner in 1945, Lilac's Luck. Photo: GRA.

something of his tremendous speed. He won the final from Western Dasher, also by five lengths, in 40.06 secs.

Joint favourite for the Derby, he reached the final only to come up against Monday's News at the height of his form, who beat him into second place in a new final record of 29.34 secs, with those outstanding trackers Plucky Hero, Celtic Chief, Dante II and Shannon Shore finishing behind him in that order. Made favourite before the race, Lilac's Luck thus came within an ace of adding the English Derby to his Irish success, and no greyhound has ever equalled his record of winning one and being runner-up for the other. Soon after the Derby final he won the second July Stakes at West Ham, covering the 700 yds course in a new record time of 39.88 secs and being the first to break 40 secs over this distance at West Ham or at any track, for it was a world record for the distance.

To show how versatile he was, he then went back to Ireland to contest the National Sprint, run over 435 yds, and again reached the final but had to be withdrawn because of an injured foot. It was then decided that he should be retired to stud, having proved himself one of the greatest dogs over all distances in the history of the sport.

Throughout 1946 he was, with Monday's News, the best dog in training. At Hull in April he set a new track record over 700 yds, beating Alvaston Lulu Belle by two and a half lengths in 41.32 secs, and at Shawfield he ran up to Mad Midnight when that dog set a new track and world record over 700 yds with a time of 39.55 secs.

Lilac's Luck was kennelled at Doncaster, where he was trained by R. Jones and owned by Major A.E. Allnatt.

LOCAL INTERPRIZE

This black dog by Ruby Border out of Mystical Daisy had as his grand sire the famous Creamery Border, through whom he was endowed with amazing speed from the traps and intelligence in his running. Owned by Mr E.W. Goddard, a Sheffield butcher, Local Interprize was trained at Clapton by Stanley Biss and by his consistent running during 1948 and 1949 won more than £6,000 in prize money. He was considered by many who saw him run in the postwar years the greatest sprinter of all time and one of the best dogs ever to race in Britain. It is not known what Eric Goddard paid for him – possibly no more than a few hundred pounds. For some years he had owned the best dog at the old Darnall track, Jacob Retires, who won more than £2,000 in prize money from graded races alone. When that dog was retired Mr Goddard's ambition was to replace him with one whom after the war he could enjoy seeing run for top open events.

Local Interprize had his first race in Britain at Powderhall, Edinburgh, when towards the end of 1947 he ran up to that outstanding bitch Sheevaun for the Scottish Puppy Derby. It began two years of continuous success, repeating the 1946–7 successes of Monday's News, a dog endowed with similar intelligence and speed from the traps. When Monday's News finished, Eric Goddard's black dog took over, and he drew the crowds, then usually about 50,000, at the top London tracks wherever there was racing. Both these dogs appeared at exactly the right time, when the sport was enjoying its greatest popularity, and they were followed by Priceless Border, then Endless Gossip, two other all-time greats.

Like Mick the Miller and Wild Woolley and Monday's News and Dante II later, Local Interprize was a trim, compact animal and was a neat and tidy runner. Not for him running out at the bends. He trapped like lightning and looked for the slightest space to move into the rails where he stayed, keeping tight to the inside position throughout the race.

He did little to impress during the early months of 1948, and when he appeared at Catford in May for his first classic, the Gold Collar, few gave him a second look. But those who saw him win his heat by three lengths from the favourite, Royal Canopy, were much impressed by his tidy running and he was made favourite to win his semi-final. This he did, beating Tell Nobody by an amazing eight lengths, and he had little difficulty winning the £600 prize (more than his purchase price) by beating that good dog Kerry Rally by almost a yard. The 400 yds race had been tailor-made for the young dog on his first appearance in London.

In June he was at the big White City track for the Derby. He ran up his heat to

Mazurka and was runner-up to Priceless Border, the only dog who could beat him, in his semi-final. Mr O'Kane's great brindle was to beat him again to win the final by two lengths in a record 28.78 secs. It was almost three lengths faster than the record time of the previous year, and so Local Interprize as runner-up had himself also bettered the previous record. Two lengths behind him in third place was the brilliant Sheevaun, kennelled and trained in Scotland, who had beaten him in his first race at Powderhall.

A month later he was at Clapton, his home track, for the Scurry Gold Cup, run over 400 yds. Though Stanley Biss thought the shorter distances were exactly right for him he was beaten in both his heat and semi-final by Ironmonser, who was made favourite to win the event, but in the final it was Local Interprize who reached the front first and made all the running to win by an incredible eight lengths from Clonroche Lad in 23.04 secs. It was the biggest winning margin in the history of the event and the fastest time in the twenty-years history of the Scurry Cup. Just four days later he was at Cardiff for the Welsh Derby, winning his heat and final by seven lengths from West End Dasher in a record time for the event of 29.32 secs, which was also a new track record. Some years later the Welsh Derby was rightly given classic status, so it may be said that in his first three months' racing of the new season Local Interprize had won three classics and had run up for the Derby, a record of victories in important events which has never been equalled at any time. The dog always saved his finest performance for the final, the big occasion. He was like Mick the Miller in this respect; Monday's News was similar, and he had a trainer who always got his charges on peak form exactly at the right time. Local Interprize had now won £600 for the Gold Collar; £300 as runner-up for the Derby; £600 for the Scurry Cup; and £500 for the Welsh Derby. If the prize money had been the same as it is today, Local Interprize would have collected a record sum in just three months. As it was, he had won £2,000.

His next race was the Stewards' Cup at Wembley. He won his heat but was only third in his semi-final and did not get a place in the final. He put up a similar performance in the Laurels at Wimbledon, over a course that was thought to be ideal for his style of running, but again he disappointed, finishing third in his heat and semi-final, and although he reached the final he did not get a place. It was thought that by his tremendous efforts earlier in the year he had shot his bolt for the time being and should be given a winter's rest. But Stanley Biss had other ideas. Local Interprize's next run was for the Essex Vase at Romford, where he won his heat by five lengths from the Laurels winner Good Worker, but lost the final by a short head, Trev's Idol beating him on the line.

It was now well into October and he had been running without a break since early summer. But before the year ended Stanley Biss thought he should be tried over a longer course to prove his staying powers. At that time the Cesarewitch was run over 550 yds (later it went back to its original 600 yds) and at West Ham the dog came right back to form. Winning his heat, he ran up to Whiterock Abbey in his semi-final, but once again a final saw him on peak form and he took the event by almost two lengths from Freckled Major in 30.88 secs. He had confounded his critics by winning over 550 yds and had won his fourth classic in the year, a feat never accomplished before or after in England or Ireland. But he still had the Pall Mall to contest in December. He won his heat and semi-final and was installed 2–1 for the final but was beaten into third place. During the year his prize money amounted to £4,000 and swelled the total won by Stanley Biss for his patrons to more than £20,000, a total never before achieved by any trainer.

Local Interprize was then given the long rest he had earned and came out again in May 1949. On 14 May, in a 'loosener' at Stamford Bridge, he defeated a greyhound new to Great Britain called Ballymac Ball, who finished one and a half lengths behind him. Few who saw the race could have had any idea that they had seen the Derby winner of 1950 beaten by the champion of 1948–9.

A week later, at Catford, he began his efforts to retain the classic Gold Collar and, as usual for a big event, he finished third in his heat and ran up his semi-final, beaten

Local Interprize, winner in 1948 of three classic events, the Cesarewitch, the Gold Collar and the Scurry Gold Cup. Photo: GRA.

three quarters of a length by Killure Lad, the 20–1 outsider. In the final, however, Local Interprize was again at his best, winning by four and a half lengths from Laughing Grenadier in 25.88 secs. So he had become the first and only greyhound ever to have won the event twice. It was his fifth classic, a record which no other dog racing in Britain has ever equalled.

The heats for the 1949 Derby began on 11 June; Local Interprize finished third in heat 7 and occupied a similar place in heat 4 of round 2, won by the champion hurdler Dangerous Prince. In his semi-final he ran up to Glencloy Regent with Dangerous Prince behind him, to go through to the final for the second successive year. But he was now not quite the force he was the year before; if he had been he would have won, for this time there was no Priceless Border to compete against. Glencloy Regent was favourite but it was the bitch Narrogar Ann, English-born and -bred, who won, beating Dangerous Prince by one and a half lengths, and Local Interprize finished fourth.

He was then entered for the Stewards' Cup at Powderhall, where he had run his first race more than two years before. After winning his heat he went through to the final, but was beaten into third place, Eastern Madness winning the event. In July he was again entered for the Scurry Gold Cup, like the Gold Collar the sprinters' classic. He had already won two Gold Collars and one Scurry Cup; could he do the impossible and add another Scurry Cup to his formidable array of classics? No other dog had won two Gold Collars, and none up to them had won the Scurry twice. The excitement was intense when the heats began on 9 July, but it was 14 July before his own, heat 6, was to be run. Against him was the flying Irish dog Burndennet Brook, made 6–1 on favourite, and both shot from the traps like bullets. But it was Local Interprize who was the winner by three and a half lengths, in 23.13 secs, which was by far the fastest of the eight heats. The two fliers were in different heats of round 2, Burndennet Brook finishing third in his and being lucky to qualify for the semi-finals, but Local Interprize won his from Magna

Leader in what was again by far the fastest time of the heats. In the semi-finals they were again drawn in different races and both won, Local Interprize by an amazing ten lengths in 22.99 secs, which was the first time 23 secs had been broken in the event. As they lined up for the final on 23 July 30,000 people crowded into the Clapton Stadium, for everyone now expected Local Interprize to do the impossible. He was 6–4 on favourite and the two left the traps as if shot from a gun as a tremendous roar went up from the crowd. Burndennet Brook was in the favourable trap 1; Local Interprize in trap 6. At the first turn Burndennet Brook was in front but Local Interprize never gave up. Neck and neck the two dogs raced; as they came round the final bend there was scarcely an inch between them and they crossed the line together. It appeared to be a dead heat and it seemed an age before the lights flashed on the tote board – first no.1; second no.6. Burndennet Brook had won by the shortest of short heads.

In August Local Interprize was at Wimbledon for the Laurels, an event he had not won, and it was ominous for him when Ballymac Ball, whom he had beaten at Stamford Bridge earlier in the year, won his heat in the fantastic time of 28.03 secs, but the other heats were won by Local Interprize, Magna Hasty, Good Worker and Flintfield Grosvenor. In a semi-final Local Interprize once again met the rising new star Ballymac Ball, who won by a fantastic twelve lengths and breaking 28 secs for 500 yds at Wimbledon for the first time ever, with a time of 27.99 secs. Made 5–4 on favourite for the final, Ballymac Ball won by two lengths from Magna Hasty and was immediately installed favourite for the 1950 Derby.

Both Ballymac Ball and Local Interprize were then entered for the Thames Silver Salver at Southend and drawn together in heat 1. Ballymac Ball won comfortably, while Local Interprize was unable to get a place in the semi-finals. But he still was to have another crack at winning his second Cesarewitch. In his heat, however, he came up against Sailing at Dawn at his best, and this dog set a new track record with a time of 30.77 secs. Local Interprize progressed no further. Both he and Ballymac Ball were then at Harringay for the Pall Mall, but neither gained a place in the final and Local Interprize was clearly past his best. Quoted at 33–1, he was the outsider of all the contestants and one felt sad at his being kept in training after his wonderful effort for the Scurry Gold Cup. It would have been better if he had gone out on a high note. His Harringay run on 25 November 1949 was his last, but he had proved himself the greatest sprinter in the history of greyhound racing.

Eric Goddard did not buy another greyhound. He had no need to for he had enjoyed a lifetime's excitement in just two years and for an outlay of a few hundred pounds.

Local Interprize was to sire little at stud but his best was his daughter Monachdy Girlie, owned by Mr W.E. Carter, who in 1952 became the first bitch and one of only two ever to win the Scurry Gold Cup, which her sire, the only Scurry Gold Cup winner to sire another winner, had won four years previously. Monachdy Girlie was Jimmy Jowett's first classic winner, his success coming only a few weeks after he joined Clapton as a trainer.

LUCKY HI THERE

By Hi There out of Olive's Bunny and whelped in 1962, he was one of Hi There's greatest sons, a dog possessing tremendous courage and stamina. He was unbeaten in 1964 in sixteen consecutive races in top class which were run on seven different tracks, during which he broke six track records including the 525 yds at Limerick when only eighteen months old; the 700 yds at Wembley; and the 760 yds at Clapton which he smashed by more than eight lengths when winning the Orient Cup. In addition he won the Cambridgeshire, run over 600 yds; the 700 yds Wimbledon Spring Cup; and the Wembley Gold Cup over a similar distance. He also became the first and only dog to win both the English and Scottish St Legers. In the English event he clocked 39.90 secs in heavy going and was only the sixth dog to break the 40 secs barrier since the event was inaugurated in 1928. He was also a finalist in the 1964 Laurels and Gold Collar and in 1965 won the TV Sportsview Trophy, run over 880 yds. In all he won over £6,000 in prize money and was at his best over the longer distances. He was, with Model Dasher, perhaps the greatest stayer of all time.

At stud he was as successful as when racing, and one of his first sons to race was Monalee Peter, bred at Mr Hatton's kennels in Enniscorthy from his famous dam Kitty at Last. Her mother was the equally famous Sheila at Last, one of the greatest dams in the history of track racing. Monalee Peter showed the same liking for the Wembley track as his sire had done before him, and reached the final of the 1969 St Leger, won by Crefogue Dancer. In taking the Gold Cup, however, he emulated his famous sire, and in 1970 he once again reached the final of the St Leger, being one of the few dogs ever to do so in successive years. Unfortunately he was knocked over at the first bend and suffered injuries which resulted in his retirement to stud.

MAD TANIST

He was to succeed his sire, Tanist, as the greatest sire of fast-breaking greyhounds in the sport's history, and the combination of Mad Tanist's offspring and those of Castledown Lad, which possessed great staying power, was to transform the breeding of racing greyhounds from the early 1950s. Like his sire, Mad Tanist was so quick away that he was almost unable to control his terrific pace, and unlike slower dogs from the traps he moved so fast to the first bend that he was often in dire trouble. Yet though knocked over, as he was on occasions, he had such enormous pace and courage that he was able to come again when lengths behind and still win comfortably. This he did when winning the National Sprint in 1943, in which he set up a new track record at Dunmore Park with a time of 23.89 secs. He won by twelve lengths after winning his semi-final by a margin of fourteen lengths! In 1945 he reached the final of the Trigo Cup at Celtic Park, which he lost by inches to Fair Brook after being knocked over again and having to make up ten lengths on the final straight. Contesting the 1945 Derby at Shelbourne Park he set a new track record in his early heat, but in the semi-final was again in trouble and so severely injured himself that he was unable to contest the final. He was retired to stud, though his owner had been offered £1,750 for him after his Derby tragedy. A black dog with white feet and whelped in July 1942, his dam was Mad Darkie. He was a lightweight in comparison with many other dogs, weighing only 65 lbs when racing, but at stud he was to transmit his terrific pace to many of his offspring, like Mad Prospect, dam of Crazy Parachute; and The Grand Champion, who from a mating with Quare Fire produced The Grand Fire, sire of so many outstanding dams.

In one year alone, 1951, he sired the winners of the Irish, English, Scottish and Welsh Derby, the first of these being won by Carmody's Tanist and the others by one dog, Ballylanigan Tanist. He was also sire of that great all-rounder Sandown Champion, unbeaten on the coursing field and winner of the Easter Cup after winning all his heats. He also won the National Sprint at Dunmore Park, in which he broke the track record with a time of 23.86 secs for the 435 yds course. At stud Sandown Champion was to sire two great dams, Kentucky Duchess, dam of Himalayan Climber, and Lisabelle, dam of Solar Prince, sire of Supreme Witch who gave birth to that great litter which included Tric Trac, Spectre II and Forward King. Mad Tanist was owned by Mr Jack McAllister of Ballymena and stood at the kennels of Mr Paddy Kelly at Celbridge. The dog died in 1953 aged eleven, having perpetuated his sire's name and laying such excellent foundation for the future success of greyhound racing that we will remain in his debt as long as the sport continues.

MAGHEREAGH SOLDIER

Whelped in January 1934, he ran most of his races at Celtic Park, where in the Trigo Cup, now the Guinness Ulster Derby, he set up a record of three consecutive wins which only Spanish Battleship by his three Derby wins and Special in the Grand National have ever equalled in a major event in Ireland. The dog ran his first race at Celtic Park in May 1935, when he beat Queen of the Rocks' 525 yds record with a time of 30.37 secs. Five days later he won his heat of the Trigo Cup, this time breaking the 550 yds record in 31.67 secs. A week later he reduced this to 31.50 secs and ten days later took the Trigo Cup in 31.45 secs, again setting a new record. Before the end of the summer of 1935, he had also broken his 525 yds record, so that within two months he had set new times for the 525 yds and 550 yds courses on no less than five occasions, a record without precident in greyhound racing. Maghereagh Soldier won the Trigo Cup again in 1936 and 1937, and was almost unbeatable at his home track, Celtic Park. This great dog was trained by Mick Horan, first trainer of Mick the Miller.

MAGOURNA REJECT

By Astra's Son out of Saucy Dame, he is considered by some greyhound racing enthusiasts to be one of the best ten dogs ever to have raced in Britain. He was a brindle of handsome appearance, possessing the stamina and speed of his grand dam Astra, whose mating with the great Castledown Lad sire Paddy the Champion produced another outstanding sire, Astra's Son.

Magourna Reject was bought by Mrs Frances Chandler who placed the dog with Miss Noreen Collin, the Walthamstow trainer, who handled him brilliantly. He was to follow and rival Ballymac Ball and Endless Gossip in his ability to draw and enthral the crowds. Then came Duet Leader, Ford Spartan, Pigalle Wonder and Mile Bush Pride, greyhounds who made their contribution to a golden era of racing in the 1950s.

Magourna Reject was at his best over the longer distances, and his time of 39.88 secs when winning the 1953 St Leger over 700 yds was bettered by only one dog, Dante II, in the first twenty-five years of the race. In the Cesarewitch, run at West Ham over 600 yds, he ran brilliantly, his time of 33.24 secs being the fastest to date over that distance. Later trained by Tommy Reilly, the dog won the Coronation Cup at Monmore Green and the Stewards' Cup at Gloucester, beating Dashing Ash and Galtee Cleo by two lengths and setting a new track record. He was the first greyhound to win a televized race, which was the 1953 St Leger.

Magourna Reject was to become sire of Chittering Hope, dam of the 1965 Derby winner Chittering Clapton from a mating with Noted Crusader, but surprisingly sired little else of note.

MICK THE MILLER

It was a parish priest in Ireland who was to give greyhound racing its brightest jewel, for it was from his bitch, Na Boc Lei, that the great dog Mick the Miller was whelped from a mating to Glorious Event. Little credit has been given to Father Brophy's choice of bitch which was to give him in the same litter not only the greatest dog to run on the flat, Mick the Miller, but one of the best over hurdles, Macoma. But Father Brophy knew exactly what he was about when selecting Na Boc Lei, for not only was she a fine upstanding greyhound, ideal for breeding, but her sire had been one of Father Brophy's favourite coursing dogs, the unlucky Let 'Im Out – unlucky because the dog had reached the finals of the Irish Cup, the Tipperary Cup, the Cork Cup and the Greenall Cup by his determination and courageous running, only to find that when he had reached the last hurdle he had taken too much out of himself to bring off the prize. Let 'Im Out was to pass on this same courage to his grandsons, Mick the Miller and Macoma, two of the greatest the sport has known.

They were in a litter of twelve born in June 1926 and when the pups were about twelve months old one of them, the weaker, seemed unlikely to recover from a bad attack of distemper for which there were then no reliable vaccines. But the manager of Shelbourne Park when the track opened was Arthur Callanan, who had qualified as a veterinary surgeon some years before and was known to Father Brophy and other greyhound breeders. When he took the pup to him Arthur Callanan could see that, in spite

Arthur 'Doc' Callanan, who saved Mick the Miller's life. Photo: Mrs M. Callanan, MB, DPH.

Mick the Miller after winning the 1930 English Greyhound Derby for Mr and Mrs Arundel Kempton (centre). Sidney Orton, Mick's trainer, is on the left. Photo: GRA.

of its obvious frailty, it had an outside chance of surviving. Working day and night, Arthur Callanan managed to save the pup, and after several months returned it to Father Brophy with the advice not to put him in trials for some months but to give the dog a long period of convalescence. This accounts for Mick's late start on a race track.

When Mick was eighteen months old Father Brophy took him back to Shelbourne Park for his first trials and placed him with Mick Horan to train. Mr Horan has said that he also schooled the two dogs over hurdles, and found that Mick was quite as accomplished as his brother and would have performed equally well if he had been entered for hurdle events throughout his career. In fact the two dogs were able to perform well anywhere, over all distances and in all types of racing, but it was decided to allow one to race on the flat and the other over hurdles, which they continued to do throughout their careers.

Mick the Miller ran his first race, which he won, at Shelbourne Park on 18 April 1928, and his last at Wembley on 3 October 1931, which he also won. That last race was the St Leger, run over 700 yds, when Mick was more than five years old, an age when most greyhounds are long past their best let alone expected to win this long-distance event. Mick ran on twenty occasions in Ireland, mostly at Shelbourne Park, and only five times was he defeated, the last being in the final of the Easter Cup in April 1929, when he ran up to Odd Blade, who had won the first Easter Cup the previous year. Father Brophy was, of course, delighted with the greyhounds he had reared, and when Mick Horan suggested that Mick the Miller should have a crack at the English Derby in June that year the priest was absolutely over the moon.

Mick came to England with Father Brophy and Mick Horan in May 1929, and his first trial, at White City, caused tremendous excitement by the way he ran and the time he achieved. He was certainly favourite to win the Derby. As soon as the trial was over, Father Brophy was approached by several people who offered as much as £500 for the dog, money that could be spent by a poor parish priest in so many ways. His conscience told him he should not refuse, and there and then he asked the White City racing manager to put Mick up for auction on the terrace steps. The dog made the incredible price for a novice greyhound of 800 gns, and that night the London evening papers were full of it. Such money had never before been paid for a greyhound, and any dog worth so big a sum must be something quite outstanding. His new owner was Mr A.H. Williams, a London bookmaker, and the dog's first race in England was his first round heat for the Derby, run on 16 July which he won in 29.82 secs, then a national record, and the first time 30 secs had been broken over this course. His followers now began to realize that here was indeed a dog possessing special qualities. After winning his second round heat and semi-final he lined up for the final and was made favourite at 7–4 on, but was unsuccessful. It was, however, declared 'no race' and in the re-run he beat Palatinus who had won the first time by three lengths in 29.96 secs. Mr Williams' prize money amounted to only £700, the lowest sum awarded to a Derby winner, but even so he had recovered most of his purchase price within a few weeks and, always with an eye to business, he sold Mick to Mr Arundel Kempton who bought him as a present for his wife for 2,000 gns.

Once again the dog had made the headlines. It was the first time a dog had been sold for more than £1,000 and in a year of disquiet (the Wall Street crash was only twelve weeks away) Mick had come at just the right time to take people's minds off their troubles, while he gave the new sport just the boost it needed to enable it to establish itself. After their champion had won the Derby, Father Brophy and trainer Horan went back to Dublin rather richer than when they set out. Mick the Miller was henceforth kennelled at Wimbledon in the capable hands of Sidney Orton.

Mick's great asset was his wonderful trackcraft and his tranquillity. Not for him the over-excitement which was to cause so many good greyhounds to lose races which were well within their capabilities. He was not one of the quickest from the traps; indeed this may have been a good thing, for when others were hurtling along the straight to the first turn Mick was always just behind, ready to cut in to the rails at the slightest opportunity when faster dogs ran wide, and he had the stamina to come again and again if he was denied the chance of getting to the rails. He was at his best in 525 yds events and up to 700 yds. Anything less than 525 yds was not for him, which is why he did nothing in the Laurels at his home track, nor would he have achieved anything if he had contested the Gold Collar or Scurry Cup. These were for sprinters and that was not his forte. He liked the big, galloping tracks with wide turns as at West Ham, White City and Wembley, and his trainer was astute enough to select most of his races at these tracks. His home track never saw him at his best.

After his first Derby win he contested the International at West Ham, run over 600 yds, and won his heat and final, then back to the White City he went in November for the London Cup. He won his first and second round heats and semi-final, but was beaten a short head in the final. He saw the year out by winning his heat and semi-final for the Champion Stakes at Wimbledon over 550 yds, but after being badly baulked again finished second in the final. He was back at Wembley in March to win the important Spring Cup, and in June was at White City for the 1930 Derby. As was to be expected, he had little difficulty in again winning the event, an achievement equalled by only one other greyhound, Patricia's Hope in 1972 and 1973. On neither occasion did that dog start favourite, as did Mick the Miller. In the 1930 final Mick won by three lengths from the great bitch Bradshaw Fold, the only greyhound that year able to give him a run for his money.

It is not generally realized that not only did Mick win the Derby on successive occasions, but he also went through both events by winning every heat and his semi-finals, and apart from one single occasion he started from traps 1 or 4.

Just two days after the Derby Mick was at West Ham for the Cesarewitch, run over 600 yds, and once again he won every heat and the final and twice set a new national record for the course, clocking 34.01 secs in his semi-final. Also in July he was at the White City, Cardiff, for the Welsh Derby (later given classic status) and as usual won every heat and the final, in which he set a new national record of 29.55 secs, beating his national record of the previous week when winning his first round heat. Thus in six weeks he had set four national and world records for 600 yds and 525 yds, a feat which has never been equalled. Later that month came the Laurels at Wimbledon, in which he finished sixth in his heat and took no further part. He was clearly tired and given a long rest, after which he came out in March 1931 to contest the Spring Cup again at Wembley. Once more he won every round and the final, his time of 30.04 secs equalling the track record. In almost two years, from his first race in England on 16 July 1929 until 16 May 1931, when he won an open race at the White City, he took part in twenty-five races and nine match races, winning all but five, and in four of these he finished second, by a neck or short head. This period covered his sequence of nineteen wins in a row. This sustained success was equalled by only two greyhounds in the sport's history: by Ballynennan Moon, who between 28 February 1942 and 1 February 1943 ran forty-six races and won forty, and two matches, winning one; and over hurdles, between 9 May 1969, and 1 May 1972 (three years) when Sherry's Prince contested sixty-six races of which he won all but twenty and achieved this after recovering from a broken hock sustained when running in only his fifth race.

Mick was again entered for the 1931 Derby but was clearly beginning to lose some pace, for he was now almost five. Once again, however, he came through to the final and won it, making three in a row, but as on the first occasion, it was declared 'no race' and the re-run told against a dog of his age. He could only finish fourth behind the West Ham-trained Seldom Led, a dog that had been bought for a £5 note! The race, however, had been rightly won by the best dog of the year. In his career Seldom Led ran in sixty-two races and won exactly half of them, over all distances and on all tracks.

It was thought that Mick would have been retired after the Derby, but this was not so. He again contested the Cesarewitch, though without success, and was beaten in the first round of the Welsh Derby. It was clear that his best days were behind him. It was, however, decided to give him one more race, the St Leger, over a longer course than he had ever before attempted. Many thought it was asking too much of a dog over five, who had given so much. But Mick had other ideas. He loved racing and throughout the race he pulled out every ounce of his strength which enabled him to get home by a length from Virile Bill to the thunderous cheers of a packed stadium. Once again he had won a classic event after winning all his heats and semi-final. In the five classics he had won he remained unbeaten throughout, a record without parallel in the history of the sport. The St Leger final was run on 3 October 1931 and it was Mick's last race. He had taken his bow like the champion he was and never would we see his like again.

In 1935 Gainsborough Films gave him the lead in a film called *Wild Boy*, for he was still looked upon as a star in his own right. He lived on in happy retirement until he died on 5 May 1939. After his death it was found that his heart weighed 1½ ozs more than normal for a racing greyhound. His body was embalmed and placed in the Natural History Museum in London where it may be seen to this day. In all, Mick won £10,000 in prize money, a huge sum in those days, and his record reads

Ireland	20 races	15 wins and 3 2nds
England	61 races	46 wins and 10 2nds

Only on five occasions in eighty-one races was he out of the first two, a truly wonderful performance from a dog who possessed a very fine intelligence.

At stud he was nothing like the success that Macoma was, but in those days he was asked to serve bitches that had never seen a race track and were often of haphazard breeding. Among his best sons were Glen Ranger and Mick the Moocher, and his best daughters were Gallant Ruth, Oaks winner of 1934, and Greta's Rosary (from a mating with the Derby winner Greta Ranee, the first bitch to win the event), who emulated her sire in winning the 1938 St Leger.

One is often asked how the dog got his delightful name. He was named after Mick Miller, the odd-job man about Father Martin Brophy's vicarage and his church who looked after Mick when a puppy, during the days of complete freedom which the dog enjoyed before beginning serious training.

MILE BUSH PRIDE

By The Grand Champion out of Witching Dancer, the great brindle was bred by Mrs Nora Johnston of Campile, Co. Wexford and reared by Mrs Hannah Malone. Whelped in 1956, he was to set the racing world alight by his amazing speed and track sense, the like of which had not been seen since Mick the Miller and Future Cutlet. Each decade seems to produce champions of outstanding quality. In the early 1930s they were Mick the Miller, Wild Woolley, Future Cutlet, Creamery Border and Brilliant Bob; a decade later Ballyhennessy Seal, Monday's News, Trev's Perfection and Local Interprize. The 1950s produced Ford Spartan, Pigalle Wonder and Mile Bush Pride, and ten years later came Tric Trac, Spectre II, Faithful Hope and Sand Star. They stand out above all others in their speed and courage, consistency and track sense, which was more highly developed than in other greyhounds.

After many years trying to win the Greyhound Derby and having spent tens of thousands of pounds in the purchase of some outstanding greyhounds, Noel Purvis, a shipowner and fanatical greyhound-lover, obtained Mile Bush Pride early in 1958 and took him to Jack Harvey at Wembley to prepare for that year's event. That the dog lived up to everything his owner expected of him was entirely due to Mr Harvey's wonderful care and ability to bring out the best in his charges. The dog was not yet two years old when he did reach the final, and if he had won he would have been the youngest ever to win the Derby, but he

Mile Bush Pride, 1959 English, Scottish and Welsh Derby winner. Photo: GRA.

found his great rival Pigalle Wonder, drawn in trap 1, just too good for him. This equally great dog won for Mr Al Burnett by two and three quarter lengths from Northern Lad, with Mile Bush Pride a neck behind. The race was won in 28.65 secs, a photo-timing record for the Derby. Mile Bush Pride raced but little for the rest of the year, for both owner and trainer knew they had a dog who would be at his best the following year and would then stand a wonderful chance of winning the sport's premier event. Running through the 1959 Derby undefeated, he was even-money favourite to win and did so by inches in the most thrilling final ever seen, for three dogs crossed the line virtually together. The photo, however, showed that Mile Bush Pride had beaten Snub Nose by a neck, with Crazy Parachute a short head behind. The racing manager at the White City has said that it was as near to a triple dead heat as he had ever seen, but justice had been done for the dog and his owner and trainer and there was never a more popular win for Mr Purvis had at last achieved his life's ambition. A week or so later Mile Bush Pride took the Scottish Derby at Carntyne in 29.41 secs and equalled Trev's Perfection in the grand slam by winning the Welsh Derby at Arms Park, Cardiff, for which his track record of 28.00 secs was never beaten. Then, to complete an amazing year, Mr Purvis's dog won the Cesarewitch at West Ham in 32.66 secs, the fastest time ever recorded for the event when run there. As the Welsh Derby was later given classic status, the dog can be said to have equalled Brilliant Bob's record in winning three classics in the same year, but Brilliant Bob did not win the Derby and Mile Bush Pride's record must rank as the greatest ever in a single year.

By the time of the 1960 Derby Mile Bush Pride was almost four, but once again he showed just how good he was as, for the third successive year, he reached the final for which he was 5–4 on favourite. That he found himself crowded at the first turn and, having to check, allowed the outsider Duleek Dandy to move to the rails and win by two lengths from Clonalvy Romance, a length in front of Mile Bush Pride, is known to all followers of the sport. Afterwards Noel Purvis decided that his great dog had done enough, and retired him.

MODEL DASHER

A son of Model Whiskey out of Dashing Comet, he was bred 'in the purple', his sire being by Danielli (sire of Tokio, sire of Bah's Choice), his dam by Dasher Lad out of Dancing Comet. Castledown Lad's dam and Dancing Comet's sire were litter brother and sister, so this all-white dog, whelped in June 1942, was destined to show great stamina if nothing else.

Born and reared in Ireland, he was sent to Perry Barr, Birmingham, as an untried sapling for his first trials, together with his litter brother Model Chaser, where they were seen by Mr Frank Bithel, always on the look-out for a top-class greyhound. He immediately purchased the two dogs for £100 and must have had an eye for a good one for neither dog had done anything sensational in his trials, but their make-up appealed to him. Though it is usually said that luck was on their side, great credit must be given to Frank Bithel in this instance and to Fred Trevillion a few years later, who saw a potential Derby winner in Mott's Regret, a very moderate chaser, and after buying him very cheaply was proved correct.

Model Dasher was placed in the care of the Perry Barr trainer Tommy Baldwin, and had his first important race at Coventry at the age of seventeen months. Starting at long odds, he confounded many by winning the event in impressive style. His next race was the Midlands Puppy Championship for which Allandstown Playboy and Ballyhennessy Seal were entered. This he also won with similar ease by no less than six lengths, and it was then decided to take him to London for several open events, but like Disputed Rattler before him the dog was unimpressive, though at Wembley he was beaten by that great black bitch, then at the top of her form. After a rest during the winter of 1944 he came out in April and by mid-summer had set a new 500 yds record at Perry Barr of 28.24 secs; at Eastville, where he won the Golden Crest, he covered the 600 yds course in 35.11 secs. During the same period he contested ten open events throughout the country, eight of which he won and another he dead-heated. He won the Gold Cup at Wembley by the big margin of eight lengths, his first success in the metropolis, and when winning the Stayers' Stakes at the same track his time of

39.73 secs for the 700 yds course was a new world record for the distance. Again the experiences of Disputed Rattler were being repeated with Model Dasher, who found his true form at Wembley Stadium after many had written him off. Shortly after his great run he lowered the 750 yds record at Coventry with a time of 43.65 secs, and at Wimbledon in October 1944 he set a new record for 700 yds when winning the Key; at Walthamstow he was quoted 8–1 on to win the Test and duly did so. His dead heat was at the White City, in a race that included Laughing Lackey and the expensive Fawn Cherry. In his first time round the track he was knocked off his feet and was at one stage twenty lengths behind, yet recovered to dead-heat with Laughing Lackey, the dog who had beaten Ballynennan Moon on two occasions. He was rested during January and February of 1945 and then won the April Stakes at Coventry over 750 yds from a top-class field. In doing so he lowered Unwin Beauty's record by more than four lengths with a time of 43.65 secs.

No matter what the distance or where he was to run, the great white son of Model Whiskey performed with the greatest courage; he never ran a poor race, and never gave up when he often looked beaten. He ran just as convincingly on hard, dry grounds as he did in winter mud, revelling in everything he did. He was also a great traveller, making long journeys by train to arrive as fresh as a daisy just before he was due in the racing kennels.

After the April Stakes at Coventry the dog was entered for the Perry Barr Cup and, starting as usual odds-on favourite, won his first heat, but in his second heat tragedy struck. Coming from behind on the second straight he pulled up suddenly, rolled over and had to be carried from the track by his trainer. His leg was broken and he never raced again. He was at the peak of his form and in two years' racing had proved himself one of the greatest long-distance dogs of all time, some say the finest. In all he won over £2,000 in prize money and fourteen trophies at a time when no classic events were being held and when travelling conditions were extremely difficult. Out of forty-seven races he won twenty-seven times, and Mr Bithel was offered £10,000 for him but would never part with the dog he loved so much.

It is sad that Model Dasher met his death in a tragic way in 1951, straying on to the railway line near his home close to Perry Barr and being hit by a train which killed him instantly. But he will never be forgotten by those who saw him race. His only offspring of note was the unlucky Magna Hasty, from his mating with May Hasty. Their son three times reached the final of the Laurels, only to be beaten on each occasion; he also got to the final of the 1950 Derby, in which he was again beaten. From a mating with Mythical Rose he was to sire Deeps Dasher who ran up for the 1950 Irish Derby, won by Crossmolina Rambler at Shelbourne Park.

MONARCH OF THE GLEN

This brindle by Carolina Prince out of Turn of the Glen weighed 76 lbs when at his racing best and was whelped in 1940. He ran during the war years when classic events were few but was one of only two greyhounds to win the Irish St Leger on two occasions. This he did in 1942 and 1943, at Harold's Cross and Celtic Park, for it was not until 1944 that the race was permanently allocated to the Limerick track. When he won the Easter Cup at Shelbourne Park in 1943 his time of 30.12 secs was the fastest since Tanist's record in the 1940 Derby, while he set a new record for 550 yds at Harold's Cross the same year with 31.28 secs. He was then purchased for £2,000 by Miss G. Stockman to race in England, but in his first major event, the Scottish Derby final, he injured a thigh muscle so badly that he could never race again and was retired to stud. His running in Ireland in 1942 and 1943, however, stamped him as a greyhound of exceptional quality.

It is of interest that Cook, dam of Creamery Border, was also dam of Black Warrior who won the Wembley Spring Cup in 1934 and who in turn sired Turn of the Glen, dam of Monarch of the Glen, from a mating with Carolina Prince. Cook passed on to her sons the tremendous pace of her own sire, a champion of the coursing field, Guiding Hand.

MONDAY'S NEWS

This dog was a brindle weighing only 64 lbs, by Orluck's Best out of Monday Next. Not since Mick the Miller had appeared on the scene almost twenty years earlier had the

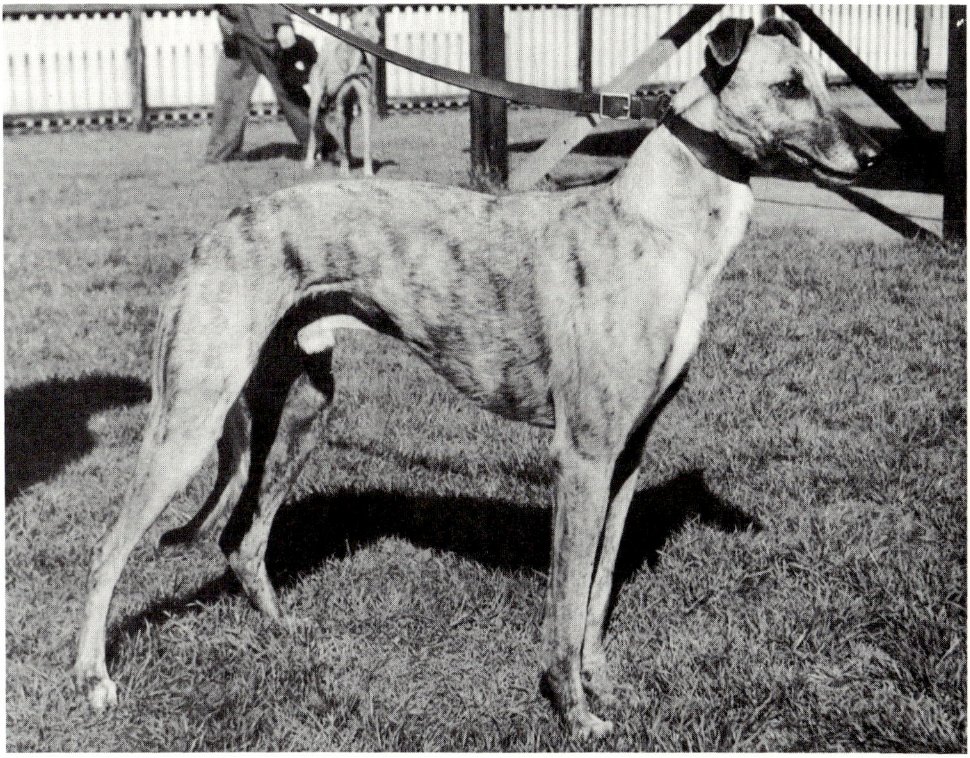

Monday's News, winner of the English Greyhound Derby 1946 and the Pall Mall 1947. Photo: GRA.

racing public taken to their hearts any greyhound in quite the same way, for like Mick he possessed superlative intelligence and never acknowledged defeat. He came on the scene (again like Mick) at exactly the right time, just after the war ended and with it five long years of black-out and rationing. Now the public were attending greyhound racing as never before or since (50 million attended the 100 tracks during 1946) and were looking for a new star to help them forget the lean war years.

That Monday's News was expected to possess speed from the traps was almost a foregone conclusion, for his sire had won the Scurry Gold Cup in 1938 and was one of the fastest ever over the shorter-distance races. The same combination of sire and dam had also produced an outstanding son in Monday's Son, whelped in 1942, winner of the Scottish Derby and the St Mungo Cup, who had finished third in both the Gold Collar and Scurry Cup. Monday's Son had been raised at Killenerry, Co. Tipperary by Mr John Maher, and when his brood bitch was ready for a second mating he decided to take her to Orluck's Best once more. In April 1944 she had her litter and the two dog pups were raised at Mr Maher's home until they were about nine months old, having the free run of his land and the best food of all for young greyhounds, a plentiful supply of cow's milk. By now he had named his pups Monday's News and Monday's Times, and although he had great hopes of their emulating the Scottish Derby winner from an earlier mating, he had no hesitation in accepting the £200 he was offered for the two pups with a view to their racing in England. The buyer was Mr D.T. Stewart and they were left with Mr Maher until they were ready for their trials.

Placed at Harringay, neither performed any better than dozens of others kennelled at the track and who took part in graded racing, but at this point Mr Stewart made a move he never had cause to regret. He placed the two dogs with Fred Farey, a private trainer at Shenfield in Essex. They were to bring fame and fortune to both their owner and trainer.

After undergoing a number of trials during which they improved all the time, it was decided to enter the dogs for an open race at Southend and Monday's News gave a surprising performance by not only winning but also lowering the track record which had stood for many years, clocking 28.22 secs for the 500 yds course. It was his first race in public and he never looked back. Entered for the 1946 May Stakes at Wembley, Monday's News created a sensation by the manner in which he left the traps and led all the way to beat the world's fastest at the time, the great Bah's Choice. It was at this moment that he was entered for the Derby and was quoted by leading bookmakers at 200–1 since his chances were considered so remote. Yet in the final of the Circuit at Walthamstow he again ran brilliantly, to be beaten only by a short head by Gullane Idol.

The contestants for the Derby were of outstanding quality. There was the English-bred Bah's Choice, the first to break 29 secs for 525 yds, and Quare Times, for whom his owners, Mr and Mrs Quinn of Co. Tipperary, had refused £10,000 before the premier event. Others taking part were the Irish Derby winner Lilac's Luck; Celtic Chief and Shannon Shore; Plucky Hero and Dante II – all greyhounds of the highest class. After reaching the final, before which Bah's Choice and Quare Times were eliminated, Monday's News, in the difficult trap 3, came out like a rocket and moving in to the rails at the first turn was never headed. He won by seven lengths from Lilac's Luck in the fastest time for the event. During the rest of the year he took part in twenty events, winning fifteen of them in perhaps the most successful six months' running of any greyhound in the history of the sport. He was well nigh invincible, and apart from his speed from the traps he kept clear of trouble, as Mick the Miller did, by his wonderful intelligence.

In the All-England Cup at Brough Park he won his semi-final in 29.87 secs and defeated the Scottish Derby winner Latin Pearl by a short head in the final in 29.55 secs, a new record. Then he went to Perry Barr where he won his heat of the Birmingham Cup and the final by a length from the £3,000 dog, Lemon Flash, in 30.35 secs.

For the St Leger at Wembley, run over 700 yds, there were those who thought the distance too much for him, but he won his heat and ran up to Call Maggie in his semi-final, only to be crowded at the first turn in the final, won by Bohernagraga Boy with Dumbles Maid in second place. He was, however, back to winning form for Charlton's Cloth of Gold, run over 600 yds, winning both his heat and semi-final, from Tinock Brigade and the final by two lengths from Bright Oak in 35.10 secs, confounding those who thought he could not achieve the longer distances.

In the Grand Prix at Walthamstow he won his heat by four lengths from Dante II in 30.14 secs, but could only finish third in the final. However for the Test, run over 700 yds, he won his heat in 41.94 secs and the final by two lengths from Missouri, winner of the Cobb Marathon, in 42.27 secs. Still on top of his form in December, he won his heat for the Gilbert Trophy at Hackney by half a length from Col. Skookum and then took the final, and before the year ended had won his heat in the International at Wimbledon from Mrs Dent's Tonycus, though he was beaten by this dog in the final.

During 1946 he had won £3,636 in a year when only £1,000 was awarded to the Derby winner, and he was given a well-earned rest during the first months of 1947 when the whole country was encased in snow and ice. He came back to racing in time to contest the April Stakes at Walthamstow and took up where he had left off, winning by one and a half lengths from Floating Dinghy in 30.50 secs. Then he went to Catford for the classic event, the Gold Collar, where for the first time he came up against the new champion, Trev's Perfection. 'Monday', as he was affectionately called, won his heat by ten lengths from Trev's Al in 25.81 secs, the fastest time for any of the eight heats, and in his semi-final set a new track record when beating Trev's Perfection by five lengths in 25.41 secs. (The previous record had been set by Fine Jubilee twelve years earlier.) In the final, for which he was made favourite, he met his match in Trev's Perfection, the first time this great dog was to show his enormous ability. He beat Monday's News by three lengths in 25.52 secs.

Quoted at 33–1 against his winning the Derby for a second time, he went near to equalling Mick the Miller's record of winning in consecutive years. He won his heat from Quinn's Selection in 29.36 secs and ran up to Lacken Invader in his semi-final, won in 28.97 secs. In the final, however, drawn in an outside trap, he ran into trouble in his efforts to get to the rails and was beaten two lengths by Trev's Perfection in a new final record of 28.95 secs, this being the first time 29 secs had been broken in the final. No other dog in Britain could have beaten him and behind him were Slaney Record, Trev's Jackie, Lacken Invader and Patsy's Record, all outstanding performers.

Entered for the Scottish Derby he was again defeated by the Derby winner in his heat, by a head in only one tenth of a second outside the track record. In the final, won by Trev's Perfection, he finished fourth. Afterwards Mr Stewart caused a sensation by taking the dog away from Fred Farey and placing him with Sidney Orton at Wimbledon, an unusual decision in view of the great success Farey had enjoyed with the dog the previous year, but clearly Trev's Perfection was the rising star.

In October Monday's News was selected to contest the England v Ireland International at Shelbourne Park, and after winning his heat he defeated the favourite, Dante II, by three lengths, with Ireland's Little Arthurstown a further one and a half lengths behind. His time of 29.93 secs was only half a length outside Smartly Fergus's track record.

Back in England he was entered for the Grand Prix at Walthamstow, winning his heat from the 1948 Derby winner Priceless Border, who was to become the new sensation. He again defeated him in the final by two and a half lengths in 30.41 secs to win his second classic, worth £500. For this event he again started the outsider, which was usual throughout his career, and yet no dog since Mick the Miller had won over the racing public to a greater extent, for no matter where he raced, nor how good the contestants, he always gave a performance way above what was expected of him.

In December 1947 he was still on brilliant form, winning his heat for the Pall Mall by one and a half lengths from Dan Bedam in 30.05 secs and his semi-final by five lengths from the same dog. He also took the event for the second year in succession by defeating Pilgrim's John in 30.10 secs. He had completed another wonderful year by winning his last five races, worth over £1,300 in prize money, and to the end of 1947 in two years he had amassed a total of £6,500.

In 1948 he again took his winter's rest in the early months and came back in March to contest the Wembley Spring Cup. Finishing third in his heat, he qualified for the final which was won by Don Gipsy and Whiterock Abbey in a dead heat. He then contested the 1,000 Guineas at Park Royal, winning his heat from Trev's Castle in 22.65 secs and his semi-final by three quarters of a length from Tonycus, but in the final he could only finish third behind Jack's Arrow, the winner, and Tonycus.

Entered for the Spring Stakes at Wandsworth on 1 May, he ran up in his heat to Ala Mein but won the final by two lengths from Tell Nobody in 25.12 secs for the 440 yds course. It was his last race, and he ended his career as he began it at Southend back in April 1946 – on a high note. In all he won more than £7,000 in prize money and must be considered one of the ten best greyhounds ever to race in Britain. Mr Stewart's investment had paid handsome dividends but he knew a good puppy when he saw one, and when the dog began his trials and gave a very ordinary performance he backed his judgement by placing him with the best private trainer he could find.

MUTT'S SILVER

By The Grand Silver out of Simple Pride, this outstanding fawn dog was whelped in April 1974 and handled throughout his career by Phil Rees at Wimbledon. Mr Ray Lancaster, who purchased Mutt's Silver for £1,250 in partnership with five others, including Lord Wigg, obtained one of the outstanding bargains in the sport's history, for in 1976 alone he won £22,500 which made him one of the biggest winners of prize money in any one year.

After setting a new track record at Wimbledon over 460 m, his first classic was the 1976 Scurry Gold Cup in which he was beaten in the final by his kennel companion Xmas Holiday. The distance was perhaps a little too short for him, but in the Derby, in the difficult trap 4 position, he found the 500 m course just to his liking and he won a thrilling race by a head from the favourite, Ballybeg Prim, in 29.36 secs. The line-up at the White City that June evening included the Scurry Cup winner Xmas Holiday in trap 1; Jackie's Jet in trap 2; Westmead Champ in trap 3; Mutt's Silver in trap 4; Ireland's greyhound of the year of 1975, Ballybeg Prim, in trap 5; and Myrtown's first daughter, Westmead Myra, in trap 6. Although Xmas Holiday was, as usual, quickest away, by the halfway stage Mutt's Silver was comfortably in the lead. Though Ballybeg Prim kept up the challenge throughout Mutt's Silver crossed the line a comfortable winner by two and a half lengths and he was on offer at 300–1 in the ante-post betting.

He then took the Double Diamond Select Stakes at Wembley; the Thames Silver Salver at Southend, a sprinters' race run over 277 m; and the Cambridgeshire at the White City. He also ran up for the Gold Collar to complete a magnificent year's racing.

Entered for Carroll's International at Dundalk, he took the winner's prize of £2,500 for this prestigious event. After a winter's rest he was entered for the 1977 Derby and after winning his first three heats in convincing style was expected to emulate Mick the Miller and Patricia's Hope by winning a second time. However, badly crowded at the first turn in his semi-final, he was narrowly eliminated and was retired to stud. His sire, The Grand Silver, was also sire of Little County who ran up in the 1970 English Derby, won by John Silver, and many other star performers. Mutt's Silver's pedigree reads:

Winner of the 1976 English Greyhound Derby, Mutt's Silver. Photo: GRA.

NAMELESS PIXIE

A black bitch by Monalee Champion out of Itsastar and owned and bred by Mr and Mrs McAuley of Dublin, she raced with such distinction during 1979 that she will go down in the history of the sport as one of the greatest of her sex. Her grand-dam was the wonderful Itsamint, owned by Leslie McNair, and Pixie was trained throughout her career by Ger McKenna.

Whelped in January 1977, Pixie first began racing towards the end of 1978 and, by the time the 1979 Irish Derby was to be run, she had contested some twenty races, winning half of them, and was coming into top form at just the right time. In the Cambridgeshire in May, at her home track,

Mutt's Silver	The Grand Silver	Prairie Flash	Hi There
			Prairie Peg
		April Twilight	Solar Prince
			The Grand Dancer
	Simple Pride	Clonlavy Pride	Solar Prince
			Asmena
		Simply Dandy	Dandy Man
			Simply Terrific

Shelbourne Park, she reached the final in which she finished fifth and it was thought that, like so many black bitches in the sport's history, she would be at her best over the longer distances, from 550 to 750 yds. A well-built powerful animal, she always put in a tremendous finish and often won in the last two strides, still going strong when the others were fading.

More than a hundred greyhounds contested the eighteen first-round heats for the 1979 Irish Derby, Nameless Pixie winning her heat with comparative ease in the fast time of 29.27 secs for the 525 yds course. She performed even better in her second-round heat, coming from behind the field to beat Carlin Shamrock in a devastating finish in 29.25 secs. In her quarter-final, she was left in the traps and was so far behind on the back straight that her chances of going through to the semi-finals looked to have gone, yet again she gave all she had and, coming from last place on the run-in, finished second behind Rathvilly Night to go through to the semi-finals. In her semi-final she again finished second, this time to Airmount Champ who beat her by four lengths in 29.16 secs.

Six outstanding greyhounds lined up for the final. Indian Joe was in trap 1; Distant Clamour in trap 2; Airmount Champ in trap 3; the great Malange, in his second final, was in trap 4; Nameless Pixie in trap 5; and Penny County in trap 6. The race took place in torrential rain but it was all over seconds after the traps went up, for Penny County came out like a flash of lightning with Distant Clamour some three lengths behind and they led throughout the race, with Penny County beating Distant Clamour by three lengths and with Nameless Pixie, running powerfully at the finish, a further length behind in third place. For the first time two bitches had finished in the first three in Ireland's premier event and a first prize of £20,000 went to the winner.

Pixie's next race was the now famous Carrolls International (open to all comers), held in August each year at Dundalk and worth £3,000 to the winner. After the classics this is one of the most prestigious events in Ireland and attracts the best greyhounds from across the Irish Sea. On this occasion, the English challenger was Monday's Bran, the 500 m world record holder from Brighton. Also in the race were Hunday Dook and Irish Derby finalist Distant Clamour. Mr Blackburn's English dog (in trap 6) was quickest away and led throughout the race until almost the end when Pixie, gaining on him all the time, pulled in front along the final straight to win by two lengths with Distant Clamour seven lengths behind in third place. But this great dog was to tip the scales in the Respond Stakes, sponsored by Kerry Co-operative Society with £5,000 in prize money, when he defeated a top-class field which included Nameless Pixie, Indian Joe, Tough Decision, Airmount Champ and Desert Pilot. Indian Joe was second and Nameless Pixie third.

Nameless Pixie's outstanding performance was still to come, however. This was in the Irish Oaks run at Harold's Cross in September. Also taking part in the event was Derby winner Penny County, who was at her brilliant best when winning her first-round heat but came 'in season' the following day which deprived her of the chance of becoming the first greyhound bitch ever to win the Derby and the Oaks. Much of the disappointment of those who had come to see Penny County attempt this feat was forgotten when Nameless Pixie produced magnificent running, winning all her heats and semi-final, always with her terrific finishing. When Penny County pulled out she was made favourite to win the event and did so, though in the final she had to recover from a severe bumping at the first bend and her courage alone pulled her through as she crossed the winning line two lengths in front of Surfing Maid with Say Ship only a short head behind. Her win gave Ger McKenna his first Oaks success and, to crown a wonderful evening for him, he also trained the runner-up.

Nameless Pixie was rightly chosen as the Greyhound of the Year (1979), an honour she richly deserved. After her winter rest she came over to contest the 1980 English Derby, and in her first-round heat ran up to Commutering Kid, being beaten by only a short head. She won her second-round heat, beating Redshot by a length, but in round 3 she was badly hampered and was beaten into fourth place by three outstanding dogs in Knockrour Slave, Young Breeze and Indian Joe, though the latter went through by only a short head. He was to go on and win the event: such is the luck of the game.

A few weeks later Pixie again reached the final of the Irish Derby, sponsored by Carrolls with a record sum of £22,000 for the winner, in which she finished third behind Suir Miller and Another Trail. She was the first bitch ever to contest two Derby finals either in Britain or in Ireland, and she became one of the few greyhounds of either sex to contest two Derby finals, a feat which established her as one of the greatest ever to grace an Irish racecourse.

NARROGAR ANN

This fawn daughter of the Waterloo Cup winner Dutton Swordfish out of the Beef Cutlet bitch Winnie of Berrow was whelped in May 1946, one of a litter of ten, six bitches and four dogs, all of them fawns and all of which performed with distinction during the latter weeks of 1947 and in 1948 and 1949. They began their careers at Oxford where Ann ran her first race on 7 March 1948, when she finished second. In May she was eliminated from the Regency Produce Stakes at Brighton after finishing fourth in her heat and when starting at 33–1. In July at Wembley she reached the final of the Coronation Stakes, in which she finished fourth behind Major Movement, then in two further events at her home track, Oxford, she was again well beaten but by late July she had won her heat, semi-final and final of the Western Two-year-old Produce Stakes, when three from Winnie of Berrow's wonderful litter took the first three places.

She was now beginning to show something of her potential and was sent to Leslie Reynolds, which proved to be the turning-point in her career. After her seasonal rest she was entered for an open event at Stamford Bridge, losing by only a short head, and she next contested the Derby Trial Stakes at White City, winning her heat by three lengths. Leslie Reynolds must have been quietly confident about her chances in the premier classic. She won her first round heat and also her heat in round 2, defeating that honest performer Whiterock Abbey. In her semi-final she ran up to Sailing at Dawn but won the final by just over a length from the outsider, Dangerous Prince, who had previously run up for the Grand National. Entered for the Cesarewitch, she ran well in her heat, to be beaten by Drumgoon Boy in 30.54 secs, a new track record; since this dog went on to win the event and also the Pall Mall, Narrogar Ann was in no way disgraced. She was back at the White City in November for the O.A. Critchley Memorial Stakes, winning her heat and final by nine lengths from such outstanding greyhounds as Red Wind, Sheevaun, Behattan Marquis and Sailing at Dawn and in the fast time of 29.31 secs. Later that month she contested the Gilbert Trophy at Hackney, winning her heat and final by six lengths which made her the biggest prizewinner that year and one of the outstanding bitches ever to race. She was then retired and, coming in season early in 1950, was bought by Mr H.E. Gocher who took her to be mated to Priceless Border, who had won the Derby in 1948. The result was a litter which included Endless Gossip, who was to win the Derby in 1952 in the fastest time for the event of 28.50 secs; and Edgerley's Gloria, who when mated to Sandown Champion whelped Elphin Girl, dam of Holystone Elf who won the Waterloo Cup in 1958.

The mating of Narrogar Ann and Priceless Border was one of the most important in the history of greyhound breeding, for from a mating to Castle Yard, Endless Gossip sired Sally's Gossip, dam of Printer's Prince, who from a mating with Yellow Streak sired the Irish Derby winner, Yellow Printer, the world's fastest greyhound; and when mated to Pardee sired Newdown Heather, who was to become the world's greatest sire of track and coursing stock of the 1970s. Mr Reid's mating of his bitch Winnie of Berrow to Dutton Swordfish back in 1946 was certainly one of the most important in the history of greyhound racing and the sport was to benefit for years to come.

Romance surrounds Winnie of Berrow for it was never intended to race her and she did not begin racing until she had whelped a litter of six pups by Grand Victor which sold at auction in England for £1,200. One was the ace stayer of the 1940s, Victory of Waterhall.

Winnie, like her daughter, was English-born and -bred and cost only £70 when bought at auction. Whelped in October 1940, when five years old she won the famous

Eclipse Stakes at Coventry, beating the Derby winner of that year, the flying Ballyhennessy Seal. A week later she set a new record at her home track, Oxford, and went back to Coventry to win the November Stakes by three lengths. In all she won nearly £2,000 in prize money when £50 was the usual amount for an open event winner. She was one of the all time greats, for besides her courage and ability on the track she was able to pass on to her daughter the tremendous pace of her sire, Beef Cutlet, which was transmitted through Narrogar Ann to her son, Endless Gossip, and in turn through Sally's Gossip to Printer's Prince, sire of Yellow Printer and Newdown Heather. Winnie of Berrow was one of the great foundation dams of modern greyhound racing, probably the greatest, and her name should never be forgotten.

Early in 1945 she was again mated to Grand Victor and whelped seven puppies, then when almost five she travelled to Carntyne for the Scottish Derby and only just failed to gain a final place. Back at Oxford, after a journey of fourteen hours, she set a new track record, then contested the Summer Cup at Wembley, finishing third in the final. Shortly afterwards, she came in season and was put to Dutton Swordfish, which resulted in the famous litter that included Narrogar Ann.

OREGON PRINCE

By the great Knockhill Chieftain out of Burleigh's Fancy, this outstanding greyhound was trained by Phil Rees and when a puppy clocked 27.16 secs around the 500 yds circuit at Stamford Bridge to become the fastest in the world over this distance. A brindle whelped in 1958, he won Wimbledon's Puppy Derby in 1950 in 28.59 secs, and the following year, when winning the Chelsea Cup at Stamford Bridge, clipped .01 secs off his world record for 500 yds. That year, when favourite for the Derby, he reached the final but was surprisingly beaten by one and a quarter lengths by Palm's Printer. Shortly afterwards he won the Welsh Derby in 28.86 secs, a time bettered only by Mile Bush Pride.

Retired to stud, he was an outstanding success. Mated to Wild Countess he was to sire Pool's Punter, who was to win the Irish St Leger for his owner, Mr George Adams of Sheffield, who became the first English owner ever to win this event. Another of Oregon Prince's outstanding sons was Prince of Roses, who like his sire set a world record for 500 yds at Stamford Bridge and who in turn was sire of that fine English-bred tracker Forest Noble, one of the most consistent dogs to run in recent years. A brindle weighing 77 lbs and whelped in July 1970, he was a finalist in ten major open events during 1972 and 1973 and was unfortunate never to win a classic. He was outstanding in the 1973 Derby, winning his semi-final in the fastest time; in the final he finished fourth, beaten only half a length, a neck and a neck by Patricia's Hope, Softly and Say Little in one of the closest finals for years, contested by six outstanding greyhounds. In two years' running he never once gave a poor performance.

Oregon Prince was also sire of Land Rail, dam of Sugarloaf Bunny, who from a mating to Jimsun sired the 1979 English Derby winner Sarah's Bunny; and of One for Minnie, dam of the Scurry Cup winner Don't Gambol. But his greatest son was Carry on Oregon, who ran undefeated through the 1967 Scurry Gold Cup which he won in 22.62 secs, a new track record. He also took the Chelsea Cup, as his sire had done before him, and the Laurels in 27.89 secs. He was owned by Mr Frank Newton and trained by Clare Orton. Although the dog had only eight months' racing during his career (1967), he won sixteen of the twenty-four races in which he took part and £5,000 in prize money. He was retired aged only two years three months after breaking a hock, and there is no knowing just how good he might have been.

Carry on Oregon was to transmit his own tremendous pace and that of his sire to Westmead Valley, a brindle whelped in 1971 who won the Scurry Gold Cup in 1975 and was one of the fastest sprinters of his day, while Oregon Prince was sire of Val's Prince, sire of Beachwalk Lady, dam of Backdeed Man from a mating with Flaming King. Backdeed Man ran up for the 1978 English Derby, won by Lacca Champion.

At stud, Oregon Prince produced stock that broke more than 100 track records. When eleven years old he went to the USA to continue his stud duties, where he died aged

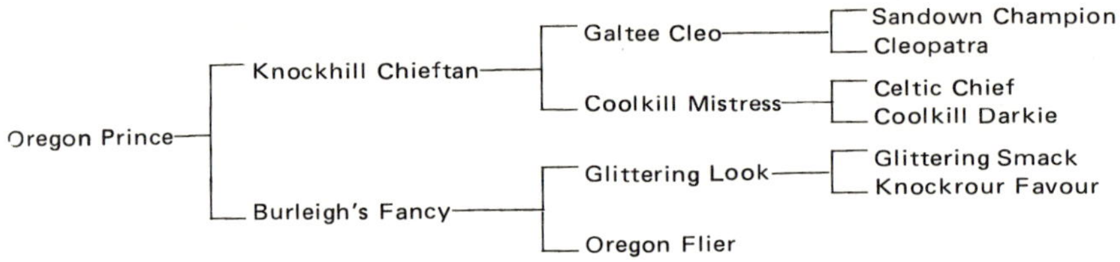

thirteen. The pedigree of this remarkable greyhound is given above.

Oregon Prince's dam, Burleigh's Fancy, was also dam of Top Note, winner of the Irish Oaks, and who in turn was dam of the great Supreme Fun from a mating with Newdown Heather.

OWN PRIDE

By the Irish Derby winner Always Proud out of the Crazy Parachute bitch Kitty True, he came within an ace of twice winning the Irish Derby which no other dog has achieved except the great Spanish Battleship, who won it three years in succession. A brindle dog bred by Ignatius Kelly and owned by Mr Tom O'Doherty of Co. Clare, he was trained by Ger McKenna of Co. Tipperary and won his semi-final for the 1969 Irish Derby by a short head from Finola's Yarn in what some believe to have been one of the finest contests ever seen at Harold's Cross. In the final he won by two and a half lengths from Monalee Gambler in 29.20 secs, the fastest time recorded at the track. In the 1970 event this great dog again won his semi-final and, made favourite for the final, was fast away. However he was hampered at the first turn and beaten into second place by Monalee Pride (Prairie Flash–Sheila at Last) owned by Mr Cahill, an Irishman resident in Chicago, who flew over for the event.

Besides his wonderful contest with Finola's Yarn, Own Pride figured in another event which had his followers biting the edges of their race cards. This was the final of the 1969 Guinness 600 run at Shelbourne Park in which Own Pride, Sports Ban and the bitch Itsamint flashed over the winning line together. The photo-finish apparatus, however, revealed that Itsamint had won by a short head (about two inches) from Own Pride, with Sports Ban another short head behind. But for the two losers bumping into each other when coming out of the final bends it is more than likely that one of them would have won the event. A month later Own Pride was made a 2–3 on favourite to take the St Leger at Limerick, and after winning each round and his semi-final won the final by three lengths from Tender Heroine in 30.95 secs, which no other Derby winner had ever done, to complete a wonderful year at the end of which he was rightly elected Champion Greyhound. After the 1970 Irish Derby he was retired to stud after a career that earned him the right to be classed with the greatest of all time. His pedigree reads:

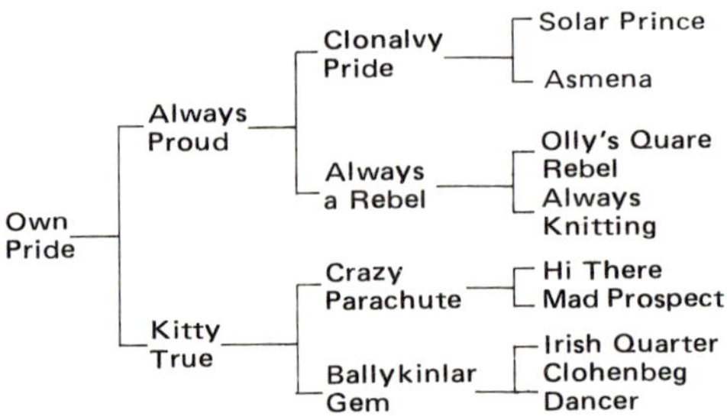

His breeding was outstanding, for his sire also won the Irish Derby and of his grand sires, Clonalvy Pride won the English Laurels, St Leger and Pall Mall, while Crazy Parachute was one of the greatest sires of all time, by Hi There out of Mad Prospect.

One of Own Pride's first sons to run was Flip Your Top, whose dam was Whittle Off, 820 yds record holder at Tralee. Her sire was the Irish St Leger winner Movealong Santa. Flip Your Top is a brindle weighing 80 lbs and was whelped in July 1973. After winning his first race in Ireland by twelve lengths and showing amazing pace, he was purchased to race in England where in April 1975 in his first race he created a sensation by breaking the track record at Brighton. Just three nights later, in his first heat for the Laurels, he broke the Wimbledon 500 yds record the first time round the track and went on to reach the final, in which he was beaten into second place three quarters of a length by the great bitch Pineapple Grand. A half share in the dog was then sold for £4,500 before the Derby, but after being knocked over at the first turn he failed to qualify for the semi-final by only a short head. In 1976 he won the Winter Cup at Wembley; the Evening Standard Cup; and the Scottish Derby; he also reached the final of the Wembley Spring Cup; the Pall Mall; the Edinburgh Cup; and the St Leger. He was a semi-finalist in both the English and Irish Derbys and with a bit more luck could well have set up a record number of classic wins. In less than two years' racing he won more than £8,000 and was then returned to stud, a great champion of impeccable breeding.

Own Pride, one of the greatest of modern sires, sired Cameo Colonel, a brindle who won the Welsh Derby in 1975 but then broke a hock and was retired to stud long before the great things expected of him could be fulfilled. Own Pride also sired Dromlara Flash from a mating with Monalee Last (Prairie Flash–Sheila at Last), a brindle who won the 1975 Scottish Derby; also the Bass Cup at Owlerton where he broke the track record on his first run. In addition Dromlara Flash was a finalist in the Welsh Derby that year. Another of Own Pride's excellent sons was the 1977 Irish St Leger winner Red Rasper, trained by Ger McKenna who also trained his sire to win the St Leger. Red Rasper's victory was Ger McKenna's eleventh St Leger since Prince of Bermuda won in 1959, a record which may never be broken, for he has been able to get the best out of stayers as no one has ever done before. His English counterpart is Mrs Natalie Savva who has the same wonderful ability with her Westmead greyhounds.

Own Pride also sired Mrs M. Wichello's Bansha Pride, trained by Phil Rees, who in 1975 won the Wimbledon Gold Cup over 460 m hurdles by six lengths in 28.24 secs, a track record for the new distance and perhaps equalling Ballinatona Special's amazing 28.37 secs done over the 500 yds course in May 1961, which was never beaten until the track changed to metres in 1975.

PALM'S PRINTER

Two greyhounds dominated the year 1961 on English racecourses: one was Clonalvy Pride, and the other Palm's Printer, owned by Mr Alf Heale; he was the first and only greyhound ever to win the Derby and the Scurry Gold Cup, the classic event for sprinters, which he won in 22.63 secs. Previously that time had only been bettered by one other, the great Gorey Airways, who had clocked 22.48 secs the previous year. In the 1961 Derby Palm's Printer defeated Oregon Prince, then the fastest dog in the world over 500 yds, by one and a quarter lengths, both dogs being made joint favourite in the ante-post betting.

Sired by The Grand Champion, Palm's Printer was trained at Clapton by Paddy McEvoy and gave this popular trainer his third Derby winner in nine years, a record only bettered by Leslie Reynolds who had trained five winners in the previous eight years (1948–55), a record which may stand for all time.

PAT SEAMUR

By Tullig Rambler out of Dainty Black, this white and blue dog whelped in May 1975 was one of the most consistent but unluckiest ever to race in Britain. Owned by Mrs H. Tasker, he was handled throughout his career by Geoff de Mulder and his first big event was the 1977 Derby in which he reached the final, only to be beaten into third place. He repeated his performance in the St Leger, the Gold Collar and Grand Prix of that year, running up for the Gold Collar which he could well have won but for being badly obstructed at the first turn. He came out again in 1978 after his winter rest and at Shawfield over the 500 m course at last won a classic event, an achievement so often been denied to him. Showing devastating early pace in his first round heat for the Scottish Derby, in which he defeated Rum Please by five lengths, he finished third in his semi-final, being beaten by Kentim Khan, but in the final he reversed this result, winning by a length in 30.52 secs. His next event was the Cambridgeshire at the White City. In this he was again successful, winning from a top-class field which included the Derby winner Lacca Champion. He also won the Summer Cup and Prince Philip Stakes to complete another outstanding year. So consistent were his performances that he was kept in training for another year and contes-

Pat Seamur	Tullig Rambler	Monalee Champion	Crazy Parachute
			Sheila at Last
		Yurituni	Pigalle Wonder
			Rather Fancy
	Dainty Black	The Grand Silver	Prairie Flash
			April Twilight
		Dainty Beauty	Myross Again
			Graceful Beauty

ted the 1979 Derby; he won his first round heat but, badly baulked in the second round, he failed to qualify for the semi-finals and was retired to stud. He was the modern equivalent of Bah's Choice, a strong dog renowned for his tremendous middle pace, and he was able to run all distances up to the St Leger course, never giving a poor performance whatever the state of the ground.

The pedigree of Pat Seamur is shown above.

PATRICIA'S HOPE

A white and fawn dog by Silver Hope out of Patricia and owned by Mr Gordon and Mr Basil Marks, he was whelped in July 1970 and came over to England to contest the 1972 Derby. After winning his heats and finishing third in his semi-final, he was quoted at 7–1 against his winning the final. Yellow Printer's only outstanding son, Super Rory, was made 9–4 odds-on favourite after he set a new world record in his semi-final. The moment the traps went up, however, there was only one dog in the hunt, Patricia's Hope, who made all the running to cross the line almost four lengths in front of Bally Larder, with Mick's Pride a short head behind. He next contested the Welsh Derby at Arms Park and had no great difficulty in adding this to his owners' endeavour to win the triple crown, which the dog accomplished when winning the Scottish Derby at Shawfield, bringing his winnings in just over a month's racing to £14,000. Once again his old rival Super Rory was made odds-on favourite, and when he set a new track record in his second round heat, clocking 28.74 secs for the 525 yds course, it seemed that on this occasion the bookmakers had got it right, especially when Patricia's Hope finished third in his semi-final and only just qualified for the final. With Super Rory first from the traps in the final, it appeared that Patricia's Hope's chances had gone, but as always he never gave up and had three quarters of a length to spare over Priory Hi at the winning line, with Mrs Thurlow's Super Rory, the 6–4 odds-on favourite, the same distance away in third place. During the dog's great triumph he was handled by the Clapton trainer Adam Jackson, who was given a special award for his great work by the Clapton management.

After his great feat it was decided to retire Patricia's Hope to stud, and he was sent back to Ireland to stand at the kennels of Mr Jimmy O'Connor. During the next six months, the dog served more than sixty bitches, so highly thought of was he by Irish breeders, but when his owners decided that he should return to try to emulate Mick the Miller's feat of twice winning the Derby, Jimmy O'Connor, who was now his trainer and who had purchased a one third share in the dog, believed that a second success was well within the dog's capabilities. He was proved entirely correct, but once again the bookmakers believed that Patricia's Hope's chances of achieving the dual success were far from attractive and it was the Perry Barr champion, Say Little, who was made favourite. But winning his first round heat from Forest Noble by one and a half lengths in 28.81 secs, the fastest of the eight heats, Patricia's Hope gave some idea of his amazing speed and stamina. In his second round heat, however, he was beaten by Say Little and in his semi-final finished third, only just in front of Shara Dee, but qualified for the final. Once again Patricia's Hope was to rise to the great occasion. As usual his amazing speed from the traps took him into the lead at the first turn, but then Say Little gained ground and at the half-way mark was only a length behind. But it was the bitch Softly who was to make the challenge in the final run to the line, gaining ground with every stride on Patricia's Hope who held on gamely to win by half a length, the bitch just getting to the line a neck in front of Say Little, with

Black Banjo only a neck behind, in the closest Derby for years.

The great Patricia's Hope was an example of the power of Pigalle Wonder (*see also* entry under his name) to perpetuate his own amazing speed through the dam line. His pedigree reads:

Patricia's Hope	Silver Hope	Clonalvy Pride	Solar Prince
			Asmena
		Millie Hawthorn	The Grand Fire
			Glittering Millie
	Patsicia (Patricia)	Odd Venture	Glittering Look
			Blarney Groves
		Helena's Gossip	Pigalle Wonder
			Sally's Dreamer

PENNY COUNTY

One of the fastest greyhounds ever to leave the traps and one of the sport's finest bitches, she was the only one of her sex in a litter of six born to the dam Columbcille Aim, by Sole Aim out of She's Silver, a litter sister of the 1971 English Oaks winner Shortcake. Columbcille Aim was one of two pups purchased by Richard Moore for his teenage son, Con, of Thomastown, Co. Kilkenny, and when Columbcille Aim had finished a short career on the track, they took her to Yanka Boy's son, Dark Mercury, through their first choice of a sire, another of Yanka Boy's offspring, Clashing, being unavailable. It was one of the quirks of fortune for the only bitch of the litter born to Columbcille Aim in March 1977 and named Penny County turned out to be one of the best of all time.

As is usual practice in Ireland, Penny County spent her first winter on the coursing field and performed with distinction at the N. Kilkenny meeting in December, qualifying for the Oaks at Clonmel. During the winter she won nine of her eleven courses. It was at this point that she was sold to Sean Dunne and Patrick Hurney of Lucan who in April placed her with the Dublin trainer Matt Travers. The handsome fawn bitch, now weighing around 56 lbs, made a quick impact with some excellent times at Harold's Cross which were to qualify her for the 1979 Derby at Shelbourne Park. This was her first major event on the track and she won her first-round heat by two lengths in 29.12 secs, one of the fastest times of the heats. In the second round she started at 2–1 on her winning but was beaten by half a length by Moonshine Again. In her quarter-final she was again the 2–1 on favourite and, trapping with her usual brilliance, was an easy winner, beating Allemaine by five lengths in 29.44 secs. In her semi-final she was on equally devastating form, winning by four lengths in the fast time of 29.30 secs, and behind her was Indian Joe who was to go through with her to the final.

For Carroll's Irish Derby final and a first prize of £20,000, the line-up included six of the best greyhounds in Ireland, amongst which were two of the finest bitches of all time in Nameless Pixie (trap 5) and Penny County (trap 6). The first four traps were occupied by Indian Joe (trap 1); Distant Clamour (trap 2); Airmount Champ (trap 3); and Malange (trap 4). When the traps went up, Penny County was out like a bullet and, cutting inside at the first bend, was several lengths ahead of her nearest rival, Distant Clamour, along the back straight with Nameless Pixie just behind. This in fact was how it finished, with Penny County winning by three lengths, a big margin for a greyhound Derby, and Nameless Pixie a length behind in third place. She raced no more until the Oaks, run at Harold's Cross in September. On her home track, this was an event she was expected to win, to become the first bitch to do the 'double' and in the same year. But it was not to be, for after winning her first-round heat in 29.30 secs, she came 'in season' and took no further part. It was left to her great rival, Nameless Pixie, to take the honours and even Penny County's withdrawal could not detract from her success.

PERUVIAN STYLE

A light brindle dog by Kilbelin Style out of Russian Boots and whelped in 1973, he made headlines in the sporting press when set to make a new record of twenty-one wins in consecutive races, but, having equalled the record of twenty in a row set by Westpark Mustard, he was beaten in a race at Galway by a length when not fully recovered from an injured foot.

Owned by Miss Deirdre Hynes and trained by Tony Fahy of Portumna, the dog had his first race at Navan in

September 1974 when he finished fourth. Then after several wins at Harold's Cross and Cork early in 1975 he won his heat for the 1,000 Guineas at Dundalk but was beaten in the final by the outstanding Lively Band.

Towards the end of July he went through the Tipperary Cup at Thurles undefeated and won the final and £1,000 in 29.48 secs, until then the fastest for the event. Next he went to Cork for the Laurels, and after winning his two heats in a fast time he was beaten in the semi-final. From there he contested the Harp Lager Stakes at Dundalk, winning his heats, semi-final and the event in 29.80 secs; he was next at Waterford for the Waterford Glass Stakes. Again he won his heats, semi-final and the final, setting a new track record of 29.34 secs for 525 yds. This was his eighth consecutive win, and his tenth from eleven starts. November saw him take the Shelbourne Leger, run over 550 yds, which some thought might be too far for him, but once again he made short work of his task, winning his heats, semi-final and final which was his twelfth consecutive win.

After his winter rest, his first run in 1976 was for the Callanan Cup at Harold's Cross and there were many followers of the sport who came specially to see him run, for twelve wins in a row was no mean feat. After his first heat it was obvious the dog was on better form than ever before, and it caused no surprise when he went through the event, winning the final in 29.30 secs and taking the first prize of £1,000.

Sixteen consecutive wins now brought him in sight of Mick the Miller's nineteen and Westpark Mustard's twenty in a row, which had been achieved in England in 1974. In April he was at Waterford again, winning the Truboard Gold Cup and setting a new track record of 29.28 secs which took his total to eighteen consecutive wins. But in the final he injured a foot and was off racing for almost six months. By October it seemed that he was fully recovered and he was entered for another attempt to win the Waterford Glass Stakes. He had no trouble in winning his first-round heat but pulled up lame and had to be withdrawn.

He had now equalled Mick's record, though it must be said that Mick's run included the Wembley Spring Cup, the 1930 Derby, the Cesarewitch and the Welsh Derby – eleven wins in a row including three classics, and no dog has ever done that before or since. Peruvian Style was now again in sight of equalling and then beating Westpark Mustard's record twenty in a row but this did not include a classic nor an event of major importance. Even so, it was a wonderful achievement. After a month's rest, Peruvian Style was thought to be ready for his attempt at the record and was duly entered for the Federation Championship held at his home track, Galway. He won his heat and when a week later he contested the final the Stadium was packed to capacity, some travelling 100 miles or more to see the dog set an all-time record which he was fully expected to do. But it was not to be, for he was beaten a length by Pet Ace, much to the disappointment of all who had followed his wonderful achievement. He had won twenty races in a row, the most ever by a greyhound in the Irish Republic, for Westpark Mustard had set her record in England. Peruvian Style had set the record for a dog and Westpark Mustard for a bitch. She raced over longer distances but Peruvian Style had to contend with much stronger opposition, so it is perhaps right that the record for most wins in succession is held jointly by these two outstanding greyhounds, both so ably handled by two great trainers.

After losing at Galway, Peruvian Style was retired to stud.

PIGALLE WONDER

This great dog, by Champion Prince out of the famous dam Prairie Peg, was bred and reared in Co. Kilkenny by Mr Tom Murphy, who originally named him Prairie Champion, a name which would have suited him better for he was indeed a champion in every respect. A brindle, he rivalled Future Cutlet and Endless Gossip in his appearance; with his sleek, graceful lines he looked every inch a champion and, like those other winners of the premier classic, would have taken all before him on the show bench if he had not been employed doing other things. Whelped in March 1956, he ran his first race at Kilkenny in a heat for the famous McCalmont Cup on 10 October 1957, which he won by ten lengths in 29.80 secs; he went on to win the final, showing just how good he was when only eighteen months old. He was bought by Mr Al Burnett, owner of the Pigalle Club in London, after clocking 29.10 secs in a 525 yds trial at Harold's Cross and he was renamed Pigalle Wonder.

He was indeed a wonder and during a career which lasted three years won almost £8,000 in prize money, when £1,500 was awarded to the Derby winner; and while £35,000 was awarded to the winner of the 1980 Derby, he must have earned considerably more than that sum at stud. Wherever he ran, his fantastic speed and track sense drew the crowds as no dog had done since Mick the Miller and Monday's News. He was a law unto himself, handsome, with a sharp intelligence and capable of amazing speed from the traps; in addition he never knew when he was beaten, which he rarely was. All tracks came alike to him and he set new track records on seven of the most important courses in Britain, his 28.44 secs run made in his Derby semi-final standing until Yellow Printer did 28.30 secs in 1968, ten years later. It is not generally realized that in his first-round heat for the Derby, this great dog went through by no more than an inch for he was awarded third place, only a nose in front of the fourth dog, when the order of finishing was shown on the photo-finish camera, it being impossible for the judge to separate the two dogs.

Pigalle Wonder's pedigree reads:

Pigalle Wonder (Prairie Champion)	Champion Prince	Bella's Prince (Castledown Lad)
		Sallywell
	Prairie Peg	The Grand Champion (Mad Tanist)
		Prairie Vixen

He was placed with Jim Syder Jnr at Wembley, and his first big event was the 1958 Derby. He won his second-round heat and semi-final (in which he set the track record referred to) and went on to win the final by three lengths from Northern Lad, with Mile Bush Pride, winner the following year, a neck behind in third place. He had started 5–4 on, and in the first photo-timed Derby his time of 28.65 secs was only two lengths slower than Endless Gossip's hand time of 28.50 secs.

His next contest was for the Pall Mall at Harringay, which he also won comfortably, and his time of 29.03 secs for 525 yds was not beaten while the event was run over this

Al Burnett (second from left) receiving the J.H. Balfour Trophy at the White City, won by his dog Pigalle Wonder. Trainer Jim Syder is on the left.

distance until Local Motive clocked 28.86 secs ten years later. This time stood until the distance was changed to metres in 1975.

Showing himself outstanding over middle distances, Pigalle Wonder was to end a wonderful year by dead-heating with Rylane Pleasure for the Cesarewitch, the only time a classic event in England has ended in a dead heat. That year on every track he raced he set new fast times, his 28.78 secs for 525 yds at Wembley on 26 May 1958 never being beaten over that distance; it stood for almost twenty years until the distance was changed to metres.

His last race was at Shelbourne Park on 13 August 1960 when, in the final of the Irish Derby, which he reached by running up to Perry's Apple in his semi-final, he was again beaten by this dog and also had The Black Ranger in front of him after running into trouble at the first bend. But he was then four and a half years old and had done enough to ensure that his name was to occupy a top place in the hall of fame of racing greyhounds. Yet his career was only just beginning; he still had nearly ten years at stud, during which time his influence on modern greyhound racing was to be considerable.

Early in 1963 Mr Burnett sold his champion to Mr A.S. Lucas of Bray, Co. Wicklow, to stand at stud in Ireland, for the then amazing sum of £3,500, the highest price ever paid for a dog whose racing career was over, yet Pigalle Wonder must have earned his new owner many times that sum and was to become as famous as a sire as he was when racing. It was as a sire of bitches that Pigalle Wonder, like Brilliant Bob twenty years earlier, was to become famous, for it was mostly through the dams he produced that his own phenomenal speed and trackcraft were perpetuated. He himself had several of the greatest dams in his pedigree and so was well equipped to pass on their wonderful qualities. Only Macoma and Brilliant Bob in earlier years and The Grand Fire and Pigalle Wonder of the 1950s and 1960s have been able to pass on their own superb qualities through the female line through the many bitches they served, which, more than anything, has contributed to the great improvement of the average racing greyhound of today. The champions of the past, from Entry Badge, Mick the Miller and Brilliant Bob to Sand Star and Patricia's Hope of more recent times were as good as, if not better than, the champions of today, but the average greyhound of those earlier days could not have stood comparison with those of the past decade and much of the credit for this is due to The Grand Fire and Pigalle Wonder. Like those dams of Macoma and Brilliant Bob breeding of earlier years, a dam with the blood of The Grand Fire or Pigalle Wonder in her pedigree is worth her weight in gold. Irish breeders in particular were quick to realize this and could never be persuaded to part with one of them.

One of Pigalle Wonder's finest offspring, however, and one of his first, was a dog, not a bitch, and he was to perpetuate his sire's outstanding qualities on the track and later to transmit them to his own offspring. His name was Wonder Valley, the winner of the Irish Derby. Wonder Valley has also left a great impression on the coursing field. The winner, Kyle Guest, and runner-up Ballyard Jumbo, of the Irish Coursing Derby run at Clonmel in 1979 both descended from Wonder Valley, and likewise the winner and runner-up for the Coursing Oaks, won by Little Treasure. Both she and Kyle Guest were sired by Wonder Valley's outstanding son Woodford General, but out of different bitches though both were by Newdown Heather. So on the race track and coursing field Wonder Valley has passed on the devastating pace of his sire, Pigalle Wonder, whose pace he was to inherit from the mating with Racing Millie.

Mated to Shandaroba, Pigalle Wonder produced the great Russian Gun, winner of the 1968 Irish Derby and who ran up to Yellow Printer in the final the following year. In turn Russian Gun was sire of An Tain, dam of Tain Mor, who won the Irish Derby in 1976 and who in turn sired Desert Pilot. Russian Gun, mated to Sheila's Prize gave Pampered Peggy, dam of Pampered Rover.

From his mating with The Grand Fire bitch Survival, Pigalle Wonder was to sire Martin's Pigalle, dam of Highland Finch, who in turn was dam of Lacca Champion, the English Derby winner of 1978 and runner-up of 1979. A litter sister of Martin's Pigalle was More Wonder, dam of Kilmagoura Fair, in turn dam of the 1978

Oaks and 1979 St Leger winner Kilmagoura Mist. Then from a mating to Rather Fancy Pigalle Wonder sired Yurituni, dam of the litter brothers Cobbler and Sole Aim, the Irish Derby winner of 1971, who in turn sired Columbcille Aim, dam of the flying bitch Penny County who won the Irish Derby in 1979. Mated to Red Caviar, Pigalle Wonder sired Paradise Wonder, dam of Paradise Spectre, twice winner of the Grand Prix; and with Narod Queen he was to sire Sabrina, dam of the Welsh Derby winner Instant Gambler.

A later son was Fantastic Prince, sire of the 1972 Irish Derby winner Catsrock Daisy, one of the fastest bitches ever to run. Thus his influence on modern greyhound racing was as great as that of Monalee Champion and Newdown Heather. Pigalle Wonder was also sire of Shady Begonia, who reached the final of the 1968 English Derby and the Cesarewitch that year and won the Midlands St Leger and 1968 TV Sportsview Trophy. Owned by Mr Bob Dinning and trained at Brough Park by Norman Oliver, he was a white and fawn dog, whelped in May 1966, and was out of the dam Castle Swan. Shady Begonia won on every track he raced and collected over £6,000 in prize money during 1968 and 1969. He was the greatest dog ever kennelled at Brough Park and ran his last race at Owlerton when he won for the fifty-eighth time in his two-year career.

If one had to name the greatest racing greyhound(s) in fifty years of the sport, taking into consideration all things – racing ability, appearance and performance as a sire – the answer must be Brilliant Bob and Pigalle Wonder, the two names coupled together, and more recently Sole Aim and Russian Gun, both from Pigalle Wonder. Pigalle Wonder died during the first days of January 1969 aged nearly thirteen, and lucky indeed are those who saw him race.

PINEAPPLE GRAND

By The Grand Silver out of Pineapple Baby, this fawn bitch was whelped in October 1972, not the best time of year for a greyhound to be born, having to face the cold weather after she was weaned, but in her case it made little difference for she was the outstanding greyhound of 1975. Owned by Mr Michael Cleary, she was trained by Frank Baldwin at Perry Barr and after winning the handsome Monmore Green Bookmakers' Trophy and the Trafalgar Cup at Wembley she next contested the Wembley Spring Cup in April. Installed as even-money favourite, she made no mistake and won by three quarters of a length from Sampson Flash in 29.78 secs for the 490 m course. Her next race was for the Laurels in May and, winning her heat, she also won her semi-final starting 2–1 on favourite by three quarters of a length from Hillside Kuda and running from trap 6. But all traps came alike to her, for in the final she came from trap 1 and, keeping close to the rails throughout the race, forced her competitors to cover more ground. In one of the best Laurels finals ever seen she again won by three quarters of a length from another outstanding greyhound, Flip Your Top, to give trainer Baldwin and the Perry Barr track their first-ever Laurels win. Nor must the name of her kennel man, Bill Phillips, be forgotten for he was never far away from the great bitch during her stay at Perry Barr. She had only a short period of racing but proved to be one of the greatest of her sex to race in England. This outstanding bitch reached the final of the 1975 Derby in which she finished third, behind Tartan Khan, the 25–1 outsider, and Sally's Cobbler. Two lengths behind her was the even-money favourite Myrtown, contesting his second final.

POOR MICK

This black dog, by Crazy Parachute out of Dearnside, was whelped in 1965 and was one of the greatest marathon stars since Model Dasher. Kennelled at Harringay, where he ran his first graded race in January 1968, he won the Gold Vase at his home track, run over 900 yds, when he beat Forward King, and then took the Will's Silver Rose Bowl at Powderhall over 880 yds. Later that year he won the Gold Cup at Wembley and the GRA Stakes at the White City (run over 880 yds), and during the year set five new track records covering each event in which he took part. He was beaten by a short head for the 1968 TV Sportsview Trophy at Romford, won by Shady Begonia. The following year he won the Gold Vase at his home track by an amazing sixteen lengths and the Pontin Stakes at White City over 880 yds. To these he added the Ray Jackson

Stakes and the Halbert Marathon, both run over 900 yds at Wembley, and in April was at the Dorchester Hotel in London where he was presented with a special award for his most consistent running in marathon events. If ever a dog ran his heart out, it was Poor Mick.

POSTAL VOTE

Owned by Mrs Betty Hastings and trained by Ger McKenna, he was one of the fastest and gamest dogs ever to race in Ireland, though most of the classic events eluded him for he was twice beaten by Sole Aim, winner of the English Laurels and the Irish Derby in 1971, on the latter occasion in the fast time of 29.12 secs. He first came into prominence when he won the 1970 Irish Cesarewitch, run over 600 yds at Navan, when he set a new track record of 33.08 secs in the final after winning his earlier heats. In December that year he won the £500 Pigalle Wonder Stakes at Shelbourne Park by one and a half lengths from Gentle Lady in 29.35 secs. In April 1971 Postal Vote won the important Easter Cup at the same track, and in the Derby that year he finished in second place, one and a half lengths behind Sole Aim, after leading throughout until the last turn. His last race was the Guinness 600. After winning his heat he was made odds-on favourite to take the final, which he did in 33.27 secs for the 600 yds course.

A brindle dog by Dusty Trail out of Paddistarr, he was one of the fastest greyhounds ever to race and his purchase by Mrs Hastings at the Shelbourne Park sales for £500 must be one of the all-time bargains. His sire Dusty Trail, whose dam was the Knockhill Chieftain bitch Dolores Daughter, was Greyhound of the Year for 1966 for he finished third in the English Derby; second in the Welsh Derby; and won the Scottish Derby, in which event he covered the 525 yds at Powderhall in 28.54 secs to better the time done by Pigalle Wonder. Mated to the bitch Will Hire, the result was Kirkland Darkie, whose 28.79 secs in the McAlevey Gold Cup semi-final was the fastest over 525 yds ever recorded in Ireland.

PRANCING KITTY

By Tanist out of Be Careful Kitty, she was a fawn bitch, weighing 55 lbs. Her owner was Mr R.G. Hills, who also owned her litter brother, Newtown Defender. Whelped in March 1943, Prancing Kitty first contested the 1944 Puppy Derby at Wimbledon which she won, her time of 28.84 secs being the fastest recorded. She reached the final of the Trafalgar Cup and the eleventh Two-year-old Produce Stakes which was won by her litter brother. In the final of the Midlands Puppy Championship at Perry Barr, she was beaten only a short head by Country Life. Next year she ran a dead heat with another great bitch, Robeen Printer, for the Coventry Eclipse Stakes, both finishing eight lengths in front of Wandering Lad. On 7 July she won the Coronation Cup at Wembley, a race for bitches, beating Coonvincent Betty in 29.26 secs, and in the 1945 Oaks at the White City she ran up to Trev's Fashion in her heat and, after winning her semi-final, defeated her great rival Robeen Printer to win the final in the fast time of 29.54 secs.

The 1945 Oaks was contested by what many followers of the sport believe to be some of the greatest bitches ever to have taken part in this event. These included (with their ante-post quotations): Awful Foolish, 25–1; Bradwell Cutlet, 14–1; Disputed Rattler, 40–1; Hurry Kitty, 5–1; Lady Grosvenor, 6–1; Mudinuri, 8–1; Prancing Kitty, 4–1; Robeen Printer, 2–1; Ryan's Rose, 6–1; and Trev's Fashion, 12–1.

In the November Stakes at the White City, run over 550 yds, she defeated Race Day in 31.14 secs. In the same year her litter brother won the Wembley Summer Cup from the great Shannon Shore and proved what a fine investment the two Tanist offspring were to their owner, for Newdown Defender had been purchased at Aldridges for 100 gns. Both were trained by Paddy Fortune at Wimbledon.

PRICELESS BORDER

A brindle whelped in June 1945, by Clonahard Border out of Priceless Sandhills, he first made headlines when in 1947 he won the third Home-bred Produce Stakes at Celtic Park in a new track record of 29.54 secs, beating the Mad Tanist pup Aura Monarch by five lengths. Priceless Border was owned by Mr W.P. O'Kane, an Ulster poultry farmer who decided to enter his dog for the 1947 English Derby and took

Mr W. P. O'Kane (left) and Priceless Border.

him to Leslie Reynolds at Wembley. After winning his first round heat in 29.18 secs, which was easily the fastest time for any of the heats, and beating Slaney Record by eight lengths, he was made odds-on favourite. However before the next round, possibly because of a change of climate and diet, he went down with a severe attack of enteritis and could take no further part in the event, which was won by Trev's Perfection from Monday's News, with Slaney Record in third place.

After recovering from his illness he contested the Thames Silver Salver at Southend and there showed just how good he was, winning his heat by seven lengths from the great Rimmell's Black and his semi-final by nine lengths from Trev's Castle in 28.07 secs, a new track record. In the final he beat the bitch Izadaisy by eight lengths and improved upon his track record with a time of 28.04 secs. Two days before he had beaten the same bitch by an astonishing twelve lengths when winning the Autumn Stakes at the White City, and in doing so had broken Quare Times' world and track record for 525 yds with a time of 28.75 secs, a speed of almost 40 mph.

In the fourteenth International run at Wimbledon on 27 December 1947 he beat Rio Cepretta by four lengths with Monday's News two and a half lengths behind. The *Greyhound Review* said: 'No one will ever forget his fantastic run to catch and overtake the fastest trapper of the time – Monday's News.'

After his winter rest he came out for the 1948 May Stakes at Stamford Bridge exactly where he had left off, for he defeated that excellent dog Whiterock Abbey by eight lengths in 27.60 secs which was a new world record for 500 yds. He was quoted 12–1 at odds on on his winning!

This amazing run gave some idea of his

Derby potential and in June he set a new 525 yds world and track record when winning his heat in 28.64 secs. He went on to win the event by two lengths from one of the best greyhounds ever to race, Local Interprize, and in a new final record of 28.74 secs, a time which only he had set when winning his heat. The great bitch Sheevaun was third, a further two lengths behind.

Priceless Border was beaten by only one dog, Monday's News, twice in the 1947 Grand Prix, and after eleven successive wins he was retired to stud. He had won £4,000 at a time when £1,500 was the amount awarded to the Derby winner, and his trainer said that he was the nearest to the perfect racing dog he had ever seen. Throughout the 1948 Derby he was quoted odds-on his winning, the first and only time this has happened. He won from trap 1 at 2–1 on and made all the running from trap to line, never being headed throughout the race.

At stud at the kennels of his owner at Ballymena, Co. Antrim, he was something of a disappointment, although he served the finest bitches of the time in Robeen Printer, Hurry Kitty, Coyne's Castle and Narrogar Ann. But if he had done nothing else his son Endless Gossip, from a mating with another Derby winner, Narrogar Ann, carved his name and that of his sire for ever in the hall of fame. Endless Gossip proved a worthy son of two outstanding Derby winners and was perhaps the greatest of all English-bred racing greyhounds, for he too won the Derby, the first son of a previous Derby winner to do so, and when mated to Castle Yard fathered Sally's Gossip, who from her mating with Hi There produced Printer's Prince, sire of Newdown Heather and Yellow Printer, the world's fastest greyhound.

PRINCE OF BERMUDA

A brindle dog by Champion Prince out of Sunora, a bitch whose grand sire was Ruby Border, sire of the brilliant Local Interprize, 'The Prince' as he was affectionately called inherited the same amazing speed as his great grand sire on his dam's side and of his sire Champion Prince, also sire of two great English Derby winners, Pigalle Wonder and The Grand Canal, and of the Irish Derby winner Sir Frederick, a dog virtually unknown to modern followers of the sport.

Whelped in August 1953, Prince of Bermuda was owned by Mrs E. Buckley of Nenagh and over middle distances was one of the fastest ever to run. He came on the scene exactly as Spanish Battleship was finishing, so he had much to live up to. He first hit the headlines with several fast times when contesting the Irish Derby of 1956, reaching the final in which he ran up to another outstanding dog, Keep Moving, probably the only one capable of beating him. The time of 29.18 secs was not only the fastest up to that date but was not beaten until Yellow Printer knocked .07 secs off it some twelve years later. It was indeed a fabulous time when it is considered that Spanish Battleship was about twelve lengths slower when winning his second Derby at Shelbourne Park two years previously.

Trained by Ger McKenna, 'The Prince' next contested the Laurels at Cork where he showed his amazing speed and trackcraft, though in this event too he had to be content with second place. In a heat run on 12 September he became the first dog to break 28 secs for the 500 yds course when winning in 27.95 secs, a record which stands to this day. In the final he was beaten a neck by Rather Grand, a dog he would have beaten nine times out of ten.

But it was in the 1956 St Leger at Limerick that he reached his peak. Winning his heats, he took the final in a record 30.66 secs which was not bettered until Time Up Please clocked 30.56 secs (just over a length faster) some fifteen years later and which is the only final to have been run in a faster time than that clocked by Prince of Bermuda. His St Leger win was the first of twelve that dogs trained by Ger McKenna were to achieve and the event has come to be known as 'Ger's Leger'.

Prince of Bermuda possessed the same phenomenal pace as did Brilliant Bob and Quare Times, and Yellow Printer and Bashful Man of more recent times. When winning the Leger he was four or five lengths in front at the first turn, and more often than not began his races in a similar way, moving from the traps like lightning. He was also endowed with great intelligence, for whenever there was the slightest opportunity he would move inside to the rails, almost brushing them as he flew past. When he retired to stud great things were expected from him but he was disappointing. He did, however, sire a little-known bitch, Little Puss, dam of Little Baytown who was to sire Highland Finch, dam of the great Lacca Champion. He was also sire of another obscure bitch, Market Beauty, dam of Market Green, sire of Flaming King, the Irish Laurels winner of 1968, himself sire of Backdeed Man who ran up to Lacca Champion for the English Derby of 1978. Perhaps if he had been mated to bitches such as Survival, Don't Bet and Sheila at Last he would have produced some pups endowed with his own amazing pace.

QUARE TIMES

A blue dog weighing 67 lbs, he was one of the fastest ever to race on any track and was the first to break 29 secs for the 525 yds course in a race, though Bah's Choice had done so previously in a trial at the White City.

By Ballydancer, Irish 550 yds National record holder, out of the dam Quite Welcome, and whelped in 1944, he first came into prominence when finishing runner-up to Shaggy Lad for the 1945 Irish Puppy Derby which was won in the record time of 27.98 secs, the first time 28 secs had been broken. In round 2 for the National Puppy Cup at Clonmel he had clocked an amazing 29.75 secs to set a new track record, and in the final of the 1946 Easter Cup at Shelbourne Park he ran up to the bitch Astra, having previously beaten her in the second round by six lengths.

Owned, bred and trained by Mr and Mrs Quinn of Killenaule, Co. Tipperary, Quare Times was the fastest since Mr Quinn's star of earlier days, Brilliant Bob, but his early races set the pattern for his whole career – the dog had amazing speed but no trackcraft when compared with champions such as Mick the Miller, Wild Woolley, Ballynennan Moon and Monday's News, none of which was as fast from the traps as he was. So many times he appeared to have an event at his mercy, yet was beaten only by himself. Like Yellow Printer, who came later, he was too fast to the first turn and tended to run out, thus allowing a dog with trackcraft to move in to the rails and so cover less ground during a race. Yet he came on to the greyhound racing scene at the end of 1945, at a time of rationing and petrol shortages, and was just what the sport required to create excitement.

Coming to England in May 1946 after

Quare Times. Photo: GRA.

his Easter Cup run, he was placed with Sidney Orton and entered for the Derby. It was in heat 4 of the second round that he clocked a new world record time of 28.95 secs (Bah's Choice had done 28.99 secs in a trial), and though reaching the semi-finals he was unable to get through to the final much to everyone's surprise, for he was then favourite to win the event. In the Derby Consolation Stakes, however, he won by four lengths from Bah's Choice in 28.82 secs to improve on his own world record, and this was a much faster time than that done by Monday's News when winning the Derby that night.

In the Laurels at Wimbledon his running followed a similar pattern, for he won his heat by four lengths from Shannon Shore but was beaten by the same distance by that great dog in his semi-final when he finished third. In the final, however, he was again beaten by Shannon Shore, a dog with a flair for the big occasion. A few days later at the White City, in an England *v* Ireland match against Bah's Choice on Bank Holiday Monday for £500 a side, run over 550 yds, Quare Times was the winner by three and a half lengths in the world's fastest time for the distance of 30.38 secs. It is said that Mrs Quinn was offered £10,000 for the dog but would not accept the offer, and the Quinns never did part with him. Instead he was retired to stud and, although he sired few outstanding greyhounds, his mating with Negros Fire produced Quare Fire who, from a mating to The Grand Champion, produced The Grand Fire who was to have as great an influence on the dam lines of modern greyhounds as did Brilliant Bob twenty years earlier. The Grand Fire was sire of Millie Hawthorn, dam of the English Derby winner Faithful Hope, who in turn was sire of another Derby winner, John Silver. The Grand Fire was sire of Technician, dam of Booked Six; and of Finola, dam of Finola's Yarn; of Clomoney Grand from a mating with Last Landing and who, in turn, was dam of Clomoney Jet, so that the influence of Quare Times on modern greyhound racing has been enormous, from that one mating to Negros Fire.

See also Bah's Choice.

QUARTER DAY

A black bitch whelped in 1935, by Lawyer's Fee out of Housekeeper, she was trained in turn by Stanley Biss and Joe Harmon and was owned by Mr George Flintham. Her dam, Housekeeper, was Creamery Border's litter sister so Quarter Day inherited the tremendous speed of this famous dog. Housekeeper was also dam of Roving Spring who broke five track records and reached the final of the Laurels and Pall Mall and is frequently thought to be the best greyhound never to have won a classic event.

During her career Quarter Day won more than £4,000 in prize money and in the late 1930s drew the crowds wherever she raced. Her first race was for the 1937 Trafalgar Cup at Wembley, which she won in fast time, and then took the Oaks in 29.49 secs, a time beaten on only a few occasions during the next twenty years. She followed this by winning the Coronation Stakes at Wembley and won the event again the following year. Her time of 29.34 secs on this occasion was a track and world record, and so amazing that it was not beaten in the event until Breda's Feathers won the Cup thirty years later, while it stood as a track and world record until July 1943 when Jubilee Time

Quarter Day, winner of the 1938 English Oaks. Photo: GRA.

clocked 29.20 secs. Between the end of August and the end of October 1938, in eight weeks of sustained running, Quarter Day amassed a total of almost £2,500 and nothing like her running had ever been seen before.

Still running well in her third season on the track, she won the 1939 Thames Silver Salver at Southend; the Invitation Stakes at Wolverhampton; and the White City Stakes, valued at £2,000, until the 1960s the highest prize ever to be won on the track. She then came in season and was retired.

QUEEN OF THE SUIR

By Mutton Cutlet out of the Melksham Tom bitch Burette, and whelped in May 1930, she came from one of the greatest litters of all time which included Beef Cutlet and the bitch Bella, and for three years, from early 1932 until the end of 1934, she completely dominated track events contested by her sex. Her grand sires Jamie and Melksham Tom not only produced the finest coursing stock of the time but also the best racing greyhounds. Melksham Tom was to sire Other Days, sire of Brilliant Bob and of the bitch Banriogan Dann, dam of Ballynennan Moon from a mating with Mutton Cutlet's son Mr Moon, and many of the finest performers during the first twenty years of the sport were of this breeding. It was the solid foundation on which greyhound racing developed in the British Isles and in America, combining speed, stamina, track sense and courage, the attributes of top-quality greyhounds.

The litter was bred and reared by Mr J.A. Byrne of Co. Tipperary, and after selling Beef Cutlet he retained Bella and Queen of the Suir as it was his intention to breed from them if they proved a success on the track. Entered for the first Irish Oaks at Clonmel in 1932, the only time it was run over 550 yds, Queen of the Suir won convincingly from Silvery Sail and it was decided to send her over to Stanley Biss with a view to her competing for the English Oaks, then run at White City. Here, too, she was successful, becoming the first and only bitch to win both the English and Irish Oaks. She was also the first greyhound to win a classic race in both countries, and no bitch has ever done so since.

After her seasonal rest she was entered for the 1933 Coronation Stakes, an event for bitches, at Wembley which she won in the fast time of 30.06 secs. Again entered for the Oaks at the White City, she ran with greater brilliance than the year before and made it two in a row, an achievement equalled only by Ballinasloe Blondie in 1961 and 1962 and Cranog Bet in 1963 and 1964, but with her win in Ireland she was now a triple Oaks winner, something no other bitch has ever accomplished. She was off racing all winter but again came back in February 1934, when almost four years old, and once more won the Coronation Stakes, the premier event for bitches after the Oaks. Her time of 30.03 secs was equalled only by Quarter Day four years later and who set a new record the following year when she too won for the second year. In her three years' running, contesting only a few top events, Queen of the Suir won more than £2,000.

After being served by a number of important sires and producing little of note she was put to Maiden's Boy, twice winner of the Wembley Gold Cup and the St Leger in 1930. She was then nine years old and Maiden's Boy was almost eleven when in 1939 she whelped Brave Damsel, one of the few bitches to win the Irish Derby, which she did in 1941 at Shelbourne Park, beating another bitch, She's Tidy, into second place. It was 'The Queen's' last litter and she had proved herself both on and off the track.

RED WIND

A fawn dog by Dysertmore Prince out of Light Biddy and whelped in April 1948, he had his first race in England in July 1949 at Southend and amazed everyone by beating the outstanding Ballycurreen Garrett by an astonishing seven lengths. It was obvious that a new champion had arrived on the scene. Next, entered for the important Thames Silver Salver at the track in early September, he won his heat by ten lengths and the final by three lengths, defeating next year's Derby winner, the fabulous Ballymac Ball, in 27.87 secs which was a new record for the 500 yds course. Red Wind was clearly one of the fastest puppies ever seen and in his next race, his heat for the Walthamstow Grand Prix, he was expected to do something dramatic. This he did, winning by eight lengths from the St Leger runner-up Rio Cavallero. The final appeared to be a foregone conclusion. He won his first classic by two lengths, beating another outstanding dog, Drumgoon Boy, who was to win the Cesarewitch a few days later.

Red Wind was then entered for the Midland Puppy Championship at Perry Barr and he was again in devastating form, winning his heat by seven lengths in 28.98 secs, easily the fastest time of all the heats, and he took the final by three lengths from Richmond Tanist. But he had still not yet reached his best. His next outing was for the Wimbledon Puppy Derby, run in November, when he showed even more fantastic speed, winning his heat by nine lengths in the fast time of 28.45 secs and starting at 5–1 on. In his semi-final he beat the same dog he had beaten in his heat, Red Teddy, but this time by an incredible sixteen lengths in a 500 yds race. He took the final by eight lengths in 28.61 secs when starting at 7–1 on, defeating Ballycurreen Garrett who had won the Trafalgar Cup the previous week and was thought to be the fastest puppy in training.

Red Wind still had one more outing before the year ended, when in the Boxing Day Stakes at the White City he met his only defeat since coming to England in early July, when he was beaten a neck by Ballymac Ball over 550 yds in 30.27 secs after missing his usual bullet-like exit from the traps. But in just six months' racing he had taken the greyhound racing world apart, for nothing like his speed had ever been seen before on a track, and in his only defeat, on Boxing Day, both Ballymac Ball and Red Wind had broken the track record by more than a length.

Red Wind was owned and trained by Mr Fred Davis who also owned another outstanding dog of 1949, Drumgoon Boy, winner of the Cesarewitch and Pall Mall. When taking the Cesarewitch, this dog had set a new track record at West Ham over the 550 yds course when winning his heat, beating that year's Derby winner, Narrogar Ann, by six lengths in 30.54 secs; in his semi-final when beating Captured Dick by the same distance, he lowered his record by .01 secs. He was to win the final by two and a half lengths from that fine bitch Quare Caltha, who was to win the Test at Walthamstow.

RIMMELL'S BLACK

Owned by Miss Jean Collins, the actress, he was whelped in April 1944, and was by the famous Manhattan Midnight, his dam the two-year old Drishogue. He was one of the greatest sprinters in the history of the sport and first came into prominence in April 1946 when he set up a new 500 yds record at the Norwich track with a time of 28.40 secs. Later that year he qualified for the Scurry Gold Cup, losing by only half a length from another of Manhattan Midnight's sons, Mischievous Manhattan, in 23.40 secs. He also reached the final of the Laurels, won by Shannon Shore. But it was in the Golden Crest at Eastville that he ran his greatest race that year. He ran up to Shannon Shore when that great dog set a new track record in the semi-final, but won the final by a neck from Tan Gent in 28.69 secs. At the White City he won the A.O. Critchley Memorial Stakes by eight lengths from Listry Laddie in 29.06 secs and the following week reached the final of the Pall Mall.

In 1947 he was in equally good form. He won the Walthamstow March Stakes by nine lengths from Trev's Al in 31.07 secs and then ran up to Mr Flintham's dog Rowley for the Hunt Cup at Reading, won in 22.32 secs. Then in June he set a new track record at Southend, covering the 525 yds course in 29.57 secs. At Clapton for the Scurry Gold Cup he won his heat by six lengths in 23.13 secs, the fastest of the six heats. In his semi-final he finished third behind Kerry Rally and Terry's Monarch, and was then purchased by Mr J. Byrne of Cahir, his breeder, to stand at stud, though he promised Miss Collins the Scurry Cup and winnings if the dog was successful. He was indeed. After running up in 1946 he won the final by a length from Kerry Rally in 23.11 secs, to reward his trainer, Stanley Biss, with his first Scurry Cup. Stanley Biss always said that he was the fastest dog he ever trained.

Within weeks Rimmell's Black had won his second classic. After running up to Tonycus in the final of the Chelsea Cup, won in 27.71 secs, he was contesting the Laurels at Wimbledon, winning his heat by two and a half lengths from Monday's News; although only third in his semi-final he won the final by a short head from the unlucky

Slaney Record in 28.77 secs. Entered for the Golden Crest at Eastville, he set a new track record when winning his heat, covering the 500 yds in 28.65 secs and beating Funny Mick by two and a half lengths. However he was beaten into second place by this dog in the final. In the Thames Silver Salver at Southend he defeated the Trafalgar Cup winner Mad Birthday by five lengths, but met his match in the final, won by Priceless Border who was to win the Derby the following year. At Coventry for the Eclipse Stakes he won his heat by a length from the locally trained bitch Simone, but was beaten into second place in the final, won by another fine bitch, Castledown Tiptoes. He was then chosen to represent England in the international against Ireland, but on reaching the final he broke a toe and was retired to stud after winning more than £3,000 in prize money and trophies to the value of over £1,000.

RIO CEPRETTA

A handsome fawn bitch weighing 56 lbs, by Flying Dart out of Rio Czarina and whelped in February 1945, she was owned by Mr A.R. Tuck and had her first race in 1947 at New Cross for the 1st April Stakes, which she won by seven lengths in 35.97 secs. It was obvious that here was a new bitch destined for stardom. The 1940s were dominated by a number of the greatest bitches ever to race in England. Here now to join them was Rio Cepretta, English-born and bred by Mr and Mrs R.A. Cordwell and trained at Clapton by Stanley Biss, who could manage a bitch better than anyone.

Her next race was at Harringay, which she also won comfortably, and then came the thirteenth Two-year-old Produce Stakes at Wimbledon. Winning her first and second round heats, the latter by nine lengths, she also won her semi-final and the final by a handsome six lengths from Mrs Ivy Regan's Shadowlands Delight in 28.82 secs. In the Derby she reached the semi-final and was expected at least to make an appearance in the final, but she ran into early trouble and did not get a place.

Her next race was at Wembley for the 1947 Coronation Cup, but although she reached the final she could only finish as runner-up to Crissie Tanist who beat her by six lengths. Then she went to Reading for the Berkshire Summer Stakes, run over 550 yds, she won her heat and then the final by four lengths from Come Up First in 31,56 secs.

She then went back to Wimbledon, scene of her early success in the Produce Stakes, this time to contest the Laurels. She ran up in her heat to Tonycus, but, finishing fourth in her semi-final when favourite to win, she did not get a place in the final which was won by Rimmell's Black whom she had beaten so decisively at Coventry. She did, however, win the consolation final in 28.64 secs, a faster time than that made by the Laurels winner.

Then to the White City for the Oaks where she ran brilliantly, winning her heat from another outstanding bitch, Izadaisy. Both won their semi-finals by a wide margin and the final was one of the best ever seen. It was a contest between these two fine performers who raced neck and neck the whole way round, neither yielding an inch of ground, but it was Rio Cepretta who crossed the line first, a head in front of Izadaisy in 29.32 secs. Earlier in the year Izadaisy had beaten the virtually unknown Mott's Regret at West Ham by four lengths. It caused little comment at the time, but six months later Mott's Regret was to win the Derby as Trev's Perfection. Izadaisy was the only bitch ever to beat Mr Trevillion's champion, who also won the Scottish and Welsh Derbys in the same year.

Still at the top of her form, Rio Cepretta was next at Wembley for the St Leger where she was beaten a short head in her heat by Canada's Glory in a thrilling finish, for behind her and only a neck away was Come Up First in third place. She won her semi-final from Trev's Jackie, but in the final found Dante II on tremendous form and she was beaten eight lengths by the Wayne brothers' great black and a short head by Shadowlands Delight, who took second place. It was, however, a most creditable performance.

Before the year ended she still had the Cesarewitch, and though beaten in her heat by Parish Model she won her semi-final by three lengths from her old rival Izadaisy, who also went through to the final only to be beaten a neck by Red Tan, with Rio Cepretta close behind her.

During the Christmas holidays she was

still racing with her usual brilliance. In an open event at Wembley she defeated Western Post and Tonycus, two of the best dogs in the country, by five lengths, and at Wimbledon on 27 December for the International she was beaten into second place by the new wonder dog from Northern Ireland, Priceless Border, who was to go on to win the Derby next year. Behind her, though, were Monday's News, Castledown Tiptoes and Rimmell's Black, which gives some idea of her ability.

Before the winter was over she won at New Cross and Perry Barr and at Stamford Bridge, where she beat Jersey Creamery, a new star from the White City, Manchester, by a short head over 700 yds in what was described as one of the most thrilling races ever seen there. She then went in season and raced no more that year.

By early January 1949 she was back again and contested the Longcross Cup at White City but did not get a place in the final which was won by the new wonder bitch Sheevaun. Next she was at Wandsworth for the Wandle Cup and, qualifying for the final, finished third. At Harringay on 16 February over 700 yds she ran a magnificent race to beat Ballybeg Printer by a length in 41.26 secs. Then at Wembley, for the New Year Stayers' Stakes, also over 700 yds, she won her heat by a head from Northam Star but was beaten in the final three lengths by Baytown Whitethorn. For the Wimbledon Stayers' Plaque she failed by inches to reach the final, being beaten in a thrilling finish, a head and neck by Olive's Ivy and Northam Star (winner of the Clapton Cup). She next contested the Catford Cup, run over 600 yds at that track, reaching the final which she won in 36.12 secs by one and a half lengths from My Crash.

She was then rested until the Oaks in which she ran up to Lady Maud in her heat and to Still Drifting in her semi-final, but in the final, won by Still Drifting, she finished third, with Baytown Stream the runner up by a head. Entered for the St Leger at Wembley in September, she won her heat by five and a half lengths and failed by only a neck in her semi-final to go through to the final, won by Lovely Rio. She did, however, win the consolation final, the St Leger Plate, in a faster time than for the St Leger. In October she was at Belle Vue for the Northern 700, and in her heat beat the St Leger winner Lovely Rio by five lengths. She ran up her semi-final and, running brilliantly, took the final and £250 prize beating Mayfair Mite by a head in 40.99 secs. In November she was at Wimbledon for the Key, run over 725 yds. She ran up in her heat but had to be content with third place in the final, won by Drastic O'Leer. That same month she contested the Test at Walthamstow, again running up in her heat, but she finished last in the final which was won by Quare Caltha. Her last race was at Stamford Bridge on 15 December, after which she was retired after three years of wonderful running.

RITA'S CHOICE

A black dog weighing 70 lbs, he was sired by the great Spectre II out of Toffee Apple II and inherited the tremendous staying powers and courage of his great sire, which he in turn is now passing on to his offspring.

Whelped early in 1972, Rita's Choice first came into prominence when winning the important Corn Cuchulainn at Harold's Cross in 1973, run over 750 yds, which always attracts the best stayers in Ireland. His time of 42.40 secs when winning the final was and is the fastest done in the event and was a national record over the distance.

He next contested the Irish Derby held at Shelbourne Park in August, and by superb running reached the final. Others taking part were Black Banjo, Itsawitch, Heavy Sleeper, Kal's Daisy, and Bashful Man, and it was expected that a fast time would be recorded for the event had brought together six of the finest greyhounds in all Ireland. The Dublin track was packed to capacity that night and those who had come expecting to see something sensational were not disappointed. First into the lead, as if catapulted from the traps, was Bashful Man, the favourite, owned by Miss Hynes and trained by Ger McKenna. By the first bend he had a lead of at least four lengths but Rita's Choice never gave up and, though unable to reduce the commanding lead, finished in second place. The time of 28.82 secs was the fastest ever done in the Derby and the first time 29 secs had been broken in the final. Rita's Choice had also crossed the line in a calculated 29.10 secs, faster than had ever been achieved in the final before, so he was in no way disgraced.

Still on magnificent form, Rita's Choice next contested the Cesarewitch at Navan and again reached the final which he won in 33.04 secs, creating a new track record which still stands and which is the fastest time ever done for the event and a national record over 600 yds. At the end of the season Rita's Choice was retired to stud and was soon to show the same qualities as a sire as did his own sire, Spectre II, for the fawn dog Nameless Star, owned by Mrs Rita McAulay of Shankill, Co. Dublin, became the first dog to win the Irish St Leger and Laurels which he did in the same year, 1976, and two of his sons reached the 1979 English St Leger final.

His pedigree reads:

Rita's Choice	Spectre II	Crazy Parachute	Hi There
			Mad Prospect
		Supreme Witch	Solar Prince
			Witching Grand
	Toffee Apple II	Kileden General	The Grand Fire
			Kilcomney Mistress
		Stiff Toffee	Carmody's Tanist
			Judy's jet

ROBEEN PRINTER

This beautifully made light fawn bitch, sired by Creamery Border's son, the great Printer, out of Deoc Deireannach and whelped in April 1942, was bred and reared by Mr Arthur Probert and was one of the best racing bitches of all time. The Laurels, run at Cork in 1944 for the first time, was also her first race on this or any other track, and to have gone through to the final and to have won it, beating Shannon Shore and breaking the track record at Cork, stamped her as a bitch quite out of the ordinary. Then in the McAlinden Gold Cup at Shelbourne Park she clocked 29.90 secs in her heat, which was the fastest time ever done by a bitch at the track, and she went on to win the final in 30.17 secs. In the Easter Cup, also at Shelbourne Park, she ran up to Empor Lassie and reached the final of the Oaks at Harold's Cross, which was won by My Little Daisy. She also ran up for the Irish Cesarewitch to crown a magnificent year. On the coursing field she won a trial stake and ran up in the Belton Cup at St Margarets.

Put up for auction at Shelbourne Park sales at the year end, bidding stopped at 1,650 gns when she was bought by Mrs Hilda Sanderson to race at Coventry where her husband was managing director of the track. To that time, and for many years later, it was the highest price ever paid for a greyhound at public auction in Ireland.

She was trained by George McKay, and her first race in England was the Coventry Eclipse Stakes, one of the most important of provincial events, in which she dead-heated for first place with another wonderful bitch, Prancing Kitty, after a most thrilling race in which they were neck and neck from start to finish. She had arrived in England at exactly the right time for the war had almost ended and the classic events were about to be restarted. In April 1945, in a trial at Wimbledon over 725 yds, she broke the existing track record by twenty lengths, clocking the amazing time of 41.56 secs, and a day or two later she lowered this to 41.52 secs when winning the ninth Stayers' Plaque there. Seven days later over the same distance she knocked one-thousandth of a second off her record when beating Bonny Brae by sixteen lengths, and nothing like her had ever been seen before. Yet she had been equally impressive when winning the Irish Laurels over 500 yds and she was made favourite to win the 1945 Oaks at Harringay. She comfortably won her heat and semi-final, beating Cassa's Spotlight, but was beaten in the final by her old foe Prancing Kitty. In September she contested the 1945 St Leger at Wembley, run over 700 yds, and put up a wonderful performance throughout, winning the final by three and a half lengths from Cherry's Equal in 40.03 secs, exactly the same time clocked by Dolores Rocket, another wonderful bitch, when winning the event twenty-six years later. She than contested the tenth Key at Wimbledon, run over 725 yds, in which she defeated the impressive stayer Kampion Sailor by six lengths. Then to the White City for the October Stakes, in which she defeated Ryan's Rose by twelve lengths in 41.48 secs over 750 yds. Yet at Coventry, her home track, she held the 310 yds record for many years and all distances came alike to her.

After her seasonal rest she again came back to racing in 1947, aged five, and in January won the Winter Stayers' Stakes at

Stamford Bridge by a short head from Trev's Docket, and the Ivybridge Stayers' Stakes at Wembley by three lengths. At Coventry in February she was well beaten by Shaggy Lass, who set a new track record of 40.87 secs for 700 yds. A new star had appeared and it was decided to retire Robeen Printer. Those who saw Quarter Day immediately before the war thought she was the best, but no bitch had a better record in England and in Ireland than Robeen Printer, who must be one of the six best bitches of all time.

RUSSIAN GUN

By Pigalle Wonder out of Shandaroba, this great dog, his sire's finest son, was whelped in 1965 and after showing tremendous speed in his trials was purchased by the late Mr Hugh Marley of Portadown, Co. Armagh, for a four-figure sum said to be £1,200. Within months he had won the 1967 Irish Derby at Harold's Cross in 29.44 secs, and the following year came within an ace of winning two in a row. After winning his first and second round heats he was beaten into second place by Yellow Printer. After his winter rest he began 1968 by contesting the Easter Cup at Shelbourne Park, and after a magnificent race was beaten a short head by his great rival Itsamint, with another wonderful bitch, April Flower, a short head behind him, the three finishing virtually together.

The 1968 Irish Derby final was one of the best ever contested, for in trap 1 was Clinker Flash; trap 2, Itsamint; trap 3, Drumna Chestnut; trap 4, Yellow Printer; trap 5, Ballybeg Flash; and trap 6, Russian Gun — each a champion in his or her own right. Yellow Printer was quoted 6–4 and Itsamint and Russian Gun 5–2 just before the hare was due to start. Ballybeg Flash was first away but at the first turn moved wide into Russian Gun's path which allowed Yellow Printer the space he needed to move to the front, a position he held to the finish, though Russian Gun, forced to run out wide with Ballybeg Flash, came again on the back straight like the champion he was and had closed to within a length behind Yellow Printer as he crossed the winning line. He also ran up the Ulster Derby at Celtic Park, beaten only a short head by Drumna Chestnut, but won the Guinness 600 at Shelbourne Park and was chosen Greyhound of the Year for 1968, being unplaced only once in nineteen starts.

In the National Sprint at Dunmore Park Russian Gun again was just pipped at the line in yet another triple dead heat, or so it looked to those who were there. The photo-finish, however, showed that Newhill Printer and Dry Flash, litter brothers, whose sire was Prairie Flash and were owned by Mrs Kitty McBride, had dead-heated, with Russian Gun just a short head away. It was the great dog's last race.

Retired to stud, he was to sire An Tain, the bitch who, from a mating with Monalee Champion, produced Tain Mor, who won the 1976 Irish Derby and was the outstanding tracker of that year. Russian Gun inherited the tremendous pace of his sire and throughout his career was trained by Tom Lynch of Blanchardstown, Co. Dublin. Russian Gun was Pigalle Wonder's best son.

SAND STAR

His career was short but during that time he did enough to show that he was one of the all-time greats. A white and black dog, he was by Bauhus, a son of the peerless Solar Prince out of the magnificent dam Direct Lead, and was whelped in 1967. Direct Lead's mating with Bauhus was her last litter. She was then eleven and died in 1969 aged thirteen. She was sister to Mad Era, sire of Sherry's Prince, and in the same litter as Sand Star was Cloudbank, who set a new track record at Walthamstow in 1969 when fifteen months old and won the Puppy Derby at Wimbledon shortly after. The mating of Direct Lead to Jockey's Glen in 1964 produced the Trigo Cup winner Woodlawn; and to Knockhill Chieftain resulted in Booked Out, sire of Booked Six, so she was one of the great dams of greyhound racing.

Owned, bred and trained by Mr Hamilton Orr in Northern Ireland, Sand Star showed something of his quality in his first engagement, winning his first round heat of the Irish Puppy Derby at Harold's Cross in 1968, his time of 29.58 secs being the fastest of the heats, but he was surprisingly beaten in his semi-final. Coming to the White City, London, for the 1969 Derby, he won every heat, his semi-final, and the final by two lengths from Kilbelin Style. In doing so he broke 29.00 secs on every occasion, the first time this had ever been done. After his triumph Mr Orr took the dog back to Ireland to compete in the Irish Derby, but in a trial at Harold's Cross he pulled up lame and was immediately retired to stud. His death shortly afterwards robbed breeders of the services of what would surely have been an exceptional sire.

Sand Star's pedigree reads:

Sand Star	Bauhus	Solar Prince	Champion Prince
			Lisabelle
		Lovely Sister	Fourth of July
			Shannon Sister
	Direct Lead	Hi There	Slaney Record
			Dublin Red
		Drumlock Sheevaun	Mad Tanist
			Sheevaun

SAY LITTLE

By Albany out of Newhouse Blue, he was owned by Mr A.L. Cox, a Lincolnshire corn merchant, and trained by Colin McNally at Perry Barr. His sire, Albany, a black dog weighing 70 lbs, was by Prairie Flash out of The Grand Fire bitch, the blue Clomoney Grand, one of Ireland's greatest, while Prairie Flash was by Hi There and that outstanding dam Prairie Peg. Albany was from a second mating between his sire and dam, and the litter included the Derby runner-up Kilbelin Style and Kilbelin Grand, who contested the final of the 1969 Irish Derby. When only fifteen months old Albany won the 1968 Thurles Puppy Derby, a seventy-two dog event, and was the youngest-ever winner. Say Little's dam, Newhouse Blue, was by the record-breaking Derby winner Faithful Hope and the Hi There bitch Grange Liner, so her pedigree included the greatest sires and dams of modern times.

A blue brindle (there was blue on both sides of his family), Say Little was British-bred and -trained and during two years (1972 and 1973) he won more than £5,000 in prize money and established himself as one of the best British-bred dogs ever to run. His racing weight was 69 lbs and he was equally consistent over 500, 525 and 880 yds. He set a new track record at Walthamstow, clocking 28.83 secs in his heat for the Circuit, and won the final by three lengths from the great Skyhawk in only .02 secs slower than his heat. At Powderhall, in the Edinburgh Cup, in his first run round the track he covered the 500 yds course in 27.80 secs and won the final in 27.91 secs, beating Shortcake by two lengths. He was selected Midlands Greyhound of the Year for 1972. The following year saw him contest the Derby, after winning the Select Stakes at Wembley by eight lengths from Mel's Pupil and Forest Noble. In the Derby he won his first and second round heats and in his semi-final was beaten only a neck by Forest Noble. In the final, won for the second year running by Patricia's Hope, he was beaten only half a length by that great dog after starting a 6–4 favourite and was a neck behind Softly to take third place; Forest Noble was a neck behind him. He next contested the Welsh Derby; he won his heat but after making a rare slow start was beaten a length in the final by Silly Rocket, a dog who ran through the event undefeated. Chosen to represent his country in the Anglo–Irish international, Say Little won his first-leg race easily but in the return at Shelbourne Park broke a toe and was retired to stud.

His pedigree reads:

Say Little	Albany	Prairie Flash	Hi There
			Prairie Peg
		Clomoney Grand	The Grand Fire
			Last Landing
	Newhouse Blue	Faithful Hope	Solar Prince
			Millie Hawthorn
		Grange Liner	Hi There
			Imperial Peg

SHADY PARACHUTE

A white and brindle bitch by Crazy Parachute out of Shady Contempora, and whelped in 1965, she came over to England in May 1967 to contest the Derby, and after showing impressive form in her heats and semi-final reached the final. Here she was beaten by the great litter brothers Tric Trac and Spectre II and by Mel's Talent, but in trap 3 she had the worst of the draw and was hampered at the first turn.

After her seasonal rest during the winter, she was on devastating form during 1968. Trained at Wimbledon by Phil Rees, she took the International at her home track in 27.57 secs and the Playfield Cup, also over 500 yds, in 27.79 secs. By the time of the Derby she was made favourite. Once again she reached the final, becoming the first bitch to do so in successive years; starting 6–4 on, she again had to be content with fourth place. The Oaks at Harringay, however, saw her at her best, winning her heats and final in 29.38 secs; later at the White City she won the Sir Joseph Simpson Memorial Stakes in 28.68 secs for 525 yds, one of the fastest times ever done by a bitch. Afterwards she was chosen top racing bitch of 1968 and she well deserved the honour.

SHAGGY LASS AND SHAGGY LAD

They were litter brother and sister from the famous Castledown Lad–Shaggy Shore mating, whelped in February 1944, and were among Castledown Lad's last offspring, for he was then in his twelfth year and, after Mutton Cutlet, had established himself as the greatest of track sires. Shaggy Lass was a fawn weighing 55 lbs, and after showing exceptional promise in her early trials was purchased by Mr Leslie Hamilton for 1,500 gns. Her first race was the 1945 Derby at the White City. After winning her heat, in which she beat Bah's Choice, she was unfortunate in not getting through to the final, but in the Welsh Derby she made no mistake, winning by three quarters of a length from Duffy's Arrival in a new track record time of 29.75 secs. She next contested the Puppy Oaks, winning by ten lengths from Trev's Ensign in 28.67 secs, and without a previous trial set a new record at Walthamstow with a time of 28.55 secs in her heat for the £200 Puppy Sweepstakes. Afterwards the *Greyhound Express* said that she was 'the finest bitch puppy that has ever raced in this country'.

After her seasonal rest she was ready to race again for the First May Stakes at the White City, which she won by one and a half lengths from Model County to set a new record for 700 yds with a time of 41.43 secs, and in the Welsh Derby she won her first heat by nine lengths but was beaten in the final won by Negro's Lad. In the same week she won the Second July Stakes at Eastville over 700 yds, beating Diamond Jim by twelve lengths in the record time of 40.61 secs.

Again she was off for her seasonal rest during the winter, but was back in time to contest the forty-first Coventry Trophy on 4 February 1947. On a rain-sodden track she covered the 700 yds course in a new record time of 40.87 secs, beating another great bitch, Robeen Printer, by six lengths. Throughout 1947 she was in magnificent form. She won her heat for the twelfth Stayers' Plaque at Wimbledon by two lengths from Pearl's Choice in 43.89 secs, and the final by five lengths from Dumble's Maid in 42.25 secs, which was near the track record. In the Catford Cup she was beaten in her heat and then in the final by Riac's Gift in 35.65 secs. Then she went off for her seasonal rest. She was mated to Bah's Choice and did not race again.

Shaggy Lad won the Puppy Derby at Harold's Cross in 1945, beating Quare Times in what was the fastest time ever recorded for a puppy, for he covered the 500 yds course in 27.96 secs, a track record. Astra won the previous year in 28.52 secs and she was no loiterer. Those who saw the race and have seen every top-class greyhound since have no hesitation in declaring him the fastest ever to race. Indeed, in his heat for the event he set a new record with a time of 28.21 secs. This he beat in his semi-final when he became the first ever to break 28 secs at the track when clocking 27.98 secs, which he bettered in the final.
No more amazing display by a young dog has ever been seen before or since. A fawn weighing 70 lbs, he was retired to stud shortly afterwards and sired winners from every bitch he mated, including Prince Palatine, winner of the McAlinden Cup, and Spanish Lad, the Irish Laurels winner. Shaggy Lad was also sire of Knockrour Again, sire of Kilbeg Kuda, who has played an important part in the breeding of modern racing greyhounds.

SHANNON SHORE

Purchased for a large sum after he ran up to Robeen Printer for the first Irish Laurels, run at Cork in 1944, this black dog by Well Squared out of Second Row, whelped in January 1943, drew attention when, in his first race at Tralee, he set a new track record with a time of 30.35 secs for 525 yds and went on to prove one of the most consistent runners in the history of the sport. In the same litter was another excellent dog, Celtic Chief, but neither enjoyed their fair share of luck. Reaching England in time to contest the Derby, he was eliminated in his semi-final and ran up to Fair Brook in the consolation final. Then in the Laurels he won his heat and ran up to Burhill Moon in his semi-final, but on the day of the final had to be withdrawn as he was suffering from enteritis, and Burhill Moon, trained by Sidney Orton, won the event. Shannon Shore was fully recovered in time to contest the Golden Crest at Eastville, and after winning his heat and semi-finals won the final by an amazing ten lengths from Magic Beau in a new track record of 28.76 secs for 500 yds. He was equally at home on every track he ran on, and at Harringay on 26 November 1945 he won the £500 Pall Mall after winning his early rounds, to defeat Race Day by two and a half lengths in 29.80 secs with Hurry Kitty, Kilpeacon Bride, Burhill Moon and Tough Hill behind.

After a short winter rest he began 1946 where he left off, winning his heat of the Kent Championship at Rochester in a record 29.89 secs and the final by two lengths from Trev's Fashion in 30 secs. For the Derby at White City he won his first round heat from Kilcora Master by one and a half lengths and in round 2 was beaten only a neck by Bah's Choice. In his semi-final he defeated his litter brother Celtic Chief in 29.20 secs to reach the final, which was won by Monday's News from Lilac's Luck; others in the race were Celtic Chief, Plucky Hero and Dante II, each an outstanding greyhound. It was Celtic Chief's second successive final and he was later to sire one bitch who came to play an important part in the breeding of modern greyhound champions. His mating to Coolkill Darkie produced Coolkill Mistress, who from a mating with Galtee Cleo whelped the great Knockhill Chieftain, sire of Cranog Bet, dam of Itsachampion and grand dam of Lacca Champion. Knockhill Chieftain was also sire of Oregon Prince, sire of Land Rail who was dam of Sugarloaf Bunny, dam of Sarah's Bunny. So Celtic Chief had a great deal to do with the best dams and sires of modern greyhound racing.

It was in the 1946 Laurels (which he might so easily have won the previous year but for illness) that Shannon Shore reached his peak. Though narrowly beaten in his heat by Quare Times and by Plucky Hero in his semi-final when he badly injured a foot, he was again a dubious contender for the final and only at the last moment was he pronounced fit to race. After a careful examination the Wimbledon vet passed him fit and the dog won the event by three quarters of a length from Tan Gent in 28.26 secs, the fastest time then achieved for a Laurels final.

Then he went to Eastville for the Golden Crest, and after setting a new track record of 28.26 secs in his semi-final he was beaten a neck in the final by Rimmell's Black. Still running with brilliance, he next contested the Thames Silver Salver at Southend, which he won by six lengths from Tan Gent in a new track record of 27.89 secs, and before his retirement at the end of 1946 he won the Legion Stakes at Breck Park by six lengths from Alvaston Lulu Belle and in the same week his heat for the Pall Mall, winning by eight lengths, though in the final he was badly baulked and finished third. It was his last race, but for two years only Monday's News could beat him on level terms. He was owned by Mrs R.H. Dent and trained by Leslie Reynolds, and as an inside trap specialist he must rank with the greatest. He was bred and reared by Mr R. Sheehy in Co. Limerick.

SHEEVAUN
A fawn bitch by Bella's Prince out of Honey Gale, whelped in March 1946, she first came into prominence when winning the 1947 Scottish Puppy Derby at Powderhall by two and a half lengths from her great rival-to-be, Local Interprize. She started 5–2 on to win the event and did so in 29 secs for the 500 yds course. Owned by Mrs Mary Thomson of Glasgow, she was then sent to Wimbledon to be trained by Paddy Fortune, as Mrs Thomson realized she had a bitch of more than average ability. January 1948 saw her contesting the White City Longcross Cup and winning her heat in a full second faster than the other heats; it was no surprise when she started 7–4 on for the final, which she won by eight lengths from another wonderful bitch, the previous year's Oaks winner Rio Cepretta, with Castledown Tiptoes, purchased for £3,000, twenty lengths behind. It was an amazing performance, but she then came in season. However she was ready to race again in time to tackle the Derby in June.

In this event she ran up to Shadowlands Delight in her heat and won her semi-final by seven lengths in 28.74 secs, the fastest time ever recorded for 525 yds by a bitch. Priceless Border won his semi-final in 28.76 secs but in the final he was too good for her, winning it by two lengths from Local Interprize in 28.78 secs with Sheevaun two lengths behind in third place. She was beaten by the two fastest dogs in the world at that time and she had been back on the track only a few weeks, so was anything but disgraced. She was not to race again for some time, but began 1949 by winning the fifteenth International at Wimbledon on New Year's Day by eleven lengths from that fine dog Whiterock Abbey in 28.84 secs. Once again entered for the Longcross Cup, she won her heat by seven lengths and the final from Romantic Nigger by eight lengths. She was quoted 3–1 on before the race. Her next race was for the Inaugural Sweep at Wembley, in which she ran up to West End Dasher with that year's Derby winner, Narrogar Ann, two lengths behind her. Then, after winning her semi-final for the Wimbledon Spring Cup, she was again runner-up in a final, this time to Olive's Ivy. After her seasonal rest she was back to contest the O.A. Critchley Memorial Stakes at White City, but was again beaten in the final which was won easily by Narrogar Ann. She had a few races early in 1950 and was then retired, after winning more than £2,000 in prize money at a time when prizes were low after the war but when the sport was at its peak of popularity.

She was to be as successful as a brood bitch as she was on the track. From a mating to Mad Tanist she whelped the bitch Drumloch Sheevaun, who from a mating with Hi There produced Direct Lead, dam of the English Derby winner Sand Star.

SHOVE HA'PENNY

To finish runner-up in three classics in three successive years must stamp him as one of the unluckiest dogs ever to race, but in most instances it was of his own doing, for no dog found himself in more trouble and had to extricate himself by great courage and determination, which happened in almost every final he contested. A grandson of Mutton Cutlet, his sire was Town Treasure and he was whelped in 1932, so that when he ran up to Wattle Bark in the 1937 Derby he was five years old. He was owned by Mr C.C. Keen, who also owned his kennel companion Ataxy, and only that dog was his equal for speed. Ataxy possessed greater trackcraft, and Shove Ha'penny was so often beaten by an inferior dog that his followers were reduced to despair.

In his first important race, the Pall Mall at Harringay, he put up a magnificent performance, for after winning his heats he defeated the dog who was to become his great rival, Grand Flight II, in the final by a head after being baulked on the first bend. In the 1935 Cesarewitch, however, the order was reversed, although Shove Ha'penny had again won every round and had broken the track record in doing so. Made favourite for the final, he was beaten by a dog who could not match him for speed yet possessed greater trackcraft, for Shove Ha'penny ran into the rear of a dog in front of him and was thrown completely off balance, though he had the courage and speed to come again and lose by only inches. Next year he won the Wood Lane Stakes at White City, the West Ham Spring Cup, and the Daily Mirror Championship, beating outstanding greyhounds in doing so. In the 1936 St Leger he was again beaten into second place, this time by his kennel-mate Ataxy, and did not reach the Derby final although he was expected to win it. Yet he was still going as strong as ever in 1937 and reaching the Derby final. Drawn in trap 1 and made 6–4 favourite, he was beaten into second place by Wattle Bark whom he would have beaten nine times out of ten. The time of 29.26 secs was a national and track record, and he lost by just over a length, which gives some idea of his speed.

Jack Harvey, his trainer, looked after him until the dog died in 1946 aged fourteen, and he endeared himself to all the kennel staff for he always appeared so grateful for little kindnesses. He sired Flying Dart II, sire of Magic Buttercup, dam of Magic Bimbo, sire of Waterloo Cup winner, Magical Lore.

SKYHAWK

A brindle, whelped in August 1970, by Monalee Arkle out of Little Playgirl, his sire was by Prairie Flash out of the great dam

Skyhawk	Monalee Arkle	Prairie Flash	Hi There
			Prairie Peg
		Sheila at Last	The Grand Prince
			Last Landing
	Little Play Girl	Kilbeg Kuda	Knockrour Again
			Burmuda's Glory
		Newpark Edna	Clopook (The Grand Fire)
			Belle of Ballymac (Ballymac Ball)

Sheila at Last. He was purchased by a Watford businessman, Mr Tony Fisher, for, it is said, only 165 gns, and was placed with the Wembley trainer Tommy Johnston. The dog won his first race at Wembley in 29.80 secs, which he reduced to 29.65 secs in his next outing. Entered for the Circuit at Walthamstow, he won his heat and semi-final but was beaten in the final by Say Little, whose 28.85 secs was a new track record. In the 1972 Laurels he reached the final, but missing his break had to be content with third place behind Cricket Bunny and Priory Hi, but in the final of the White City Championship he completely outclassed the dual Derby winner Patricia's Hope and the Oaks winner Short Cake, to win by an astonishing three lengths in 28.65 secs. In October he again met these outstanding greyhounds in the Supreme Champion Stakes at the White City and won again, this time in 28.44 secs. Reaching the final of the Pall Mall, he was badly hampered at the first turn and was well beaten, but the following week, in the Anglo-Irish International, again at the White City, his favourite track, he once more defeated Patricia's Hope. In December he won the Ladbroke Stakes which was televized on ITV. In March 1973 the dog won the Wood Lane Stakes at his favourite track, but in a race at Brighton in April he pulled up lame and was retired to stud at a fee of £65. In just twelve months he ran in thirty-four races and won twenty of them, collecting £2,500 in prize money, many times the price his owner had paid for him, and he always raced in top-class events, in which he invariably gave everything he had. No more genuine performer ever raced on a greyhound track.

His pedigree is shown above.

SLANEY RECORD

A fawn dog by Rare Record out of Honey Gale and whelped in October 1944, he was considered one of the best dogs never to win a classic event, and at stud his mating with the Bella's Prince bitch Dublin Red was to bring about a tremendous improvement in track racing in the years ahead, for their son was Hi There, winner of the National Sprint in 1954, who was to become sire of Crazy Parachute. He in turn sired Kitty True, dam of Own Pride, winner of the Irish Derby and St Leger, and of Tric Trac and Spectre II, first and second in the English Derby, and who in turn were to sire some of the greatest dogs of modern times. Crazy Parachute was also sire of Monalee Champion, who in turn passed on the terrific pace of Hi There and Crazy Parachute to some of the best modern greyhounds including Sole Aim, winner of the Irish Derby, who in turn was sire of Columbcille Aim, dam of Penny County, winner of the Irish Derby in 1979; and of Tain Mor and Linda's Champion, both of whom won the Irish Derby.

Hi There was also sire of Prairie Flash, sire of the English Derby winner, Camira Flash; of Sally's Yarn, sire of Finola's Yarn; of the Irish St Leger winner Powerstown Prospect, sire of Trojan Silver, dam of the 1970 Derby winner John Silver; and of Printer's Prince, sire of the world's fastest greyhound, Yellow Printer. Hi There was the greatest sire of the past twenty years, who produced champions from every bitch he mated. His progeny won every classic on both sides of the Irish Sea, and it should never be forgotten that his sire was Slaney Record.

Weighing 70 lbs when racing, Slaney Record was purchased by Mr Bithel at Shelbourne Park Sales for £1,500 after showing promise in his trials, and within a year had earned more than his purchase price in prize money. Coming to England, he first contested the 1,000 Guineas at Park Royal, run over 400 yds, winning his heat and semi-final by eight lengths from

Lights of Midnight. Quoted 2–1 on for the final, he won by four lengths from Munday in 22.67 secs. His next race, at West Ham, was the Spring Stakes, also over 400 yds; he won his heat by a head from Trev's Perfection and the final by a short head from Terry's Monarch in 22.20 secs, with Trev's Perfection in fourth place at 10–1.

In May he contested the Perry Barr Cup at his home track, winning his heat but running into trouble in the final in which he was beaten into second place by Humming Bee. Then he went to Catford for the Gold Collar, but here he did not reach the final, which was won by Trev's Perfection.

In June he was at the White City for the Derby and ran up to Priceless Border in his heat, only for that great dog to go down with enteritis and to take no further part in the event. In his semi-final, Slaney Record ran up to his old rival Trev's Perfection, with Dante II and Humming Bee well behind him, to qualify for the final. Once again, however, he found Mr Trevillion's dog too good for him and had to be content with third place, with Monday's News, winner the previous year, one and a half lengths in front of him as runner-up. It was the first time the final had been run in less than 29 secs, and Slaney Record was only three and a half lengths behind the winner.

After a short rest he contested the Northern Flat at Belle Vue, won by Tonycus, and was back at his home track for the August Cup, winning his heat and then the final by two lengths from Hepicoleum in 28.61 secs for 500 yds. From here he went to Wimbledon for the Laurels, winning his heat; in his semi-final he dead-heated with Lisanley Bobby as runners-up to qualify for a place in the final. Again he ran brilliantly but without luck, and once again a classic eluded him for he was beaten by an inch or so, a short head separating him from Rimmell's Black who won in 28.77 secs.

The following year, 1948, after a winter rest, he again contested the 1,000 Guineas, but failed by only a head to reach the final. In the Perry Barr Cup he again reached the final but without success. He continued to race until almost the end of 1950, without ever winning a classic and the large winnings that went with it. However he amassed £2,150 for his owner before being retired to stud in Ireland at a fee of 15 gns. Slaney Record was a thoroughly honest dog, always competing in top company and his name (from his mating to Dublin Red) figures in the pedigree of the greatest of modern greyhounds.

Slaney Record x Dublin Red (B)

Hi There x Mad Prospect (B)

Sheila at Last (B) x Crazy Parachute x Supreme Witch (B)

Monalee Champion — Tric Trac, Spectre II

Sole Aim (Rhu), Linda's Champion, Tain Mor, Itsachampion, Jimsun — Black Andrew, Spectre Jockey, Glin Bridge, Tartan Khan, Rita's Choice

Burniston Jet, Sarah's Bunny — Nameless Star, Black Earl

SOLE AIM

By Monalee Champion out of the Pigalle Wonder bitch Yurituni, he was whelped in July 1968 and was to become one of only three greyhounds to win classic races both in England and in Ireland – Brilliant Bob and Queen of the Suir were the other two. Sole Aim was purchased as a puppy by Mrs Frances Chandler and when just two years old contested the thirty-seventh Laurels at Wimbledon. Trained by Dave Geggus at Walthamstow, Sole Aim was to win every round of the Laurels. He won his heat by four lengths in the fastest time for any of the eight heats, and in the second round he again won his heat, this time by four lengths from Idle Thoughts. After winning his semi-final he took the final, for which he was made favourite in one of the most exciting races ever seen. Coming from well behind, he defeated Always a Monarch by a short head (1 in.) in 28.04 secs, with The Other Green, whom he defeated in his semi-final, in third place. It was Mrs Chandler's fourth Laurels victory.

The Other Green was an outstanding tracker, by Prairie Flash out of The Other Flash, a black bitch owned by Mr Matt O'Donnell of Killenaule and a granddaughter of Ballymac Ball. He won the 1970 Northern

Flat at Belle Vue, twice breaking the 500 yds record in doing so, and in the Laurels, in which he finished third, he won his first and second round heats. He then took the Edinburgh Cup at Powderhall by five lengths from Brenda's Pick, and after earning £2,500 that year was retired to stud.

Sole Aim returned to his native Ireland for the 1971 Derby after being eliminated from the English event through being badly hampered in his semi-final. In the Irish Derby he defeated the odds-on favourite Postal Vote to win his semi-final, and repeated the performance in the final, beating Postal Vote by one and a half lengths in the second fastest time ever recorded for a Derby final at Shelbourne Park. His time of 29.12 secs was only bettered by Yellow Printer and Lively Band, who clocked one-tenth of a second faster.

Sole Aim was bred and reared in Co. Clare by Mr Jimmy Burke and in the same litter were two other outstanding greyhounds. One was Mic Mac, who won the Guinness 600 at Shelbourne Park and the Will's 700 at Dunmore Park; the other was Cobbler, who in 1971 reached the final of the English Derby, ran up the Pall Mall, and won the Circuit. He in turn was to become sire of Sally's Cobbler, who when handled by John Bassett, then a private trainer, broke six track records over all distances in England and was described in *Sporting Life* as the all-time 'king of the railers'.

Retired to stud, Sole Aim fathered one of his first and finest sons in Rhu. Owned by Mr Denis Diffley and trained by Matt O'Donnell of Killenaule, Rhu won the 1978 Irish St Leger at Limerick and was undefeated through his heats and semi-final. Though this great dog's time was one of the slowest recorded for the Irish St Leger in recent years, he showed just how good he was when he contested the English St Leger, run over 655 m. From trap 5, from which no greyhound has ever won the event, he finished second to Westmead Power who won in 39.67 secs. If more favourably drawn, Rhu might well have become the only greyhound ever to win the English and Irish St Leger.

Another of Sole Aim's sons is Knockrour Slave, who won the Guinness Trophy at Cork in 1979 by ten lengths after winning his heats and semi-final by a similar margin and equalling Allemaine's track record for the 525 yds course. He was the fastest to race in Ireland during 1979, and his owner, Mr Denis Lynch, is known to have been offered and refused a staggering £50,000 for him.

Sole Aim is now taking over from his sire and passing on to his sons those same qualities which made his sire and dam so outstanding at stud in the early 1970s. He was the first of Monalee Champion's sons to win a classic, and ten years later, in 1979, he sired the Irish Oaks winner and Derby finalist, the black bitch Nameless Pixie. Monalee Champion was perhaps the greatest sire of track champions of all time, for among his progeny were Linda's Champion, the 1977 Irish Derby winner; Jimsun, the English Derby winner the previous year; and Rhu. Sole Aim was also sire of Columbcille Aim, dam of Penny County, a bitch who won the Irish Derby in 1979 and whose pedigree is worth giving (below). She combines the greatest track blood of modern times. An Tain was dam of the 1976 Irish Derby winner Tain Mor and her grand sire, Yanka Boy, was out of the greatest dam of all time, Millie Hawthorn. An Tain was by Russian Gun, whose sire was Pigalle Wonder, and Pastorville Badge was by another great track sire, Prairie Flash, by Hi There out of another great dam, Prairie Peg. Monalee Champion was by Crazy Parachute out of another outstanding dam, Sheila at Last. Sole Aim's dam Yurituni was also by Pigalle Wonder,

Penny County	Dark Mercury	Yanka Boy	Clonalvy Pride
			Millie Hawthorn
		An Tain	Russian Gun (Pigalle Wonder)
			Pastorville Badge
	Columbcille Aim	Sole Aim	Monalee Champion
			Yurituni
		She's Silver	The Grand Silver
			She's Landing

who was a son of Prairie Peg, this time from a mating with Champion Prince. Thus the greatest sires and dams of modern track racing have combined to produce those champions of the 1960s, in Pigalle Wonder, Russian Gun and Clonalvy Pride, and of the early 1970s, Yanka Boy, Dark Mercury and Sole Aim. Now in the 1980s we have Penny County and the 1979 Irish Oaks winner Nameless Pixie, another bitch, who is of similar breeding, by Monalee Champion out of Itsastar, by Yanka Boy out of another Oaks winner, Itsamint, who was by Prairie Flash out of the English Oaks winner Cranog Bet.

SPANISH BATTLESHIP

A fawn brindle dog, he was born of the bitch Ballyseedy Memory, owned by Tadhg Drummond of Tralee, who had leased her to Tim O'Connor, the owner of a public house of Killorglin, to mate with his dog, Spanish Chestnut. Tim had enjoyed considerable success in the 1950s with his two dogs. Spanish Lad had won the Irish Derby in 1949 and had run up in the same year for the Laurels, which had been won by Tim O'Connor's other champion, Spanish Chestnut, who was to win the Laurels again in 1950 and become the only dog to win the Irish classic on two occasions. It was from a mating of Ballyseedy Memory to Spanish Chestnut that Spanish Battleship was born in August 1951, one of four dogs and three bitches. The pup who was to win an unprecedented three Derbys was the weakest of the litter, like Mick the Miller twenty years earlier and the champion bitch Clomoney Grand twenty years later. The Irish do not put down the weakest, but give them more care than the others, and Tim O'Connor spent every spare moment with the little dog in the back parlour of his public house, coaxing him to drink milk and Guinness from a baby's bottle. He reared the pup although it always remained a dog of slight build compared to the others of the litter. When Tim took him for his first trial at Tralee, the dog weighed less than 60 lbs; he was no bigger than the bitches of the litter and there must have been several present at the trials that day who were in no way impressed by the appearance of Tim's puppy, although they knew he was no fool with a greyhound.

Spanish Battleship did not unduly impress in his first trial, but won his first race at Tralee early in 1953 chiefly by his amazing track sense, which surprised those who saw him run for it was as highly developed as in a dog with a year's experience of track racing. Now weighing about 60 lbs, Tim's puppy had caused a number of eyebrows to be raised by the manner of his win, and when he also won his next race at Limerick, over 525 yds, it seemed that Tim O'Connor could well have a third champion performer. Entered for the St Leger at Limerick, he did not find the distance to his liking and did not proceed beyond the first round. Few could have contemplated all that was to come.

It was at this point that Tim had a brainwave, and sent him to his friend Tom Lynch, the legendary trainer of Blanchardstown, in the hope that in more experienced hands and with someone who could devote more time to him the puppy would make some headway. Tom Lynch has said that the dog required the minimum of training for he never put on weight, remaining at about 60–62 lbs throughout his career. He was also a wonderful traveller and distances never worried him. Like Model Dasher, racing in England just before him, he could travel 100 miles and go into the traps as fresh as a daisy. Nor was he in any way highly strung. All traps and all tracks were the same to him. He just got on with the job he was expected to do. He ran just as well in the wet as on turf baked hard by midsummer sun; as well in the cold as in great heat.

Entered for the 1953 Derby at Harold's Cross, Spanish Battleship won his heats and the final, beating Smokey Glen by about a length in 29.78 secs. It was run in August when the dog was just two years old, the youngest winner of the Irish Derby, and he earned his owner £500 compared with the £20,000 he would have won today.

Rested over the winter, he next contested the Easter Cup at Shelbourne Park and was again successful, although the odds of 2–1 against his winning did not make him favourite to do so. Then he went to Harold's Cross, scene of his Derby triumph the previous year, but he was well beaten in the final of the Callanan Cup. Back at Shelbourne Park for another crack at the

Derby he set a new track record in his heat with a time of 29.50 secs, and at 3–1 on his winning the final he did so in no uncertain manner, beating the dog Dignity by three lengths in 29.64 secs. He was then at Thurles for the Tipperary Cup which he won, and in so doing broke the track record twice in four days. Then at Kilkenny he won the McCalmont Cup by six lengths, showing devastating speed and his usual wonderful trackcraft. He was always in full control of the task he had in hand, and in this respect resembled Mick the Miller.

When he came out from his winter rest Spanish Battleship was to win a second Easter Cup also by six lengths, in 29.72 secs, but he failed to win the Corn an Tostail a few weeks later and it was thought he was past his best. However he was never happier than when racing, and was again entered for the Derby which he won for a record third year in succession. No other greyhound has ever won the Irish Derby even twice. In the final he left the traps like a rocket. By the first bend he was at least two lengths in front and he led all the way, beating Crosty's Bell by the same margin in 29.53 secs. Not only had he won the event three times in a row but had amazingly improved upon his times on each occasion, and he was now four years old. Many thought that Tim O'Connor would now retire his champion, who was now the most popular greyhound ever to race in Ireland, but Tim had other ideas for he thought his dog still capable of winning the 1955 Laurels. He was not to be disappointed for 'The Battleship', as he was now affectionately called by Dubliners, won comfortably, beating Wild Pilot in 28.35 secs, a time which was beaten only once, by Last Lap in 1960 when the Laurels was run over 500 yds.

Now in his fifth year, Spanish Battleship was, like Mick the Miller at the same age, still at his peak, and at Kilkenny in October he was to win the prestigious McCalmont Cup for the second time, beating Coolagh Record by a short head. Before October was out he had broken the track record at Galway, dead-heating with Portahard Boy in 29.98 secs, the first time that 30 secs had been bettered for the 525 yds course. He might then have been retired, for he had done enough to carve his name for all time in the annals of Irish greyhound racing, and when Tim O'Connor decided to send him to England at the end of 1955 many thought it was inadvisable. This was proved so, for in several races at Romford and the White City his form was far from impressive, and he ended the year and his career on a low note when he should have gone out on a high, for he had become a legend in his lifetime, acclaimed the length and breadth of Ireland.

At stud he was a complete failure; like Mick the Miller (who did, however, sire a St Leger and an Oaks winner) he had possibly raced too much and too long, for the successes at stud have been those sires and dams which have been lightly raced and for no more than two years.

In more than three years' racing Spanish Battleship won more than £6,000 in prize money at a time when £500 was awarded to a classic winner. If racing today he would have won around £100,000.

SPANISH LAD and SPANISH CHESTNUT

A fawn dog by Shaggy Lad out of the great brood bitch Cordial Moonlight, 'Lad' was whelped in February 1947 and was the first of Mr T. O'Connor's wonderful dogs, each of whom had the prefix 'Spanish', who were to dominate the Irish racing scene during the 1950s. None of them raced in England very often. In the Irish Derby of 1949 Spanish Lad won his first and second round heats, being the only dog to break 30 secs on each occasion. In his semi-final he ran up to Mr F. Johnson's Rushton News, but made no mistake in the final which he won from Merry Courier in 29.87 secs, with Rushton News in third place. He next contested the Laurels at Cork in August, where one opponent was his half brother Spanish Chestnut, a white and brindled dog whelped in March 1948, from the same dam but by the great coursing dog Rebel Abbey. In the Laurels Spanish Lad won his heat in 28.60 secs, but Spanish Chestnut was lucky to go through, finishing well third in his heat. In the second round heats Spanish Lad was again successful, this time in 28.50 secs, and Spanish Chestnut came second in his heat. In the semi-finals both dogs were successful and ensured that they would be there to battle it out in the final. Sure enough this was so, for from the start there were only two dogs in it. Spanish Chestnut won a great race from his half brother, who finished in second place with Musical Charles third, the winning time being 28.55 secs. The following year Spanish Chestnut was again successful, winning from Ella's Ivy, and five years later his son Spanish Battleship won the event to crown a magnificent career.

Mr O'Connor might also have taken the St Leger that year, 1949, for the fawn dog Spanish Emperor, litter brother to Spanish Lad, reached the final after winning his heats and running up his semi-final. However in the final he was beaten into fourth place, with the even-money favourite, Ballybeg Surprise, winning.

SPECTRE II

A black weighing 73 lbs, whelped in February 1965 at the kennels of Mr Leo Stack at Duagh, Co. Kerry, he was one of the greatest litter in the history of track racing, which included Tric Trac, winner of the 1967 English Derby, and Forward King, winner of the 1968 English St Leger and more than £5,000 in prize money. Forward Flash was also in the litter and but for injury might well have been the best of them all, for in the few months of 1966 in which he raced he won the Juvenile Stakes at Wembley; the Manchester Cup at White City, Manchester; and the Mackeson Cup at Walthamstow; further great things were expected of him. The litter, of five dogs and four bitches, was by Crazy Parachute out of Supreme Witch. The dam was one of a litter that included Mile Bush Pride, whelped in 1956, who won the English Derby in 1959 and four other classics in that year.

The 1967 Derby which Spectre II contested was sensational in that one owner, Mr Nat Pinson of Sheffield, and one trainer, Ron Hookway of the Owlerton Stadium, had the first two in the Derby. It was also the first time that two from the same litter finished first and second in a classic event. Although Spectre II was made favourite Tric Trac was in trap 1, and as an excellent railer he made full use of his position to win by a length. This was a Derby final of outstanding greyhounds, for the race included Shady Parachute, who also contested the 1968 final and again finished in fourth place when 6–4 on favourite; the great sire of the future, Silver Hope; and the Laurels winner Ambiguous. Tric Trac was retired to stud after his great win but was brought out of retirement the following year and won the Wimbledon Champion Stakes. This return to racing after a year's lay-off may have contributed to his early death, for he died shortly afterwards. He was track record holder for many years over 525 yds at Owlerton, his home track.

Spectre II continued to win in top company during 1967, taking the BBC TV Trophy at Brighton, run over 880 yds, in a record time of 50.09 secs, and the Midlands St Leger at Wolverhampton. Retired to stud in 1968, he was to prove one of the greatest sires in track racing. One of his first sons was Black Andrew, who won the 1971 Laurels. Another was Spectre Jockey, who ran up to Down Your Way in the Gold Collar and in the same year, 1971, won the prestigious Evening Standard Cup and All-England Stakes. He is now making as famous a name at stud as his sire, who must rank with Monalee Champion, Newdown Heather, Clonalvy Pride and Westmead County as the most outstanding of the late 1970s. Spectre Jockey is sire of the game Langford Dacoit, who ran up in the Cesarewitch and who in turn is now retired to stud.

Among Spectre II's other famous offspring was Tartan Khan, who in 1975 won the Derby and St Leger, emulating Dolores Rocket; he won £23,000 in that year alone. Then there were Stormy Spirit, winner of the 1977 St Leger; Glin Bridge, who won £8,000 in prize money; Paradise Spectre; and Rita's Choice, one of Spectre's greatest sons. A black dog like his sire, Rita's Choice was to earn himself the title of best Irish track greyhound of 1973, in which year he won several major long-distance events, including the Corn Cuchulainn at Harold's Cross; the Cesarewitch at Navan; and the Sean Graham 700 at Dunmore Park. From his mating to Itsastar he was to sire in April 1974 Nameless Star, who in 1976 won the Irish Laurels at Cork; the St Leger at Limerick; and the Hurst Cup at Kilkenny, thus perpetuating the great speed and stamina of his sire and grand sire. Some of Spectre's outstanding sons now at stud include: Crown Walter, Glin Bridge, Millcock, Paradise Spectre, Rita's Choice, Shamrock Sailor, Spectre Jockey, Stormy Spirit, Tartan Khan and Tullig Doctor.

Forward King, the other excellent mem-

Spectre II Tric Trac Forward King Forward Flash	Crazy Parachute	Hi There	Slaney Record Dublin Red
		Mad Prospect	Mad Tanist Caledonia Desire
	Supreme Witch	Solar Prince	Champion Prince Lisabelle
		Witching Grand	The Grand Champion Witching Dancer

ber of Leo Stack's wonderful litter, won the St Leger and the Scottish St Leger, the only dog ever to do so. He also won the Wembley Gold Cup and the Stewards' Cup, and in seventy top-class open events won half of them. Yet he might never have reached a race track at all, for when twelve months old he escaped from his kennels and lived wild on the Yorkshire moors for nearly a year before being recaptured! He was none the worse for his escapade.

The litter brothers' pedigree is above.

SPORT PROMOTER

Owned and trained by Pat and Linda Mullins who also bred him, this outstanding brindle dog was whelped in June 1978 and in little more than twelve months' racing established himself as one of the finest of all British-bred greyhounds. By Breakaway Town by Kensington Queen, whose dam Kensington Lil was by the great Oregon Prince, he began his career by winning the 1979 British Bred Greyhound Championship sponsored by Spratts Ltd and run over 500 m at the White City in November. In his heat, semi-final and final, each of which he won, he defeated the game little bitch How Much who had won the event in 1977 and 1978 and who was only just back from a six-month lay-off through injury when she contested the event. This time she met a puppy who was destined to win two classics within the next ten months.

Always running around the outside of the track and so covering more ground than the other dogs, Sport Promoter next contested the 1979 Romford Xmas Puppy Stakes during which event he improved all the time. He only just qualified for the semi-final in which he was beaten by half a length by Fast Talker but made no mistake in the final, and he also won the Sporting Life Juvenile Championship at Wimbledon.

He began 1980 by winning a few top class 'open' races, and by the time the Gold Collar came to be run at Catford -- an event sponsored by John Humphreys – Sport Promotor was in superb condition, going through the event undefeated, winning his first and second round heats and semi-final by six lengths from Westmead Echo, with Owner's Guide in third place. This dog had also reached the final the previous year. Sport Promoter was to win the final, for which he was made 2–1 on favourite, and the £5,000 first prize by beating Owner's Guide again, this time by two lengths in 35.06 secs to give him his first classic win.

SUPREME FUN (SUPER FUN)

By Newdown Heather out of Top Note, this outstanding white and black dog was firstly in the ownership of Mr Alf McLean, and then of Mr Harry Gover of Southend, who purchased him for £2,000. The dog was whelped in March 1969, his dam, an Irish Oaks winner, being by the great bitch Burleigh's Fancy, dam of Oregon Prince, one of the fastest greyhounds ever to run, and she passed on her tremendous powers to her first grandson.

Originally named Super Fun, he had his first race at the Dungannon track in September 1970, when he clocked the fast time of 18.03 secs for the 325 yds course. Entered for the Nursery Cup at Dundalk, a seventy-two-dog event, he won the final comfortably and was then entered for the Sporting Life Puppy Championship at Wimbledon. The first three to finish in the final were to become three of the finest greyhounds of their time, and only inches separated them as they crossed the winning line. They were Dolores Rocket, Crefogue Flash and Supreme Fun, in that order. It is said that after the race Mr McLean parted with his great dog for £2,000, and as there was already a dog named Super Fun racing in England his name was changed to Supreme Fun. He was soon to earn his new owner his purchase price.

Placed in the kennels of the Hertfordshire trainer S. Ryall, the dog began by contesting the 1971 English Derby, one of the strongest entries in years, for among those taking part were Postal Vote; Crefogue Flash; two recent Laurels winners, Sole Aim and Black Andrew; Dolores Rocket; Clohast Rebel; and Ivy Hall Flash, who beat Supreme Fun into second place in their semi-final, with Dolores Rocket third. In the final, too, Supreme Fun met one too good in the wonder bitch Dolores Rocket and had to be content with second place, losing by half a length. From there he took the Charlton Olympic, breaking the track record in 34.16 secs, and later came within .04 secs of equalling the 550 yds record at the White City. He then won the Edinburgh Cup at Powderhall and in Wembley's Select Stakes had his revenge on his great rival Dolores Rocket, this time beating her by half a length. After his Derby defeat he had a run of twelve consecutive open race victories and reached his third classic final that year, only to be beaten in the Cesarewitch. In six months, from contesting the Derby until his Cesarewitch defeat, he won more than £3,000 and was then retired to stud through injury. Printer's Prince was his grand sire (also sire of Yellow Printer), being a son of the Derby winner Endless Gossip, whose sire was another Derby winner, Priceless Border.

One of his first sons to run was Xmas Holiday, a white and brindle out of the dam Mary's Snowball. Whelped in January 1974, he won the 1976 Scurry Gold Cup, now run at Slough, and also the Laurels. In July 1975, from his mating to Gormanstown Aye, Supreme Fun sired Brush Tim who ran up for the 1977 Irish Derby and won Carroll's International at Dundalk the same year before being retired to stud through injury. His dam's sire, Silver Hope, was by Clonalvy Pride out of Millie Hawthorn.

TAIN MOR

By Monalee Champion (Sheila at Last—Crazy Parachute) out of An Tain and whelped in 1973, this great dog made his first appearance on a race track in the 1976 Irish Cambridgeshire, run over 600 yds at Shelbourne Park, and went through the event undefeated. This must surely be the only instance of a dog whose first race was a classic, and which he won. He then contested the Irish Derby and repeated his performance, winning the final from Corn Top in the fast time of 29.35 secs. In the Shelbourne 600 he was eliminated in his semi-final by two short heads, the three dogs crossing the winning line virtually together, and from there he took the Shelbourne Leger. In only fourteen races he won eleven times, and those races he lost were by two short heads and a neck. He could so easily have won on every occasion he ran, and was elected Champion greyhound of 1976.

At the beginning of 1977 Tain Mor was retired to stud. During his racing career he ran in the name of Affric Campbell, daughter of Sean and Peggy Campbell, who purchased An Tain, his dam, at an early age. Both Tain Mor and his dam were looked after by Peggy Campbell's brothers, Jack and Paddy Nolan of Enniscorthy.

Paddy Nolan, trainer of Tain Mor.

Tain Mor's pedigree contains the greatest dams and sires in modern greyhound racing, and one of his first sons to run was Desert Pilot, from a mating to Dark Hostess; he reached the final of the 1979 English Derby but, drawn in trap 3, was crowded at the first turn and was unable to show his tremendous speed and track sense.

Tain Mor's dam An Tain was to make her influence felt on track racing although she bred only two litters. She was herself the product of a mating of Pigalle Wonder's greatest son, Russian Gun, to the Prairie Flash bitch Pastorville Badge. The mating of An Tain to Yanka Boy produced the Trigo Cup winner Dark Mercury who was sire of the bitch Penny County, winner of the 1979 Irish Derby. An Tain's grand

1976 Irish Greyhound Derby winner Tain Mor.

dam was by The Grand Fire, who has had the strongest influence on the dam lines of the greatest of modern track greyhounds, while Prairie Peg figures on both sides of her pedigree.

Tain Mor's pedigree reads:

Tain Mor	Monalee Champion	Crazy Parachute	Hi There
			Mad Prospect
		Sheila at Last	The Grand Prince
			Last Landing
	An Tain	Russian Gun	Pigalle Wonder
			Shandaroba (Odd Venture)
		Pastorville Badge	Prairie Flash (Hi There)
			Badge of Greatness

TANIST

A brindle whelped in March 1938 by the flying Inler out of the dam Tranquilla, he was one of the fastest trackers the sport has known and was one of the foundation sires of modern racing greyhounds. His sire was ten when Tanist was born, and he had been one of the first Irish dogs to reach Britain in the early years of the sport. Kennelled at Clapton, Inler was endowed with tremendous speed but, like so many blessed in this way, found it difficult to manage the turns, running out wide as did his sons Tanist and Ataxy. They moved too fast down the straights and were unable to control their running not only at the turns but whenever they were in trouble. Like a car being driven too fast, there was no room for error or correction. Yet Inler and then his son Tanist, and in turn his son Mad Tanist, have provided the sport with the fastest greyhounds ever and that excitement that only comes with breath-catching speed. The staying power was provided by Melksham Tom and Mutton Cutlet and by their sons Beef Cutlet and Castledown Lad, but the real excitement came from Inler and Tanist and Creamery Border at a later date.

It was in April 1940 that Tanist first gave his owner, Arthur Probert, some idea of his potential, when the dog reached the final of the important Easter Cup at Shelbourne Park, won by Shy Sandy. He immediately sent Tanist to Paddy

McEllistrim at Wimbledon with the idea of entering him for the Derby. But here he found it almost impossible to circumnavigate the sharp turns, and if he did not run wide he tended to check and was not able to win a single race at Wimbledon by the end of June. On Mr McEllistrim's advice Tanist was recalled to Ireland and was given a trial at Shelbourne Park where he had run so well in the Easter Cup. Within a week of his return he had set a new Irish national record for 525 yds and was entered for the 1940 Irish Derby. Here was a dog who only a few weeks before was not able to win a race at Wimbledon in the poorest company, yet in every heat of the Derby he set a new track record and by the time of the final was favourite. Up against the best dogs in Ireland he made no mistake, winning from Another Dancing Willie in 29.82 secs, the first time 30 secs had been broken in the final and which stood as the fastest time for a decade. Tanist had proved that he was the fastest greyhound in the world, though only a month before he had been a laughing stock, which only goes to show how easy it is to write a dog off when it fails at the first attempt. During that summer Tanist had reduced the track record at Shelbourne Park to 29.66 secs and he was also the first to break 30 secs at Clonmel to set a new record in his only race there.

With the Irish tracks then closing for the winter he did not race again, but knowing how greatly Tanist enjoyed running his owner entered him for the Irish Cup, Ireland's premier coursing event. Could Tanist do the double by taking Ireland's premier track and coursing events? The whole greyhound world waited for the outcome, and on that cold February day at Clounanna, thousands stood with bated breath as Tanist and Ocean Blend were slipped together. But Ocean Blend was adjudged the winner after a most unsatisfactory trial, and Tanist was retired to stud. He died in January 1948, after standing at stud for six years at a record fee in Ireland of 60 gns, and after siring a long list of the fastest greyhounds the sport has known. Among his stock were the famous brother and sister Mad Tanist, winner of the National Sprint in 1944, and Astra, who won the Easter Cup in 1945 and 1946; also Cold Christmas, winner of the 1946 Irish Oaks; Smartly Fergus, who broke track records everywhere; Lemon Flash, sold for £3,000; Prancing Kitty, winner of the 1945 English Oaks; and many more. Mad Tanist in turn was sire of The Grand Champion, sire of The Grand Fire who sired some of the finest dams the sport has known and who after more than twenty years still held the 525 yds record at Clonmel with a fantastic 29.40 secs, while Astra, one of the fastest bitches of all time, from her mating to Paddy the Champion gave birth to Astra's Son, sire of Prairie Vixen, dam of Prairie Peg, in turn dam of Pigalle Wonder, sire of the Irish Derby winner Russian Gun. It should also be noted that The Grand Fire was sire of Millie Hawthorn, dam of the 1966 English Derby winner Faithful Hope, who in turn sired the 1970 Derby winner John Silver. But for Arthur Probert never having lost faith in Tanist when all but he had written him off as almost useless, the dog would never have won the Irish Derby and might never then have been so well patronized at stud. He was one of the great foundation sires of modern greyhound racing.

Tanist was bred and reared by an Irish priest, Father Browne of Bray, Co. Dublin. Thus perhaps the two most famous of Ireland's track greyhounds were trained by members of the Catholic Church.

TARTAN KHAN

He did not run for long but in one year alone, 1975, proved himself the best dog on either side of the Irish Sea and won £23,000 in prize money. A brindle whelped in November 1973, he was by Spectre II out of Chilled Sweet. His dam's sire was the Wembley St Leger winner Clonalvy Pride, whose time for the event was never beaten, so on both sides of his pedigree he inherited great staying power and remarkable track sense which enabled him to make full use of every opportunity to get to the front in every race he ran, yet he always started the outsider!

As a puppy he was kennelled at Perry Barr and reached the finals of four major events there during 1974. After his winter rest his owner, Mr D.M. Law, placed him at White City to prepare for the 1975 Derby, but in March the dog was seriously ill and there seemed little hope of his competing.

Tartan Khan.

It was a shrewd move of his owner to place him with Mrs Lynds as soon as the dog was well enough to be moved. By magnificent running he reached the final of the 1975 Derby, for which he was the 25–1 outsider, but, fast away and running brilliantly, he won from a top-class field, beating Sally's Cobbler by a length, with Pineapple Grand in third place and Myrtown two lengths behind her. From there he went to Wembley for the St Leger and once again, although he was thought to have little chance, he came through a top-class field to win and stamp himself as a great competitor. In a letter to the author, his owner said: 'The dog's great asset was his magnificent temperament and his great courage. I can best sum up by saying that if he was human we could agree that he was the perfect gentleman.' Just how good he would have been but for his serious illness, one will never know.

TIME UP PLEASE

Whelped in January 1970, this black dog by Newdown Heather out of Dogstown Fame proved himself in a short career one of the greatest stayers in history. He first contested the Guinness Puppy Stakes, in which he was beaten by only a short head, and he than went on to win the Spring Cup at Mullingar. Clocking 29.04 secs at Shelbourne Park over 525 yds, he reached the final of the Irish Derby in 1971, won by Sole Aim, and at Limerick in the fastest time ever done in the St Leger over 550 yds he won the event in 30.56 secs from Ivy Hall Flash. The following year he became only the second dog in the sport's history to win the Irish St Leger twice remaining unbeaten throughout the event and winning the final by four and a half lengths. But for losing his semi-final in the 1971 Leger, beaten a short head, he would have gone through both events undefeated. In 1972 this outstanding dog also won the important Carroll's International at Dundalk and reached the semi-final of the Irish Derby, in which he was badly hampered. Retired to stud after his second St Leger win, he was to sire Pampered Rover who won the 1978 Irish Derby for Mr Joe Phelan and for his trainer Paddy Keene, who became one of the few to train an English (Faithful Hope) and Irish Derby winner.

The pedigree of Pampered Rover reads:

Pampered Rover	Time Up Please	Newdown Heather	Printer's Prince
			Pardee
		Dogstown Fame	Wonder Valley (Pigalle Wonder)
			Yoblestrap
	Pampered Peggy	Russian Gun	Pigalle Wonder
			Shandaroba
		Sheila's Prize	Prairie Flash
			Sheila at Last

TOUGH DECISION

A fine upstanding brindle of 74 lbs by Minnesota Miller out of track record holder Carter's Drain and whelped in March 1977, he is yet another example of Pigalle Wonder's influence coming through on the female line, for his dam was out of a bitch called Avenue Maggie whose sire was Russian Gun, a son of Pigalle Wonder. The dog was well named for he was tough in the extreme, never had a day off because of illness, and all tracks and all weather conditions came alike to him. 1979 was a vintage year for Irish greyhounds with Nameless Pixie and Penny County, two outstanding bitches, and Distant Clamour, Knockrour Slave, Indian Joe, Hume Highway and Tough Decision, there being little to choose between them.

Tough Decision's first race was at Lifford in October 1978 when he won the Abraham David Trophy, run over 575 yds, to earn £2,500 for his owner, Mrs Owens of Belfast. He was trained by Harry McLarnon of Ballymena, home of that all-time 'great',

Priceless Border. Two weeks later, he reached the final of the Shelbourne Leger, run over the same distance, in which he finished third and was running so strongly at the end that those who saw him thought he would do even better over 600 yds.

The dog was then bought by his trainer, Harry McLarnon, in co-ownership with Ronny Barber who placed him with Tommy Kane at Galtrim in Co. Meath, and in February he was to show just how good he was by taking the Bookmakers Championship at Shelbourne Park and at Harold's Cross the following week to bring his winnings to £10,000. In May he added £3,500 to his total by taking the Guinness 600 (run over 600 yds) at Shelbourne Park when he beat a top-class field. In the same month, at the same track, he won his heat and the final of the Cambridgeshire, also over 600 yds, in a time of 33.61 secs.

He then came over to contest the English Derby and, in his qualifying heat run at Shawfield, defeated Fulmax Boy by four lengths. In round 2 at the White City, London, he again won by four lengths, this time beating Design Council, but in round 3 he was badly baulked and ran up to Greenville Boy. In his quarter-final he was again in early trouble and finished third. In his semi-final he was drawn against Sarah's Bunny, the winner, and Desert Pilot who ran up, but he took third place to go through to the final. As usual in recent finals, it was the 'seeded' greyhounds in traps 5 and 6 who had a clear run throughout, the inside dogs in traps 1 and 2 being badly baulked at the first turn which prevented them from taking much part in the rest of the race. The bitch Tyrean in trap 1 finished in fifth place and Tough Decision in trap 2 was last.

Shortly afterwards at White City, Manchester, the dog injured a leg and, failing to respond to treatment, was retired to stud early in 1980. In a little over twelve months he had won twenty top-class events and taken his earnings up to £17,000. He had the heart of a lion and always came from behind to win when the odds looked to be stacked against him.

His pedigree includes Bauhus, sire of Sand Star; Clonalvy Pride; and Explosive Gilbert, litter brother of Endless Gossip who was to pass on to future stock many of the outstanding qualities of Endless Gossip when that great dog was exported to the USA.

The Pedigree of Tough Decision reads:

Tough Decision	Minnesota Miller	Bright Lad	Rocket Ship
			July Joan
		Letesia	Bauhus
			Goldie's Fancy
	Carter's Drain	Ivy Hall Flash	Proud Lincoln
			Ivy Hall Rose
		Avenue Maggie	Russian Gun
			Backford Jill

TRAIN

A brindle whelped in June 1938 at the kennels of Major Tennyson, he was by the great sire Danielli out of the dam Tiang. Danielli was to sire Model Whiskey, sire of the great stayer of the war years, Model Dasher; and Tokio, sire of Bah's Choice; also Chancellor, sire of the Waterloo Cup winner Countryman. All of them possessed outstanding courage and stamina. At the start of the war Major Tennyson felt he could retain in his kennels only a few of his best brood bitches as a foundation for breeding when the war was over, and so Train was sold to a Mr Harris for about £50, and he in turn let him go to Miss Lambert for, it is said, £80. It was one of the biggest bargains in the history of greyhound racing.

Miss Lambert took the dog for his first trials at Harringay where, in the capable hands of trainer Campbell, the dog gave early indications of his ability and on August Bank Holiday 1940 scored his first win from a good-class field. In his second race he injured a toe and was off racing until October, when at the White City he won in 29.52 secs which stamped him above the ordinary. Then at Clapton in November he won a 550 yds race in 32.90 secs and great things were expected of him, yet lameness again prevented his running over that winter and it was six months before he was ready to race again. This was in the 1942 Cambridgeshire at West Ham, and in his heat was the great Ballynennan Moon. Showing amazing courage and stamina, Train not only beat 'The Moon' in his heat but again in the final, and became the first dog to beat the champion twice. Train was more than five years old when he was put in the hands of trainer Appleton at West Ham, and within a few weeks had won the West Ham Winter Stakes. On 2 January 1943 he was defeated by Ballynennan Moon for the Red Cross Stakes at Wembley. Their meetings, however, had created great interest and another match was arranged for the following week at Wembley where they would be joined by the home-trained bitch Satin Beauty, winner of the Coronation Stakes in 1942. She was, however, past her best and never really in the reckoning as the two champions raced neck and neck to the shouts and cheers of the crowd. But it was Train who crossed the line first, about three quarters of a length in front of Ballynennan Moon, and it was the third time he had done so in four meetings.

Train next contested West Ham's second Winter Stakes, this time run over 400 yds, which he won in 22.16 secs, and then the Easter Stakes there, over the same distance, which he also won in his stride. Miss Lambert then decided that her dog should be retired to stud, for he had established himself as one of the best English-bred greyhounds ever to race, well able to take care of anything matched against him, but there were no classics for him to win during the war years.

TREV'S PERFECTION

The story of this dog is one of the most romantic in the history of greyhound racing. This brindle, whelped in April 1944 by Trev's Dispatch out of a Beef Cutlet bitch, the curiously named Friar Tuck, was to become one of the greatest in the history of the sport after a change of name and ownership. He was bred and reared in the keen air of the Cumberland Fells by Mr H.G. Nunn who named him Highland Perfection and from whom he was purchased, when ready to race, by Miss Nora Roth. During 1946 he won a number of open races for her under the name of Mott's Regret. Indeed in June of that year he was entered for the Derby at the White City (as Mott's Regret) and, a 50–1 outsider in his heat (8) of round 1, was well beaten into fourth place, after which he took no further part in the contest. Later that year the dog went down with distemper and pneumonia at the GRA kennels at Northaw, and at one time his life was despaired of, but after a long convalescence he reappeared on the track and reached the final of the Wandsworth Spring Stakes in which he ran up to Balmaha, Ballynennan Moon's last son. Later that month he was beaten eight lengths by Izadaisy in a race of 500 yds and gave little insight as to his capabilities.

One person, however, must have been impressed with the dog's running and that was Mr Fred Trevillion, a haulage contractor from Dartford in Kent, who was a licensed greyhound trainer with a number of good dogs in his kennels each of whom carried the Trev prefix. The price he paid for Mott's Regret was £900, which many considered a huge sum for so mediocre a performer. Yet within six months the dog's new owner is on record as saying that 'It was the best £900 worth I ever had,' and indeed it was. The dog was then three years old and his name was changed yet again, this time to Trev's Perfection. Even at that stage, without the dog ever having won a race in eighteen months, and many thought perhaps he never would do, Fred Trevillion must have seen something special in the dog that others did not, to have given him this new name. It soon proved well chosen.

His first big race for his new owner–trainer was on 22 March 1947 at White City, when he beat Parish Model by one and a half lengths. He was next at Walthamstow for the Circuit, which he won in 28.80 secs, a fast time for a dog who was only a few weeks over serious illness, and his form so far must have impressed his new owner. Then, early in June 1947, he contested the Gold Collar at Catford. After winning his heat he was beaten in his semi-final by Monday's News when that fine dog set a new track record, but took the final by three lengths in 25.52 secs to give his owner–trainer his first classic success, which was the start of a series of triumphs the like of which had never been seen before. From Catford the dog took on the cracks of England and Ireland lined up at the White City for the Derby, in which he showed devastating form. He won his heat by five lengths from Mad Midnight in 29.50 secs and his semi-final by three lengths from Slaney Record in 29.30 secs, to qualify for the final in which he was the only English-bred dog. This, too, he won by two lengths from his great rival Monday's News, winner the previous year, in the fastest time yet recorded for the event,

28.95 secs, also the first time 29 secs had been broken in the Derby final. It was the first time the Derby had been won from trap 2 and he earned £1,400 for his owner.

The following week Trev's Perfection went to Glasgow for the Scottish Derby at Carntyne and again beat Monday's News by a head in his heat in 29.10 secs; he won the final by three lengths from two outstanding dogs, Dante II and Monday's News, in 29.25 secs. In one week he had won £2,000, and had earned £600 for his Gold Collar win the previous week. The following week he accomplished what no greyhound had ever done before: by winning the Welsh Derby he achieved the grand slam, the triple crown. Winning his heat, he went on to win the final by two lengths from Spring Ruler in 29.74 secs, which brought his earnings in seven months of 1947 to £3,500, and he earned more than £4,000 in that year. After his defeat by Monday's News in his Gold Collar semi-final he went unbeaten until he retired to stud at the year-end. He had won every race for his new owner except that semi-final and the final of the Private Trainers' Championship at Coventry. The dog owed his success to his devastating speed from the traps, and for his courage and trackcraft. Like Mick the Miller, he never knew when he was beaten and rarely was.

As the Scottish and Welsh Derbys were later given classic status, it can be said that Trev's Perfection had won four classics in successive races he contested, which was and remains an all-time record.

On 1 April 1948 Fred Trevillion, his head kennel-man Arthur Hancock and Trev's Perfection left on the *Queen Mary* for the USA where the dog was expected to make new headlines. They were accompanied by three other dogs, Trev's Key, Trev's Harlequin and Trev's Harvest, each attired in a handsome coat bearing the Union Jack emblem, and their destination was Raynham Park, Boston, Massachusetts. But after his many successes in England Fred Trevillion's departure for America was a step he was much to regret, for the dog was a comparative failure and in five races did not win one. Fred Trevillion returned home early in July and after the great dog's death several years later Fred returned to the USA to try his luck as a trainer but died there greatly disillusioned. Yet he will for ever be remembered as a great trainer of a great greyhound and one who could see a diamond in a slag heap when no one else could.

The pedigree of Trev's Perfection is of great interest. Jamie figures in the ancestry of his sire and dam lines on three occasions. His sire, Trev's Despatch, was by Silver Seal, whose sire was Mick the Miller's litter brother Macoma, but the dam line of Trev's Perfection is of even greater interest. His dam, Friar Tuck, was by Beef Cutlet (by Jamie's son, Mutton Cutlet), but it is not generally realized that Friar Tuck's dam was Wild Woolley's litter sister Wild Winnie, a brindle bitch whose sire, Hautley, was also a son of Jamie. This is yet another instance of outstanding breeding showing itself in the pedigree of a superlative dog like Trev's Perfection. The dam of Wild Winnie was Wild Witch, by Gip's Pride, an almost unknown sire, but who was by the great Osprey Hawk, sire of Glorious Event, whose most famous sons were Mick the Miller and Macoma.

Trev's Perfection's pedigree reads:

Trev's Perfection	Trev's Despatch	Silver Seal	Macoma
			Yatton Tiny
		Lady Moonshine	Brutus (Jamie)
			Lady Christobelle
	Friar Tuck	Beef Cutlet	Mutton Cutlet (Jamie)
			Burette
		Wild Winnie (litter sister Wild Woolley)	Hautley (Jamie)
			Wild Witch

WESTMEAD CHAMP

Though this outstanding fawn dog, by Clonalvy Pride's son Westmead County out of Hacksaw (Hack up Chieftain–Meteoric) was beaten by Mutt's Silver in the final of the 1976 English Derby, he ran so well to take the St Leger and Gold Collar that year that he was elected by the press joint Greyhound of the Year, together with Mutt's Silver, a very popular choice. In the Derby he won each of his three heats, but in the final was badly baulked at the first turn and did not get a place. But to show that this was not his true form he then won every heat and the final of the Gold Collar,

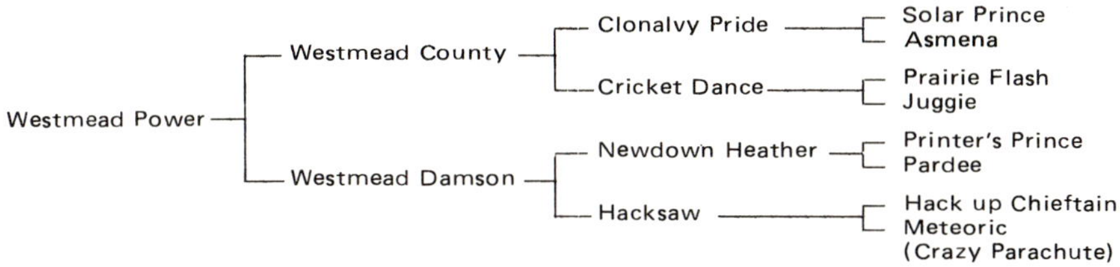

during which he set a new track record of 34.65 secs, and later that year won the St Leger at Wembley. In two years' racing he won £11,000 in prize money and was retired to stud at a fee of £200.

His sire, Westmead County, was also sire of another great stayer, Westmead Power, who repeated the dual classic wins of Westmead Champ in winning the 1977 Gold Collar and the 1978 St Leger, a record without parallel in the history of these events. Westmead Power's breeding was similar to that of Westmead Champ, for his dam, Westmead Damson, was the result of a mating of Hacksaw to Newdown Heather. Westmead Power won nearly £15,000 in prize money.

Their pedigree is given above.

WESTPARK MUSTARD

This bitch by Newdown Heather out of April Merry was owned by Mr Cyril Scotland (alias Cyril Young) and trained by Tommy Johnston at Wembley. One of Newdown Heather's finest daughters, she made national headlines in 1974 when she went twenty races without defeat, beating Mick the Miller's nineteen successive wins in 1930. Mick achieved his within six months; Westpark Mustard did hers in ten months (though this included her four months' seasonal rest), and whereas Mick's total included three classic events Westpark Mustard's were in open events but included no classics. It was not her fault, though, for she was expected to win the 1974 St Leger at her home track but came in season just before and so could take no part. She did most of her running over long distances, though she began her great winning sequence over 525 yds at Wembley for the Abbey Cup on 7 January, not a suitable time of year to begin her career, but by the time she was in season early in May she had won on fifteen consecutive occasions, a tremendous achievement during the winter months. She was chosen Greyhound of the Year for 1974, an award well deserved.

Her pedigree reads:

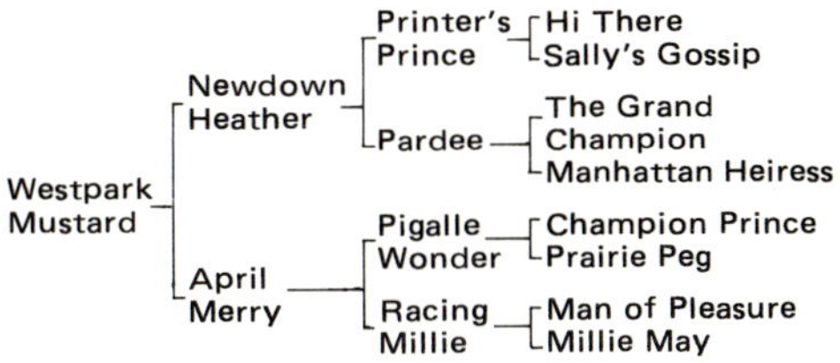

The mating of Pigalle Wonder and Racing Millie was one of the most important in the history of greyhound racing, for April Merry was also dam of another outstanding bitch, April Flower, winner of the 1969 Irish Cesarewitch, and the litter born to Racing Millie included Wonder Valley and Lucky Wonder, two sires who were to have a great influence on modern racing. Wonder Valley was to become sire of Dogstown Fame, dam of Time Up Please, in turn sire of the 1978 Irish Derby winner Pampered Rover, while Lucky Wonder sired Broadford Boy, sire of Malange, who was also a finalist in the same Irish Derby. Note, also, that Racing Millie's sire, Man of Pleasure, was also sire of Last Landing, dam of Sheila at Last; and of Clomoney Grand.

WILD WOOLLEY

This brindle son of Hautley out of Wild Witch was whelped in January 1930 and trained at White City, Manchester, by Jimmy Rimmer for the dog's owner Mr Sam Johnson. He began his career early in 1931 by winning the Northern Flat Championship, run at Belle Vue over 500 yds, in the wonderful time of 28.49 secs. He then contested the Trafalgar Cup at Wembley which he won in 30.84 secs, and Londoners began to take notice of this champion from the north who came on the scene soon after

Mick the Miller had finished and was a worthy successor. From Wembley he moved to the White City to contest the 1932 Derby. His trainer feared only one dog, the equally outstanding Future Cutlet, and he was right. Both won their heats, and when they reached the final both were quoted 5–2 against and no other dog was considered to have much of a chance. The race was one of the finest ever seen, only the two dogs, Wild Woolley flashing over the line just a neck in front of Future Cutlet, with the next dog, Fret Not, an incredible ten lengths behind with the others as far away again. Wild Woolley had also set a new 525 yds track record with a time of 29.72 secs.

He was given a long rest and came out the following spring in time to have a few runs at his home track before contesting the first Gold Collar at Catford, then run over 440 yds. In this event he showed something of the exceptional pace for which he had now become famous. Winning his heat and semi-final by six lengths after being badly hampered early in the race, and in a new track record of 25.95 secs, he was quoted 3–1 on his winning the event, the shortest odds ever placed on a dog to win the Gold Collar. In trap 4, he was again badly baulked at the first bend by Luttrell and Warrior Guide, but lying close behind them at the last turn he moved to the rails and managed to squeeze through them, crossing the line a length in front of Deemster's Mike to win in 26.63 secs. After a short rest he won the Spring Cup at Wimbledon, and then began his attempt to emulate Mick the Miller in winning his second successive Derby. Again he had his great rival Future Cutlet to contend with, and there had also appeared on the scene another great star, Beef Cutlet. All three champions safely reached the final, but it was Future Cutlet and Beef Cutlet, Mutton Cutlet's two sons, who fought it out, Future Cutlet getting the decision by the shortest of short heads from Beef Cutlet, with Wild Woolley a creditable third.

After the Derby he ran the first of his three famous matches with Brave Enough, each over a different distance and each of which he won, and in August he contested the Laurels. The dog was now kennelled at Belle Vue and trained by Jimmy Campbell, and once again he had a resounding success, following Beef Cutlet who won in 1932 and Future Cutlet in 1931. These dogs were the champions of 1931–3. After his Laurels victory he had a long rest but came back for the 1934 Derby. Again he won his way to the final but, now four and a half years old, could not sustain his early pace as in previous years and was beaten into third place by Davesland and Grey Raca. To finish in the first three in three consecutive Derbys was a magnificent effort, quite apart from his other wonderful achievements, and he must certainly go down in history as one of the ten best greyhounds ever to race in England. He combined tremendous early pace with great courage and trackcraft, all the attributes which combine to make a champion.

It is interesting that in each of his Derby finals he was drawn in trap 6 and seeding was not then done. Being a railer, he had the worst of the draw on every occasion.

XMAS HOLIDAY

A white and blue dog by Supreme Fun (Super Fun) out of Mr A. Wichello's bitch Mary's Snowball, he was bred in England by Phil Rees who had the added satisfaction of training him to win two classics and a host of open events. Though both sire and dam were registered with the Irish Stud Book and likewise their son, Xmas Holiday was English-bred and -trained and Phil Rees has said that he classed him with Oregon Prince and with those wonderful bitches Cranog Bet and Shady Parachute whom he also had the privilege to train. The dog was born on 1 January 1975, and was owned throughout his career by Mr Arthur Wichello.

Xmas Holiday had his first run at Romford over 425 m in their Xmas Puppy Stakes of 1975, which he won with ease, and he then took the *Sporting Life* Juvenile Championship at Wimbledon where he was kennelled. Then came the Scurry Gold Cup of April 1976, run at Slough, which he took in his stride. After winning his heats, he defeated his kennel companion Mutt's Silver, who was to win the 1976 Derby, by four lengths, one of the biggest margins in the history of the event. In May followed the Laurels at his home track, which he also won comfortably in 27.66 secs, and he was made second favourite to win the Derby.

Xmas Holiday	Supreme Fun	Newdown Heather	Printer's Prince
			Pardee
		Top Note	Chieftain's Guest
			Burleigh's Fancy
	Mary's Snowball	Yanka Boy	Clonalvy Pride
			Millie Hawthorn
		Noinin Deas	Printer's Prince
			Dainty Princess

Away to a flying start, he was unable to maintain his speed over the longer distance and in the run-in was passed by his companion, Mutt's Silver, who won by a head from Ballybeg Prim, with Westfield Myra in third place and Xmas Holiday close behind. In the same year Xmas Holiday won the Essex Vase at Romford and the Champion of Champions Race, and in 1976 alone won over £12,000 in prize money. After his winter rest he again contested the Scurry Cup in 1977 and reached the final, but found the younger Wired to the Moon his better. He was then retired to stud.

His pedigree (see above) includes the top sires and dams of modern track racing.

YANKA BOY

A fawn dog weighing 77 lbs during his racing days and whelped in March 1965, he was voted champion racing dog of 1967 in Ireland and was especially prominent over longer distances. His first important win was in the Guinness Puppy Derby, over 525 yds, which he won by a comfortable margin; he then took the Irish St Leger, run at Limerick over 550 yds, and also the Cesarewitch over the 600 yds course before being sold by his owner, Mr Mick Laughnam, to Mr Matt Costello for stud purposes.

The first of his progeny to run was Gabriel Boy, owned by Mr P. Dalton and trained by Ger McKenna to win the 1970 Irish Laurels. Since 1961 this classic has been run over 525 yds, and his time of 29.25 secs was the fastest recorded for the longer course. He had previously taken the Ryan Memorial Trophy, also run at Cork. Another outstanding son, Gaultier Swank won the 1970 National Sprint, and two years later Tom's Pal, whelped in April 1969, won the 1972 National Sprint.

Yanka Boy was by Clonalvy Pride out of Millie Hawthorn, who was also dam of the English Derby winner Faithful Hope from a mating to Solar Prince and of Finola's Yarn from a mating to Finola, proving herself to be one of the best dams of all time. Clonalvy Pride's grandson was the Irish Derby winner Own Pride, who was Ireland's champion greyhound of 1969. Clonalvy Pride was an outstanding greyhound in his own right, winning the English St Leger in 1961 in 39.64 secs which has been bettered on only one occasion, by O'Hara's Rebel in 1967. Clonalvy Pride also won the Laurels in the same year, again in the fastest time recorded for the event until that date and which has never been equalled. In 1960 he reached the final of the English Derby, which was won by Duleek Dandy. Besides siring Yanka Boy, Clonalvy Pride sired Always Proud who won the Irish Derby in 1966, and who in turn was to sire Own Pride.

Yanka Boy's influence on modern greyhound racing was noticeable in the pedigree of the winner of the 1979 Irish Derby, Penny County, and of Nameless Pixie who finished third. From his mating with An Tain he was sire of Dark Mercury, sire of Penny County, and from his mating with Itsamint he produced Itsastar, dam of Nameless Pixie.

Yanka Boy's pedigree is given below.

YELLOW PRINTER

He was perhaps the fastest dog ever to race and won the Irish Derby in 1968 which is sufficient to give him immortality, but like

Yanka Boy	Clonalvy Pride	Solar Prince	Champion Prince
			Lisabelle
		Asmena	Westbury Sonny
			Leading Lady
	Millie Hawthorn	The Grand Fire	The Grand Champion
			Quare Fire
		Glittering Millie	Glittering Look
			Millie's May

Yellow Printer, the fastest Irish Greyhound Derby winner when he won in 1968. Photo: GRA.

Ataxy, Quare Times and Tanist he was almost too fast for most greyhound tracks with their sharp turns and did not possess the same ability to make the best of many attributes as did Mick the Miller, Monday's News and Pigalle Wonder and others noted for their trackcraft.

A fawn dog whelped in March 1966, he obtained his tremendous speed from his grand sire, Hi There, and his great grandsire through his grand dam, Sally's Gossip, whose sire was the great Endless Gossip. Owned by Sir Robert Adeane and Miss Pauline Wallis, the dog hit the headlines when making an early exit from the 1968 English Derby yet won the Irish Derby at Shelbourne Park in 29.11 secs, a time never beaten for this event and equalled only by Lively Band six years later. Yellow Printer won the final when beating Russian Gun, an equally fine greyhound, who had won the event the previous year. It was in a heat for the Derby that Yellow Printer was to become the first greyhound to break 29 secs for 525 yds at Shelbourne Park, when he won by nine lengths and clocked 28.83 secs which was unbeaten until Tantallon's Gift clocked 28.73 secs on 24 July 1976. Previously, in the Easter Cup run at the same track in April, Yellow Printer had reached the final, won by Itsamint, and gave some indication of his Derby potential. His fantastic run when winning his Derby heat made him the biggest favourite to win the event for years.

Once again in the final of a big event he came up against the great bitch Itsamint, owned by Mr Leslie McNair; also in the final were Hugh Marley's Russian Gun; Mr Carroll's Clinker Flash; Mr McCusker's Drumna Chestnut; and Ballybeg Flash. The race that night drew a huge crowd, since not for some years had the Derby been contested by such outstanding greyhounds. First from the traps were Ballybeg Flash and Russian Gun, both of whom occupied the outside traps and moved slightly wider at the first turn. It was then that Yellow Printer, in trap 4, moved inside and yielded not an inch until he had crossed the line one and a half lengths in front of Russian Gun, who hung on to him the whole way round and only conceded his crown to a younger dog after a tremendous effort. It was Yellow Printer's finest hour. In third place was another great dog, Drumna Chestnut, who was to beat Russian Gun by a short head to win the Ulster Derby at Celtic Park later that year.

Early in 1969 Yellow Printer again showed his amazing speed when winning the Sir Billy Butlin Stakes at White City when he clocked 28.38 secs, a time which was beaten only by himself. He again showed his liking for this track when winning the Wood Lane Stakes in 28.91 secs after being badly hampered at the first bend. He also won the Summer Cup at Wembley in 29.20 secs. In the Pall Mall at Harringay he won his heat in 28.71 secs to set a new track record, which he lowered to 28.60 secs when winning his semi-final in which he defeated the ultimate winner, Local Motive, by as much as six lengths but lost to him by a neck in the final. He was then flown to Shannon to represent England in the international at Limerick on 30 November, but he was beaten four lengths by Flaming King in 29.24 secs. He was elected Greyhound of the Year in 1969 and retired to stud to stand in Ireland at a fee of 75 gns, yet his name does not figure in any pedigree of present-day champions which is surprising for his own pedigree was outstanding:

Yellow Printer	Printer's Prince	Hi There	Slaney Record
			Dublin Red
		Sally's Gossip	Endless Gossip
			Castle Yard
	Yellow Streak	Odd Venture	Glittering Look
			Blarney Groves
		Shane's Judy	The Grand Fire
			Racing Boy

He was trained during most of his career by John Bassett at Clapton, who said of him: 'Placid types are best: they take nothing out of themselves and Yellow Printer is the perfect example.. He is quiet, placid, nothing ever disturbs him. He is the perfect gentleman at all times – an aristocrat of the canine world.' No words could better sum up this great champion.

YANKEE EXPRESS

His winning of the Scurry Cup three years in succession 1982, '83 and '84 earned him a place in the Hall of Fame and established him as one of the fastest over this distance (442 m) ever to run. It also established his trainer, George Curtis of Brighton as one of the greatest handlers of sprinters in the history of the sport for he had trained Wired to the Moon when this dog won the event in 1977.

A brindle dog whelped in October 1980 and British bred, his sire was the American bred, Pecos Jerry, his dam the bitch, King's Comet. Made favourite for the 1982 Scurry, he was beaten by 3½ lengths in his 1st round heat but won his 2nd round heat by 8 lengths and easily accounted for Decoy Ranch in his semi-final. In one of the closest finals ever, he defeated Lannon Lass by a short head with Decoy Ranch only a head behind, centimetres separating the three.

He took the 1983 Scurry in amazing style, winning his 1st round heat by 4½ lengths and his 2nd round heat by the same margin. Winning his semi-final by 6 lengths, he beat Squire Cass in the final by almost as much, in 26.84 seconds. There was only one dog in the event and it was his 17th win in 18 races. In that year, he also won the Pall Mall at Harringay in 28.55 secs and when 5/4 odds on favourite and in October at the same track, the Classic Select Stakes in 28.22 second and was chosen Greyhound of the Year for 1983.

Though entered for another attempt at the Scurry in 1984, he was not expected to win, yet he did. Opening up an early lead, he had a length to spare when crossing the line in front of Karina's Pal in 27.03 secs to become the first British greyhound to win the same classic flat race three times. Only a short head deprived the sport of a unique 'double' when his litter brother King's Merlin was beaten by Easy and Slow in the 1983 St. Leger.

FIGHTING

The term refers to the aggressive interference by one greyhound with another, during a race or trial. The local stewards will disqualify a greyhound which fights or turns its head against another greyhound. The owner of the disqualified greyhound forfeits all rights in the race, though the result of the race stands.

FILM APPEARANCES

The popularity of the sport and the Irish and English love of dogs was recognized by the film industry shortly after the advent of 'talkies'. In 1930, when Mick the Miller was a household name, he was invited to appear in the film *Wild Boy*. In America shortly afterwards the film *Dark Hazard*, starring Edward G. Robinson, centred on the career of a racing greyhound, its success and failure, which were coupled with those who had an interest in the dog. Another film depicting greyhound racing in America was *Johnny Eager*, which starred Robert Taylor and Edward Arnold. In England, shortly after the war, Daphne du Maurier's novel *Hungry Hill* was filmed; 'Greyhound John', its main character, forsakes his father's business for coursing. In 1947 that fine dog Rimmell's Black appeared in *The Turners of Prospect Road*. It was a time when the sport was enjoying its greatest popularity and any film with a greyhound in it was certain of success at the box office.

FIRST RACE IN BRITAIN

The first official race meeting was held at Belle Vue, Manchester, on 24 July 1926, under the auspices of the Greyhound Racing Association. The north was chosen for building the first track as whippet races had been run by the miners of Lancashire and Yorkshire and Derbyshire for many years and it was thought that greyhound racing would have a large following. Yet a crowd of only 1,600 witnessed the first meeting, and of these only about half paid for admission, but before the end of the year the sport was attracting crowds of 30,000 at Belle Vue and those who had faith in the venture were fully justified.

The first race, run over a distance of 440 yds on the flat, was won by eight lengths by a red dog, Mistley, carrying the blue coat from trap 2, in 25.00 secs. He was by Jack-in-Office out of a dam named Duck. The meeting consisted of six races, eight dogs taking part in each, for the rule limiting each race to a maximum of six greyhounds was not brought in until 1 January 1927. In this first meeting the programme consisted of three races over 440 yds; two over 500 yds; and one over 440 yds hurdles. This last was won by Melksham Autocrat by ten lengths in 27.80 secs. The judge's box was on the inside of the track and the hare was on the outside.

At the beginning racing was confined to the afternoons of the summer months since there was no overhead lighting for winter and evening racing. Three meetings were held each week, the last on 9 October.

The first meeting in London took place at White City on 20 June 1927, and in Northern Ireland (*see* First Race in Ireland) at Celtic Park on 18 April of that year.

FIRST RACE IN IRELAND

The first race run in Ireland was over 600 yds and took place at Celtic Park, Belfast, on Easter Monday 1927. The line up was as follows:

Trap 1	Mr S. Kissock's fwd Master Adams
Trap 2	Mrs P. Carson's wbld Calvo
Trap 3	Mr J. Tuite's fd Mutual Friend
Trap 4	Mr C. Sullivan's fd Strange Barry
Trap 5	Mr J. Fraser's bdd Gift
Trap 6	Mr R. Matthews bkd Real McCoy

The race took place at 3.30 and was won by Mr Jim Tuite's Mutual Friend (by Three Speed out of Lady Peggy) in 34⅔ secs. The dog was exactly four years old. In second place was Real McCoy. The dogs were wearing differently-coloured coats from those of today. They were: trap 1, purple; trap 2, cerise; trap 3, tangerine; trap 4, yellow; trap 5, green; and trap 6, white. The sum of £15 was given to the winner, a generous amount and worth £150 today. The second race was won by Mr A. McAlister's fawn dog Altmore, sired by the great Staff Officer, from trap 4.

The first race to be run in the Republic of Ireland took place at Shelbourne Park, Dublin, on 14 May 1927, and was run at 7.30. This was the first evening meeting in Ireland.

FLAPPING TRACK

A term used for those tracks which number about 100 and operate outside the jurisdiction and supervision of the NGRC. Owners who use them are disqualified from running greyhounds on all tracks licensed by the NGRC.

Flapping tracks must be licensed by the local authority before racing can take place, and they must operate within the terms of the Betting and Lotteries Acts. They mostly cater for the owner–trainer of one or two greyhounds and are frequented by those who keep a greyhound at home, while whippets are also raced on them. They are situated mostly in the industrial areas of the north, where people have traditionally kept a racing dog at home and where they can be easily reached on foot. These tracks have few amenities, but contrary to popular belief are conducted fairly. Anything detrimental to the running and health of the dogs is not tolerated, though the security and codes of racing are nothing like as strict as where racing is under NGRC rules.

FLAT RACE

A race run on the flat, not over hurdles. No more than 6 greyhounds may complete in a flat race, which may be a graded or handicap race. Smaller tracks, which have only limited kennelling, usually run five-dog events, omitting trap 6.

FOG

So great was the enthusiasm for the sport in the immediate postwar years, before TV kept people at home in the evenings, that so as not to disappoint the large crowd gathered at Wembley on 19 January 1946, when such dense fog came down that the dogs were unable to follow the hare, a light was fixed to the tail of the lure and racing continued normally, although neither spectators nor the dogs could see anything of the hare except the light! The full programme was completed and the results of each race flashed on the totalizator.

FOSTER MOTHER

Some breeders obtain the services of a foster mother if the bitch has more pups than she can manage, say more than eight or nine, or if she is unwell after whelping a litter. It is never advisable to kill any of the pups, however weak they may be. So often, the weed of the litter turns out to be the best, possibly because it receives the most attention.

If a bitch appears heavy in whelp it will give an indication of how many pups she will have and it will enable her owner to contact a breeder or to insert an advertisement in the local paper perhaps two weeks in advance, asking for the use of a foster mother who may have lost her own pups or have had only one or two, to take over several of the greyhound pups. The better the bitch has been looked after, the better will she be able to manage a large litter. Some can look after ten or eleven pups without undue strain, especially if the pups are assisted to lap as soon as possible.

Field dogs such as retrievers and spaniels, and sheepdogs, make the most suitable foster mothers. She must have the pups brought to her gradually, and if her urine is first rubbed on to them or they are allowed to lie on sacking which the foster mother has laid on she will take to them more readily. Do not leave her with the strange pups until you are quite sure she has taken to them. If she has one or two of her own she will usually take to them better. It is, however, important that the pups are not removed from their own mother until after the third or fourth day, for her milk will contain colostrum immediately after she has given birth and this acts as a mild purgative on the whelps.

The pups are weaned from the foster mother in the same way as they would be from their own mother.

See Bitch; Brood Bitch; Weaning.

G

GLASGOW RACECOURSE
See under British Greyhound Racecourses.

GLOUCESTER AND CHELTENHAM RACECOURSE
See under British Greyhound Racecourses.

GOLD COLLAR
See under Classic Events in Great Britain.

GOLDEN JUBILEE

The fiftieth anniversary of greyhound racing in Britain was on 24 July 1976, fifty years after the first track opened in Britain at Belle Vue, Manchester. The fiftieth anniversary of the opening of the first track in London, White City, was commemorated on 18 June 1977, just two days short of its fifty years.

The golden jubilee of the first meeting held in Ireland, at Celtic Park, was on 15 April 1977. On 14 May 1927 the first meeting was held in the Irish Republic, and on 21 May 1977 the president of Ireland, Dr P.J. Hillery, unveiled in the Shelbourne Park Stadium a plaque which reads: 'To commemorate fifty years of Greyhound Racing in Ireland, 1927–1977.'

GOSFORTH RACECOURSE
See under British Greyhound Racecourses.

GRADED RACE

A race in which greyhounds kennelled at a track are selected or graded as to their trial performances. Before a dog runs in its first graded race it must have run at least three trials at the track on separate days. This allows the racing manager to assess the dog's capabilities, fitness, and freedom from any interference with other dogs taking part in the same trials. In graded races greyhounds of a certain standard race together, with the starting boxes (traps) in a row.

In the rules of racing, a licensed trainer must have had charge of a greyhound for at least seven days prior to his final trial and before its first race.

GRADING

In every race run by greyhounds kennelled on a track (not open races) the dogs will be graded or grouped into sections so that in each race, except in handicap races, there will be dogs of similar ability. Usually the first two events will be composed of those greyhounds that may be new to the track and to racing, young dogs that run somewhat 'green' and have not yet developed any real track sense. The next two races will be for a better class or for more experienced dogs and may include a top-class bitch just back from her seasonal rest. There will usually be a race for hurdlers, one for long-distance runners (stayers) and one for sprinters, with the remaining event perhaps an open race for outside-kennelled greyhounds.

The racing manager must know the capabilities of every greyhound in the kennels including those that are back after a rest or injury, to give them a reasonable chance when first back to racing and in a lower than usual grade. He must know the wide runners and the sprinters, and those that cannot do more than the shorter distances. The weather and state of the track plays an important part in compiling his card, for certain dogs will run better in soft going than in hard going and vice versa; while some dogs run better in certain tracks than in others. If you know that a dog is in its favourite trap, back him to win. The racing manager must also consider a succession of wins or losses, lifting a dog with a number of wins to a higher grade or putting a dog with a succession of failures in a lower grade until it recovers its confidence. It is the aim of every racing manager to grade the dogs in every race so that they finish together. Even so, a dog's determination to reach the hare first may upset the most careful grading, and there are other factors such as a dog's failure to trap well, or it may slip on a wet surface or bump into another dog on a bend. If a dog is off colour just before a race, however slightly, it will affect his running.

Perhaps the finest grader in the history of the sport was Con Stevens, for many years racing manager at Wimbledon Stadium; because he was rarely known to be swayed by his emotions, however exciting the racing, he came to be known as 'The Sphinx'. When making up his card he gave each greyhound a class figure, beginning with A1 for the top race; A2 for a slightly lower grade, and so on all the way down to A8 which was allotted to the lowest-class dogs. After every race he awarded points to each of the six dogs taking part in relation to the position in which they finished. A league points table for each dog enabled him to see at a glance how the dogs moved up or down the table each week and he could grade them accordingly. So meticulous was Con Stevens in his efforts to please everyone and to give his patrons the best possible racing that he placed staff around the track at each meeting to note the position and running of each dog every few yards. This information was taken into consideration when making up his card for future meetings. Indeed, nothing at all was left to chance.

See Racing Manager.

GRAND NATIONAL

See Classic Events in Ireland.

GREATEST TRACK GREYHOUNDS

A personal choice of the best to have raced in Britain and in Ireland:

BRITAIN

DOGS	*BITCHES*
Ballymac Ball	Ballinasloe Blondie
Beef Cutlet	Bradshaw Fold
Brilliant Bob	Cranog Bet
Endless Gossip	Disputed Rattler
Future Cutlet	Dolores Rocket
Junior Classic	Hurry Kitty
Local Interprize	Kitshine
Mick the Miller	Narrogar Ann
Mile Bush Pride	Prancing Kitty
Monday's News	Quarter Day
Patricia's Hope	Queen of the Suir
Pigalle Wonder	Rio Cepretta
Priceless Border	Robeen Printer
Sherry's Prince	Shady Parachute
Trev's Perfection	Shaggy Lass
Wild Woolley	Sheevaun

IRELAND

DOGS	*BITCHES*
Abbeylara	Astra
Ballybeg Prim	Baytown Ivy
Lively Band	Catsrock Daisy
Own Pride	Clomoney Grand
Postal Vote	Cold Christmas
Prince of Bermuda	Fair Mistress
Rita's Choice	Hairdresser
Russian Gun	Itsamint
Shaggy Lad	Last Landing
Sole Aim	Mad Printer
Spanish Battleship	Monologue
Spanish Lad	Nameless Pixie
Tain Mor	Peaceful Lady
Time up Please	Penny County
Wonder Valley	Prairie Peg
Yanka Boy	Romping to Work

GREYHOUND BREEDERS' FORUM

It was founded on 1 January 1969 by Dr Richard Handley, who died shortly afterwards. It was his idea that greyhound breeders should meet as often as possible to discuss modern breeding methods with a view to improving the quality of greyhounds for track racing in Britain, and he envisaged an annual Breeders' Festival. This now takes place at Harringay on a Sunday in September, and attracts many breeders from all parts of Britain and Ireland and those who have an interest in promoting their products. The trainer Noreen Collin was for ten years secretary of the Breeders' Forum, and since its inauguration it has played an important part in greyhound racing. At the Festival there are classes for retired greyhounds and a parade of famous stud dogs, as well as numerous events for a dozen or so trophies, including the Dick Handley Memorial Stakes. *Greyhound Magazine* makes an award for the best one-year-old sapling registered with either the NCG or ICC, but not necessarily named. Mr David Poulter succeeded Dick Handley as chairman of the Greyhound Breeders' Forum.

GREYHOUND PRESS

Followers of the sport have been fortunate in that those who have written professionally about its many facets have become as widely respected as those who have covered the other British national sports of football and cricket. From the beginning the *Sporting Life, Daily Mirror, Daily Express* and London *Evening Standard* have been generous in their coverage, indeed they were among the very first sponsors, presenting handsome trophies to be won at the leading London tracks and which through the years have become prestige events (*see* Sponsorship).

The *Sporting Life* has through the years been well served by its writers, who are always fair and most knowledgeable. There was Leo Wilson in the 1930s and 1940s and later came Charlie Maskey, Archie Newhouse and Reg Potter, three of the most respected of all writers on the sport, the former now *Sporting Life's* greyhound editor. But by far the longest serving member of the greyhound journalists with *Sporting Life* was Albert Bright who retired in August 1980 after more than thirty years on the staff. It was in 1937 that he joined the *Greyhound Express*, serving them until 1948 except for wartime service abroad.

At the *Evening Standard* the greyhound editor is Jack Osborne, whose 'Greyhound Standard' gives in detail each Friday the weekend programmes for all the London tracks. At the *Evening News* Bob Richardson, now retired, was greyhound editor for many years. In 1928 William Wicks joined the *Evening Standard* as a junior reporter and saw Mick the Miller win his first Derby in 1929. Thirty years later he became greyhound racing editor, a position he held until his retirement twenty years on. He was founder chairman of the Greyhound Writers' Association, a position he also held until his retirement. Alf Hitch, 'King Cob' of *Sporting Life*, also made a considerable contribution to greyhound racing in its early days. He took over from the late Gerry Fitzgerald, who became greyhound editor of the *Evening News* in 1930 and remained so for many years.

In Ireland great pleasure has been obtained through the years by the informative writings of John Comyn of the *Irish Independent*, Harry Duff of the *Belfast Telegraph*, Tom Higgins of the *Cork Examiner*, who must have seen more Laurels run than anyone, Noel Anderson of the *Irish Times*, Mike Fortune of the *Irish Press* and John Martin of the *Dublin Evening Herald*. Each of these gentlemen of the press has rendered as great a service to Irish greyhound racing as have those of Fleet Street.

During its early years greyhound racing was covered in considerable detail by the *Greyhound Mirror and Gazette* whose chief correspondent was Isidore Green; and by the *Greyhound Evening Mirror*. The subscription was one shilling (5p) a week for the six daily issues, which also included postage! After fifty years they make interesting reading and show how well the sport was served by the press in those days. Present to see Mick the Miller win the 1931 St Leger at Wembley was Trevor Wignall, then sports editor of the *Daily Express*, who devoted a column of his famous Daily Sportlight to a description of the dog's amazing performance, while on the leader page of the *Daily Express* there appeared a special article about the most famous greyhound that ever lived. Other members of the press present at Wembley on that great occasion were L.V. Manning, sports editor of the *Daily Sketch*, and 'Dragoman' of the *Daily Express*.

Early in 1946 appeared *The Greyhound Owner*. A newspaper-style weekly, it cost 6d (2½p), a three months' subscription (thirteen issues), including postage, costing 8s (40p). The paper carried articles on young stock by Reg Sheath and on greyhound trainers by Bill Shepherd. The salerooms were covered by Harry Carpenter who periodically did a saplings sale analysis of considerable interest.

The issue for 7 April 1949 carried a large number of advertisements of dogs at stud, among which were Celtic Chief, at Stanley Biss's kennels at Waltham Cross, and Rimmell's Black, both at a fee of 25 gns. At Dartford Trev's Perfection stood at a fee of 50 gns, and Shannon Shore with Leslie Reynolds at the same fee. With Sidney Orton stood Burhill Moon at a fee of 35 gns, and at the same fee was Magic Bohemian, Jesmond Cutlet's greatest son.

The first issue of the *Greyhound Review* appeared in April 1946, with Frank Dowd as its editor and publisher. It continued to be published every month for four years. The first edition contained magnificent photographs of four of the finest bitches ever to race, Prancing Kitty, Shaggy Lass, Robeen Printer and Disputed Rattler, each of whom were racing between 1941 and 1945. The dominant theme was the perilous state of greyhound breeding in Britain after the war. The magazine cost 1s 6d (7½p) a copy, or £1 for a year's subscription, post free.

In 1932 appeared the *Greyhound Express*. It was published daily for the Greyhound Bureau Ltd from Fleet Lane, Farringdon Street, EC4, and cost 2d (1p). Most days the edition was of sixteen pages and on Saturdays contained the full programme for meetings at the London tracks. It also included advertisements for stud dogs and information articles. It closed down at the end of 1969. On the staff was Neil Martin who, during the mid-1960s, when sales of the *Greyhound Express* were declining in line with attendances at the tracks, had the idea of starting a monthly magazine to be devoted to the sport, with stories about famous greyhounds, events and personalities, for example owners and trainers. Backed financially by Norman Bowl, an estate agent and keen greyhound owner, Neil Martin and his friend the late John Bower launched the *Greyhound Magazine* in October 1968 and today it is still flourishing. Yet three years after its launching, the magazine found the going so difficult that a buyer was sought and found in John Jenkins, deputy night editor of the *Daily Telegraph*, who still retains control with Neil Martin as editor. Amongst its knowledgeable contributors each month are Archie Newhouse, Reg Potter and Harry Lloyd, who was in at the beginning and whose 'Mainly Personal' column provides readers with all the off-track information of interest. Alan Lennox covers the breeding of greyhounds with great interest and Bob Greeves writes from Northern Ireland, with Tom Kelly covering the Republic. Other popular contributors are Dennis Wray, Adrian Hunt and Bob Richardson.

In the Republic of Ireland the Coursing and Racing Calendar was formed in June 1926, with T.A. Morris as editor. The official organ of the Irish Coursing Club, it cost 3d (1½p) weekly and covered all aspects of coursing and track racing with the results of every race run in Ireland (including the North) during the previous week. It was superseded in December 1951 by the *Sporting Press* which incorporated the Coursing and Racing Calendar and became the official organ of the Irish Coursing Club and Irish Kennel Club. It also covered horse racing in Ireland, foxhound meetings, and Kennel Club meetings throughout the Republic, but to the greyhound lover it was nothing like so good as the old Coursing and Racing Calendar, since the greyhound coverage was considerably less. Thirty years on, the *Sporting Press* is again fully devoted to greyhound coverage, though sadly Jim Murphy, for long its editor, died in 1978. A kind and considerate man, he has had much to do with the success of the *Sporting Press* in recent years and is greatly missed.

GREYHOUND RACING ASSOCIATION

Known for short as GRA, this limited company was formed in 1926 with Sir William Gentle, a retired chief constable of Brighton, as its first chairman. Together with Brig.-General Critchley and an American,

Charles Munn, he put up the £22,000 needed to float the company and to build its first track. The head office was originally at Belle Vue, Manchester, where the first race took place on 24 July 1926. The company took over the White City Stadium, Shepherd's Bush in 1927 and in 1938 the company was granted a Stock Exchange quotation for its shares. In March 1972 the company took over Wimbledon Stadium, several of whose directors joined the GRA board. At present the GRA own the following tracks:

London (Harringay, Wimbledon, Catford); Birmingham (Hall Green); Manchester (Belle Vue); Glasgow (Shawfield); Edinburgh (Powderhall); Slough; Portsmouth.

At Northaw near Potter's Bar the GRA have their rest and breeding establishment, which consists of 150 acres with kennels grouped according to the tracks operated by the company. Here each trainer has his own block of kennels, assisted by a number of kennel lads and kennel maids.

During the 1970s the GRA had a chequered history, and the property boom of the early 1970s brought about a revaluation of the large areas of land held by the company situated in many of Britain's largest industrial cities. In 1972 the GRA renamed itself the GRA Property Trust with a view to redeveloping certain tracks as shops and flats. The result was that famous tracks at West Ham, where the Cesarewitch was held, and at Clapton, venue of the Scurry Gold Cup, were closed for racing, likewise that excellent venue Stamford Bridge. There were fears that if this was to continue the finest tracks in London and in the provinces would soon be lost to the sport. Then, with great suddenness, the bottom fell out of the property market, the shares of all property companies plummeted, and the GRA Property Trust found itself in grave financial difficulties. Early in 1975, with debts said to be near £20 million, for a time the company's Stock exchange quotation was suspended. Mr Jack Aaronson, who had a reputation in the City as one who could sort out the troubles of a company and put it back on its feet again, was called in and given a place on the board of directors. This meant that those tracks which had been under the threat of closure for some years because of their high redevelopment potential were enabled to continue the sport for another ten years but after the race meeting on September 22nd, 1984 an unexpected announcement from the GRA chairman, Mr Isadore Kerman said that the track had closed.

GREYHOUND RACING IN AMERICA

The first track was opened by Mr O.P. Smith and his partner George Sawyer at Tulsa in 1921, followed a few months later by one at Hialeah, Florida, which state has since been to the forefront in its promotion of greyhound racing. There are now twenty-five racing venues in Florida, the most important track being the West Flagler at Miami, a quarter-mile track with an inside hare. Equally important is the Miami Beach Kennel Club Stadium. At these two tracks annual attendances have passed the million mark, with tote takings of more than 50 million dollars. Similar figures may be quoted for the Southland Park Stadium at West Memphis, Arkansas; for the Wonderland Park Stadium, Revere, Boston; and for the Taunton track – the last two of which both opened in 1935. Multonomal in Oregon opened a year later.

In the USA, except in New York State, there is no legalized off-course betting as in Britain, so that track attendances are very much higher and tote takings amount to more than 100 million dollars annually. The seven states which permit greyhound racing collect some 70 million dollars each year in tax, the state of Florida contributing about half. More tracks continue to be opened, and for the past twenty years attendances have increased by 8 per cent annually, 20,000 for a meeting now being common, and the sport and all connected with it now earn some 1½ billion dollars annually.

In 1946 the American Track Operators' Association came into being with its headquarters at Miami, to provide a common meeting ground for all track operators and for discussion to assist in track management.

It is however, surprising that so few states (only seven) have recognized greyhound racing, of which Florida, Massachusetts, Arizona and Arkansas are the most important. The Wonderland Park Stadium was the first of the Massachusetts tracks, where greyhound racing is held under the auspices of the State Racing Commission who have representatives in attendance at every meeting. They also supervise the working of the totes and the kennelling of the greyhounds, which are privately trained under the contract system as now used in Britain. By law all greyhounds running at a meeting must be handed over to state officials two hours before each meeting to check the health of each dog and its identity. No dog whose weight varies by more than 1½ lbs at each weigh-in is allowed to take part.

Before a contract is signed with a trainer to provide greyhounds for a particular track, the track will inspect the kennels and equipment to ensure that it is of the highest standards. The track must also be certain that the trainer is able to provide at least thirty greyhounds for each meeting, which means, that allowing for bitches in season and injured dogs, a kennel must have in training at least fifty greyhounds. In America ten races make up a meeting, and each race has eight greyhounds.

The contract kennels deduct a percentage of prize money for handling expenses, for often the dogs have to be transported 100 miles or more to the tracks. The larger tracks have as many as thirty kennels under contract and perhaps 1,200 or more greyhounds permanently available. With prize money high and competition keen to provide the tracks with top-class dogs capable of winning considerable sums, owners are always on the look-out for good dogs and racing is of a high standard. In any case a good greyhound will eat no more than a poor dog, and will take the same amount of time in training and handling. The dogs are graded into four categories, those in A class running in top races and earning most prize money, so the kennels are keen to supply as many top-class dogs as possible. If they do not maintain a high standard they may lose their license, for others are always waiting to obtain one of the lucrative contracts.

Racing kennels at the tracks have glass doors through which the public can view the dogs during a meeting. All races are electric ray-timed and finishes are photographed. This is even more important than in Britain, since eight dogs make up a race and the tote pays out on the first three. It would be difficult for a judge to declare the first three in a close race without the aid of cameras. By state law it is laid down that unless there is a length's difference between each greyhound for the winner and second and third place, only a photo shall determine the positions.

The state commissioners, who have the power to draw up the rules and regulations for the tracks under their jurisdiction, also keep an account of the books and tote receipts, to ensure that the state is receiving the correct percentage of takings. State auditors work out the exact amount of tote deductions as soon as each race is finished.

Win and place betting is done with two and three dogs; also what is known as 'daily doubles' which takes into consideration winners of first and third races, second and fourth, and so on. With eight dogs taking part tote takings are larger than in Britain and the pay-outs considerably more.

Automatic all-glass starting boxes are used so that the dogs can be seen when in the traps. The hare runs either inside or outside. The colours for each dog are: no.1, red; 2, blue; 3, white; 4, green; 5, black; 6, orange; 7, green and white; 8, black and yellow.

Though most of the racing takes place in the eastern states, most greyhounds are bred and reared some 2,000 miles from the main centres, in the middle western states where food is cheaper and more easily obtained and where the flat country is ideal for rearing puppies. Before being sent to the contract kennels the puppies are trained on home-made tracks to chase a dummy hare fastened to the end of an arm about 40 ft long. The puppies are first slipped by hand, then placed in starting boxes which are hand-released, so that by the time they are old enough to race they are thoroughly used to the procedure.

The first greyhounds to reach America went over with the early settlers, for they were needed to catch hares and rabbits for meat just as they did in Britain. The mid-western states, where hares were plentiful, remain the centre of the breeding industry and from the beginning of track racing many top-class dogs have been introduced from Britain and Ireland. The rise in exports from Ireland in the past twenty years has been considerable. In 1959 seventeen greyhounds valued at £2,500 were exported to the USA: in 1969 300 went, valued at £100,000; and in 1977 807 greyhounds were exported to the USA, valued at £360,000.

One of the important early importations was from Australia, however. He was a sire called Just Andrew who, when mated to an Irish-bred bitch called Mustard Roll, produced Lucky Roll, sire of Lucky Sir. For some years he stood at the kennels of Ohlinger and Blair at Jewels, Kansas City, and was the first to command a stud fee of 100 dollars. He was to sire Flashy Sir, winner of the American Derby and who was to dominate track racing there in the 1940s as Mick the Miller had done in Britain a decade earlier. Flashy Sir's pedigree went back to Mutton Cutlet and his sire Jamie on the dam's side, so that these great sires were to play as important a part in the early years of track racing in the USA as they had done in Britain. From eighty starts Flashy Sir won on sixty-two occasions and was second ten times, setting track records wherever he ran, several of which remain unbeaten after nearly forty years.

Another of Lucky Roll's offspring was Never Roll, a dog which at one time held two world records and who is still considered to be the fastest dog ever to race. He was to become sire of Lucky Pilot, owned by Mr Holmes of Revere, Boston, and his great record of sixty-one wins and ten seconds from eighty-four starts was bettered only by Flashy Sir. A brindle, he had Just Andrew on both sides of his pedigree. This great Australian sire was the foundation stone upon which American greyhound racing was built.

At about the time Just Andrew had reached the United States, Upside Down also arrived from Australia, and he too had Mutton Cutlet as his sire. It was through the female line that he was to pass on his wonderful speed, and among his offspring were Thrilling Sport, dam of Mixed Harmony; Johnny Leonard; Great Valor; and Fieldcrest. Lucky Bannon, too, could trace his ancestry to Upside Down and he was to win the American Derby and become a force at stud. His sire was Michigan Jack, who was a son of the Bella's Prince dog Julius Caesar, an Irish importation in the 1950s.

Never Roll's outstanding son was the brindle Real Huntsman, whelped in February 1948 out of the bitch Medora. He was to become the only greyhound ever to win the American Derby twice, which he did in 1950 and 1951, having been voted in 1949 the outstanding puppy of the year. He also holds the world record for consecutive wins, having won twenty-seven races in succession between 1 April 1950 and 3 June 1951, most of them in eight-dog races.

Another of the early stars was Traffic Office, owned by Mr Art Wilson, who sold him when his racing days were over to Mr George Oswald, for whom the dog earned more than 30,000 dollars in stud fees.

In more recent years the bitch Miss Whirl has captured the hearts of racegoers in the USA by her gameness and won over 100,000 dollars in her career, while Mortar Light, a son of Newdown Heather, won 60,000 dollars and reached the final of the American Derby in 1971 and 1972. Another outstanding recent greyhound to race in the United States was Rocking Ship, bred and reared in Co. Kerry, Ireland, by Mr Jimmy Lyne. After winning the Rose of Tralee Cup in 1970, the dog was purchased by Mr David Cahill, an Irishman living in Chicago, and placed with Pat Dalton, an Irish-born trainer at the Flagler track in Florida. There he was to break Flashy Sir's twelve consecutive wins and over the marathon course bettered his own record on three occasions and twice at the Biscayne track. In all he ran fifty-four times, winning forty-four, and was second on five occasions; in two years he won over 100,000 dollars in prize money.

Later Don Cuddy of Boston was to train the great black, who won the Irish–American Marathon by eleven lengths. When the dog retired he was expected to earn at least a further 100,000 dollars in stud fees. But shortly after running his last race he was bitten by either a snake or a spider when out exercising and died within twenty-four hours.

GREYHOUND RACING IN AUSTRALIA

At about the same time that greyhound racing was starting in England an attempt was made to start the sport in Australia, the instigator being an American, a Mr Swindell, and an Irish priest, Father Meaney, living in New South Wales and who was a keen follower of coursing there. They were able to obtain valuable backing for the new sport with the result that the Greyhound Association was formed and was granted a licence by the New South Wales government to hold greyhound meetings. The first meeting took place on 28 May 1927, only a fortnight after the first meeting at Shelbourne Park, Dublin. But there were difficulties, for the government would not at first license the tracks for betting. Soon, however, Mr Andy Lysaght declared that the new sport should be fully recognized and the Games and Betting Act was passed by which the tracks were granted betting licences.

Mechanical hare racing as it was called was first legalized in New South Wales and Tasmania, with evening racing and totalizator betting, control of which was in the hands of the Greyhound Racing Board of New South Wales, a body which included owners of greyhounds and trainers. From the beginning the principal state for greyhound racing has been New South Wales, where the first track to open was Harold Park, Glebe. Other tracks in the state are at Sydney, which claims the world record for 500 yds with a time of 26.90 secs and where ten-dog races are normally held; and the Iklawarra track, where eight-dog races are run, which is more usual in Australia. Here racing takes place on Saturday evenings over 500 yds and 710 yds.

All track racing in New South Wales comes under the control of the Greyhound Racing Council, similar in its functions to the British NGR Society, while the National Coursing Association of New South Wales controls the registration of greyhounds, transfers, etc. When a stud dog serves a bitch the NCA must be informed within seven days and given the name of the bitch, that of her owner, and her pedigree and markings.

Stringent rules and regulations govern the running of a meeting. All dogs must be in the racing kennels at least an hour before racing starts; the dogs are weighed and if found to be 2 lbs over or below their last running weight they are disqualified and their owner fined. All dogs are examined by a vet in attendance and identity cards must be lodged with the racing manager seven days before they take part in a race.

Fighting is not tolerated and any dog which does so is suspended for a month and for two months for a second offence. Stewards appointed by the GRC have powers to enter kennels to inspect the dogs and to report on any irregularities.

Bookmakers, who have first to obtain a licence from the state authorities, are subject to the jurisdiction of the GRC and betting tickets must contain details of the bet made, otherwise in a dispute judgement may be given against the bookmaker.

Throughout Australia the states have established Totalizator Agency Boards. By law they are required to include all money wagered off-course in the on-course pools before racing commences. All off-course investments are required to be added to the totalizator on each course fifteen minutes before each race commences. The information is telephoned from each Agency direct to the course, where it is received by a TAB agent who informs the tote operator. The bets placed on each dog (or horse) are shown before the on-course investor places his bet. Off-course betting with a bookmaker is not allowed.

The legalized control of tote betting throughout Australia has resulted in a new interest in the sport, and with it has come a demand for better performances by the greyhounds and increased prize money. The tracks normally hold one meeting each week of ten races, each with eight dogs which are privately owned and trained. At the Melbourne tracks, Sandown and Olympic Park, attendances of 10,000 for a meeting are usual, but the New South Wales tracks draw crowds of up to 15,000, especially at the Sydney tracks of Wentworth and Harold Park, where prize money averages £5,000 a meeting. The photo-finish is not used in Australia; the judge's decision is final.

One of Australia's finest racing greyhounds was Chief Havoc, at one time holder of ten track records over all distances. Romance surrounds the champion for he was purchased as a puppy for only £9 by a small boy who had never before owned a dog. Chief Havoc won on eleven tracks and of his first twenty-two races he won seventeen. It was as a stayer that he will be remembered. At the Maitland track over

740 yds he clocked 40.70 secs, then the fastest time in the world over this distance, and knocking ten lengths off the previous record. Another world record was set at Harold Park when he clocked 44.50 secs for the 800 yds course. The Harold Park track is one of the fastest as well as being one of the longest, for over the 500 yds course there is only one bend.

The outstanding bitch of recent times was Zoom Top, owned and bred by Mr Hector Watt. In a career lasting two and a half years she won more than £30,000 for her owner. By Black Top out of Busy Beaver, she was a fawn, whelped in August 1966, and she had her first race late in October 1967. When she retired in June 1970, out of 137 races she was first or second on ninety-three occasions and set new records on twelve different tracks. At the Wentworth Stadium she twice set a new record for 790 yds. When she retired her place was taken on the tracks, though not in the affections of Australian race-goers, by the black bitch Tara Flash, by Spotted Lightning out of Banner Maid. She was chosen Greyhound of the Year for 1970, when in twenty-two races she was first or second on seventeen occasions. Her great rival was the bitch Shapely Escort, owned and trained by Mrs Drady. At the Harold Park track she won eight races from nine starts over all distances.

GREYHOUND STUD BOOK

The Waterloo Cup had been inaugurated twenty-three years when, in 1858, the first official body, the National Coursing Club was formed. This was following the first sixty-four-dog stake event, for by then the Waterloo Cup had earned worldwide recognition in the coursing calendar. Henceforth all greyhounds taking part in any coursing event anywhere in the British Isles had to be registered with the NCC. The 1859 Waterloo Cup meeting at Altcar was the first held under NCC rules but it was not until 1881 that the NCC decreed that all greyhounds running at any meeting held under its rules were to be registered after 15 July 1883, and by that date nearly 1,000 entries had been received.

The first Stud Book appeared in 1882 and contained entries received up until early that year. Of these 351 greyhounds registered were black or black and white and only 68 were of the now common brindle colouring which was bred into the breed from Lord Orford's bulldog crossing which had taken place a century before.

The second Stud Book, published in 1883, contains 5,766 entries and a list of stud dogs. One of these was the blue dog McPherson whose fee was 7 gns, and another was the famous Misterton, a black and white dog who had won the Waterloo Cup in 1879 and was standing at a fee of 15 gns.

For a decade J. Brown was keeper of the Stud Book. When W. Lamonley took over in 1892, he introduced the system of entries we know today. The issue of 1894 stated that henceforth all litters were to be registered within two months of the date of birth.

From 1917 to 1932 the Stud Book was compiled by H.A. Groom whose successor was S.H. Dalton, a man of Kent and a keen cricketer who was secretary of the NCC and Keeper of the Stud Book until 1964 when T.H. Ball took over. Already in the office of the NCC with Mr Ball was Olive Turner, working as a junior clerk, and it was this lady who took over from Mr Ball upon his retirement in 1976.

It was Mrs Olive Turner who, in 1980, introduced a new Greyhound Identity Card which is sent to all those registering a litter or a greyhound with the English Stud Book. It contains the name of the greyhound, its earmark and certificate of registration number and is issued with the seal of the Greyhound Stud Book. There is a page for a greyhound's identification markings and space for registering transfer of ownership.

GREYHOUND TRACKS

A greyhound track can be of any size and shape. Certain tracks are almost circular, while others are more oval, but to enable the spectators to see the dogs throughout the race, which mostly takes about 30 secs to complete, the track must not be too large. Running tracks are mostly constructed with two straights of about 100 yds long, which are joined together to make up the track by two almost half circles or arcs (known as ends) which are banked to prevent the greyhounds running off the track when reaching high speeds at the end of the straights.

Of two famous tracks which are now closed down, West Ham had a circumference of 562 yds with 123 yds straights and was the fastest track in Britain, while Clapton had only 75 yds straights and very long bends of 103 yds, making the circumference about 365 yds. Today the White City, London, has the largest circumference in Britain, of 500 yds, with 120 yds straights, while Southend is almost a replica of the old Clapton Stadium with 75 yds straights and bends of about 150 yds.

There is a wide variation between all tracks, the smaller tracks best suiting the smaller dog and the one which prefers to run on the inside. Wide runners rarely do well on such a track. There have always been greyhounds which have their favourite tracks, and those kennelled at a certain track soon become used to them. If successful, they should not be moved to another track, possibly with sharper bends, unless for a definite reason. The privately trained dog, though it will have its favourite tracks, because it contests events all over Britain which appear most suited to its capabilities will not get used to any particular track.

Overhead lights enable the entire race to be seen at night when meetings are frequently held. The running surface is of grass (in winter, often covered with peat which makes for slower times) which is the best surface for the feet of greyhounds since it is free of grit and shingle which would make their feet sore, as would a concrete or asphalt surface. A grass track also has a certain amount of 'give' which protects a greyhound's legs.

GUINNESS NATIONAL SPRINT
See Classic Events in Ireland.

GUINNESS ULSTER DERBY
See Classic Events in Ireland.

HACKNEY RACECOURSE
See under British Greyhound Racecourses.

HALIFAX RACECOURSE
See under British Greyhound Racecourses.

HALL GREEN RACECOURSE
See under British Greyhound Racecourses.

H

HANDICAP RACES

These have been popular in the north since the start of greyhound racing, but not in the south where patrons prefer to have all the dogs starting from level traps (six in a row) with the dogs suitably graded. Staggered traps are frequently seen on northern tracks where the front trap is on the outside and may be several yards in front of the back marker. Usually, 1 m is allowed between each trap, so that the front runner may be 5 m in front of the back marker in a six-dog race. The elimination of first bend congestion is the chief advantage of staggered races. A well-graded staggered race often ends in an exciting climax, with the back marker often giving 5 m start to the front dog but just managing to pass the other dogs at the finishing line.

HARE CONTROLLER

After the racing manager, his is the most important job in track management. He is appointed by a race track with the approval of the stewards of the NGRC, who will grant him a licence annually. He must be present at all trials and races and is responsible for starting the hare from a position out of the direct vision of greyhounds in the starting traps; the hare must be kept within reasonable distance of the greyhounds during a trial or race. This calls for a great deal of experience since acceleration and deceleration need split-second judgement. The dogs leave the traps when the hare is about 10 m in front of them and should be kept at about this distance throughout the race. There are difficulties when the leading dogs may bump together at a bend and lose speed or where the going is heavy and the dogs may begin to fade; in such instances the hare must be slowed down in case the dogs lose sight of it. The hare must never be allowed to pass the starting traps twice before the dogs are released. After the race the hare continues round the course and into its box, hidden from the dogs.

The hare controller is situated high above the Stadium so that he can watch the race throughout. In front of him is a speedometer which enables him to keep the hare at a given speed except when difficulties arise, such as bumping or a leading dog falling at a hurdle; or if a trackless hare is in use, rain may cause the driving ropes to stretch and slip so that more power in necessary to keep the hare at its usual distance of 10 m in front of the leading dog. Co-ordination of hand and eye is essential to the correct working of the hare, and this comes only with long experience. The trackless hare, which is silent in its running and provides greater flexibility in its control, is now the most popular type.

HARE, ELECTRIC

The lure or mechanical hare which replaced the live hare of coursing. The first recorded instance of greyhounds following a dummy hare took place more than 100 years ago, at the Welsh Harp, Hendon, when *The Times* for 11 September 1876 carried a report headed 'Coursing by Proxy', and described the use of the mechanical hare:

> For a distance of 400 yds, a rail was layed on grass in a straight line and on it was mounted an artificial hare on wheels. It was made to travel at any required pace and so resembles the living animal, that it is eagerly pursued by greyhounds. On Saturday afternoon at 3.30, the meeting was due to commence and when the time came, all that was seen was the artificial hare bounding out, followed at once by the greyhounds.

The report concluded: 'the new sport is undoubtedly an exciting and interesting one.' The hare was operated by a windlass and the race was run on a straight 400 yds course. It was watched by a small crowd who were most enthusiastic.

In 1890 a patent was taken out for a circular track and mechanical hare but nothing happened after the event at Hendon until 1920 when O.P. Smith, an Oklahoma sportsman, took up the idea of greyhounds chasing an artificial hare in an enclosed space and the idea quickly snowballed. Within twelve months several tracks had opened in the USA which led Mr Charles Munn to believe that by 1926 there would be a commercial future for the sport in Britain. His meeting early that year with Major Lyne-Dixon resulted in the formation of the GRA, and the first meeting of greyhounds chasing an electric hare was held at Belle Vue, Manchester, on 24 July.

The electrically operated hare runs either on the inside (near the inner fence) or the outside of the track, and is usually one of three types: M.S. Cable, Sumner, or McWhirter trackless. The hare or lure is made to look as much like a live hare as possible but hare skins, used in the early days of the sport, are not now used as they will not stand up to the intense vibration, the weather, or the dogs if they catch it when there is a mechanical failure. If the hare is let into the ground it is not made in an arc at the bends but in short straights, which gives the hare an erratic movement like the running of a live animal.

Automatic starting is done by a simple mechanism attached to the rail on which the hare runs, whereby a trigger or rangement is attached by a wire to the starting boxes which open at the passing of the hare. Automatic starting assures race-goers that the hare controller plays no part in the result of a race by giving a late start. The dogs leave the traps when the hare is about 10 m in front of the traps, or in a graded race about 8 m in front of the dog allocated the front trap or with the biggest lead.

The Sumner hare is mounted on a trolley and moves in a zigzag fashion as well as making some noise as it travels round the track, while the trackless McWhirter is silent when running. Few dogs show fighting tendencies when following the Sumner hare. They do so only when they lose interest.

At the first meeting at Wembley Stadium, on 10 December 1927, the dog Palatinus caught the hare and there had to be a re-run.

HARE PATH

This is the position of the electric hare on a track and it varies; sometimes it is on the inside (near the rails) where it favours dogs drawn in trap 1, and sometimes on the outside where it favours dogs in trap 5 or 6. On smaller tracks and those with short straights and sharp bends the hare is usually on the outside. This lessens the convergence on the bends and also enables the dogs to keep it in sight, which would be difficult if it was on the inside. The position of the hare is important to those who attend race meetings for betting purposes, and where the hare is on the inside, dogs in traps 1 and 2 are most likely to succeed except when the going is soft in wet weather. The inside track is usually muddy and those dogs from the outside traps (4 and 5 or 5 and 6), where the ground is less churned up, will stand a better chance of winning especially where the race is over 500 m. Against this, however, it must be remembered that a greyhound running in the outside position round a track of 500 m circumference has to cover an extra 15–16 m. This does not have the same effect in a long-distance race as it does over a short distance – an important point for the punter.

HARE STARTER
He is a different official from the hare controller. The starter sees that each greyhound is in its trap and in a comfortable position. When he is quite sure that each greyhound is safely in the traps, without further delay he gives the signal for the hare to be released. The same official is in attendance during trials.

HARRINGAY RACECOURSE
See under British Greyhound Racecourses.

HENLOW RACECOURSE
See under British Greyhound Racecourses.

HODDESTON RACECOURSE
See under British Greyhound Racecourses.

HULL RACECOURSE
See under British Greyhound Racecourses.

HURDLES RACES
No more than five greyhounds compete in a hurdles race and there must be at least four hurdles in a race of more than 400 m and three hurdles in one of up to 400 m. If a hurdle falls during a race it should be replaced if possible, but any greyhound that takes advantage of a fallen hurdle is not disqualified.

The first race over hurdles took place at Belle Vue, Manchester on the opening meeting on 24 July 1926, and was won by Melksham Autocrat by ten lengths in 27.80 secs. The second track to hold hurdles racing was Celtic Park, Belfast, and the classic event for hurdlers, the Grand National, was first run at the White City, London in 1927 and is permanently allocated to that track.

It is surprising how many greyhounds debarred from racing on the flat because of fighting tendencies or interfering with another dog have taken to hurdling without the slightest trouble and have raced for years perfectly cleanly. The future hurdles champion Blossom of Annagurra, disqualified on the flat, was to become a champion over hurdles, winning more than £2,000 in prize money and setting up a new hurdles record at Wembley Stadium after the war.

The Grand National is the first of the year's classics, run in April over 500 m with a first prize of £2,000 and is now sponsored by the *Daily Mirror (see under* Classic Events in Britain). Then follows Wimbledon's important Gold Cup, which has been contested since 1929 and takes place late in April. Most of the great hurdlers have won this event including Long Hop, Sprightly Peter and Sherry's Prince, three times winner of the Grand National. The winner of the Gold Cup in 1978 was Moreen Penguin, the 12–1 outsider, privately trained by Miss Godwin. The dog had in the previous month won the William Hill Hurdles at Watford. March and April are busy months in the calendar for hurdlers. In March is run the Yorkshire Hurdles at Leeds, an event now sponsored by Britvic who also sponsor the Britvic Hurdles Cup run at Crayford in October. This was won in 1978 by Topothetide, who in the same year had won the Yorkshire Hurdles and the Grand National. At Crayford in February is run the *Daily Express* Hurdles and in March the *Daily Mail* and *Evening News* Hurdles is held at the White City. In 1978 this was won by Mr P. Leeper's Out All Night, who also took the *Daily Mirror* Hurdles at Harringay earlier in the month. In July the Whitbread National is held at Brighton over 500 m, and in August the Heart Foundation Hurdles at the White City over a similar distance. In September comes the important Midlands Grand National, sponsored by Courage's brewery, and which is run at Hall Green.

The Wimbledon Perpetual Challenge Trophy, run in September, is unique in that a hurdler kennelled at the track is selected to run against five others selected by a panel of pressmen. Then, to complete the year, the long-established Christmas Vase is run at the same track. Fastest time for this event was the 28.99 secs done by Innsbruck in 1966.

Great hurdlers of the past include Stylish Cutlet, Long Hop, Scapegoat, Juvenile Classic, Printer, Gypsy Win, Blossom of Annagurra, Macoma, Derryboy Jubilee, Sherry's Prince, Topothetide and Bobcol.

HURDLERS

BLOSSOM OF ANNAGURRA

This brindle dog by Speedy Danger out of Orchard Blossom was whelped in June 1945 and was to become one of the most consistent over hurdles in the history of the sport. Early in his career, when running the flat races, he was disqualified for fighting but when tried over hurdles he showed no tendencies to interfere with other dogs and soon earned the applause of all who followed the sport in the immediate postwar years. He raced almost twice a week during 1949 and won nearly £2,000 in prize money for his Ramsgate owner, Mr A.W. Wood. After showing great ability over hurdles in the early weeks of 1949 he was entered for the Grand National, the first of the season's classics. Almost unknown, his chances of winning were not considered great and in his heat he was quoted 16–1. He won this by four lengths from Ross Abbey, and won his semi-final by three lengths from the same dog. He continued to show exceptional form and won the final by two and a half lengths from the favourite, Dangerous Prince.

He next contested an open event at White City and again beat Ross Abbey, this time by ten lengths. A week later he set a new record at Wembley for the 525 yds hurdles with 29.94 secs, the first time that 30 secs had been broken at the track. In early July he was back at the White City and in an open beat Sprightly Peter. In the Hackney Cup at Clapton in August he was once again to defeat his old rival, this time by two and a half lengths. During 1949 he was one of the outstanding performers over hurdles.

After his second Grand National win at the White City in 1950 this great dog contested the Irish Grand National at Kilkenny and became the first dog (Queen of the Suir won the English and Irish Oaks) and only the second greyhound in the history of the sport to have won the same classic event in both Britain and in Ireland. The dog was more than five years old when he won the Irish Grand National and is the oldest greyhound ever to have won a classic event there.

Blossom of Annagurra was one of the outstanding bargains in the whole history of greyhound racing, for he was bought for £100 and before his heat for his first Grand National he was quoted at 16–1 against; though he won his heat and semi-final by a comfortable margin he was quoted at 8–1 against for the final which he won.

DANGEROUS PRINCE

Trained by Ken Appleton at West Ham, he was perhaps the greatest all-rounder in the history of the sport, good over all distances, on any track, and as good over hurdles as on the flat. Wherever he ran, he never gave a poor performance and those who saw him remember him with great affection. 1949 was his best year. He began at West Ham, his home track, in the April Stakes over 550 yds hurdles which he won by six lengths from Ross Abbey. It was a loosener for the Grand National in May, and in winning his heat by fourteen lengths he set a new track and national record of 29.39 secs. In the semi-final, however, he could only finish third and lost the final to his old rival Blossom of Annagurra, who beat him by two and a half lengths. Next came the White City Derby trials in June, which he won by seven lengths on the flat in 29.07 secs, only one or two dogs having improved on this; he won his heat in the Derby by two and a half lengths from Sailing at Dawn, with Local Interprize third, four and a half lengths behind.

Dangerous Prince was third in his semi-final and was the 14–1 outsider for the final, in which he followed Narrogar Ann all the way round and was closing on her as she crossed the line one and a half lengths in front of Dangerous Prince who took second place after a magnificent effort. After a rest he was in action again in October when he won over 525 yds hurdles at Harringay by ten lengths from Baytown Fox, and he next contested the Millfield Cup at Clapton, winning his heat and semi-final from

Blossom of Annagurra, an equally reliable performer, but once again was beaten in a final, this time by Ross Abbey. At West Ham in December he won the 550 yds hurdle event by five lengths from Creamery Lieutenant, and just before the year ended he won his heat for the Xmas Vase at Wimbledon but again was beaten in the final, this time by Sprightly Peter who thoroughly deserved his success. Throughout the year Dangerous Prince had raced almost twice weekly, over all distances, and on all the London tracks. Never once did he give a poor performance. He would have been a worthy Grand National winner but it was not to be. He ran up in the two premier classic events, which no other dog ever did.

DERRY PALM

This fawn dog, by O'Leary out of Fannie Caesar, was whelped in May 1967 and was one of the greatest hurdlers of all time. He broke track records over hurdles at Charlton, Catford and Romford and twice won the Midlands Grand National at Hall Green and the Thameside Hurdles at Charlton. He also won the Welsh and Scottish Grand Nationals, the Wimbledon Gold Cup and Christmas Vase and the Cobb Hurdles at Catford. In 1969 and 1970 he won nearly £6,000 in prize money and sixty-four open events. Rarely was he out of the first two.

DERRYBOY JUBILEE

This outstanding dog was born in 1941 and as there were no classic events during the war years he had no opportunity to win a Grand National, yet he was one of the greatest jumpers in the history of the sport. By Fine Jubilee out of Swiss Miss, he was descended through Fine Jubilee's Silver Seal II from Macoma, Mick the Miller's litter brother, from whom most of the sport's finest hurdlers were descended.

Originally owned by Miss Gertrude Stockman, Derryboy Jubilee was purchased by Mrs Sanderson for 1,250 gns, the highest price paid for a greyhound at public auction (Aldridge's) in England up to that time, 1943. The following year he showed what a bargain he was for he won the Silver Plume at Eastville; the Chase at Walthamstow; the Empire Stakes at Wembley; and the Catford Hurdles Stakes where he set a new 600 yds hurdles record with a time of 36.31 secs. In 1945 he won the Wimbledon Gold Cup from his great rival Wandering Lad, and in 1946, when five years old, won his first round heat of Wimbledon's Christmas Vase by twenty lengths from Nilo in 30.07 secs and the final by a neck from Witchford First in 30.17 secs, to end a great career during which he won over £4,000 in prize money when £100 was the maximum for most events.

FACE THE MUTT

Owned by Mr Vic Thirwell and trained by Nora McEllistrim, this son of Mutt's Silver and Mill Road Cast was whelped in June, 1979 and is a fawn dog weighing 70 lbs. His record over hurdles is without parallel in the history of the sport for in 1981, he won the Irish Grand National at Thurles and the 1982 Daily Mirror National at White City. Beaten by a neck in his 1st round heat by Westmead Prince, he reversed the decision in his semi-final and won in 30.09 seconds, a new track record. He again beat this fine hurdler by 2 lengths when winning the final after leading all the way. He thus became one of the few dogs to win a classic in two countries and in July 1982, he became the first greyhound to win the same event in three countries when he took the Scottish National, though not classic status, beating Power's Pride by 2 lengths in 28.99 secs. For this event he was trained by Alex Race of Middlesborough.

JUVENILE CLASSIC

By Beef Cutlet out of Lady Eleanor, a combination of classic breeding certain to bring success, this brindle dog was litter brother to one of the greatest of all, Junior Classic, and was whelped in 1936 from a second mating of sire and dam. Lady Eleanor's sire was the great hurdler Macoma, litter brother of Mick the Miller, and her dam was Nanki Poo. Owned by Mr J.J. Cleaver, in less than three years' racing the two sons of Macoma won more than £7,000 in prize money when £100 was the sum usually awarded to a winner of a top event.

In his short career Juvenile Classic won over £2,700 and seventeen trophies, which gives some idea of his ability. He twice won the Grand National, in 1938 and 1940, the last time at four years old when his time of 30.23 secs was faster than on the first occasion; only Sherry's Prince has a better record in this event. In three years he set up five national hurdles records over all distances, including a time of 25.58 secs over 440 yds and 31.40 secs over 550 yds, both of which were made in 1938. At one time, he held seven track records over hurdles and for three years was invincible, rarely stumbling over the hurdles while possessing the speed and stamina of Beef Cutlet, his sire. Trained at Wembley by Joe Harmon, the great dog died in his sleep at Christmas 1942, shortly after retiring from racing, and before he could pass on his wonderful ability to any offspring.

LONG HOP

A magnificent white and brindle dog by Macoma out of Bright Emblem, he was whelped in 1930 and his breeder was Mr L. Lake who owned his dam. Long Hop was from the first mating of sire and dam and he raced with the same distinction over hurdles as Mick the Miller did on the flat. Both were at their peak together. In 1932 Long Hop took the Grand National, the Empire Stakes at Wembley, and the Challenge Trophy at Wimbledon, all over hurdles, and during the last six months of the year he won sixteen consecutive hurdles events in top class, a winning sequence never before or since equalled.

From a second mating to Macoma, in 1931, Bright Emblem produced an equally fine jumper, Scapegoat, who was to win the Grand National in 1933 for his owner, Mr Lake. No one else has won the premier hurdles event with two different greyhounds.

PRINTER

By Creamery Border out of the bitch Dumont, he was the first of his sire's sons to show that Creamery Border was destined to become as great a force at stud as he was on the track. Printer began his career on the Dublin tracks in sprint events since he possessed his sire's tremendous speed from the traps, but it was as a hurdler, when sent to England, that he was to amaze those who saw him and to stamp his name on the annals of the sport. He was one of that great trio of Printer, Juvenile Classic and Valiant Bob (winner of the 1939 Grand National) who raced during what has been described as the golden age of hurdle racing. Printer was whelped in 1936 and was at his finest as a hurdler in 1939 when he won the Wimbledon Gold Cup and Empire Stakes at Wembley. In taking the Gold Cup he set a new track record over the 500 yds course (hurdles) of 29.00 secs, and at Wembley his time of 30.11 secs over 525 yds was also a new track record. At the end of 1939, with Britain at war, he was returned to Ireland, having set up three national and four track records over hurdles, and was retired to stud, soon becoming as prepotent as his sire in the quality of track greyhounds he produced.

The first of his wonderful offspring was one of the outstanding bitches of all time, Robeen Printer, whelped in 1942, who after winning the Irish Laurels at Cork and the McAlinden Cup at Shelbourne Park in 1944 was sold for 1,650 gns, then the highest price ever paid in Ireland for a greyhound at public auction. She was worth every penny and took the English St Leger in 1945. In that year Lilac's Luck, a son of Printer, won the Irish Derby, and Mad Printer the Irish Oaks.

SHERRY'S PRINCE

A brindle whelped in April 1967, by Mad Era out of Nevasca, he was owned by Mrs R. Matthews and with Juvenile Classic must be rated the finest and most consistent hurdler in the sport's history. He ran his first race on 9 May 1969 at West Ham, and his last in May 1972, when winning his third Grand National. In those three years from 106 starts he won seventy-one times and was second fifteen times. Over hurdles he set new track records wherever he ran, on fourteen occasions. His time of 29.81 secs at Wembley over the 525 yds course, made in October 1969, was never beaten. At Harringay he clocked 29.02 secs for the 525 yds hurdles, the world's fastest time for this distance, but which he was to better.

In April 1970 he won the Long Hop Hurdles at the White City and then contested the Grand National, winning his heat and semi-final and the final. Soon afterwards, in the final of the Scottish Grand National, he broke a hock, yet was able to finish in second place though his career seemed over. However by October he was back to running and in January 1971 won the New Year Hurdles at Wembley, so it was decided to run him again in the Grand National. Once again he won his heat

The great hurdler Sherry's Prince in a trial at the White City.

and semi-final and took the final in 29.22 secs. Thus he equalled Juvenile Classic in winning the event twice. He then took the Gold Cup at Wembley, setting a new world record with 28.83 secs, and once again the Long Hop Hurdles. In January 1972 he won the Cobb Marathon Hurdles at Catford, run over 810 yds, by eight lengths from Adamstown Valley in a new record. Then he went down with a kidney infection. Once again his racing days seemed over, yet within two months he was running again. Entered for his third National he again won his heat, semi-final and the final to make three in a row, a record which must surely stand for all time. He was trained and kept at the White City by Colin West who looked after him for his second and third Grand National wins. Mr West trained four Grand National winners in six years (1971–6 inclusive), an unsurpassed record.

Sherry's Prince died in 1978, aged eleven. Known as 'Nooky' to those who looked after him, he was so attached to his trainer Colin West and the kennel staff that on the rare occasions when he left them he fretted so much that even in old age he spent his whole time in the track kennels, where he was given the loving care he had come to expect and deserve.

Between April 1971 and April 1972 he ran forty-three times (almost once a week), and won thirty-three races and was second on five occasions.

His pedigree reads:

Sherry's Prince	Mad Era	Hi There	Slaney Record
			Dublin Red
		Drumloch Sheevaun	Mad Tanist
			Sheevaun
	Nevasca	The Grand Canal	Champion Prince
			The Grand Duchess
		Shangri	Keep Moving
			Hopalong Olly

TACT

By Inler out of the great dam Tranquilla, he was from the great litter that also included Tanist, the 1940 Irish Derby winner; Talon; and Tempestuous. Always in the care of Paddy McEllistrim, the dog was three years old before he arrived in England, a year after his brother Tanist had won the Irish Derby. He was immediately tried over hurdles, with considerable success, especially at Wimbledon, his home track. Here he won the important Perpetual Challenge Trophy, defeating Juvenile Classic; at Wembley he won the Empire Stadium Stakes, and at Gloucester the West of England Grand National. At both the White City and Wandsworth he set a new track record over the 525 yds course, but had no opportunity to add the Grand National to his many successes for it was not run between 1941 and 1945. Tact raced for only one year in England before returning to Ireland and being retired to stud. His best son was

Bohernagraga Boy, who won the 1946 St Leger in 39.92 secs, the first to break 40 secs for the event.

TALL MAJOR
By Tall Boy out of Rosy Miller, whose sire was the great hurdler Macoma, Tall Major defeated the great Juvenile Classic on seven of their twelve meetings and in his seventy-nine races over hurdles was first or second on forty-four occasions. His greatest success was the Wimbledon Gold Vase, in which he defeated Captain Moonlight, another great hurdler, and set a new track record over 500 yds with a time of 29.83 secs. He won on every track on which he ran, setting many new records over hurdles, and though he never won the Grand National his performance stamped him as one of the best hurdlers of all time.

TOPOTHETIDE
This dog was the outstanding hurdler of 1978 and 1979 and the best for a decade, since Sherry's Prince won his third Grand National. Owned by Mr and Mrs Denis Parrish, the dog was first kennelled at Harringay and trained there by Tim Foster. His first open over hurdles was at Romford, which he won in convincing style, and in March 1978 he contested the Britvic Yorkshire Hurdles at Leeds. Starting at 3–1 on he had little trouble in winning the event, and when appearing at the White City the next month for the Grand National he again showed himself to be an outstanding jumper, winning this classic event at 6–4 on. Two weeks later the dog was at Powderhall for the Scottish National, for which he was quoted 9–4 on; he had no trouble in winning, clearing the hurdles with feet to spare. All tracks seemed alike to him, and when taking the Britvic Hurdles at Crayford in early October he had taken his winnings that year to more than £5,000, which included £2,000 for the *Daily Mirror* Trophy at Southend. After a winter's rest he was more than four years old by the time he contested the Grand National at White City in April 1979. The dog was now kennelled at Southend and trained by T. Lanceman. Age was no obstacle to another great performance, and Topothetide refuted those who doubted whether he could defeat younger dogs by winning his second classic with apparent ease, to prove worthy of comparison with the greatest hurdlers in the history of the sport.

WANDERING LAD
By Kilrea Lad out of Midas Jason, this brindle was trained by Stanley Biss and first caught the attention of racegoers when winning the Trafalgar Cup in 1944. But Biss believed he had a champion hurdler in the making and he was proved to be correct. Entered for Walthamstow's main hurdles event, the Chase, in April 1945, Wandering Lad defeated the great Derryboy Jubilee, the previous year's winner, and clocked 31.04 secs for 525 yds, failing by only half a length to lower the track record. He was then bought by Mrs Sanderson, who also owned his arch rival Derryboy Jubilee, and for his new owner he won the Downs Plate at Eastville and ran up (beaten a length) to Country Life for the 1945 Scurry Gold Cup, won in 23.50 secs. Equally good on the flat as over hurdles, he contested the 1945 Laurels, winning his heat and semi-final in which he defeated Country Life, but he was beaten by half a length into third place in the final by Burhill Moon and Country Life, who with Ballyhennessy Seal and Robeen Printer were the best in Britain that year.

HURDLES
For many years track hurdles were a hazard for greyhounds, causing considerable injuries, and few owners allowed their dogs to compete in these events although they provided variety and excitement. It was not until Con Stevens, racing manager at Wimbledon, who always championed hurdles events, invited Jim O'Connell to devise a more satisfactory type of hurdle that fear of injury to dogs was virtually eliminated. Working to Mr Stevens' suggestions, Jim O'Connell devised what is known as the Conal hurdle, which was hinged; when hit by a dog it would topple over and remain flat on the ground. The hurdles were also covered in plastic foam to act as a cushion if the hurdles were knocked over, thus eliminating serious leg injuries.

The hurdles used on greyhound tracks racing under NGRC rules must conform to the requirements of the Club. They are made of brushwood and must be 2 ft 6 ins high and slope at an angle of 75–80°

I

IDENTIFICATION

A registered greyhound is identified by comparison of its markings with those stated in its identity book, and the racing manager of an approved racecourse appoints one or more licensed officials to be in charge of the identification of each greyhound kennelled at the track or which is brought in for trials.

See Markings.

IDENTITY BOOK

Each greyhound has its identity book, containing its identification markings, without which it is unable to take part in any graded or open race on any track under the auspices of the NGRC. Entered in the book are the colour, sex and toe markings which appear on the registration form, and the identity book is marked up by the racing manager when he has made a careful examination of the greyhound. After completion the identity book, together with the English or Irish Stud Book documents, are sent to the NGRC who will seal the identity book and return it to the racing manager of the track where the greyhound is kennelled. Until the identity book is sealed, no greyhound can take part in a race anywhere. Where a dog is contesting an open event at another track, the dog's identity book is sent to the racing manager before the dog arrives so that he can check the dog's identification upon arrival. At no time does the identity book reach other hands apart from the racing managers of the tracks on which the dog performs.

During the dog's racing career, the racing managers enter:

(1) details and dates of inoculations,
(2) The name of the dog's trainer(s),
(3) Details of each trial and race,
(4) Dates of arrivals and departures from all tracks,
(5) If a bitch, dates when in season,
(6) Any suspensions and disqualifications.

An identity book is the sole property of the NGRC and no one except an NGRC steward, a racing manager, assistant racing manager, local steward, paddock steward, judge, or other person authorized by the NGRC or racing manager may be in possession of it. It is the public's safeguard against malpractice, for an unscrupulous person in possession of an identity book could quite easily change the markings of a dog.

INOCULATION

All greyhounds should be inoculated against distemper when twelve weeks old and for distemper, hardpad, viral hepatitis and leptospira canicola before starting racing or being placed with a trainer. A certificate signed by a veterinary surgeon should confirm this and accompany the greyhound throughout his life. Greyhounds racing on licensed (approved) tracks are required to have booster inoculations at intervals of not more than twenty-four months.

Inoculation should never be neglected. You may possibly have a greyhound worth more than £1,000 or one that, although still a puppy, may eventually become a champion and earn many more times that sum on the track and later at stud. Inoculation of pups at twelve weeks should be done as routine, and even if immunization is not complete, the chances are that the dog will contract only a mild attack of distemper, whilst the Epivax-TC plus (tissue culture) vaccine will give immunity also against viral hepatitis and heptospiral jaundice. The modern tissue vaccines give more rapid and effective immunization than the older vaccines.

Inoculation will usually put a dog off its food for two or three days and he may have a bout of shivering. Keep the dog in his kennel with plenty of water available, for he will drink frequently, and give only wholemeal bread and warm milk and very little exercise until he has fully recovered.

See Ailments and Diseases.

IPSWICH RACECOURSE

See under British Greyhound Racecourses.

IRISH CESAREWITCH

See Classic Events in Ireland.

IRISH DERBY

See Classic Events in Ireland.

IRISH GREYHOUND RACECOURSES

BELFAST RACECOURSES
See Celtic Park; Dunmore Park.

CELTIC PARK (Closed October 31, 1983)

It was two Belfast bookmakers, the late Joe Shaw and Hugh McAlinden, who after a visit to Belle Vue in 1926, together with their friends Paddy O'Donoghue and James Clarke, formed the National Greyhound Racing Company and held their first meeting in Ireland at Celtic Park on 18 April 1927. Hugh McAlinden was elected chairman of the company and P.J. Ryan secretary. McAlinden was also a director and chairman of Belfast Celtic Football Club and he was able to persuade his co-directors to grant them a lease to stage greyhound racing at the ground. Six races made up the first meeting, but the attendance on that opening afternoon proved a big disappointment and some people gave the sport only a few months. Despite these misgivings the ground is now closed for football but greyhound racing still flourishes there, and many of the finest track greyhounds have performed at Celtic Park. The first meeting was held under the jurisdiction of the Irish Coursing Club, the official body for the sport in the whole of Ireland until the Bord na gCon took over the running of greyhound racing in the Republic in 1959, but with the ICC still in charge of racing in the North.

Among the six races at the first meeting were two hurdles events. One race ended in a dead heat between Imperial Jimmy and Keep Whistling. Each event was run over 600 yds and one hurdles race was won by Strange Baird, a dog that was to become a favourite over hurdles at the track.

Celtic Park was the first track to have a trophy presented for competition when, later that first summer, the *Belfast Telegraph* presented a magnificent cup. The first winner was Duneynie Castle, a dog that endeared himself to followers of the sport at Celtic Park with his amazing finishes, always coming from behind to win with the last stride.

Many outstanding greyhounds have run at Celtic Park since 1926. Among the first to achieve fame were Beaded Biddy and Cruseline Boy, the latter coming to England in 1928 to contest and win the first Scurry Gold Cup at Clapton. English Derby winners to have run with distinction at Celtic Park were Mick the Miller, Dunmore King, Sand Star and Priceless Border.

In 1929 the Trigo Cup (now the Guinness Ulster Derby) was inaugurated and was the first classic to be run in Ireland, though the important Easter Cup, run at Shelbourne Park, preceded it by a year and the Trigo Cup was not given classic status until 1944. The actual Cup was presented to the track in 1929 by Mr William Barnett of Co. Down, in honour of his great horse Trigo, who won the Epsom Derby and St Leger that year. For the first three years the Trigo Cup was run over 640 yds, and Black Scab was the first winner. The next two years saw the event reduced by 40 yds and in 1935, when Magheragh Soldier won the first of his three consecutive Cups, it was run over 550 yds. Since 1944 it has been run as a classic event over 525 yds, the fastest time being put up in 1959 when Bermuda's Cloud did a fantastic 29.19 secs.

In 1938 the McAlevey Gold Cup was introduced, and first won by Leo's Gift. It was won in 1946 by Mr Jack McAllister's famous Mad Midnight; he also won the Trigo Cup the same year with Miltiades. The following year the great Priceless Border won the event and went on to take the English Derby. In 1956 Mr McAllister's outstanding dog Dunmore King was to win the event and, like Priceless Border, he was to win the English Derby in the same year. Dunmore King was a son of Shaggy Lad whose sire was the great Castledown Lad, and his dam was Shaggy Shore. Kirkland Darkie won in 1970, and two years later it was Itsachampion, winner of the Guinness 600 at Shelbourne Park the same year, and who was to become an outstanding sire. His son Lacca Champion was to win the 1978 English Derby, and he ran up the following year. The 1970 event was won by Mr W. Anthony's Kirkland Darkie with a time of 29.27 secs for the 525 yds course. Two of the greatest to win were sons of Pigalle Wonder. In 1964 Millie's Dandy won for Jack Mullan and in 1966 Dillie's Pigalle, who set a national record in doing so, also won the Irish Coursing Derby.

Other great dogs to perform at Celtic Park were Smartly Fergus, one of the fastest in the history of the sport, who was the first to break 34.00 secs over 600 yds with a time of 33.99 secs which he achieved in 1945; it remained a record for many years. In 1947 Ballymore Cottage made a new 525 yds record with a time of 29.38 secs when winning the Trigo Cup; this remained unbeaten for nine years. Another favourite at the track was Fair Mistress, who covered the 375 yds course in a record 20.52 secs, and here and at Dunmore Park no greyhound ever enjoyed greater popularity.

If Fair Mistress was the greatest bitch to have raced at Celtic Park, maybe Lilac's Luck was the greatest dog, for after winning the Trigo Cup in 1945 he went to Dublin to beat Gun Music in the Derby. Next year he almost did the impossible in his attempt to win the 1946 English Derby and so become the first ever to win both events. He was beaten into second place (though he was the 2–1 favourite) by the outstanding dog Monday's News. No greyhound has ever won the two major track events.

At Celtic Park the Jim Rice Memorial Trophy is held each year to commemorate the track's first racing manager, and of many fine greyhounds to have won it none was better than Mr and Mrs Marley's Mark Antony, trained by Tom Lynch, who won in 1970 and took the Irish St Leger at Limerick in the same year. Since 1959 the Ulster St Leger has been run at Celtic Park over the 550 yds course. In fact the first Irish St Leger classic was run at Celtic Park in 1932. That year it was won by Castle Eve, and eleven years later Monarch of the Glen, one of only two dogs to win the St Leger twice in Ireland, achieved the second of his great wins at Celtic Park. The following year the St Leger was run at Limerick, where it has been held ever since.

The Ulster Sprint, run here in October over 375 yds, is also long established and was first run in 1930 when it was won by Mountsandal. The 1936 event was won by the outstanding Lone Keel, who two years later was to win the English Derby when more than four years old, beating Wattle Bark and Manhattan Midnight, the favourite, in the final.

It was at Celtic Park on 24 October 1955 that Spanish Battleship ran his last race on Irish soil. The dog was more than four years old by then and had three Irish Derbys to show for his endeavours, but Tim O'Connor, his owner, was delighted for his champion to run his last race on the track where it all began in Ireland. Against him were lined up Claremont John, Captain's Keeper, Pleasure Garden and Imperial General, and the race was to be known as the Champion Stakes. As usual, Spanish Battleship was away like lightning and stayed in front throughout, to beat Pleasure Garden by three lengths in 29.48 secs with Captain's Keeper third. It was a wonderful end to a magnificent career, and like Mick the Miller who won the English St Leger on his last appearance, Spanish Battleship had finished on a high note.

It was on 1 January 1978, that a new board of directors took over Celtic Park, determined to return it to its former glory. Amongst the new directors were Sean and Brian Graham and Jim Delargy. During 1978 the track was closed for racing as it needed complete restoration, and after many years as racing manager Eddie O'Hagan retired. New kennels have been built, new restaurant accommodation provided and new starting boxes installed. Celtic Park has also followed Dunmore Park's example in that the running track now has an all-sand surface. Amongst those officials who were there on the opening night in 1927 were Mr Paddy Murray of Ballymena and Eddie O'Hagan and they are still at Celtic Park as stewards for the Irish Coursing Club. Mr Joe Duffy is the new racing manager. The longest-serving member of any racetrack anywhere is Paddy Murray who was appointed control steward at Celtic Park in 1928 and still served in this capacity when the track closed fifty years later. Now he is back again to continue where he left off at the re-opened track.

Sadly, Celtic Park closed its doors on October 31st, 1983, the site being purchased by Brookmount Properties for use as a supermarket. The last race, run over 550 yds was won by Helen Roger's bitch, Azure Yard of Bangor, Co. Down in a photo finish from Dunham Park in 31.70 secs. So ended Paddy Murray's 56 years association with the track.

Track Records (1950)

Fair Mistress	375 yds	20.52 secs
Ballymore Cottage	525 yds	29.38 secs
Mazurka	550 yds	30.98 secs
Smartly Fergus	600 yds	33.99 secs
Ilene Darling	860 yds	51.55 secs

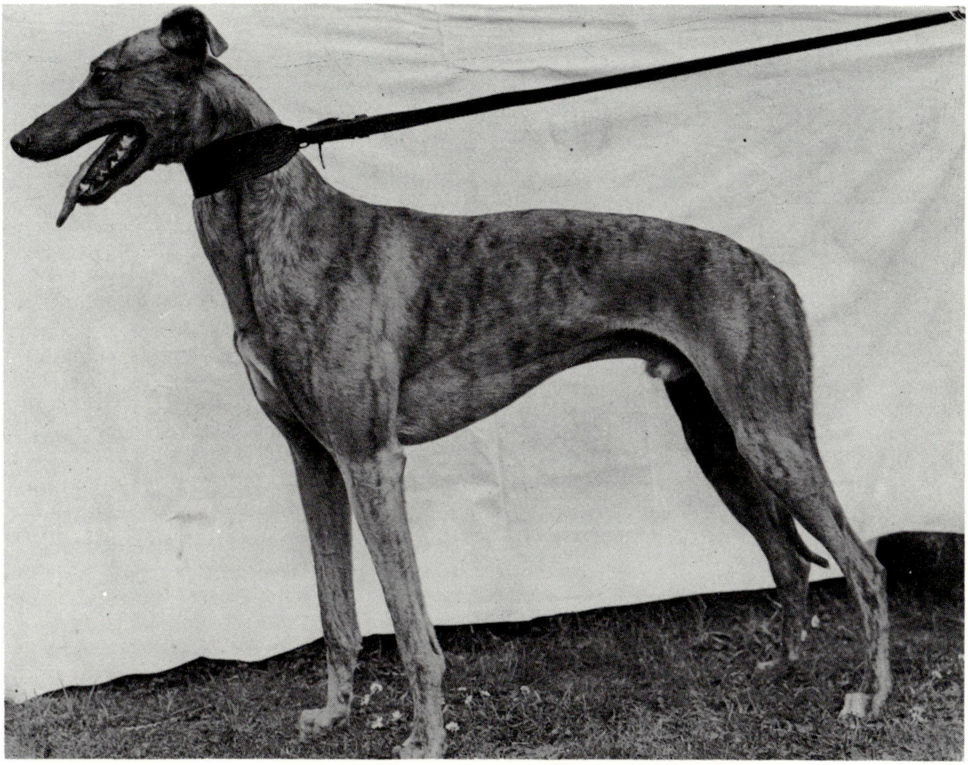

Smartly Fergus, one-time holder of the 600 yds record at Celtic Park and the 525 yds record at Shelbourne Park.

Track Records (1960)

Fair Mistress	375 yds	20.52 secs
Northern Customer	525 yds	29.14 secs
Smartly Fergus	600 yds	33.99 secs
Ilene Darling	860 yds	51.55 secs

Track Records (1970)

Every Effort	1965	375 yds	20.37 secs
Jemmy John	1970	525 yds	28.61 secs
Blissful Pride	1970	600 yds	32.90 secs
Ilene Darling	before 1950	860 yds	51.55 secs

Track Records (1980)

Kirkland Darkie	375 yds	19.94 secs
Jemmy John	525 yds	28.61 secs
Sulky Mac	550 yds	30.38 secs
Blissful Pride	600 yds	32.90 secs
Ilene Darling	860 yds	51.55 secs

Winners of the McAlevey Gold Cup

1938	Leo's Gift	30.21 secs
1939	Myroe Roving Boy	30.12 secs
1940	Munster Hills	30.36 secs
1941	Carnagh Moon	30.14 secs
1942–4	not run	
1945	Kilrea Try That	30.34 secs
1946	Mad Midnight	30.12 secs
1947	Priceless Border	29.54 secs
1948	Newhill Rose Again	30.12 secs
1949	Lone Train	29.54 secs
1950	Creole Fair	29.49 secs
1951	Aughaway	29.49 secs
1952	Clongorey Nina	30.24 secs
1953	Racing Snob	29.61 secs
1954	Coolkill Chieftain	29.75 secs
1955	Tully Jokes	29.76 secs
1956	Dunmore King	29.44 secs
1957	Cleo's Sprig	29.32 secs
1958	Imperial Ivan	29.82 secs
1959	Northern Customer	29.14 secs
1960	Rockmount	29.33 secs
1961	This is Broadway	29.51 secs
1962	Marie	29.62 secs
1963	Right Choice	29.68 secs
1964	Millie's Dandy	29.14 secs
1965	Billy Gale	29.51 secs
1966	Dillie's Pigalle	28.86 secs
1967	Prince Queensil	29.48 secs
1968	Rapid Streak	29.22 secs
1969	Piper Play	29.52 secs
1970	Kirkland Darkie	29.27 secs
1971	Rapid Brandy	29.51 secs
1972	Itsachampion	29.72 secs
1973	Killybrick	29.55 secs
1974	Lucky Mint	29.23 secs
1975	Win Sam	28.86 secs
1976	Garford Maxi	29.34 secs
1977	Macash Queen	29.38 secs
1981	Cloghogue Lady	29.69 secs

Winners of the Trigo Cup (now Guinness Ulster Derby)

1929	Black Scab	37.00 secs
1930	Filon	37.40 secs
1931	Bright Brindle	37.67 secs
1932	Jack Knows	35.15 secs
1933	Rustic Martin	34.63 secs

Winners of the Trigo Cup (Guinness Ulster Derby)

1934	not run	
1935	Magheragh Soldier	31.45 secs
1936	Magheragh Soldier	31.40 secs
1937	Magheragh Soldier	31.80 secs
1938	Strong Mutton	31.34 secs
1939	Fearless Gaughan	31.72 secs
1940	Fearless Gaughan	31.56 secs
1941–3	not run	
1944	Fair Brook	29.95 secs
1945	Lilac's Luck	29.65 secs
1946	Miltiades	29.62 secs
1947	Ballymore Cottage	29.38 secs
1948	Manley Creamery	29.66 secs
1949	Astra's Nephew	29.90 secs
1950	Fine Sprig	29.85 secs
1951	Lucky Blackbird	29.72 secs
1952	Outcast Surprise	29.69 secs
1953	Flashy Name	29.79 secs
1954	Moyala Flash	29.39 secs
1955	Shaun's Tip	29.42 secs
1956	Howardstown Tonic	29.29 secs
1957	Nimble Star	29.70 secs
1958	Drumskea Chieftain	29.70 secs
1959	Bermuda's Cloud	29.16 secs
1960	Laurdella Prince	29.58 secs
1961	Ashley Park Ranger	29.20 secs
1962	Ballyshoneen Plucky	29.62 secs
1963	Memory Lane	29.60 secs
1964	Coolkerane Prince	29.38 secs
1965	Montorte Malina	29.42 secs
1966	Woodlawn	29.40 secs
1967	Super Quick	29.15 secs
1968	Drumna Chestnut	29.27 secs
1969	Bill of Sale	29.57 secs
1970	Jemmy John	28.61 secs
1971	Super Trust	29.54 secs
1972	Clackmore Island	29.73 secs
1973	Itsawitch	28.80 secs
1974	Moordyke Maxi	29.16 secs
1975	Piping Rock	29.60 secs
1976	Croft Lass	29.40 secs
1977	Backdeed Man	29.40 secs
1978–9	not run – track closed	

1929, 1930, 1931 run over 640 yds; 1932 and 1933 run over 600 yds; 1935–1940 run over 550 yds

Winners of the Ulster Sprint Cup

1954	Creevy Lily	21.35 secs
1955	Pleasure Garden	20.29 secs
1956	Jeff's Fun	20.81 secs
1957	Obedia's Son	20.70 secs
1958	Drumna Nut	21.25 secs
1959	Tomadilly Prince	20.40 secs
1960	Rockmount	20.90 secs
1961	Aye Rather	20.85 secs
1962	Tanyard Chef	20.47 secs
1963	Pleasure Gleam	20.69 secs
1964	Creggan Bush	20.47 secs
1965	Fiery Effort	20.37 secs
1966	Shaun's Ticket	20.75 secs
1967	Filipino	20.60 secs
1968	Flying Pigalle	20.43 secs
1969	Rockeel Brae	20.53 secs
1970	Rapid Smokey	20.53 secs
1971	not run	
1972	not run	
1973	Moygara Sligo	20.10 secs
1974	Well My Pal	20.57 secs
1975	Rapid Roger	20.30 secs
1976	Garford Streak	20.47 secs
1977	Gullion Lad	20.44 secs
1978–9	not run – track closed	

Winners of the Jim Rice Memorial Trophy

1970	Mark Antony	29.86 secs
1971	Prince Saffron	29.03 secs
1972	not run	
1973	Moordyke Maxi	29.60 secs
1974	Croft Lass	29.64 secs
1975	Donard Arkle	29.48 secs
1976	Racing Tip	30.84 secs
1977	Noble Brigg	30.92 secs
1978–9	not run – track closed	
1980	Ballinfonta Hero	29.37 secs
1981	Big Smile	29.40 secs

CLONMEL

One of the largest of Ireland's towns, since 1921 it has been the home of the Irish Coursing Club, of which the late Tom Morris was for many years secretary. He was also the first managing director of the Clonmel racecourse when it opened in March 1931, with Tim Rice racing manager. The track, of 480 yds circumference, possesses excellent facilities for patrons and is one of the best for racing in all Ireland with a long run to the first bend, while the turns are suitably banked to make for trouble-free running. Racing takes place on Monday and Thursday each week.

Hurdle racing has always been a feature of racing here. The classic National Breeders' Produce Stakes is run here, which began in 1939 as the National Sapling Stakes and then became the National Puppy Cup. Its first winner was Sporting Fancy, and in 1947 the great Priceless Border first showed his tremendous speed. In 1943 the event was won by Mr Billy Quinn's Britannia's Son. In 1944 it was renamed the National Breeders' Produce Stakes and is now one of the richest races in Ireland. Mr Quinn of Killenaule was later to breed and train those two champions Brilliant Bob and the flying 'blue' Quare Times, and for many years was one of the greatest names in greyhound circles. In at the start of track racing, he trained the great Tanist to win the 1940 Irish Derby and at one time the dog held the 525 yds record at Clonmel with a time of 29.85 secs. Mr Quinn also trained another great star of track and coursing field, Brilliant Bob, perhaps the greatest of them all, who won the Irish St Leger at Clonmel on the only occasion it has been run there.

The first year in which the newly named National Breeders' Produce Stakes was run, 1944, the winner was the great sire The Grand Fire, son of The Grand Champion and Quare Fire, and from him have come many champions of the past thirty years, mostly through the dam line, for Quare Fire was one of the greatest dams of all time.

All greyhounds bred by Mr Paddy

Dunphy were given the prefix The Grand, and most began their racing career at Clonmel. Mr Dunphy owned that great sire The Grand Champion, and in 1962 he bred, trained and owned the English Derby winner The Grand Canal. The Grand Silver was another wonderful sire, one of his best sons being Little County who ran up in the English Derby to the great John Silver. The Grand Prince was equally famous, being sire of the great Sheila at Last, dam of Monalee Champion.

For twenty-two years, The Grand Fire's Record for 525 yds stood undefeated until in September 1979 The Potman, a black dog owned and trained by Ronnie Chandler, clocked 29.34 secs to win his race by an amazing twelve lengths. Afterwards, he was sold to Belfast bookmaker Alf McLean for a large sum. The Potman was by Mortar Light out of Sky Banner and was only twenty months old when making his fantastic run.

The great sire Odd Venture set the 500 yds record in 1961 over 500 yds with a time of 28.25 secs, which was not bettered for more than ten years.

The National Breeders' Produce Stakes for 1979 was won by Hume Highway, owned by Mrs Patricia M'Grath of Cahir. Her outstanding dog was whelped in May 1977 by Free Speech out of Coaster, and he defeated Tsetse Choice by a length in 30.16 secs. Free Speech ran up in the 1977 Scurry Gold Cup, now run at Slough, and set a new track record at Slough of 26.37 secs when winning his semi-final. He is also sire of Carhumore Speech, winner of Wimbledon's Puppy Derby.

Clonmel was in 1932 and 1933 the venue for the Oaks, the first winner being Queen of the Suir, Beef Cutlet's litter sister.

During 1979 Christy Mulcahy, long associated with the track and for the past decade its racing manager, retired. Sean Bourke is Clonmel's general manager.

Among other events run at Clonmel are the Tommy Murphy 525 and the Munster Cup.

Main Events Run at Clonmel

National Breeders' Produce Stakes	525 yds
Tommy Murphy 525	525 yds
Munster Cup	525 yds

Track Records (1950)

Brilliant Tulip	330 yds	18.30 secs
Barna Derg	525 yds	29.65 secs
Fair King	525 yds H	31.00 secs
Flighty Rover	550 yds	31.30 secs
Quarter Cross	550 yds H	32.55 secs

Track Records (1960)

Brilliant Tulip	330 yds	18.30 secs
Odd Venture	500 yds	28.28 secs
Knockdrina Ranger	500 yds H	29.95 secs
The Grand Fire	525 yds	29.40 secs
Flighty Rover	550 yds	31.30 secs

Track Records (1970)

Quiet Spring	1970	300 yds	16.50 secs
Odd Venture	1961	500 yds	28.25 secs
Knockdrina Ranger	1957	500 yds H	29.95 secs
The Grand Fire	1957	525 yds	29.40 secs
Jerry's Wonder	1963	525 yds H	30.90 secs
Unguarded Moment	1963	525 yds H	30.90 secs
Lady Bon	1961	700 yds	40.40 secs

Track Records (1980)

Odd Venture	1961	500 yds	28.25 secs
Knockdrina Ranger	1957	500 yds H	29.95 secs
The Potman	1979	525 yds	29.34 secs
Jerry's Wonder	1961	525 yds H	30.90 secs
Lady Bon	1961)	700 yds	40.40 secs
Unguarded Moment	1963)		

Winners of the National Breeders' Produce Stakes

1939	Sporting Fancy	30.20 secs
1940	Landy's Style	30.30 secs
1941	Botley's Best	29.95 secs
1942	not run	
1943	Britannia's Son	30.30 secs
1944	Lotty's Gay Boy	30.35 secs
1945	Victory Star	30.45 secs
1946	Crissie Tanist	30.40 secs
1947	Priceless Border	29.54 secs
1948	Something Short	29.90 secs
1949	Esso Major	30.15 secs
1957	The Grand Fire	29.45 secs
1958	Summerhill Reject	30.20 secs
1959	Toast the Champ	29.70 secs
1960	Springvalley Grand	29.95 secs
1961	Kiledon General	29.55 secs
1962	Rattle the Key	29.45 secs
1963	Piper Apache	29.85 secs
1964	Motel Chief	29.70 secs
1965	Kileden Guest	29.76 secs
1966	Happy Thadie	29.70 secs
1967	Whiteless Gift	29.90 secs
1968	Sally's Chance	29.85 secs
1969	Right o' Myross	29.90 secs
1970	Gentle Lady	29.90 secs
1971	Westpark Anti	30.18 secs
1972	Rathokelly Gem	30.05 secs
1973	Big Kuda	29.98 secs
1974	Quote Me	29.96 secs
1975	Kaiser Bill	29.64 secs
1976	Cill Dubh Darkey	29.64 secs
1977	Greenane Decca	29.68 secs
1978	Alway's Kelly	30.34 secs
1979	Hume Highway	30.16 secs
1980	Flying Marble	30.02 secs
1981	Calandra Champ	29.66 secs

Winners of the Munster Cup

1970	Woodman Jim	29.85 secs
1971	Newdown Master	30.14 secs
1972	Big Kuda	30.08 secs
1973	Miles Apart	30.30 secs
1974	Monday's Glamour	30.26 secs
1975	Mons Pride	30.30 secs
1976	Easter Week	29.80 secs
1977	Malange	30.52 secs
1978	Field Service	30.26 secs
1979	The Potman	29.38 secs
1980	Ron Hardy	29.64 secs

CORK

Capital of the largest of Ireland's four provinces, Munster, it has one of the finest greyhound racing tracks. The classic Laurels is run here, and was won for the first time in 1944 by the wonder bitch Robeen Printer, who in the following year won the English St Leger, the only greyhound ever to achieve this double. In the final of the first Irish Laurels Robeen Printer narrowly defeated that great dog Shannon Shore who, had he been successful, would have been the only dog ever to win the Irish and English Laurels for he won the latter event in 1946 after contesting the final the year before. From its inauguration and until 1961, the Laurels was run over 500 yds; the fastest time for the event and the track record of 28.15 secs was achieved in 1960 by Last Lap. From 1961 the event has been run over 525 yds. In 1969 it was first won by an Englishman, when the dog Skipping Tim was successful for his Lincolnshire owner, Mr R. Marshall, who took the first prize of £1,500 when his dog won from a top-class field.

Greyhound racing began at Cork on 13 June 1936 with Pat O'Brien as the track's first manager. Two years before, his dog Ocean Monarch had won the Irish Cup for coursing. Since then the greatest dogs ever to race in Ireland have contested the Laurels and other events at Cork. Only one dog, Spanish Chestnut, has won the Irish Laurels twice. He was also sire of the immortal Spanish Battleship, the only dog ever to win the Irish Derby more than once – he did so three times, in 1953, 1954 and 1955. In 1955 he also took the Laurels at Cork. In 1971 Ivy Hall Flash set a new 525 yds record here when winning in 29.10 secs, and won the Laurels in the fastest time ever for this event of 29.15 secs.

The only dog ever to win the Irish St Leger and Laurels was Nameless Star, who accomplished this wonderful feat in 1976. By Rita's Choice out of Itsastar, and owned by Mrs R. McAulay of Dublin, he was whelped in May 1974.

The 1977 Laurels was sponsored by a firm of Cork bookmakers, the Liam Cashman Organisation. That year for the first time the winner's prize was £5,000. It was increased to £5,500 in 1978 when it was won by Denis Lynch of the famous Knockrour kennels with his Knockrour Girl, who won from Gay Corner; Knockrour Jet was in third place. In the 1951 Laurels his father, Jack Lynch, had bred and trained the first and second, Knockrour Favourite and Knockrour Bella.

For the second year (1979), Denis Lynch was again successful with his Knockrour Slave whom he also bred, owned and trained at his Aghabullogue kennels. This great dog had previously won the Guinness Trophy at Cork by an amazing ten lengths from Black Colina, after which Lynch was offered £50,000 for the dog but he would not sell. This is believed to be the highest price ever offered for a greyhound anywhere in the world. In 1979 Lynch achieved another unique distinction in that he also won the classic Irish coursing event, the Irish cup with Knockrour Tiger. To win a classic event on both racetrack and coursing field in the same year is without precedent.

Another classic, the Oaks, has twice been run at Cork, the first occasion being in 1939 and the second in 1943 when it was won by Mad Printer. She was in the care of the great trainer of coursing greyhounds, Mick Horan, trainer of Mick the Miller when he began his career in Ireland. Her dam had previously set up a new 550 yds record at the track, showing some of the fantastic speed she was able to pass on to her sons and daughters.

To the greyhound enthusiasts of Cork the Pegasus Cup, later named the Perpetual Challenge Cup and still later the Guinness Trophy, is second only to the Laurels in importance. The Cup is the largest and most valuable in Ireland and was originally made for a special race to be run on the Cork Park horse-racing track in 1900, between two horses representing Ireland and the USA. The silver trophy was first contested by greyhounds in 1939.

It was at Cork that the 1978 English Derby winner Balliniska Band won his only race in Ireland, by twelve lengths, and was afterwards sold for £2,500 to race in England – one of the all-time bargains.

Racing takes place on Monday, Wednesday and Saturday and one of the most popular events is the sweepstake sponsored by the city's Windsor Hotel and worth £1,500 to the winner. The Ryan Memorial Trophy is held each year; in 1978 the valuable Smirnoff Gold Collar was won by Keen Truth in 29.75 secs. Another event which carries a £1,500 prize and for which a large number of entries is always received is the Guinness Trophy. The Cork Bookmakers' Stakes and the British and Irish Line Gold Cup, with prizes of £1,000, also creates much interest. The Bass Ale Cup, inaugurated in 1970 with a prize of £1,500, was won in 1978 by Nameless Light who also won the Windsor Hotel event that year. Mrs McAulay's dog was one of the best greyhounds to run here in recent years.

A number of outstanding greyhounds have held track records here. In 1949 Spanish Lad did 31 secs for 550 yds, which was not bettered in twenty years. Prince of Bermuda clocked 27.95 secs for 500 yds in 1956, being the first to break 28 secs; this, too, was not beaten for twenty years. Ivy Hall Flash did 29.10 secs for 525 yds in 1971, a record which she kept until 1978.

Greyhound racing has never enjoyed greater popularity in Cork than at present. In the 1980s a new track with better amenities will probably have to be built to accommodate all those who come here for the more important events, of which no track stages a greater number. The present track is of 445 yds circumference with long straights and well-banked bends which makes for fast times. Noel Holland is racing manager.

Main Events Run at Cork

Guinness Trophy	March	525 yds
Windsor Hotel Stakes	April	525 yds
Bass Ale Stakes	May	525 yds
Cork National	June H	525 yds
B & I Line Gold Cup	July	525 yds
Cashman Laurels	August	525 yds
Smirnoff Gold Collar	September	525 yds
Ryan Memorial Cup	October	525 yds

Track Records (1950)

Blondsman	310 yds	17.50 secs
Double Shadow	500 yds	28.82 secs
Clogher Cross	525 yds	29.96 secs
Deputy Lieutenant	525 yds H	30.74 secs
Gorriencoona Border	550 yds	31.40 secs
Muskerry Cream	700 yds	40.85 secs

Track Records (1960)

Prince of Bermuda	1956	500 yds	27.95 secs
Spanish Lad	1949	550 yds	31.00 secs
Muskerry Cream	1950	700 yds	40.85 secs

Track Records (1970)

Lucky Blunder	1967	300 yds	16.60 secs
Tanyard Heather	1964	525 yds	29.20 secs
Ashgrove Look	1966	525 yds H	30.15 secs
Spanish Lad	1949	550 yds	31.00 secs
Lucky Break	1964	700 yds	40.00 secs

Track Records (1980)

Odd Crest	1975	310 yds	17.20 secs
Prince of Bermuda	1956	500 yds	27.95 secs
Knockrour Slave	1979	525 yds	29.00 secs
Race Riot	1973	525 yds H	29.75 secs
Spanish Lad	1949	550 yds	31.00 secs
Lucky Break	1964	700 yds	40.00 secs

Winners of the Bass Ale Stakes

1970	Westpark Fiona	29.50 secs
1971	Pardon Lad	29.65 secs
1972	Muskerry Border	29.75 secs
1973	Scintilla's Fred	29.65 secs
1974	Mountleader Omar	29.55 secs
1975	Moonshine Bandit	29.80 secs
1976	Spotlight Swanky	29.15 secs
1977	Valiant Band	29.45 secs
1978	Nameless Light	29.65 secs
1979	Carrick Chance	29.50 secs
1980	Gentle Star	29.20 secs

Winners of the Guinness Trophy

1964	Aheramore	29.45 secs
1965	Annard	29.60 secs
1966	Red Barrell	29.50 secs
1967	Ardralla Wonder	29.65 secs
1968	Brendan B	29.45 secs
1969	Mountleader	29.50 secs
1970	Hack It Lee	29.95 secs
1971	Woodman Jim	29.60 secs
1972	Kilnaglory Spot	29.80 secs
1973	Hay Win	29.45 secs
1974	Ballymaclune	29.50 secs
1975	Splendid Silver	29.35 secs
1976	Mountleader Omar	29.90 secs
1977	Granure Aim	29.90 secs
1978	Mr Jester	29.80 secs
1979	Knockrour Slave	29.15 secs
1980	Oakdene Sonny	29.40 secs

Winners of the Laurels

1944	Robeen Printer	28.98 secs
1945	Munster Hotel	29.20 secs
1946	Ballinrea Express	28.80 secs
1947	Careless Border	28.80 secs
1948	Double Shadow	28.33 secs
1949	Spanish Chestnut	28.55 secs
1950	Spanish Chestnut	28.70 secs
1951	Knockrour Favourite	28.85 secs
1952	Tragumna Dasher	28.70 secs
1953	Templenoe Rebel	28.55 secs
1954	Come on Bella	28.90 secs
1955	Spanish Battleship	28.35 secs
1956	Rather Grand	29.00 secs
1957	Kilcasey Streak	28.80 secs
1958	Brook Prancer	28.43 secs
1959	Celbridge Chance	28.50 secs
*1960	Last Lap	28.15 secs
1961	Round Tower Rose	29.80 secs
1962	Dark Baby	29.40 secs
1963	Powerstown Proper	29.75 secs
1964	Tanyard Heather	29.20 secs
1965	Boro Parachute	29.60 secs
1966	Westpark Ash	29.40 secs
1967	Philotimo	29.65 secs
1968	Flaming King	29.25 secs
1969	Skipping Tim	29.50 secs
1970	Gabriel Boy	29.25 secs
1971	Ivy Hall Flash	29.15 secs
1972	Dublin Eily	29.70 secs
1973	Kilbracken Style	29.10 secs
1974	Silent Thought	29.50 secs
1975	Moonshine Bandit	29.30 secs
1976	Nameless Star	29.30 secs
1977	Ashleigh Honour	29.15 secs
1978	Knockrour Girl	29.40 secs
1979	Knockrour Slave	29.45 secs
1980	Knockrour Slave	29.00 secs
1981	Knockeen Master	29.50 secs

*Until 1960 run over 500 yds; thereafter 525 yds

Winners of the Ryan Memorial Cup

1970	Gabriel Boy	29.50 secs
1971	Real Gem	29.50 secs
1972	Spring Life	29.70 secs
1973	Deise Recker	29.95 secs
1974	Cos Abu	29.50 secs

Winners of the Ryan Memorial Cup

1975	Cos Aroon	30.05 secs
1976	Fifth of June	30.20 secs
1977	Kispeam Jim	30.00 secs
1978	Allemaine	29.40 secs
1979	Wyoming Baby	29.85 secs
1980	Ballygarvan What	29.50 secs

DERRY

This track is in the second largest city in Ulster, also known as Londonderry. Though one of the smallest tracks in Ireland the bends are not sharp and the running surface is good, so that fast times are recorded. It was through the untiring work of the late Hugh Duffy that the track was opened, and racing takes place on Mondays, Wednesdays and Fridays. The Irish Derby Trial Stakes are run here in June, followed by the important James Corry Marathon, run over 720 yds, a recent winner of which was Four of Spades. Derry Festival Derby also attracts some outstanding greyhounds; Drumawhiskey Champ won in 1978, equalling the track record for 500 yds, and he also set a new record for the 525 yds course. Also run here is the Ulster 500.

Main Events Run at Derry

Festival Derby	June	500 yds
James Corry Marathon	August	720 yds

Track Records (1950)

Currowgariff Border	300 yds	16.83 secs
True Record	440 yds	25.56 secs
Hale Farloe	525 yds	30.64 secs

Track Records (1980)

Bright Oliver	300 yds	16.45 secs
High Footstick	440 yds	25.05 secs
Clackmore Island	500 yds	27.98 secs
Drumahisky Champ	525 yds	29.51 secs
Leck Venture	600 yds	34.20 secs
Atomic Rebel	720 yds	40.96 secs

DUBLIN

See Harold's Cross; Shelbourne Park.

DUNDALK

The name of Dundalk (a corruption of Dun Dealgan) is situated in Louth, of which it is the county town, not far from the glorious Carlingford Lough. In the churchyard lies the body of Agnes Galt, elder sister of Robert Burns. The town is famous for its tobacco and brewing industries which provide its prosperity.

Dundalk is fifty miles from both Dublin and Belfast, and attracts greyhound enthusiasts from both sides of the border. The track opened as early as 1930, with Paddy Martin as founder director and first racing manager. Since 1957 Jimmy Martin, his son, has been racing manager and has done much to make this one of the pleasantest and most efficiently run tracks in Ireland, with several important sponsored events.

The Major Extra Size International, sponsored by Carroll's, is the highlight of the year, in August. Inaugurated in 1968, it is limited to six outstanding greyhounds and usually attracts the best dogs in Ireland and Britain. Those who have taken part include Time Up Please, Lively Band, Ivy Hall Flash and Mutt's Silver, all well able to negotiate the unusually sharp bends which make for slow times compared to Dunmore Park.

Racing takes place on Monday, Friday and Saturday each week over 325 yds, 525 yds and 760 yds, the record for the last of these distances being held by Miss Pauline Wallis's Quakerfield Boy, who shortly afterwards went with her to the USA where he won more than £5,000 in prize money. Track affairs are in the hands of Dr N. McGahon and his brother, H. McGahon, who with Gerry Kerley and Jimmy Martin are the track's directors.

At Dundalk is held the 325 yds Sprint Cup, won in 1969 by Mr Woods' Easter Lad, whose time of 17.97 secs was then the fastest for the event and the first time 18.00 secs had been broken. The Dundealgan Trophy is presented by the Dundealgan Greyhound Racing Co. who hold the track's licence. One of its early winners was Mr J. Mullen's magnificent Newdown Heather bitch April Flower. Among other important events held at Dundalk are the McLarnon Junior Cup and the Sharp Lager 525, whose winner receives £2,000, but it is the Carroll's International that creates so much enthusiasm. With the exception of the classics and the top events run in Dublin, no fixture draws a larger crowd or finer greyhounds. The 1978 event included the English Derby winner Lacca Champion and the Irish Derby winner Pampered Rover, but they had to be content with second and third place behind Mr B. McElholm's strangely named Hunday Dook who took the £3,000 prize.

Another big attraction here is the 1,000 Guineas which is run in May and is a valuable pointer to those dogs which will contest the Irish and English Derbys. One of the outstanding dogs to win this event was Lively Band in 1974, who also won the Irish Derby and St Leger and was elected greyhound of the year. The Dundalk Marathon and Michael Kerley Memorial Trophy are both run over 765 yds, the bitch Kilcam Lady being a recent winner of the Dundalk Marathon. The Spur Nursery Championship, with £1,000 going to the winner, attracts the best puppies from all over Ireland.

Main Events Run at Dundalk

1,000 Guineas	May	525 yds
Ballygall Spring Cup	June	325 yds
Michael Kerley Memorial Cup	June	765 yds
Carroll's International	July	525 yds
Guinness Harp Lager Stakes	September	525 yds
Matthew Harvey Memorial Trophy	October	550 yds
Spur Nursery Championship	November	525 yds

Track Records (1970)

Grisette	1969	500 yds	28.47 secs
April Flower	1969	525 yds	29.38 secs
Right o' Myross	1970	525 yds H	30.72 secs
Twelfth Man	1967	700 yds H	40.20 secs

Track Records (1980)

Mourne Return	1958	325 yds	17.85 secs
Why Me	1974	500 yds	28.38 secs
April Flower	1969	525 yds	29.38 secs
Right o' Myross	1971	525 yds H	30.73 secs
Calypso Melody	1969	550 yds	31.02 secs
Pick Me	1977	550 yds H	31.90 secs
Full Book	1971	765 yds	44.48 secs

Winners of the Carroll's International 1971–80

1971	Ivy Hall Flash	29.62 secs
1972	Time Up Please	29.60 secs
1973	Bashful Man	29.70 secs
1974	Nelson's Blast	30.30 secs
1975	Main Avenue	29.74 secs
1976	Mutt's Silver	29.80 secs
1977	Brush Tim	29.72 secs
1978	Hunday Dook	29.76 secs
1979	Nameless Pixie	29.82 secs
1980	Jelly Crock	29.80 secs

DUNGANNON

This Co. Tyrone town first opened its greyhound track in May 1930. The track is a fast one, 485 yds in circumference, and is always well maintained with an all-sand surface that dries out quickly after heavy rain. Racing takes place on Tuesdays, Thursdays and Saturdays. The Ulster Oaks, run here since 1970 over 525 yds is sponsored by Guinness. Its first winner was Mr D. Kernan's bitch Tyrone Street in the fast time of 29.64 secs. The 1978 winner was Mr T. McHugh's Sole Aim bitch Palestine Pride. Here, too, are run the Mick Horan Puppy Championship over 325 yds, inaugurated as a memorial to Mick the Miller's first trainer who died in 1962; and the Tuborg Viceroy Cup, which attracts the best greyhounds in Northern Ireland. The Harry McCrory Memorial Trophy was contested for the first time in 1978, as a memorial to the Irish Coursing Club steward who was at the track for more than thirty years. Tommy McCombe is Dungannon's racing and general manager, moving here in 1962 when the Clones track closed.

Main Events Run at Dungannon

Tuborg Viceroy Cup	May	500 yds
Guinness Ulster Oaks	June	525 yds
Bacci Cup	August	550 yds
Mick Horan Puppy Championship	September	325 yds

Track Records (1950)

Millionaire	325 yds	18.11 secs
Head Over	500 yds	29.96 secs
Maggie's Pup	525 yds H	31.75 secs
Kilcool Mounty	550 yds	31.97 secs

Track Records (1960)

Millionaire	325 yds	18.11 secs
Calrossie Morning Star	325 yds H	19.39 secs
Pauline's Pal	525 yds	29.18 secs
Maggie's Pup	525 yds H	31.71 secs
Rose Velvet	600 yds	33.78 secs

Track Records (1970)

Cornetto	325 yds	17.62 secs
Stoneville Queen	500 yds	28.17 secs
Newdown Son	550 yds	31.33 secs
Rose Velvet	600 yds	33.78 secs
Twelfth Man	780 yds	45.29 secs

Track Records (1980)

Cornetto	325 yds	17.62 secs
Kensington Lil	500 yds	27.64 secs
Paula's Pal	525 yds	29.18 secs
Merchant Bound	550 yds	30.75 secs
Rosevale Desire	780 yds	44.67 secs

Winners of the Ulster Oaks

1970	Tyrone Street	29.64 secs
1971	Kilwoney Rose	30.45 secs
1972	Trace of Red	30.07 secs
1973	Ashling Ban	29.80 secs
1974	Rokeel Rebel	29.78 secs
1975	Bright Evening	29.38 secs
1976	Kisses for Me	29.98 secs
1977	Kisses for Me	29.78 secs
1978	Palestine Pride	29.31 secs
1979	Shanes Rocket	29.68 secs

DUNMORE PARK

The track opened its gates for greyhound racing at Antrim Road on 6 June 1928, a year after the other Belfast track, Celtic Park, began racing and so is one of the oldest in the British Isles. It is the largest and fastest track in Britain and here is held the classic sprinters' event, the National Sprint, now known as the Guinness National Sprint, run over the 435 yds course since its inception. The fabulous Fair Mistress won this event in 1943, the year after she won the Oaks at Limerick, the only occasion it was run at this track. In the National Sprint she defeated Munday in a thrilling race to equal the track record of 24.03 secs set up by Farloe Border. Three years after this an equally famous greyhound and future sire,

Mad Tanist, improved upon her time when he won the event in 23.89 secs, being the first to break 24.00 secs – a new national and world record. It was an amazing performance, for twenty-five years later Gaultier Swank won with a time of 24.00 secs.

In three seasons (1942, 1943 and 1944) Fair Mistress ran thirty-four times on the two Belfast tracks, winning twenty-four times and being second on seven occasions, and those who saw her believe her to have been the greatest bitch in the history of track racing. Other famous winners of the National Sprint were Sandown Champion in 1950, Hi There and Bauhus, also to become wonderful sires, the latter siring Sand Star, winner of the 1969 English Derby. Bauhus was sired by Solar Prince, whose sire Champion Prince was by Bella's Prince, a son of Castledown Lad. Sandown Champion followed in the footsteps of his sire, Mad Tanist, in winning the National Sprint. Sandown Champion was sire of Lisabelle, dam of Solar Prince from a mating with Champion Prince, thus combining the speed of Tanist with the staying powers of Castledown Lad. Solar Prince, with The Grand Fire bitch Millie Hawthorn, gave Faithful Hope, who in turn sired the Derby winner John Silver. Solar Prince was also sire of Supreme Witch, dam of Tric Trac, Spectre and Forward King. The winners of no other classic event have contributed more to producing the champions of modern track racing: first Mad Tanist, then Sandown Champion, followed by Hi There and Bauhaus, all of them champions on the track and sires without rival. Add to them Wonder Valley and Newdown Heather, winners of the Dunmore Puppy Cup in 1963 and 1965, and it will be seen that Dunmore greyhounds have done more to produce modern champions than the winners of all other classics put together.

Only one dog to win the National Sprint has also won the Irish Derby – Keep Moving, who won both events in 1964. His time of 29.18 secs in the Derby was the fastest until Yellow Printer did 29.11 secs twelve years later, and shows just how good a dog he was.

Mad Tanist's record was later broken by Move Gas, who did 23.60 secs when winning the event in 1969; this, too, was later lowered by Irish Rain who recorded 23.52 secs. The previous year, 1968, saw one of the greatest National Sprint finishes in its history, when Prairie Flash's litter brothers Neohill Printer and Dry Flash crossed the line together to record one of the rare dead heats in a classic race; the great Russian Gun, then four and running in his last race, was only a short head behind – a magnificent effort by this great champion who had won the Irish Derby the previous year.

Over the same course are run the Smirnoff Puppy Cup for greyhounds not yet two years old, and the Dunmore Spring Cup. The Dunmore 700 has been run over 780 yds since 1961; originally sponsored by Wills, the cigarette manufacturers, it is now sponsored by Sean Graham, the Belfast and Dublin bookmakers. Probably the two best-known winners of the Puppy Cup are Wonder Valley, the Pigalle Wonder son who won in 1963, and Newdown Heather who won two years later and was only the second dog to break 24 secs. His time of 23.71 secs has never been beaten and gives some idea of his potential, which was never realized owing to injury; however he was to become the greatest sire in the history of modern greyhound racing and coursing since Mutton Cutlet fifty years before him. Only five puppies have broken 24 secs for the event since the race was inaugurated in 1951, the first being Lovely Language who did so in the first event. Wonder Valley went on to win the 1964 Irish Derby and also sired a number of outstanding greyhounds. Only one greyhound has won both the National Sprint and Puppy Cup at Dunmore Park – Hairdresser, who won both events in 1966.

It was at Dunmore Park in the early 1930s that James McKee and Jim Scott improved upon the pulley hare with a wire cable fixed below ground, and set up the M.S. Cable Hare Co. This type of hare has since been taken up by many Irish tracks. It was McKee who also devised the automatic trap release when the hare passed the starting boxes, which was a great improvement over releasing the traps by hand.

On 1 April 1977 a group of Belfast businessmen including James Delargey, Jack

McKee, Jack Hynds and the brothers Sean and Brian Graham formed a new board of directors at Dunmore Park as the track was in urgent need of revitalization. They also took over Celtic Park on 1 January 1978.

Now that there is greater interest in winter racing in Ireland, coursing, as in England, taking a back seat, the Irish tracks are turning to sand instead of turf for their running surface because it ensures better drainage in wet weather. Dunmore Park changed to a sand surface in 1978, the first track in Ireland to do so. The track surface was removed to a depth of 10 ins and sand brought from the Republic to replace the soil and turf. Provided the sand is watered and rolled during dry weather, it provides a better running surface than turf. Faster times are achieved, and as there is little or no slipping at the turns there are fewer injuries to the dogs.

As tote betting is not permitted on the Northern Ireland tracks (the only part of Britain and Ireland where it is not allowed) and with the track not being eligible for any Bord na gCon grants, the Stadium is supported entirely by its patrons and by those who bring greyhounds for trials. Racing takes place on three nights a week – Tuesdays, Thursdays and Saturdays – while trials are held on Monday and Friday and schooling on Wednesday and Saturday. The fee is £1 per dog, and as more than a hundred dogs a day use the track it brings in a useful income, while 156 meetings take place each year. The sand surface stands up to this hard usage and can be in daily use whatever the weather.

At Dunmore races still take place over 435, 525, 550, 600 and 700 yds. These are the most popular distances, and the new management have sensibly retained them. For more than thirty years Ian Ross has been a popular racing manager, and did much to maintain high standards.

When the track reopened in 1978 after extensive alterations and modernization it was the track's fiftieth anniversary year. The superb Noble Brigg won the National Sprint. Owned by Mr Arthur McGookin, he was sold to Mr B. Eastwood, the Belfast bookmaker, for £10,000 a day or two before the final. Noble Brigg's sire was Faction Fighter who was also sire of Racing Tip, winner of the Jim Rice Memorial Stakes. But perhaps the most exciting event of the year was the long awaited match for £5,000 a side over 700 yds between Yellow Band from Enniscorthy, owned by an American, and Northern Ireland's Townview Man from Newry. The race was won by Townview Man by two lengths after coming from the traps like a bullet and leading all the way.

Main Events Run at Dunmore Park

Bass Stakes	February	435 yds
Allwood Electric Stakes	May	550 yds
Guinness National Sprint	August	435 yds
Sean Graham 700	October	700 yds
Smirnoff Puppy Cup	November	435 yds

Track Records (1950)

Mad Tanist	435 yds	23.89 secs
Coolagh Ration	525 yds	29.40 secs
Carrie's Ferry	525 yds H	30.78 secs
Hatton Black	600 yds	34.52 secs

Track Records (1960)

Keep Moving	435 yds	23.65 secs
Carstown Boy	435 yds H	24.94 secs
Coolagh Ration	525 yds	29.40 secs
Hatton Black	600 yds	34.52 secs

Track Records (1970)

Move Gas	435 yds	23.60 secs
Blissful Pride	525 yds	28.88 secs
Westpark Quail	700 yds	39.13 secs

Track Records (1980)

Mister Colm	435 yds	23.31 secs
Blissful Pride	525 yds	28.88 secs
Ballydonnell Sam	600 yds	33.53 secs
Westpark Quail	700 yds	39.13 secs

Winners of the Sean Graham 700

1961	Ballinaclougher Champion	40.48 secs
1962	Poma Bocka	40.50 secs
1963	Drishane Wonder	40.53 secs
1964	Westpark Quail	39.65 secs
1965	Twisting Charlie	40.31 secs
1966	Gazarra	39.34 secs
1967	April Merry	40.38 secs
1968	Nimble Queen	40.09 secs
1969	Meadowbank Joe	40.18 secs
1970	Mic Mac	40.90 secs
1971	Tornado Tootsie	40.08 secs
1972	Rita's Choice	39.56 secs
1973	Feakle's Record	40.56 secs
1974	Rayhill Joe	41.05 secs
1975	All Shook Up	40.17 secs
1976	Garford Maxi	40.26 secs
1977	Bendradagh Dart	39.88 secs
1978	Yellow Band	39.42 secs
1979	Ballydonnell Sam	39.72 secs

Winners of the Smirnoff Puppy Cup

1951	Lovely Language	23.95 secs
1952	Cheeky Tippy	24.19 secs
1953	More Tea	24.66 secs
1954	Flying Champion	24.33 secs
1955	Major of Pleasure	24.97 secs
1956	Frisky Look	24.20 secs
1957	Drummullagh Tower	24.37 secs
1958	Glittering Brook	24.43 secs
1959	Greenane Sunrise	24.58 secs
1960	Grazy Motto	24.19 secs
1961	Tanyard Chef	24.17 secs
1962	Monday's Ranger	24.41 secs
1963	Wonder Valley	24.06 secs
1964	Alpine Message	24.03 secs
1965	Newdown Heather	23.71 secs
1966	Hairdresser	24.41 secs
1967	Graham's Cuff	24.50 secs
1968	Winter Hope	23.96 secs

Winners of Smirnoff Puppy Cup

1969	Wonder Lannon	24.41 secs
1970	Silver Plassey	24.38 secs
1971	Ballylander	23.98 secs
1972	Mister Colm	24.34 secs
1973	Empty Pride	24.40 secs
1974	Glory Boy	24.44 secs
1975	Cairn Pride	24.32 secs
1976	Carmoni Mint	24.44 secs
1977	Glenroe Hiker	24.61 secs
1978	Carlin Minstrel	23.94 secs
1979	Maireads Style	23.92 secs
1980	Please Retain	24.16 secs

Winners of the Guinness National Sprint

1943	Fair Mistress	24.03 secs
1944	Mad Tanist	24.11 secs
1945	Oranmore Bandit	24.08 secs
1946	Count Lally	24.56 secs
1947	Fair Moving) Hockfield Light)	24.32 secs
1948	Leamas Sport	24.66 secs
1949	Burndennet Brook	23.99 secs
1950	Sandown Champion	23.86 secs
1951	Mad Companion	23.88 secs
1952	Kilrid Blackbird	23.90 secs
1953	Mushera Shaggy	23.99 secs
1954	Hi There	24.51 secs
1955	Claremont John	23.77 secs
1956	Keep Moving	23.65 secs
1957	Coalfield Here	24.04 secs
1958	Obedia's Son	23.89 secs
1959	Clougharevan Boy	23.84 secs
1960	Skip's Choice	23.92 secs
1961	Highland Fame	24.22 secs
1962	Tanyard Chef	23.96 secs
1963	Melody Wonder	24.17 secs
1964	Dorade	24.08 secs
1965	Bauhus	23.73 secs
1966	Hairdresser	23.89 secs
1967	Mullaghroe Hiker	23.72 secs
1968	Dry Flash) Newhill Printer)	24.10 secs
1969	Move Gas	23.60 secs
1970	Gaultier Swank	24.00 secs
1971	Benbradagh Luck	23.74 secs
1972	Clashing	23.72 secs
1973	Get the Point	23.87 secs
1974	Empty Pride	24.05 secs
1975	Rapid Roger	23.58 secs
1976	Thurles Yard	24.04 secs
1977	Land Power	23.97 secs
1978	Noble Brigg	23.76 secs
1979	La Cosa Nostra	23.82 secs
1980	Blue Train	23.77 secs
1981	Noble Legion	23.78 secs

ENNISCORTHY

On 3 August 1933 greyhound racing started at Enniscorthy, the first provincial track in Ireland, and its directors were Denis O'Brien, J. McCrea, W.K. Stamp and Tim Larkin. Mr O'Brien was still a director more than forty years later at the age of ninety, and the track is flourishing as never before. Racing takes place on Monday and Thursday each week, over 525 yds, 550 yds and 600 yds, and the slight incline at the start makes for slower times than at most tracks. The track has a circumference of 480 yds. Sean McCrea, son of James McCrea, is racing manager, and Mr O'Brien's daughter Kathleen Prendergast is the official timekeeper, the only woman official on any greyhound track. She is also a director, as is Harry Larkin, son of the late Tim Larkin; Sean McCrea; and Billy Stamp, son of the late W.K. Stamp. So the track's affairs are in the hands of the sons and daughter of the founders.

Here are staged the Grand Prize (the counterpart of Britain's Grand Prix) and the Leinster Puppy Stakes, both prestige events in the Irish racing calendar. The latter was won in 1940 by the wonderful bitch Brilliant Gay who in the following year ran up for the Coursing Oaks. She was to enjoy even greater fame as the mother of Hurry Kitty, one of the greatest bitches of all time, and of Paddy the Champion, one of the greatest sires. He sired Astra's Son, who in turn was sire of Magourna Reject.

Two greyhounds to win the English Derby, Mile Bush Pride and Palm's Printer, began their careers at this track, as did the 'Monalee' greyhounds which are bred nearby, where the great dam Sheila at Last was the foundation of the line. Mated to Crazy Parachute, she produced Monalee Champion, who with Newdown Heather was the greatest sire of the 1970s. Among his sons were Itsachampion, sire of Lacca Champion, winner of the 1977 Irish Derby; and Jimsun, who in turn sired another Derby winner, Sarah's Bunny. He also sired Cobbler, sire of Sally's Cobbler; Wired to the Moon; and Tain Mor, yet another Irish Derby winner.

In 1963 the Wexford (now the Guinness Wexford) Leger was inaugurated, run over 550 yds, the first winner being Mr Hatton's famous bitch Sheila at Last, who from a mating with Odd Venture whelped Monalee King who was to win the Wexford Leger in 1965 and for several years held the 550 yds record there. His daughter Monalee Leader was to win the event in 1971. No other important event has been so dominated by the progeny of one dam in the history of the sport.

Winner of the Guinness Wexford Leger in 1972 was Mr Paddy Nolan's black bitch Quick Thought, who broke two track records in one week, lowering the 550 yds to 30.80 secs and becoming the first to break the 31 secs barrier. She was by Yanka Boy out of Nolan's famous dam An Tain.

Coupled with the Grand Prize is the name

of the late W.K. Stamp, and the event is worth £1,250 to the winner. It is now sponsored by Guinness. A similar sum is awarded to the winner of the Champion Puppy Stakes, won in 1978 by Bregate who was one of the few puppies to better 30 secs for the 500 yds course. Hurdle racing has always been a feature here and one of the outstanding bitches to race over hurdles was Dogstown Fame, who in 1968 set a new record of 30.60 secs for the 525 yds hurdles course. She was to become famous as the dam of Time Up Please, sire of the 1978 Irish Derby winner Pampered Rover.

Main Events Run at Enniscorthy

April Stakes	April	525 yds
Guinness Wexford Leger	May	550 yds
Grand Prize and W.K. Stamp Memorial Cup	July	525 yds
Leinster Puppy Stakes	September	525 yds

Track Records (1950)

Carlow Printer	525 yds	18.15 secs
Millugh Fairy	325 yds H	18.78 secs
Carlow Joe	525 yds	30.00 secs
Kuadza	550 yds	31.68 secs

Track Records (1960)

Pleasure Flight	1957	325 yds	18.05 secs
No Play	1957	325 yds	18.05 secs
Palm's Sonny	1956	325 yds H	18.55 secs
Fitz's Chariot	1956	325 yds H	18.55 secs
Precious Princess	1958	500 yds	28.70 secs
Carlow Joe		525 yds	30.00 secs
You Dropout	1947	525 yds H	31.40 secs

Track Records (1970)

Pleasure Flight	1957	325 yds	18.05 secs
No Play	1957	325 yds	18.05 secs
Palm's Sonny	1956	325 yds H	18.55 secs
Fitz's Chariot	1956	325 yds H	18.55 secs
Precious Princess	1958	500 yds	28.70 secs
Next Round	1968	500 yds H	29.55 secs
Cross Mistress	1965	525 yds	29.50 secs
Dogstown Fame	1967	525 yds H	30.60 secs
Monalee King	1965	550 yds	30.60 secs

Track Records (1980)

No Play	1957	325 yds	18.05 secs
Pleasure Flight	1957	325 yds	18.05 secs
Palm's Sonny	1956	325 yds H	18.55 secs
Fitz's Chariot	1956	325 yds H	18.55 secs
Precious Princess	1958	500 yds	28.70 secs
Next Round	1968	500 yds H	29.55 secs
Rail Ship	1973	525 yds	29.20 secs
Supreme Blue	1974	525 yds	29.20 secs
Hillville Harry	1975	525 yds	29.20 secs
Dogstown Fame	1967	525 yds H	30.60 secs
Yellow Band	1978	550 yds	30.60 secs
Get Going	1974	600 yds	33.40 secs

Winners of the Grand Prize and W.K. Stamp Memorial Cup

1960	Sandown Dick
1961	Moyne Rocket
1962	Toast the Prince
1963	Jumbo Valley
1964	Barrow Prince
1965	Brandon Jungle
1966	Kiddie Kut
1967	Shean Ransom
1968	Whiteoaks Lady
1969	Roiterri
1970	Ballybush Flyer
1971	Day Di
1972	Daddy's Chick
1973	Rail Ship
1974	Coras Skip
1975	Kenler Darkie
1976	Jiggins Best
1977	Luminous Rory
1978	Kylehill Gem
1979	Altitude
1980	Black Arkle

Winners of the Guinness Wexford Leger

1969	Rich Tea	31.10 secs
1970	Monalee Leader	31.15 secs
1971	Ask Goodness	31.00 secs
1972	Aquaduct Lady	31.00 secs
1973	Solid Hit	31.00 secs
1974	Millie's Express	30.70 secs
1975	Christmas	31.00 secs
1976	Cecil's Delight	31.20 secs
1977	Slip over Sabot	31.20 secs
1978	Quarrymount Jack	30.85 secs
1979	White Ferrari	31.15 secs
1980	Another Trail	31.25 secs

GALWAY

It is the most westerly city in Ireland to have a greyhound track, and racing takes place on Tuesday and Friday each week at the new venue in College Road, built at a cost of some £500,000 and opened in May 1979. Races are run over 325 yds, 525 yds, 550 yds and 700 yds, while hurdles events are also popular over these distances. The main events are the O'Droighnean Cup and the Galway Sprint, the former run over 525 yds, the latter over 325 yds.

One of the finest greyhounds to race at Galway in the early years was Marching Through Georgia, who set a new 525 yds record here in 1939 and went on to defeat Irish Rambler to win the Derby on the only occasion it was run at Limerick. Another great dog was the hurdler Bay Moon, who set a new hurdles record at Galway shortly afterwards.

During 1978 the track was closed for modernization and improvements. A new stand with bars and tote facilities was built, while the bends have been banked and the track resurfaced. The newly modernised track was ready for racing again on 25 May 1979, after renovations costing nearly half a million pounds. Tom Holland is the racing manager here.

Main Events Run at Galway

O'Droighnean Cup	May	525 yds
Galway Sprint	July	325 yds
Galway Marathon	July	810 yds

Track Records (1950)

Hello, Guy	325 yds	18.61 secs
Gambling Editor	330 yds H	19.75 secs
Marching through Georgia	525 yds	30.00 secs
Bay Moon	525 yds H	31.00 secs

Track Records (1960)

Hello, Guy		325 yds	18.15 secs
Levally Roe	1958	325 yds H	19.00 secs
Golden Victory	1951	500 yds	28.52 secs
Marching through Georgia	1940	525 yds	30.00 secs
Golsto	1956	525 yds H	30.55 secs
Gorman's Fancy	1950	550 yds	32.90 secs
Farmhill Prince	1950	600 yds	35.05 secs
Rambling Customer	1960	700 yds	41.12 secs

Track Records (1970)

Ardrine Belle	1970	325 yds	17.88 secs
Levally Roe	1958	325 yds H	19.00 secs
Move Handy	1966	330 yds	18.05 secs
Golden Victory	1951	500 yds	28.82 secs
Marching through Georgia	1940	525 yds	30.00 secs
Golsto	1956	525 yds H	30.55 secs
Gorman's Fancy	1950	550 yds	32.90 secs
Rambling Customer	1960	700 yds	41.12 secs

Track Records (1980)

Patricia's Champ	1976	325 yds	17.95 secs
Levally Roe	1958	325 yds H	19.00 secs
Move Handy	1966	330 yds	18.05 secs
Golden Victory	1951	500 yds	28.82 secs
Splendid Silver	1976	525 yds	29.50 secs
Golsto	1956	525 yds H	30.55 secs
Fealeside Duke	1977	550 yds	31.28 secs
Rambling Customer	1960	700 yds	41.12 secs
Skilful Story	1975	810 yds	46.80 secs

Winners of the O'Droighnean Cup

1970	Elegance	30.02 secs
1971	Winterfield Hero	30.30 secs
1972	Glamorous Hero	30.30 secs
1973	Prince Owen	30.20 secs
1974	Clomboo Castle	30.00 secs
1975	Don Quixote	30.00 secs
1976	Splendid Silver	29.75 secs
1977	Reward the Black	30.50 secs
1978	not run	
1979	Brandy Express	30.25 secs
1980	Queen's Town	29.86 secs

HAROLD'S CROSS

About three miles from the centre of Dublin, this track is pleasantly situated and may be likened to the Catford Stadium in London, with Shelbourne Park the counterpart of the White City. It opened on 10 April 1928, a year after Shelbourne Park, with John O'Riordan as its first racing manager, followed by his son John F. who continued in office for more than thirty years, to be superseded by his son, Kerry, and more recently by George Deegan. The veterinary surgeon at the track when it opened was Arthur Callanan, more familiarly known as 'Doc' Callanan, for by his great ability and untiring care he saved many greyhounds at a time when veterinary science was in its infancy and vaccination almost unknown. He looked after Mick the Miller and Creamery Border at the start of their racing careers, and without his great skill these champions might never have reached a racecourse. Later he was to become a trainer at Wembley, but his days at Harold's Cross have never been forgotten and his memory is perpetuated by the Callanan Cup, one of the most popular events held at the track. Arthur owned the little black bitch Nanny Goosegog, who was never beaten in her thirty-two races and became as popular in Dublin as her contemporary Mick the Miller was in England. As a number of her races were handicap events, her record has never been given the attention it deserved, for she was the first to draw the crowd to the Dublin track, as did Astra and Baytown Ivy in later years. The Callanan Cup is run over 525 yds and in importance is the counterpart of Shelbourne Park's Easter Cup. It takes place in March, just before the Easter Cup is run. One of the outstanding winners of the Callanan Cup in recent years was Finola's Yarn who won in 1969. After winning his first heat, the dog was purchased by Cyril Young and he went on to win his semi-final and final when he was quoted at 6–4.

The Oaks, a race confined to bitches, is the classic run at Harold's Cross in early September. At one time the Derby and Oaks alternated between the two Dublin tracks, but now the Derby is run at Shelbourne Park and the Oaks here, though the Oaks was run at the sister track in 1977 and 1978 when Harold's Cross was undergoing modernization. This included the building of a new stand with excellent restaurant and tote facilities, though some people feel it has lost something of the atmosphere of the older stand. But modernization was necessary and Harold's Cross was never a track to fall behind the times.

The first Oaks was run at Clonmel in 1932, over 550 yds, and it was again run at Clonmel the following year but this time over 525 yds, over which distance it has since been run. In 1934 it was first run at Harold's Cross, and was won by Chocolate Kid in the slowest time ever recorded for the event. The 1946 Oaks, run here, is generally conceded to be the best ever seen, from the heats right through to the final, for it was dominated by the two brilliant bitches Baytown Ivy and Cold Christmas. When winning her semi-final 'Ivy', as she was affectionately known to Dubliners, set a new track record which was broken just a few days later when Cold Christmas took the final, with 'Ivy' in second place, in 29.89 secs, the fastest time recorded for the final and one which was not beaten until ten years later when Prairie Peg clocked 29.55 secs at Shelbourne Park, and at Harold's Cross when Ballet Festival recorded 29.73 secs in 1958. Apart from this one occasion, Cold Christmas's time was unbeaten by a bitch at Harold's Cross until 1966 when Hairdresser clocked 29.40 secs, twenty years after the great encounter between those two outstanding greyhounds of the first post-war years. The 1979 Oaks was sponsored by the Lyon Industrial Estate, with £10,000 going to the winner.

Until 1969 Harold's Cross alternated with Shelbourne Park in staging the Derby. The 1934 event, held here, was won by Frisco Hobo. Abbeylara won the 1938 Derby here and went on to win the St Leger that year, and in 1945 Lilac's Luck was victorious beating the courageous Gun Music. Four years later came Spanish Lad, whose son Spanish Battleship won in 1953 the first of his three crowns, two of them at this track. The Grand Fire, who passed on his great speed and track craft through many dams and was one of the most influential sires of modern track racing, came here in 1957 to run up to Hopeful Cutlet, and in 1967 Russian Gun, to become an equally famous sire, won the Harold's Cross Derby. Two years later the last Derby held here was won by Own Pride, who ran up the following year at Shelbourne Park. His time of 29.20 secs was the fastest ever for a Derby final at this track.

The Puppy Derby, which has always been run at Harold's Cross, is now sponsored by the Burmah Castrol Co. From 1943 to 1950 it was run over 500 yds, with Fawn Cherry the first winner and Astra the following year. The 1945 event was dominated by two of the fastest dogs in the history of the sport – Shaggy Lad, Castledown Lad's finest son, and Quare Times. Those who saw them race are in no doubt that these two were the two fastest ever to race in Ireland. Shaggy Lad was owned by Mr Arthur Probert, an Englishman who went over to Ireland in 1939 and purchased the champion hurdlers Printer and Tanist – the latter won the Derby for him in 1940. Shaggy Lad was to become sire of the Derby winner Spanish Lad and other outstanding greyhounds. Shaggy Lad, litter brother to Shaggy Lass, just had the better of Quare Times in that great final, to win in 27.96 secs, the only occasion 28 secs had ever been broken in the final; it was the second time during the event that he had broken the 28 secs barrier, believed to be impossible. By far the fastest time for the 525 yds course was the 29.08 secs recorded in 1976 by Glen Rock when winning from Game Parachute. The Puppy Derby is run in the autumn, and a month later the Haughey Stakes is contested over 580 yds to conclude the racing year.

The first Grand National, now held at Kilkenny, was run at Harold's Cross and won by Cowboy. Three years later Orluck was successful here; The Gunner won in 1941. This was the last occasion on which it was run here, though Harold's Cross has always staged races over hurdles.

In 1944 automatic starting traps were installed here, the first on any track in Ireland. Racing takes place over 330, 525, 580 and 750 yds on Tuesday, Thursday and Friday evening, and the track, of 500 yds circuit, is one of the fastest in the world. Bord Na gCon took over its running on 1 January 1971.

Main Events Run at Harold's Cross

Callanan Memorial Cup	March	525 yds
Islandbridge Open Sprint	April	330 yds
Corn Cuchulainn	June	750 yds
Irish Oaks	September	525 yds
Auctioneer's Stakes	September	580 yds
Burmah Castrol Puppy Derby	October	525 yds
Haughey Stakes	November	580 yds

Track Records (1950)

Sky Patrol	350 yds	19.20 secs
Printer	350 yds H	20.36 secs
Shaggy Lad	500 yds	27.96 secs
Inly	500 yds H	30.08 secs
Cold Christmas	525 yds	29.86 secs
General Kildare	525 yds H	30.72 secs
Dee Diabolo	580 yds	33.35 secs
Druze	580 yds H	34.73 secs
Yardley Whistler	600 yds	34.00 secs
Soaring Leary	750 yds	45.30 secs

Track Records (1960)

The Mall	325 yds	18.26 secs
Shaggy Lad	500 yds	27.96 secs
Spanish Battleship	525 yds	29.53 secs
Make Sure	525 yds H	30.65 secs
Yardley Whistler	600 yds	34.80 secs
Soaring Leary	750 yds	45.30 secs

Track Records (1970)

The Mall	1958	325 yds	18.26 secs
Clomoney Grand	1966	525 yds	29.03 secs
Make Sure	1960	525 yds H	30.65 secs
Mile Bush Pat	1964	550 yds	30.75 secs
Seskin Mist	1968	550 yds	30.75 secs
Hurry Guy	1968	580 yds	32.30 secs
Ballybeg Pride	1968	750 yds	42.15 secs

Track Records (1980)

Bay Vale	1978	330 yds	17.76 secs
Romping to Work	1973	525 yds	28.86 secs
Keeragh Sambo	1975	525 yds H	29.90 secs
Move First	1975	550 yds	30.48 secs
Rail Ship	1973	580 yds	31.82 secs
Dark Cowboy	1975	580 yds H	32.88 secs
Rita's Choice	1973	750 yds	42.10 secs
Ballygall Point	1978	830 yds	47.32 secs

Winners of the Irish Oaks

1932	Queen of the Suir	30.80 secs	Cl
1933	Loophole	30.55 secs	Cl
1934	Chocolate Kid	31.18 secs	HX
1935	The Fenian Bride	30.73 secs	SP
1936	Chicken Sandwich	30.73 secs	HX
1937	Godiva's Turn	30.61 secs	SP
1938	Gentle Sally Again	30.13 secs	HX
1939	Janetta Hunloke	30.47 secs	C
1940–1	not run		
1942	Fair Mistress	30.10 secs	L
1943	Mad Printer	30.05 secs	C
1944	My Little Daisy	30.08 secs	HX
1945	Paladin's Charm	30.70 secs	SP
1946	Cold Christmas	29.86 secs	HX
1947	Belle o' Manhattan	30.46 secs	SP
1948	Lovely Louisa	29.90 secs	HX
1949	Coolkill Darkie	30.36 secs	SP
1950	Celtic Gem	30.00 secs	HX
1951	Glenco Pearl	30.23 secs	SP
1952	Peaceful Lady	29.95 secs	HX
1953	Peaceful Lady	30.11 secs	SP
1954	Wild Iris	30.04 secs	HX
1955	Prairie Peg	29.55 secs	SP
1956	Baytown Dell	29.99 secs	HX
1957	Gallant Maid	30.02 secs	SP
1958	Ballet Festival	29.73 secs	HX
1959	Last Landing	30.09 secs	SP
1960	Tristam	30.03 secs	HX
1961	Just Sherry	29.95 secs	SP
1962	Purty Good	29.78 secs	HX
1963	Cherry Express	29.87 secs	SP
1964	Knock Her	29.98 secs	HX
1965	Drumsough Princess	29.76 secs	SP
1966	Hairdresser	29.40 secs	HX
1967	Kevinsfort Queen	29.79 secs	SP
1968	Orwell Parade	29.96 secs	HX
1969	Itsamint	29.35 secs	SP
1970	Rosmore Robin	29.60 secs	HX
1971	Blissful Pride	29.30 secs	HX
1972	Brandon Velvet	29.45 secs	HX
1973	Romping to Work	29.20 secs	HX
1974	Fur Collar	29.40 secs	HX
1975	Main Avenue	28.98 secs	HX
1976	Clashing Daisy	29.64 secs	HX
1977	Snow Maiden	29.09 secs	SP
1978	Hail Fun	29.40 secs	SP
1979	Nameless Pixie	29.34 secs	HX
1980	Strange Legend	29.34 secs	HX
1981	Claremount May	29.52 secs	HX

Those run at Harold's Cross shown HX; those at Shel. Pk SP; Clonmel, Cl; Limerick, L; Cork, C

Winners of the Sean Kelly 750 and Corn Cuchulainn

1961	Special Move	42.78 secs
1962	The Fixer	43.05 secs
1963	Tracy Crisps) Danton)	42.80 secs
1964	Chieftain's Envoy	42.70 secs
1965	Westpark Quail	42.42 secs
1966	Radiographer	42.77 secs
1967	Proud Molly	43.40 secs
1968	The Saint	43.20 secs
1969	Hat Band	43.10 secs
1970	Quakerfield King	42.54 secs
1971	Fleur de Lis	43.27 secs
1972	Keeragh Bluff	42.93 secs
1973	Rita's Choice	42.40 secs
1974	Purple Sun	43.04 secs
1975	Cricky Choice	42.72 secs
1976	Lord of Moray	42.62 secs
1977	Rathdaniel Irene	42.74 secs
1978	Orient Champ	42.58 secs
1979	Yvonne's Glory	42.60 secs
1980	Dolittle Sarah	43.10 secs
1981	Kilnaglory Pearl	42.72 secs

Opposite: Wembley trainer Bob Burls with Irish Oaks winner Drumsough Princess.

Winners of the Burmah Castrol Puppy Derby

1943	Fawn Cherry	28.36 secs
1944	Astra	28.52 secs
1945	Shaggy Lad	27.96 secs
1946	Ten Derry's	28.54 secs
1947	Fearless Invader	28.70 secs
1948	Buzz on Train	28.91 secs
1949	For Sure	28.60 secs
*1950	Sealed Castle	28.51 secs
1951	Odile's Latch	29.97 secs
1952	Olly's Pal	29.89 secs
1953	Baytown Colt	30.30 secs
1954	The Grand Streak	30.12 secs
1955	Master of Me	30.00 secs
1956	Leg it Lucy	29.93 secs
1957	Prince Olly	30.11 secs
1958	Balrath Flute	30.18 secs
1959	Choc Ice	29.80 secs
1960	King Niall	30.68 secs
1961	Wild Spark	29.75 secs
1962	Kudas Tiger	29.55 secs
1963	Fleadh Music	29.40 secs
1964	Wonder Guest	29.96 secs
1965	Prince of Roses	29.40 secs
1966	Little Kate	30.17 secs
1967	Quarrymount Prim	29.70 secs
1968	Always Keen	29.75 secs
1969	Ballad	29.64 secs
1970	Hey Dizzy	29.74 secs
1971	Luminous Lady	29.70 secs
1972	Clane Royal	30.20 secs
1973	Blessington Boy	29.68 secs
1974	Shamrock Point	29.48 secs
1975	Elsinore Silver	29.40 secs
1976	Glen Rock	29.08 secs
1977	Hammond	29.46 secs
1978	Greenhill Paddy	29.40 secs
1979	Tivoli Cant	29.88 secs
1980	Killahora Champ	29.42 secs
1981	Greenwood Robic	29.86 secs

* 1943–50 run over 500 yds; thereafter over 525 yds

Winners of the Callanan Memorial Cup

1970	Rosmore Robin	29.40 secs
1971	Lucky Punter	29.58 secs
1972	Eighthouses	29.62 secs
1973	Ardrine Moss	29.54 secs
1974	Tommy Astaire	29.26 secs
1975	Tommy Astaire	29.36 secs
1976	Peruvian Style	29.30 secs
1977	Cautious Cal	29.56 secs
1978	not run	
1979	Matlock	29.80 secs
1980	Endless Star	30.24 secs
1981	Blue Stone	30.18 secs

KILKENNY

The track opened on 5 June 1946. Racing takes place here on Wednesday and Friday each week, and the track is the largest and one of the fastest in Ireland.

Among the events run here are the McCalmont Cup, worth £1,000 to the

winner; the Hurst Cup; and the Great Whistler Cup – each of these events over 525 yds. At Kilkenny are also run the Friends of the CBS Perpetual Challenge Cup and the Friends of the Social Services Cup, both of which carry a first prize of £1,000. The McCalmont Cup was first contested in 1947 and was won by the bitch Lady Maud, who set a new track record. Four years later it was won by Mad Tanist's son The Grand Champion. In 1954 and 1955 the McCalmont Cup was won by the great Spanish Battleship who took all before him during those years and established himself as one of the outstanding racing greyhounds of all time. Another first-class greyhound who won the Hurst Cup was the blue bitch Clomoney Grand, later an excellent dam also. On 28 May 1966 she clocked 29.00 secs for the 525 yds course, to set a new track record which was not beaten until thirteen-years later, when the black dog Lax Law (Tain Mor–Miss Rowley) clocked 28.98 secs in round 2 of the McCalmont Cup, the first dog to break 29.00 secs at Kilkenny. In 1968, from a mating with Prairie Flash, Clomoney Grand whelped that great litter which included Albany, Kilbelin Style who was to be second in the English Derby, and the Irish Derby finalist Kelbelin Grand.

Clomoney Grand put up several of her finest performances here, including her win in the first Waterford Glass International in which she made a new track record. In 1976 another outstanding greyhound came here to win the Hurst Cup. His name was Nameless Star and he was to become the only greyhound in England or Ireland to win a St Leger and a Laurels, which he did in Ireland in the same year.

The racing manager at the track since its opening until his death in 1978 was the much respected James Kinahan, a great coursing man who made the track one of Ireland's best. The new racing manager is John Flynn, who was to see some outstanding greyhounds perform during his first year there, one of the best being Alert Bell, trained by David Flynn for his mother. The dog was to win the McCalmont Cup in the fast time of 29.35 secs. Only two or three greyhounds have ever beaten this time while the Hurst Cup was won by Mr D. Comerford's Ivy Hall Dasher.

Main Events Run at Kilkenny

Ossory Stakes and Hurst Cup	June	525 yds
McCalmont Cup	September	525 yds
Great Whistler Cup	October	525 yds
Racewell Stakes	November	525 yds

Track Records (1960)

Verboden	1960	300 yds	16.50 secs
Singing Border	1952	300 yds H	17.35 secs
Clopook King	1959	550 yds	31.50 secs

Track Records (1970)

Verboden	1960	300 yds	16.50 secs
Singing Border	1952	300 yds H	17.35 secs
Magic Hands	1962	500 yds	28.30 secs
Clomoney Grand	1966	525 yds	29.00 secs
Tropical Splendour	1961	525 yds H	29.95 secs
Clopook King	1959	550 yds	31.50 secs
White Sails	1966	700 yds	41.00 secs

Track Records (1980)

Magic Hands	1962	500 yds	28.30 secs
Lax Law	1979	525 yds	28.98 secs
Ballybeg Maid	1975	525 yds	29.00 secs
Nameless Star	1976	525 yds	29.00 secs
Tropical Splendour	1961	525 yds H	29.95 secs
Clopook King	1959	550 yds	31.50 secs
The Knack	1966	700 yds	40.85 secs

Winners of the McCalmont Cup

1963	April Twilight	29.60 secs
1964	Good Brandy	30.00 secs
1965	Come on Baunie	30.20 secs
1966	Brandon Jungle	30.30 secs
1967	Hack 'em Jo-Jo	30.40 secs
1968	Limestone Castle	29.65 secs
1969	Seafield Mink	29.60 secs
1970	Ballyea Hope	29.20 secs
1971	The Grand Light	29.60 secs
1972	Grey Light	29.60 secs
1973	Tain Rua	29.75 secs
1974	Shady Ruffian	29.70 secs
1975	Goodbye John	29.70 secs
1976	Antone Wonder	29.85 secs
1977	Jolly Youth	29.65 secs
1978	Alert Bell	29.35 secs
1979	Lax Law	29.35 secs
1980	Flying Marble	29.70 secs
1981	Anner Duke	29.60 secs

Winners of the Great Whistler Challenge Cup

1970	Lincoln's Faith	30.90 secs
1971	Regent Cindy	29.85 secs
1972	Midnight Trip	30.50 secs
1973	Solar Silver	30.60 secs
1975	Play Silver	30.20 secs
1976	Foot it Ramdeen	30.10 secs
1977	Ballyneale Boss	30.00 secs
1979	Doire Garb	31.10 secs
1980	Pope's Bridge	29.90 secs

LIFFORD

This small town in Co. Donegal in Eire is not far from Derry in Ulster, which also has a greyhound track, so that this rather remote part of Ireland has two tracks within easy reach of each other. Both draw 90 per cent of their support and their greyhounds from the North. Lifford has been open only twenty years as a licensed track – in 1959 a cattle dealer called James Magee built the track here on land grazed by his bullocks, and he became the first director. Since his death in 1971 his sons Cathal and Seamus have administered the track as racing manager and general manager respectively. A new stand, with a glass-enclosed bar, was erected in 1971, when the first inside hare in Ireland was also installed. The track is large, almost 500 yds in circumference. Racing takes place on Tuesday, Thursday and Saturday each week over 325 yds, 500 yds and 575 yds, with an occasional race over 790 yds. The track record for the 790 yds course (almost twice round the track) is held by the bitch Barrick Maid, who in 1978 clocked 45.03 secs for what is one of the longest races on any track in Ireland.

The Irwin Cup and Harp Lager Stakes are the premier events which draw many entries each year. Another prestige event here is the Abraham David Trophy which carries a prize of £2,500 for the winner, the biggest amount for any non-classic race in Ireland outside the Dublin tracks. Run over 575 yds, it was won in 1978 by Mrs Owen's Tough Decision. He was the first of Minnesota Miller's sons and litter brother to Moss Fairy. The Border Trophy is also run here and the Duffy Greenbrae Sweepstake with its prize of £1,000, as well as the North-west Leger. Indeed, few other provincial tracks enjoy better patronage. Here Yellow Printer and Top Note began their careers as puppies, when they were unknown outside this little town. But no greyhound caused more excitement at the track than the bitch Marina's Crazy, owned by Ronnin McKeown, who on 18 August 1979 flew round the 525 yds course in the amazing time of 29.18 secs, to lower Palestine June's 29.35 secs which had stood for several years. Marina's Crazy is by Supreme Fun out of Marina's Magic, and was whelped in October 1977.

Main Events Run at Lifford

Lifford Derby	April	525 yds
Matchabelli Cup	May	525 yds
Duffy Greenbrae Sweepstake	July	525 yds
James Magee Memorial Trophy	August	525 yds
Border Trophy	August	525 yds
Irwin Cup	September	525 yds
Abraham David Trophy	September	575 yds
Harp Lager Stakes	October	325 yds

Track Records (1970)

Golden Ram	1961	325 yds	17.94 secs
Taxi Dancer	1970	525 yds	29.52 secs
Bowe Princess	1962	550 yds	31.08 secs
Duel	1967	575 yds	32.46 secs
Bowe Princess	1962	780 yds	45.10 secs

Track Records (1980)

Fulmax Fever	1976	325 yds	17.84 secs
Marina's Crazy	1979	525 yds	29.18 secs
Bowe Princess	1962	550 yds	31.08 secs
Tour Valley	1977	575 yds	32.11 secs
Barrack Maid	1978	790 yds	45.03 secs

Winners of the Irwin Cup

1970	Lee Fee Pois	30.03 secs
1971	Bits and Pieces	30.19 secs
1972	Free Mission	29.91 secs
1973	Jon Chuck	30.34 secs
1974	Kensington Park	29.90 secs
1975	Bann Blue	29.85 secs
1976	Clady Blue	29.82 secs
1977	Kisses for Me	29.60 secs
1978	Friendly Lawyer	29.45 secs
1979	Prince of Gold	29.70 secs
1980	Alone Solo	30.31 secs
1981	Brogan's Gem	29.89 secs

LIMERICK

The city is situated in the lush green province of Munster, near to Shannon Airport and the plains of Clounanna where the Irish Coursing Cup is contested annually. The greyhound racecourse opened in 1933; its directors were T.F. Ryan and J.P. Frost. In the early years of the sport no classic event was allocated to this track, and it was not until 1944 that the Irish St Leger was run here on a permanent basis, though it was staged here in 1940, when it was won by Cherrygrove Cross. The first St Leger was in fact run at Celtic Park in 1932, when Castle Eve was the winner, and the next year Brilliant Bob won the event at Clonmel on the only occasion it was run at this track. Celtic Park staged the 1943 Leger, won for the second time by Monarch of the Glen. The previous year he had won the event at Harold's Cross.

The 1944 Leger was won by No Relation, who defeated the Irish Derby winner of that year, Clonbonny Bridge. The first dog to cover the St Leger course in less than 31.00 secs was Doonmore Dreamer, who recorded 30.98 secs in 1955. The following year Prince of Bermuda won the Leger in the amazing time of 30.66 secs, which was not bettered for fifteen years and then only by one tenth of a second, when Time Up Please recorded the first of two successive wins with a time of 30.65 secs. Only on eight occasions since its inauguration has 31.00 secs been broken for the St Leger, and among other dogs to have done so are Movealong Santa, Yanka Boy, Own Pride and Pools Punter. The last dog, a son of Oregon Prince, was owned by Mr George Adams of Sheffield who won it in 1968 to become the first Englishman ever to win this classic event.

Since 1965, when Lovely Chieftain won the St Leger with a time of 30.92 secs, being only the third dog to break the 31 secs barrier, every greyhound winning the event had proved an all-round champion, winning other classics or events of almost classic status while also proving himself a top-class sire. Among them were Movealong Santa, Yanka Boy, Own Pride, Lively Band and Time Up Please, and more recently Ballybeg Prim, Nameless Star and Rhu. For the past fourteen years the St Leger has been won by truly great dogs.

Time Up Please won in 1971 and 1972, being one of only two dogs in Ireland or in England ever to win the event twice. A black, by Newdown Heather, he was originally owned by Mr Pat Browne, a Limerick bookmaker who sold him to Mr Michael Loughnane whose Yanka Boy had won the Leger in 1967. The 1971 race, however, ended in tragedy, for Mr Loughnane collapsed and died on the track before he could receive the trophy.

Since he trained Prince of Bermuda to win the 1954 St Leger, Ger McKenna has virtually made the race his own, having trained eleven winners in twenty-five years. In addition to Time Up Please, Mr McKenna trained Ballybeg Prim, Yanka Boy, Own

Irish National Greyhound Racing Award winner Ballybeg Prim (winner of the 1975 Irish St Leger and Cesarewitch), pictured with Mrs G. McKenna, who received the trophy on behalf of John Bullen. Photo: Bord na gCon.

Pride, Rita's Choice and Bashful Man, among the greatest greyhounds in the history of the sport in Ireland, perhaps in the world, for all were equally successful at stud and have had a greater influence on modern greyhound racing than any others.

Only twice has the Irish Derby been run out of Dublin, once at Cork and once at Limerick, when Marching through Georgia won in 1939. The Oaks was run here in 1942, when it was won in 30.10 secs by the great Fair Mistress who in an earlier round had set a new track record with a time of 29.98 secs, the first to beat 30.00 secs.

One of the greatest of all races to take place at Limerick was run in November 1968, when Mr F. Moran's Flaming King defeated the great Yellow Printer in 29.24 secs. Flaming King was to break his track record over 525 yds again in the same event when he covered the distance in 29.15 secs, and he also did the 550 yds Leger course in 30.48 secs. Though he did not win the St Leger, this great dog took the Cork Laurels in 1968. No dog has ever won both these classic events. Only three have ever won the Irish Derby and St Leger – Abbeylara in 1938; in 1969 Own Pride, who ran up for the Derby the following year; and Lively Band in 1974. Prince of Bermuda came near, for he ran up in the Derby in the year he won the Leger.

The track record for the 315 yds course was set up in 1938 by Well Squared and remains unbeaten, though it must be said that this distance has been superseded in recent years by the 300 yds race. For the 550 yds St Leger course, the 30.44 secs put up in the 1975 Leger final by Ballybeg Prim remains unbeaten. When Rhu won in 1978 it was in the slowest time since Brook Jockey won in 1964, but the going was heavy.

Also run at Limerick are the Bulger Cup over 550 yds, and the Kennedy Memorial Cup over 525 yds and worth £750 to the winner. The Guinness Puppy Sweepstake is also run over 525 yds. In 1979 Top Customer (by Monalee Champion out of Gruelling Point), after clocking a new record of 29.27 secs in the Guinness Sweepstake which he won by ten lengths, was purchased on behalf of a Belfast bookmaker, Alf McLean, for £6,000. This was the highest sum known to have been paid for a greyhound, though others may have changed hands for a greater amount which has not been publicized. It was at Limerick in 1968 that the previous highest price for a greyhound was paid. After he had beaten her dog Yellow Printer in an international event at the track, Flaming King was bought by Miss Pauline Wallis for £5,000. The dog went on to win the Laurels that year. The Hi-Way Hurdles Championship is another popular event at Limerick.

In 1966 the Limerick track opened its new stand, built at a cost of over £60,000, enabling its patrons to place their bets and view the racing in the comfort now expected by greyhound followers everywhere. The track is of 465 yds circuit and tends to be on the slow side. Racing takes place here on Monday, Friday and Saturday and the 550 yds St Leger course is the most popular, for it gives those dogs with stamina and track sense plenty of time to prove themselves. The racing manager for the past fifteen years has been Brendan O'Connell, who is kept fully occupied with the increased number of trials which take place daily throughout the year.

Main Events Run at Limerick

Bulger Cup	April	550 yds
Kennedy Memorial Cup	May	525 yds
Bass Ale Stakes	June	525 yds
J.P. Frost Memorial Sweepstake	August	550 yds
Guinness Puppy Sweepstake	September	525 yds
St Leger	October	550 yds
November Sweepstake	November	700 yds
Garryowen Sweepstake	December	525 yds

Track Records (1950)

Well Squared	315 yds	17.84 secs
Fair Mistress	525 yds	29.98 secs
Dark Shadow	550 yds	31.37 secs
Maiden's Beach	600 yds	35.25 secs

Track Records (1960)

Well Squared	315 yds	17.84 secs
Fair Mistress	525 yds	29.98 secs
Prince of Bermuda	550 yds	30.66 secs
Maiden's Beach	600 yds	35.25 secs

Track Records (1970)

Well Squared		315 yds	17.84 secs
Flaming King	1968	525 yds	29.15 secs
Jerry's Memory	1966	525 yds H	30.95 secs
Flaming King	1968	550 yds	30.48 secs
Greenville Queen	1970	700 yds	40.07 secs

Track Records (1980)

Lazuli Mountain	1971	300 yds	16.45 secs
Well Squared	1938	315 yds	17.84 secs
Flaming King	1968	525 yds	29.15 secs
Silver Light	1976	525 yds H	30.10 secs
Ballybeg Prim	1975	550 yds	30.44 secs
Nancy's Laurel	1952	600 yds	34.70 secs
Dromlara Champ	1975	700 yds	39.75 secs

Winners of the St Leger

1932	Castle Eve	32.08 secs
1933	Brilliant Bob	31.53 secs

Winners of the St Leger

1934	Chicken Sandwich	31.59 secs
1935	Carra's Son	31.82 secs
1936	Moresby	31.68 secs
1937	Cheers for Ballyduff	31.42 secs
1938	*Abbeylara	31.61 secs
1939	Negro's Crown	31.77 secs
1940	Cherrygrove Cross	31.82 secs
1941	not run	
1942	Monarch of the Glen	31.28 secs
1943	Monarch of the Glen	31.48 secs
1944	No Relation	31.48 secs
1945	Dark Shadow	31.37 secs
1946	Star Point	31.55 secs
1947	Pouleen Boy	31.92 secs
1948	Beau Lion	31.52 secs
1949	Ballybeg Surprise	31.55 secs
1950	Maddest Daughter	31.55 secs
1951	Ella's Ivy	31.08 secs
1952	Silver Earl	31.25 secs
1953	Gortaleen	31.26 secs
1954	Mount Nagle Surprise	31.10 secs
1955	Doonmore Dreamer	30.98 secs
1956	Prince of Bermuda	30.66 secs
1957	Kilcaskin Kern	31.05 secs
1958	Firgrove Snowman	31.28 secs
1959	Ocean Swell	31.18 secs
1960	Swanlands Best	31.60 secs
1961	Jerry's Clipper	31.10 secs
1962	Apollo Again	31.26 secs
1963	General Courtnowski	31.12 secs
1964	Brook Jockey	31.66 secs
1965	Lovely Chieftain	30.92 secs
1966	Movealong Santa	30.92 secs
1967	Yanka Boy	30.77 secs
1968	Pools Punter	30.88 secs
1969	*Own Pride	30.95 secs
1970	Mark Antony	31.02 secs
1971	Time up Please	30.56 secs
1972	Time up Please	31.05 secs
1973	Romping to Work	31.04 secs
1974	*Lively Band	31.20 secs
1975	Ballybeg Prim	30.44 secs
1976	Nameless Star	30.62 secs
1977	Red Rasper	31.15 secs
1978	Rhu	31.44 secs
1979	Airmount Champ	31.20 secs
1980	Rahan Ship	30.72 secs
1981	Oran Jack	30.62 secs

1932, 1943 run at Celtic Park; 1933, Clonmel; 1934, 1936, 1938 and 1939, Shelbourne Park; 1935, 1937 and 1942, Harold's Cross. The event has been run at Limerick since 1944, but it was also staged here in 1940 for the first time.
*also won the Irish Derby

Winners of the Guinness Puppy Sweepstake

1962	Hack it About	29.87 secs
1963	Kylepark Choice	29.73 secs
1964	Sherry Wind	29.99 secs
1965	Kilmagoura Trail	30.08 secs
1965	Rambling Wonder	30.08 secs
*1966	Movealong Santa	30.92 secs
1967	Garry Lower	29.78 secs
1968	Clinker Flash	30.05 secs
1969	Mountleader	29.75 secs
1970	Atlas Range	29.82 secs
1971	Easy Slip	29.73 secs
1972	Clerihan Venture	29.26 secs
1973	Karty's Gold	29.44 secs
1974	Black Sole	29.82 secs
1975	I Say Moss	29.56 secs
1976	Wolseley's Jet	29.78 secs
1977	Daring Dandy	29.88 secs
1978	Funny Idea	29.82 secs
1979	Lisamote Sailor	30.16 secs
1980	Traffic Survey	29.58 secs

*550 yds

Winners of the Kennedy Memorial Cup

1970	That's Bonkers	29.60 secs
1971	Bold Invader	29.36 secs
1972	Navy's Beauty	29.62 secs
1973	Faction Fighter	29.60 secs
1974	Scaragh Prairie	30.15 secs
1975	Antone Wonder	29.72 secs
1976	Pack Leader	29.88 secs
1977	Ballinter Star	29.52 secs
1978	Mount Nagle Joy	29.80 secs
1979	Flowers Prince	29.82 secs
1980	Camp Fisher	30.08 secs
1981	Careless Sonny	29.80 secs

LONDONDERRY

See Derry.

LONGFORD

About sixty miles west of Dublin, this town opened its greyhound track in May 1939, and in recent years it has enjoyed increased patronage. Mr M.J. Lyons, a local businessman, was one of the pioneers of track racing here and was at one time secretary to the track, while Mr J.E. Doris remains as managing director, with Jim Conroy racing manager and Anna Stritch secretary.

Racing takes place on Monday and Friday and is attended by enthusiasts from Co. Roscommon and Co. Cavan for the track is situated almost in the centre of Ireland and is well attended. Hurdles events are also staged and young dogs are always given a chance to show their paces. The circuit is a large one, of 485 yds circumference.

The most important event here is the Padian Cup, run over 525 yds and won in 1978 by Mrs Lane's Indian Sign. The Longford Puppy Derby is also run here and Smithwick's 550, a race run over 550 yds and worth £500 to the winner. The winner of the Puppy Derby in 1979 was that outstanding bitch April May, who also won the Guinness Puppy Stakes at nearby Mullingar. Owned by Mr Larry Clancy, she was by Westpark Mint out of May Venture, and in that year also reached the final of the Callanan Cup in Dublin and with Penny County and Nameless Pixie was the outstanding bitch of 1979.

Main Events Run at Longford

Longford Puppy Derby	June	525 yds
Padian Cup	September	525 yds
Smithwick's 550	October	550 yds

Track Records (1950)

Richmont Mick	330 yds	18.69 secs
Bena's Gift	330 yds H	19.95 secs
Cooleeny Twister	525 yds	29.98 secs
Fortwilliam Pagan	525 yds H	31.44 secs

Track Records (1970)

Portumna Bouncer	1969	330 yds	18.64 secs
Cave View Clipper	1959	330 yds H	19.48 secs
Lovely Rambler	1965	525 yds	29.38 secs
Fortwilliam Pagan	1946	525 yds H	31.44 secs
Claddagh Quail	1970	550 yds	31.04 secs
Danba	1967	600 yds	34.67 secs

Track Records (1980)

Scaragh Prairie	1971	330 yds	18.32 secs
Cave View Clipper	1959	330 yds H	19.48 secs
Sampson Flash	1974	525 yds	29.28 secs
Fortwilliam Pagan	1939	525 yds H	31.44 secs
Danba	1967	600 yds	34.67 secs

Winners of the Longford Puppy Derby

1970	Hilda Go By	29.50 secs
1971	Lyneen Gun	30.00 secs
1972	Bold Invader	29.47 secs
1973	Sona's Flyer	30.24 secs
1974	Sampson Flash	29.28 secs
1975	Tubbercurry Son	29.94 secs
1976	Sound Performer	30.20 secs
1977	The Shrew	29.90 secs
1978	Air Pirate	30.20 secs
1979	April May	29.86 secs
1980	Pinchbeck	30.10 secs
1981	Jaime Starlight	29.64 secs

Winners of the Padian Cup

1970	Liver Lover	30.19 secs
1971	Belmont Gun	30.28 secs
1972	Inny Winter	30.40 secs
1973	Dear Lundy	30.54 secs
1975	Joseph's Choice	30.02 secs
1976	Count Alacard	30.26 secs
1977	Kenny Rambler	30.24 secs
1978	Indian Sign	30.32 secs
1979	Corboy Roller	30.18 secs
1980	Ougham Tory	30.22 secs
1981	Time Ash	30.14 secs

MULLINGAR

In this pleasant town, forty miles west of Dublin, stood those two great stud dogs Castledown Lad in the 1940s and later Newdown Heather (bred by Miss O'Reilley from her dam Pardee). The race track, at Ballinderry, opened on 16 August 1932. The first racing manager was Billy Bligh, whose dog Splonk was a winner at Shelbourne Park on the day the track opened. Mr Bligh was to be racing manager until his retirement in 1978, which makes him the longest serving official on any track anywhere. His place has been filled by Peter Kenny.

Mullingar is not a fast track, the times returned being similar to those at Thurles, Youghal and Longford. For several years in the 1930s the 525 yds record was held by Managha Boy who covered the distance in 30.28 secs, an astonishing time when it is realized that in 1970 Blackrath Santa won the Guinness 1000 here in 30.30 secs. Since the 1950s the track had been considerably improved on the running surface and banking of the bends. A new stand and club house were opened in 1972, and Mullingar's amenities now compare with the best of the provincial tracks in Ireland. Racing takes place on Tuesday and Saturday and the track is well patronized by Dubliners for it is within an hour's car or train ride. The track is large 500 yds in circumference.

Shortly after the track opened the great sire Castledown Lad raced here, as did later his two wonderful offspring, Shaggy Lass and Shaggy Lad, both out of the dam Shaggy Shore. Shaggy Lass defeated Robeen Printer by an astonishing six lengths on one occasion, but she did most of her running in England during the war years when no classic events were held. Shaggy Lad achieved fame as sire of Dunmore King, who won the English Derby in 1956 for Mr Jack McAllister of Belfast.

At Mullingar in May is run the Midland Puppy Stakes, sponsored by Guinness. In 1967 it was won by the dual classic winner Yanka Boy, in 1969 by the late Hugh Marley's fine dog Monalee Gambler, and in 1978 by Ivy Hall Solo, who won the Guinness 600 that year. Here too are run the Joe Clyne Memorial Stakes and the Midland Cesarewitch, the last open event of the season. The winner of the 1979 event was the consistent dog Count Alacard, who had previously won the Midlands St Leger. Owned by Mr J. McAuliffe of Strokestown, Co. Roscommon, the dog had won the Padian Cup at Longford in 1977 and was more than four years old when he turned in his wonderful performances two years later. Hurdle racing is a feature of most racing programmes, and Mullingar is the venue for the longest race run on any track, the 810 yds marathon. As would be imagined, the track record for this distance was made many years ago by a bitch, the wonderful stayer Comagh Beauty who recorded 47.90 secs. It has never been equalled.

Another outstanding dog to run here in the late 1930s was Fearless Gaughan, who set new track records for the 360 and 525 yds courses and went on to win the classic event of the north, the Trigo Cup, in 1939 and 1940. He is one of the few Irish greyhounds to win a classic event twice. The Joe McCormack Memorial Trophy is run here and is worth £500 to the winner.

Main Events Run at Mullingar

Guinness Puppy Stakes	April	525 yds
Dwan Midlands St Leger	July	550 yds
Joe Clyne Memorial Trophy	September	525 yds
Midland Cesarewitch	October	600 yds

Track Records (1950)

Fearless Gaughan	1939	360 yds	20.30 secs
Fearless Gaughan	1940	525 yds	30.30 secs
Hello King	1942	550 yds	31.97 secs

Track Records (1960)

Clonmeen Garden	1958	360 yds	20.01 secs
Quiet Sergeant	1958	360 yds H	21.05 secs
Fearless Gaughan	1940	525 yds	30.30 secs
Hello King	1942	550 yds	31.97 secs
Comagh Beauty	1960	810 yds	47.90 secs

Track Records (1970)

Red Menace	1964	330 yds	18.55 secs
Clonmeen Garden	1958	360 yds	20.01 secs
Quiet Sergeant	1958	360 yds H	21.05 secs
Rex Again	1964	525 yds	29.55 secs
Man Friday	1964	525 yds H	30.98 secs
Butterfly Billy	1965	600 yds	33.61 secs
Comagh Beauty	1960	810 yds	47.90 secs

Track Records (1980)

Kilmagoura Again	1971	300 yds	17.00 secs
Clonmeen Garden	1958	360 yds	20.01 secs
Quiet Sergeant	1958	360 yds H	21.05 secs
Rex Again	1964	525 yds	29.55 secs
Man Friday	1964	525 yds H	30.98 secs
Twitters	1972	550 yds	31.15 secs
Butterfly Billy	1965	600 yds	33.61 secs
Comagh Beauty	1960	810 yds	47.90 secs

Winners of the Guinness Midland Puppy Stakes

1964	Kylepark Chieftain	29.98 secs
1965	Dumbles Rose	30.00 secs
1966	Spid's Pride	30.45 secs
1967	Yanka Boy	30.46 secs
1968	Kylera Chieftain	29.95 secs
1969	Monalee Gambler	30.11 secs
1970	Blackrath Santa	30.30 secs
1971	Brackbawn Pat	30.20 secs
1972	Baylough Jet	30.23 secs
1973	Lyons Tune	30.30 secs
1974	Pass me Not	30.10 secs
1975	Broken Leg	30.38 secs
1976	Right Moordyke	30.36 secs
1977	Gullion Lad	30.56 secs
1978	Ivy Hall Solo	30.58 secs
1979	April May	30.18 secs
1980	Only Three	30.31 secs

NAVAN

The racecourse here was opened as recently as 1950, with the late Johnny Cantwell as racing manager. Some twenty years later the track was fully modernized, yet it has maintained its friendly atmosphere and racing there is of the highest class. Johnny Cantwell's sons John and William are now racing manager and general manager respectively and are continuing the work of their father who did so much for greyhound racing in the town.

The most important events are the Tara Puppy Cup, inaugurated to stimulate interest in local breeding, and the classic event, the Irish Cesarewitch, now run here over 600 yds. The Cesarewitch was first competed for at Navan in 1960, when it was won by Pocket Glass. One of the greatest of Navan's greyhounds was Yanka Boy, winner of the event in 1967 when owned by Mr M. Loughnane, for whom he also won the St Leger and Guinness Puppy Derby and was chosen champion of 1967. Here in September 1970 came the great Postal Vote to win the Cesarewitch with a time of 33.08 secs from a top-class field. This was a new track record, which remains unbeaten. Three years later came an equally fine greyhound, Rita's Choice, to win the event. In his semi-final he was only half a length outside Postal Vote's record, and in the final he set a new record of 33.04 secs when defeating Mr Leslie McNair's Itsawitch, who had won the previous year. Top greyhound of 1973 in Ireland, Rita's Choice ran up for the Derby to Bashful Man and won the Bord na gCon TV Trophy and Corn Cuchullain at Harold's Cross, where his time of 42.10 secs was another track record. A son of Spectre, he now stands at stud and is siring some oustanding greyhounds. The 1978 Cesarewitch, worth £2,000 to the winner, was won by Bright Lad's son Gullian Lad, who had previously won the Midland Puppy Stakes at Mullingar and the Ulster Spring Cup at Celtic Park. He beat Solitary Aim to win by a neck. With the Cesarewitch now goes the Johnny Cantwell Memorial Trophy.

It was from Navan that Duleek Dandy, bred by Mr J. Owens, the track's chairman, crossed the Irish Sea and, although the outsider, won the 1960 English Derby from such champions as Mile Bush Pride and Clonalvy Pride.

Also run at Navan are the Paddy Barry Memorial Cup, over 525 yds; the Matthew Bruton Cup, over 550 yds; and Open Sprint, over 350 yds.

Main Events Run at Navan

Paddy Barry Memorial Cup	May	525 yds
Cesarewitch	September	600 yds
Matthew Bruton Cup	October	550 yds
Tara Puppy Stakes	December	525 yds

Track Records (1960)

Oagham Doreen	1954	350 yds	19.15 secs
Sarsfield Castle	1951	550 yds	31.20 secs
Five Arrow	1956	550 yds	31.20 secs

Track Records (1970)

Oagham Doreen	1954	350 yds	19.15 secs
Little Kim	1966	525 yds	29.17 secs
Sarsfield Castle	1951	550 yds	31.20 secs
Five Arrow	1956	550 yds	31.20 secs

Track Records (1980)

Never So Gay	1975	350 yds	19.04 secs
Little Kim	1966	525 yds	29.17 secs
Murphy's Arkle	1973	550 yds	30.72 secs
Rita's Choice	1973	600 yds	*33.04 secs

*also a Cesarewitch record

Winners of the Cesarewitch

1960	Pocket Glass	33.85 secs
1961	Perry's Orchard	34.00 secs
1962	Harem Queen	34.35 secs

1963	Motel Chief	33.71 secs
1964	High Note	33.80 secs
1965	Butterfly Billy	33.26 secs
1966	Pendant	33.59 secs
1967	Yanka Boy	33.38 secs
1968	Young Ferranti	33.88 secs
1969	April Flower	33.32 secs
1970	Postal Vote	33.08 secs
1971	Rapid Maxi	33.22 secs
1972	Itsachampion	33.48 secs
1973	Rita's Choice	33.04 secs
1974	Ballinattin Boy	34.06 secs
1975	Ballybeg Prim	33.30 secs
1976	Murray's Turn	33.46 secs
1977	First Debenture	33.70 secs
1978	Gullion Lad	33.76 secs
1979	Loman's Lad	33.90 secs
1980	Rahan Ship	38.78 secs

Winners of the Paddy Barry Memorial Cup

1970	Sterling Romeo	29.75 secs
1971	Serjeant Pepper	29.62 secs
1972	Arle Lad	30.16 secs
1973	Lively Solo	29.58 secs
1974	Dark Mercury	29.50 secs
1975	Denis Auburn	29.90 secs
1976	Coolock Mermaid	29.92 secs
1977	Stylish Gorse	29.54 secs
1978	Minorcas Rosie	29.76 secs
1979	Laundry Basket	30.00 secs
1980	Endless Star	29.54 secs

NEWBRIDGE

The greyhound track opened here on 21 June 1950, and racing takes place on Monday and Friday each week, mostly over 525 yds. A new track was opened in 1972 with up-to-date kennels, weighing room and lighting system. The Texacloth Puppy Stakes, worth £1,000 to the winner, is one of the most important events. The Cox Cup, also worth £1,000 to the winner, is another popular event, as are the Rosebran Sweepstake and Kelly's Red Seal Sweepstake, worth £600 to the winner.

One of the outstanding greyhounds of recent years to win the Cox Cup was the black dog Point Duty, who also won the Harp Lager Stakes at Dundalk in 1978. In the Taxacloth Puppy Stakes that year Mr Harry Barry's bitch Shady Lilac won from her litter brother Shady Bunch in 29.48 secs.

1978 was a year of changes at the track when improvements were made to the main stand, and after many years as racing manager Denis Brennan retired, his place being taken by Christy Connolly. The track, one of Ireland's largest, is 520 yds in circumference.

Main Events Run at Newbridge

Kelly's Red Seal Stake	May	525 yds
Cox Cup	June	525 yds
Texacloth Puppy Stakes	October	525 yds

Track Records (1960)

Feale Ranger	1960	310 yds	17.65 secs
P for Poor	1963	350 yds	19.88 secs
Chestnut Bridge	1950	350 yds H	21.08 secs
Jigger Lee	1950	350 yds H	21.08 secs
Claverstown Flower	1957	550 yds	31.89 secs

Track Records (1980)

Clane Mint	1976	300 yds	16.50 secs
Some Skinomage	1977	525 yds	29.02 secs
Moreen Flamingo	1977	525 yds H	30.08 secs
Red Smoke	1976	600 yds	33.34 secs

Winners of the Cox Cup

1972	Ashley Prince	29.56 secs
1973	Pearl Ring	29.56 secs
1974	Nelson's Belle	29.64 secs
1975	Newpark Twilight	29.72 secs
1976	Stop It	29.26 secs
1977	Master Kim	29.51 secs
1978	Point Duty	30.02 secs
1979	Blushing Spy	29.78 secs
1980	Brindle Choice	29.98 secs
1981	Mistress Post	29.82 secs

SHELBOURNE PARK

Situated in Dublin's busy dockland, it was the first track to open in the Republic, on 14 May 1927, and has remained the premier track, within easy reach of buyers and enthusiasts from Britain and Europe. The track was opened at the instigation of Paddy O'Donoghue, Jerry Collins, Patsy McAlinden and Jim Clarke, who witnessed the first meeting of six races, including hurdles. Jerry Collins began hurdles events and was later to enjoy success with his dog Stylish Cutlet, winner of the English Grand National in 1930, but the dog had first made his name over hurdles at Shelbourne Park.

There was an interval of four years before the first classic, the Irish Greyhound Derby was inaugurated and was won by Guideless Joe. The first 'Derby' had been run in 1928 at Harold's Cross and won by Tipperary Hills, trained by Bill Quinn but it was 1932 before given classic status. Guideless Joe was owned by champion Irish jockey, Jack Moylan, who was to win the Irish Horse Racing Derby on Slide On in 1944 achieving a unique 'double'. He was also successful on Piccadilly and in England won the 1000 Guineas for Atty Pearse on Resplendent which was to enjoy even greater fame as the dam of Windsor Lad. Jack Moylan might easily have added to his unique 'double' by winning the 1925 Aintree Grand National for he was on Fly Mask when narrowly beaten into 3rd place. Moylan, who died in 1949 was the grandfather of champion jockey, Pat Eddery.

1933 saw the great Monologue win, bred by John Hughes of Fenniscourt, Co. Carlow and owned by Luke Maher. She had won the Irish Coursing Oaks and she, too, achieved a great 'double'. She also won the 1932 Easter Cup and on the coursing field, An Corn Osruighe at Sevenhouses. The 1936 Derby was won by Minstrel Rover who cost Michael Sheehan, a Cork coalmerchant, £85 and was his first greyhound. In the 1937 final were two bitches from the same litter, one of which, Muinessa won the event. She defeated Tom Black's Western Skipper by 2 lengths but Black was successful the following year with Abbeylara, bred by Larry Kiernan. He was to win the Derby by a record 8 lengths.

The 1939 event was held in Limerick and was won by Marching thro' Georgia, owned by J.J. Doran, who went through undefeated. 1940 saw the great Tanist win. By Inler out of Tranquilla, he was bred by Father Browne, parish priest of Bray, Co. Wicklow who raced him in the name of "W. Twyford". The year before, Father Browne had sold him to Arthur Probert for £200 with the proviso that if he won either the English or Irish Derby, there would be another £100 to swell the parish funds. Tanist won by 6 lengths from Prince Norroy and he was to become the first Irish Derby winner to sire a winner, Daring Flash, who won in 1947 and was bred, owned and trained by Mary d'Arcy. Steve won for Mrs Yate in 1946 who became the first person to own an English and Irish Derby winner.

The 1949 Derby, won by Spanish Lad ushered in a new era when dogs bred and owned by 'Chubb' O'Connor took all before them for 1953 saw the first of Spanish Battleship's three successive wins. Another outstanding dog, Keep Moving, bought at Shelbourne Park sales in June 1956 by Mrs McBride of Belfast for 700 gns was to win the Derby a few weeks later. 1961 saw the first of Leslie McNair's champions, Chieftain's Guest win the event and three years later the great Wonder Valley. Next came Ballyowen Chief trained by Gay McKenna to begin a unique decade for Gay and his cousin Ger who trained Bashful Man to win the 1973 Derby in the fastest time for the event.

One of the greatest races ever seen at the track was when Linda's Champion (a son of Monalee Champion) beat Brush Tim by inches, the judge giving his decision after calling for a photo of the finish. Linda's Champion was owned, bred and trained by

Opposite: Wattle Bark, pictured with owner Mrs R. H. Dent after he won the 1937 English Greyhound Derby in record time. Only the previous year the dog had been close to death. Photo: GRA.

twenty-one-year-old Michael Barrett of Crohane, Co. Tipperary, who became the first person to achieve the feat of owning, breeding and training a winner.

The Oaks was inaugurated in 1932 also, but was not run at Shelbourne Park until 1935. Only one bitch has won the Oaks twice -- Peaceful Lady in 1952 and 1953, the second time at Shelbourne Park. Two years later came Prairie Peg to win in 29.55 secs on this track. She was to become the mother of Pigalle Wonder from a mating to Champion Prince and of Prairie Flash from a mating to Hi There. With Sheila at Last and Millie's Hawthorn she was one of the foundation dams of modern track racing. Another great bitch to win the Oaks at Shelbourne Park was Itsamint. She was the last until 1977 and 1978, when Harold's Cross was closed for modernization, for since 1970 the Derby has been run at Shelbourne Park and the Oaks at Harold's Cross. Since 1978 the Oaks has been sponsored by the Sean Kelly Organization, Dublin bookmakers.

In its early years the Grand National was also run here on several occasions, Hot Shot winning in 1933 and 1934. The first race was run at Harold's Cross in 1932. The third St Leger was run at Shelbourne Park and Abbeylara won the event in 1938, the year he took the Derby at Harold's Cross. He was one of the finest dogs ever to run in Ireland.

Every champion raced at Shelbourne Park. Mick the Miller had his first race here and in 1929 ran up to Odd Blade in the second Easter Cup before he left for England to win his first Derby two months later. Others to run up for the Easter Cup were Ruby Robert, Mad Tanist and Model Whiskey, sire of Model Dasher.

The Easter Cup, inaugurated to commemorate the Rising of 1920 in Dublin, is the oldest race in Ireland's track history and has been run each year without a break since 1928. The Trigo Cup, the next oldest, was first run at Celtic Park the following year and the Irish Derby was first run at Shelbourne Park in 1932.

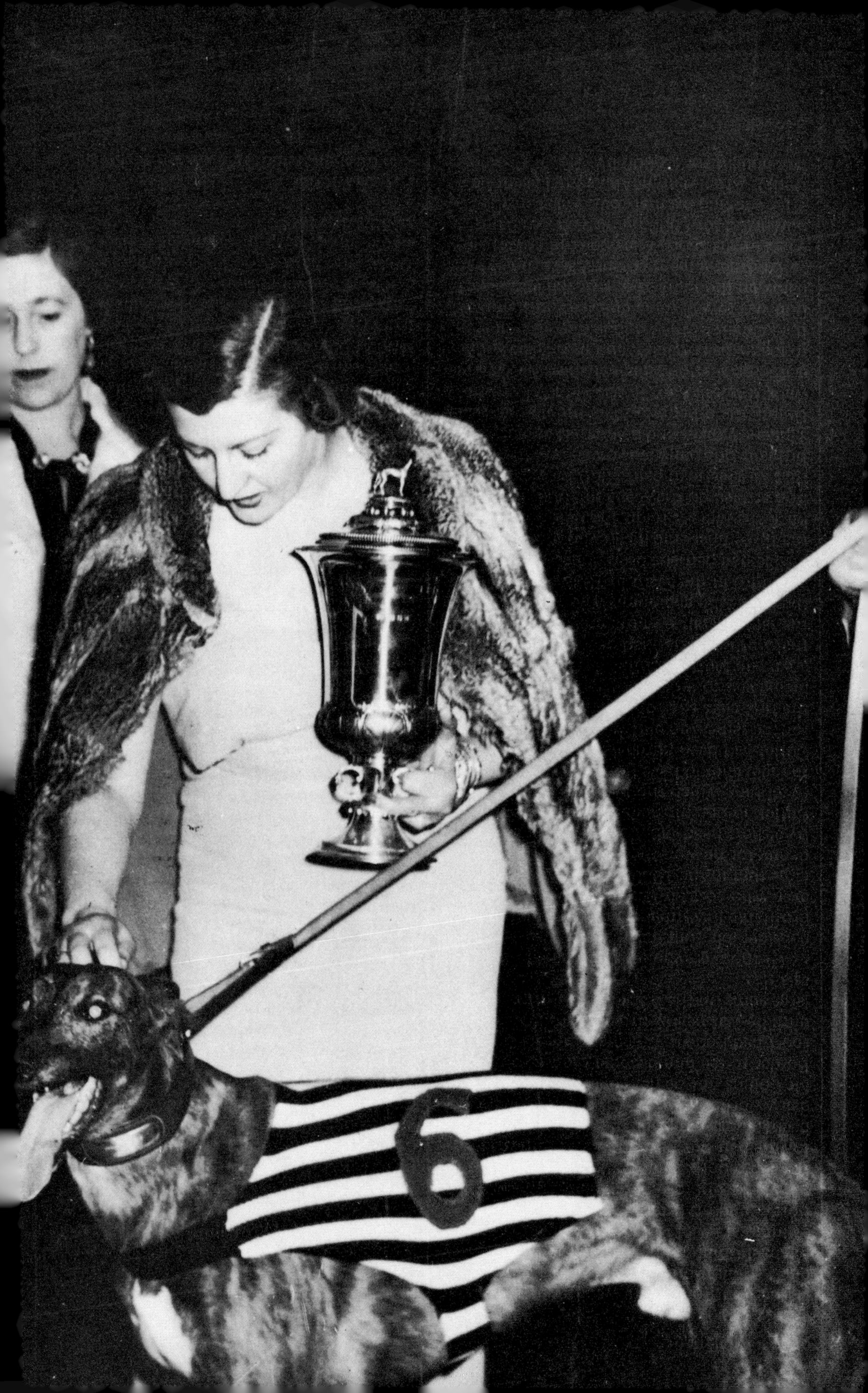
6

Many outstanding greyhounds have won the Easter Cup. Odd Blade was the winner for the first two years and any dog to beat Mick the Miller was a good one. In 1932 the great bitch Monologue won and she was to take the Derby the following year. In 1934 it was won by Billy Quinn's well-named dog Brilliant Bob, one of the all-time 'greats'. Billy Quinn had won the 1927 Horse Show Cup at the track with the bitch Beaded Biddy, and trained Tanist to win the 1940 Irish Derby. He also bred and trained Quare Times, in the postwar years, the fastest ever to race. He trained Britannia's Son to win the National Produce Stakes in 1943 too. Quinn was one of the greatest handlers of track and coursing greyhounds ever known. In 1939, another equally fine dog, Abbeylara, won. He also won the Derby that year and had won the St Leger the previous year, as Brilliant Bob had also done. The dual St Leger winner, Monarch of the Glen, won the Easter Cup in 1943, and in 1945 and 1946 the great blue bitch, Astra, was successful. Sandown Champion, later to win the National Sprint and in due course to become an outstanding sire, won in 1950, and in 1954 and 1955, the victor was the one and only Spanish Battleship who also won the Derby three years in succession. The Grand Canal, winner of the English Derby in 1962, also took the Easter Cup that year, and four years later the great bitch Clomoney Grand, another blue, won. She was followed in 1968 by another fine bitch, Itsamint, and four years later by Irish Derby-winning bitch Catsrock Daisy.

The 1969 Easter Cup winner, Move Gas, proved one of the fastest dogs ever seen on any track. He was owned by R. Liffey who also bred and reared him. A fawn dog, he had raced only twice before appearing in the Easter Cup and went through undefeated to the final, finishing one length in front of the favourite, Clever Kid. In the same year he also won the National Sprint at Dunmore Park, his time of 23.60 secs being the fastest for the event.

Also held at Shelbourne Park is the McAlinden Gold Cup, first run in 1939 over 525 yds when it was won by Nore Prince. In 1942 it was won by Uacterlainn Riac, winner of the Derby that year, the only time it was run in Cork. Mad Printer won the following year when My Little Daisy, the Oaks winner, ran up; she died soon afterwards. Bitches have always run well in this event: in 1944 Robeen Printer was successful, and the next year Baytown Ivy ran up. In 1946 the event was won by Lemon Flash, who shortly afterwards was sold at the Shelbourne sales for £3,000 to race in England but died without doing so.

The Cambridgeshire, over 600 yds, is run here; it was won in 1971 and 1972 by the outstanding stayer Kerryman and in 1976 by the Derby winner Tain Mor. In 1963 the Shelbourne Leger was inaugurated. The choice of name is unfortunate for it is often confused with the classic St Leger run at Limerick, and a more original name could surely have been chosen. Until 1977 it was run over 550 yds, and since then over 575 yds. Its first winner was Motel Chief, who was to win the Cesarewitch later that year and the National Breeders' Produce Stakes in 1964. A succession of outstanding greyhounds have won this event: Clomoney Jet in 1968; followed by Finola's Yarn; Ivy Hall Flash and his son Tommy Astaire, national record holder for 550 yds; Peruvian Style in 1975; and Tain Mor the following year.

In 1979 the richest one-race event ever contested was run here. This was the Respond Champion Stakes inaugurated by the Kerry Co-operative, entry being open to 'all-comers'. The line-up included Desert Pilot; Nameless Pixie, the Irish Oaks winner; Tough Decision, winner of the Irish Cambridgeshire; Airmount Champ, 1979 St Leger winner; Indian Joe; and in the no. 6 coat, the ever reliable Distant Clamour, runner-up in the 1979 Irish Derby and Cox Cup at Newbridge. The race was won by Distant Clamour (Here Sonny—In Gear), owned by Mr Jack Hogarty and trained by Pat Jones, with Indian Joe half a length behind. The prize of £3,500 took the winner's earnings to more than £16,000 during that year, and without a classic win to boost the amount.

In 1964 the Guinness 600 was first run here, when it was won by that outstanding bitch, twice winner of the English Oaks, Cranog Bet, said by some to be the finest bitch that ever raced in England. In 1965 Faithful Hope won the event; he went to England the next year and left as winner of the 1966 Derby. The Irish Derby winner Russian Gun won in 1968; Itsamint in 1969;

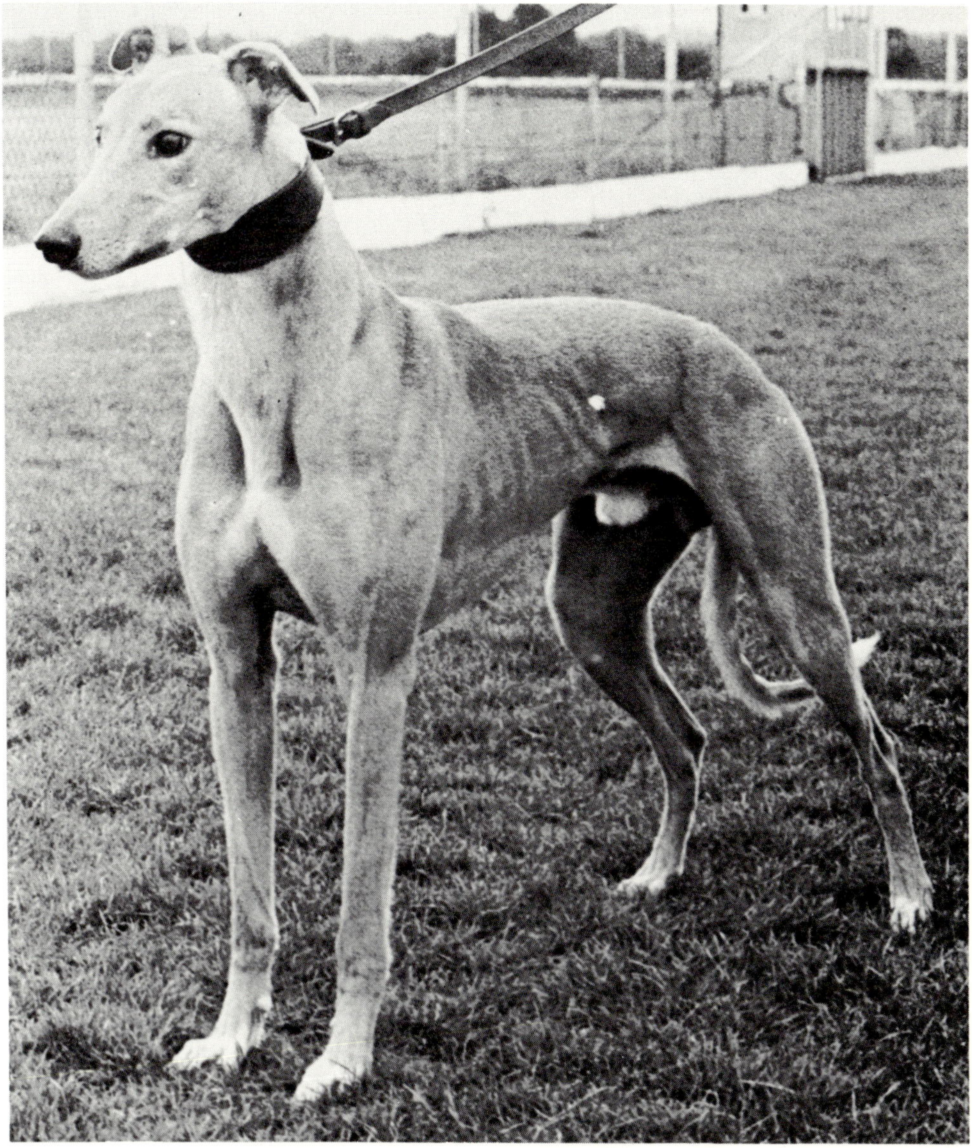

Lively Band, winner of the 1974 Irish Greyhound Derby. Photo: Bord na gCon.

and Postal Vote in 1971. The following year Itsachampion took the trophy, and in 1975 and 1976 Ballybeg Prim became the first to win two years in succession. In 1977 Here's Tat won in 33.26 secs, the fastest time for the event which was inaugurated to commemorate Mr Paddy O'Donoghue, popular racing manager here for many years. The 1980 Guinness 600 was won by Ballarat Prince, litter brother of Hume Highway who was bred and owned by Patricia McGrath of Outrath, Co. Tipperary.

Since its beginnings, those in charge at Shelbourne Park have never thought it necessary to change the distances of the races nor to move the starting traps or finishing line, so that for the past half century those who have watched racing and trials here know exactly how good a dog is from the times recorded when compared with those of any other race winners, and one may readily assess speed from the traps and finishing power. This greater standardization of distances and their measurement in yards rather than in metres has done much to answer those who wonder why attendances have continued to fall in Britain and have risen in Ireland. Change for the sake of it, as on the British tracks, rarely proves successful. Older followers of the sport look forward to visiting the Irish tracks for they can compare times and the running of present-day champions with those of fifty years ago. Only the right things have been changed, such as improved amenities and running conditions.

On two days each week auction sales of greyhounds are held at Shelbourne Park, when more than 150 dogs are entered and a high proportion are always sold. They range from brood bitches, many of excellent breeding, through untried saplings, to winners of important events, and buyers come from Britain and all parts of the world where greyhound racing is legalized.

Late in 1969 a magnificent new stand capable of accommodating 15,000 in comfort was opened shortly after Bord na gCon took over the track. The Long Bar on the first floor has no equal for atmosphere and for viewing a race; food is available, and closed circuit TV gives betting prices from the comfort of easy chairs. A first-class restaurant is situated on the ground floor. The track lighting here is outstanding; it is supplied by Philips 'Sun' lamps which give a brightness at night as good as sunlight. Racing takes place on Monday, Wednesday and Saturday evenings, and Pat Ryan is the much respected racing manager. The general manager here and at Harold's Cross is Louis McGauran, who was appointed by Bord na gCon when they took over Harold's Cross in 1965 and Shelbourne Park six years later.

Main Events Run at Shelbourne Park

Easter Cup	April	525 yds
Cambridgeshire	May	600 yds
Carroll's Irish Derby	July	525 yds
McAlinden Gold Cup	August	525 yds
Guinness 600	October	600 yds
Shelbourne Leger	November	575 yds
Pigalle Wonder Stakes	December	525 yds
Eddie McWilliams Memorial Trophy	December	525 yds

Track Records (1950)

Count's Cure	360 yds	20.10 secs
Smartly Fergus	525 yds	29.60 secs
Table Cut	525 yds H	30.98 secs
Ballydancer	550 yds	31.25 secs
Galloping Home	600 yds	33.95 secs

Track Records (1960)

Kilbelin Battleship	360 yds	19.80 secs
Prince of Bermuda	525 yds	28.98 secs
Table Cut	525 yds H	30.98 secs
Ballydancer	550 yds	31.25 secs
Galloping Home	600 yds	33.95 secs

Track Records (1970)

Portumna Wonder	1970	360 yds	19.80 secs
Kilbelin Battleship	1957	360 yds	19.80 secs
Yellow Printer	1968	525 yds	28.83 secs
Hillcrest Pride	1969	525 yds H	30.71 secs
Ballydancer		550 yds	31.25 secs
Lazy Tim	1968	600 yds	33.07 secs

Track Records (1980)

Tom's Pall	1972	360 yds	19.50 secs
Tantallon's Gift	1976	525 yds	28.73 secs
Knockreigh Dawn	1975	525 yds H	29.68 secs
Jerpoint Paris	1976	550 yds	30.35 secs
Tommy Astaire	1974	550 yds	30.35 secs
Lax Law	1979	575 yds	31.79 secs
Lazy Tim	1968	600 yds	33.07 secs

Winners of the Carroll's Irish Derby

1932	Guideless Joe	30.36 secs	SP
1933	Monologue	30.52 secs	SP
1934	Frisco Hobo	30.45 secs	HX
1935	Roving Yank	30.18 secs	SP
1936	Minstrel Rover	30.48 secs	HX
1937	Muinessa	30.83 secs	SP
1938	Abbeylara	30.09 secs	HX
1939	Marching through Georgia	30.05 secs	L
1940	Tanist	29.89 secs	SP
1941	Brave Damsel	30.64 secs	SP
1942	Uacterainn Riac	30.22 secs	C
1943	Famous Knight	30.26 secs	HX
1944	Clonbonny Bridge	30.55 secs	SP
1945	Lilac's Luck	30.12 secs	HX
1946	Steve	30.20 secs	SP
1947	Daring Flash	30.04 secs	HX
1948	Western Post	29.90 secs	SP
1949	Spanish Lad	29.87 secs	HX
1950	Crossmolina Rambler	29.70 secs	SP
1951	Carmody's Tanist	29.64 secs	HX
1952	Rough Waters	29.95 secs	SP
1953	Spanish Battleship	29.78 secs	HX
1954	Spanish Battleship	29.64 secs	SP
1955	Spanish Battleship	29.53 secs	HX
1956	Keep Moving	29.18 secs	SP
1957	Hopeful Cutlet	29.60 secs	HX
1958	Colonel Perry	29.79 secs	SP
1959	Sir Frederick	29.30 secs	HX
1960	Perry's Apple	29.55 secs	SP
1961	Chieftain's Guest	29.45 secs	HX
1962	Shane's Legacy	29.58 secs	SP
1963	Drumahiskey Venture	29.60 secs	HX
1964	Wonder Valley	29.30 secs	SP
1965	Ballyowen Chief	29.42 secs	HX
1966	Always Proud	29.44 secs	SP
1967	Russian Gun	29.44 secs	HX
1968	Yellow Printer	29.11 secs	SP
1969	Own Pride	29.20 secs	HX
1970	Monalee Pride	29.28 secs	SP
1971	Sole Aim	29.12 secs	SP
1972	Catsrock Daisy	29.20 secs	SP
1973	Bashful Man	28.82 secs	SP
1974	Lively Band	29.11 secs	SP
1975	Shifting Shadow	29.35 secs	SP
1976	Tain Mor	29.35 secs	SP
1977	Linda's Champion	29.52 secs	SP
1978	Pampered Rover	29.23 secs	SP
1979	Penny County	29.28 secs	SP
1980	Suir Miller	29.18 secs	SP
1981	Bold Work	29.32 secs	SP

SP signifies run at Shelbourne Park; HX at Harold's Cross; C at Cork; L at Limerick

The finish of 1976 Irish Greyhound Derby, won by Tain Mor. Photo: Bord na gCon.

Winners of the Easter Cup

1928	Odd Blade	30.64 secs
1929	Odd Blade	30.71 secs
1930	Hannah's Pup	30.59 secs
1931	Lion's Share	30.71 secs
1932	Monologue	30.78 secs
1933	Rustic Martin	30.59 secs
1934	Brilliant Bob	30.29 secs
1935	Khun Khan	30.54 secs
1936	Mooncoin Captain	30.54 secs
1937	Cardinal Puff	30.50 secs
1938	Pagan Miller	30.27 secs
1939	Abbeylara	30.27 secs
1940	Shy Sandy	30.34 secs
1941	Prince Norroy	30.32 secs
1942	Wayside Clover	30.39 secs
1943	Monarch of the Glen	30.43 secs
1944	Empor Lassie	30.35 secs
1945	Astra	29.86 secs
1946	Astra	30.40 secs
1947	Patsy's Record	30.15 secs
1948	Castlecoman	29.90 secs
1949	Flashy Prince	29.85 secs
1950	Sandown Champion	29.85 secs
1951	Clogher McGrath	30.03 secs
1952	Wee Chap	30.12 secs
1953	not run	
1954	Spanish Battleship	30.17 secs
1955	Spanish Battleship	29.72 secs
1956	Baytown Duel	29.67 secs
1957	Doon Marshall	30.41 secs
1958	Sharavogue	29.96 secs
1959	War Dance	29.76 secs
1960	Springvalley Grand	29.92 secs
1961	Tiny's Trousseau	29.66 secs
1962	The Grand Canal	29.93 secs
1963	General Courtnowski	29.98 secs
1964	Ballet Dante	30.27 secs
1965	The Grand Time	29.83 secs
1966	Clomoney Grand	29.50 secs
1967	Tiny's Tidy Town	29.59 secs
1968	Itsamint	29.63 secs
1969	Move Gas	30.29 secs
1970	Monalee Gambler	29.52 secs
1971	Postal Vote	29.36 secs
1972	Catsrock Daisy	29.00 secs
1973	Newpark Arkle	29.40 secs
1974	Aquaduct Rosey	29.52 secs
1975	Tantallon's Flyer	29.60 secs
1976	Cindy's Spec	29.20 secs
1977	Weigh in First	29.58 secs
1978	Rokeel Light	29.50 secs
1979	Shady Burch	29.42 secs
1980	Indian Joe	29.16 secs
1981	Murray's Mixture	29.15 secs

Winners of the Guinness 600

1964	Cranog Bet	33.60 secs
1965	Faithful Hope	33.51 secs
1966	Val's Prince	33.30 secs
1967	Limits Crackers	33.50 secs
1968	Russian Gun	33.48 secs
1969	Itsamint	33.69 secs
1970	Mic Mac	33.65 secs
1971	Postal Vote	33.27 secs
1972	Itsachampion	33.45 secs
1973	Case Money	33.68 secs
1974	Tommy Astaire	33.56 secs
1975	Ballybeg Prim	33.40 secs
1976	Ballybeg Prim	34.05 secs
1977	Here's Tat	33.26 secs
1978	Ivy Hall Solo	33.47 secs
1979	Tough Decision	33.72 secs
1980	Ballarat Prince	33.54 secs

Winners of the Cambridgeshire

1964	Tommie Spot	34.06 secs
1965	Giggler	34.04 secs
1966	Val's Prince	34.22 secs
1967	Blackwater Park	34.05 secs
1968	Proud Lincoln	33.72 secs
1969	Orwell Parade	33.35 secs
1970	Hurling Flash	34.00 secs
1971	Kerryman	33.57 secs
1972	Kerryman	33.80 secs
1973	Here Sonny	33.55 secs
1974	Laroline	33.68 secs
1975	Sunday Chimes	33.93 secs
1976	Tain Mor	33.50 secs
1977	not run	
1978	Cautious Cal	33.83 secs
1979	Tough Decision	33.61 secs
1980	Squeeze the Blue	33.58 secs

Winners of the Shelbourne Leger

1963	Motel Chief	31.38 secs
1964	Jaime Can Can	31.00 secs
1965	Boro Parachute	31.53 secs
1966	Web Offset	31.42 secs
1967	not finished	
1968	Clomoney Jet	31.31 secs
1969	Finola's Yarn	31.27 secs
1970	Ivy Hall Flash	31.34 secs
1971	Lucky Again	32.08 secs
1972	Congress Daisy	30.82 secs
1973	Wind Jammer	31.09 secs
1974	Tommy Astaire	30.58 secs
1975	Peruvian Style	30.62 secs
1976	Tain Mor	30.71 secs
*1977	Shady Bait	32.20 secs
*1978	Witch's Champion	32.91 secs
*1979	Corlecky Glory	33.00 secs
1980	Ballarat Prince	32.52 secs

* Pre-1977 run over 550 yds; since 1977 run over 575 yds

THURLES

At the greyhound racecourse in Town Park, which opened in April 1950, are staged several important events, including the Tipperary Cup; the Puppy Stakes; the Guinness 575; and the classic event, the Grand National, which attracts the finest hurdlers in Ireland and carries a first prize of £1,000. It was at Thurles in 1972, 1973 and 1974 that the great hurdler Special equalled Sherry's Prince's record of winning three English Grand Nationals in a row, and so became one of only four greyhounds to win one classic event three times and in consecutive years. When winning the event in 1973, Special set a track record that remains unbeaten. Special's great record was almost equalled when Pick Me won in 1976 and 1977, and reached the final again the following year when Mr Peter Jones's Bowery Music won the event in only his third race over hurdles. With the Grand National goes the W.J. Dawn Memorial Trophy.

No event creates more interest than the Puppy Stakes, one of the most popular winners of which was the black dog Albany, one of that great litter which included the Irish Derby finalist Kilbelin Grand and other outstanding trackers, as was to be expected from parents such as Prairie Flash and Clomoney Grand. Another great dog, the Sheffield-owned Flaming King, came here in 1968, having won the Laurels, and set a new track record when covering the 525 yds course in 29.25 secs.

At Thurles, where Eamonn Bourke is racing manager, racing takes place on Tuesday and Saturday over the 330 yds, 525 yds, 575 yds and 700 yds course, with hurdle events over 330 and 525 yds. It shares with Tralee the honour of providing Irish patrons with the greatest variety of racing, though many of the Irish provincial tracks offer a greater variety of racing than do most English tracks. The Thurles track is one of the largest and prettiest in Ireland, with a 510 yds circumference. Its running surface is watered by the River Suir in summer by means of a modern sprinkler system, and though it may be considered a slow track compared with most others, it is so well constructed that it brings out the best in a greyhound, whether running on the flat or over hurdles.

At Thurles is run the Champion Bitch Stakes, worth £1,000 to the winner. Donegal Burgess won in 1978, covering the 525 yds in 29.72 secs; it is not often that 30.00 secs is broken here. Another to achieve this in the same year was Laundry Basket, winner of the Tipperary Cup, with a time of 29.68 secs. In 1966 Movealong Santa was successful; and soon afterwards he won the St Leger and then became one of the greatest sires of the early 1970s. Peruvian Style won in 1975, and in 1977 Linda's Champion, Derby winner that year, was successful. The 1979 winner was Racing Prince, who only a few weeks before had been beaten by Knockrour Tiger in the final of the Irish Cup at Clounanna. Owned by Messrs Chandler and O'Brien, Racing Prince turned the tables on Denis Lynch on that day at Thurles when their dog defeated Mr Lynch's great Laurels winner, Knockrour Slave, by three lengths to take the £1,250 winner's prize. Here in 1978 to run over the 575 yds course came the great Rhu, trained by the renowned Matt O'Donnell, to win the open 575 for Mrs Franchetti. He then went on to win the St Leger for Mr D.J. Diffley, his new owner, and ran up for the English St Leger at Wembley. Had he won, he would have been the first ever to win the two St Legers.

Main Events Run at Thurles

Thurles Open 575	June	575 yds
Tipperary Cup	July	525 yds
Renault Stakes	July	525 yds
Grand National	August	525 yds H
Puppy Stakes	September	525 yds
Champion Bitch Stakes	October	525 yds

Track Records (1960)

Rambler Tonic	1960	330 yds H	18.80 secs
Listoney			
Groxvenor	1960	360 yds	20.20 secs
July Sister	1960	600 yds	33.90 secs
Cool Lad	1960	600 yds	33.90 secs

Track Records (1970)

Move Handy	1966	330 yds	18.05 secs
Rambler Tonic	1960	330 yds H	18.80 secs
Flaming King	1968	525 yds	29.25 secs
Oliver's Leader	1966	525 yds H	30.20 secs
Ballybeg Pride	1968	575 yds	32.00 secs
Orwell Wonder	1964	700 yds	40.00 secs

Track Records (1980)

Top Customer	1976	330 yds	18.04 secs
Rambler Tonic	1960	330 yds H	18.80 secs
Flaming King	1968	525 yds	29.25 secs
Special	1973	525 yds H	29.75 secs
Ballybeg Maid	1975	575 yds	31.94 secs
July Sister	1960	600 yds	33.90 secs
Cool Lad	1960	600 yds	33.90 secs
Orwell Wonder	1964	700 yds	40.00 secs

Winners of the Grand National

1960	Dawn Dancer	31.40 secs
1961	Tropical Splendour	31.15 secs
1962	Indoor Sport	30.85 secs
1963	Trojan Van	30.85 secs
1964	Ashgrove Chief	31.10 secs
1965	Bolshoi Prince	30.65 secs
1966	Oliver's Leader	30.20 secs
1967	Bandit	30.95 secs
1968	Rusheen Rhythm	30.85 secs
1969	Hillcrest Pride	30.65 secs
1970	Fire Hunter	30.95 secs
1971	Getaway Buff	31.04 secs
1972	Special	30.85 secs
1973	Special	29.75 secs
1974	Special	30.95 secs
1975	Own Kuda	31.00 secs
1976	Pick Me	30.14 secs
1977	Pick Me	29.96 secs
1978	Bowery Music	30.40 secs
1979	Kerragh Sambo	30.20 secs
1980	Killerisk Prince	30.42 secs
1981	Face the Mutt	30.16 secs

Tipperary Cup

1963	April Twilight	29.85 secs
1964	Good Brandy	29.55 secs
1965	Knock Late	30.10 secs
1966	Movealong Santa	30.10 secs
1967	Gortkelly Hope	30.05 secs
1968	Roundtower Ville	29.45 secs
1969	Clonsherry	29.80 secs
1970	Paddock Judge	29.85 secs
1971	Bold Invader	29.28 secs
1972	Westpark Ceylon	29.80 secs
1973	Caulstown Rose	29.50 secs
1974	Miller's Express	29.90 secs
1975	Peruvian Style	29.48 secs
1976	Stop It	29.38 secs
1977	Linda's Champion	29.44 secs
1978	Laundry Basket	29.68 secs
1979	Racing Prince	29.54 secs
1980	Carrick Chance	29.50 secs
1981	Bally Echo	29.72 secs

TRALEE

The greyhound track opened at Oakview Park in 1930. It is surprising, considering the track's remoteness, how many of the sport's champion greyhounds first began racing here. Ballyhennessy Seal had his first run at the track, after which he was sold to Mrs Stowe for £100 and went on to become an English Derby winner and one of the fastest in the history of greyhound racing. Here, too, began those equally talented champions, both to win the English Derby – Ballymac Ball and Priceless Border – and Mr Tim O'Connor's fabulous Spanish Battleship. Patricia's Hope, twice winner of the English Derby, started his impressive career at Tralee; his dam, Patricia (spelt Patsicia in error in the Stud Book) was bred here by Mr James Burke.

The track is a fast one, 475 yds in circumference. Racing takes place on Tuesday, Wednesday and Friday each week over 325 yds, 525 yds and 525 yds hurdles, 550 yds, 600 yds and 820 yds. The track record for the last distance mentioned is held by Whittle Off, dam of the fast Flip Your Top who broke the track record at Brighton in his first race in England. The Hannafin Cup is run here as a memorial to the late M.J. Hannafin, for many years racing manager and timekeeper, and brother of the highly respected Wimbledon trainer Jerry Hannafin. The event was won in 1978 by the most consistent tracker that year at Tralee, Macari Boy, who also took the April Stakes and the Harp Lager Stakes.

The most important event run here each season is the Bloom 500, run over 500 yds and sponsored by Kerry Co-op Creameries; £3,000 is awarded to the winner. Lena's Honour received first prize in 1978, while

Orange Prince won in 1979. Owned by Mrs Mary Kenny, this fine dog set a new record when winning his semi-final in 30.72 secs. The Clarke Cup is run over the same distance, as is the Corn Chiarrai, of which Attractive Lad was a recent winner of the £675 prize when he set a new track record. This was broken in the same event by Killaclug Jet, who won his semi-final in the amazing time of 30.52 secs, which may stand for many years. He did so only twenty-four hours after setting a new track record at Youghal in the Paddy Stakes.

As with many English greyhound tracks, the sport in Ireland has been fortunate in having had so many long-serving officials of great integrity and capability, and Tralee is no exception. On M.J. Hannafin's retirement, after serving for twenty years, his job as racing manager was given to Kevin Laide, who has been at the track for thirty years. Only recently another long-serving director, John Roche, died, whilst Tom Banbury, control steward since the track opened, only retired early in 1978.

Main Events Run at Tralee

Kerry Co-op Creameries Bloom Stakes	April	550 yds
M.J. Hannafin Cup	May	525 yds
Monalee Hiker Stakes	June	570 yds
Clarke Cup	July	550 yds
Harp Lager Stakes	August	525 yds
Rose of Tralee Cup	August	550 yds
Kerry National	September	525 yds H
Kingdom Puppy Derby	September	525 yds
Clayton Love Puppy Stakes	October	525 yds
Corn Chiarrai	November	525 yds

Track Records (1950)

Annagh's Pride	315 yds	17.65 secs
Roman Emperor	525 yds	30.20 secs
Pouleen Boy	525 yds	30.20 secs
Hobo's Choice	525 yds	30.20 secs
Another Hi Jack	550 yds	31.10 secs

Track Records (1960)

Ballyard Dick	1958	315 yds	17.45 secs
Lamond Laddie	1958	315 yds	17.45 secs
Sugar Prince	1958	500 yds	28.55 secs
Another Hi Jack	1960	550 yds	31.10 secs
Glittering Smack	1960	600 yds	33.65 secs

Track Records (1970)

Upourdat	1968	325 yds	17.95 secs
Sugar Prince	1958	500 yds	28.55 secs
Tellus	1964	525 yds	29.12 secs
Nervy Peggy	1961	525 yds H	30.68 secs
Sirius	1969	570 yds	31.34 secs
Glittering Smack	1960	600 yds	33.65 secs

Track Records (1980)

Ballyard Dick	1958	315 yds	17.45 secs
Lamond Laddie	1958	315 yds	17.45 secs
Rosslyn Raider	1980	325 yds	17.90 secs
Gina Girl	1973	525 yds	29.11 secs
Ballyard Hurdler	1980	525 yds H	29.10 secs
Pineapple Kuda	1973	550 yds	29.85 secs
Killaclug Jet	1979	550 yds	30.52 secs
Glittering Smack	1960	600 yds	33.65 secs

Winners of the M.J. Hannafin Memorial Cup

1970	Noel's Fortune	29.58 secs
1971	Hopeful Hope	29.47 secs
1972	Upton Song	29.45 secs
1973	Flesk Bridge	29.25 secs
1974	Break the Bottle	29.54 secs
1975	Deise Dreams	29.38 secs
1976	Killerisk Boy	29.74 secs
1977	Laughing Sea	29.60 secs
1978	Macari Boy	29.76 secs
1979	Atlantic Expert	29.94 secs
1980	Hidden Shadow	29.90 secs

Winners of the Monalee Hiker Stakes

1973	Brisla Chief	31.62 secs
1974	Gigli's Glitter	30.96 secs
1975	Hi Doris	31.28 secs
1976	Duval King	31.12 secs
1977	Gillie's Black	31.42 secs
1978	Luanda	31.20 secs
1979	Jemmy Jed	31.30 secs

Winners of the Rose of Tralee Cup

1970	Shankill Flash	32.15 secs
1971	Rocking Ship	32.10 secs
1972	not run	
1973	Well To Do	31.72 secs
1974	Tullig Master	31.62 secs
1975	Brian's Hope	31.06 secs
1976	Tullig Champion	31.80 secs
1977	Una's Swallow	32.10 secs
1978	Real Rory	30.86 secs
1979	Heather Daisy	31.92 secs
1980	Boha's Tim	31.06 secs

Winners of the Harp Lager Stakes

1970	Oaklawn Motel	29.90 secs
1971	Shankill Flash	29.88 secs
1972	Venture Darling	29.56 secs
1973	Pacific Treasure	29.18 secs
1974	Dungeel Check	30.02 secs
1975	Dromlara Turn	29.86 secs
1976	Free Estimate	29.56 secs
1977	Snow Maiden	29.58 secs
1978	Macari Boy	29.52 secs
1979	Shelyn Lass	29.60 secs
1980	Cloghercannon	29.74 secs

Winners of the Clarke Cup

1971	Flesk Queen	32.22 secs
1972	Jim's Right	31.96 secs
1973	Kerry Gambler	31.60 secs
1974	not run	
1975	Black Abbey	31.28 secs
1976	Pier Phantom	31.32 secs
1977	Candy's Rejection	30.84 secs
1978	Hoffeen	31.30 secs
1979	Putney Bridge	31.12 secs
1980	Buff's Point	30.84 secs

Winners of the Kingdom Puppy Cup

1970	Woodman Jim	30.05 secs
1971	Midi Tail	30.10 secs
1972	Broadford Boy	29.70 secs
1973	Bansha Jet	29.84 secs
1974	Dungeel Check	29.76 secs
1975	Eagle King	30.02 secs
1976	Sting Ray	29.70 secs
1977	Manhattan Bell	29.78 secs
1978	Knockeen Mint	29.38 secs
1979	You Genius	29.72 secs
1980	Chemist Boy	29.58 secs

WATERFORD

The track, at Kilcohan Park, was opened in May 1947 and is one of the smallest of the Irish provincial tracks, of 460 yds circumference. Racing takes place on

Tuesday and Saturday each week, over 525 yds, 525 yds hurdles, and 770 yds. The main events are the Waterford Glass Sweepstake, with £1,200 for the winner, and the Truboard Gold Cup, originally the Marquis of Waterford Cup, both run over 525 yds. Both events are sponsored by the Waterford Glass Co. It was in the 1975 Waterford Glass Stakes that Peruvian Style began his great run of twenty consecutive wins which beat Mick the Miller's nineteen in a row of 1930 and equalled the twenty of Westpark Mustard made in 1974. Another important event, run over 770 yds, is the Hughie Sauvage Memorial Stakes, worth £500 to the winner.

In September 1978, encouraged by consistently increasing attendances, the management opened a magnificent new stand with excellent restaurant and tote facilities. Paddy Grant is the racing manager, backed by a fine team of directors at the track, which is owned by Waterford Greyhound Racing Co.

Through the years many fine greyhounds have raced here, but none better than those favourites of 1978, Gala Display, Quarrymount Jack – winner of the Guinness Leger at Enniscorthy – and the litter sisters Tain Nua and Tain Gerty. The latter reached the final of the Oaks and won the Waterford Glass Stakes that year. The Quarrymount greyhounds have long raced here with distinction and are bred at the kennels of Mr Jack Mackey.

Main Events Run at Waterford

News and Star Cup	June	525 yds
Marquis of Waterford Cup	August	525 yds
Waterford Glass Stakes	October	525 yds

Track Records (1950)

Square Kid	310 yds	17.89 secs
Cookhouse	525 yds	30.20 secs
Chancellorstown Lad	525 yds H	31.30 secs

Track Records (1960)

Square Kid	310 yds	17.89 secs
Cookhouse	525 yds	30.20 secs
Tropical Splendour (National Record)	525 yds H	29.90 secs

Track Records (1970)

Prince Kay	1968	300 yds	16.75 secs
Good Stayer	1965	525 yds	29.40 secs
Trop. Splendour	1980	525 yds H	29.90 secs
Local Minnie	1963	700 yds	40.35 secs
Kon Tiki Lady	1964	700 yds	40.35 secs

Track Records (1980)

Last Landing	1959	310 yds	17.25 secs
Olly's Prince	1960	310 yds H	17.85 secs
Slippery Sam	1961	500 yds	28.80 secs
Peruvian Style	1976	525 yds	29.28 secs
Lady Referee	1976	525 yds	29.28 secs
Trop. Splendour	1980	525 yds H	29.90 secs
Tain Nua	1978	770 yds	44.02 secs

Winners of the Marquis of Waterford Cup (Truboard Gold Cup since 1976)

1970	Kevinsfort Star	30.40 secs
1971	Star Mise	30.10 secs
1972	Dark Treasure	29.85 secs
1973	Speck of Luck	30.30 secs
1974	Tory Snowball	30.18 secs
1975	Peruvian Style	29.34 secs
1976	Melody Shine	29.60 secs
1977	Bins Bridge	29.38 secs
1978	Gala Display	29.76 secs

YOUGHAL

The track opened on 30 July 1948, the first race being won by Mr James Power's dog Hackles Sprig. Mr. Power later became chairman of the Youghal Racing Co. and remained there until it was taken over by Bord na gCon twenty-four years later. Finbarr Coleman is racing manager. Racing takes place on Tuesday and Friday on the very fast, almost circular track of 464 yds circumference.

The main events are the Guinness Blackwater Cup, run over 525 yds during August and won in 1978 by Always Kelly; the Aherne Memorial Trophy, run over 550 yds in early July; and the Southern Sprint, sponsored by a bookmaker, John Graham, which takes place in September. One of the most successful greyhounds in these events was Mr D. Cashman's Skipping Flash, track champion in 1970, but the record for the 550 yds course is held by the 1968 Irish St Leger winner Pool's Punter, who in the same year covered the distance in 30.85 secs, being the first dog to break 31.00 secs at the track. He was to set track records at Ballybunion (now closed) and Tralee soon after.

Also at Youghal is held the Paddy Stakes, sponsored by Irish Distillers; it is run over 550 yds, and worth £1,000 to the winner. In 1976 the event was won by Stormy Spirit, Spectre's great son, who went on to win the English St Leger the following year. Three years later the event was won by Killaclug Jet, winner of the Irish Consolation Derby and owned by Miss Kate Murray. He won by ten lengths in a new track record of 30.60 secs; the record was previously held by Blanco Kerry. Next night Killaclug Jet was to set up a new record at Tralee which may stand for years. Another race here is the Murphy's Brewery Stakes, won in 1978 by Mrs T. O'Connor's Blanco Kerry.

On 1 January 1972, the Bord na gCon took over the track, purchasing the 15,383

£1 shares at par value, and so ensured the continuation of racing.

Main Events Run at Youghal

Murphy's Brewery Stakes	March	525 yds
J.J. Ahern Memorial Stakes	April	550 yds
Jim Parker Memorial Trophy	May	550 yds
Irish Distillers' Paddy Stakes	June	550 yds
Guinness Blackwater Trophy	July	525 yds
Southern Sprint	August	325 yds
Coleman Memorial Trophy	September	550 yds
Bookmakers' Trophy	October	525 yds

Track Records (1970)

Wonderful Era	1968	325 yds	17.80 secs
Speedyman	1968	525 yds	29.45 secs
Pools Punter	1968	550 yds	30.85 secs
Rovigno	1969	790 yds	45.70 secs

Track Records (1980)

Basking Shark	1974	325 yds	17.70 secs
Special Check	1976	525 yds	29.00 secs
Super Fellow	1962	525 yds H	30.70 secs
Killaclug Jet	1979	550 yds	30.60 secs
Man of Ice	1980	700 yds	40.20 secs
Whittle Off	1972	760 yds	45.30 secs

Winners of the Guinness Blackwater Trophy

1970	Skipping Flash	29.95 secs
1971	Eastpark Star	29.80 secs
1972	Muskerry Rambler	29.90 secs
1973	Scintilla's Bud	30.10 secs
1974	Uno Best	29.60 secs
1975	Millie's Express	29.44 secs
1976	Special Check	29.25 secs
1977	Imperial Frog	29.85 secs
1978	Always Kelly	29.80 secs
1979	Dangan Honour	29.75 secs
* 1980	Gold Flight	30.80 secs
1981	Beautiful Choice	29.55 secs

* Run over 550 yds

Winners of the Paddy Stakes

1970	Gurteen Daisy	31.50 secs
1971	Fly Clown	31.50 secs
1972	Hopeful Sergent	31.10 secs
1973	Kilnoglory Spot	31.00 secs
1974	Uno Best	30.85 secs
1975	Captain Larry	31.30 secs
1976	Clashing Breeze	30.90 secs
1977	Castlerichard	30.90 secs
1978	Glorious Champ	30.75 secs
1979	Killaclug Jet	30.50 secs
1980	Gold Flight	30.75 secs

IRISH ST LEGER

See Classic Events in Ireland.

J

JACKET

Each greyhound taking part in a race must wear an approved jacket from the time of parading until the end of the race. The jackets fit over the back and around the sides of the dog and are held in place by tapes made sufficiently secure that the jackets will not come off during a race or cause the dog difficulty in running. The jackets have the colours and trap numbers clearly visible on both sides, and are standard on all NGRC tracks. Trap 1 is red; 2 is blue; 3 is white; 4 is black; 5 is orange; 6 is black and white stripes. R is the reserve dog.

It is to be regretted that Britain and Ireland do not standardize the jacket colours, for in Ireland the dog in no.1 trap has a red jacket, no.2 is blue and no.3 is white as in Britain, but no.4 trap has a red and white jacket while no.5 is black and trap 6 is orange. This tends to be confusing to those who watch racing in both countries.

In the USA, no. 1 dog wears a red jacket, no. 2 blue, no. 3 white, no. 4 green, no. 5 black, no. 6, orange, no. 7 green and white and no. 8 black and yellow. (Eight-dog races are run in the USA.)

JUDGE

An official appointed by the stadium and confirmed by the NGRC to judge the races, he must occupy the judge's box during the entire race. He must declare the greyhound whose nose first reaches the winning line to be the winner, and must announce the result at once, together with the placing of other dogs. It is the nose only of the winning dog which determines the result of a race; the legs play no part in deciding the winner, even if they reach the line first.

It is a judge's duty to watch carefully the distances between the dogs as they finish, for the racing manager will grade each dog on the distance it was behind the winning dog when he next includes them in his programme. In his calculations 0.06 secs represents 1 yd; 0.05 secs represents 1 m.

At every meeting a press agency representative is in attendance to note the starting price of a race. The moment the dogs are in the traps and the hare moves off, he notes the prices of at least three bookmakers and hands them to a 'runner' to take to the judge's box. The judge enters the prices on his card, together with the exact time the hare was released and the result and times of each dog in the race. Copies are then sent to the press, the racing manager, and the stewards of the NGRC. The information is final and binding.

K

KENNELS

Race tracks have their own kennels, either close to the track or a short distance away, where the greyhounds are housed and exercised. These are different from the racing kennels, which are reached from the paddock close to the track and where the dogs are housed during a meeting or trials. Private trainers have their own range of kennels, and anyone rearing greyhounds should have suitable accommodation for them.

The greyhound is believed by some to be a delicate breed, requiring more than average care in its feeding and housing, but this is not so. I have seen magnificent young greyhounds in Ireland allowed to roam about the fields and farmyards in bitterly cold weather, and crunching between their teeth old wireless batteries which they apparently enjoyed. They looked the picture of health. This is how the Irish raise their greyhounds, in no way pampering them, but they are always housed in a dry, airy shed or barn. Greyhounds are never harmed by the cold but damp housing must be avoided and so must draughts.

Kennels may be of three types:

(1) Suitable outbuildings such as a barn or shed built of brick or stone which are warm in winter and cool in summer. These are excellent conditions under which to keep greyhounds, especially if they have a concrete floor.

(2) A wooden shed such as an old garden tool shed or henhouse, now disused.

(3) A specially constructed kennel or range of kennels, made of brick, or breeze blocks, or timber and asbestos (brick or breeze blocks will be more durable).

On most farms there is often a barn to spare to house a brood bitch or young greyhounds where the dogs can have the freedom of the place. This is the ideal way to rear good greyhounds and is why they do particularly well on the North Country Fells, where many of the finest coursing and track dogs have been reared. The housing is warm and dry, while complete freedom ensures good bone formation and strong hind quarters.

Often the walls of an old barn will be more than 15 ins thick, but if the inside is in a rough condition it will be advisable to cement-render the surface. This will fill up any holes which might let in draughts and will discourage pests which might prove troublesome to the dogs. A reasonably smooth surface will also enable the walls to be washed down with disinfectant after illness. This will prevent outbreaks of mange which causes irritation and loss of hair and makes a dog go off his food and lose condition quickly. (*See* Ailments and Diseases.) It is just as important to provide greyhound kennels with a concrete floor. Most farm sheds have floors of earth or cobblestones which cannot be properly washed down. An earth floor will be damp and will harbour worms which are also picked up from farmyards and from anywhere there is soil or grass, such as earth run for the dogs to exercise. Tapeworms are also carried by fleas which inhabit the earth floor and rough walls of farm sheds, and ticks which suck the blood, causing irritation and making the dog go off colour.

Where there is an earth floor, remove the top 6 ins of soil and put down a 3 in. layer of crushed brick or shingle; make it compact and cover it with the same depth of concrete. This is made by mixing two parts sand to one part cement and working it into a smooth consistency (but not too sloppy) so that it can be easily spread over the layer of stones to a uniform depth and made as level as possible. Do this by moving a length of 1 in. thick board edgewise over the surface. Begin at the back of the room and work towards the front or entrance. Make sure that the door will open, but do not leave too much space at the bottom or it will be draughty. Make sure to fill in all holes around the base of the walls with cement so as to prevent rats entering, for they carry infective jaundice (heptospirosis). As a further precaution, have all dogs and pups immunized with an Epivax-TC vaccine. (*See* Ailments and Diseases.)

At the back of the barn or shed fix a wooden bench for the dogs to sleep and rest on. This should be not less than 6 ft wide and 5 ft from back to front, and it should be about 12 ins above floor level. Being made of wood it will be warmer than the floor, and the dogs will be protected from draughts. Use ¾ in. timber for the bench, with supports at the centre to carry the 60–70 lbs weight of a greyhound. Plenty of fresh straw, which can be purchased by the bale from a local farmer, should be put down on the bench, though not on the floor. The straw should be changed twice a week to keep it free from ticks and fleas. The floor of the kennel should be swilled out every day to maintain hygienic conditions.

A kennel should have ample ventilation. If possible, put in wall vents well above ground level. The best doors are the stable type, made in two parts, so that on most days, except during severe weather, the top portion can be left open in the day and closed in the evening. If this type of door is not fixed, a window opening from the top should be inserted into a wall about 5 ft above ground. This will let in additional fresh air and light.

Fresh water should be available at all times, for greyhounds are big drinkers. Remove all feeding utensils and clean them immediately the dog has finished its food. Dirty dishes are a cause of many illnesses.

The size of a kennel or shed in which one dog or a brood bitch and her litter are kept should be not less than 12 ft from back to front and 6 ft wide. It should be about 8 ft high, so that one may enter to attend to a bitch and her pups and clean the kennel out without difficulty.

A brood bitch in whelp or with her litter should always be kennelled on her own; she needs complete quiet and privacy. Two young or older dogs, though, can be housed together, provided they get on well with each other and do not fight over their food. Most will enjoy each other's company, but some (like humans) are bad-tempered, and an older dog may prevent another from sharing its sleeping quarters and may take another's food if it has a more timid disposition. You will soon know how they get on together.

A stud dog, too, should be given a kennel or compartment on its own. He may be of considerable value and earning big fees from his services, perhaps mating two bitches each week at anything from £50 to £200 a service, and he needs to be given extra care in his daily routine. Kennelled on his own, he will have no interference from other dogs when feeding after a service and taking a little sleep, and there will also be less risk of infection.

If you are keeping a brood bitch and raising her pups for sale at twelve to sixteen weeks old, she will need the same kind of attention. It will be advisable to board up the front of her sleeping bench to prevent the pups from going underneath, in which event she will not be able to get to them for feeding, washing, etc.

A wooden hut such as a garden shed or henhouse is ideal for a brood bitch, being warm, but it should never have a corrugated iron roof which becomes extremely hot in summer if in direct sun, and is just as cold in winter. There will also be condensation on the underside, causing the greyhound's bedding to get damp with the falling moisture. If a shed has an iron roof, remove it and replace it with one of wood covered with bituminous felt. This will be waterproof and warm in winter, and there will be no condensation. If the shed can be lined with hardboard it will give additional warmth.

A shed is best in semi-shade to prevent it from becoming too hot in summer, causing distress to the bitch, while excess sunlight is harmful to pups. If the shed can be placed beneath mature trees, so much the better. If not, plant a few poplars on the sunny side; these will grow quickly and soon provide the necessary protection. A shed will require ample ventilation in summer and should have a small run attached, to enable the bitch and her pups, or a stud dog, to obtain plenty of exercise and to lie out in good weather. The run can be enclosed by chain-linked fencing or wire netting supported by strong wooden posts, and it must be at least 6 ft high because greyhounds, especially when between one and three years old, can jump almost to this height.

I have seen excellent pups reared to twelve months old in the yard of a town house, where they were housed in an old wash-house or shed. The concrete yard will often be surrounded by a 6 ft wall which will give protection from cold winds. Greyhounds may be kept in a town garden if the shed is sited at the end of the garden and the pups have a grass run. Better still, give them a concrete run, for this is easier to clean and will prevent the animals picking up parasites from soil or grass. In addition the concrete will harden the pups' feet and legs, which is most important for track greyhounds. Old flagstones placed close together over a 2 in. base of sand will be just as good, and have the advantage that they can easily be removed. Even a single row of flagstones placed close to the fence down one side will help the pups harden their feet, as they will usually jump up against the fence whenever anyone approaches to have a word with them.

Always choose a well-drained site for kennels. We get plenty of rain in the British Isles, and wet ground not only encourages parasites but gives the dogs rheumatism. Cold does not harm greyhounds, but wet does. At all times they should be kept as dry as possible, but artificial heat is not necessary except for young pups in very cold weather. Even so, the best way to protect the pups will be to put down fresh straw over the top of the old while the weather is very bad. The heat from their urine and droppings (due to bacterial activity) will provide the extra warmth.

Those breeding on a larger scale or keeping older greyhounds for racing in open events will need a private trainer's licence, renewed annually. It is granted only after an inspection of the kennels by a steward of the NGRC, who will visit the kennels annually to ensure that they are kept up to the required standard. If you do not wish to train racing greyhounds but to keep a stud dog of your own, or for another owner, and one or more brood bitches to breed either for sale or for the pups to be placed with a farmer when six to eight months old, you do not need a licence.

A small breeding establishment can be formed for a limited sum provided there is land on which to do so or a large barn that can be converted to house a number of dogs. This is done by inserting wooden partitions over a concrete floor, each section being entered through a door made of a wooden frame covered by wire netting. A passage along the front of the inside of the barn will enable each compartment to be easily reached and cleaning to be done under cover. If there is no existing structure available, a group of wooden kennels can be constructed, possibly four, back to back, each 6–7 ft high, 6 ft wide, and 8 ft from back to front. Each should have a window, ample ventilation and a door, but a single flat roof covered with bitumen-treated felt will cover the four kennels.

Building the kennels back to back will keep construction costs to a minimum. The kennels should be constructed of ½ in. boarding, and 2 x 2 in. timber used for the supports. The kennels can have a wooden floor, or one made of flagstones or concrete, and the usual bench for the dogs to sleep on. All timber should be treated with wood preservative after construction. Leave the kennels for several weeks before any dogs are housed, to enable the fumes to escape.

Around the kennels should be a 6 ft high chain-link fence with places for entry, and if flagstones are available a row should be put down inside the fence all the way round if you are rearing the pups to a reasonable age. Outside the fence should be a garden shed with a table or bench where medicines, coats, leads and muzzles are kept and where the paperwork is done, for there will be mating certificates to fill in and NCC forms for registration of whelping.

The work shed will be always in use and therefore needs electricity laid on. Alternatively an efficient battery lamp will enable work to go on after dark in winter and help you give the dogs attention whenever necessary during the night. Greyhounds are like children – one never knows just when they need care, and one must be prepared to attend to them at all times. Because of this the kennels should be as close to one's home as possible.

A supply of fresh water will be necessary, to provide water for the dogs at all times, also for washing down the kennels and treating the dogs for, or as a preventative against, sarcoptic mange (*see* Ailments and Diseases). Water is also required for preparing the dogs' food, for stewing horse meat and for washing the hands after attending the dogs. A tap (preferably indoors) and a good-sized bowl are essential in all kennels.

An efficient mincer will be necessary to mince the meat; also a strong table to cut up the meat and prepare the vegetables which should be included in every greyhound's diet.

Medicines should be kept on a shelf away from the reach of any children. Nail scissors will be required to trim the dogs' toe nails and coats, and leads for taking the dogs out to exercise. Leather leads look so much better than chains when taking a dog to a racecourse for trials or a bitch for service. Much time will be spent in collecting and returning bitches to put to one's stud dog, and a small car or van will be necessary if the kennels are any distance from a railway station.

There is always a demand for boarding greyhounds which may be off racing because of illness or injury, and time will be taken up in collecting the animals and taking them to the tracks when they resume trials. This must be taken into consideration when charging for a dog's keep and kennelling.

The rearing of greyhound pups for sale is a profitable business if stock of the right breeding is obtained. A stud dog, too, can be equally profitable, as is the kennelling of dogs for owners, but it must be realized that it will occupy all your time. Boarding and breeding is a twenty-four-hours-a-day job. You may be up all night nursing a sick animal or attending to a bitch when whelping, for you will be dealing with expensive stock. A champion brood bitch of the right breeding may have cost several hundred pounds and there may have been a £100 stud fee.

To keep them really fit, racing greyhounds require more care and attention than any other breed. They need daily grooming and massage of the hind quarters to keep the back muscles supple; their feet need regular attention and they are prone to skin troubles if not kept under the cleanest conditions. They will suffer from stomach upsets if not given the correct food, and being a highly-strung sporting breed they use up a great deal of energy which needs to be replenished constantly, while the brittleness of their bones causes them to injure themselves much more readily than other breeds.

A great deal of pleasure and satisfaction can be obtained from attending greyhound tracks just to see the magnificent condition in which the dogs are turned out, week in week out, and one is filled with admiration at the dedication of the trainers and their staff. Everything is done to keep their charges in peak condition, and when a well turned out greyhound is brought into the arena there is no finer sight.

L

LADY OWNERS

Since that first meeting at Belle Vue in 1926, when Lady Stanley had a greyhound on the card, women have taken as great an interest in the sport as men, and as owners and trainers have met with equal success. The winner of the second Greyhound Derby (1928), Boher Ash, was owned by Mrs M. Stokes, and two years later Mrs Arundel Kempton won with her famous Mick the Miller for whom she had paid 2,000 gns (a large sum in 1930) shortly after Mick had won the 1929 Derby. In 1936 Mrs M. Yate became the only woman ever to own the Derby winner (Fine Jubilee) and also to breed and train him to win the premier event. In 1937 Mrs R.H. Dent won with Wattle Bark in the fastest time (29.26 secs) then recorded over the 525 yds course. This gave her considerable satisfaction for only the previous year, when this great dog's life was despaired of, a veterinary surgeon had devoted twelve months to saving him, at a cost to his owner of more than £200. Both were amply rewarded for their patience.

In 1946 at Shelbourne Park Mrs Dent became the first person to win the English and Irish Greyhound Derby when her dog Steve won from Manhattan Seal. Her success was repeated in 1966 when Faithful Hope won the English Derby for Sir Richard Adeane and Miss Pauline Wallis, and two years later their dog Yellow Printer won the Irish Derby.

Only four years after Wattle Bark's achievement Mrs Stow's flyer Ballyhennessy

Seal, whom she had bought for £100 after winning a race at Tralee, won the 1945 Derby, and in 1960 Mrs B. Dash's Duleek Dandy won the first £2,000 Derby prize. The dog was trained by her husband.

Women have been equally successful in other major events. Besides winning the Derby, Mick the Miller won the Cesarewitch and St Leger for Mrs Kempton and in three years' racing took more than £10,000 in prize money. Mrs Vera Cherry reared that fine greyhound Cockeyed Cutlet in the back yard of her town house, and he won for her the Cambridgeshire and Thousand Guineas. More recently Hard Held, which cost Mrs Corbett only 200 gns at auction, reached the final of the 1969 Greyhound Derby.

In the early years of greyhound racing, when Mick the Miller was doing so much to popularize the sport, the performances of Beef Cutlet were almost as remarkable. He was owned by Miss J. Merritt and was undoubtedly the fastest dog during the first ten years of the sport. When in 1944 Ballyhennessy Seal set up a new national record of 27.64 secs for the 500 yds course, it was not generally realized that on a specially constructed Blackpool course in May 1933 Beef Cutlet had clocked 26.13 secs, a time never beaten.

During the 1930s and 1940s Mrs Cearns, wife of the then managing director of the Wimbledon track, owned many famous greyhounds, none finer than Ballyhennessy Sandhills (whose national record for 500 yds put up in 1938 stood for many years) and Ballynennan Moon, whose popularity equalled that of Mick the Miller in the previous decade and who was the first dog to command a stud fee of 100 gns. Ballyhennessy Sandhills was the first dog to win the Laurels twice, and the racing public had to wait nearly twenty years before Duet Leader achieved the same distinction for Mrs Frances Chandler, wife of the managing director of the Walthamstow track. Mrs Chandler owned many fine greyhounds, the best of whom was Magourna Reject, winner of the Wembley St Leger in the fast time of 39.88 secs. Mrs Chandler's dogs won three Laurels, the first occasion being with Polonius in 1951, a dog who was to sire an English Derby winner, Ford Spartan. She also won the Irish Derby with Sole Aim.

Another famous woman owner was Mrs Hilda Sanderson, whose husband Alan was managing director of the old Coventry track. Her finest greyhound was the great Robeen Printer, winner of the St Leger and of the Eclipse Stakes at Coventry which she divided in a dead heat with an equally wonderful bitch Prancing Kitty.

Another great bitch during the 1940s was Disputed Rattler, owned by Mrs Robinson and her friend Mrs Gilhooley. The bitch was to endear herself to race-goers much as Quarter Day and Bradshaw Fold did in the previous decade, and gave her owners several years of the greatest pleasure when seeing her run. Miss Gertrude Stockman was a successful owner during the same time and won the Wimbledon Puppy Derby in 1943 with Allardstown Playboy, trained by Stanley Biss.

The first race run at Wembley, on 10 December 1927, was won from no. 4 trap by a dog called Spin owned by Mrs Allcoat. Wembley Stadium was the venue for the famous match between Miss Lambert's dog Train and Mrs Cearns' Ballynennan Moon. It took place on 16 January 1943, and the bitch Satin Beauty also contested it. The match was run over 525 yds and it was Train, bred from the famous coursing sire, Danielli, who was the winner. Women owners have always played a big part in the success of Wembley as a greyhound venue, for there in October 1969 the great hurdler Sherry's Prince, owned by Mrs R. Matthews, clocked 29.81 secs for 525 yds. The record has never been beaten. In more recent years racegoers have seen the wonderfully consistent running of Mrs Lily Aubrey's white and black bitch Miss Taft, trained at the Stadium by Mr Bob Burls. In 115 races she won on fifty-five occasions and was second twenty-five times. After a winning sequence of ten she was elected best bitch for 1967, an honour well deserved.

What must be a unique record took place at Perry Barr in September 1945 when all five greyhounds running in the final of the Birmingham Cup were owned by women. The race was won by Mrs Hilda Sanderson's dog Duffy's Arrival.

The blue riband event for puppies, the Trafalgar Cup, run at Wembley, was won in 1932 by Mikado Beauty, trained by Jim Syder Snr and owned by a Japanese lady.

The 1947 Irish Derby was won by Mary d'Arcy's, Daring Flash when she became the first and only woman to train, breed and rear the winner of this event.

In 1981, Mrs Grace Costello had a runner in both the English and Irish Derby finals (different dogs). In the Irish event, both she and her husband, Eddie had a dog running in the final.

A feat unique in the history of Irish greyhound racing occurred in 1982 when Mrs Mary McGrath of Coalisland, won the Racing Derby with her dog Cooladine Super and in the same year, the Mulvaney Coursing Derby with Martry Scotch.

LEASE

An owner may assign an interest in a registered greyhound for any period to a lessee, provided that the lease is registered on the appropriate form by the NGRC and is to the satisfaction of the stewards of the course. The lessor will retain the greyhound in his or her name in the English or Irish Stud Book.

LICENSED TRACK

Before it can start operating a greyhound racecourse (a track) must be licensed under the Betting, Gaming and Lotteries Act, 1963 (or any amendments) and the NGRC must approve its amenities and jurisdiction. It will then be known as an approved licensed racecourse.

LIGHTS

The first meeting to be held under artificial lighting was at Belle Vue, Manchester, on the opening night, since when racing has generally taken place in the evening, to encourage larger crowds after the working day has ended.

On every track the tote, traps, hare and lighting of the track and club house are electrically controlled and each comes under a separate official. The lighting round the track is of great importance and a big item to be placed against profits. At the Perry Barr Stadium, for example, there are sixty overhead lights, each of about 200 candle-power. At night the lights are switched on around the track just before each race starts; this lighting consumes about 170 units during a meeting while other lighting accounts for about 300 units. The tote consumes seventy to eighty units and the hare only two units.

LITTER

Pups born to a bitch are known as a litter. The size of a greyhound litter varies considerably. A bitch may have a single pup, particularly if she is old, or she may have as many as eleven or twelve, which is quite normal. The largest litter known to have been whelped to a greyhound is seventeen, born to Dew Wall in April 1944, though all of them died soon after birth. Fly Joan, dam of the excellent long-distance runner Rushton Ranger, whelped thirty-five pups in two and a half years from three matings; all lived. It is usual for a bitch whose first litter was a large one to continue having large litters, but perhaps one of six to eight pups is ideal as too many take too much from the bitch and are more difficult to manage. The number of dog and bitch pups in a litter also varies greatly. Of twelve pups born to the bitch Becker's Tea, eleven were dogs.

Some litters have been remarkable in the number of high-class greyhounds they have produced. An outstanding example was the litter of five dogs and four bitches born at the kennels of Mr Leo Stack in Ireland from a mating of Supreme Witch and Crazy Parachute. Among them were Tric Trac and Spectre II, who finished first and second in the 1967 English Derby, the only occasion on which two greyhounds from one litter did so. Of the others, Forward King won the 1968 English St Leger; while Forward Flash was the fastest of them all but had to be retired early due to injury. Other outstanding examples were Junior Classic and Juvenile Classic who were from the same litter; so were Shannon Shore and Celtic Chief. The great Beef Cutlet and Queen of the Suir were litter brother and sister, while Clomoney Grand, from a mating with Prairie Flash, produced from one litter Kilbelin Style (ran up in the 1969 English Derby), Kilbelin Grand (Irish Derby finalist), Clomoney Jude (winner of the Pigalle Wonder Stakes), Albany and Albany Grand, both outstanding trackers.

There have been even more outstanding examples on the coursing field. In 1956 Elphin Girl had a litter of four, one of which, Holystone Elf, won the 1958 Waterloo Cup while the others won the International Cup and the Barbican Plate and ran up for the St Leger. There was the famous litter of Inler May, who from a mating to Border Cutlet produced from one litter Sneem (winner of the Irish Coursing Oaks), Shule Aroon (Irish Cup winner), Salisbury (Irish Coursing Derby winner), and Spring of Shillalegh (Connaught Cup winner). Probably the greatest litter of all time, though, from a mating of Tender Heart with Newdown Heather, consisted of Tender Hero, Tender Heather and Tender Honey, who were to take the three major Irish Coursing events of the 1968–9 season, the Irish Cup, Derby and Oaks.

Remember to register every litter before it is four weeks old with the National Coursing Club or Irish Coursing Club. Which of the two will depend upon the registration of the dam. To register a litter up to the age of eight weeks with the English Stud Book, a fee of £4 is currently charged; £10 thereafter. On the form provided, the colour and sex of each puppy is shown, with the predominating colour first. Attached to the form is a certificate to be filled in by a veterinary surgeon to the effect that he has inspected the pups and is able to confirm that the number of each sex is correct as stated by the owner on the form. On the reverse is a mating certificate to be signed by the owner of the sire. The sire should be registered with both coursing clubs; otherwise to transfer the bitch from one club to the other, to coincide with that of the sire, a fee of £5 is charged.

It was usual to register a litter when about six to seven weeks old, for the colours may change slightly after birth and as the pups get older. If an alteration or correction is necessary, inform the coursing club as soon as possible. No extra fee is required if this is done within six months of whelping.

LITTER BROTHERS AND SISTERS

Since the start of greyhound racing there have been many instances of greyhounds from the same litter proving outstanding performers on the flat or over hurdles. The first were the two litter brothers Mick the Miller and Macoma, raised in Ireland by Father Brophy. They were by Glorious Event out of Na Boc Lei and were whelped in 1926, when greyhound racing had just started. Mick the Miller was to become the greatest ever on the flat, twice winning the Derby; the Welsh Derby; the Cesarewitch; and St Leger over a period of three and a half years. He won his last race, the St Leger, when more than five years old, being the oldest dog to win a classic event. Macoma was equally brilliant over hurdles, and at stud was one of the first important sires of racing greyhounds. He sired Kitshine, winner of the Oaks, and Long Hop and Scapegoat, who excelled over hurdles. Both were out of the same bitch, Bright Emblem, but from different matings. Macoma also sired two remarkable bitches, both born in 1931; one was Lady Eleanor, who from her mating with Beef Cutlet whelped in 1936 Junior Classic and Juvenile Classic. The former was one of the greatest sprinters of all time, winner of the 1938 Gold Collar and holder of the world record for 500 yds at Stamford Bridge; the latter was twice winner of the Grand National, the premier event for hurdlers.

The other great Macoma bitch was Wonderful Expression, who from a mating to Golden Hammer produced in 1935 Grosvenor Bob and Grosvenor Edwin, two of the finest stayers in the sport's history. 'Bob' won the Trafalgar Cup, ran up the Cesarewitch and won the St Leger, while 'Edwin' won the Wembley Gold Cup (like the St Leger run over 700 yds) and the Stayers' Plaque. Thus Macoma, himself one of a famous litter, had produced two bitches who were to whelp litter brothers of equal fame and who were at their peak at the end of the 1930s.

Before those great litter brothers to the two Macoma bitches, there had appeared in 1932 a litter brother and sister the like of whom were not to be seen again until Mad Tanist and Astra in 1942. Beef Cutlet and Queen of the Suir were born in the kennels of Mr J. Byrne in Co. Tipperary from a mating of Mutton Cutlet to the bitch Burette. Beef Cutlet was the fastest dog of his time, and in May 1933 made the fastest run over 500 yds ever recorded. He also won the Laurels. He is remembered, too, as the sire of Junior Classic and Juvenile Classic and of Winnie of Berrow, dam of the Derby winner Narrogar Ann. His sister, Queen of the Suir, was the most outstanding bitch of the early years of the sport, winning the Irish Oaks in 1932 and the English Oaks the following year, being the only bitch ever to do so. She again won the English Oaks in 1934.

Astra and Mad Tanist, by Tanist out of Mad Darkie, came ten years later and were the fastest brother and sister ever to be whelped in the same litter. To give some idea of Astra's amazing speed, she twice won Ireland's most important event after the classics, the Easter Cup, the first time beating her brother Mad Tanist and another wonderful bitch, Hurry Kitty; on the second occasion she beat the world's fastest, Quare Times. She also finished third in the Irish Derby of 1946. To show that he was just as fast from the traps, Mad Tanist won the Irish National Sprint (the equivalent of England's Scurry Gold Cup) at Dunmore Park in 1944. Mad Tanist was to become the most important sire of the 1950s, while Astra, from her mating to Paddy the Champion, whelped Astra's Son, sire of Prairie Vixen, dam of Pigalle Wonder, one of the greatest of all greyhounds, and of Prairie Flash, sire of the English Derby winner Camira Flash. From a mating to Clomoney Grand she whelped that excellent litter which included Albany, Clomoney Jet and Kilbelin Style, who ran up to Sand Star for the Derby. Mad Tanist was sire of Sandown Champion, sire of Lisabelle, dam of Solar Prince, sire of the Derby winner, Faithful Hope; and of The Grand Champion.

One of the greatest litters of all time was that born to Deemster's Olive in 1936. Creamery Border was their sire and it was his first after being retired to stud. He was one of the fastest from the traps of all greyhounds, and his sons in this litter all inherited his tremendous speed. Roeside Creamery was a blue, like his sire, and for seven years was recognized as the fastest dog in the world after covering the 500 yds course at Stamford Bridge on 28 July 1938, in 27.68 secs or 37 mph. In the same year he won the Pall Mall and Chelsea Cup, while his litter brother Roeside Scottie ran up to Ballyhennessy Sandhills for the Laurels and won the Scottish Derby. The third litter brother, the blue Manhattan Midnight (originally named Roeside Prince), was perhaps the fastest of the three but injury early in his career forced his retirement to stud, where he was to rival his sire in the outstanding stock he produced. Favourite for the 1938 Derby, he won his heats and semi-final with the greatest ease, but in the final, won by Lone Keel, he broke a hock and was carried from the track. He was to sire the bitch Caledonian Desire, dam of Mad Prospect, dam (from a mating with Hi There) of Crazy Parachute who in turn was sire of probably the greatest litter in the history of the sport – the one that included Tric Trac and Spectre II, first and second in the 1967 Derby, and Forward Flash and Forward King, the latter winner of the 1968 St Leger and the Scottish St Leger. Spectre won the BBC Sportsview Trophy in 1967 and was to become one of the leading sires of modern greyhound racing. His son Black Andrew won the 1971 Laurels and another son, Tartan Khan, won the English Derby, while Stormy Spirit took the 1977 St Leger. With Monalee Champion Spectre was the greatest sire of the 1970s; both were sired by Crazy Parachute, whose great grand sire on the dam's side was Manhattan Midnight.

In 1944 Humming Bee and Maesydd Michael, sons of April Burglar who was a son of Lord Rosebery's great sire Danielli, were born. April Burglar had won the Laurels before being retired to stud shortly after with a broken hock. Of his sons from the same litter, Maesydd Michael won the Waterloo Cup in 1946 and Humming Bee performed with great ability on the track, reaching the semi-finals of the Gold Collar and the Derby in 1947 and winning the Essex Vase and Perry Barr Cup in addition to many other important events.

In more recent times, one of the best litters included Sole Aim, winner of the 1971 Irish Derby in record time, and Cobbler. Both were to become famous sires, Sole Aim being sire of the Irish St Leger winner Rhu out of Columbcille Aim, dam of the 1979 Irish Derby winner Penny County.

Another outstanding litter of recent times was that whelped in 1975, by Lively Band out of Certral, a Newdown Heather bitch. The greatest of the litter was Balliniska Band, winner of the 1977 Derby and holder of the 500 m record at the White City with a time of 29.16 secs. During three years' racing he was almost unbeatable, winning the Manchester Puppy Cup in 1976; the Derby in 1977; and the Wimbledon Winter Cup in 1978. Almost as successful was Linacre, who in two years won £12,500 and twenty-three open races from thirty starts. These included the Edinburgh Cup, the Wembley Spring Cup and the Sussex Cup, while he ran up in the 1977 Welsh Derby and the Laurels.

See under Famous Racing Greyhounds.

LOCAL STEWARD

Three local stewards are appointed to each racecourse. They have the authority to make and, if necessary, vary all arrangements for the running of a trial or race, and to abandon a trials or race meeting if necessary. Should the local stewards not be satisfied with the running of a greyhound in a trial or race, or if they are notified of a complaint or objection, they will hold an enquiry and inform the NGRC. They will reach a decision as soon as possible and this will be final for the purpose of that particular trial or race.

LONDON RACECOURSES

See under British Greyhound Racecourses.

LONG ODDS

Antrim Seal was quoted at 100–1 for the 1949 Chelsea Cup at Stamford Bridge and came close to winning, running up to Eastern Madness by half a length. When winning the 1951 Orient Vase at Clapton the bitch Castle Tina was quoted 100–1. She had cost Mr Alf Vango £50.

When winning the 1971 Cesarewitch at West Ham Whisper Billy, owned by Lady Houstoun Boswell, was 50–1 against, and the dog who ran up, Rosemount Gunner, was 33–1. The sum paid out by the tote for 'win and place' is believed to be the biggest in the history of greyhound racing in Britain.

The longest odds for an English Derby winner was 25–1 against, given for Duleek Dandy who won in 1960, and for Tartan Khan, the 1975 winner. The latter went on to win the St Leger the same year.

LONGEST RACES

In Britain the longest classic event is the Cesarewitch, now run at Belle Vue over 815 m in October. In Ireland it is also the Cesarewitch, run over 600 yds at Navan.

One of the longest races is the Dorando Marathon, which takes place on Derby night at the White City early in July and is run over the 962 m course. The BBC TV Trophy, staged at a different track each year, is also a marathon and is usually run over 820 m (previously over 880 yds).

Catford have always staged top-class events over long distances. The Catford Marathon, once run over 1,180 yds, is now run over 1,000 m, while the Cobb Marathon, formerly run over 810 yds, now takes place over 850 m. It was at Catford in September 1971 that Spot of Luck covered the 1,180 yds course in 70.94 secs to establish a track record for the distance, this being one of the longest times ever recorded.

The Key is run over the 868 m course at Wimbledon in June, and amongst recent winners (1978) was Langford Dacoit, owned by Mr R. Andrews and Mr D. Allen and trained at Brighton. This dog was quoted 4–1 on before the race, as he was established as the best stayer in Britain.

The Crayford Marathon is run over 880 m in February, and the Wembley Marathon in May over 850 m. Romford holds the Wheatley–Triad Stakes over 750 m in September. At one time Western Dasher held the record over this distance, with a time of 74.42 secs.

In Ireland the longest race is for the Galway Marathon Trophy, run over 810 yds, while the Michael Kerley Memorial Trophy is run at Dundalk over 765 yds and the Corn Cuchulainn at Harold's Cross over 750 yds. Rita's Choice won the latter event in 1972 in 42.10 secs, the fastest time recorded in Ireland over this distance.

One of the longest races to have been run on a greyhound track was over 1,180 yds at Catford, twice round the track, in February 1948. It was won by the bitch Maggie Sally, who finished sixteen lengths in front of her nearest rival in a time of 76.42 secs, believed to be the longest time ever taken to complete a race in Britain. One of the longest races in Britain is the 1,068 m event run at Crayford each year. It was won in 1978 by the bitch Brookfield Sarah, kennelled and trained at Yarmouth.

M

MANCHESTER RACECOURSES

See under British Greyhound Racecourses.

MATCH

A match is a race between two greyhounds in the charge of different licensed trainers and the property of different owners, on terms to be agreed by the latter. A match requires the approval of the NGRC before it can be included in a meeting.

One of the greatest matches was between Leslie McNair's dog Knockhill Chieftain and Al Burnett's Pigalle Wonder run at White City in 1958 over 550 yds. It was won by Knockhill Chieftain by 2½ lengths after leading all the way.

MATING

A bitch will be ready to put to a stud dog about twelve days after the first discharge is seen, perhaps a day or so earlier or later. She should be left at the sire's kennels for at least a full day for a satisfactory service to take place. First allow the dog to get the scent of the bitch; the best way is to kennel the bitch overnight and let the dog spend a few minutes around the straw bed, when he will usually take to the bitch as soon as they are brought together. If not, give them ample time in comparative isolation, for they may not mate if there are people about whom they do not know.

The animals will be locked together for fifteen to twenty minutes in a normal service, after which care must be taken to prevent either from trying to break away, in which event serious damage may be caused to the dog. After a normal service the dog will be tired and gradually break away, but it may be wise to have dog and bitch on leads held by those who know them or who are used to the procedure, so that some control can be exercised concerning the beginning and end of the service. The bitch must also be muzzled, unless you know her well, for almost invariably she will turn on the dog at the start of her service. The whole procedure takes about an hour, after which both dog and bitch should be placed in separate kennels, the dog given a feed of meat, brown bread and broth, the bitch one of warm milk and biscuit. Then allow both to rest overnight, or the bitch for at least two hours before taking her home.

It used to be general practice to give the bitch a second mating on the following day, but nowadays this is thought unnecessary and may in fact harm the bitch. A second service, however, may be given if it was thought that the first one was unsatisfactory – that the time was too short or if the bitch was still showing excessive discharge. In this rare event she may be served again, possibly two days later. If she conceived the first time, she will not do so again and will have her pups in sixty-three days, the normal period of gestation.

After the service, the owner of the bitch will be given a certificate of mating, showing the date of service (which can be checked when the pups are born, after sixty-three days) and the earmarkings (in Ireland) of dog and bitch. A stud dog should be registered with both the English and Irish Stud Books, so that bitches registered with either club can be mated and their offspring registered without paying a transfer fee. Books of mating certificates are signed by the stud dog's owner, and a certificate must also be made out and signed if mating one's own bitches to one's own stud dog.

Before a mating takes place, a bitch must be examined by a veterinary surgeon who will issue the owner with a certificate of her freedom from venereal disease. If she is not clear, she must not be used. Likewise the owner of a stud dog must have it examined and certified clear before he can be used to serve bitches. In Ireland, any owner of a stud dog that accepts an unexamined bitch who has not been declared free of the disease is liable to have his dog removed from the register.

See Bitch; Brood Bitch; Dam; Sire.

MIDDLESBROUGH RACECOURSE
See under British Greyhound Racecourses.

MONMORE GREEN RACECOURSE
See under British Greyhound Racecourses.

MOST CLASSIC WINS IN GREAT BRITAIN

5	Local Interprize	Cesarewitch 1948 Gold Collar 1948, 1949 Scurry Cup 1948 Welsh Derby 1948
5	Mick the Miller	Cesarewitch 1930 English Derby 1929, 1930 St Leger 1931 Welsh Derby 1930

4	Mile Bush Pride	Cesarewitch 1959 English Derby 1959 Scottish Derby 1959 Welsh Derby 1959
4	Future Cutlet	Cesarewitch 1931, 1932 English Derby 1933 Laurels 1931
4	Patricia's Hope	English Derby 1972, 1973 Scottish Derby 1972 Welsh Derby 1972
4	Trev's Perfection	English Derby 1947 Gold Collar 1947 Scottish Derby 1947 Welsh Derby 1947
3	Brilliant Bob (also 1 in Ireland)	Cesarewitch 1934 Laurels 1934 Scurry Cup 1934 Irish St Leger 1933
3	Ballymac Ball	Laurels 1949, 1950 English Derby 1950
3	Rushton Mac	English Derby 1954 Scottish Derby 1954 Welsh Derby 1955
3	Sherry's Prince	Grand National 1970, 1971, 1972
3	Wild Woolley	English Derby 1932 Gold Collar 1933 Laurels 1933
3	Yankee Express	Scurry Gold Cup 1982, 1983, 1984

MOST CLASSIC WINS IN IRELAND

4	Spanish Battleship (also won Easter Cup 1954, 1955)	Derby 1953, 1954, 1955 Laurels 1955
3	Magheragh Soldier	Trigo Cup* 1935, 1936, 1937
3	Special	Grand National 1972, 1973, 1974
2	Abbeylara	Derby 1938 St Leger 1938
2	Ballybeg Prim	Cesarewitch 1975 St Leger 1975
2	Fair Mistress	Oaks 1942 National Sprint 1943
2	Fearless Gaughan	Trigo Cup* 1939, 1940
2	Hairdresser	Oaks 1966 National Sprint 1966
2	Hot Shot	Grand National 1933, 1934
2	Keep Moving	Derby 1956 National Sprint 1956
2	Knockrour Slave	Laurels, 1979, 1980
2	Lilac's Luck	Derby 1945 Trigo Cup 1945
2	Lively Band	Derby 1974 St Leger 1974
2	Monarch of the Glen	St Leger 1942, 1943
2	Motel Chief	Cesarewitch 1963 National Produce Stakes 1964
2	Nameless Star	Laurels 1976 St Leger 1976
2	Own Pride	Derby 1969 St Leger 1969
2	Peaceful Lady	Oaks 1952, 1953
2	Pick Me	Grand National 1976, 1977
2	Rahan Ship	St Leger 1980 Cesarewitch 1980
2	Romping to Work	St Leger 1973 Oaks 1973
2	Spanish Chestnut	Laurels 1949, 1950
2	Time up Please	St Leger 1971/2
2	Yanka Boy	Cesarewitch 1967 St Leger 1967

*Trigo Cup given classic status in 1944

The following greyhounds won classics in both Britain and Ireland:

Burndennet Brook	Scurry Gold Cup 1949 National Sprint 1949
Face the Mutt	Irish Grand National, 1981 English Grand National, 1982
Priceless Border	National Breeders' Produce Stakes 1947 (Ire) English Derby 1948
Queen of the Suir	Irish Oaks 1932 English Oaks 1933, 1934
Robeen Printer	Irish Laurels 1944 English St Leger 1945
Sole Aim	English Laurels 1970 Irish Derby 1971
I'm Slippy	English Derby 1983 National Sprint 1983

Brilliant Bob also did so.

MOST EXPENSIVE RACING GREYHOUND

The most expensive greyhound to race in Britain was Indian Joe, winner of the fiftieth Greyhound Derby who was purchased by Mr Alf McLean, a Belfast bookmaker, for a sum believed to be in excess of £40,000 after winning its first-round heat. It won from trap 6 in 29.68 secs, beating Hurry on Bran by one length to win £35,000, the biggest amount ever put up for a race in Britain.

MOST RACES
The greyhound believed to have run most races in London is the bitch Miss Taft (whose kennel name was Kitty) owned by Mrs Lily Aubrey and trained by Bob Burls at Wembley. In four years she ran 115 races, mostly open events, winning fifty-five of them and being second on twenty-five occasions. Nor must it be forgotten that Miss Taft ran over the marathon distances and in 1967 set a new record for the 880 yds course at Wembley with a time of 50.78 secs which stood for many years. She was then more than four years old.

Ballynennan Moon ran ninety-one times in Britain and Ireland and won on sixty-five occasions. Mick the Miller ran sixty-one times (including match races) and was first forty-six times and second ten times.

In hurdle events, Sherry's Prince took part in 106 opens between May 1969 and May 1972, winning seventy-one times and being second on fifteen occasions. One of the finest hurdlers of recent years was Try It Blackie, a black dog whelped in May 1971 who set a new world record for the 525 yds hurdles course at Brighton with a time of 28.88 secs. He was the first dog to break the 29 secs barrier for 525 yds hurdles. His sire was Russian Gun (by Pigalle Wonder), his dam Gurteen Daisy, by Shaggy Lad's grandson, Kilbeg Kuda, out of The Grand Fire bitch Daisy Charm, so his breeding involved a combination of the greatest sires of modern times. In his career Try It Blackie ran 130 races, winning fifty-one and being second twenty-nine times, winning more than £5,000 in prize money. For consistency he was difficult to beat.

Of his 181 races at the Darnall track, Sheffield, Jacob's Return won forty-eight times and was second forty-eight times. He was one of the most consistent greyhounds ever to race and in graded races, always from scratch, often gave up to 10 yds start.

In three years' racing (1935–7) Border Mutton ran 166 open events, winning seventy of them and being second on forty-one occasions. He raced over hurdles and on the flat, and over all distances. He made four new track records on the flat and four over hurdles, and was one of the most consistent performers in the history of the sport.

One of the most durable of racing greyhounds was the bitch Tell You What, who did most of her racing at Eastville where she was trained by Ernest Wilson. She took part in 123 races, winning forty-three times and earning £6,500 in prize money, proving a wonderful investment to Mr Alex Coombs, her owner. She also set seven new track records, mostly over longer distances. Also at Eastville, Strong Jack, owned by Mr Con Stevens, ran 147 races between 1942 and 1945, winning thirty-two of them. At Cleveland Park, Middlesbrough, in the 1940s, Cheerful Chinaman took part in more than two hundred races and won on 126 occasions, amongst the greatest number of wins ever recorded by a greyhound.

N

NAMING A GREYHOUND
In the case of duplication of names in the English or Irish Stud Book, the name of the second or subsequent greyhound registered with the NGRG shall have its name changed. If the name of a greyhound carries any advertisement, the stewards of the NGRC may charge an extra fee for registration, or require the name to be changed.

Any name of more than sixteen letters is not acceptable. Thus Mischievous Manhattan, a popular dog of the 1940s, and even that great sire, Manhattan Midnight, would find their names unacceptable.
To name a greyhound within twelve months the ICC charge £5, and £20 to change a name.

NATIONAL BREEDERS' PRODUCE STAKES
See Classic Events in Ireland.

NATIONAL COURSING CLUB
Though the first Waterloo Cup was run in 1836, it was not until 1858 that the first official body, the National Coursing Club, came into being. 'Why do not the coursing public have a tribunal of appeal similar

to the Jockey Club?' wrote Thomas Thacker in 1830, but there was a delay of nearly thirty years before it was so. It was inaugurated after the first sixty-four-dog stake event at Altcar, for by then the Waterloo Cup had earned world-wide recognition. It was decreed that henceforth all greyhounds taking part in events under the auspices of the NCC should be registered, and a code of conduct was drawn up, to be upheld at recognized coursing events throughout the British Isles.

In 1881 the NCC decided that all greyhounds running at coursing meetings anywhere in the British Isles must, after 15 July 1883, be registered, and almost 1,000 entries were received before that date.

In 1882 the first Greyhound Stud Book appeared; of the entries recorded 351 were of black or black and white greyhounds and only 68 were brindles, which is now the most common colour. The second Stud Book contained 5,766 entries. The list of dogs at stud included the blue dog MacPherson at 7 gns and the black and white Misterton, winner of the Waterloo Cup in 1879, standing at 15 gns, a large sum in those days.

In 1892 Mr Lamonby took over the Stud Book and introduced the system of entries we know today, for although track greyhounds may never have seen a coursing field every dog must be registered with either the English or Irish Coursing Club. Which of the two will depend on the Stud Book with which the dam who whelped the litter had been registered.

Coursing in Ireland was under the jurisdiction of the NCC of Britain until 1916 when Mr Dan Irwin, secretary of the South Clare Coursing Club, pressed for control of the sport in Ireland to be taken from the NCC. At a meeting in Thurles Mr Irwin was given full support and asked to go ahead. He counted the number of owners in Vol. 34 of the Greyhound Stud Book and found that most were Irish, and with this information he asked T.A. Morris, Tom and Hugh McAlinden, J.J. Quaid and several others to accompany him to a meeting of the NCC in Liverpool on 12 September 1916. There he was told by the Earl of Sefton that they would be given full control of coursing in Ireland. On their return Phil O'Sullivan was elected president and Tom Morris secretary and keeper of the Irish Greyhound Stud Book.

Unlike those in Britain, the Irish dogs perform with equal distinction on coursing field and track. The two sports are inter-related and many dogs run on the tracks in summer and on the coursing field in winter, so that the stamina needed to win a coursing event is passed on to those greyhounds running on the tracks, and there is no deterioration in standards. In 1932 Kerry's famous Kingdom Cup was won by the future track star Creamery Border, and the following year Brilliant Bob was successful in the Tipperary Cup. Both dogs were to become among the most famous of track greyhounds when racing in England in the early years of the sport, and both were to become brilliant sires, passing on to their progeny their staying powers combined with outstanding speed. They figure in the pedigree of many of today's finest greyhounds.

NATIONAL GREYHOUND RACING CLUB

Known in short as the NGRC, it was formed on 1 January 1928. At a meeting at Wembley Stadium it was decided that a controlling body was needed to protect the sport and its large following, since when the rules of the NGRC have acted in the same way that the Queensberry Rules have for boxing. On the same day the National Greyhound Racing Society came into existence to protect the public against speculators, while the Racing Club was set up to organize the sport, to formulate the rules of racing and to register the tracks, the greyhounds, the trainers and staff. On 1 March 1976 the NGRC became a limited company.

The first stewards of the NGRC were Capt. E.A. Stanley, Lieut-Gen. Bethune and Major Corbet, and the members included Sir Harry Brittain and Professor Hobday. On 28 April 1928 all tracks licensed by them came under their rules. Capt. Stanley was the senior steward, and the immediate duties of the Club were to inaugurate the rules of racing and to register all greyhounds on their tracks, bringing into use identity books stating the markings of every greyhound, so that all dogs on their tracks could be checked when necessary. Trainers and all other officials had to be registered with the Club. At that date only six tracks operated under NGRC rules but by 1948, a time when over 50 million enthusiasts were attending meetings each year, there were seventy-seven tracks. There was also an equal number of tracks operating that did not meet the requirements of the Club and were not licensed by them. They became known as 'flapping' tracks, and it was illegal for dogs registered with the NGRC to take part in events at any unlicensed track, the penalty being disqualification from racing greyhounds with a registered track.

Many problems confront this vast industry which employs many thousands of people. Technical details such as the working of the tote, the electric hare and traps have to be dealt with; the identity of every greyhound has to be filed as a precaution against unscrupulous dealers; and precautions must be taken against doping. That the sport since its beginning has been run in so excellent a manner is due in great part to the NGRC and to the hard work and impeccable character of all who have worked in it.

Every week of the year a calendar of open races is published by the NGRC, and a dog may be entered well in advance for those events thought most suitable for its capabilities. Particulars of an open race will be advertised by the racecourse executive in an issue of the NGRC calendar so as to allow at least seven days between such an issue and the closing date of the race.

There are 184 rules of racing drawn up by the NGRC, and in the 'rogues' gallery' at headquarters is the name of every person and every dog who has, at some time, broken one or other of these rules. One of the strictest is Rule 152 which states that 'a greyhound is not qualified to be entered or raced if it has run at an unrecognized meeting', and on all tracks not run under NGRC rules representatives of the Club keep a strict look out for owners or their dogs which have been registered with the Club and which may have a dog entered under an assumed name for a race.

On 1 March 1977 the new British Greyhound Racing Federation took over most of the duties of the NGRC and the NGRS, with Lord Mancroft as its first chairman and Mr Fred Underhill, secretary of the NGRC for many years, as its executive director. But the NGRC remains responsible for the rules of racing and discipline.

See Open Races; Rules of Racing.

NATIONAL GREYHOUND RACING COMPANY OF IRELAND

Track racing had not been long established in England when news spread across the Irish Sea. Hugh McAlinden and Joe Shaw, both Belfast bookmakers, paid a visit to Belle Vue before the track closed for the season on October 1926, and returned much impressed with all they had seen. With Paddy O'Donoghue and James Clarke, keen sportsmen in the North, they founded the NGR Co. Ltd, whose first arena, at Celtic Park, Belfast, opened on 18 April 1927.

The chairman of the NGR Co. was Hugh McAlinden, and P.J. Ryan was secretary. McAlinden, already a director of Belfast Celtic Football Club, was able to persuade his co-directors of the tremendous impact the new sport was bound to have and to stage greyhound racing at that famous ground. There was therefore no need to build a new track and both time and money was saved. Six races made up the card at the first meeting, one of which ended in the first dead heat in track racing, between Imperial Jimmy and Keep Whistling. One meeting a week soon became two and then three, and in May that year the first meeting took place at Shelbourne Park, Dublin, where attendances were very much larger than at Celtic Park.

Little did they realize at the time that their venture was to bring much wealth to a poor country. Indeed, the sale of good greyhounds from Ireland to Britain and the USA from the late 1920s kept the country's economy afloat until new industries were set up some fifty years later. During the war years alone, from 1940 to 1945 more than 15,000 greyhounds were exported to Britain, at a value of more than £1 million, and at the end of the war Ireland became the centre of attraction to many lovers of the sport in Britain who had obtained much pleasure and relaxation from greyhound racing during those years. This resulted in many millions of pounds going into the Irish economy in the immediate postwar years, not only in the purchase of greyhounds but from those who spent considerable sums during their visits to Dublin and other Irish racecourses.

NATIONAL GREYHOUND RACING SOCIETY
On 30 December 1927 two days before the formation of the NGRC, the Society came into being, chiefly to protect the public against the speculator, and through the years, until the British Greyhound Racing Federation was inaugurated on 1 March 1977, it has been in regular consultation with the government of the day in all matters concerning the public interest and the sport. It was the Society who, in 1932, when a royal commission was set up to look into the question of betting in Britain, put forward a strong recommendation for the totalizator to be installed on all tracks, in spite of a strong objection from the Bookmakers' Association. This was legalized in the Betting and Lotteries Act of 1934, which put the sport on a recognized basis.

By the time track racing had got under way there were two influential bodies to see to the interests of all concerned. By 1932 seventy tracks had applied for affiliation but only twelve were accepted unless the venue could be brought up to standard. The following year sixty tracks were thought to be of a sufficiently high standard and were accepted.

The Society stipulated that if a track was to be accepted it had to prove, or comply with, the following:
(1) The directors were of the highest integrity.
(2) Finances were sound and, if a public company was proposed, the prospectus must be approved by the Society.
(3) The proposed track was to be built only where there was a need for it, a matter to be decided on population density and easy access by public transport.
(4) The proposed track should not be built near another existing one.

At first it was not considered commercially viable to build a track in a town of less than half a million inhabitants, and in these towns, e.g. Manchester, Birmingham, Sheffield and Bristol, two tracks were eventually built and were well supported until 1950 when television and other sports took away many followers and one track in each of these towns closed down. Other towns with small populations, however, e.g. Leicester, Swindon and Oxford, took up the sport and healthy attendances were reported. Within ten years of the start of track racing in Britain, 25 million were paying to see the racing each year, and ten years later this had doubled, to reach a peak in the immediate postwar years. By 1946 tote takings amounted to more than £200 million. But by 1970 the amount spent on the tote was less than £50 million, and with ever-increasing overheads the NGRS pressed the government to allow the tracks to retain more than the 6 per cent permitted under the Betting and Lotteries Act of 1934. When the Act was amended, the tracks were allowed to retain 12½ per cent for expenses and profits, which was later increased to 15 per cent. However, this is still insufficient to allow for feeding and veterinary costs, high electricity bills, staff wages, rates and printing, all of which increase each year.

From 1 March 1977, the British Greyhound Federation took over most of the duties of the NGRS, and will be in close touch touch with the Royal Commission on Gambling and with the government of the day about the future of the sport in Britain.

NEWCASTLE RACECOURSE
See under British Greyhound Racecourses.

NO RACE
The NGRC rules of racing stipulate that the local stewards may declare 'no race' or 'no trial' if:
(1) There is a mechanical defect of the hare or starting traps.
(2) There is outside interference with the race or trial.
(3) The hare is not kept within reasonable distance of the leading greyhound.
(4) No greyhound completes the course in reasonable time.
If the race is to be re-run, at least fifteen minutes must elapse. The words 're-run' are to be included in the identity book of the greyhounds taking part. Though a greyhound may be disqualified for fighting after a race, the result of the race shall stand. Originally this was not so.

Perhaps the most famous 'no race' incident in the history of the sport was the 1929 English Derby, when Palatinus, fast away and hugging the rails all round the corner, won the event in 30.16 secs only for the race to be declared void. This was due to Beadsman running wide at the first bend into the path of Mick the Miller and En Tomb in the four-dog race, causing them to be badly hampered. There was nothing in the rules of racing to suggest that there was any reason for the local stewards to declare 'no race', but half an hour later the four dogs were in the traps again. Once more Palatinus was fastest away, but due to his age faded towards the finish, allowing Mick the Miller to overtake him and achieve his first classic success. Palatinus, who finished second, was decidedly unlucky, for he had won perfectly fairly if somewhat fortunately. The same thing happened to Mick the Miller two years later, when in the 1931 Derby Ryland R was disqualified and the event declared 'no race' after Mick had won. (*See* Disqualification.)

In the early years of the sport a klaxon horn was sounded for a 'no race' decision. A red light is now shown on the tote board.

NORTON CANES RACECOURSE
See under British Greyhound Racecourses.

NOTTINGHAM RACECOURSE
See under British Greyhound Racecourses.

O

OAKS
See under Classic Events in Great Britain; Sean Kelly Oaks *see* Classic Events in Ireland.

OFFICIALS

Each greyhound racecourse approved by the NGRC shall appoint three stewards, known as local stewards; a racing manager; judge; timekeeper; paddock steward; security officer; hare controller; starter; and a veterinary surgeon who must be a member of the Royal College of Veterinary Surgeons.

OLDEST RACING GREYHOUND

This distinction must surely go to the black Jacob's Return, who was the most consistent dog ever to race at the defunct Darnall Stadium, Sheffield, and ran almost once a week until he was eight years old. He took part in more than 200 graded races and won more than 100 of them. He reigned supreme at the track from 1940 to 1945, and so fierce was he in his kennel that his trainer said that anyone apart from himself who could go in and bring him out could have him! There were no takers, yet once outside he was as gentle as a lamb and there never was a more honest dog.

Miss Taft was still running in top-class open events at the age of six, and so was the Oxford-trained Prince Harry. Both remained as fresh as puppies until the end of their careers.

See Racing Age.

OPEN EVENTS

In addition to the classics, there are at least 2,000 open events for top-class greyhounds run in Britain each year. Each carries a winner's prize ranging from £200 to £30,000 for the winner of the Derby, and as racing takes place throughout the year a calendar of open events is issued in January each year by the NGRC. The entry forms must be correctly filled in well in advance. Racing takes place over all distances from 277 m for the Thames Silver Salver at Southend and 280 m for the Sovereign Stakes at the Rye House track to the 820 m for the BBC Television Trophy which has become established as the most important event for stayers. Trainers of open race class greyhounds know exactly the length of race best suited to their charges and will enter them accordingly.

To enter a greyhound for open events it is to one's advantage to kennel the dog with a private trainer, licensed by the NGRC as being competent to train and race greyhounds, and whose kennels will be regularly inspected by NGRC officials. A private trainer has more time to concentrate on the limited number of greyhounds he will take, and so bring them to the peak of fitness necessary to compete in top-class open races. It is advisable to select a trainer as near to one's home as possible, so that you can visit the kennels regularly to discuss the events for which the dog may enter. In addition to a yearly calendar of events, the NGRC publishes each week a calendar of open races due to take place in a few weeks' time. The trainer will receive the calendar of events in time to allow at least seven days before the closing date for the race. Full details are given on:

(1) The name of the track where the event is to be staged, its address and telephone number.
(2) The dates of heats (if there are any).
(3) The distance of the race.
(4) Number of entries required.
(5) Title of the race.
(6) Method of qualification.
(7) Prize money allocated (the event may be sponsored).
(8) Closing date for entries and date of the draw for traps (there may be seeding for wide runners which will be allocated outside traps at the racing manager's discretion).
(9) Reference as to whether standard conditions of entry apply.
(10) Details of any special conditions of entry.

Entry forms for any event in which your dog is to be entered should be obtained in plenty of time and also sent in early, for if the field is limited the first entries received will make up the number required.

These are some of the more important events and their prize money:

These are some of the more important events and their prize money:

January	Mecca Winter Stayers	740 m	£1,000	Hackney
	Longcross Cup	680 m	£300	White City, London
	William Hill Sixer	484 m	£800	Hackney
	Empire Hurdles	490 m	£600	Wembley
February	Inaugural Sweepstakes	490 m	£300	Wembley
	William Hill Hurdles	475 m H	£500	White City, London
	Ladbroke Golden Jacket	660 m	£1,500	Harringay
	Daily Mirror Hurdles	475 m	£1,000	Harringay
	Winter Cup	460 m	£800	Wimbledon
	Coronation Stakes	490 m	£500	Wembley
	Hunt Cup	635 m	£500	Reading
March	Greenwich Cup	555 m	£750	Catford
	Ladbroke Golden Sprint	304 m	£1,000	Hackney
	Manchester Cup	485 m	£600	White City, Manchester
	Spring Cup	660 m	£500	Wimbledon
	Greater London Challenge Cup	750 m	£500	Romford
	Britvic Yorkshire Hurdles	460 m H	£300	Leeds
	Daily Express Trophy	680 m	£250	White City, London
	Courage Spring Trophy	650 m	£250	Crayford
	Wood Lane Stakes	500 m	£750	White City, London
	William Hill Hurdles	410 m	£600	Watford
April	*Grand National	500 m H	£2,000	White City, London
	Northern Stayers' Stakes	654 m	£400	Belle Vue
	Spring Cup	490 m	£600	Wembley
	BBC TV Trophy (final)	815 m	£2,000	various
	Pall Mall	475 m	£1,500	Harringay
	William King Cup	500 m	£1,000	Shawfield
	Steel City Cup	500 m	£1,000	Owlerton
	Gold Cup	400 m H	£500	Wimbledon
	Midlands Grand Prix	385 m	£500	Leicester
	Mullard Stakes	730 m	£2,000	White City, London
	Scottish Grand National	465 m H	£300	Powderhall
May	*Laurels	460 m	£3,000	Wimbledon
	Evening Standard Cup	500 m	£1,500	White City, London
	Coral Regency	680 m	£650	Brighton
	Marathon Stakes	850 m	£500	Wembley
	Britvic Midland Marathon	813 m	£300	Wolverhampton
	St Mungo Cup	480 m	£500	Shawfield
	Wilkinson Sword Stakes	650 m	£500	Crayford
	Whitbread Trophy	603 m	£500	Portsmouth
	Gold Cup	655 m	£500	Wembley
June	Perry Barr Trophy	650 m	£500	Perry Barr

	Courage's Midland Sprint	370 m	£250	Willenhall
	The Key	868 m	£250	Wimbledon
	The Test	540 m	£1,000	Walthamstow
	*Derby	500 m	£20,000	White City, London
	Ebor Stakes	650 m	£1,000	Leeds
July	Thanet Gold Cup	465 m	£1,000	Ramsgate
	Thames Silver Salver	277 m	£1,000	Southend
	Summer Cup	490 m	£500	Wembley
	Whitbread National Hurdles	500 m H	£250	Brighton
	Skol Champions Stakes	484 m	£3,000	Wolverhampton
	Coral Essex Vase	575 m	£3,000	Romford
	Whitbread National Hurdles	550 m H	£250	Brighton
	Summer Cup	490 m	£500	Wembley
	Northern Flat	460 m	£2,000	Belle Vue
	*Scurry Gold Cup	442 m	£5,000	Slough
	Golden Crest	470 m	£2,000	Bristol
	Double Diamond Stakes	490 m	£750	Wembley
	Gold Vase	660 m	£500	Harringay
	Holsten Circuit	475 m	£2,000	Walthamstow
	Midlands St Leger	647 m	£500	Wolverhampton
	William Hill Sprint	300 m	£500	Shawfield
August	Midland Flat	475 m	£2,000	Hall Green
	W.J. Cearns Memorial	660 m	£600	Wimbledon
	White Rose Trophy	650 m	£500	Owlerton
	Trinity Marathon	792 m	£250	Portsmouth
	Courage Crayford Vase	462 m	£1,000	Crayford
	Buckinghamshire Cup	593 m	£400	Slough
	*Harp Scottish Derby	500 m	£3,000	Shawfield
	Eclipse Stakes	460 m	£500	Coventry
	Coral Sussex Cup	500 m	£500	Brighton
	Northern Hurdles	460 m H	£500	Belle Vue
	*Ladbroke's St Leger	655 m	£10,000	Wembley
	Challenge Trophy	460 m H	£250	Wimbledon
September	Arkell's Silver Plume	480 m	£350	Swindon
	Berkshire Cup	465 m	£2,000	Reading
	Birmingham Cup	475 m	£1,000	Perry Barr
	British Breeders' Produce Stakes	385 m	£250	Catford
	Edinburgh Cup	465 m	£2,500	Powderhall
	National Sprint	414 m	£500	Harringay
	Courage's Midland Grand National	474 m H	£400	Hall Green
	East Anglian Derby	462 m	£2,500	Yarmouth
	*Gold Collar	555 m	£2,000	Catford
	Scottish St Leger	650 m	£2,500	Powderhall
	Trafalgar Cup	490 m	£500	Wembley
	Haig Cambridgeshire	500 m	£500	White City, London
	Northumberland Cup	484 m	£300	Brough Park
October	Bass Charrington Cup	500 m	£1,000	Owlerton
	Sovereign Stakes	281 m	£400	Rye House
	*Ladbroke Cesarewitch	815 m	£5,000	Belle Vue
	*Grand Prix	640 m	£8,500	Walthamstow
	1000 Guineas	484 m	£1,050	Hackney
	Empire Stakes	490 m H	£300	Wembley
	Ben Truman Stakes	555 m	£600	Catford
	Cock o' the North	670 m	£600	White City, Manchester
	All England Cup	484 m	£1,000	Brough Park
	The Marathon	830 m	£500	Harringay
	Victoria Sporting Stakes	490 m	£600	Wembley
	Oxfordshire Stakes	450 m	£1,000	Oxford
	Alliance Bldg Society Trophy	680 m	£500	Brighton
November	*The Oaks	475 m	£1,750	Harringay
	Puppy Oaks	460 m	£500	Wimbledon
	Stow Marathon	820 m	£800	Walthamstow
	William Hill Championship	500 m	£500	White City, London
December	Sporting Life Juvenile	460 m	£500	Wimbledon
	British Breeders' Championship	500 m	£500	White City London
	Winter Trophy	663 m	£500	Hall Green
	Boxing Day Marathon	715 m	£500	Catford

* Classic event

There may be an alteration from year to year in the month in which these events are staged. The prize money for the winning greyhound has been increased for several events since the time of writing

OPEN RACE

A race for greyhounds of above-average ability and not necessarily kennelled at the track where the event is to take place. Conditions of entry can be obtained from the racing manager at the track where the race will take place.

Rule 64 (section a) of the NGRC rules of racing states that 'an open event shall be a race or series of races, particulars of which are advertised in the calendar and for which entries are normally received for greyhounds in the charge of any racecourse trainer, private or owner-trained or of a "C Licence" or regional trainer eligible to train greyhounds under rule 8'.

The best tracks usually include an open race at each meeting, because it creates greater interest among both owners and spectators, for dogs can be entered against others of good class from another track, while new dogs are an extra stimulus at any meeting. Some open events are run over several rounds, culminating in the final of a classic or some other important event.

The first open race was run at Wembley in 1928.

ORDER OF FINISH

The result of a race means the order in which the noses of those greyhounds which have completed the course reach the winning line, subject to any amendment because of disqualification which will move other dogs up in their placings.

ORIGINS OF THE SPORT

Mr O.P. Smith, an Oklahoma sportsman, evolved the idea of greyhounds chasing a mechanical hare, for it was illegal to hold coursing meetings in the USA in an enclosed space. As early as 1912 he applied for a patent for a dummy hare; some five years earlier he had promoted a coursing meeting in Salt Lake City and it had given him the idea of holding a meeting in a confined space with the dogs chasing a dummy hare. Shortly afterwards he was in Tucson, Arizona, where he met another enthusiast, an Irishman called Tom Keen, and after the two had invented a mechanical hare they tried out the idea in a field outside New Orleans, but without success. Smith, however, was not easily put off and for several years worked hard on his ideas. In 1920 he built a crude track at Emeryville, California, to try out his idea.

He was now helped by George Sawyer, and a year later they were to open a better track in Tulsa, but Smith was now down to his last dollar after spending more than ten years and a small fortune on the idea. But Americans returning after war service were looking for excitement and at Tulsa the sport took off. The first greyhound meeting was definitely a success and each week more and more came to see greyhounds chasing O.P. Smith's mechanical hare. Within six months the new sport had become so popular that Smith was encouraged to open another track, this time at Hialeah in Florida. When he died in Miami in 1927 he had become a rich man, the owner of twenty-five tracks in the southern United States capitalized at the dollar equivalent of over £1,000,000.

The name of O.P. Smith is perpetuated in America by the O.P. Smith Classic, which is run at the track of the Miami Beach Club each year. He had lived to see the new sport become established in various parts of the USA and also in England and Ireland, where it was soon to become the second most popular sport after association football.

OWLERTON RACECOURSE
See under British Greyhound Racecourses.

OWNING A GREYHOUND

Many enthusiasts who have followed the sport for a number of years may want to own their own greyhound, for there is no greater thrill than seeing one's own dog run in and win a race, especially if the dog is of good enough quality to win open events in the best company. If you are buying a greyhound, some thought must be given to what type of dog you most enjoy watching, a fast breaker or a sprinter, capable of showing the others a clean pair of heels over a short distance, or a stayer, one able to come from behind to win a long-distance race when its chances halfway seemed anything but promising. If a stayer, it should have coursing blood in its pedigree for a good coursing dog needs to have a stout heart.

After deciding the type of greyhound you would like to own, you will want to know how to set about buying a greyhound. Trainers at the various tracks will often know of genuine greyhounds for sale – good, honest dogs with a clean record, for sale at a reasonable price. It is often possible to buy one that is not too old and has several more racing years in front of it. The track may also be prepared to keep the dog in its kennels, with the same trainer to which it has become accustomed.

One is often asked at what age a greyhound should be bought for racing and how long it will continue to race. Officially, the age of a greyhound is taken from the first day of the month in which it was born, and the minimum age at which it may run on tracks controlled by official bodies in England and Ireland is fifteen months; not until then will the dog be fully developed. At that age it commences trials and if it shows ability to follow the hare and does not interfere with other dogs it may be sold for £200 or more, for it will have cost almost that amount to rear it to this stage and it may have up to five years of racing in front of it. Some greyhounds reach their best quickly, while others develop late and are often sold by their owners as disappointing only to develop into champions when long past the age at which they would normally be expected to do so. The celebrated Bah's Choice, for instance, won only one of his first ten races and was sold for a small sum by his owner, Mr E.W. Bah, yet was later to set up a new national record for the 525 yds course at Wembley. Dolores Rocket, on the other hand, was only two years three months when she won the English Derby in June 1971, and was six months younger than this when first showing her amazing speed, winning the 1970 Puppy Oaks at Wimbledon in the fast time of 28.31 secs for the 500 yds course.

Those who have connections in Ireland may ask a friend or relative to find a greyhound at the price one is prepared to pay. Those which have not raced should be no more than eighteen months old before being placed on a track since it will take several months for the dog to become acclimatized and for its form to be ascertained from its trials. A dog over that age without a track record should be avoided, because there will usually be a reason why it has not raced. Perhaps ill health has left its mark on the dog, or it may have been tried and found to be a fighter.

A reliable way of obtaining a greyhound in Ireland is to have the daily papers sent over and to follow the performances of the dogs at the varous tracks. Full details are given of times and winning distances, the length of races and the dogs taking part. The date of whelping of each dog is also given. You will then be able to pick out one or two about which a friend could make enquiries at the track where it has raced with a view to contacting the owner and asking whether he or she is prepared to sell. Or you could write to the track manager yourself and ask for details about the dog and for the name and address of the owner. An advertisement could be inserted in the *Sporting Press,* the official organ of the Irish Coursing Club, describing the type of greyhound required, whether a fast starter or a stayer or a dog which is at its best over the middle distances for which the tracks here and in Ireland mostly cater. Then, if the price seems reasonable, ask for a veterinary surgeon's certificate of its health to ensure that its teeth are good and its ear markings are correct, and for a guarantee from the owner that the dog is a non-fighter. You will need the dog's identity papers, and a transfer of ownership form signed by the vendor. All this is most important, for without its papers, a greyhound will be ineligible to run on any NGRC registered track in England or on a licensed track in Ireland. Greyhounds entered in the Irish Stud Book need not be registered in the English Stud Book and vice versa before being accepted for racing on licensed tracks here (or in Ireland), but must have their markings taken for registration with the NGRC. Remember that you will be purchasing a greyhound worth anything from £100 to £1,000 or more, depending on its age, form and breeding, and it will be advisable to go to a little trouble to get everything right before handing over your money. Also, have the dog insured before it is sent over. This will cost only a small sum, but is necessary, for it may be injured during a rough crossing or for other reasons.

Have a word with your local track manager before bringing over the greyhound, to see if there is a vacancy in the kennels of one of the trainers. Alternatively you may want to place it with a private trainer and to enter the dog for open events all over Britain if it is good enough to be accepted. But first you must be sure that the trainer has a vacancy. If your greyhounds show above-average performances there will always be a welcome for them on most tracks, except where the stadium runs only their own dogs, but this is rare and over the years there a close relationship will be built up between owner, trainer and racing manager where good-class greyhounds are introduced. A good greyhound will be popular with patrons, and anybody who has one will be given all possible encouragement to bring in another. There is great satisfaction, too, in seeing a dog perform well, while financial rewards, especially for winners of open events, can be considerable. There is always room in kennels for the best and most tracks welcome such animals.

Usually about 200 dogs are required by the tracks to fill the meetings in any one year. Six greyhounds is the normal number to contest an event, and there are now ten races during each meeting, so that sixty dogs are needed. With two meetings a week, that means more than 120 greyhounds; others will be contesting open races elsewhere, while yet others will be sick, injured or in season. For this reason some tracks do not favour bitches, which will be out of racing for about two months each year. It is a point to be considered when obtaining a greyhound. Against this, the enforced lay-off acts as a useful rest period, and a bitch will retain her racing powers up to two years longer than a dog. Some tracks appreciate the racing qualities of a bitch more than others. Perry Barr, Birmingham, comes into this category, and of forty greyhounds (five in each event) taking part in the meeting on 3 February 1972 exactly half were bitches.

It is usual for a dog to be at his peak when between three and four years of age. He may well go on racing after that time but his performances usually decline and he will be given a lower rating whenever he runs. It is therefore not advisable, unless he is required for stud purposes, to purchase a dog more than four years old; it is preferable to buy one at only half that age. A bitch will still be at her best for another year. When a greyhound has reached four years old its value will be considerably less than it was when two or even three years old, and it may have little more racing left. A dog bred in the purple, however, which was a litter brother to a famous performer or brother (from a different litter) to a famous sire, could well be purchased when four years old with a view to racing him for another year before retiring him to stud.

Get a veterinary surgeon to ensure that the greyhound you are about to buy is thoroughly fit for racing, is sound in limb, free from skin troubles, and has good eyes and teeth. The teeth will reveal a dog's age and whether he has had distemper or any other severe illness, but only a qualified, experienced vet will be able to decide whether a greyhound is fit for racing or not. His services are not expensive and he will protect the buyer from unscrupulous dealers.

Another way in which a greyhound can be bought is through an auction, of which several are held every week in England and Ireland (*see* Auction Sales). Before parting with your money, decide the type of greyhound you want and weigh up all the pros and cons about the dog that takes your fancy.

If you have placed a greyhound with a trainer to a certain track and it does not prove successful, do not write him off until you have tried him on some other track to which he may be more suited. A big, well-proportioned dog will rarely do well on a small track; he will not be able to master the bends (turns) as well as a small dog or bitch, or he may follow better an outside hare rather than an inside hare, or vice versa. If he is disappointing, try him at a track which is differently constructed and the result may surprise you. Bah's Choice, already mentioned as a late developer, first ran on the Catford track, one of the best in Britain. Evidently, however, it did not suit his style of running, for when transferred to Wembley he soon began to make a name for himself and he was equally successful on the White City track where he was the first dog to break the 29 secs barrier for the 525 yds course on any track in Britain or Ireland.

Always persevere with what appears to be a good greyhound. Try him on more than one track until he finds one to suit his running; or remember that he may be a late developer. The reverse holds true of those greyhounds which are successful at a certain track and should be left there. Do not chop and change, for a dog may have become fond of his trainer and kennel maid who are able to get the best out of him, while the track may suit his style of running. So when a dog is running well, leave well alone, even though another track may be paying a little more prize money. Remember, a dog will run well only where he is happy.

OXFORD RACECOURSE
See under British Greyhound Racecourses.

P

PADDOCK

A small area of grass or concrete in front of or near the racing kennels where most of the action takes place before and after every race or trial. It is the hub of any race meeting, where owners gather to see the various new dogs brought in for trials and old favourites having a trial after injury or lay-off after a long period of racing. Here each dog is weighed before being placed in its allotted kennel before the meeting or trial and where it remains until required to run. When the race has ended the kennel lads capture the dogs, put on a leash and lead them back to the racing kennels where they stay until the meeting has finished. When those dogs taking part in a race have been returned to the kennels, the ones to perform in the next event are brought out into the paddock. After the coats with the trap numbers are fitted the dogs are again inspected by the vet to make sure that all is well and that the jackets have been correctly fixed before being taken on to the track to parade in front of the main stand for several minutes before they are placed in the traps and the hare released.

The paddock is always a hive of industry. Those leading out the greyhounds are smartly and correctly attired to conform to regulations and the greyhounds are (or should be) in the peak of condition. Owners will gather in the paddock to discuss their respective greyhounds among themselves and with their trainers, for a great deal of pride is taken in owning a good racing greyhound – one that gives its owner and the patrons a good run for their money even if it does not win. Those who do not go into the paddock arena (and the paddock is always fenced off from the public) miss much, for that is where all the work behind the scenes goes on during every meeting.

A meeting will last for about three hours, but each of the ten races will take only thirty seconds or a little more for long-distance events – say about five minutes during each meeting – so that those who are more interested in the dogs than in betting will obtain their enjoyment in the paddock.

PADDOCK STEWARD

It is the responsibility of this official to see that all dogs are placed in their correct racing kennels at the track before the meeting starts. These kennels are used only to house the dogs while awaiting their races, and it is to these kennels that they are returned after each event. At the end of the meeting the dogs are returned to their training kennels which are often some distance from the track and to which the dogs are taken by van.

It is also the responsibility of the paddock steward to see that each dog is inspected by the veterinary surgeon before racing begins, so that any greyhound declared unfit can be replaced by one of the reserves selected for that race. The paddock steward must also see that before a race each dog is given its correct coat to coincide with the trap number the dog is allotted on the race card. Before the greyhounds are kennelled for trials or for racing, the kennels and any material used in them are examined by the paddock steward or security officer, and throughout a meeting or trials a paddock steward must be in attendance.

PARADE

Every greyhound taking part in a race must be paraded round the track before being placed in the traps, unless the weather is so bad that it might be harmful to the dogs, a matter that can only be decided by the local steward. The dogs, in their jackets, are led on their leashes by kennel maids, always in trap order. This allows the public to have a last-minute look at the dogs and assess their chances before the dogs are placed in the traps.

Each dog wears a jacket represented by

a different colour (*see* Jacket) and number for each of the six traps. The parading enables spectators to become familiar with the dogs and their numbers so that they may readily be spotted during the race. This is important, for the dogs run at almost 40 mph and the race will be over in 30 secs.

The behaviour of the dogs when paraded always creates interest. Some dogs love it: Mick the Miller was never as happy as when being led around the track, his head held high, his tail swishing. On the other hand that equally fine tracker, Brilliant Bob, hated the experience. All the time he would bark furiously, pull at his lead and try to push off his muzzle (with which all racing dogs are fitted before an event) with his front paws. He was impatient to get his race over and done with and be back into his kennel which he loved, away from the crowds which Mick the Miller so much enjoyed. Mick was so free of nervous tension that he always seemed half asleep during the parade, as if he couldn't care less. This can be confusing to punters, who are usually on the look-out for a dog showing alertness, which some believe is essential to winning a race.

The condition of a dog is all-important and is best observed in the paddock. The coat should be glossy and sleek, not dull and staring, and he should step in a sprightly manner rather than be in an excited condition. But all dogs behave differently, and one needs to look for any peculiarities in the behaviour of those dogs with which one is familiar, for changes of behaviour can be helpful in assessing a dog's chances. If attending a track regularly, take note of all the track-kennelled dogs, how they behave in the paddock and on parade, as well as their favourite traps, which really means whether a dog likes to run on the inside or outside of a track or if it runs better in hard or soft going. Some dogs win more often in winter than in summer and vice versa; the big, strong dogs usually do better in heavy going, when the ground is wet through rain. The order of racing can make a difference to a dog's ability to perform well; often a big, sturdy greyhound, running in one of the last races when the track is cut up and mud flying in all directions, will revel in such conditions and show the stamina to defeat all his rivals. Some dogs are even put off by high winds and show their dislike during the parade. Even aircraft noise may cause some to be put off the task in front of them, whereas others take little notice of any adverse factors.

PARTNERSHIP

When two or more persons have an interest in the same greyhound they shall be considered part owners who will be jointly and separately liable for upholding the rules of racing. Any reasonable number of people can own a greyhound: three is quite common and two even more so. In 1976, when Mutt's Silver won the Derby, Mr Ray Lancaster and five others had a share in him. 1,760 partnerships were registered with the NGRC during 1979.

PERRY BAR RACECOURSE
See Under British Greyhound Racecourses.

PHOTO-FINISH

It is laid down under NGRC rules that where the photo-finish apparatus is called into use to show the first dog past the winning post, though it may assist the judge in deciding the order of finishing it shall in no way alter his own decision, which shall be final. The photo-finish apparatus was installed for the first time in Britain at White City, London, and used for the first time on 18 October 1945, since when every licensed track has installed the apparatus which is used to photograph the finish of every race.

The photo-finish camera was the invention of an American called del Riccio, who a few days before the outbreak of war in September 1939 came to London at the invitation of the GRA with his moving-strip camera. After his return the Photo Chart Co. of America carried on working with his blueprints. After the war del Riccio returned with his modified camera, which the GRA officials found entirely satisfactory and installed at once at White City.

It is the nose only of the winning dog which decides a race; the feet and legs are not taken into consideration even though the front leg of a dog has crossed the winning line before the nose of the declared winner. This factor often causes controversy among followers of the sport.

Though the photo-finish camera serves a useful purpose, especially when determining the finish of a race when perhaps three greyhounds reach the winning line together, it is not infallible, for so often the dog on the outside (nearest the camera) gets the decision when closer inspection of the photo may show the inside dog to be fractionally in front. Without the photo-finish camera the judge would most certainly have given a dead heat, the best result. The camera is there to confirm the judge's decision and not to replace him, and unless one is standing right in front of the winning line, as the judge is, it is not possible to decide the winner of a close race. The result of a race is flashed up on the tote within seconds — there can be no delay — together with the dividends for the various forecasts made.

POINTS OF A GREYHOUND

When showing or buying a greyhound, these are the points to consider.

HEAD and NECK

Before Lord Orford's bulldog cross, the greyhound was of finer proportions than we know it today, nor had it the stamina which the bulldog bred into it. The head, as Dame Juliana Berners said, was long and narrow, like that of a snake with the jaws terminating almost at a point. Dr J.H. Walsh, one of the founder members of the National Coursing Club, writing in *The Field* magazine under the pseudonym of 'Stonehenge', said that a greyhound's head should be wide between the ears and that of a fully grown dog should measure, between the eyes and ears, about 15 ins in circumference. The head should be broad and flat, not arched, and the muzzle long and firm, with muscular jaws and a pointed nose. The cheeks should also be firm and muscular. These features were passed on by the bulldog, with its larger head and bigger brain, while it also brought about earlier maturity. Before Lord Orford's experiments in breeding, greyhounds did not mature until almost three years of age, whereas today a greyhound is able to compete in classic events before it is two years old. The head, from forehead to nose tip, should measure about 10 ins.

The teeth should be strong and level when they meet. Overshot or underhung teeth will prevent a dog from holding a hare when coursing, and it will not be able to chew its food correctly.

The eyes should be clear and bright, neither too large nor too small, while they should not be set too deep. The darker in colour they are the better, and they should have an intelligent look about them. The ears must be set well back and be quite small. They should be thin and softly textured, falling back with a half fold to expose the inner surface.

The neck, as Dame Juliana said, should be like that of a drake, long and supple. Stonehenge, whose book *The Greyhound,* published in 1853, was the most important work on the greyhound ever published, and still accepted as such in greyhound circles today, said that the length of the neck should be the same as that of the head. It should be slightly arched over the windpipe and gradually swell out to meet the shoulders. Fifteen points are awarded on the show bench for the various aspects of the head, and ten for the neck.

SHOULDER and BACK

The chest, shoulders and forelegs are considered together as they are dependent upon each other. The chest must be deep and wide, with good heart room to contain the lungs in full development. If the chest is too narrow and not of sufficient depth, there will not be enough room for the heart and lungs to develop fully, to give a dog staying power. All the great long-distance champions of the sport have had well-developed chests, and when breeding for stamina select a dog and bitch with well-developed chests.

The shoulder must be oblique so that the forelegs can be stretched well forward. The arm from shoulder to elbow and the forearm from elbow to knee must be of good length and short from the knee to the ground; the pasterns slightly sprung but strong, for then the forelegs will come well forward when galloping, while the shoulder blade will play freely on the ribs and not be confined by an out- or in-turned elbow. A greyhound 'tied at the elbow' cannot gallop freely. The shoulder muscles should be strong and well developed; the legs strong, with the knees close to the ground. Twenty points are awarded on the show bench for these features.

The back should be like a beam, said Dame Juliana, and it should be broad and square, supported by slightly rounded sides. A slightly arched back, as noticeable in Future Cutlet, provides additional strength. The loin muscles must be strongly attached to the ribs above the shoulders, showing a prominent edge at the junction with the blade. There is no better comparison, said Stonehenge, than that the slightly rounded sides should resemble the sides of a beam. The loins should be wide. For these considerations, fifteen points are awarded on the show bench.

The hindquarters should be broad and powerful with the stiples well bent and set widely apart. For great speed there should be more than average length to the upper and lower thighs so that the hind legs will be 'well bent'. This is achieved only when greyhounds have been given full freedom when puppies, and is the main reason behind the success of Irish-bred greyhounds and those reared in England on the Cumberland Fells.

FEET, LEGS and HOCKS

The first and second or upper and lower thigh should be muscular. The lower thigh is that part of the leg below the hams which will show prominently if the dog has been well walked and massaged. 'The lower thigh can scarcely be too muscular', wrote Stonehenge, and this point must be carefully noted when buying or judging a greyhound on the show bench.

When standing, the legs should be wide apart and if a dog does not show this at the time of judging he should be helped to take up this stance which will show off his strong hindquarters to advantage. Well-developed muscles here are necessary for the propulsion of the dog and to enable a track greyhound to take the bends at speed. Twenty points are awarded for outstanding hindquarters on the show bench.

The hocks should be long and strong, and nearly but not quite upright. A dog with long hocks is able to maintain high speed for a much longer time than one with short hocks. The hocks should be well down and nicely separated from the leg bone.

The feet, says the *Booke of St Albans,* should be like those of a cat, with the toes well arched, drawn up together and not splayed, and the pads arranged almost in a circle; this is achieved only by hard exercise from an early age. If the toes are flat and extended, not drawn up together, do not purchase the dog for track racing, though in a bitch of good breeding lines this fault will not be passed on to her offspring, for bad feet are caused by neglect in exercising. It is also necessary, through exercise, to build up a hard covering to the pads as far as the back of the pasterns, so that the pads cannot be torn away with hard running. Ten points are awarded for the feet when the dog is shown.

TAIL and COAT

The tail, as the *Booke of St Albans* says, should be thin and tapering to a point, like that of a rat, but should be thick at the root, then after 2–3 ins it should continue almost to the end about as thick as a man's thumb, before finishing in a point. It has been said that the tail acts as a rudder on the coursing field and race track, though White Sandhills won the coveted Irish Cup for coursing with only half a tail and there are instances of track greyhounds winning top-class events after losing the end of their tail. But it does add to the dog's appearance and is essential on the show bench, where five points are awarded.

The coat should be fine, close, glossy, and silky when stroked, leaving the hand covered with a greasy film which signifies a dog's good health. A dog that has been ill or has received little grooming will have a staring coat. When walking, a greyhound should show a regal deportment, striding out with a sprightly movement, its head held high, but should not be of a nervous disposition, jumping at the least sound. Noise should not worry it.

For showing, a dog should be 29–30 ins high at the shoulder, and a bitch 27–28 ins, but smaller animals have won honours on the track and coursing field (*see* Weight of a Greyhound), whilst the colour of its coat, wrote Stonehenge, is such that 'a good dog cannot be a bad colour' (*see* Colour of a Greyhound).

POOLE RACECOURSE

See under British Greyhound Racecourses.

PORTSMOUTH RACECOURSE

Sec under British Greyhound Racecourses.

POSTAGE STAMPS

The fiftieth anniversary of the first greyhound race meeting to take place in the

Republic of Ireland, that at Shelbourne Park on 14 May 1927, was commemorated by the issue of a 17p postage stamp.

The issue of a set of dog stamps by the GPO in February 1979 did not include a greyhound though could well have done so since greyhound racing is Britain's second most widely attended sport. However at the suggestion of Des Nichols, racing manager at Brighton, the Post Office agreed to issue a first day cover envelope designed by Mr Nichols which showed the Brighton Stadium and the hurdler County Prince, and on which the four dog stamps could be franked on the day of issue.

POWDERHALL RACECOURSE
See under British Greyhound Racecourses.

PREFIX

Subject to the approval of the NGRC stewards and of the English and Irish Coursing Clubs, an owner of the greyhound may register for five years, at a fee of £20, a prefix to be used in naming a greyhound, and after payment of the registration fee no other owner will be permitted to use the same prefix. The prefix may be disposed of by the executors of an owner subject to the approval of the NGRC. The following prefixes belonging to breeders are well known in the greyhound racing world.

Ballyard	Mr Michael Daly, Ballyard, Tralee, Co. Kerry
Baytown	Mr Paddy Barry, Baytown, Co. Westmeath
Breach's	Mrs Judy Pattinson, Uppingham, Rutland
Dunmore	Mr J.J. Mooney, Dunmore, Co. Galway
Chittering	Mr W.E. Creek, Waterbeach, Cambridge
Greenane	Mr P. Nugent, Greenane, Clonmel, Co. Tipperary
Hack Up	Mr Frank Tynan, Johnstown, Co. Kildare
Itsa	Mr Leslie McNair, Co. Down
Knockrour	Mr Denis Lynch, Knockrour, Aghabullogue, Co. Cork
Mad	Mrs McCarthy, Abbeyfeale, Co. Limerick
Minnesota	Mr Jim Ryan, Cashel, Co. Tipperary
Monalee	Mr B. Hatton, Enniscorthy, Co. Wexford
Priceless	Mr John Enright, Dromerin, Co. Kerry
Quare	Mr and Mrs. Billy Quinn, Killenaule, Co. Tipperary
Quarrymount	Mr John Mackey, Quarry-mount, Co. Waterford
Rushton	Mr and Mrs Johnson, Rushton, Cheshire
Sandown	Mr James Killeen, Moyvalley, Co. Kildare
Shady	Mr Harry and Mrs Noreen Barry, Delvin, Co. Westmeath
Silver	Mr Reg Young
Spanish	Mr Tim O'Connor, Killorglin, Co. Kerry
Tain	Mr J.P. Nolan, The Moyne, Enniscorthy
Tender	Mr and Mrs Hayes, Newbridge, Co. Down
The Grand	Mr Paddy and Mrs Moira Dunphy
The Great	Mr Matt O'Donnell, Killenaule, Co. Tipperary
Townview	Mr Brendan Matthews, Townview, Doran's Hill, Newry, Co. Down
Trev's	Mr Fred Trevillion, Dartford, Kent
Tullig	Mr P. Ahern, Tullig South, Abbeyfeale, Co. Limerick
Westmead	Mr and Mrs Savva, Westmead Kennels, Eddlesborough, Beds

Several owners have now died and their prefix is no longer in use, but each left its indelible mark on the greyhound racing scene.

See Naming a Greyhound.

PRICES PAID FOR GREYHOUNDS

(1926–80)

These are the sums believed to have been paid for racing greyhounds at auction and privately. Prices of the latter, however, may not be entirely correct in all cases.

Allardstown Playboy £1,000; Balliniska Band £2,000; Ballybeg Era £2,000; Ballyhennessy Sandhills £2,000; Ballyhennessey Seal 100 gns; Bigaroon 1,800 gns; Blue Mercedes 200 gns; Boher Ash £25; Bokassa £4,000; Brilliant Bob £800; Brilliant Paddy 2,000 gns; Bubbling Away £3,000; Burhill Moon 700 gns; Cairnville Pilot 4,750 gns; Cal's Invader £2,000; Cal's Pick £1,400; Camira Story £700; Carrowkeel Star 4,759 gns; Clohast Rebel £2,000; Cold Christmas 3,000 gns; Cormorant £1,000; Cosha Orchis £300; Cranog Bet 300 gns; Crefogue Flash 325 gns; Darkie's Gift 1,000 gns; Defence Leader £650; Derry Palm 300 gns; Derryboy Jubilee 1,250 gns; Derry's Son £1,400; Discussion £3,500; Disputed Rattler £50; Distant Clamour 1,050 gns; Don't Gambol 1,100 gns; Ella's Champion 3,100 gns; Fair and Handsome 1,500 gns; Fair Brook 1,500 gns; Famous Knight 1,500 gns; Fawn Cherry 1,700 gns; Finola's Yarn £2,500; Fluster 1,400 gns; Future Cutlet £600; Gale Display £4,000; Garrane Cropper 300 gns; Glenco Mill 4,000 gns; Golden Hammer £3; Grand Flight £36; Hattan Black 900 gns; Hurry Kitty £2,000; Jack of Diamonds £5,000; Killoran Castle 100 gns; Kitshine 3½ gns; Latin Pearl 500 gns; Lemon Flash 3,000 gns; Lilac's Luck £400; Lissarda Bar £2,500; Lively Band £300, £2,500, £10,000; Lively Breeze 800 gns; Lone Seal £60; Master Myles £30,000; Maverick Chaser 1,775 gns; May Hasty 14 gns; Melody Wonder (renamed Lucky Wonder) £4,000; Mick the Miller £800; Mile Bush Pride £2,500; Model Chaser, Model Dasher £100; Model County 1,300 gns; Monday's News 100 gns; Mutt's Silver £1,250; Negro's Lad 700 gns; Newdown Heather 600 gns; Nipa Lassie £2,500; Noble Brigg £10,000; Olly's Pal £3,000; Paul's Fun £1,750; Penny County £3,000; Pigalle Wonder £2,500; Pool's Punter £2,500; Postal Vote 500 gns; Red Tan 1,075 gns; Robeen Printer 1,650 gns; Sally's Cobbler £4,000; Seldom Led £5; Shady Parachute 300 gns; Shaggy Lad £350; Shaggy Lass 1,500 gns; Simone 1,450 gns; Skyhawk 165 gns; Smartly Fergus 625 gns; Snowcap 1,800 gns; Supreme Fun £2,000; Talardo £10; Tanist £200; Tonycus 2,000 gns; Top Customer £6,000; Town View Bonier 5,000 gns; Train 78 gns; Trev's Perfection £900; Wander's Luck 1,300 gns; Winnie of Berrow £70; Witches Champion £6,000; Yardley Whistler 3,000 gns.

Though a figure of £30,000 is said to have been offered for the track greyhound Knockrour Slave in 1979 and was refused, the same sum actually changed hands in 1978 when Master Myles, winner of the Irish Coursing Derby that year and the biggest and fastest greyhound ever known, was bought by Captain Tim Rogers from Mr Jerry O'Carroll. This was the highest price for which a greyhound had ever changed hands, but Master Myles was quite special. By Flying Merry (Newdown Heather) out of Better Get On (Lucky Wonder), he was a white and black dog (though almost entirely white like his grandsire Newdown Heather), whelped in January 1976 at the kennels of Mrs Mary Barrett, Monavalley, Tralee, Co. Kerry; his weight when coursing was 97 lbs. He was known as 'The Big Dog', and wherever he coursed he drew the crowds as no other dog had ever done, for he was something of a phenomenon. He won his first course at Clonmel and then at Listowel, after which, it is said, his owner refused £10,000 for him. At Abbeyfeale he again showed his devastating form, and again in the Derby at Powerstown he made mince-meat of his opponents throughout, winning the event from the outstanding Coxcomb. He was then sold for £30,000. But tragedy was soon to strike. A few weeks later, in a gallop over his new trainer's grounds at Gould's Cross, the dog suffered terrible injuries and died at the Veterinary College at Celbridge in the early hours of the morning.

Noble Brigg, owned and bred by Mr Arthur McGookin, was sold to the Belfast bookmaker Barney Eastwood for £10,000 after winning the 1978 Guinness National Sprint at Dunmore Park. Other greyhounds to change hands for large sums in recent years include Top Customer and Witch's Champion for £6,000 each; and Sally's Cobbler and Melody Wonder (renamed Lucky Wonder) for £4,000 each. With inflation continuing unabated, the price of greyhounds will soon be matching football transfer fees and we may soon see the £100,000 greyhound.

But it so happens that the least expensive sometimes proves to be the best bargain. though it is unlikely we shall see anything again like the 25s bargain Waterloo Cup winner of 1866, Brigadier, who filled a late nomination when the bitch Wild Geranium had to be withdrawn. However bargains in greyhounds remain one of the romances of the sport.

In the early days of greyhound racing there was no greater enthusiast than Mr George Flintham, who raced greyhounds for many years. One of his first purchases was the game dog Grand Flight II, who won the Cesarewitch for him in 1935 and altogether several thousand pounds in prize money – he cost George Flintham only £36. The same year the dog won the International and in 1936 reached the final of the Derby. He also won the *Daily Mirror* Trophy at the White City. An equally splendid bargain was the 3½ gns Mr Freeman paid for the bitch Kitshine at Aldridge's in the 1930s, for she was to win the Oaks and the Laurels in 1935. Another bitch, May Hasty, also purchased at Aldridge's and for only 14 gns, had within twelve months won the Stayers' Plaque at Wimbledon and had broken the great Bradshaw Fold's 700 yds record at West Ham which had stood for ten years. Two years later she was to break English Warrior's 810 yds record with a time of 48.95 secs before retiring from racing and whelping a large litter, several of which turned out to be successful trackers. But perhaps there is no more romantic story than that of the great dog Train who, in the early war years, when food was scarce, was sold by Major Tennison for a few pounds. It was decided that there was room in Major Tennison's large kennels of foxhounds and greyhounds for only a few outstanding brood bitches to maintain the strains built up over many years and for which the kennels had for so long been famous. So, reluctantly, the promising dog was sold. He went first to a Mr Harris who sent him to

Aldridge's where he was purchased by Miss Lambert for 78 gns. The dog was a son of the great coursing sire Danielli, and Miss Lambert took him to the Harringay track to see what he would do. Within three months Train had won three open events there and had set up a new 525 yds record with a time of 29.46 secs. He was to defeat the great Ballynennan Moon in three out of the four occasions on which they met, and he always showed the same tremendous pace combined with the stamina of his coursing sire. These qualities he passed on at stud, during which time he earned his owner many thousands of pounds in addition to the large sums he earned on the track. Was there ever a better investment for 78 gns?

Almost as profitable was Ballyhennessy Seal to Mrs Stowe and Mr Vivian, who purchased him for £100 after winning a race for novices at Tralee. Within twelve months the dog had set up a new national record for 500 yds at Stamford Bridge with a time of 27.68 secs, and the following year he won the Derby by five lengths. In all he won more than £3,000 on the track and at least that amount in stud fees. His sire, Lone Seal, who had been purchased for only £60 and became one of the greatest of all track sires, was equally profitable, for he earned his owner in one year alone more than £2,500 in stud fees; the dog was in such demand that he served two bitches a week at a fee of 25 gns. One of his most famous sons was Ballymac Ball, who won the Derby and was twice winner of the Laurels. Lone Seal was ten years old when the Derby winner was born, having been at stud for more than six years, during which time he must have earned his owner more than £20,000.

In more recent times Talardo, who won more than £2,000 over hurdles, was purchased for only £10 as he had done little of note when racing on the flat. In 1969, at the now defunct Clapton track, Not Permissible won six races in a row over 760 yds. He had been purchased a few months before by Mr Arthur Bryan for only £50.

Another outstanding purchase was Lilac's Luck, who was bought at auction in Ireland for £400 after showing promise as a puppy. He went on to win the 1945 Irish Derby by two lengths from that excellent dog Gun Music. He then took the Trigo Cup at Celtic Park, Belfast, beating Astra and Mad Tanist, Ireland's fastest. Within twelve months he had more than proved himself one of the best bargains of all time, but his owner sent the dog over to England where he was to reach the final of the English Derby. He came within an ace of becoming the first greyhound to win both the Irish and English events, but was beaten into second place by the amazing performance of Monday's News.

Mr Frank Bithel purchased Model Dasher and his litter brother Model Chaser for a very small sum after seeing their first trials at the Perry Barr Stadium. Within two months, when only seventeen months old, Model Dasher had beaten a host of champions to take the Eclipse Stakes at Coventry and the Midlands Puppy Championship in equally impressive style. He raced when the classic events were postponed during the war years and when prize money was small by today's standards, yet he proved himself one of the greatest stayers in the history of the sport (perhaps the greatest). Out of forty-two races he won twenty-seven, earning his owner more than £2,000 in prize money and an equally impressive amount at stud.

Many have made fortunes out of the running of greyhounds. The English bred Trev's Perfection, which cost his owner Mr Fred Trevillion £900 and was, in his words, 'the best investment I ever made', earned over £2,000 of prize money in one week in 1947 and twice that sum in the next seven months, which included £1,400 from winning the Derby — a far cry from the £17,500 awarded to the winner of the fiftieth anniversary Derby won thirty years later by Mr Raphaello Bacci and his dog Balliniska Band, and the £35,000 won by Indian Joe in 1980.

In recent years surely one of the best bargains ever was the 300 gns paid for Cranog Bet, one of the six greatest bitches ever to race in Britain, who won more than £8,500 for her owner and became one of the best dams in the history of track racing. It is said that the great Skyhawk cost only 160 gns and Cosha Orchis, a son of Own Pride, was purchased at the Shelbourne Park sales by Mr C. Gleeson for £300 and won the Scottish Derby for him soon afterwards.

Phil Rees, who trained the renowned Oregon Prince, has told of buying Can Willie, a popular Wimbledon dog for some years, for just £20 and he won more than £2,000 prize money in graded races. Another example of a profitable investment was the 300 gns paid at auction for Derry Palm, a courageous dog who earned almost £3,000 from hurdling, winning the Midland, Scottish and Welsh Grand Nationals for his owner, Mr William Perkins. This sum was only exceeded by the hurdler Tony's Friend until Sherry's Prince passed the £3,000 mark in his winnings.

In recent years it is said that Bella's Iris, who reached the final of the Irish Derby, was purchased for 1 gn at Shelbourne Park sales, and Hard Held, who reached the final of the 1969 English Derby only to be crowded and bumped at the first bend after winning his semi-final, was, I believe, purchased by his owners, Mr and Mrs Corbett for only £200.

One of the greatest of all sires, Newdown Heather, bought as an untried puppy by Mrs Kathleen McKee and Mr George Posnett of Belfast for 600 gns, showed such devastating pace on track and coursing field in his early trials that his owners were offered and refused £5,000 for him. An amputated toe soon afterwards finished his most promising career and he was put to stud, with amazing success, at Jack Mullan's kennels at Newry, Co. Down, where he sired world-beaters from every bitch put to him. One of his finest sons was Crefogue Flash, a black dog like his famous sire, who was sold for 325 gns at the Shelbourne Park sales in 1970 jointly to Mr Peter Taylor and the Williamson brothers, bookmakers. So quickly did the dog come on when brought over to England that he was widely tipped to win the 1971 Derby but had to be withdrawn owing to injury and was retired to stud in his prime. But in only eight months he won £2,000 in prize money, including the Puppy Derby at Wimbledon and the Midlands event at Wolverhampton. He reached the semi-final of the English Derby, in which he finished lame.

Of the six greyhounds to contest the final of the 1979 Derby, two were bitches and both had been purchased for a very small sum. Romance surrounds Mr Peter Horn's black bitch Tyrean, for at the beginning of the year she was running only in graded races, and in the ante-post betting was quoted at 500–1, considered to be the complete outsider among the 215 entries. In rounds 3 and 4 and in her semi-final she was first over the line, beating some dogs purchased for more than £1,000, but she failed to win the final. Sarah's Bunny won, and she, too, had been purchased for only a small sum. Discarded by her original owner, she was bought untried on the track by Birmingham businessman Mr Roy Hadley, who had owned greyhounds for less than two years. That she won the 1979 Derby by a length from the 1978 winner Lacca Champion is one of the romances of greyhound racing. She was only the fourth bitch to win in forty-nine Derby events and won for her owner the sum of £20,000. Sarah's Bunny was the daughter of the 1975 Derby winner Jimsun, owned by the late Mr Joe de Mulder and Miss Walker and trained, as was Sarah's Bunny, by Joe's son Geoffrey at Hall Green.

In the history of track racing there have been many successes which read like fairy tales for the owners of greyhounds, and one never knows just how good a greyhound will turn out to be in the hands of a top-class trainer who will play as big a part in a dog's success as will the dog itself. But credit must always be given to those who have had an eye for a good young dog or for an older one whose potential has not been fulfilled until purchased by a new owner and placed in the hands of a capable trainer. There are those who will say how lucky the owner has been, but what is usually thought to be luck is really sound knowledge of exactly what to look for in buying a greyhound, which comes only with experience or by trusting the matter to someone long connected with greyhound dealing and who may have had many successes in the sport.

Mostly the greatest successes have been with those dogs purchased for only a small sum, but one's greatest admiration is for those who have bred and reared a litter or who may have purchased a good-looking puppy perhaps twelve to sixteen weeks old and have kept it all its life, and never been tempted to sell it as it progresses to become a champion. Some owners have refused very big sums, for instance the £10,000 offered to Mrs Billy Quinn in 1946 for her dog Quare Times, bred and reared by herself and her husband in Co. Tipperary. The same sum was offered to Mr Frank Bithel for Model

Dasher, but these were wealthy people and one's admiration is felt most of all for Mr Michael Collins, a buttermaker in a creamery at Inniscara, Co. Cork, who bought Creamery Border and his litter brother Sly Mover at ten weeks old for £30, a big sum then. Fifteen months later he was offered £600 for the pair but refused it, and it must have been a most tempting offer for a young dairy worker in 1931. All credit is due to Mr Collins, for he held on to Creamery Border to see him become the fastest the sport had known. Creamery Border lived until he was nearly fifteen, earning his owner large sums on the track and during his years as a sire.

Of those greyhounds purchased for a considerable sum, few have proved to be a profitable investment. Future Cutlet, however, who cost Mr W.A. Evershed £600, a large sum in the 1930s, was worth every penny for he won the English Derby of 1933 by a short head (about 2 in.) from Beef Cutlet, in one of the most amazing finishes of all time which those who saw the race thought should have been a dead heat. Beef Cutlet had been purchased by Miss Merritt for the same sum and was to become one of the first-class sires on which modern track racing was founded. Both were sons of the great sire Mutton Cutlet. It should be said that Future Cutlet had been beaten by only the same distance in the previous Derby by the Belle Vue champion Wild Woolley, who was third in the event in 1933 and 1934, so justice had perhaps been done. These were the three finest racing greyhounds after Mick the Miller's reign and before Brilliant Bob arrived on the scene in 1934. It is said that Mr Dearman paid £800 for the great Brilliant Bob, who was owned by two Co. Tipperary men, one being the famous Billy Quinn, the other a farmer, and neither really wanted to sell him. It was Sidney Orton's gentle persuasion which enabled Mr Dearman to make his purchase, and in England, in the kennels of the famous Burhill trainer, Bob was to win three classics and stamp his name on the sport as one of the immortals.

Of other expensive purchases of the early years of the sport, Mick the Miller was also purchased for £800 by Mr A.H. Williams after winning his first round heat of the Derby. After winning the actual event he was bought for £2,000 by Mrs A. Kempton, for whom he again won the premier event. The wonderful bitch Hurry Kitty cost Miss Kwasnik £2,000 and won the 1945 Cesarewitch in record time, and Robeen Printer cost £1,650 at auction in Ireland after winning the Laurels, in which she defeated the great Shannon Shore, and the McAlinden Cup at Shelbourne Park, her time of 29.90 secs being the fastest for a bitch ever recorded up to that time. Purchased at auction by Mrs Hilda Sanderson, Robeen Printer won the English St Leger and dead-heated the Coventry Eclipse Stakes. Mr L. Hamilton gave £1,500 for another wonderful bitch, Shaggy Lass, who proved to be an equally good buy, and Mrs Cearns, wife of Wimbledon's managing director, gave £2,000 for Ballyhennessy Sandhills, twice winner of the Laurels and of over £5,000 on the track and the same sum in stud fees. More recently Cal's Pick, another wonderful bitch, cost £1,400 at the Hackney auctions and repaid her owner many times; and Supreme Fun, who cost £2,000, ran up the 1971 Derby and was well patronized at stud. Supreme Fun had twelve consecutive wins after being pipped on the line for the Derby by that great bitch Dolores Rocket and until beaten in the final of the Cesarewitch. Then in the Ben Truman Stakes at Catford he was knocked over and badly injured.

On the other side of the coin, Bigaroon also cost £2,000 and met with little success in England. Famous Knight, who cost £1,500 after winning the Irish Derby, had no success at all in Britain, neither did Fair Brook, who cost the same sum. In the 1940s the two Tanist offspring, Lemon Flash and Cold Christmas, both of which cost Mr Joseph £3,000, died shortly after arriving in England without ever having won a race, and Yardley Whistler, said to have been purchased for £3,500 in Ireland, made no impression on English tracks; nor, in more recent times, did Cal's Invader, purchased for £2,000, or Top Customer, said to have cost £6,000.

A good greyhound can be bought for a £10 note and a poor one for £1,000 or more. Those who have a good one at whatever age may obtain a bargain at whatever price is paid for it.

PRIZE MONEY

The total prize money awarded each year for

the approximate 2,000 meetings held at the eighteen tracks in the Irish Republic, which includes Bord na gCon grants, entry fees and sponsors' awards, amounts to:

1960	£112,935	1971	£320,455
1961	£138,241	1972	£358,670
1962	£146,250	1973	£481,045
1963	£155,971	1974	£525,754
1964	£210,117	1975	£641,775
1965	£267,910	1976	£776,617
1966	£277,000	1977	£778,668
1967	£280,000	1978	£928,549
1968	£241,718	1979	£1,000,000
1969	£249,936		
1970	£290,179		

In Britain, prize money for 1979 amounted to £1,255,000. This was made up of stake money put up by the contestants, amounts contributed by the tracks, and from sponsors.

R

RACE

A contest between no more than six greyhounds on an approved racecourse over a distance of not less than 230 yds or 210 m and not more than 1,200 yds or 1,105 m.

All races are run in an anti-clockwise direction, known as left-hand travel. A race takes place at a time specified on the race card, but the local stewards have full powers to change the order of racing should they think fit to do so.

Long distance. A race of more than 600 yds or 500 m, one of which is included at most meetings though there is always a scarcity of greyhounds able to compete in such events (known as stayers). They are the most interesting of all races as there is time for so much to happen between start and finish.

Middle distance. A race over 525 yds or 500 m. A middle-distance runner is a dog which does best over this distance as opposed to a stayer or a sprinter. This distance allows a good dog plenty of time to recover from a poor start and beat those which are at their best over shorter distances.

Short distance. A race run over a course of less than 500 yds or 500 m. Young dogs are started over the shorter course, to allow them to get used to the track and to gradually build up their confidence and stamina. Some greyhounds are only at their best over the shorter distances, showing tremendous pace for a short burst, before they begin to fade, and so are usually graded by the racing manager accordingly. Some of the fastest greyhounds in the history of the sport spent their entire career running short or sprint races.

The only occasion a race has been run in a clockwise direction was on Derby final night in July 1939 when the dog Scattering Illusion won this specially organized event. The greyhounds taking part navigated the course exactly as when running in the anti-clockwise direction.

RACE CARD

At each meeting an official race card is published and given to those who pay for admission. On it are the name of the racecourse, the date of the meeting, and the names of all officials licensed to act at the meeting. The names of the greyhounds making up each race must be given, together with their trap numbers and the name of the reserved dog(s) for each race. The names of the owners and trainers are printed, together with full information concerning each dog's last four races or trials. Rule 76 of the NGRC must be complied with on the card, as to whether trap numbers have been allocated or drawn. If drawn, the names of the persons witnessing the draw must be given.

Since 1976 a NGRC rule has allowed 'seeding' for wide runners in the draw for open races, including the Derby. Of all NGRC rules this has caused most controversy, for the wide runners (to lessen their running across the line of other dogs) are often allocated favourable traps while other dogs have to take their luck. But owners are unhappy about another's dog being given preferential treatment even if it is intended to improve the racing. Trap places for graded races are allocated by the racing manager, and (W) after a dog's name signifies a wide runner.

To enable the punter to read the race card, a list of abbreviations is provided:

7.23—3rd RACE - OR **500 Metres Hurdles**

THE SHERRY'S PRINCE HURDLES

AN OPEN RACE FOR SIX GREYHOUNDS AT £3 EACH

1st £120 & Trophy; 2nd £40; Others £15

	Date	Dist	G'g	Trap	Position At Quarters	Fin	Win Dist	Greyhound	Remark	Win Time	Wght	S.P.	Class	Calculated Time
1 Red	**SALERNO**							(Wembley) be.bd.d. Clerihan Venture—Fish Pond, Feb., '74						Mrs. P. M. Carter J. Coleman
	Jun 20	500h	N	T2	(03.38)			Solo Trial ....(WC)	slow away	31.34	35.1	T		31.34
	Jun 15	490h	10s	T3	1 111	4th	16¾	Craheen Magic .. (Wem)	fell 6h	30.77	35.1	10/11F	OR	32.03
	Jun 4	484h	10s	T4	5 443	4th	3½	Jimmy Trouble ......(Southend)		30.96	35.3	2/5F	OR	31.14
	May 10	500h	N	T4	1(03.16)111	1st	5½	Moon View ....(WC)	e.pace	30.38	35.0	1/2F	OR	30.38

Above: A typical race card. Details of how to read it are given below.

Al. led	Always led
B 1st	Bumped first bend
BLKD	Baulked
C/A	Come again
Ch	Checked
CWD	Crowded out
D/H	Dead heat
D/S	Distance (won by)
EC	Every chance
F	Fell
FA	Fast away
Fav	Favourite
FWW	Finished well
H	Hurdles
Hd	Head (won by)
H/G	Hard going
Hp	Hampered
HT	Hand timed (trials)
J/F	Joint favourite
K/O	Knocked over
N/G	Normal going
Nk	Neck (won by)
S	Stumbled
SA	Slow away
S/G	Soft going
SH	Short head (won by)
SLP	Slipped
S/P	Starting price
Tr	Trial
W	Ran wide
Wn W	Won well

This is how to read a race card, taking the Sherry's Prince Hurdles event, run at the White City, London on 25 June 1977, as an example. The patron is told that this race is an open event for six greyhounds at an entry fee of £3 each. It is the third race of the meeting and will be over 500 m hurdles, the winner receiving £120 and a trophy, with £40 going to the runner-up (second dog) and £15 to the others.

No. 1 dog wearing the red jacket is Salerno, a blue brindled dog by Clerihan Venture out of Fish Pond, whelped in February 1974. It is owned by Mrs P.M. Carter and trained by J. Coleman at Wembley Stadium where it is kennelled. As this is an open event the dog is on this occasion running away from his home track.

Beneath the dog's name are the four last trials or races in which he performed; the last line (the first is a trial) tells us that he ran on 10 May in a 500 m hurdles event. The going was normal (N) and he raced from trap 4. At each quarter stage of the run the dog was leading (1), and he finished first so he led all the way, beating Moon View (winning distance) by five and a half lengths. Moving further across the card, we are told that this race took place at the White City (WC) and (under Remarks) the dog showed good early pace (e. pace). His winning time was 30.38 secs and his racing weight was 35 kilos. His starting price (SP) was 2—1 on and he was favourite (F) to win. It was an open race (OR) and the calculated time (making any allowances for heavy going) was the one that he recorded.

RACING

The chief points to note in the running of the dogs around a track are the start, first bend, back straight, second bend, and run-in or finish. Not every race covers the entire course, while some may cover several parts of a track more than once, depending on the distance of a race, but for the average 500 m race on the average-sized track the dogs race once over the course, plus a few extra yards or metres for the run-in and the finishing line.

The start. A quick break or start from the traps is important for all except long-distance events. Those dogs fast away, e.g. Local Interprize, Quare Times and Yellow Printer, are soon into their stride and are usually well in front of the other dogs and out of trouble by the first bend.

First bend. By the time they reach the first bend or left turn at the end of the straight, the dogs will be moving at more than 40 mph, and only the bends slow them down a little. At this point the dogs may bump if all bunched together. That is why the fast breaker will be in front and away from the others when reaching the first bend.

Back straight. In races over shorter distances, by the time the dogs have rounded the first turn and are coming to the back straight it is usually possible to decide on the winner, for he will often be clear of the others and striding out with beautiful action and rhythm.

Second bend. The dog reaching this point first in all but long-distance races will, bar some mishap such as slipping on a wet track, reach the finishing line first, for he will be on the rails and so will have less ground to cover. Dogs running wide at this point will have little chance of winning except in long-distance races.

Run-in. By the time the dogs reach the front straight in front of the main stand, where the finishing line is found, most races will be won unless particularly outstanding greyhounds are taking part or if the race is over a long distance, where a top-class stayer, perhaps well behind at some stage, may be coming with a late burst of speed to pip the other dogs on the line. This is greyhound racing at its most exciting best. Also those stout-hearted trackers with great ability who never give up however far behind at some point during a race, perhaps through slipping or bumping on the bends, will still be battling on to the end; when their chances of winning as they round the final bend look hopeless they often come again as they approach the finishing line to take the race by a nose. This too is greyhound racing at its finest. Some dogs are never beaten until the winning line is reached and this is the one aspect of greyhound racing which makes it so exciting. There is no jockey to wield the whip to persuade his horse to make a final effort. The greyhound is on its own, propelled only by its love of racing and instinct to reach the hare first. A courageous dog will win the applause of all present, whether they have backed the winner or not.

RACING AGE

A greyhound is not permitted to run on a licensed track until fifteen months old. Some develop quickly. John Silver won the Derby at twenty-two months, whereas Future Cutlet was four and a half years old when he won. Mick the Miller at more than five years old was the oldest dog to win a classic. At Darnall, Sheffield, Mr E.W. Goddard's Jacob Retires was still winning in 1946 at the age of eight and in graded races won over £1,000. His litter brother, Jacob's Return, did the same. At Warrington, Double Twenty won in 1946 when eight and a half years old, and at New Cross Lengthy Laird was winning at the age of seven and a half. Spalding Spark was running and winning at nine years.

See Oldest Racing Greyhound.

RACING BITCH

A bitch may not take part in a race or trial after coming in season and for a minimum of ten weeks after. An attached or permit trainer must inform the racing manager when a bitch in his or her charge comes in season.

See Bitch.

RACING CALENDAR

Published by the NGRC the calendar is issued fortnightly throughout the year and costs £15, including postage. It lists all open events run on NGRC tracks, their results, stewards' enquiries and, indeed, everything that goes on at all the licensed tracks. It is indispensable to owners, trainers and serious followers of the sport as it is a complete record of events.

RACING MANAGER

A licensed official, he is the most important member of a greyhound racecourse and the sport has been fortunate in having so many racing managers of the utmost integrity who have held their important position often for more than thirty years. Major Percy Brown was racing manager at White City, London for thirty years until his retirement in July 1972, and Con Stevens was at Wimbledon from the beginning of 1936 until 1976. Captain Brice had a long career as racing manager at Wembley Stadium, and at Owlerton, Sheffield, Sam Vinter was in charge of racing from the opening of the track on 12 January 1932, until he retired in 1974. Colonel Prior was for many years racing manager at the Derby Stadium. Much of the success of the racing at these venues must be attributed to the skills and long service of their racing managers, who came to know every trainer and every owner as well as every greyhound with whom they were associated, their moods, capabilities, and problems.

A racing manager must be present at all meetings and at trials; he grades the dogs according to their ability and makes up the programme for each meeting. He must check and enter the identity book of every greyhound that runs at his stadium, whether in races or in trials, even solo trials. He must register the greyhounds and their changes of ownership and report any disqualifications for fighting to the controlling body. He also has many other duties every day of the week, except perhaps Sundays, but even then a racing manager will often be at the track until mid-day, as will the trainers at the kennels, for even on Sundays the dogs must be fed and exercised.

A racing manager must learn from his trainers the condition of each greyhound kennelled at the track, whether sick or lame, or if a bitch when in season, for each of these dogs will be off the racing strength. With dogs taking part in open events it is his job to ensure that the dog's identity book reaches the track before the dog, or if the animal is sick and it has to be withdrawn, to inform the track so that a substitute can be obtained in time. In addition the racing manager must watch the trials held at the track on most week-days before taking in new dogs and to enable him to discuss with the owners and trainers a dog's capabilities.

RACING, TERMS OF *See also* Race Card.

BAULKED
This is marked on the race card, for a greyhound may be prevented from taking advantage of an opening to move to the front by another dog moving in front of it.

BUMPING
It often happens that where there are several dogs close together as they approach the bends, especially the first bend, one or two will bump into each other, perhaps causing them to stumble or run wide, with the result that those not involved will get clear away to lead the field by several lengths. Where bumping takes place it is shown on the race card, e.g. B 1st bend.

CHECKING
When one dog runs across another, such as one from an outside trap, 5 or 6, so as to reach the rail, a dog from trap 3 or 4, in an inside position, may be checked in its stride. This will make it lose ground and it may not be able to recover in time to put in a good finish. The dogs from the inside traps suffer most in this respect.

CLUMSY RUNNER
A term given to a young dog with little track experience and which may bump or collide with another on a bend.

COMING AGAIN
The term used when a dog may have been bumped or impeded, causing it to lose ground, but will come back into the reckoning (renew its challenge) with a courageous late rally.

DOG
A word used to describe all those taking part in a race whether dogs or bitches, hence 'dog racing' and 'dog track' as against 'greyhound racing'.

EARLY PACE
Describes a dog which is quickly into its stride, usually a sprinter and one that is fast from the traps.

EVEN BREAK
Describes the situation in which all the dogs come out of the traps almost together.

FADING
The inability of a greyhound to stay the full course. This may be shown on the race card in future and the dog will be graded to race over shorter distances. But factors such as heavy going will be taken into consideration, while a dog may be having its first race after injury, or a bitch after being in season.

FAST AWAY
Describes a dog which is especially quick from the traps, a fast starter like Ballyhennessy Seal, Quare Times, Shady Parachute and Faithful Hope. A dog fast away will usually be in front at the first bend and on the rails, so that it will be in a

good position for the remainder of the race.

FAST GOING
Where the going is particularly good, the running surface being at its best, dry and firm, not after rain.

FAST STARTER
A greyhound fast to break from the traps. This is a most important factor for it will often enable a dog to reach the first bend before the others and take the inside or rails position, forcing others to run on the outside with more ground to cover during the race. A dog at the rails at the first bend will often find itself in a winning position. But fast starters do not always have the stamina to stay the 500 m (or longer) course. When they do, they have considerable value.

FIGHTING
The deliberate interference by one greyhound with another during a trial or race. The stewards will disqualify any greyhound which fights and suspend it from all trials and races for not less than fourteen days. At the end of that period, provided the dog runs at least three consecutive clear trials on separate days, it may be reinstated. A clear trial must have been run over a distance of at least 400 yds. Throughout the history of the sport, where a greyhound has fought when running on the flat it has never done so when tried over hurdles, and many top-class hurdlers which were disqualified when racing on the flat have later become household names as hurdlers.

Whenever a greyhound shows fighting tendencies, in a trial or race, its identity book will be endorsed, which will make it difficult to sell if the need arises. If it offends a second time, it will be warned off the NGRC tracks. The disqualification rule is enforced on about 500 occasions during every year's racing, about ten times a year at each track, which should be kept in perspective when it is realized that more than 1,000 races are run on each track every year.

If a dog has shown fighting tendencies on a certain track, in trials or during a race, it is advisable to take it elsewhere, for a different type of hare may have quite a different effect on the dog and he may never again be at fault. It is noticeable that greyhounds following an inside hare are less liable to show fighting tendencies than with other hares, and if a dog has proved unreliable where following an outside or centre hare, it will be advisable to take it to a track which has an inside hare.

FINISHING WELL
Describes a dog that shows speed and stamina at the end of a race when other dogs may have faded.

FORM
On all race cards, the result of the last four races in which a greyhound has taken part must be shown in detail together with the name of the tracks where the races took place, the date, distance of race, the going (fast or slow), trap number, finishing position, winning or losing distance, weight before the race, betting odds and the dog's time, so that followers of form have complete and up-to-date information of the greyhound's performances. This is necessary to weigh up the animal's chances in the race in which it is about to take part and before a bet is placed.

FREAK CONDITIONS
Sudden freak change of weather at a meeting, due possibly to a hailstorm or heavy rain after a thunderstorm which will cause the track to be waterlogged for some time, causing abandonment of the meeting or delay in the running of the races.

GALLOPING TRACK
A fast track with long straights and wide turns (bends) which allows the dogs to go flat out in long, galloping strides all the way round.

GOING
Denotes the condition of the track's running surface, such as slow going (S) after prolonged rain, when the dogs plough up the surface in their running; hard going (H) in dry weather; or normal (N). These are given on the race card.

GREEN
Describes young dogs running in their first trials and races when they show little track sense, do not take the rails when the opportunity occurs, or bump other dogs at the bends.

HAND SLIPPED
A method of schooling greyhounds, slipping them from the leash by hand and not using a starting box or trap, to allow them to have a better look at the hare as it comes round.

HITTING THE BOX
A term used to describe a greyhound that leaves the trap like a bullet, leaving the other dogs far behind.

IMPEDING
See Checking.

INTERFERING
The term used when one greyhound comes into deliberate contact with another during a trail or race, when it snaps at it as it passes, causing the dog to check in its stride and perhaps lose the race. This is classed in the same way as fighting.

KENNELLING TIME
The kennelling procedure must be completed at least thirty minutes before trials or a meeting, but those greyhounds taking part must be in the kennels at least one hour before. Any dog arriving late (such as a dog coming some distance for an open event) may be disqualified by the racing manager from taking part in the event.

MUZZLE
The trainer is responsible for ensuring that each greyhound is wearing its correct racing jacket and muzzle when leaving the racing paddock to take part in a race or trial.

The paddock steward will examine the jacket or muzzle and adjust them if necessary. The racing muzzle is of wire and must be of the required measurements for the various sizes of greyhound, and of the non-biting type.

OBJECTION
The owner of a greyhound may object to the running of another in the same race or in further rounds of an event. This must be made in writing to the local stewards, accompanied by a deposit of £25. If the objection is sustained, the greyhound shall be deemed disqualified for the race concerned.

RAILERS
Dogs which try to reach the rails (inside the track) as quickly as possible. A railer drawn in traps 1 or 2 (on the inside) will take some beating as it will cover considerably less ground that those running on the outside. Those who pay regular visits to a track will know which are the railers and when these dogs are favourably drawn will place their bets accordingly. The difference between a railer and a wide runner covering 500 m is as much as sixteen lengths or one second, a very big advantage for the dog who is first at the rails. But not all railers or those drawn in no. 1 trap leave the traps well. Perhaps the dog in trap 2 or 3 will be quickest away and may reach the inside position by the first bend and retain it throughout the race.

RESERVE
A greyhound held in reserve to replace one which may have to be withdrawn, through sickness or coming in season, from an open or graded race. The name of the reserve dog must appear on the card for each race and he will wear a jacket with the letter R.

RUNNING OUT
If a greyhound runs off the defined course, it will be regarded as not completing the course and will be disqualified. Occasionally a dog will jump into the crowd, possibly through fright at a low-flying aircraft or for no apparent reason at all.

SCRATCH DOG
The back marker in a handicap race, usually occupying no. 1 trap.

SELLING RACE
A race in which one or more of the runners is offered for sale by public auction at a reserve price stipulated by the racing manager and agreed to by the owner. No more than one selling race may be included in a meeting.

SHARP BENDS
Turns which are of an acute angle, not graduated as much as on some tracks. These are more difficult for the dogs to negotiate.

SLOW AWAY
Describes a greyhound which is slow in coming from its trap, thus allowing its rivals to make early ground and perhaps reach the

first bend before it. In a short race, the dog slow away has little distance to catch up with the others. A dog slow from the traps is said to have missed its break.

SLOW GOING
Conditions which cause the track to be slower than usual, such as after heavy rain or snow, when the dogs will churn up the surface, making for slower times. This is taken into account by the racing manager when making up his future card or programme. Slow going is marked S on the race card so that the punter will know why a dog's time is poorer than usual for a given distance.

TRACK SIZE
The circumference is measured all round the running track 1 ft (30 cm) from inside the rails, which is the track normally run by the inside greyhound.

TRAP NUMBERS
The trap numbers of all greyhounds taking part in any races have to be displayed on an indicator board in full view of all members of the public ten minutes before a race is run. They are also shown against each dog's name on the race card.

TURNING ITS HEAD
A dog which has the unpleasant habit of turning its head when another passes it during a race or trial is judged to have interfered with it and may be disqualified as a fighter. A dog which goes about its proper business of following the hare has no time to interfere with others and will not turn its head.

WEIGHT VARIATION
Any greyhound whose weight, at the time it is kennelled before a race, shows a variation of more than 1 kg from its weight shown in its identity book for a previous race shall be withdrawn, and shall run at least one trial before it is allowed to race again.

WIDE RUNNER
If the racing manager believes that a particular greyhound has a tendency to run on the outside of a track, he will mark it W on the race card. Often the racing manager will make the trap allocation so that wide runners will be in the outside traps, 5 and 6, so that they will not interfere with other dogs.

WINNING LINE
This is a clear line drawn across the track, and not a post as in horse racing.

WITHDRAWALS
The withdrawal of a dog from a race is decided by the local stewards on receipt of a veterinary surgeon's certificate of the dog's health. If a greyhound is for some reason withdrawn from an open event by its owner, this must be done in writing to the racing manager not later than 10 a.m. on the day of the race and must be accompanied by a deposit of £25. The cause of withdrawal must be reported to the NGRC stewards.

RAMSGATE RACECOURSE *See under* British Greyhound Racecourses.

RAY-START
The invention of Mr A. Mulley, it was first used at Wembley Stadium on 16 November 1946, and later came to be used on all NGRC tracks. From a control panel near the rails, an invisible ray cuts the passage of the hare 12 yds in front of the starting boxes, cuts off the current of the electro-magnet holding down the trap fronts, and so releases them.

RAY-TIMING
The first photo-electric timing gear, known as ray-timing, was first installed at Hackney Wick Stadium and was the invention of G. Crookbank, their chief electrician. From his ideas and suggestions the General Electric Co. worked to bring out the new timing equipment with a view to eliminating hand-timing by stopwatch.

The equipment is set so that the moment the traps open, an amber light shows, then a red light after 10 secs have elapsed, for the dogs to pass the ray on the off-stretch. Between this moment and the moment the first greyhound's nose passes the ray which is the winning line, the clock is stopped to record the exact time taken to run the race. To reset the clock for the next race, all that is necessary is to press a button, while the time-keeper can set the starting switch for any distance without leaving his seat. The time is also taken by hand in case of any mishap to the electric ray-timer.

Many people will be surprised to know that ray-timing is slower than hand-timing. The fastest time for the Greyhound Derby by hand-timing is the 28.50 secs by Endless Gossip when winning by four lengths in 1952. The next year, ray-timing was used at the White City, the fastest time recorded for the 525 yds event being 28.52 secs by Faithful Hope in 1966 which, if taken by hand-timing, would have been faster than Endless Gossip's Record.

READING RACECOURSE *See under* British Greyhound Racecourses.

REARING PUPPIES

At six months puppies will have come through the weaning period which is the most difficult part of their life. From now on they need plenty of sunlight and fresh air. Their kennel should be well ventilated and they should be allowed out on all days except when really cold. They love to lie in the sun and this will help to build up their bones and keep them in condition, but provide them with shade in the heat of summer and always have a bowl of fresh water available. Do not pamper them, but give them plenty of good, fresh food and exercise.

From the age of eight months the dogs must be separated from the bitches. They are then known as saplings and must now get used to walking out with collar and lead. At first put on a collar for a short time each day; they will not like this, and it takes some animals several weeks to get used to it. Not until they do is it possible to take them out on a lead. Their training is now about to begin and short distances on roads are necessary to get their feet hard and make the bones knit together. This is why on farms greyhounds are allowed to roam about hard-surfaced yards and why it is important to have a strip of concrete down one side of their run which will firm their feet from an early age. The dogs will enjoy their walks, which should be a daily routine about an hour after their 8 a.m. meal, and should last at least an hour. Then brush them down and return them to their kennels for a rest. Give them another feed of milk and brown bread or biscuit at mid-day and let them play out in their run during the afternoon. In the early evening they are given their main feed of the day and are then closed up for the night.

RECORD ENTRY

The record entry for any greyhound race is always for the English Derby. In 1976 as many as 169 greyhounds were entered by their owners, and in 1979 this had passed the 200 mark. In the ante-post betting for 1976 Mutt's Silver, the eventual winner, was quoted at 300—1 against; and in 1979 the bitch Tyrean, was 500—1 but ran so well that she reached the final in which she finished third behind Sarah's Bunny and Lacca Champion.

REGISTERING OF A GREYHOUND

All greyhounds must be registered with the English or Irish Coursing Stud Book and with the NGRC before being allowed to run on a licensed track. In 1972, earmarking became compulsory before registering a litter or a greyhound with the English Stud Book. The fee for entering and naming in the Stud Book a greyhound up to fourteen months old, which has previously been registered by 30 June following the year in which is was whelped, is at present £2. For greyhounds between fourteen months and two years of age, a fee of £3 is required, while greyhounds over two years may be named only by permission of the standing committee and then at a fee of £10.

To tighten up against unscrupulous registrations, in 1966 the Irish Coursing Club introduced earmarking of the left ear, each pup being inspected and earmarked at birth. For naming a greyhound in the Irish Stud Book a fee of £5 is charged and the earmark must be given. A greyhound is not eligible to race under Irish Coursing Club Rules until the owner is in possession of an official certificate of registration.

At the same time (1980) as the new Stud Book identity card came into use, the National Coursing Club issued a new mating certificate and registration of whelping which is completed in triplicate. One copy (a) has to be signed by the owner or his (or her) agent of the stud dog when a mating has taken place and is returned to the NCC, a second copy (b) being held by the stud dog's owner or agent. A third copy (c) is held by the owner of the bitch who fills in details of the litter when they are born. This form is signed by a veterinary surgeon confirming the birth of the litter. A separate form (I) is issued for recording the sex and colour of the whelps including the toe nails on each foot and instructions for earmarking. Form II is for naming the greyhound which is done before placing the dog with a registered racecourse. Form III is for re-registration if transfer of ownership takes place, and form IV is to register a stud dog. Yet another form (V) is for registering a greyhound with the Irish Stud Book.

RE-RUN RACE

A race declared void or no race may be re-run at the same meeting, but at least fifteen minutes must elapse between the no-race declaration and the re-run. If the re-run results in another no race decision, the race shall not be re-run a second time.

The most famous re-run was for the 1931 Greyhound Derby, when Mick the Miller won his third consecutive Derby by more than three lengths only for the result to be called no race because of interference from Ryland R who was disqualified from the re-run. Mick, now almost five years old, could finish only fourth in the re-run, behind Seldom Led, Golden Hammer and Mick's Fancy, three fine greyhounds but dogs which Mick had decisively beaten in the first race. The result caused uproar among those present who thought that the result of the first race should have been allowed to stand, since Mick was unfairly penalized because he was in no way concerned with the offence. In three Derby finals he contested, two were declared 'no race', but in 1929, in the only four-dog final ever contested, Mick was in his prime and in the re-run won by three lengths from Palatinus. This was the dog that caught the hare on the opening night at Wembley eighteen months earlier, and it is only right to mention that in the first race for the 1929 Derby Palatinus won comfortably, with Mick the Miller in second place. *See* No Race.

RESERVE

A greyhound held in reserve to replace a dog which may be withdrawn for some reason, such as illness or injury or a bitch being in season. A reserve is treated as if it were due to run in the race until it is known that it will not be called upon to do so. Reserves may be included for rounds of an open event other than the first, or for the final in which the number of runners is confined to five when the conditions of such a race may provide that one of the remaining greyhounds qualifies to be included as reserve by finishing in a specified place in the previous round. The reserve will occupy the same trap number as the withdrawn dog.

The most famous reserve dog was Rhynn Castle (Castledown Lad) who occupied trap 4 in the 1945 English Derby in place of Kilpeacon Bride who was withdrawn after coming in season. The rank outsider at 20–1 against, Rhynn Castle ran magnificently to take second place to Ballyhennessy Seal, who would have beaten any dog in the world at the time.

RETIRED GREYHOUNDS

Since track racing began, much has been done to find suitable homes for greyhounds when their racing days are over. The best dogs are retired to stud and there is always a demand for a well-bred bitch for breeding when her racing career has ended. Many owners enjoy having their greyhounds about the home for they are mostly of delightful disposition and make excellent companions, but this is not possible for those living in high-rise flats and much is done to raise money so that retired greyhounds can live in kennels in some degree of comfort. Mr Derek Roy was one of the first to open kennels for greyhounds when they had finished racing and had given so much pleasure to so many. More recently the NGRC Retired Greyhound Trust was set up with Miss Gee Lebon as resettlement officer, and the tracks are doing much to help by raising funds. Gee Lebon is also resettlement officer at Southend; this track and Brighton have been notable in their efforts and hold meetings to raise funds for this purpose. Sponsors are willing to put up extra prize money and name a race after a favourite greyhound or in honour of a past champion at the track.

In 1978 the Brighton Greyhound Owners' Association set up its own registered charity trust to care for retired greyhounds, with Mr R.N. Bruce-Lockhard, Mr S. Saxby and Mrs H. Lichfold as trustees. In the first year of its existence homes were found for more than seventy greyhounds and funds were raised to enable others to be placed with recognized kennels. At the famous Deneholme kennels, owned by Mr and Mrs Saxby, many old favourites are found a good home on a non-profit basis, and at a May 1979 meeting the Brighton track raised more than £1,000 for the trust fund. In a letter to the *Greyhound Magazine* in September 1979 Mr Bruce-Lockhart mentions the fine effort of the Brighton kennel girls who, with the help of the assistant racing manager, Philip Grimstone, staged a sponsored walk from the Stadium to their Albourne kennels and collected almost £300 for the trust fund.

Wimbledon is another track where much is done to find homes for old greyhounds. Len Carter spends most of his weekends contacting people who have offered to accommodate a greyhound and taking the dogs to them. At Wimbledon there is now a Len Carter Appreciation Trophy put up by friends who wish to show their appreciation of the excellent work he does, for during the past three or four years he has been able to find good homes for more than 200 greyhounds.

In 1973 the Animal Welfare Trust organized a scheme for finding suitable homes for retired greyhounds. A national committee was set up supported by the NGRC stewards, who made an initial donation of £500. The tracks raise funds by races and various other events.

ROMFORD RACECOURSE *See under* British Greyhound Racecourse.

ROYALTY

An illuminated manuscript in the British Museum dating from the time of Elric, a ninth-century Saxon king of Mercia, shows the chieftain and his huntsmen accompanied by two greyhounds. They were an essential requisite of the royal household, used for hunting hares, deer and wild boar in the royal forests to provide meat for man and dog. A law of King Canute dated 1016 decreed that 'none but a gentleman' should be allowed to keep a greyhound. Presumably only the king's retainers would be given the right to hunt with dogs in the royal domains, and so highly valued were greyhounds that King John would accept them in lieu of taxes. It is recorded that on one occasion he sent 'three red and three black greyhounds and a sorrel-coloured one' to one of his barons, Warren Fitz-Falcon, and it is also recorded that William de Brecosa was given three castles in Monmouthshire by John in return for ten greyhounds. Special favours were also given to those who had the knowledge and the land on which to breed to rear young greyhounds. One John Engayne was given the manor of Upminster in Wiltshire for keeping greyhounds for King John.

Queen Elizabeth I was a keen follower of coursing, and it is recorded that on a visit to Cowdray Park in Sussex in 1591 she watched coursing greyhounds from the turret of the manor after dinner. Charles II was a lover of the breed and had the greyhound incorporated into his seal. Prince Albert was rarely seen in the grounds of Balmoral without his favourite long-haired greyhound Eos, and he commissioned Sir Edwin Landseer to paint the dog in 1841. After Master M'Grath had won the Waterloo Cup for the third time, Queen Victoria commanded that the dog should appear before her at Windsor Castle.

In the present century HRH The Duke of Edinburgh graciously accepted the greyhound Camira Flash on behalf of the Water Rats' Club of Great Britain, so that any winnings and stud fees earned by the dog would go towards the Duke's special Award Scheme fund. The dog was very successful, winning more than £8,000 on the track within two years.

In 1979 His Royal Highness graciously accepted a dog appropriately named Playfield Royal on behalf of the National Playing Fields Association.

See Charities.

RULES OF RACING

There are 184 rules of racing laid down by the NGRC, a copy of which currently costs 50p and can be obtained direct from them (*see* Addresses on p. 388). Every owner, as well as trainers and staff, needs to be in possession of an up-to-date copy. Indeed, it is useful to anyone who attends meetings regularly, for it provides a deeper knowledge of the rules of the sport which makes for greater appreciation of how greyhound racing is conducted on approved tracks.

RUNNING *See* Racing.

RYE HOUSE RACECOURSE *See under* British Greyhound Racecourses.

S

ST LEGER
English St Leger *See under* Classic Events in Great Britain; Irish St Leger *see under* Classic Events in Ireland.

SAPLING

A greyhound is called a sapling from the time weaning has ended, at about five or six months when they have shed their milk teeth, until they start trials at about fourteen months old. It is a term used by breeders but has no official meaning. Officially a greyhound is known as a puppy until the end of the year following the year in which it was whelped.

SATURATION

There is a belief among some breeders that if a bitch is put to one stud dog repeatedly her offspring will become weaker and weaker, a condition known as saturation. Results, however, do not bear this out, and often when a bitch has produced top-class greyhounds from a sire she is returned again and again to that sire or his litter brother. One such instance is the proven mating of Chittering Duchess with Tokio when Bah's Choice was the result of the third or fourth mating of the two. Each time high-class greyhounds were the result, but Bah's Choice was the best of all. The great bitch Bean Dubh was put to Castledown Lad every year from 1936 to 1942 and threw better and better stock from each mating. The last litter, whelped in 1942, produced one of the finest litters of all time, including Griffinstown Lad, Castledown Bridge, Castledown Turn (who broke the 525 yds record at Mullingar), and Castledown Coup, winner of the Irish Laurels in 1943. Rather than becoming weaker, each litter was better and better. Lady Eleanor was repeatedly put to Beef Cutlet and produced champions from each litter, as did Tranquilla from her matings to Inler. If a satisfactory 'nick' in breeding is obtained, it is advisable for the bitch to return to the sire again and again or to one of similar line breeding. This 'nick' in breeding should not be discarded for any reason. It is the secret of breeding good greyhounds.

SCHOOLING

At fourteen months a well-reared greyhound will be ready to start its schooling, when it will be taught to become used to slipping if it is to be coursed or to following a hare on a track. It will, however, not be allowed to take part in official trials until fifteen months old, but if it can be given a little schooling it will come to its first trials knowing something about what is to be expected of it. Begin by asking someone to hold the sapling firmly (the best way is to place its body between one's legs and to hold its shoulders firmly) and for someone whom the dogs knows well to walk about 50 yds away. The dog is released when the person whistles and it will bound off toward towards him. Give the dog two runs a day and gradually increase the distance, using a field or common land for the purpose. Later it may be possible to take one or two saplings to a private track with an inside hare and traps so as to get them used to breaking from the traps quickly. They will then know what it is all about when taken to a track for their first trials with a view to the track accepting the dogs on its racing strength; or the dogs can be placed with a private trainer for open events if they show ability at trials.

Do not be impatient if the dog takes a little time to get used to the traps and to following the hare. At first the hare will be slowed down to enable the dog to keep its eyes on it. Even so, it may show little interest at first and it may be a month or two before it is ready for its first official trials. Even then it may show little form until taken to another track or placed with another trainer. Quickness from the trap is all-important in track racing, for this enables a dog to reach the first turn just in front of the others when it will be clear of bumping and will be well placed to win the race.

SCOTTISH DERBY
See under Classic Events in Great Britain.

SCURRY GOLD CUP
See under Classic Events in Great Britain.

SEAN KELLY OAKS
See under Classic Events in Ireland.

SEEDING

Since 1971 seeding has been in practice in open races – the racing manager has the powers to place the wide runners in traps 5 and 6. These are the outside traps and give a clear run to the greyhounds which prefer to run on the outside and do not usually move in to the rails where there is an inside hare. Though a dog running on the outside has to cover a greater distance around the track, it will often move in on the first bend, crowding the others. This favourable position does give them a decided advantage over those dogs in traps 3 and 4, in the middle positions, and since the idea of seeding was introduced a greyhound from one of the outside traps has been successful on five occasions in the English Derby. In 1971 Supreme Fun, in trap 6, almost beat Dolores Rocket in trap 2, and in 1972 and 1973, Patricia's Hope, seeded in trap 5, won. The 1979 Derby was won by Sarah's Bunny from trap 6, who at the first bend crossed in front of those in traps 3, 4 and 5, causing them to check in their stride while Sarah's Bunny went on unhampered to win the event. In greyhound racing the dogs in the two inside traps and the two outside ones have always won more times than those from traps 3 and 4, and seeding creates the impression of favouritism which is detrimental to greyhound racing. In the 1979 Derby, for example, Sarah's Bunny had the advantage of running from trap 6 in five of the six rounds, while an outstanding tracker like Desert Pilot, having to take his chance by the luck of the draw for the remaining four traps, occupied trap 3 or 4 throughout the event and did well to finish in third place in the final. At the Wimbledon Stadium during the summer of 1979 dogs occupying trap 3 had a losing sequence of thirty races, during which time the dog in that trap was not made favourite on a single occasion, and since Monday's News won the English Derby from trap 3 in 1946 a greyhound occupying trap 3 has won on only three occasions.

As with the law, greyhound racing must be seen to be fair even if it does not always work out as such, otherwise the time will come when it is treated with the contempt it deserves. As Reg Potter, the greyhound correspondent of *Sporting Life,* has said: 'Any Derby winner should be seen to have beaten his opponents on merit and without any advantage conferred by the rules.'

SHAWFIELD RACECOURSE
See under British Greyhound Racecourses.

SHEFFIELD RACECOURSE
See under British Greyhound Racecourses.

SHORTEST ODDS

The biggest favourite (shortest odds-on) to win the English Derby was Entry Badge, quoted at 4–1 on to win the first event of 1927, and he won convincingly. After his Derby win he was made odds-on favourite for every race he ran. For each round of the final for the 1935 Cesarewitch at West Ham, Ataxy was quoted 6–1 on his winning, and did so. So outstanding was Priceless Border that he was quoted 2–1 on his winning the 1948 Derby, which he did, while Balliniska Band was an odds-on favourite to win each of his heats, semi-final and final of the 1977 Derby, and he was never beaten in any round. When Beef Cutlet competed in the first round heats of the 1933 Derby he was 10–1 on his winning and did so, but in the final he was beaten a short head by his great rival, Future Cutlet. In the previous year Future Cutlet was quoted 100–1 against his winning the Derby before the heats began, yet he came within a whisker of doing so, being beaten a neck by Wild Woolley. Before the final Future Cutlet was the 6–4 on favourite!

The biggest odds-on favourite for a classic final was the 6–1 quoted for Endless Gossip on his winning the 1952 Laurels, which he did. Model Dasher was 8–1 on for the final of the 1945 Test, which he won, and Red Wind was 7–1 on for the Puppy Derby of 1949. He won by eight lengths. In a classic event the shortest odds ever were given to Dante at 10–1 on for his heat in the 1947 St Leger, which he won by fourteen lengths. He won his semi-final at 5–1 on and was again at this price in the final. All others were 25–1 against. He won by eight lengths from Shadowlands Delight in 39.70 secs, a new record, with the Oaks winner Rio Capretta a short head behind.

For the Wembley Summer Cup of 1951 Ballylanigan Tanist was quoted 8–1 on and he won in 29.04 secs to equal Bah's Choice when winning the event in 1946. So outstanding was the bitch Queen of the Suir, Beef Cutlet's litter sister, that for the 1933 Coronation Stakes at Wembley she was 5–1 on her winning and she did so.

One of the biggest odds-on favourites for an important event in the history of the sport in Ireland was the 12–1 quoted on Shaggy Lad winning the 1945 Puppy Derby at Harold's Cross, which he did, though in the final the flying Quare Times was running against him. Yet so good was Shaggy Lad, considered by many to have been the fastest greyhound ever to race, that it was almost impossible to place a bet on him. He was quoted 8–1 on for his first round heat. But perhaps the shortest of all odds on a greyhound winning a top-class event was on Knockrour Slave after he had won his first round heat for the Guiness Trophy at Cork in 1979 by thirteen lengths. To win his second heat he was quoted 14–1 on and he won by nine lengths. In the final he was 12–1 on; he won by ten lengths.

SHOWING

A greyhound with its back legs placed well apart and its head held high makes a striking appearance on a show bench, where they have enjoyed considerable popularity in recent years since Treetops Golden Falcon was declared Supreme Champion at Crufts in 1956. This was the first time a greyhound has won the coveted award. At stud he passed on his outstanding qualities to several of his offspring, especially to a grandson, Champion Shaunvalley Cavalier, who won ten challenge certificates.

Greyhounds were to the fore in the early days of showing, going back almost 100 years, when dogs owned by Dr Salter, Mr Harding Cox and Tom Ashton gained many awards; the last of these was the owner of the champion bitch Jenny Jones, who contested the Waterloo Cup in 1888 only to be defeated by the redoubtable Herschel who had divided the Cup the previous year. Another famous show champion bitch was Annie Laurie, owned by Mr Sheldon of Sheffield who bred more than one litter from Herschel and each time after returned her to the show ring to continue her successes.

Several top-class trackers have distinguished themselves in the show ring, especially in the early days of the sport, and all have been brindles. The fine, upstanding Bill Elkin was the first show winner, then came Junior Classic and Future Cutlet, both track stars and dogs of magnificent proportions. It was not generally realized at the time that the 1952 winner of the Greyhound Derby, the flying Endless Gossip, also held a number of challenge certificates which is rare for a greyhound in training which must carry no extra weight and will be more 'drawn down' than a dog kept solely for show purposes. A show dog will be exercised just enough to maintain its fitness so that its attractively rounded contours will immediately catch the judge's eye.

To enter a greyhound for a show held under the auspices of the Kennel Club it must first be registered with the Club. This presents no difficulty if the dog has previously been registered with the English or Irish Stud Book, which will hold its full pedigree. The Kennel Club, which registers all pedigree breeds, was founded in 1873 and in 1874 the first Pedigree Book was introduced, containing over 4,000 entries. Each breed has it own club and holds what are known as limited shows, held for club members only; also open shows and championship events where challenge certificates are awarded to the best dog and bitch. An animal has to win three certificates in front of three different judges before it becomes a champion.

With its soft, sleek coat, a greyhound given regular grooming can be kept in show condition even in a confined space and makes an excellent house pet and companion when its racing days are over; alternatively an outhouse will make a suitable kennel if filled with plenty of straw for winter warmth and containing a bench of simple construction for the dog to sleep on. A show greyhound can be exercised around the streets of any town on a lead; it needs open spaces to chase around only when young.

If taking a greyhound to a show do not overfeed it or it may get car-sick. Some dogs travel well, others do not. Always arrive at the show in plenty of time to attend to final preparations such as grooming, and see that the dog has a warm coat for the journey and a thin leather collar and lead. Do not use a chain at the show ring. Above all, make certain that you understand the rules, for any laxity in this respect may cause the elimination of what might have been a certificate winner. If taking a bitch, make sure she is not in season.

See Points of a Greyhound.

SIRE

A dog becomes a sire when he has served a bitch and produced a litter through her; the offspring will be endowed with the characteristics of both parents, their good qualities and their bad ones; or of those of the grand- and great grandparents. Some sires have made their excellent qualities felt for many future generations — for instance, Mutton Cutlet, Creamery Border, Inler, Macoma and Castledown Lad of nearly fifty years ago, whose progeny continue to provide the sport with the champions of today.

In the history of the sport certain sires have been able to transmit to their offspring, through dams of certain blood lines, more outstanding qualities than would normally have been expected of them. This is due to the blood lines of sire and dam, when coming together, proving most potent. All other factors being equal, such as good rearing and freedom of the offspring from serious illness and injury, the result will be a litter of above-average quality, with perhaps one or more of them capable of winning classic events in top company. This, however, will not be a guarantee that a dog will prove as outstanding a sire as his own sire, though he may be if mated to bitches of certain blood lines. This may take several years to show itself and not until then will the value of the dog as a sire be confirmed.

Greyhound breeders are forever on the look-out for a sire bred from parents of proven ability on the race track, but most important from parents who themselves were the result of certain 'nicks' in breeding, and it is this factor which has produced the champions of greyhound racing.

The first of the great prepotent sires was Mutton Cutlet and his sire Jamie, together with Melksham Tom, for each of them produced high-class greyhounds from almost every bitch put to them. Mutton Cutlet was by Jamie out of Miss Cinderella and was born and bred in the famous coursing kennels of Major McCalmont in the Cotswolds. The dog was whelped in March 1921 and after contesting the Waterloo Cup of 1923, 1924 and 1925 without success was sold to Mr T.A. Morris, keeper of the Irish Greyhound Stud Book, who believed that the dog possessed all the attributes of a top-class sire. How right he was. Perhaps if Tom Morris had not shown this interest in the dog Mutton Cutlet might have spent his last years as someone's pet on a Cotswold farm, siring no pups at all, or he might even have been put down at the end of his coursing days. At first the dog was at stud for several years at a fee of 10 gns and served few bitches, yet when he died in November 1934 at thirteen years and eight months he had sired 522 winners on the race track and coursing field, and his progeny were sent out to all parts of the world wherever greyhounds were coursed or raced.

Mutton Cutlet's dam Miss Cinderella was a bitch whose pedigree can be traced back to the Waterloo Cup winner Farndon Ferry. His sire Jamie was also sire of Dasher Lad, in turn sire of several great dams including Dashing Comet, dam of Model Dasher; and of Hautley, sire of the great Wild Woolley. Jamie also sired Five of Hearts, winner of the 1929 Cesarewitch, and of Dicentra, dam of the great coursing dog Dee Rock, who was to win the Waterloo Cup in his third season. This he did after surviving the most gruelling courses in the earlier rounds which would have finished all but the most stout-hearted of dogs. Dee Rock was to sire an equally great coursing dog, Swinging Light. Jamie also passed on his qualities to many a fine greyhound through the female line and was also sire of Baffle, whose daughter Constellation (bought by Mr Cronopolos for 5 gns) produced the Waterloo Cup winner Countryman. Indeed Jamie's influence on both track and coursing field in the 1920s was enormous. Truly it can be said of him that he was father of the first track champions including Entry Badge, the first English Derby winner, though he was only an average performer himself.

Mr Tom Morris, owner of Mutton Cutlet, always preferred to use a good coursing dog as a sire for his bitches for he believed they possessed extra gameness and stamina; only those who survived the most strenuous courses were used for stud purposes. Among the early sires, besides Jamie and Mutton Cutlet there was Danielli, sire of the great stayer Train, and of Chancellor and Tokio. Danielli had almost as great an influence on coursing and track racing as had Jamie, for of his sons Tokio was to become sire of the great Bah's Choice and Chancellor sired Countryman, who won the Waterloo Cup as a puppy in 1943.

Mutton Cutlet's sons included several greyhounds endowed with and able to pass on many of his own attributes as a sire. These qualities were stamina and stout-hearted running, combined with track sense and gameness. Of these sons the best were perhaps Beef Cutlet, Border Mutton and Mr Moon. Mr Moon was to become sire of the even greater Ballynennan Moon, and Beef Cutlet sired Epinard and the bitch Winnie of Berrow, who when put to Dutton Swordfish whelped the great Narrogar Ann, one of only four bitches ever to win the Greyhound Derby. Beef Cutlet's litter sister was Queen of the Suir, among the half dozen or so fastest bitches in the history of the sport. This litter brother and sister were from a mating with Burette, whose sire was Melksham Tom.

Border Mutton was one of the last of Mutton Cutlet's sons and one of his greatest. He enjoyed a popularity almost equal to that of Mick the Miller, whom he succeeded, for he possessed his gameness and wonderful trackcraft. He was as good over hurdles as on the flat and was sire of Country Life, winner of the Scurry Gold Cup and who was beaten only a short head by Burhill Moon in the 1945 Laurels final. Beef Cutlet's sons included Jesmond Cutlet, later to become sire of Magic Bohemian who set up a new national record at White City when covering the 525 yds course in 29.11 secs; and the litter brothers Junior Classic and Juvenile Classic, two of the finest racing greyhounds ever. Nor should it be forgotten that Beef Cutlet was sire of the bitch Friar Tuck, dam of the great Trev's Perfection and of Winnie of Berrow, dam of Narrogar Ann who, from a mating with Priceless Border, whelped the 1952 Derby winner Endless Gossip. When mated to Castle Yard he produced Sally's Gossip, dam of those outstanding sires Sally's Yarn and Printer's Prince, the latter from her mating with Hi There. Sally's Yarn was to sire the Callanan Cup winner Finola's Yarn, and Printer's Prince sired the world's fastest, Yellow Printer, and Newdown Heather, who was to become the greatest sire of his generation, parent of Dolores Rocket, the fastest track bitch ever to race.

Newdown Heather shares with Mutton Cutlet, Castledown Lad and Hi There, his grand sire, the distinction of being one of the most famous sires in the history of track racing and the coursing field too. A black and white dog, he was born in January 1964 at the kennels of Miss B. O'Reilly at Mullingar, Co. Westmeath. His sire was Printer's Prince and his dam Pardee, whose own dam was Manhattan Heiress, also owned by Miss O'Reilly. Newdown Heather first contested the Puppy Cup at Dunmore Park, which he won, and was then purchased jointly by Mr George Posnett and Mrs Kathleen McKee. The price paid was said to be £600 and within days they were offered ten times that sum for their young dog. All credit is due to them for not yielding to the temptation to earn a quick and handsome profit, and they were never to rue their decision. In May 1966 the dog was taken to England to take part in the White City Derby trials but broke a toe which had to be removed and he took no part in the event. His injury all but finished his career. Returning to Ireland, he was third in the National Sprint but pulled up lame, and was immediately retired to stud, to stand at the kennels of Mr Jack Mullan at Newry. Within two years the successes of his progeny on the coursing field and track passed the achievements of even his grand sire Hi There. The first coursing season in which his stock competed was 1969 when Tender Heather won the coursing Derby and Tender Honey the Oaks. For the trial stakes for the two events, he was sire of thirty-three winners. In 1971 he was able to improve upon this amazing performance, for he had thirty-four runners in the coursing Derby which was won by his son Hack up Fenian out of the bitch Hack 'em Nell. Her dam, Hack up Nell, was a daughter of Champion Prince, whose sire was the one-time Mullingar champion Castledown Lad. Winner of the 1971 coursing Oaks was Tearaway Bess, also sired by Newdown

Heather, out of the bitch Penny Biscuit.

But it was not only on the coursing field that Newdown Heather's stock carried off so many awards. On the track he was equally successful. One of his first sons was Winter Hope, who like his sire won the 1969 Puppy Cup at Dunmore Park and the Puppy Derby at Wimbledon, while April Flower won the Irish Cesarewitch at Navan. The following year Moordyke Spot ran through the Pall Mall at Harringay undefeated, and after winning more than £500 in that year was elected champion greyhound for 1970. Then came Crefogue Flash, winner of the Wimbledon Puppy Derby, and Dolores Rocket, the wonder bitch of 1971, winner of the English Derby and St Leger. Another of his progeny was Super Fun who, on his first run at Dungannon over 325 yds, set a new record with a time of 18.03 secs. Afterwards he was purchased for a four-figure sum by Mr Harry Gover of Southend from his owner, Mr McLean of Ballymena. Renamed Supreme Fun, he was beaten into second place in the 1971 English Derby by Dolores Rocket by half a length. Of the six finalists, five had been sired by Newdown Heather. Thus once again Mutton Cutlet, through his son Beef Cutlet, combined with the blood lines of Hi There, had made his influence felt in producing the finest of modern coursing and racing greyhounds.

Almost all the great sires of modern track racing have originated from Mutton Cutlet and it is interesting to note that Mutton Cutlet had a fourth generation cross of Farndon Ferry blood in his pedigree, a cross which appears frequently in the pedigree of the finest greyhounds. This is the time it takes to bring out the genetic qualities of the parents. Spectre II, and his litter brother Tric Trac who died young, will serve as examples. Their sire was the peerless Crazy Parachute, son of Hi There, who in turn was sired by Slaney Record, his sire being Rare Record out of the Mutton Cutlet bitch Olympic Cutlet. Hi There was also sire of Prairie Flash, sire of the 1968 Derby winner Camira Flash; and of Powerstown Prospect, a St Leger winner who in turn sired Trojan Silver, dam of the 1970 English Derby winner John Silver.

Hi There was born in the kennels of Mr A. Nugent in 1952. A red dog, he possessed tremendous speed on the track, winning the Irish National Sprint and the Wembley Spring Cup before being retired to stud, having been only lightly raced. His sire was Slaney Record, whose sire was Rare Record. One of his first daughters was Gurteen Scamp, Oaks winner in 1959, and Crazy Parachute (from a mating with Mad Prospect) followed. After a short career on the track Crazy Parachute was to become as great a sire as Hi There. Later Hi There was to sire Prairie Flash, winner of the 1961 Cesarewitch from a 1959 mating with Prairie Peg; and Greenane Wonder, a litter brother. Hi There died in 1967; Prairie Flash and Crazy Parachute in 1969.

Dee Chime, Rare Record's sire, was litter brother to the great Dee Rock and was bred from the dam Dicentra, whose sire, like that of Mutton Cutlet, was Jamie. Thus on both sides of Rare Record's pedigree he had Jamie as his grand sire, and the most prepotent of modern sires, Hi There, had a pedigree which combined the greatest of all sires of the early history of greyhound racing.

Rare Record was also sire of Good Record who, when mated to Mad Tanist, became the mother of Sandown Champion, winner of the 1950 Irish Coursing Derby and the Easter Cup and sire of the Derby winner Paul's Fun. Through the Printer bitch Cleopatra he was to sire Galtee Cleo, who ran up in the 1953 English Derby and who in turn was sire of Knockhill Chieftan. He (Knockhill Chieftan) was a fourth generation cross of Tanist on both his sire's and dam's side, and he too was one of the greatest of modern sires. Bred in the purple, his great grand sires were Mad Tanist (on both sire's and dam's side), Printer and Well Squared, famous sires of the 1940s; Printer was by Creamery Border, Well Squared by Stockwell Street.

Mr L. McNair's Knockhill Chieftain was a brindle, born in 1955; he died in 1968 aged thirteen. His sire Galtee Cleo finished second in the 1953 Derby and Knockhill Chieftain was one of his first sons. Knockhill Chieftain was to sire several of the fastest greyhounds ever to race, including Oregon Prince, second in the 1961 English Derby, and who in turn was sire of Carry on Oregon and Pool's Punter. Booked Out, sire of Booked Six, was another of his sons, as was Hack up Chieftain, the outsider who won the 1964 English Derby. Knockhill Chieftain

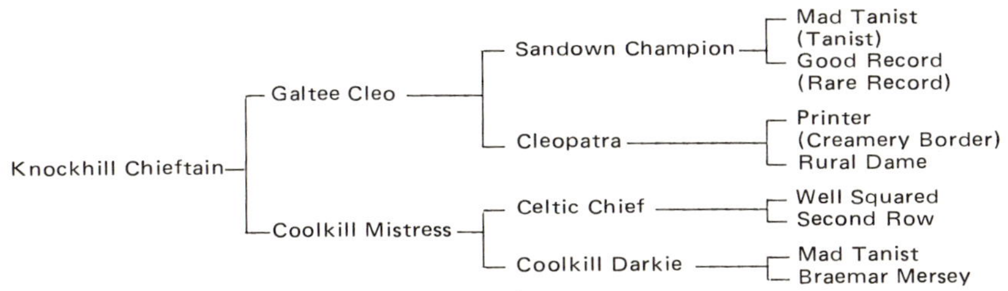

was also sire of Maryville Hi, through Hi Hook, litter sister to Prairie Flash and of one of the greatest bitches of all time, Cranog Bet, winner of the English Oaks in 1963 and 1964. He was also sire of Come on Dolores, dam of Dolores Rocket from a mating with Newdown Heather. Thus once again a combination of the Tanist—Castledown Lad blood lines had produced an outstanding star of greyhound racing.

Several of the fastest of all track runners figure in Knockhill Chieftain's pedigree, including Tanist and his son Mad Tanist and his son Sandown Champion; also Printer, Creamery Border, Well Squared and Celtic Chief, all of whom were like lightning from the traps.

Crazy Parachute was one of the most successful sires of modern times for he sired winners from almost every bitch he served and perpetuated the outstanding qualities of his sire, Hi There. Among his sons were Poor Mick, one of the greatest marathon performers of all time; Ambiguous, the 1968 Laurels winner; Val's Parachute, who won on fourteen different tracks; Forward King, winner of the 1968 St Leger and Wembley Gold Cup; Tric Trac and Spectre II, first and second in the 1967 Derby; Con's Duke, winner of over £4,000 in prize money and of the important Wembley Spring Cup and Summer Cup; Shane's Rocket, winner of the 1968 Gold Collar at Catford; and Monalee Champion, who took over from Crazy Parachute as the most prepotent of Hi There's grandsons. Though it was chiefly through his sons that Crazy Parachute made his influence felt, he was also sire of the 1968 Oaks winner Shady Parachute and of Kitty True, dam of Own Pride, winner of the Irish Derby in 1969.

Monalee Champion, from the mating of Crazy Parachute with Sheila at Last was to become one of the greatest sires in the history of track racing. During the 1970s almost all the champions were either of his breeding or were offspring of his half brother Spectre II, a son of Crazy Parachute out of the dam Supreme Witch. Monalee Champion's sons include Itsachampion, winner of the Guinness 600 at Shelbourne Park and the McAlevey Gold Cup at Celtic Park, and sire of Lacca Champion; Linda's Champion, Irish Derby winner of 1977; Tain Mor, winner of 1976; Jimsun, winner of the 1974 English Derby, and in turn sire of the 1979 winner Sarah's Bunny; Wired to the Moon, a Scurry Cup winner; Miles Apart; Here Sonny; and many others.

Spectre II, another of the outstanding sires of the 1970s and one of the great litter that included Tric Trac and Forward King, was sire of Tartan Khan, English Derby winner of 1975; Rita's Choice, Irish Derby runner-up of 1973 and in turn sire of Nameless Star, winner of the 1976 Laurels and St Leger; Glin Bridge; Stormy Spirit, winner of the 1977 English St Leger; and many others, each of whom is now sire of the finest greyhounds of the 1980s. Both Spectre and Monalee Champion have Crazy Parachute as their sire, who had Hi There as his sire and the Mad Tanist bitch Mad Prospect as his dam. The dam of Mad Prospect was Caledonian Desire from Manhattan Midnight by Creamery Border, who is still making his presence felt as a great sire of the 1930s and 1940s, second only to Mutton Cutlet in the early years of greyhound racing.

As we have seen, Hi There was also sire of Sally's Yarn and Printer's Prince, sire of Newdown Heather; so he must be acknowledged as one of the great foundation sires of greyhound racing in the past twenty years. He was from a mating of Slaney Record with the bitch Dublin Red, possibly the most important mating in the recent history of the sport. First it was Mutton Cutlet and Burette, then Macoma with Lady Eleanor and Wonderful Expression. Later came the mating of Winnie of Berrow with Dutton Swordfish which produced Narrogar Ann, dam of Endless Gossip; followed by that of Tanist and Mad Darkie; then Slaney Record with Dublin Red.

Almost as famous a sire as Mutton Cutlet, and one upon whom modern track racing was founded, was Melksham Tom, who through his son Other Days was to have so great an influence in the sport. Other Days was sire of Brillant Bob, one of the greatest performers of all time on track and coursing field and himself sire of the fastest bitches of the late 1930s, who in turn passed on the wonderful qualities of sire and grand sire to their offspring. Other Days was also sire of the famous dam Banriogan Dann, who when mated with Mutton Cutlet's son Mr Moon whelped the great Ballynennan Moon. Mr Moon was one of the greatest of the early sires; when he was mated to the Irish Oaks winner Rebel Music Mad, the litter included Rebel Light, one of the greatest of Irish coursing dogs, who won the coursing Derby in his first season and the next year the International and Connaught Cup. In his thirty-one courses Rebel Light was never led. Melksham Tom's greatest son was Melksham Nobody, sire of the 1944 Irish Derby winner Clonbonny Bridge, and of the 1946 Scottish Derby winner Latin Pearl.

It is interesting to look at the pedigree on his sire's side of one of the champions of recent years, the 1970 Derby winner John Silver. His breeding is impeccable and he was the result of a fusion of the greatest racing greyhound blood since the sport began fifty years ago. The number of outstanding sires in John Silver's pedigree would have been expected to produce a long line of champion stock, and it did. On his sire's (Faithful Hope) side are Castledown Lad, Bella's Prince, Champion Prince and Solar Prince; on the dam's male side Inler, Tanist, Mad Tanist, Grand Champion and The Grand Fire, representing a period of some forty years. The same sires figure in the pedigree of Prairie Peg, dam of Prairie Flash, sire of Camira Flash, Albany and Clomoney Jet; and of Pigalle Wonder from her mating with Champion Prince, the latter being sire of Northern King, sire of Himalayan Climber, the Waterloo Cup winner.

A look through the Derby finalists will show those which were the most effective at stud. In the first six years of the event none – and this included Mick the Miller – was very successful at stud, though the speed and intelligence of Mick were passed on through his litter brother Macoma through Lone Seal and the two outstanding bitches Lady Eleanor, dam of Junior Classic, and Wonderful Expression, dam of Grosvenor Bob and Grosvenor Edwin. Neither Future Cutlet nor Wild Woolley sired more than one or two good greyhounds, but Beef Cutlet, who ran up to Future Cutlet in 1933, was able to pass on his qualities and those of his sire, Mutton Cutlet, to many dogs and bitches, perhaps the most important being Winnie of Berrow, dam of Narrogar Ann, dam of Endless Gossip, who in turn was sire of Sally's Gossip, dam of Sally's Yarn, sire of Newdown Heather.

Of the 1934 Derby finalists it was Brilliant Bob through the female line who was the greatest success at stud. For a decade at least almost every bitch sired by the great classic winner produced outstanding racing greyhounds, usually on the female side. Of the 1938 finalists Manhattan Midnight, who did not finish owing to a broken hock, was the biggest success at stud. A son of Creamery Border, he passed on to his sons and daughters the amazing pace of his sire. He was to sire Caledonian Desire, dam of Mad Prospect from a mating with Mad Tanist, who in turn was dam of Crazy Parachute from a mating with Hi There.

Neither Ballyhennessy Seal nor Monday's News, two of the finest of all Derby winners, produced anything of note, but one dog, Celtic Chief, who appeared in both their finals, was to sire just one bitch who was to perpetuate his name. This was Coolkill Mistress, who from a mating to the Derby runner up of 1953, Galtee Cleo, was to sire Knockhill Chieftain, sire of the flying Oregon Prince, sire of Carry on Oregon and of Kilmagoura Again. The latter, from a mating with the Pigalle Wonder bitch More Wonder, whelped Kilmagoura Fair, dam of the flying bitch Kilmagoura Mist, winner of the 1978 Oaks and 1979 St Leger. She was from a mating to Yanka Boy and her pedigree contains most of the important sires and dams of modern times. One of the latter was Glittering Millie by Glittering Look, who was also sire of Burleigh's Fancy, dam of Oregon Prince from her mating with

Knockhill Chieftain. The Grand Fire, sire of Millie Hawthorn, was also sire of Survival, while the sire of Solar Prince and Pigalle Wonder, both outstanding sires in their own right, was Champion Prince. He was by Bella's Prince, son of Castledown Lad. Mad Tanists's son The Grand Champion, sire of The Grand Fire, was also sire of Prairie Peg, sire of Pigalle Wonder, and Prairie Peg's dam was Prairie Vixen, born from a mating of Astra's Son and Tae Murex. From the pedigree of Kilmagoura Mist is will readily be acknowledged that blood does count in greyhound breeding. To substantiate this still further, perhaps the fastest dog of recent years was Don't Gambol, twice winner of the Scurry Gold Cup and who finished second at his third attempt. His parents were Prairie Flash and One for Minnie, whose sire was the world's fastest, Oregon Prince, while Hi There was the sire of Prairie Flash. Hi There established himself as one of the fastest ever when winning the National Sprint in 1954, so that the combination of these flying machines could be expected to produce something equally outstanding. It did.

Oregon Prince's sire, Knockhill Chieftain, was also sire of the great bitch Cranog Bet, twice winner of the English Oaks and who was dam of Itsamint, winner of the Irish Oaks, and in turn dam of Itsastar, dam of Nameless Pixie, who won the Irish Oaks in 1979. Celtic Chief was to play an important part in modern greyhound racing through his daughter Coolkill Mistress and her son Knockhill Chieftain, who was one of the most important sires of recent years. Knockhill Chieftain's mating with the Glittering Look bitch Don't Bet produced Cranog Bet who, when mated to Monalee Champion, gave Itsachampion, a star in his own right and who in turn sired the 1978 English Derby winner Lacca Champion, surely destined to become one of the most successful sires of the 1980s. Knockhill Chieftain was also sire of Motel Chief, sire of Sabrina, dam of the 1977 Welsh Derby winner Instant Gambler.

The winner of the 1947 Derby, Trev's Perfection, produced nothing of note in Britain but he left for America with his owner soon after his retirement from racing. Third in the Derby of that year however was Slaney Record, as we have seen sire of Hi There, sire of Crazy Parachute, sire of Monalee Champion and of Spectre II, sire of Rita's Choice and Tain Mor. Slaney Record (by Rare Record) was the first of a long line of the most prepotent sires in the history of greyhound racing, each able to transmit the powers of the other to almost every bitch they mated and which was to improve the quality of greyhound racing throughout Britain and Ireland as at no other time in the sport's history.

Surprisingly, neither Priceless Border nor Local Interprize, first and second in 1948 and two of the fastest ever, produced no stock of any merit apart from Endless Gossip, the result of a mating between Priceless Border and the 1949 winner, Narrogar Ann. Their son was also to win the Derby and left behind Sally's Gossip to perpetuate his name and that of his illustrious parents. Sally's Gossip was dam of Printer's Prince, sire of Newdown Heather and Yellow Printer, the world's fastest greyhound.

In the same litter that produced Endless Gossip was the dog Explosive Gilbert. He raced but little and his only claim to fame as a sire (and it is an important one) is through his daughter Barbara Joan, for she was dam of July Joan, in turn dam of Bright Lad who in recent years has been one of Ireland's most successful sires. He was sire of the Waterloo Cup winner Minnesota Miller; more recently the English St Leger finalist Dangerous Lad; the Gold Collar finalist, Knockrour Brandy and many other champion greyhounds.

Galtee Cleo ran up to Daws Dancer in the 1953 Derby and was to sire Knockhill Chieftain, as we have seen, but the next three years saw only Barrowside sire any worthwhile stock. Ford Spartan, an outstanding tracker, left nothing as good as he was, but in 1957 came Pigalle Wonder who with The Grand Fire and Brilliant Bob was the greatest of all sires of bitches who were able to pass on the tremendous speed of their sires. Pigalle Wonder was also sire of several outstanding dogs in Russian Gun and Wonder Valley, the former being sire of An Tain, dam of Tain Mor, 1976 Irish Derby winner, but it was through the female line that Pigalle Wonder's amazing speed was passed on though Russian Gun won the Irish Derby in 1967 and ran up to Yellow Printer the following year.

Though he reached the Derby final in three successive years, Mile Bush Pride made no impact at stud even though he was sired by The Grand Champion, sire of The Grand Fire, of Prairie Peg, and of Pardee, dam of Newdown Heather. Mile Bush Pride's litter sister was Witching Grand, dam of Supreme Witch, dam of Tric Trac and Spectre II. Thus both from his record on the track and from his breeding it would have seemed that he was set for a brilliant career at stud. But this was not so. Third in that Derby final, however, only a neck and a short head behind the first two, was a dog who was destined to become one of the great sires of all time, Crazy Parachute. His exploits at stud through the bitches Sheila at Last and Witching Grand are unique in the annals of greyhound racing.

The 1960 Derby final was won by the outsider Duleek Dandy; the co-favourite and Laurels winner Clonalvy Pride finished last, some twelve lengths behind the winner, but at stud he was to become a champion, one of the greatest of all sires, whose influence is being felt to this day. He was sire of Glenogue, grand dam of the Derby winner Jimsun and, most important of all, of Yanka Boy, sire of Dark Mercury, sire of the 1979 Irish Derby winner Penny County. Yanka Boy was also sire of Itsastar, dam of Nameless Star and Nameless Pixie, winner of the 1979 Irish Oaks. In addition he sired the 1978 English Oaks winner Kilmagoura Mist, who also won the 1979 St Leger. All these outstanding greyhounds, the champions of 1978 and 1979, were bitches. After Monalee Champion, Yanka Boy has perhaps been the most important sire of racing greyhounds of the past decade.

Clonalvy Pride, when mated to Cricket Dance, produce Westmead County, sire of Westmead Champ, winner of the 1976 St Leger and Gold Collar; and with Always a Rebel he sired Always Proud, Irish Derby winner of 1966, who in turn sired Own Pride who won the Irish Derby and St Leger in 1969.

From the 1961 Derby until the 1967 event, when Tric Trac and Spectre II finished first and second, no Derby finalist made any impact as a sire. Tric Trac died young, shortly after resuming stud duties, but since 1970 Spectre II has, with Monalee Champion, been supreme in producing champions from almost every bitch he mated. His sons, and it was mostly on the male side that he fathered such outstanding stock, have already been discussed. Another of the 1967 finalists to prove himself as a sire was Silver Hope, sire of Patricia's Hope, Derby winner of 1972 and 1973, and other top-class greyhounds. John Silver produced little of note but of the 1971 finalists several have since made their name as sires, among them Cobbler, Moordyke Champion and Ivy Hall Flash. Patricia's Hope has been a disappointment as a sire, but Forest Noble and Black Banjo (Spectre II) of the 1973 finalists have sired some excellent greyhounds and Jimsun, Derby winner in 1974, sired Sarah's Bunny, winner in 1979 and other top-class greyhounds.

One sire who took no part in an English Derby final was Odd Venture, but his name recurs many times in the pedigree of the best modern greyhounds. He was sire of Shandaroba, dam of Russian Gun, sire of An Tain, and he was sired by Glittering Look, also sire of Glittering Millie, dam of Millie Hawthorn, and of Don't Bet, dam of Cranog Bet. Nor must we forget that it was Odd Venture who sired Yellow Streak, from a mating with The Grand Fire bitch Shane's Judy. Yellow Streak was to whelp Yellow Printer, the fastest since Quare Times, from a mating to Printer's Prince. Odd Venture was also sire of Dear Millie, dam of Don't Gambol, twice winner of the Scurry Gold Cup and who in turn was sire of the flying Daemonic Gambol.

In 1961 Palm's Printer won the Derby, but it was Oregon Prince, the runner-up, who was of greater importance at stud. He was to sire Kilmagoura Again, sire of Kilmagoura Fair, dam of the Oaks and St Leger winner Kilmagoura Mist; and One for Minnie, dam of the twice Scurry Cup winner Don't Gambol. He was also sire of Carry on Oregon, who won the Scurry Cup in 1967; and of Pool's Punter, who won the Irish St Leger. It is interesting that Glittering Look was also sire of Burleigh's Fancy, dam of Oregon Prince.

Solar Prince was sire of Supreme Witch, dam of Tric Trac, Spectre II and Forward King. The Mad Tanist mating with Could be Worse resulted in The Grand Champion, sire of The Grand Fire which perpetuated the Mad Tanist (Tanist) blood through a number of outstanding dams. Tanist, at one time the fastest of all greyhounds and winner of the 1940 Irish Derby, produced from a mating to Daring Lady the 1947 Irish Derby winner Daring Flash, and from a mating with Smartly There the flying Smartly Fergus. But it was from his mating to Mad Darkie that he produced Astra and Mad Tanist, through which his excellent qualities were perpetuated. Astra and Mad Tanist in turn were to pass on Tanist's great speed from the traps, which, combined with the staying power of the Castledown Lad blood, resulted in the champions of the next generation. Astra, when put to Paddy the Champion (Castledown Lad—Brilliant Gay), produced Astra's Son, sire of Prairie Vixen, dam of Prairie Peg, while Mad Tanist had as great an influence on modern breeding as any other sire. This was especially so in the female line, for he was sire of Mad Prospect, dam of Crazy Parachute and of The Grand Champion, in turn sire of the great bitch Clomoney Grand and of Millie Hawthorn, dam of Faithful Hope. In the Irish Coursing and Racing Calendar for 31 March 1951 Mad Tanist, then nine years old, was standing at a fee of 50 gns; likewise his son Sandown Champion and the equally great sire Bella's Prince. Bah's Choice and Priceless Border were also available at a fee of 50 gns, and Imperial Dancer and Monday's News stood at 30 gns. In fact Man Tanist's mating with Quare Fire produced The Grand Fire, who had more influence in modern breeding through the female line than any other sire since Brilliant Bob.

In looking for a suitable sire, and the availability of a particular sire at the time a bitch comes in season will have to be taken into consideration, one should consider not only the stud fee one is able to pay but suitable blood lines. As we have seen, a sire with the combined blood of Castledown Lad and Rare Record mated with a bitch of Tanist—Creamery Border breeding has produced the modern champions and these 'nicks' continue to give outstanding results. The Grand Fire bitches mated to Hi There and Grand Champion sires are what to look for when choosing a sire. But it may be a decided advantage to select a sire of classic breeding but which was retired to stud at an early age because of injury. The dog will not have been over-raced and, as he may be one of the same litter as a champion or Derby winner, will possess the correct blood lines. He will not be serving as many bitches as the dog who has made a household name as a classic winner and who may be serving two or more bitches each week. A consistently winning dog may have been kept in training for too long a period simply because he has been so successful, and when at last he is retired to stud his reproductive powers may have been seriously impaired. Most of the best of stud dogs through the years have been asked to prove themselves on track or coursing field and then have been immediately retired to stud. It is profitable to put a champion to stud at a fee of £100 and for the dog to serve two bitches each week. A dog of classic breeding who has proved himself on the track or coursing field will be widely patronized, especially if he is fathering large litters of big-boned pups which turn out to be champions like himself. His fee can then be increased. A sire that is well cared for during his life and who has been retired to stud early, perhaps at four or even earlier, may well have eight years left at stud, during which time he could earn £50,000 in fees. That Mick the Miller, Ballynennan Moon, Junior Classic and Future Cutlet were comparative failures at stud could be due to their long and successful racing careers. Creamery Border was still siring top-class greyhounds at fourteen, and Hi There was nearly fifteen. Age does not matter provided the sire is fit and continues to father good-sized litters of big-boned puppies.

Greyhound racing and breeding in England and Ireland are made easier owing to the small size of the two countries. The tracks are within easy reach of most large towns and a bitch can be taken to a stud dog without much trouble or expense. One may therefore select whichever sire is available and most suitable for one'e bitch. The question of weight may be a factor. It was the opinion of Stonehenge that evenly-sized litters were produced by evenly-sized parents, that a bitch should be 55—60 lbs and the sire 70—75 lbs. It is preferable to use for breeding a bitch of not less than 50 lbs weight and a sire of not less than 65 lbs, or their offspring may also be small. A bitch of 50—55 lbs should be put to a dog of not less than 68 lbs to ensure good-sized pups, but where sire and bitch are of more even size, so much the better. Mad Tanist weighed

65 lbs when at stud and Jubilee Time only 60 lbs. Trev's Perfection weighed 68 lbs; Bella's Prince and Sandown Champion 70 lbs; Paddy the Champion and Bah's Choice 76 lbs; and Spanish Lad and Smartly Fergus were 80 lbs. Confey Castle, son of Smartly Fergus, weighed 86 lbs and was one of the biggest dogs ever at stud. Joint Command, the Waterloo Cup finalist, was of the same weight. More recently Deneholme Hunter weighs 68 lbs, Forward King 73 lbs, Orwell High and Rockfield Era 76 lbs. Carry on Oregon weighed 80 lbs and was in every sense a giant, both in his performances and in his bone structure, which he passed on to his offspring. But most dogs at stud weigh 68–74 lbs, a little more than when racing, and this seems to be the ideal weight, but a dog must possess all the right qualities in his make-up and especially a calm temperament. An excitable dog rarely makes a good stud dog.

If you own a dog at stud register him with both the English and Irish Stud Books so that bitches mated to him and their offspring can be registered with either Stud Book without incurring a transfer fee. The cost of registering a stud dog with the Irish Stud Book is currently £20, with the National Coursing Club £15.

There will be other points to consider before deciding to which stud dog to take your bitch. If your bitch was fast from the traps but could not stay too well you would select a dog with stamina and staying power and vice versa. However most stud dogs of the past twenty years have possessed both quickness from the traps and plenty of stamina, a combination of the Inler–Creamery Border blood lines, through Tanist and Printer with the stamina of Castledown Lad and Rare Record. Into this category came Newdown Heather, Spectre II, Movealong Santa and Yanka Boy, the most important sires of the past decade whose sons are now standing at stud with equal success.

If your bitch is somewhat short in the back, select a dog with a long, shapely back like Pigalle Wonder and his son Russian Gun, in the hope that the pups will inherit this characteristic. Good feet are important to a racing greyhound, so avoid any sire with splayed feet. The offspring of Hi There, Pigalle Wonder and Newdown Heather were all born with the strong arched toes of their sire even when the bitch they served had less desirable toes.

It is also important to decide whether you want to rear your own litter (or putting them out to a farmer) with a view to their racing, or for sale at eight to twelve weeks soon after they have been weaned. If the latter their sire should be well known, particularly in your district. Pups from a classic winner will always make more money than those from a litter brother of the same breeding which may have been put to stud early because of injury and whose stock may well perform better than from the champion. But in selling it is the name that counts, and each dog pup will usually be worth the stud fee with bitches slightly less even though they may turn out better.

It cannot be stressed too often that one should always patronize a sire with a good female line such as Prairie Peg, Quare Fire, Mad Prospect, Witching Grand, Could be Worse, Dublin Red or Sally's Gossip. It was from these dams that the champions who later became the prepotent sires of the past twenty years were produced, the world's fastest and gamest greyhounds, as well as possessing the ability to pass on these qualities to their sons and daughters.

Dogs at stud are advertised in *The Greyhound Magazine, Sporting Life,* and in the sporting press in Ireland. Full details are usually given of the capabilities of the dog, its parents, weight and colour, together with the name and address of the owner or agent and the fee required. When you have made a decision contact the owner in plenty of time, giving some indication as to when the bitch will be in season, for a dog may be fully booked at about that time and another may have to be used. Beware of patronizing a dog known to have shown fighting tendencies or one with dubious factors in his pedigree.

If you own a stud dog, a small advertisement in a suitable magazine will bring in many enquiries, but it is advisable to take space for a reasonably long time, say a minimum of twenty-six weeks when the dog is first put to stud, in which case reduced rates will be available. The first half of the year is the most suitable time for bitches to be mated, and it will be nine weeks from the time the bitch is served until she whelps. To assist enquirers, have stud cards printed showing the track record of the dog together with his extended pedigree and his litter brothers and sisters who may have performed well on track or coursing field; a good black and white photograph of the dog should be sent with each stud card. Mention the nearest railway station and how to reach your kennels by road. If a bitch is being sent by rail make arrangements for her to be met at the station a day or so before she is due to be mated. She should rest in the kennels overnight before and after her service.

Never allow a stud dog to serve more than two bitches a week; these matings should be several days apart. Also allow him a complete rest period of a month, preferably in July or August when few bitches will be mated in any case, since the best time for a bitch to have her pups is between the end of January and late July. The pups can then spend the first weeks of their life in good weather after leaving their mother: a great help in their rearing.

It is necessary to allow a dog intended for stud at least three or four months' rest before he is asked to serve bitches if he has been racing. He should be given a roomy kennel, preferably with a grass run, but if not he must be given regular exercise to keep him at peak fitness, together with a special diet and a dry, airy kennel. His meat allowance should be generous and in winter add a little cod-liver oil to his meals or a tonic at regular intervals. He should be given three main meals daily, one being of biscuits and fresh milk. An underfed dog may be unable to mate more than one bitch a week. He will also need daily grooming and worming every six months.

To guard against the spread of venereal disease, the Irish Coursing Club has stipulated that all stud dogs must be examined by a veterinary surgeon and certified free from the disease before being registered for stud. The owner of a stud dog should ask the owner of all bitches sent for service to provide a vet's certificate of her freedom from the disease.

The age of a sire when put to a bitch has always been a matter of controversy. Some breeders contend that a sire will be most virile and produce the best stock when in his prime, aged between five and seven years, but many of the greatest sires have been very much older and have produced little good stock until well beyond that age, perhaps not until they have been standing at stud for five or six years. Tokio was almost nine when he sired Bah's Choice and his stud fee was increased from 15 to 30 gns, but he had only a year or so left as a sire. Castledown Lad reached his greatest fame at stud when ten years old, and Hi There continued to sire top-class greyhounds until he died in 1968 aged fifteen. At nine Kilrea had sired Negro's Lad, sire of the bitch Negro's Fire who, through a mating to Quare Times, produced the great dam Quare Fire, dam of The Grand Fire. Creamery Border was siring top-class trackers until he died in 1945 aged fourteen years six months.

The fees of a sire vary greatly. They would often begin at £10 or so, as did Mutton Cutlet, while Fine Jubilee, sire of many outstanding greyhounds never earned more for his services. The same may be said of Manhattan Midnight and Printer, two of the fastest trackers of all time as would be expected since they were sired by Creamery Border. They were perhaps the two most prolific sires of the 1940s. Ballynennan Moon, standing at stud at the same time, was at a fee of 100 gns, as was Ballyhennessy Seal, but neither produced any outstanding greyhounds with but one or two expections. At the same time Tanist was at stud in Dublin at 60 gns and Castledown Lad at Mullingar at 70 gns when he died in 1946. He had been retired to stud ten years before, at a fee of only 5 gns, for like Jamie and Mutton Cutlet he had done little to enhance his reputation on the coursing field or track, yet each of these superb sires was to make his mark wherever greyhounds have raced.

In more recent times Oregon Prince (sire of the flying Carry on Oregon) stood at a fee of 50 gns, as did Crazy Parachute, while Hi There and Newdown Heather commanded 100 gns for many years. Camira Flash, even after winning the 1968 Derby, stood at only 35 gns, and Kilbelin Style, who finished second to Sand Star in the 1969 Derby, stood at a similar fee.

See Blood Lines; Dam; Dogs at Stud.
See under Famous Racing Greyhounds.

SLOUGH RACECOURSE

See under British Greyhound Racecourses.

SOUTHEND RACECOURSE
See under British Greyhound Racecourses.

SPEED

On the track, where it has to get round the bends as well as run on the straights, a top-class greyhound will attain a speed of just over 38 mph. If it can run on a straight course it will exceed this speed, as did Beef Cutlet on 13 May 1933 when he ran on a specially constructed 500 yds course in 26.13 secs at Blackpool, achieving a speed of 39.13 mph. The fastest time for the old 525 yds course (now replaced by metres) was by Easy Investment on 30 June 1973, in a time of 28.17 secs or 38.12 mph. With the faster and faster times produced through the years, and improved methods of rearing and training, it is almost certain that many postwar greyhounds would have improved upon Beef Cutlet's 39.23 mph run and would have exceeded 40 mph without difficulty. This speed will almost certainly have been exceeded by top-class greyhounds running down the straights of a track in good going. In comparison a racehorse, lion or kangaroo will reach a speed of 45 mph, while the swiftest of all animals, the cheetah, can attain 70 mph. The consistency of a greyhound, however, is one of the wonders of the animal world. Pick up any race card for a track and you will notice that several dogs will on numerous occasions have covered a certain distance in a race or trial to within one-hundredth of a second, and there may be one or two dogs that will have retained exactly the same time for several consecutive races when going conditions have been similar.

A list of the national 500 yds record holders since Entry Badge clocked 29.01 secs in the 1927 Derby (then run over 500 yds) until the distance on all tracks was replaced by the metric system on 1 January 1975 may be of interest:

FASTEST TIMES OVER 500 yds 1927–62

Entry Badge	1927	29.01 secs
*Future Cutlet	1931	28.52 secs
Beef Cutlet	1933	28.46 secs
Creamery Border	1933	28.39 secs
Brilliant Bob	1933	28.39 secs
Davesland	1934	28.32 secs
Top of Carlow Road	1935	28.31 secs
Ballyhennessy Sandhills	1938	28.17 secs
Glen Ranger	1938	28.15 secs
Ballyhennessy Sandhills	1938	28.08 secs
Junior Classic	1937	27.82 secs
Roeside Creamery	1942	27.70 secs
Ballyhennessy Seal	1944	27.64 secs
Priceless Border	1948	27.64 secs
Oregon Prince	1961	27.17 secs
Oregon Prince	1962	27.16 secs

*also held the 600 yds national record

FASTEST TIMES OVER 525 yds 1930–74

Mick the Miller	29.96 secs
Mick the Miller	29.82 secs
Mick the Miller	29.60 secs
Mick the Miller	29.55 secs
Beef Cutlet	29.52 secs
Fine Jubilee	29.48 secs
Junior Classic	29.43 secs
Quarter Day	29.34 secs
Wattle Bark	29.26 secs
Grosvenor Bob	29.22 secs
Gayhunter	29.21 secs
Jubilee Time	29.20 secs
Magic Beau	29.19 secs
Magic Bohemian	29.11 secs
Duffy's Arrival	29.09 secs
Bah's Choice	29.04 secs
Bah's Choice	28.99 secs
Quare Times	29.85 secs
Trev's Perfection	28.95 secs
Quare Times	28.82 secs
Priceless Border	28.75 secs
Priceless Border	28.64 secs
Faithful Hope	28.52 secs
Endless Gossip	28.50 secs
Pigalle Wonder	28.44 secs
Yellow Printer	28.38 secs
Yellow Printer	28.30 secs
Clohast Rebel	28.28 secs
Yellow Printer	28.18 secs
Easy Investment	28.17 secs

FASTEST TIMES OVER 700 yds 1930–74

Mick the Miller	41.31 secs
Bosham	41.17 secs
Bradshaw Fold	40.04 secs
Robeen Printer	40.03 secs
Lilac's Luck	39.88 secs
Model Dasher	39.73 secs
Dante II	39.70 secs
Clonalvy Pride	39.64 secs
O'Hara's Rebel	39.54 secs
*Tartan Khan	39.45 secs

*run over 655 m

Photo-timing was inaugurated in 1953, and this has recorded slower times than hand-timing, which until then was the usual practice. In Britain the 525 yds race was replaced in 1974 by 500 m. For the 700 yds course, Bradshaw Fold's time of 40.04 secs set up in 1930 stood for sixteen years, until Lilac's Luck did a time of 39.88 secs in 1946. The fastest time ever recorded for a bitch for the 525 yds course is 28.61 secs, at the White City on 17 June 1971, by Dolores Rocket.

The fastest greyhound over hurdles was Sherry's Prince, who covered the 525 yds course in 29.10 secs at a speed of 36.90 mph. Juvenile Classic's time of 31.40 secs for a

550 yds hurdles course in 1940 was a national record.

SPONSORS

Early in the 1970s, as with many other sports a number of sponsors willing to put up greatly increased prize money for open events came into greyhound racing and gave it a much needed shot in the arm. Spillers Foods Ltd have since 1973 sponsored the English Greyhound Derby which is now called the Spillers Greyhound Derby; the original first prize money under their sponsorship was £12,500. This was later increased to £15,000, and in 1977, when Balliniska Band was successful, the dog won £17,500 for its owner. In 1978, the sum had been increased to £20,000 and was won by Lacca Champion. Total prize money for the English Derby now amounts to over £50,000, and it is the richest race in the British Isles with £35,000 for the winner.

In Britain the breweries were among the first to sponsor greyhound racing. The classic, Scottish Derby is sponsored by Harp Lager, with a first prize of £2,500, while the Bass Charrington Cup at Owlerton, Sheffield, has a first prize of £1,000. Ben Truman sponsor the Puppy Derby at Wimbledon, at Slough is run the Ben Truman Stayer's Stakes and the Sprint Trophy, and at Crayford Courage put up a prize of £1,000 for the winner of the Crayford Vase, which is one of the best supported events and takes place in August. They also sponsor the equally popular Midlands Grand National, run at Hall Green in September. Double Diamond sponsor the important Select Stakes, run at Wembley in July when the Derby has finished; it is confined to the six best greyhounds of the year. Skol Lager put up £3,000 for the winner of the Champion of Champions Trophy at Monmore Green, Wolverhampton, which makes this one of the richest events in Britain; it takes place in July. The Holsten Circuit, worth £2,000, is run at Walthamstow. The Skol Lager Stakes is run at Hall Green and the Qualifying Race, sponsored by Tetley's brewery, is held at Leeds. At Leicester is run the Worthington Bitter Trophy, while at Perry Barr Ansell's sponsor their Challenge Trophy event run over 725 m.

The second most generously sponsored English classic is the St Leger, for which Ladbrokes donate a £10,000 first prize. Besides Ladbrokes and Coral's, who are the owners of several tracks and put up special prize money for several events, other bookmakers are generous with their sponsorship. The William King Cup, run at Shawfield, Glasgow, in August, carries a first prize of £1,000, and the William Hill Sixer, run at Hackney, carries a prize of £800. William Hill also sponsor the Hornet Hurdles at the Watford track. Mecca Bookmakers put up a prize of £1,250 for the winner of the Winter Stayers at Hackney in January. They also sponsor the Christmas Marathon at White City, Manchester, run over 810 m; £1,000 is awarded to the winner and £300 to the runner-up. John Manley sponsor a hurdles event at Wembley, and Mr George Reed the Autumn Cup at Wimbledon.

The William Hill bookmaking group, part of Sears Holdings, have greatly increased their sponsorship in recent years. In January the William Hill Empire Hurdles, run at Wembley, is worth £100 to the winner. In February the William Hill Championship over hurdles is run at the White City, with £1,000 for the winning owner, and in November the William Hill Marathon takes place over 815 m at Belle Vue. In the same month is the William Hill Nationwide Championship, the heats of which are contested at six tracks after which the final is held at the White City, the winner receiving £1,500. The William Hill Sixer at Hackney is worth £800; they also sponsor the Hornet Hurdles at Watford.

Also generous in its sponsorship is the sporting press (*see* Press).

In Ireland sponsors came in earlier, and since 1970 the Irish Derby has been sponsored by the Dublin cigarette manufacturers P.J. Carroll & Co. Ltd and known as Carroll's Irish Derby. The first of their sponsored events earned the winner, Mr Cahill's Monalee Pride (Sheila at Last—Prairie Flash) the sum of £5,000 but by 1979 the winner's prize was £20,000, the same as that for the English Derby of that year.

Apart from the Carroll's Derby, another prestige event is the Laurels, run at Cork and now sponsored by the Cashman Irish organization who give a sum in excess of £5,000 to the winning owner. Also at Cork, a sweepstake sponsored by the Windsor Hotel for £1,500 attracts many top-class greyhounds, and at the same track, the British and Irish Line put up a magnificent gold cup and £1,000 to the winner of a 525 yds event. The Cork Track Bookmakers are also generous in their sponsorship. At Harold's Cross the Burmah–Castrol Puppy Derby carries a prize of £3,000, while Arrow Electric sponsor a sweepstake event; Harold's Cross is also the venue for the Sean Kelly 750 over 750 yds, with a prize of £2,000 for the winner.

But the big money sponsorship is not confined just to the Dublin and larger provincial tracks. At Tralee is run the 550, sponsored by the Kerry Co-op Creameries, with a prize of £3,000 to the winner, and at Newbridge is run Kelly's Red Seal Sweepstake and the Texacloth Puppy Stakes, worth £1,000 to the winner.

Guinness do much to encourage greyhound racing and breeding in Ireland and so ensure that spectators can see the best greyhounds in action. The Guinness 600, run at Shelbourne Park, is now given almost classic status and attracts the top greyhounds from Ireland and Britain who readily compete for the £3,000 first prize. It was one of the first sponsored races, inaugurated in 1964. Guinness sponsor a major event on every track in Ireland, including the Midland Puppy Stakes at Mullingar, worth £1,200. The Guinness Trophy run at Cork is worth £1,500. At Youghal is contested the Blackwater Trophy, sponsored by the same firm, and worth £1,000 to the winner. The Harp Lager and Guinness Trophy is run at Lifford over 325 yds and is the shortest race in the calendar; and at Dundalk is contested the Harp Lager 525, with a prize of £1,500.

Bass Ale sponsor the two important sweepstakes run at Cork and Limerick, each worth more than £1,000 to the winning owner, and Murphy's brewery a 525 yds event at Youghal. At the well patronized Cork track is also run the Smirnoff Vodka Gold Collar, worth £1,000. The Waterford track is well sponsored by the Waterford Glass Co., the sweepstakes carrying a first prize of £1,000. The TR Motor Stakes is run at Harold's Cross, and at Youghal Russell's Garages sponsor the Renault Car Stakes run over 550 yds. Irish Airlines, Aer Lingus, sponsor a 550 yds event at Navan.

In the North, the long-famous Trigo Cup run at Celtic Park is now renamed the Guinness Ulster Derby and has classic status, though to change the name of one of the oldest and most famous of all greyhound events is regrettable. But this was not the first sponsored event at Celtic Park, for as long ago as 1927 the Empire Furnishing Co. of Belfast gave a cup and £40 to the winner for a race won by the bitch Wise Kiss, owned by Mr J. Connolly of Antrim. The runner-up was the dog Benbo, whose owner issued a challenge to the owner of Wise Kiss, for £20 a side. The match took place on 28 September 1927 and Wise Kiss was again the winner. This is thought to be the first time that a match between two greyhounds was run during an organized meeting. At Dunmore Park the Dunmore 700 is sponsored by Will's cigarettes with a first prize of £1,000.

SPRINTER

A greyhound which shows early speed, which comes early into its stride after a quick break from the traps. Sprinters will reach 40 mph on the straights but usually cannot stay distances of more than 500 yds or 500 m. They race over shorter distances with tremendous acceleration. Among the outstanding sprinters were Creamery Border, Local Interprize, Don't Gambol and Palm's Printer, all winners of the sprinters' classic, the Scurry Gold Cup.

STARTING BOX
See Trap.

STAYER

The name given to a greyhound capable of staying to the end of a longer than usual course, over 600 yds or 600 m, or longer, Captain A.E. Brice, for many years director of racing at Wembley Stadium and a Waterloo Cup judge, said: 'Looking back on the sport since its inception, there is no doubt that the true staying greyhound which comes again at the end of a race with a fine burst of speed to get up at the finish to win, is held in greater affection by the public than the ordinary short-distance runner.' Bitches have always been among the greatest stayers, from Bradshaw Fold and Disputed Rattler to Lizette and Dolores Rocket, each of whom is worthy to be classed alongside those great dogs Mick the Miller, Ataxy, Model Dasher and Forward King.

STONEHENGE

This pseudonym was used by Dr J.H. Walsh, editor of *The Field* magazine (1850–60) when writing on coursing matters. Walsh was one of the founder members of the National Coursing Club in 1857. He edited the *Coursing Calendar*, published every four months by John Crockford from the office of *The Field* in the Strand, London, from 1859 to 1919 when the official *Calendar of the National Coursing Club* first appeared.

In 1853 appeared Stonehenge's book, *The Greyhound: Being a Treatise on the art of Breeding, Rearing and Training Greyhounds for Public Running; containing also Rules for the Management of Coursing Meetings.* It was published by Longman, Brown & Green and went into many editions. Revised editions appeared in 1896 and 1875. The third edition was of 485 pages and contained twenty-five wood-cuts of famous coursing greyhounds. It has remained the greyhound breeder's 'bible'.

STUD DOG

Every dog standing at stud in Britain must be registered annually with the National Coursing Club's Greyhound Stud Book at a fee of £15 before any bitch is mated by him, On receipt of the dog's registration, a supply of mating and whelping forms is issued. These are of four parts:

1(a) The mating certificate, to be completed by the owner or authorized agent and returned to the Keeper of the Stud Book within fourteen days of the date of mating, with the £1 fee.

1(b) A duplicate copy of 1(a), to be retained by the owner of the stud dog.

1(c) The register of whelping which includes a triplicate copy of the mating certificate and incorporates a top copy of the Veterinary Certificate to be completed by the Veterinary Surgeon who retains part 1(c).

1(d) The duplicate copy of 1(c) which includes a quadruplicate copy of the mating certificate 1(a). The whole of 1(d) is to be completed by the breeder and returned to the Keeper of the Stud Book within one month of the date of whelping, together with a fee of £4. For applications up to six months, the fee is £10.

SWINDON RACECOURSE

See under British Greyhound Racecourses.

T

TALLEST GREYHOUNDS

In 1933 the Catford track inaugurated a race for greyhounds not less than 27 ins tall, measured from the front feet to the shoulder. Run over 600 yds, the race was won by Top Pace, the tallest dog.

But greyhounds today are very much taller. Newdown Heather was 30 ins tall, a giant of a dog, and his grandson Cricket Bunny (Printer's Prince–Cricket Lady), winner of the 1973 Scurry Gold Cup, was 29 ins tall and weighed 80 lbs when racing. The great coursing dog Master Myles, who died of an injury soon after winning the 1978 Irish Coursing Derby, was 31 ins tall, probably the tallest ever to perform on the track or coursing field. He was known as 'The Big Dog' and his racing weight was 95–7 lbs.

TELEVISION

The first greyhound to appear on the TV screen was Trev's Perfection, when he was shown with his owner-trainer Mr Fred Trevillion and several of his other dogs in 1946. Trev's Perfection was to win the Derby in 1947. The premier track event has been featured on BBC TV from the White City since 1960, when Duleek Dandy won the first £2,000 prize awarded to the winner. At 25–1, the dog was the biggest outsider to win the event. Mile Bush Pride, who won the previous year, finished third in the first television Derby. In recent years the race commentary has been in the hands of Harry Carpenter.

The first race to be televized was the 1953 St Leger from Wembley, won by the great Magourna Reject. Wembley was also the first to put out a BBC commentary of a greyhound race.

In 1958 the BBC inaugurated their now famous TV Sportsview Trophy. From 1961 to 1975 it was run over 880 yds which made it one of the longest of all races. Since 1975 it has been run over 815 m, with a first prize of £1,750. The event is contested at a different venue each year, while the heats take place on various tracks throughout Britain. Since its inception the event has been one of the most popular in the racing calendar, seen on TV by millions of *Sportsview* followers, and the best stayers in the sport take part. The first time, the race was run at Wimbledon over 500 yds, when Town Prince won. Curraheen Bride won in 1962, also at Wimbledon. The dog had been bought for £250 and won many open events for his owner. In 1960, the race was first run over 880 yds, which Avis won, and in 1975 Lucky Hi There was the winner of a most exciting race. In 1967, after running up for the Derby to his litter brother Tric Trac, Spectre II took the first prize. Next year the race was won by the great Shady Begonia, trained by Norman Oliver at Brough Park. In 1973, Spectre's son Leading Pride landed the trophy. A black dog, like his sire, he won by a length from Westpark Dainty. He was trained by George Curtis at Brighton, where in his qualifying heat he set a new track record. Spectre also had a part in Weston Blaze's win in 1979 at Hall Green. His dam was Western Star, who had Spectre as her sire and Trojan Silver as her dam. Trojan Silver's dam was Powerstown Prospect, who won the St Leger in 1962, so Weston Star and her son were bred for marathon events.

Lizzie's Girl, who won the TV Trophy in 1975 at Monmore Green, followed in the footsteps of a long line of black bitches who were among the greatest stayers the sport has known – Bradshaw Fold, Quarter Day, Disputed Rattler, Alvaston Lulu Belle, Astra (though she was more blue than black), Cal's Pick and Dolores Rocket; the longer the race the better they performed. Each could manage 1,000 yds with ease and they were everyone's favourite because of it. Like Dolores Rocket, Lizzie's Girl was by Newdown Heather (which accounts for her stamina) out of Knockrose Lady, and she won the race by a neck from Silver Lipstick in a truly wonderful finish.

Another wonderful black bitch possessing great endurance was Montreen, who won the event in 1977. Owned by Mrs Yates, from twenty-three races the bitch had twelve wins including the TV trophy at Walthamstow; the GRA Stakes at the White City; the Northern Stayers' Stakes at Belle Vue and the Cesarewitch at that track, run over the same 815 m. By Moordyke Spot out of Avondale, she was whelped in May 1974 and won nearly £7,000 in prize money in two years' racing.

In 1972 London Weekend Television's *World of Sport* programme put out half an hour of an afternoon meeting from Harringay. The idea to use Harringay occurred when bad weather cancelled the horse racing programme and this procedure has been followed ever since. It became a regular occurrence during the severe winter of 1979 when for weeks horse racing was impossible, but greyhound racing continued to take

Winners of the BBC TV Sportsview Trophy

		Venue	*Trainer*	
1958	Town Prince	Wimbledon	L. Reynolds	28.14 secs
1959	Don't Divulge	West Ham	L. Reynolds	38.72 secs
1960	Crazy Paving	Harringay	*C.C. Payne	51.22 secs
1961	Chantilly Lace	Belle Vue	*J. Clubb	52.38 secs
1962	Avis	Wembley	J. Rimmer	51.30 secs
1963	Curraheen Bride	Wimbledon	W. Kelly	52.32 secs
1964	Hill Stride	Powderhall	T.J. Perry	51.37 secs
1965	Lucky Hi There	Wimbledon	J. Jowett	51.35 secs
1966	Bedford	Walthamstow	R. Thomson	52.46 secs
1967	Spectre II	Brighton	J. Hookway	50.09 secs
1968	Shady Begonia	Romford	N. Oliver	50.53 secs
1969	Cash for Dan	White City, London	B. Parsons	49.44 secs
1970	Hi Diddle	White City, Manchester	Miss P. Heasman	51.90 secs
1971–2	not run			
1973	Leading Pride	Wimbledon	G. Curtis	51.16 secs
1974	Stage Box	White City, London	Mrs Savva	51.75 secs
1975	Lizzie's Girl	Monmore Green	E.F. Williams	52.16 secs
1976	Aughadonagh Jock	Belle Vue	B. Jay	52.77 secs
1977	Montreen	Walthamstow	E. Bamford	52.40 secs
1978	Westown Adam	Walthamstow	Mrs Savva	52.27 secs
1979	Weston Blaze	Walthamstow	R.A. Young	53.16 secs
1980	Tread Fast	Wembley	G. Sharpe	52.20 secs
1981	Decoy Boom	Perry Barr	Joe Cobbold	54.27 secs
1982	Alpha My Son	Belle Vue	* Leon Steed	52.41 secs

*owner–trainer

place at Harringay every Saturday afternoon, much to the delight of those many followers of the sport who were unable to travel to any sporting event because of the weather.

The NGRC formed a television committee in the 1950s, which is involved in TV transmissions from all tracks. One of its most active members was Mr Reg Howell, until 1976 for thirty years chief of publicity of the GRA, who was involved in more than 100 live broadcasts and TV programmes during that time.

The first greyhound race put out in colour on television was from the Southend Stadium in 1970, after the track had installed a new system of brilliant lighting which enabled the TV cameras to cover an entire race at night, picking out the colours of the jackets worn by the dogs in a way that had not been possible before. The improved lighting has now been installed on a number of other tracks.

TERMS OF RACING
See Racing, Terms of.

TIMEKEEPER

Although timing for trials and races is done by photo- or ray-timing, the times are recorded by the official timekeeper, a licensed official appointed by the NGRC for each track who records every trial and race by a hand stopwatch. If the winning dog's time shows a wide discrepancy with the mechanical timing, the stewards must check the apparatus for any fault; if it is not working properly the time recorded by hand is taken as official.

The official winning time for a trial or race shall be that recorded by the first greyhound(s) in finishing order, from the time the fronts of the traps reach 45° from the perpendicular to the time the nose(s) of such greyhound(s) reach the winning line on completing the course.

Calculations are .01 secs for a short head; .02 secs for a head or neck; .06 for a length.

TOTALIZER (TOTE)

The tote was not legalized on greyhound tracks until the Betting and Lotteries Act of 1934, though it had been permitted on horse racing courses since the Act of 1928. The tote is not allowed to operate on greyhound tracks in Northern Ireland.

The tote is one of the wonders of the modern age. It is fully automatic in that it records, displays and prints the ticket for each bet, so that the human element is involved only in transmitting that bet by specially qualified staff who have received training for the task. Every tote must conform to the government's regulations as introduced on 1 July 1935.

At the largest tracks, 15 x 12 in. digits are used, each figure being operated by a 50 volt motor independently driven. Aggregators fitted with rear contacts are independently driven, and the aggregator mechanism, which embodies an interlocking transmission, cannot lose bets in transfer; to enable bets to be accepted at high speed a mechanical storing device is provided. This is guarded by a signal lamp mounted in the control panel which lights up when the storage is clear.

The mechanical transmission also adapts to instant mechanical zeroizing, an important feature of a totalizator. The zeroizing levers on each aggregator are actuated from one master lever which is electrically locked from the control panel until the time for its release.

Ticket-issuing machines provide for all betting facilities including Win, Win and Place, Forecast, Doubles etc. The machine is housed in a metal case which, when fitted in a bench, is supported by a flange and connected to the circuits by a telephone plug and jack. This facilitates quick removal and transfer of a machine to a different location, if necessary.

The top plate of the machine is stainless steel, with the front section, through which the ticket is issued, being easily removable for changing the code and zeroizing the veeder counters. The veeders may be read through a small aperture in the top plate.

All types of ticket-issuing machines are available; on the majority of them the printing mechanism is operated by a lever fitted on the right of the machine. The machines are also fitted with controls to change the race number and to reverse the printing ribbon.

Pressure printing for tickets, as opposed to wet rolled ink printing, is favoured because the tickets do not soil the hands or gloves of the purchaser. Furthermore, such tickets are almost impossible to forge. Another advantage is the variable code which makes it unnecessary to insert a code plate for each meeting. A door is provided in the front of the metal case so that the paper roll, which is completely enclosed, can be easily changed. Ticket-issuing machines which issue single tickets of one unit value, or multiples of the basic selling unit, can be provided, or alternatively ticket issuing machines for multi-value selling i.e. a machine which will print and issue tickets of different denominations.

The ticket operator works by pressing buttons and levers rather like using a type-writer. On receiving the signals the central apparatus directs them to the aggregator for each dog, or for a combination of dogs, and on the totalling counter. The moment the bet is recorded on the counters, it is displayed on the indicator so that the public can see the exact number of bets placed on each dog.

The tote cannot begin working without an accountant, appointed by the local council, in attendance. It is his duty to check all dividends and to satisfy himself that the figures with which he checks the dividends are also correct. He is present as a representative of the public who are placing their bets. Also in attendance is a mechanic who is available for instant consultation by the accountant if he is not satisfied that the tote is working correctly. Both officials are employed by the local authority responsible for licensing the track.

A green light after a race indicates that order of finish is final, and all totalizator dividends are declared on this. All bets are accepted on the totalizator on the terms contained in the totalizator operating rules which are displayed near the totalizator in every stadium. The operator's deductions for the various totalizator pools are 10 per cent for a win, 12½ per cent for a place, and 15 per cent forecast and multi-race pools.

Popular in totalizator betting are bets for a place (first or second), when half the starting price is paid out. A greyhound of proven ability which may be quoted at quite long odds will often be worth backing for a place, especially a big, strong dog when the going is heavy. Forecast betting is for two dogs for a win and place, which pays out higher dividends than for either a win or place bet.

It is laid down in the rules of racing that if a greyhound is disqualified for fighting or any other reason, it will not affect the 'order of finish' upon which totalizator bets are decided.

In 1975 the Owlerton track at Sheffield installed the first Data Trap Computer Tote, devised by Mr Dennis Diffley of Data-trap Electronics Ltd. The system allows for the working of up to sixty ticket-issuing machines and is based on two Digico Micro 16V computers which monitor each ticket-issuing machine and check that every aspect of the bet is correct. They drive the tote indicator board while the video-signal is fed to television screens in all parts of the Stadium which are supplied with up-to-the-moment information, for instance if a greyhound has to be withdrawn from a race and the pools odds, including forecasts, need to be adjusted. The computer calculates the number of bets and the dividends, the percentage of government tax and the Stadium's permitted deduction within seconds of the start of the race. The pay-out can then be made without delay.

TOTE BETTING

Totalizator betting was legalized on greyhound tracks with the 1934 Betting and Lotteries Act, when greyhound betting was put on level terms with horse racing which had enjoyed tote betting since 1928.

When placing a bet with the tote, it is the trap number of the dog, not its name (as given when placing a bet with a bookmaker) as it appears on the totalizator that is given to the operator, either to win or for a place, in which you will win if your dog finished first or second. Place betting is usually done on outsiders which are often quoted at quite large odds and which may be fancied as having a good chance of finishing in the first two places. This is often the case in heavy going in long-distance races, when a big, strong dog may have the stamina to hang on and win or finish second.

Regular visitors to a certain track, who may have some knowledge of how the dogs perform in heavy or soft going, or when the ground is dry and hard, may attempt to place both the first and second dog in a race, when the tote will often pay out a large sum for a small investment. This is known as a forecast betting.

The White City, London, was the first

to organize the Treble Chance Quinela stakes, by which in certain designated events for a 10p original bet with the tote two dogs are nominated for the first leg (race). If they finish first or second in either order, the winning ticket is exchanged for your similar selection in the second leg, and if successful for the third leg when a substantial amount is paid out to the successful backers. A special consolation dividend is to be won (by dividing one tenth of the treble chance pool) by those nominating the winning greyhound and that finishing third in the last leg of the pool.

The rules appertaining to the sport stipulate that no person under eighteen years of age shall make a bet on a track either with a bookie or with the totalizator. No betting shall take place on any trial race, and no person holding a licence issued by the NGRC for any purpose connected with the sport, e.g. racing manager or trainers, shall bet at any racecourse to which he or she is attached. The law also stipulates that any winnings not claimed from the tote within forty-eight hours may be retained by the tote. *See* Totalizator (Tote).

TOTE RECEIPTS

In 1946, twenty years after greyhound racing began, tote takings amounted to £200 million, and under the Betting and Lotteries Act of 1934 the tracks were allowed to retain for their expenses and profit 6 per cent of tote takings. This was a substantial amount at the time, but by 1970 tote takings had fallen to £60 million and for the tracks to survive, with ever-increasing costs, it was necessary for the 1943 Act to be amended. The tracks were then allowed to retain 12½ per cent of tote takings.

One of the main causes of the decline in attendances after 1946, besides league football and county cricket starting up again after the war, and the advent of television in the home, was the 1947 budget in which a tax of 10 per cent was imposed on the totalizator betting at greyhound tracks, deductible before the tracks were allowed to deduct their own 6 per cent. This greatly reduced the pay-out to the backers. Another reason for the continued decline has been the differential rates between on-course and off-course betting – under the 1960 Act on-course betting is taxed at 5 per cent and off-course at 6 per cent. Although the reduction in government takings from 10 per cent to 5 per cent has helped considerably, the 1 per cent difference between on- and off-course betting has not been sufficient to lure back the lost punters.

Tote takings at British greyhound tracks in recent years, from 5,688 meetings, are 1960 £55,188,302; 1967 £66,216,938; 1970 £60,000,000; 1975 £69,211,102; 1976 £65,565,333; 1977 £70,252,452; 1978 £71 504,184; 1979 £76,484,832.

In the Irish Republic (there is no tote at the four tracks in Northern Ireland) figures are as follows:

1960	£582,698	1970	£3,463,220
1961	£1,218,768	1971	£3,284,239
1962	£1,616,459	1972	£3,640,191
1963	£1,830,774	1973	£4,165,250
1964	£2,083,063	1974	£4,572,454
1965	£1,979,397	1975	£5,954,867
1966	£2,033,435	1976	£7,000,347
1967	£2,147,600	1977	£6,711,984
1968	£2,422,408	1978	£8,125,943
1969	£2,828,728	1979	£9,170,000

Approximately 2,000 meetings are held each year in the Irish Republic, attended by 1 million people, and in 1979 £20 million was staked on greyhounds in the Irish Republic, shared more or less equally between the bookmakers and the tote.

TRACK MANAGER

It is his duty to see that all things concerning the correct working of the track are functioning properly. The traps must be regularly inspected before and after each race and trials, and the track manager must supervise all other aspects of track maintenance including, most important of all, the correct running of the hare, though this comes in the first place under the aegis of the chief engineer who is usually the hare controller, appointed by the NGRC.

TRACK RECORDS

In 1972 in the Irish Republic, the dog Tom's Pal (Yanka Boy–That Maggie from Knockane) broke track records on seven occasions and at four different tracks, the most by any greyhound in one year:

13.4.1972	Harold's Cross	330 yds	18.17 secs
18.4.1972	Harold's Cross	330 yds	18.12 secs
15.8.1972	Waterford	300 yds	16.60 secs
19.8.1972	Waterford	300 yds	16.40 secs
26.8.1972	Waterford	300 yds	16.35 secs
9.9.1972	Cork	300 yds	16.60 secs
23.9.1972	Shelbourne Park	360 yds	19.50 secs

The track record which has been held for the longest period by a greyhound is the 550 yds at Cork: it was set on 7 October 1949 by Spanish Lad with a time of 31.00 secs. At the same track the 500 yds record has been held by Prince of Bermuda since 12 September 1956; and the 525 yds at Clonmel was held by The Grand Fire from 25 April 1957, when he clocked 29.40 secs, until 1979 when The Potman bettered this by one length.

On Derby night at White City, June 25th, 1983, in 'fast going', 5 track records were broken, most at one meeting anywhere. Amongst these was a new world, national and track record set by Hay Maker Mack when taking the Derby Consolation over 500 m in 28.95 seconds. This beat the national record set by Monday's Bran at Brighton in 1980. Hay Maker Mack was also sired by Brave Bran and also trained at Brighton, by Derek Knight.

TRACK SENSE

A term used to describe the ability of a greyhound to take advantage of every favourable aspect of a race such as to squeeze through an opening between other dogs; to keep clear of bunching on the bends so that the dog will not be bumped and thrown off balance; and to have the determination to get to the winning line before its rivals.

TRAINERS

A professional greyhound trainer is defined as one who trains greyhounds for any owner as a full-time occupation. The greyhounds can be track-owned or privately owned.

An 'attached' trainer is one (man or woman) who is attached to an approved racecourse and who trains greyhounds for graded or open races there.

An 'unattached' trainer trains greyhounds for any person for open races at any approved racecourse. He or she is known as a private trainer.

A 'permit' trainer is one who trains four greyhounds or fewer at a permit racecourse.

An owner-trainer is one who trains greyhounds in the ownership of himself or herself, or of his wife or her husband, or of an unmarried child over the age of eighteen. An owner-trainer may be an attached or unattached trainer.

The most famous owner-trainer in the early years of the sport was Mrs M. Yate who was the first person to train *and* own a Greyhound Derby winner. This was Fine Jubilee who won in 1936. Mrs Yate was 'unattached' to a greyhound track and so was the first private trainer to handle a Derby winner. She was also the first woman to train a Derby winner. Other owner-trainers of English Derby winners were:

- 1947 Mr Fred Trevillion with Trev's Perfection
- 1955 Mr F. Johnson with Rushton Mac
- 1960 Mr W.H. Dash with Duleek Dandy (the dog ran in the name of his wife, Mrs B.J. Dash)
- 1969 Mr H. Orr with Sand Star
- 1971 Mr H.G. White with Dolores Rocket
- 1973 Mr J. O'Connor with Patricia's Hope

Patricia's Hope ran in the joint names of Messrs G. and B. Marks and Mr J. O'Connor in 1973. Messrs G. and B. Marks are the only people to have twice won the English Derby for Patricia's Hope also won in 1972 when in the ownership of Messrs G. and B. Marks and Mr B. Stanley.

The only women to have trained an English Derby winner are:

- 1936 Mrs M. Yate with Fine Jubilee
- 1970 Mrs Barbara Tompkins with John Silver, and 1983, I'm Slippy
- 1975 Mrs Olga Lynds with Tartan Khan

It is in the NGRC Rules of Racing that every trainer handling greyhounds on a licensed track must obtain a licence before he or she is allowed to do so, whilst a person employed to handle greyhounds on parade duties for a licensed trainer must also be in receipt of a parader's licence.

The first trainer to win £10,000 with his dogs in one year was Stanley Biss, who achieved the distinction in 1933 when Queen of the Suir won on the last day. In 1948 he became the first trainer ever to win £20,000 in a year. On 28 June 1947, Sidney Orton, trainer of Mick the Miller, became the first trainer whose dogs won every race at one meeting, when he cleared the board at his home track, Wimbledon. The first person to train a Derby winner was Joe Harmon, then at White City, who had charge of Mr E. Baxter's Entry Badge when winning the

English Derby in 1927. Between 1948 and 1954 the Wembley trainer Leslie Reynolds trained five Derby winners in seven years, a feat which may never be repeated:

1948	Priceless Border
1949	Narrogar Ann
1951	Ballylannigan Tanist
1952	Endless Gossip
1954	Paul's Fun

The first Englishman to win the Irish Derby was Fred Davis in 1948 with Western Post, and he also won the Scottish Derby which has never been done before or since. In 1976 Phil Rees trained three classic winners in three months, a feat without precedent in greyhound racing. Xmas Holiday won the Scurry Gold Cup in April, and the Laurels in May; and in June Mutt's Silver won the Derby. Phil Rees is one of the few to have bred and trained a classic winner in England, for Xmas Holiday was born at his kennels in Kent. Another example is Mr H.G. White, who owned, trained and bred Dolores Rocket. Mr Hamilton Orr, owner of Sand Star, winner in 1969, is the only person to have bred, owned and trained a winner of the English Greyhound Derby. In the final of the 1978 National Breeders Two-Year-Old Produce Stakes at Clonmel, the Irish trainer Matt O'Donnell had five of the six runners, an all-time record for a classic event anywhere. His runners were Always Kelly, who won the event; Malange; Fly Future; Brilliant Champ; and Loch Bo Rover. They took the first five places.

For more general information about specific trainers, *see under* British Greyhound Racecourses; Irish Greyhound Racecourses.

TRAINING

Every trainer has his own methods of how to keep a racing greyhound in top condition and every greyhound responds in a different way to individual training methods. How often has a dog placed with another trainer responded by performing out of all recognition from his previous running? In the same way a dog which has been performing well with a trainer and has then been moved from the track or placed with another trainer may fail to live up to his earlier performances. Stonehenge has given us his ideas on how to bring a dog to a premier coursing event in top condition and the same rules hold good today for track racing.

(a) Clear the dog of worms before starting his training.
(b) Let the dog have a fast day once a week.
(c) Keep his bowels in the right condition.
(d) Give sufficient exercise for the dog to enjoy his bed.
(e) Find out his exact requirements in exercise, sleep, food and grooming.

A trainer will find out a dog's best racing weight and keep him at this. Some dogs require larger amounts of food than others to maintain their weight, while some need more exercise than others to keep them at full racing fitness. A greyhound should always come to the traps (or slips if coursing) at peak fitness, and not be over-trained in which event his muscles will be 'hard' and the dog tense. A dog should be mentally fresh and elastic, longing to chase the electric hare with everything he has got. Each dog responds in a different way. Some like to be kennelled with a companion and fret if one is taken away, which greatly affects its running. Others prefer to be kennelled by themselves in order to avoid interference from another dog when feeding. When taken by car to run in open events some dogs will travel well, enjoying every moment of the journey, while others are soon overcome with travel sickness and take several hours to recover. When taking a dog any distance, these factors must be considered and ample time allowed to a dog troubled by car sickness to recover before taking part in an event. Weather has much to do with a dog's fitness. Unduly hot weather causes distress to some dogs as it does to some humans, while others are at their best when the sun is shining Others are easier to train during cold weather.

Before serious training commences, it is advisable to allow the dog a week to do much as he pleases, then he will respond more readily when his serious training begins. Every racing greyhound should be allowed his week's 'holiday' after several months of strenuous running and before he is brought back into training again. He will then return to racing refreshed both mentally and physically.

After his rest, dose the dog for worms which will pull him down if not regularly eliminated; dose him with Epsom salts and fast him for twelve hours before giving the worming medicine. Dust his coat with derris or Pybuthin powder, rubbing it well in, to clear it of any ticks which will cause skin irritation and scratching and make the dog lose condition. Two or three days later the dog will be ready to start serious training. Begin by walking him four to five miles daily, much of the time on a hard surface, but trim his nails before doing so and regularly inspect them for any stones or flints picked up while out walking. Afterwards, dip the feet in a solution of permanganate of potash. This acts as a disinfectant and also hardens the pads. Give the dog a daily romp in a field or on common land, which will quicken him up and improve his stamina. Pay careful attention to his diet, reducing fats and carbohydrates and feeding more protein such as minced horse meat or a proprietary brand of good-quality tinned food. Mix it with brown bread soaked in Oxo. The reduction of fats will reduce the amount of body heat, so in winter he will need a coat when out exercising. Give a feed about 8 a.m. and another in the early evening before the dog settles down for the night. Remember to allow the dog two hours to digest his morning feed before beginning his exercise.

After about a month of serious training the dog will be ready to begin trials. These are usually given as solo runs over a short distance, then over longer distances. The best time for trials is between March and October when the ground is firm and the dog should give a good account of himself. This is necessary if he is to be accepted at a track, for standards are continually improving and the racing manager is always endeavouring to upgrade his race card. The dog may take some time to get used to the turns, and an inside hare is easier to follow at the beginning. Remember that a dog not quite fast enough for one track may be accepted by another, on which he may perform better in any case.

If the dog is accepted, place it with a trainer who has a vacancy in his kennels. The racing manager will take the dog's markings in accordance with National Greyhound Racing Club requirements. The dog will then be ready to race, but he may well prove 'green' and fail to put up a reasonable showing until he gets used to running in six-dog races and to the faces and shouts of the crowd. If he shows ability early, it will be possible to enter him for the British Breeders' Produce Stakes at Catford or in one of the Midlands puppy events held at Coventry, Wolverhampton and Perry Barr. For every pup born who is able to make his presence felt on a racecourse there will be many who fail to make the grade, and if yours turns out to be a game, honest dog who performs to the best of his ability in all conditions, hold on to him at all costs, for he will give several years of pleasurable racing and may then earn a useful sum as a stud dog. He will make a good friend in any case, when his racing days are over.

If the dog is with a private trainer and is to be entered for open races or is to be kennelled on a track, his day will begin at 7 or 7.30 a.m. when several dogs are let into the paddock for a romp while their kennels are cleaned out and fresh straw and water put in. From 8 to 8.30 a.m. the dogs are fed in their kennels, and at 10 a.m. are taken by a kennel lad or maid for a two-mile walk on the lead. One person can manage half a dozen dogs of racing age but no more. If the dogs are at the puppy stage no more than two should be taken, for they will pull in all directions until they are used to the lead. By 11.30 a.m. the dogs will be back for massage and grooming. A reliable massage embrocation is Alco Ectolin, with which all parts of the dog should be massaged, beginning from the neck and along the back and loin muscles, down the shoulders and thighs, always taking the hands over the various parts of the body with firm sweeps. From noon until 3.30 p.m. the dogs sleep and are then given another short walk or a romp until 4.30 p.m. when the main meal is given, consisting of minced meat with brown bread or meal. Stanley Biss, that most respected of trainers, would feed nothing but well-minced raw meat to dogs on the racing strength, and two meals a day. Fred Farey, who trained Monday's News, gave three meals daily and as he considered that, most of all, a greyhound should be mentally fit as well as physically, he would never exercise his dogs over the same ground two days in succession. Keeping a dog fresh is vital, a stale dog will never give his best on the track.

The most difficult time of year for training is from November until the end of February, when animals and humans, as well as plants, are at their lowest ebb. In bad weather it is always difficult to give the dogs sufficient exercise and change, but much can be done in keeping up their spirits by frequent changes of bedding and by giving them a more varied, liberal diet. They will, in any case, need more food in winter, owing to the need for maintaining their body temperature when it may be very cold outside.

The greatest number of winning greyhounds that any trainer has handled during any one year is 504, by Jimmy Rimmer when a trainer at the Greenfield Stadium, Bradford, in 1932. For thirty years slipper at the Waterloo Cup, Mr Rimmer was later a trainer at Slough and Clapton before moving to Wembley. He retired in 1970, shortly before Wembley moved over to contract trainers.

TRAP

The starting box into which the greyhound is placed just before the hare is set in motion. The number of boxes or traps does not exceed six and the number of each trap is shown on the race card or programme and on the dog's racing jacket, together with the colour of the jacket the dog will be wearing for identification. The traps or boxes are arranged in numerical order of trap numbers outwards, with no. 1 trap on the inside or rail.

In the early history of the sport there were eight traps in a row, but in 1927 it was decided that the number of greyhounds taking part in a race should not exceed six. At first the traps were released by hand, by a lever which was pulled down as the hare passed the traps, but in the late 1930s James McKee devised the automatic trap release which released the fronts of the traps when the hare was 12 yds in front.

At first the starting boxes were made of wood, but later came to be replaced by all-metal traps. They are aluminium-finished to prevent rust and each trap is made separately and fitted with an electric and a hand-operated release. The traps are operated by the position of the hare and may be set at any predetermined hare position. As the hare passes, the fronts fly open and above the dogs so that their vision is in no way impaired. Immediately the dogs have left the traps they are hurriedly moved away from the running track to enable the dogs to have a clear run as they come round again to the winning line.

For handicap races the starting boxes are spaced out at various distances as determined by the handicapper, but here the order is reversed compared with a graded race, the back trap (no. 1) being on the outside with the front marker on the inside to eliminate bunching at the first bend. Against this the fast breaker, who may be in one of the back traps and who likes to get his nose in front early in the race, is denied this possibility and may lose interest. Staggered handicapping is popular only in the north and in Scotland.

At most tracks greyhounds released from no. 1 trap do seem to enjoy most success, with the other traps sharing their wins about equally. This is certainly true of the Derby (*see under* Classic Events in Britain). A local steward or security officer will examine the traps immediately before a meeting or trials, and ensure that they have been correctly set up on the course.

TRIAL

A test run by one or more greyhounds on an approved course, other than a race. A greyhound is not allowed to run in a trial:

(1) Unless it is registered by name in either the English or Irish Stud Book.

(2) If it is disqualified, except for fighting, or is a confirmed fighter.

(3) If disqualified for fighting or has not been reinstated, except that it may run solo trials.

(4) Unless in charge of a licensed trainer or a responsible person known to the racing manager.

A greyhound's initial trial should have been run twenty-one days before its first race, and it may run only two initial trials before its identity book is sealed, provided those trials were run at the track where the dog's registration markings were taken. These initial trials are known as preliminary trials and must take place with at least two other greyhounds undergoing preliminary trials.

Before a greyhound can run in a race at a particular track, it must first have run at least three trials at that racecourse on separate days. The results of all trials are entered in the greyhound's identity book and trials are conducted in the same way as races.

The racing manager is always ready to give a dog a trial, either solo or with others, for he is continually on the look-out for greyhounds of top class to run at his track, and no dog will be placed on the racing strength unless he has shown up well in his trials as a non-fighter and one which shows a reasonable time comparing favourably with those of the other dogs kennelled at the track. The age of a greyhound is taken into consideration in trials and young, 'green' dogs which show a reasonable turn of speed will be given every encouragement.

TRIGO CUP
See Classic Events in Ireland.

TRIPLE DEAD HEAT

The first triple dead heat ever recorded in greyhound racing took place in 1939 in the USA, when at the Town and Country Kennel Club, Bayshore City, three dogs, White Flash, Lags Rogo and White Sox, crossed the winning line together. The first ever recorded in England was at the Doncaster track on 20 October 1945, when in the first race of the meeting Vengeance, Parkhaven and the bitch Miss Chat crossed the line together. In Scotland the first and only triple dead heat took place at Shawfield, Glasgow, on 20 March 1972 over 525 yds, when Turkish Maid, Thurles Queen and War Girl finished together. No triple dead heat has been recorded in Ireland.

There was nearly a triple dead heat at Wembley for the *Evening Standard* Cup in 1970 when Paramugs, Glebe Dandy and Barrack Street crossed the line together. The photo-finish camera, however, gave the verdict to Paramugs by a short head with the other two dead-heating for second place. It was the closest finish ever seen in a race at Wembley.

Cleveland Park Stadium, Middlebrough, on 29 January 1949 was the venue for the only triple dead heat for second place. This was confirmed by the newly installed photo-finish equipment and the race was won by Lone Craft from trap 5 by a neck, with Sun-Kit, Nafferton and Master Turk in second place, the tips of the noses of all three touching the line together.

At Wimbledon in 1933, for the Record Stakes run over 500 yds, there was almost a quadruple dead heat, a short head separating the first four to finish; Beef Cutlet defeated Future Cutlet by that margin, with Fallinga in third place and Brave Enough fourth. Less than 12 ins separated all four dogs and there was no photo-finish!

See Dead Heat.

U

UNLUCKY LOSERS

One of the unluckiest of all greyhounds, who reached the final of the Laurels on three occasions without winning once, was Model Dasher's finest son, Magna Hasty, born of the long-distance star May Hasty. He also reached the English Derby final in 1950, when he was the 50—1 outsider; from the difficult trap 3 (which was usually his lot) he finished fifth, though in front of the favourite, Ballycurreen Garrett.

Perhaps even more unfortunate, in that he reached the final of at least four important events without winning one, was Melksham Numeral, born and reared at the famous kennels of Mr Henry Sawtell in Wiltshire. Whelped in February 1936, he first contested the 1937 British National Produce Stakes and reached the final in which he finished third. Later that year he also reached the final of the Puppy Derby at Wimbledon, and in early 1938, the final of the Two-year-old Produce Stakes. From there he contested the 1938 Derby and amazed many followers of the sport by running brilliantly and reaching the final, only to be beaten once more at the last hurdle into second place by Lone Keel, who won by half a length. Melksham Numeral was a thoroughly genuine performer but always the big prize eluded him.

Another dog who reached many finals without winning a classic event was the 1970 Derby finalist Hymus Silver. One of Oregon Prince's finest sons, he was a brindle dog whelped in June 1968 and one of the most consistent dogs ever to race. He reached the final of the Midland Puppy Derby; the Wimbledon Puppy Derby; the Longcross Cup; and the White City, Wood Lane Stakes. When leading in the 1970 Derby he suffered a toe injury which compelled his retirement.

In Ireland, perhaps the most outstanding greyhound not to win a classic was the bitch Baytown Ivy. A handsome brindle, weighing 58–60 lbs when racing, she must be ranked with the half dozen best bitches who did all their racing in Ireland. By Manhattan Midnight out of the dam Ulster Row, 'Ivy' was whelped in 1943 and owned by Mr Paddy Barry. In her heat for the McAlinden Cup at Shelbourne Park she ran up to Soft Day Matt. Her running in the 1946 Derby was equally impressive. She reached the semi-finals in which she defeated the ultimate winner, Steve, and recorded easily the fastest time of the three semi-finals, but, made favourite for the final, she failed to gain a place. For the Oaks at Harold's Cross she was on brilliant form, winning her first round heat by four lengths; in the second round, which she won by many lengths, she beat Astra's track record of 29.88 secs (the first bitch to beat 30 secs at Harold's Cross) by 0.01 secs, a success she was to enjoy for only a few days. Made favourite once again to win the classic, she was pipped at the line by Cold Christmas, who in winning clipped .01 secs off her recent record. This time was not beaten until Prairie Peg clocked 29.55 secs ten years later. Though the classics eluded her, in October 1946 Baytown Ivy contested the Ossory Cup at Kilkenny in which she set a track record of 29.87 secs, being the first bitch to break 30 secs there, and she won the trophy by five lengths in 30.03 secs. It was her sixth appearance in a top-class event, after which the Irish Racing and Coursing Calendar said: 'She is the fastest bitch of her generation.' She was also the unluckiest.

One of the finest and unluckiest greyhounds never to have won a classic event was Kilbelin Style, a brindle by Prairie Flash out of the immortal Clomoney Grand and one of an amazing litter that included Kilbelin Grand and Albany. Bred by Mr George Kidd of Co. Carlow, the dog was purchased by Mr Cyril Young, a Berwickshire businessman, who placed him with the Wembley trainer Tommy Johnston. His first race in England was his first round heat of the 1969 Derby. He came up against the flying Sand Star who defeated him by four lengths, but in their second round heat by only a short head. The two were to meet in each round, including the final, when once again Sand Star was the winner by two lengths with Kilbelin Style in second place. From there he contested the Edinburgh Cup at Powderhall, winning his heat, but in the final he again had to be content with second place. Then, contesting the Kennedy Memorial Stakes in his native Ireland, he won his heat and semi-final yet lost the final by a length, beaten by Finola's Yarn. He won the Anglo-Irish Stakes at White City in great style and, entered for the Pall Mall at Harringay, he was made favourite and expected to win. Once again he won his heat and semi-final, but in the final was badly bumped which caused him to fall and he finished last.

In Ireland Mr L. Cullen's bitch Geraldine Silver was a game but unlucky finalist. In the 1970 Oaks she was beaten a short head by Rosmore Robin when the two appeared to have crossed the line together, and she also reached the final of the Irish Derby and Guinness 600. She is the only bitch to have reached the final of the Derby and Oaks in the same year.

Of owners, George Flintham had a runner in 12 English Derby finals without ever winning the event.

W

WALTHAMSTOW RACECOURSE
See under British Greyhound Racecourses.

WEIGHTS

All greyhounds are weighed in the paddock shortly before every race or trial, and trainers will frequently weigh greyhounds in their care, especially after lay-off through illness, so that a dog can be brought back to his racing weight before beginning trials again.

There is an old saying among coursing men that 'a good big 'un will always beat a good little 'un', but this is not always confirmed. The greatest of all coursing dogs, Master M'Grath, weighed only 55 lbs at the peak of condition and was one of the lightest dogs ever to win the Waterloo Cup. On the track Jubilee Time weighed only 60 lbs when beating the unbeatable Ballynennan Moon, and Monday's News 64 lbs when winning the 1946 Greyhound Derby. At the peak of his career Mick the Miller was the same weight, as was Sand Star when winning the 1969 Derby. Faithful Hope weighed 68 lbs when winning the 1966 Derby and the Irish St Leger winner Ballybeg Surprise was 70 lbs. One of the lightest of all classic winners was Pouleen Boy, who won the Irish St Leger in 1947; he was equalled in weight by Dante the Great who was only 59–60 lbs when racing.

In contrast Yanka Boy weighed 77 lbs when winning the Irish St Leger 20 years later. The 1950 English Derby winner Ballymac Ball, and John Silver who won twenty years later, turned the scales at 72 lbs. Sandown Champion and Daring Flash weighed 74 lbs; and Astra's Son, Bah's Choice and Clonahard Border, were 76 lbs. Among the heavyweights were Flip Your Top, Smartly Fergus, Carry on Oregon, Cricket Bunny and Noble Brigg, all at 80 lbs, and the son of Smartly Fergus, Confey Castle, weighed 86 lbs, as did Cash for Dan, winner of the BBC Trophy in 1969. Gayline, the Irish Coursing Derby winner, and Rushing to Work, twice winner of the Tipperary Cup, also weighed 86 lbs. Another great coursing dog, Rebel Abbey, tipped the scales at 90 lbs. But probably the heaviest dog ever to win on the track or coursing field in Britain was Captain Fuller's Tearing Anzac, which he bred from an Australian-imported bitch. The dog weighed 95 lbs when at peak fitness and several pounds more when at stud. (This was the weight of Newdown Heather when at stud, and of his grandson Master Myles who won the Irish Coursing Derby in 1978 and was known as 'The Big Dog').

Bitches are of lighter build. The great long-distance runner of the 1940s, Alvaston Lulu Belle, weighed only 45 lbs, as did Lady Steele II and Debbie Law, the marathon midget, who died in 1969 aged twelve. Bradshaw Fold and Quarter Day were 50 lbs. Unwin Beauty (Stanley Biss's favourite) was of the same weight when winning the Cobb Marathon at Catford. Shady Parachute was 52 lbs. Shaggy Lass and the 1979 Irish Derby winner Penny County were 55 lbs. Hurry Kitty and Cranog Bet were of the same weight, which seems to be the ideal one for a racing bitch and to breed from, while a weight of 68–76 lbs is ideal for a stud dog, though several of the most successful dogs at stud were considerably lighter and some were heavier.

See Sire.

DOGS	
Astra's Son	76 lbs
Bah's Choice	76 lbs
Balliniska Band	77 lbs
Ballybeg Surprise	70 lbs
Ballymac Ball	72 lbs
Ballynennan Moon	64 lbs
Carry on Oregon	80 lbs
Cash for Dan	86 lbs
Clonahard Border	76 lbs
Confey Castle	86 lbs
Cricket Bunny	80 lbs
Dante the Great	59 lbs
Daring Flash	74 lbs
Dusty Trail	72 lbs
Faithful Hope	68 lbs
Flip your Top	80 lbs
Gayline	86 lbs
John Silver	72 lbs
Jubilee Time	60 lbs
Mad Midnight	72 lbs
Master Myles	95 lbs
Mick the Miller	64 lbs
Monday's News	64 lbs
Newdown Heather (at stud)	95 lbs
Noble Brigg	80 lbs
Quare Times	67 lbs
Rebel Abbey	90 lbs
Rita's Choice	70 lbs
Rushing to Work	86 lbs
Sand Star	64 lbs
Sandown Champion	74 lbs
Saucy Buck	66 lbs
Shaggy Lad	70 lbs
Smartly Fergus	66 lbs
Spanish Battleship	60 lbs
Spectre II	73 lbs
Tearing Anzac	95 lbs
Tough Decision	74 lbs
Yanka Boy	77 lbs
BITCHES	
Alvaston Lulu Belle	45 lbs
Bradshaw Fold	50 lbs
Cranog Bet	55 lbs
Debbie Law	45 lbs
Hurry Kitty	55 lbs

Lady Steele II	45 lbs
Penny County	55 lbs
Rio Cepretta	26 lbs
Quarter Day	50 lbs
Shady Parachute	52 lbs
Shaggy Lass	55 lbs
Unwin Beauty	50 lbs

Though in Ireland, where the world's finest greyhounds are raised, they are still weighed in lbs, since 1975 in Britain greyhound weights have been given on race cards in kilos, in line with EEC regulations (1 kilo = 2.20 lbs; 1 lb = 0.45 kilos). Yet apart from Britain only Ireland among EEC countries has legalized track racing at present, and rightly sticks to pounds which everyone understands.

WEANING

If the mother is a good one, still with an adequate supply of milk (this will depend on how well she has been cared for up to the time she has had her pups and afterwards – *see* Brood Bitch), and she still enjoys being with her litter, she should be allowed to remain with them until they are at least eight weeks old when the pups are gradually taught how to manage without her. This process is known as weaning and is perhaps the most difficult and important part of a greyhound's life. Often a pup will be advertised for sale at seven or eight weeks old, but this is too young and it will have a better start in life if it is allowed to spend at least some time with its mother up to the age of eight or ten weeks. This will depend upon the condition of the bitch, for unless she is physically strong and is given ample supplies of nourishing food she will not be fit enough to be with the pups for that length of time. It is preferable not to part with the pups (if sale is intended) until they are eleven or twelve weeks old, by which time they will be fully weaned.

Weaning must be done gradually. After seven weeks the bitch is taken from the pups for an hour or so daily, though if the weather is severe she is best left with them until it becomes warmer. This is why weaning is best done after early March when the weather improves, so that it is better if the litter is whelped in early January or later, rather than in November or December. Each week, take away the bitch for a longer time each day, but always return her to her pups by evening. As her own milk supply gets shorter, she will vomit some of her well-digested food for her pups to eat and larger quantities if her milk stops entirely, thus making sure the pups are always fed. The greatest trouble the pups have at this time is digesting their food, and if their mother is able to help them it will be a decided advantage. She will bring back her partly digested food shortly after being fed, and when the pups are satisfied she must then be given another light feed which she will keep down. At this time feed her four times a day, every four hours from 8 a.m. with her last feed at 8 p.m. before she settles down for the night. Always go back to remove her dish or any left-over food some five minutes after feeding her, so that when the pups are back with her they cannot find any stale food. Always keep a bowl of fresh water for the pups and their mother to drink at will.

After eight or nine weeks she is taken away from the pups entirely. Her milk should have dried off, but if not give her a dose of Epsom Salts to clear her out, keep her on reasonably dry food for a few days and rub her breasts with camphorated oil. At the end of a week her milk secretion will have ceased, which is necessary if she is to have a satisfactory flow of milk for a future litter.

The weaning must be done gradually, or the pups will take unkindly to leaving their mother and they may not survive. It is important to feed them plenty of full-cream milk to prevent a sharp fall-off in nutritional value, for a bitch's milk is of high fat content, containing 15 per cent butterfat compared with the 4–5 per cent of cow's milk. Feed the pups little and often rather than two or three large meals a day, so as not to extend their stomachs which will cause flatulence and scouring. Stay with the pups while they are feeding to ensure that each gets its fair share of food. At nine or ten weeks give the pups their first worming, using one of the oil preparations and following the maker's instructions. Give them a large marrow bone once a week which will sharpen and clean their teeth and keep them amused for hours.

At eleven to twelve weeks they will be ready for sale, but if you are rearing them until they reach six months of age the puppies should be given complete freedom to go in and out of their run as they wish, being kept in only on the coldest days of winter. It is essential that they are allowed to run out on grass, which is why they do best when reared on farms or at kennels in the country where they can pick up the minerals in the soil and in the grass which they eat. Fresh milk augmented by dried milk is the most important food, supplying the calcium necessary for correct bone formation, while it also prevents acidity of the stomach which causes hysteria. Provide them with milk at least twice daily, augmented with brown (wholemeal) bread or biscuit. Never feed white bread, for this too causes hysteria. If feeding oatmeal, see that it is well cooked. If it can be obtained, feed the pups on goat's milk which has a higher butterfat content than cow's milk. The coursing men of old would feed liberal quantities of milk right up to the time the dogs ran their first trials. It is advisable to give a change of food every so often, which will stimulate the pups' appetite; the secretion from their salivary glands helps the digestion. Give them an occasional raw egg beaten into their milk, but not too many which will upset the digestion. To correct this put a little bicarbonate of soda into their drinking water.

One feed a day should be of minced meat to provide the protein necessary for healthy muscles and bone tissue. Feed horse meat passed fit for human consumption or meat of a proprietary make, used with brown bread or oatmeal. The daily addition of cod liver oil to the meat meal is important, and should be given to all greyhounds whatever their age for it gives protection against colds, keeps the bowels nicely free and gives the coat a beautiful gloss. It also protects the pups against rickets. The Irish breeders feed large quantities of potatoes, well boiled, and usually mix them with brown bread. A little salt added stimulates the pups' appetite. It is not, however, advisable to feed many potatoes until the pups are six months old, since younger dogs find them more difficult to digest. Add a calcium-phosphorus and vitamin D concentrate to the daily feed to assist with bone formation. In Ireland, puppies are fed sloppy food from weaning until six months old, one of the chief foods being carragheen moss, a product of seaweed which nourishes the glands controlling the digestive system.

The pups will shed their milk teeth after five months, and when six months old their permanent teeth will have formed. At this time they may suffer some loss of weight and bouts of hysteria. For a week or two feed non-heating foods and the condition will soon right itself. It is advisable to let the pups pass through this part of growing up before having them inoculated against the various greyhound diseases, for this too may pull them down for a week or two and may cause mild fever as in humans.

Mr K.D. Steadman, who bred and raised the 1946 Waterloo Cup winner Maesydd Michael and was one of the most experienced breeders of coursing dogs, contended that all pups should be allowed the freedom to exercise themselves as they wished from the age of nine to ten weeks, as soon as they had been weaned. An enclosed run attached to their kennel is ideal or, if they are housed in a barn or shed, it may be possible to make an opening in one wall and put in a small door through which the pups can go in and out to a wired run outside.

Do not forget to register the pups with either the National Coursing Club or the Irish Coursing Club within one month of birth.

See Ailments and Diseases; Bitch; Brood Bitch.

WELSH DERBY
See under Classic Events in Great Britain.

WEMBLEY RACECOURSE
See under British Greyhound Racecourses.

WEST HAM RACECOURSE
See under British Greyhound Racecourses.

WHELPING
The act of giving birth to a litter. A bitch will have her pups sixty-three days or thereabouts after being put to a sire, and on account of the thin, long legs of a greyhound pup, birth usually presents no problems to the brood bitch. She should be settled down in her kennel several hours before due to whelp and provided with clean straw over which sacking is spread. This will prevent the pups becoming buried in the straw, when she may lie on them, causing them to suffocate. If there is a large litter,

whelping may take several hours, but unless she appears to be straining and having difficulty (when the vet should be called) leave her to herself, looking in occasionally to see that all goes well. When the last of the pups is born, wash her vagina with warm water containing a little Dettol and give her a bowl of warm bread and milk with a teaspoonful of brandy added. For the next few days feed her on warm bread and milk into which a raw egg is beaten, then gradually introduce her to more solid food. Give her a pint of milk early in the morning with brown bread or biscuit, and the same at noon, with meat or fish for her evening meal. If horse meat is used, it must have been passed fit for human consumption and it must be minced, after removing most of the fat. Alternatively feed tinned meat of a proprietary brand.

When the pups begin to form their teeth, the bitch's breasts may become inflamed; the pups may also scratch her with their nails. Friar's balsam rubbed on will soon take away the inflammation. Also give her an occasional dusting with delousing powder, for continual scratching will soon pull her down, but keep the powder away from her breasts.

The pups will begin to open their eyes after about ten days and after fourteen days each pup in the litter will have its eyes open. They must then be shown how to lap milk, for if the litter is a large one this will greatly relieve the bitch. Add to cow's milk a little full-cream dried milk diluted with water. Use one-third, and of a recognized proprietary brand. See that the cow's milk is quite fresh and make up the powdered milk fresh whenever used. It should be fed lukewarm and it may take a few days before the pups learn how to lap. Take one at a time to the shallow bowl, holding the pups firmly with one hand; let the fingers of your other hand dip into the milk, so that the pup gets the taste of the milk as it licks your fingers. Some pups will begin drinking almost at once, while others may take a few days before they begin lapping it up. They are best shown how to lap if the bitch is taken out for a half hour's exercise by another member of the household or kennel staff, so that she does not interfere with the pups. Remove the feeding utensils immediately the pups have finished and clean them. Stale food and dirty utensils can cause the dreaded scour — the utmost cleanliness is necessary in their feeding.

Continue to give them a twice-daily ration of milk for another four weeks until the pups are six weeks old, during which time they will stay with their mother at all times except when lapping. From then onwards add a little crushed biscuit to their meals, and one feed should then be of broth and finely minced meat. From this time and until they are weaned give each pup two Abidon tablets daily.

See that the bitch and pups are provided with fresh straw almost daily, though breeders of old would leave down the bedding for sometime if the weather was unduly cold as it was thought the droppings and urine would cause the straw to heat up and keep the pups warm.

WHELPS

Newly born pups. When a bitch gives birth to a litter of pups it is known as whelping.

WHITE CITY RACECOURSE, LONDON
See under British Greyhound Racecourses.

WHITE CITY RACECOURSE, MANCHESTER
See under British Greyhound Racecourses.

WIDE RUNNER

A greyhound classified as a wide runner, one running on the outside of the course, is indicated on the racecard by W. The racing manager is entitled to 'seed' wide runners in outside traps if he considers that it will make for better racing.

WIMBLEDON RACECOURSE
See under British Greyhound Racecourses.

WINNING DEBUT

Many greyhounds have won on their first official outing in public but only on rare occasions set a new track record. The dog, Up Early a son of Ivy Hall Flash, did this at Tralee in 1977 when he covered the 500 yds course in 29.12 secs.

WINNING MARGINS

The biggest winning margin for a classic race was the eight lengths by Ballyhennessy Seal, which was the margin each time when winning his heat, semi-final and final for the 1945 Gold Collar at Catford. On each occasion he was quoted 9–2 on. When taking the London Cup at Clapton in 1943 Blackwater Cutlet covered the 550 yds course in 31.80 secs to win by twelve lengths from Ballykildare, with whom he had dead-heated for the Stewards' Cup at Walthamstow the previous week. In 1945, in the final of the important Golden Crest at Eastville, Bristol, Shannon Shore won by ten lengths from Magic Beau in a new record time of 28.76 secs for 500 yds. At Dagenham on 1 May 1948 Local Interprize won an open event over 460 yds by twenty-three lengths, surely the largest winning margin over a race of less than 500 yds. When winning the 1947 Cobb Marathon over 810 yds at Catford, Missouri beat Ben Silver by fourteen lengths.

WINNINGS OF SOME FAMOUS GREYHOUNDS

Ballyhennessy Sandhills	£5,000
Ballyjoker	£4,000
Black Andrew	£6,500
Dale Lad	£7,250
Flip Your Top	£8,000
Forward King	£5,000
Glin Bridge	£8,000
Knockrour Bank	£5,000
Linacre	£12,500
Pigalle Wonder	£8,000
Shady Begonia	£6,000
Shady Parachute	£8,500
Spanish Battleship	£6,000
Tell you What	£6,500
Tric Trac	£10,000
Try it Blackie	£5,000
Westmead Champ	£11,000
Westmead Power	£14,500
Xmas Holiday	£12,000

WOLVERHAMPTON RACECOURSE
See under British Greyhound Racecourses.

WORLD GREYHOUND FEDERATION

Established in Dublin on 16 October 1971, its objective was greater co-operation among those countries in which greyhound racing takes place. The founder members were Ireland, the USA, Australia, Spain and Mexico. Britain joined later. The headquarters of the WGA are at the Bord na gCon's headquarters at Limerick. Its first president was Mr Jack Ledoux of the USA, and the vice-presidents were Mr Des Hanrahan, chairman of Bord na gCon, and Mr Jack Fell of the Australian Coursing Club, with Mr Seamus Flanagan chief executive officer, a position he also occupies with Bord na gCon.

The Federation places great importance on veterinary science and research and a special committee under Mr Oliver Graham-Jones has been set up to look into many aspects of greyhound diseases and methods of treating injuries. Considerable attention is being given to the introduction of new vaccines, which it is hoped will reduce the need for such long periods of quarantine and all dogs will benefit accordingly.

Attention is also being given to running surfaces; the construction of hurdles to eliminate injury; and simple methods of testing for the doping of greyhounds. Indeed every aspect of greyhound racing is now being covered at international level by all those countries in which racing takes place.

Y

YOUNGEST CLASSIC WINNER

John Silver, best son of Faithful Hope out of Trojan Silver, owned by Mr Reg Young and trained by Barbara Tompkins was just 20 months old when winning the 1970 English Derby, the youngest winner of the event. Raised in his owner's garden in Buckinghamshire, he won for him more than £10,000 in that year alone. Yankee Express was 21 months old when winning his first Scurry Cup in 1982. But the youngest of all classic winners was the ill-fated Marbella Sky, owned by Mrs Rita Hare and trained at Halifax by Ray Andrews. A red fawn dog by Weston Blaze out of Marie's Kate and whelped in February, 1980 he was just under 18 months old when winning over 500 m at Shawfield to take the Scottish Derby in 30.66 secs and it was only his fourth race. Shortly after, he ran up to Deel Jocker in the Edinburgh Cup but in his heat for the Puppy Derby injured a toe and was withdrawn. He never raced again as shortly after, he was stolen from his kennel and disappeared without trace, his full potential never realised.

YARMOUTH RACECOURSE
See under British Greyhound Racecourses.

BIBLIOGRAPHY

The books are listed chronologically according to year of publication.

The Greyhound, 'Stonehenge' (Longman, Brown & Green, London, 1853, revised editions 1875, 1896). *See* entry for 'Stonehenge' in text.

The Greyhound: Its History, Points, Breeding, Rearing, Training and Running, Hugh Dalziel (Upcott & Gill, London, 1888). This volume went into many editions over a period of fifty years, the last (ninth edition) which appeared in 1938 containing an interesting chapter on track racing by Leo Wilson.

Greyhound Racing, 'Leveret' of the *Star* (Fleetgate Publications (*Daily News*), London, 1927). Thirty-eight pages. The first book to appear on the new sport of track racing with descriptions on the greyhounds running at White City, London, that year.

All About Greyhound Racing, A.R. Cardew (*Daily Mail,* London, 1928). Eighty-eight pages. A.R. Cardew was greyhound correspondent of the *Daily Mail* at the time.

The Book of the Greyhound, Edward C. Ash, (Hutchinson & Co., 1933, with a second edition later the same year). A volume of 351 pages, with 120 illustrations, it remains the best book on the greyhound published this century but it makes no mention of track racing. For the breeder and trainer, however, and those interested in pedigrees, it is indispensable.

Greyhounds and Greyhound Racing, Mrs Carlo F. Culpeper Clarke (Methuen & Co., London, 1934). A volume of 140 pages and containing many excellent photographs of Future Cutlet, Mutton Cutlet, Wild Woolley, Creamery Border, etc. This was the first authoritative book on the early years of the sport in Britain. It is sub-titled 'A Comprehensive and Popular Survey of Britain's latest Sport, with a Foreword by Professor Sir Frederick Hobday'.

The Greyhound: Coursing, Racing and Showing, Edward C. Ash, (published in The Dog Owner's Handbook Series, 1936). A small volume which appeared shortly after Edward Ash's monumental work.

Greyhound Racing for Profit. The 'Dos' and 'Don'ts' of Betting, 'Professional Backer' (Sporting Handbooks Ltd, 1945). Forty pages.

Modern Greyhound Racing, Roy Genders (Sporting Handbooks Ltd, London, 1946). A book of 164 pages covering the history of the first twenty years of track racing in Britain and Ireland with track records and the results of important events, together with chapters on training, breeding and owning a racing greyhound. A second revised edition called *Modern Greyhound Racing and Coursing* appeared in 1949 with 301 pages and sixteen photographs. This book remained in print for twenty-five years.

The Greyhound Stud Dog Annual, Thomas H. Ball and Leonard C. Makin (Makin & Ball, Harrow, Middx, 1946). This valuable publication of seventy-eight pages first appeared as Vol. I but no further editions were published. It gives the pedigree of every greyhound at stud in England and Ireland in 1946; also the addresses where they were kennelled and the fees charged. It was invaluable for greyhound breeders of the time.

The Modern Greyhound, H. Edwards Clarke (Hutchinson & Co., London, 1948). Dedicated jointly to the Earl of Sefton and J.V. Rank, Esq, Presidents of the Altcar and South of England Coursing Clubs. A handsome volume of 224 pages and twenty-three full-page illustrations, the book is an outstanding contribution by the greatest of modern greyhound authors and covers the breeding and performances of the finest track and coursing greyhounds of the period 1918–48.

Greyhounds, Roy Genders (W & G Foyle Ltd, London, 1960; reprinted 1963, 1964, 1970; revised edition 1973). This 104-page illustrated book, in the Handbooks for Dog Lovers Series, deals with the buying of greyhounds, their care, training and breeding.

The Greyhound and Greyhound Racing,

Roy Genders (Sporting Handbooks Ltd, London, 1975). A volume of 345 pages dealing with greyhound racing and coursing from the earliest times to the present day, with particular emphasis on track racing.

Trap to Line: Fifty Years of Greyhound Racing in Ireland, ed. John Comyn (Aherlow Publishers Ltd, Dublin). 288 pages with numerous photos, and chapters by many Irish authorities on coursing and track racing.

ADDRESSES

Bord na gCon,
104 Henry Street,
Limerick, Eire

Irish Coursing Club
Davis Road,
Clonmel,
Co. Tipperary, Eire

National Coursing Club
35 Grosvenor Gardens,
London SW1

National Greyhound Racing Club
24–28 Oval Road,
London NW1

Retired Greyhound Trust,
24 Oval Road,
London NW1 7DA

World Greyhound Racing Federation,
1065 N.E. 125th Street,
Suite 219,
North Miami,
FL 33161
U.S.A.

INDEX

The index is divided into the following sections: Breeders, Main Events, Owners, Racing Greyhounds, Racecourses, Racecourse Officials, Sponsors and Trainers.

OWNERS

RACING GREYHOUNDS

RACECOURSES

GREAT BRITAIN

REPUBLIC OF IRELAND

NORTHERN IRELAND

UNITED STATES OF AMERICA

AUSTRALIA

RACECOURSE OFFICIALS

SPONSORS